Jimb Moore

D1738915

The World in Their Minds

THE WORLD IN THEIR MINDS

Information Processing, Cognition, and
Perception in Foreign Policy Decisionmaking

Yaacov Y. I. Vertzberger

STANFORD UNIVERSITY PRESS, STANFORD, CALIFORNIA

Stanford University Press, Stanford, California
© 1990 by the Board of Trustees of the Leland Stanford Junior University
Printed in the United States of America

CIP data appear at the end of the book

Published with the assistance of the Leonard Davis Institute,
The Hebrew University of Jerusalem.

*In memory of my grandparents and members of the family
who perished in the Holocaust, and
with hope for a more enlightened future for humanity*

Acknowledgments

It is a pleasure to acknowledge the many debts of gratitude I owe to the individuals and organizations that helped make an abstract idea into this book. Michael Brecher read the whole manuscript carefully and made extensive critical comments, encouraging me to rethink, rephrase, and polish concepts, arguments, and reasoning. Yehudit Aurbach, Ernst Haas, Robert Keohane, Maurice White, and Aaron Wildavsky read earlier versions of some of the chapters. Their responses proved to be helpful in calling my attention to flaws and specific problems in those chapters. Over the years I have discussed the general ideas and concepts underlying this book with Alexander George, and his broad expertise in the subject matter was a source of insightful suggestions that were incorporated in this study. The reviewer for Stanford University Press made very useful, detailed structural and specific suggestions.

I am indebted to many of my students, who provided research assistance at various phases. They include Smadar Bar-Akiva (Dreiman), Rachel Blumenfeld, Miriam Fendius, Efrat Elyashar, Aryeh Green, Michal Halevi (Even-Chen), Yoseph Meir, Michal Navot, Yael Shalgi, Smadar Shilo, Yaacov Tiegel, Omri Yadin, and in particular Shimon Arad. A preliminary draft of some of the chapters was translated from Hebrew to English by Dafna Alon. Special thanks are due to Sara Lehman, who tirelessly and skillfully typed and retyped numerous drafts, meeting impossible deadlines. David Hornik, my editor in Jerusalem, did an outstanding job on the first draft in making the writing accessible to professionals and the general public alike. The librarians at the Social

Sciences Library, the Hebrew University, Jerusalem, and the Resource Materials Collection, East-West Center, Honolulu, were eager to assist in locating any published material required.

Part of Chapter 6 appeared in my article "Foreign Policy Decision-makers as Practical-Intuitive Historians: Applied History and Its Shortcomings," *International Studies Quarterly*, 30 (1986): 223–47, and is reprinted by permission of the International Studies Association, Byrnes International Center, University of South Carolina.

This book could never have been completed without the generous financial assistance of the S. A. Schonbrunn Research Endowment Fund, the Authority for Research and Development, the Research Fund of the Social Sciences Faculty of the Hebrew University, and the Basic Research Foundation administered by the Israel Academy of Sciences and Humanities. I am also grateful to the Harry S. Truman Research Institute, its former director Zvi Schiffrin and his successor, Ben-Ami Shiloni, and to the Leonard Davis Institute of International Relations and its former director, Yehoshafat Harkabi, for their support.

My work on the project began during a sabbatical in 1983–84, when I was a fellow at the Institute of International Studies at the University of California, Berkeley. I am grateful to the director of the institute, Carl Rosberg, for inviting me and to the institute's staff for their assistance in launching the project. The final version of the book was prepared in 1987–88 while I was a research fellow at the East-West Center. I am grateful to President Victor Li and to Norton Ginsburg, Charles Morrison, and Seiji Naya for making it possible for me to spend a year at the center, which provided an excellent research environment. The staff of the International Relations Program at the center—Dorine McConnell, Sherée Groves, and Dorothy Villasenor—were friendly, helpful, and efficient, and I am indebted to them for helping me accomplish more than I had hoped for. The East-West Center Graphics Production Services prepared the figures. A short-term residency in 1989 at the Rockefeller Foundation's Bellagio Study and Conference Center, the Villa Serbelloni, where the director, Roberto Celli, and the staff created ideal working conditions, allowed me the opportunity to give the text its final polish.

Last but not least I would like to express my appreciation to Grant Barnes, the director of Stanford University Press, who showed interest in the project from the early stages and who nursed it through to its conclusion. At Stanford University Press I also had the good fortune of working with John Feneron, who supervised the production of the book, and Mary Pasti, the copy editor who did a most excellent, thorough, and conscientious job.

None of the above carry any responsibility for the views expressed or for possible errors.

Y.Y.I.V.

Contents

Figures and Tables

The World in Their Minds

Introduction

....

History in general and diplomatic history in particular are the story of human aspiration, achievement, adaptation, and survival. But they are also the tale of human error and fallibility. A common element in many failures is that they did not stem from a dearth of information but rather from incorrect judgment and evaluation of available information. Each particular error in the march of folly is often labeled by both historians and laypeople as avoidable or unavoidable; yet these labels are neither correct nor incorrect, just meaningless, if not coupled with an understanding of how errors could be avoided or why they could not be avoided. To achieve that understanding, to learn useful and accurate lessons from the past, and to cope more effectively with the present and future, information processing has to be analyzed at all levels—individual, small-group, organizational, and societal; we have to comprehend how information becomes available and is attended to, analyzed, integrated, and interpreted—in other words, how decisionmakers construct a view of the world in their minds. To achieve this understanding is the subject and purpose of this book. The term information processing is treated here as an organizing concept for understanding a broad but interrelated range of cognitive and motivational phenomena of great significance in human judgment and decisionmaking in general and foreign policy decisionmaking in particular. It is used as a comprehensive rubric for many variables and processes.

Besides the academic, detached rationale for this study there is also a personal motive. My interest in the subject matter reflects the reality of growing up and living in the Middle East, a region rife with conflict and war, and in Israel, a state under permanent threats to its security. All this is bound to affect a scholar's focus of interest, or at least it affected mine. The conception of the national leadership walking a tightrope, having to fine-tune its defense and foreign policies, to decide when a threat is real, acute, and imminent, when preemptive violence is called for and when it should be avoided, has been part of the political socialization and daily awareness of every Israeli. This conception has been accompanied by the realization that the misjudgment, misevaluation, and misperception of external threats may either cause unnecessary bloodshed or possibly lead to a repetition of the Holocaust. The image of the Holocaust is particularly vivid even for my generation, not only because of the terrible human costs but also because of the serious misjudgments and misperceptions regarding the intentions, capabilities, and fanatical dedication to evil of the Nazi leadership and its followers and accomplices, which helped make the catastrophe possible. These misperceptions were shared by world leaders, the public, the media, and the Jewish leadership in Europe, America, and Palestine.

That basic awareness at the state leadership level fostered in Israel, from the early days of statehood, a determination to develop an efficient intelligence community; Israeli intelligence has in fact acquired a reputation as one of the finest. But the Yom Kippur debacle and the related intelligence failure highlighted its fallibility—and the crucial importance of information processing. The obvious conclusion was that information processing by the intelligence community and other decisionmaking bodies had left much to be desired and that the failure in the Yom Kippur case was not an exception to the rule. Even what was considered a major intelligence coup, the Six Day War of 1967, was actually a failure of information processing, which, owing to luck and other favorable circumstances, was turned into a brilliant military victory.[1] I thus began to seek an answer to two universal questions: What affects information processing? And why is it that decisionmakers go wrong so often, even when all the information necessary for an appropriate analysis of the situation is available?

The ability to distinguish appearance from reality is an integral aspect of the human developmental process (Flavell, Flavell, and Green, 1983). Yet immaturity in this regard remains widespread among decisionmakers, albeit asymmetrically, particularly in those areas where available information is characterized by attributes that make the distinction prone to error as well as to conscious and unconscious manipulation by the self and others. Learning in such contexts frequently proves ineffective or even countereffective, and what is learned does not always promote accurate distinctions between appearance and reality and in fact may have regressive rather than progressive effects.

Why does not an "orderly" developmental process occur, and why, instead, do errors in distinguishing between appearance and reality recur? Why do actors not only repeatedly make the same types of error made by others—which they already know something about and should apparently have been able to avoid—but also seem unable to escape repeating their own errors?

The existing literature on the subject suggested two conclusions. One was that the available answers are plausible but not satisfactory, sometimes simplistic and reductionist; the second, that a deductive, interdisciplinary, multivariate research effort could be productive. My realization that the emergent theoretical framework has become increasingly complex represented an important step toward developing a general theory. It seemed, however, to require rigorous testing of its applicability before it could be amplified any further. That was done by applying the theoretical framework to a detailed analysis of a crucial case history,[2] India's China policy in the period 1959–62 (Vertzberger, 1984a), and indeed the framework has proven to be a useful and effective one. To me it indicated that the path taken was in the right direction and that the natural next step was to extend and fully develop the existing theoretical framework. What resulted is the current study.

Since the efficacy of the framework has already been demonstrated, applying it in full to additional case studies was not necessary, nor would the scope of this study allow it. On the other hand, since a purely theoretical study might have caused difficulties to at least some of the potential readers, I preferred to take the middle road. Two current case histories of the failure of information processing—American intervention in the Vietnam War (1964–75) and Israeli surprise in the Yom Kippur War of 1973—were chosen as the main, although not the only, sources for illustrative examples but were not used as formal case studies. Those events seemed well suited to my purpose for a number of reasons.

In the first place, the two failures in question involved open societies, and their magnitude inspired much soul searching at the national level. The relevant information uncovered in the process found expression in the available accounts of the Vietnam and Yom Kippur wars. The richness of detail provided a gold mine of illustrations for my theoretical analysis.

No less important was the second consideration—the effect on the reader. To make the theoretical-deductive variables, arguments, and reasoning readily understandable, it was necessary to use short, empirical illustrations. Unfortunately, not many readers can be expected to be intimately acquainted with the history of the last two centuries, from which most examples in current international relations literature are taken. The impact of a given example is lost when the reader is not sufficiently familiar with its general historical context. Very few readers, however, will be unaware of the context of the Vietnam and Middle East conflicts because they are both so prominent in current history. Occasionally, when a satisfactory example could not be found in one of the two case histories, examples from some other case histories were used (particularly in Chapters 5 and 6). But as a rule arguments are followed by examples (not necessarily in chronological order) from the Vietnam and Yom Kippur wars. A note of caution is warranted, however: these examples are not, and should not be interpreted as, evidence for the validity of the theory, but as illustrations of it.

The structure of the book reflects the comprehensive multidisciplinary approach chosen. Chapter 1 explores the notion of information processing, and the nexus between it and cognition and perception, and suggests a typology of perceptual outcomes and their dynamics. Chapter 2 presents the effects of the type, quality, and quantity of information on its processing and the impact of the nature of interacting with the information. Chapter 3 discusses the impact of personality variables on the quality of information processing. The variables include beliefs, values, attitudes, personality traits, and biophysiological conditions. Chapter 4 analyzes social (organizational and small-group) effects on information processing, including the effects of organizational structure and role, interorganizational and intraorganizational interaction, as well as small-group dynamics. Chapter 5 establishes the societal-cultural influences, such as national role and status conceptions, and the relevance of typical societal-cultural attributes and behavior patterns. Chapter 6 deals with the role of learning from the past and using history as an instrument of information processing. Chapter 7 summarizes the main themes of the theoretical analysis and suggests how to limit the potential negative consequences of faulty information processing, thereby reinforcing the relevance of this study to policymaking. Since it is difficult, almost impossible, to always draw a sharp line between the different variable-sets, there is some overlap between chapters. But I tried to make the distinctions between variable-sets clear and to keep overlaps to a minimum.

This book's main audience is students of foreign policy and foreign policy decisionmakers and executives at all levels, as well as their advisers and direct and indirect staff members. But the book is not intended just for students and practitioners of foreign policy decisionmaking. It is also for fellow academic social scientists and decisionmakers in all fields who are dealing with information processing and operating in environments that have the attributes of complexity, uncertainty, ambiguity, overload, high risk, and issue interdependence. Although the illustrations reflect my area of specialization, i.e. international politics, the study is interdisciplinary, in methodology, in approach, and in terms of target audiences, hence the general main title and the reference to foreign policy only in the subtitle.

I am also aware that not many readers read books from cover to cover but read selectively for lack of time, interest, or both. That is why I wrote the book modularly. Although it should be read as a whole to get a full understanding of information processing, each chapter can be read and understood on its own.

I would like to think of this study as another brick in the wall humanity must erect against critical errors in judgment and inference, which have resulted in so much human misery. In the nuclear age even the worst past horrors, brought about by total war, pale when compared with the potentially disastrous consequences of errors in judgment and inference that lead to a nuclear confrontation. I believe that an integrated, interdisciplinary approach provides a broad understanding of how information is used and abused and could improve decisionmakers' capabilities to minimize errors in judgment and inference by understanding their causes and taking preventive measures.

CHAPTER I

Information Processing, Perception, and Misperception

....

"Appearances to the mind are of four kinds. Things either are what they appear to be; or they neither are, nor appear to be; or they are and do not appear to be; or they are not, and yet appear to be. Rightly to aim in all these cases is the wise man's task." EPICTETUS

The Notion of Information Processing

Our world is one of growing complexity, increasing uncertainty, and diminishing capability to anticipate and control outcomes. Foreign policymaking is oriented toward coping with the environment—political, social, and physical—to at least minimize risk and damage to the national interest, as the decisionmaker perceives it, or to at best maximize benefits. Coping is, then, the process of consciously attempting to manage complexity and uncertainty and of striving for accurate anticipation and effective control of outcomes in a milieu, characterized by actor-interdependence, where relations among actors are mainly of the strategic-interaction type. Coping is reactive if it is a response to an acute problem, proactive if it is intended to preempt anticipated future occurrences or to hedge against unanticipated ones. Social interaction, such as foreign policy, is best described not only as a process of strategic interaction but also as one of symbolic interaction in the sense that "human beings interpret or 'define' each other's actions instead of merely reacting to each other's actions. Their 'response' is not made directly to the actions of one another but instead is based on the meaning which they attach to such actions" (Blumer, 1967: 139).

Consequently, the process we deal with here can be broadly described as having three interrelated stages in which (1) information is gathered and interpreted; (2) alternative courses of action are derived and evaluated in terms of some comparative cost-benefit calculus or in some other, less analytic manner and a choice is made among them; and (3) the preferred alternative is implemented or at least formally becomes the preferred action orientation even when domestic or external constraints prevent its actual implementation. The process within each of the stages and the transition process from one stage to the next do not necessarily unfold consciously. Nor are they necessarily rational-analytic processes; they may be cybernetic or cognitive ones (Stein and Tanter, 1980; Steinbruner, 1974). The results of each stage constrain, condition, and shape the possible outcomes of the next stage. The grand architecture of coping is consequently formulated at the first and hence most critical stage, that of information processing. The definition of the situation affects not only foreign policy behavior but also the structure of the decisionmaking unit and the process of choosing (Brady, 1978). Accumulated misjudgments, misevaluations, wrong inferences, and simple unawareness of relevant data are likely to carry over to the next stages, with negative ramifications for the quality of the overall coping process. Still, because of the possible discontinuity between process and outcome, the effects of nonoptimal coping processes do not always carry the sanction of negative outcomes and vice versa.

Recognizing successes and failures in information processing is sometimes tricky because of their disguised manifestations. When a failure in information processing does not produce high-cost outcomes because external circumstances intervene, significant failures may go unnoticed and the failure may even be mistaken for a success. Similarly, when a success in information processing is not utilized and policy and policy implementation consequently produce high-cost outcomes, the success may be mistaken for a failure. In both cases feedback produces the wrong kind of learning because the inferences from outcomes are misleading. We shall come back to these points later in the chapter. Nonetheless, the ability to cope effectively with any given situation will on the whole be greatly affected by the quality of information processing.

What is information processing? It is the plethora of activities, performed individually and collectively, through which decisionmakers strive for an accurate and sophisticated understanding of their social, political, and physical milieu in terms of the issues they face and the environmental constraints on the range of available responses open to them. It may not necessarily involve uncertainty reduction, as argued by some (e.g. Garner, 1962: 3). On the contrary, information processing may actually lead to the introduction of uncertainty into our knowledge of the world around us; recognizing structural and situational uncertainties is part of a realistic perception of the world. Thus, uncertainty reduction and coping are not the same, though sometimes they may converge when coping implies imposing warranted or unwarranted (more often the last) certainty on ambiguous information.

What does information processing entail? It involves recognizing and attending to information, interpreting it, assessing its relevance to problems at hand, evaluating the importance of new data within the existing information set, integrating the various information ingredients into the knowledge base by synthesizing, updating, expanding, abstracting, or transforming them substantially, and finally going beyond the information given and drawing inferences. Information processing is, then, not just a passive response to stimuli but also an active process of constructing reality.

The end product of information processing is knowledge that can be applied to the users' tasks and will affect the processing of future information. This knowledge has two dimensions—its specific content and the validity with which it is held. Knowledge does not necessarily have an absolute value; information may be given plausible alternative interpretations, to each of which a level of validity is attached. The interpretation preferred is the one that is given the highest validity at a particular time. New information or reevaluation of old information may result in attaching new validity values to the same set of plausible alternative interpretations, which could then lead to a choice of a different interpretation as the most valid. Updating validities is more common than adding completely new interpretations; it demands less transformation of mind-sets, since it is based on knowledge that already exists in memory storage and has been earlier accepted as at least plausible.

Information processing is symbiotically related to the issues of cognition, perception, misperception, and image formation and transformation (cf. W. L. Bennett, 1981, 1982). Hence, an analysis of information processing and the evaluation of its quality should deal with the image of the world the decisionmaker has at a given time and its change over time. The first question—How comprehensive and accurate is the decisionmaker's understanding and knowledge?—is concerned with the gap between the real and psychological environments. Organically following is the second question: What happens to this gap over time? Do the quality and quantity of knowledge improve or deteriorate?

Four typical modes of information processing can be detected; they represent various combinations of data-driven and concept- (or hypothesis)-driven knowledge-acquisition activities, which range along the continuum from direct knowing (perception-based knowing) to indirect knowing (cognition-based knowing) that involves more and more complex inference tasks (Baron and Harvey, 1980; Harris, 1981; Lindsay and Norman, 1977: 488–89; Taylor and Crocker, 1981).

1. *Thinking* is a deductive process focused on concept formation and elaboration. It relies on propositional structures.

2. *Sensing* is an inductive process focused on observable sensory inputs and their meaning. It relies mainly on non-propositional knowledge structures.

3. *Symbolizing* involves the use of symbols and rites to represent and give meaning to reality. It is metaphorical or analogical by definition and uses non-propositional knowledge structures (March, 1982: 37; Royce, 1974: 153–54).

4. *Intuiting* draws unconsciously on a person's store of knowledge structures and experience and is actually an associative act of recognition (Bastick, 1982: 61–62, 77–83; Bowers, 1981; Simon, 1981: 105; Westcott, 1968: 40, 79).

Through the different stages of the process, which yields an image of the environment as its product, different combinations of the modes can be dominant. Each carries its own dangers of distorting reality, as we shall see in the following chapters, and each is related to the variable-sets used to explain the dynamics and outcomes of information processing. In fact, the information processing variable-sets influence the preference—conscious or unconscious—for any one or any combination of the modes, and that preference affects the outcomes, at least to some extent.

Finally, as a task that is directed toward goal achievement and oriented toward knowledge acquisition, information processing spans past, present, and future. Knowing and understanding the past is one of the many instrumentalities for making sense of the present. Similarly, anticipating the future or forecasting alternative futures also relies on knowledge structures that are based on memory-stored cognizance and interpretation of the past and present.

A Critical Review of Selected Literature

Before further outlining the major conceptual terms of this study and dealing with some related epistemological questions, I shall briefly survey a selection of the pertinent literature in the field of international relations. The literature on information processing is rich and instructive. This short overview does not pretend to reveiw all of it but rather to use the prominent and illustrative writings that focus directly on information processing. The purpose in indicating what in my view are the main flaws in the literature is to illuminate the rationale for and objectives of this book.

Much of the early literature concentrated on demonstrating that information processing is imperfect and that it often produces misperceptions that play an important role in shaping international politics. The focus was natural in that the literature accompanied the emergence of the mediated stimulus-response model as an alternative to the simple stimulus-response model. It called attention to the highly relevant and virtually neglected perceptual-psychological aspect of such major foreign policy inputs as threat and hostility and to such outcomes as conflict, crisis, and war. The Stanford school studies of the 1914 crisis and the Cuban missile crisis are some of the best known in this category (e.g. O. R. Holsti, 1972b; Holsti, North, and Brody, 1968; Holsti, Brody, and North, 1969; North, 1968; Zinnes, 1968; Zinnes, North, and Koch, 1961). These and other studies, however, have a number of flaws and limitations.

First, many of the research questions focus on international crises. But crises, although fairly frequent in the history of state relations, dramatic in their effect, and hence salient, are, in the long perspective, only spasmodic; by definition they are activities that take place in a short or finite time (Brecher with Geist, 1980; C. F. Hermann, 1969; Hermann and Brady, 1972). The ability of the early researchers to observe and analyze long-term dynamics of perceptual continuity and change was constrained, because perceptual change and learning are usually long-term phenomena. Most of their studies are unavoidably centered on the static and short-term aspects of perceptual behavior and neglectful of long-term processes. This flaw is aggravated by another—that of using perception or misperception as an explanatory variable but in general treating the variable itself descriptively rather than analytically. I shall elaborate this point later.

Second, focusing on crisis situations has led to an emphasis on explaining misperceptions in terms of the "bad faith model" (O. R. Holsti, 1967a,b, 1969; Stuart and Starr, 1981–82), in which a crisis is seen by each participant as proof of the opponents' bad faith. Not much attention, however, has been devoted to perceptual errors springing from the adoption of a good faith model.

The preference for an explanation of the bad-faith-model type often dovetailed with the value system of the scholarly community. To allow explicitly that a display of good faith toward other countries is likely to be no less dangerous and ineffective than a display of bad faith in influencing their policies contradicted the prevailing norms. The norms postulated that ultimately improvements in relations between states are solely a function of the goodwill and peaceful intentions of those concerned, even to proposing a unilateral display of good faith as a strategy that will finally oblige the other side to respond in the same manner (e.g. Osgood, 1960b). Some social scientists felt a moral obligation to be the vanguard of a movement for reeducating national decisionmakers to think in terms of displaying more good faith and less suspicion toward other states.

Another corollary of the focus on the bad faith model was that the impact of variables not directly connected with good or bad faith—the motives and interests of the organizational system, bureaucratic infighting, and so on—was overlooked and underplayed, a situation that lasted till the late 1960's. What is more, bad faith and good faith are not by themselves variables that provide an explanation for erroneous information processing but a symptom of it, and their use is an exercise in labeling, not explaining.

Third, insofar as the Stanford school researchers attempted to explain the sources of misperception, they often did so in terms of a single, predominant variable, such as stress. For example, the tendency of the actor to perceive the number of alternatives as fewer than they in fact are, or to perceive the need to reach a decision as more pressing than it in fact is and the time available to do so as shorter than it really is, are all explained as effects of stress (e.g. O. R. Holsti, 1971, 1972a,b). But can such a complex phenomenon be explained in terms of one variable? We shall return to this point later on.

Flaws of this type were not the sole preserve of quantitative research on perception and do not reflect the limitations of only the quantitative approach (which dominated the Stanford school studies) in measuring and detecting motivations and cognitive processes, as some proponents of the traditional approach argued (Bull, 1969). For example, Stoessinger's (1968) study of the Sino-American conflict emphasizes description rather than causal explanations of perceptual distortions; in this particular case the sources of Sino-American mutual misunderstanding are traced to different world views. The argument is simplistic, running more or less thus: "World views were different, hence perceptions of the world's particularities were different and remained different." It describes and posits the existence of a phenomenon; it does not contribute much to the understanding of when and under what circumstances different world views might become the source of long-lasting misconceptions with little or no regard for dissonant information. Further, different world views have not inevitably led to a single outcome, conflict.

Another example is a study (S. Hoffmann, 1968a) that attempts to explain misperceptions in Franco-American relations and succeeds in defining the relation between the dependent variable (misperception) and the independent one (national style) with some precision; but this study, too, does not define the contingencies under which differences in national style lead to misperceptions. This type of univariate explanation is bound to confuse rather than enlighten. Few nations have identical national styles. If difference in national styles is the single most influential causal variable, that is, if misperceptions are not dependent on additional variables or conditions qualifying the relevance of the national-style variable, then constant misperceptions between any two nations with different national styles are inevitable; but that is not how things are.

Similar single-variable explanations are offered by researchers from other disciplines who ventured into the mine field of foreign policy decisionmaking. For example, Janis's (1982) influential groupthink theory, which has already been criticized on a number of other counts (e.g. Flowers, 1977; Longley and Pruitt, 1980), explains misperception and related policy fiascos as engendered by a single specific structure of the decisionmaking group and the group dynamics resulting therefrom. "The exclusion of factors is certainly a valid practice in scholarly work. One frequent psychological side-effect, however, is exaggeration of the importance of those factors which are included" (Fischhoff and Beyth-Marom, 1976: 392). Moreover, Janis's study presents an explanation in terms of an extreme case of group conformity—groupthink—which reduces its external validity. Nor do all cases of groupthink necessarily produce failure because of cognitive rigidity and closure. Rigidity and closure can also act to cancel the effect of deceptive information. Nor are most manifestations of groupthink unique to the insular cohesive group; they can be found in decisions made by isolated individuals, which raises the problem of how to differentiate individual-based from group-based effects on the quality of decisions. These arguments do not discount the relevance of the groupthink syndrome; they indicate that groupthink is a sufficient, but not a necessary, condition for flawed information processing (Abelson and Levi, 1985: 292–93).

A fourth difficulty has to do with the failure to distinguish between the symptoms of misperception and the causes for their existence, a failure that is sometimes bound up with tautological explanations. The problem is exemplified by R. K. White (1966, 1970), who deals with the misperceptions resulting from information processing during the Vietnam War. He contends that the misperceptions were linked with a demonic image of the enemy, a positive self-image of virility and morality, overconfidence, selective inattention to information, and lack of empathy with the adversary. But all of those are either symptoms or descriptions of misperceptions, not variables that explain why inattention was selective and how information processing ended with misperceptions. Furthermore, as correctly noted by J. S. Levy (1983: 79–80), images of one's own character and the adversary's are not misperceptions but beliefs that may affect the direction of information interpretation and that cannot be falsified because they are based on normative judgments for which no logical or empirical standard of comparison exists.

Fifth, the studies mentioned are insensitive to variations between the static aspects of perceptual outcomes and the dynamic varieties of perceptual-cognitive processes. The lack of analytical differentiation between types of misperception and types of perceptual dynamics of change over time has contributed to the non-emergence of a typological theory of misperception as well as to the tendency toward overgeneralization.

Another important category of literature dealing with information processing and its failure is on military and diplomatic surprise and deception. In terms of explanatory power, however, these studies fare little better. For example, Whaley (1973) attempts to explain the surprise achieved by Operation Barbarossa, the German invasion of Russia in June 1941. He contends that Stalin's failure to perceive the impending attack stemmed from his assumption that a German attack would necessarily be preceded by an ultimatum; only that indicator would turn the accumulated signals of Hitler's intentions into certainties. Thus, Whaley argues, the German surprise succeeded because of German intelligence's effective deception in support of the mistaken expectation of an ultimatum and because of the Russian preconception that the German army was not prepared to fight on two fronts simultaneously. But does preconception or successful deception really provide an explanation? Is it not a tautology to contend that a statesman was deceived because he accepted a mistaken assumption? The crucial question is why the mistaken assumption was not corrected, even when strong contrary information was available as in this event. Moreover, in instances of successful deception, the information supporting the deception has to counter contradictory information; otherwise, successful deceptions would not be that difficult to perpetrate and would occur much more often than they do. The successful deception leads to acceptance of supporting information and rejection or neglect of contradictory information. Why did the information supporting the successful deception win out? The elegance and sophistication of a deception are simply factors that may increase the capability of the information they are supporting to counter contradictory and often more reliable information, but they do not necessarily accord it preference.

The same considerations apply to the attempt to explain misperceptions springing from the difficulty of distinguishing between noises and
signals (Wohlstetter, 1962). This problem does indeed exist, given the
nature of information in the international arena. But what about instances where the information does make this distinction possible? It is
not a sufficient explanation to suggest that the difficulty of distinguishing
between noises and signals is maintained by the adversary's intentional
deception (Wohlstetter, 1965). This is so for the reasons already given
showing the unsatisfactory nature of the argument about deception and
also because it does not cover situations where the adversary made no
attempts at deception and yet misperception did occur. A case in point is
Nehru's misperception of the likelihood of attack on the eve of the war
with China in 1962, when the Chinese made no attempt whatsoever to
conceal their intentions or their preparations. Still, he was taken completely by surprise when, in October 1962, the Chinese army struck from
Tibet into the disputed areas (Vertzberger, 1984a).

The inadequacy of surprise-attack studies is further borne out by a
comparative, comprehensive analysis of the subject by Betts (1982). Although the chapters attempting to provide a causal explanation of surprise contain important insights, they incoherently introduce a list of
possible explanatory variables at different levels of aggregation (the individual, the organization, the state) ranging from prominent to marginal
ones without an effort to systematically evaluate the importance of each
in different contingencies. The explanations go back and forth between
information processing variables (the surprised) and behavioral variables
(the surpriser) and do not distinguish between causes and symptoms. We
remain in the dark with regard to which variables explain what type of
surprise, because the author fails to produce a significant typology of
cases or explanations except for the most rudimentary one.

In this sense Kam's (1988) multiple case analysis as well as Handel's
(1976, 1977) and Shlaim's (1976) single case studies appear to be more
satisfactory, presenting analyses that are methodologically sounder in
that they define explicitly the different levels of explanation, the independent variables, and the causal links; the same applies to a more general analysis of surprise by Morgan (1983). But these studies too have
one or more of the lacunae discussed above.

Two recent studies attempt to avoid information processing variables.
Hybel (1986) traces the logic of surprise to provide both would-be surprisers and would-be victims a handle on how to surprise the rival or
avoid being surprised. The key variables explaining the disposition to
resort to surprise and the achievement of success are the surprisers' beliefs in their capability to control the victims' sense of vulnerability and

level of mistrust and the surprisers' ability to accurately estimate their adversaries' sense of vulnerability. But how do they make an accurate assessment? What are the obstacles to judging accurately? And when are surprisers able to affect their adversaries' perceptions of self in the desired direction? Without answering these questions, the prescription for successful surprise is not likely to be practical, and the answers are missing from the study.

Analyzing the causes for success or failure of surprise, Levite (1987) rejects the findings indicating that pathologies in information processing are responsible for the success of surprise on the ground that the researchers assume that a warning was indeed available to the target but that barriers to receptivity operated. How is it possible, he argues, that the same barriers operated to cause surprise in some cases but not in others? This argument misperceives the nature of information processing pathologies. The fact that sources of such pathologies exist does not mean that the pathologies will be present in every single instance of information processing, but only that they may be present. He is correct, however, in saying that the available literature on surprise does not specify the conditions under which pathologies will be present. Moreover, as will be maintained later in this chapter, misperceptions sometimes do not lead to policy failures (e.g. Israel's intelligence failure preceding the Six Day War), so surprise does not always bring the expected benefit to the initiator.

Levite's emphasis on the quality of strategic warning raises the same question he raised with regard to other studies: How can cases of surprise be explained where a high-quality strategic warning was available to the target (e.g. India's surprise by China's attack in 1962 or U.S. surprise by the Tet offensive in 1968)? He could respond that in those cases the strategic warning was not high quality, because his notion of the quality of warning is fuzzy. Levite recognizes the quality of warning only in retrospect; where a surprise did not work, the quality of strategic warning was not of high enough quality. Such ex post facto reasoning is not useful to explantion, prediction, or prescription.

Levite argues further that rational incentives for avoiding strategic surprise because of its high cost necessarily cause decisionmakers to be receptive to hard intelligence data. This flies in the face of a growing body of literature in the social sciences refuting that argument and stressing the impact of motivational and unmotivational biases causing errors and closed-mindedness. Finally, he emphasizes how critical the reliability attributed to the source of warning by the warned is, but as we know, judgments of credibility are manipulable by the adversary and are highly subjective; the interesting question is, When and how can an adversary manipulate a target's perception of the reliability of particular sources? This by necessity should lead us back to information processing variables that Levite attempted to avoid.

In the final analysis, surprise is a by-product of information processing and hence should be treated as such and not as an independent issue. A logical follow-up of this argument is that diplomatic surprise is in the same category of faulty information processing as military surprise and falls under the same general rubric of outcomes, namely, surprise. It is then self-evident that the causes for diplomatic surprise are much the same as those for military surprise and that the two are equally difficult to anticipate. Hence the conclusions to this effect in Handel's (1980, 1981) painstaking comparative studies are hardly unexpected.

The seminal works of Jervis (1969, 1970, 1976) substantially advanced our understanding of information processing and perception in international politics. As such, his studies are a category in themselves and are of indispensable importance. Still, they too contain a number of significant problems that should be noted. First, Jervis makes no clear or systematic distinction between the static aspects of perception and the dynamic ones; that is, there is no systematic analysis of the pattern of change over time. Nor does Jervis clearly distinguish between sources and symptoms of misperception. The line between the descriptive aspect of his theory and its explanatory aspect is often blurred. For example, certain hypotheses (Jervis, 1969) say that states tend to see other states as more hostile than they actually are and their behavior as more organized and coordinated than it really is. Both cases are symptoms and descriptions and not, as the author implies, sources of misperception.

Another study (Jervis, 1970) focuses on the dynamics of the signaling system between actors in the international arena and on manipulation of this system to influence the adversary's perceptions. It does not, however, deal adequately with the essential questions, What renders such manipulation possible, and why do certain manipulations succeed and others do not when the same quantity and quality of relevant information are at the actor's disposal? This study, then, is concerned mainly with characterizing different patterns of signaling behavior without actually explaining systematically the causes governing the failure or effectiveness of signaling patterns and the consequent changes in each actor's image of the other.

Second, precisely because of the author's implied aspiration, in his most comprehensive effort (Jervis, 1976), to present a general theory of perception in international politics, it is all the more striking that basically the study remains eclectic. This is best exemplified by Chapters 8 and 9, where Jervis deals with common misperceptions but does not relate them to the sources and explanations analyzed in the preceding chapters. Since the causal links between dependent and independent variables are not fully specified, what he ends up with are sets of hypotheses that are additive but do not come together in an integrative form.[1] It is no wonder that although Jervis's studies contain numerous historical examples, neither he nor any other scholar using his theoretical framework has attempted a case study in depth. What was used in explaining case histories were portions of the mentioned studies by Jervis. Taking into account the loose structural coherence in these studies, their use in full as a theory for analyzing a particular case study is highly problematic.

Third, Jervis's study of perception and misperception is unidimensional on a number of counts. Its explanatory variables are all psychological, whereas social (group and organizational) and societal-cultural variables have been ignored. Jervis also attributes the major explanatory power to a single human need—the drive for balance and order—which in turn leads to the development of simple rules for processing information. This is an overgeneralization (cf. Nisbett and Ross, 1980: 234–35; M. Steiner, 1983: 411) as well as a reductionist approach. The human psyche is too complex to be described as dominantly motivated by a single need; sometimes it may be but not as a rule. Attribution theory, which Jervis utilizes only marginally, could attest to this point, not to mention needs that have their source in social pressures and cultural socialization. Moreover, if, as some studies suggest (e.g. Hiniker, 1969), cognitive consistency is a cultural trait, it cannot be treated as a general explanation without taking the cultural context into account.

Mandel looks to the cluster phenomena of misperceptions, faulty decisions, and conflicts for an explanation and asserts that "those [tensions] generating distorted perceptions, inappropriate decisions and severe conflict are quite similar and are readily grouped together" (1979: 11). The strength of his study lies in its recognition of the need to integrate the effects of individual, group-level, and societal-level processes. But on the whole, the elaboration of this insight is vague and problematic on a number of counts. In the first place, it is not clear what exactly is explained, that is, what such a general term as distorted perceptions entails and how different types and levels of distortion cause inappropriate decisions and severe conflicts. Nor are inappropriate decisions specified. How inappropriate is inappropriate? What are severe conflicts? How can they be distinguished from ones that are not, or does it make a difference at all?

Second, in Mandel's analysis severe conflicts are invariably associated with misperceptions; but, as I have already contended, misperceptions can also lead to conflict avoidance.

Third, Mandel uses a typology of sources of pernicious outcomes that differentiates temporal tensions (between present and past) from spatial tensions (between the self and others) but neglects to deal with tensions within the self; the last are discussed only in passing in the context of temporal tensions. In focusing on tensions, he also fails to deal with inherent human cognitive constraints, which have little to do directly with tensions of one type or another. In the same manner the analysis of consequences of information, which are the building blocks of perception, is limited to a discussion of ambiguity; ambiguity, however, is only one aspect of the problems arising from the nature of information in general and from international-politics-related information in particular.

Finally, the core typology of two types of tension has only limited value as an organizing concept and little descriptive or explanatory power and utility. On the whole, the study does not manage to integrate the different sources of pernicious outcomes. What emerges is an incohesive study that does not provide a comprehensive approach, as could have been expected from the author's declared intention.

Lebow's (1981) work on misperceptions in crises is significant for a number of reasons. He recognizes the need to reconcile and integrate various psychological perspectives (e.g. the cognitive and motivational) and emphasizes the different levels of explanatory variables: individual, bureaucratic-organizational, and national. But like other studies already mentioned, his too takes an undifferentiated approach to misperception and cognitive closure. Furthermore, in spite of the comprehensiveness of the study's empirical case histories, it lacks theoretical and conceptual rigor and elaboration. Lebow does not go beyond outlining the explanatory variables in general terms, which makes his study less instructive in this sense than could have been expected from his broad overall approach.

J. S. Levy (1983) recognizes the need for a typology of the forms of misperception and specifies the causal links between misperceptions and their outcomes, but the study is limited to war-related perceptions. As a consequence, his typology consists of a distinction between misperceptions of intention, capability, and third-state behavior, but it fails to encompass the whole potential range of perceptual distortions; it is in fact not a typology of misperception phenomena but rather of the specific content of misperceptions, which is a completely different thing and which by definition has limited external validity.

The earlier works by De Rivera (1968) and the important study by George (1980a) are both comprehensive and attuned to the need to deal with the multiple variables affecting information processing at the individual, group, and organizational levels. Yet whereas De Rivera deals in some detail with group and organizational variables, but only very generally with their core element, the individual, George considers the individual decisionmaker in more detail, but group and organizational processes only briefly. Both, however, pay insufficient attention to, or neglect altogether, the attributes of the information itself as well as the societal context and its effects on information processing and choice. De Rivera's study poses another problem, of making only fuzzy distinctions about which variables and explanations refer to the information processing stage of decisionmaking and which to the choice stage.

To sum up, then, international relations research on information processing and its perceptual consequences is flawed in a number of areas. First, it fails to distinguish between descriptive analysis and causal explanation. That is, some of the studies that profess to explain the phenomenon merely describe it without outlining its causes.

Second, some of the research is reductionist in nature (cf. Ben-Zvi, 1976–77) and propounds single-variable explanations. But even most multivariate studies are unidimensional in the sense that all the variables are drawn from one context of human activity or one discipline.[2] Complex situations are thus reduced to one dimension as though that dimension alone could explain much of the phenomenon under study or could exist independent of the broad aspects of the problem.

A third shortcoming is overgeneralization. Variables are presented in the most general way, lacking precision, and often without clarifying exactly what they include. The meaning and scope of variables like personality and national style are so broad that they end up having limited utility as explanations of particular cases. At the same time, using such umbrella variables provides a false sense of parsimony. Another aspect of overgeneralization is the failure to distinguish between the static and dynamic aspects of misperception and the various forms each can take, that is, between different types of outcome and adaptation process.

The fourth type of shortcoming, eclecticism in research, appears to be linked in some way with the preceding one. Even multivariate studies often fail to bind the different variables together into a coherent conceptual system. Whereas a rich, albeit disparate, accumulation of research efforts on information processing, cognition, social perception, and misperception exists, research as it applies to foreign policy is additive rather than integrative. Furthermore, overgeneralization and lack of a more differentiated approach to such a complex and diversified phenomenon as information processing hinders the emergence of a typological theory, which is a necessary condition for an accurate description and a powerful and sophisticated explanation (George, 1979a: 59) of information processing and the quality of its outcomes. Thus there has been a failure to improve the descriptive and explanatory power of the theory and make it more policy relevant (George and Smoke, 1974: 511; George, 1980a: 243) through contingent predictions and discriminating diagnoses.

Having demonstrated the need for an integrated theory of information processing, I can now outline briefly the aim of this study: to draw together various threads of arguments, approaches, and explanations and weave them systematically into a comprehensive explanatory theory that could provide practical guidance for further empirical and theoretical research (Kuhn, 1970: 10). Information processing cannot be understood by means of a single-variable or unidimensional approach. The study will attempt, therefore, to treat variables and rationales advanced by diverse and different perspectives and disciplines, not separately or in competition with each other, but as complementary multicausal explanations and sources of information processing behavior. This approach should make it possible to formulate an effective, multidisciplinary gestalt theory.

Spreading such a wide net contravenes the prevailing emphasis on parsimony. However, when dealing with the complex, multifaceted, social-cognitive activity of information processing and the variety of related contingent outcomes, parsimonious theoretical elegance may have to be sacrificed for the sake of the internal validity and reliability of the explanatory theory. The true nature of the elephant of information processing cannot be grasped if one is overinfatuated with parsimony.

The Attributes of Foreign-Policy-related Information

Information processing is a human activity as universal, natural, unavoidable, and continuous as breathing. It is performed by every individual, group, and organization and is in all fields of endeavor. But different issue-areas, subjects, and circumstances call for different degrees of sophistication in information processing and emphases on different processing modes or combinations of modes and consequently for different types and combinations of variables to come into play; they also create possibilities for error, for cognitive avoidance and conservatism, and for inappropriate adjustment to new information. Even the scientific community, supposedly socialized to be open-minded toward new information, has had difficulties following this norm in its search for scientific truth (Broad and Wade, 1982). As the physicist Max Planck cynically observed: "An important scientific innovation rarely makes its way by gradually winning over and converting its opponents: it rarely happens that Saul becomes Paul. What does happen is that its opponents gradually die out and that the growing generation is familiarized with the idea from the beginning"(quoted in Broad and Wade, 1982: 135). Foreign policy, then, is not the only, and perhaps not even the main, area affected by imperfect information processing (and hence by misperception), but it is one that offers an important and instructive demonstration of the problems involved. Relations between actors in the international arena take place in conditions that make information processing tasks particularly prone to bias and error; misperceptions are propagated and sustained with particularly serious consequences, such as loss of life, material damage, and wounded national morale. The price may be exacted not only from the nation whose leaders erred but, in an international system marked by mutual interdependence, also from other nations that are unavoidably entangled.

Decisionmakers are aware that knowledge is power and, like power, can be distributed asymmetrically. They may wish to preserve a distribution of knowledge that favors their interests or change it if the current balance is perceived to favor the adversary. Since the balance of knowledge can be affected through the denial or manipulation of information, a number of situations can be distinguished. In one prototype Actor A assumes or knows that an opponent, Actor B, has acquired information, but this information is not perceived to affect the outcome of issues in dispute. Nonaction is the most likely reaction. A second prototype is when Actor A is aware of Actor B's attempts, or assumes that Actor B may make attempts, to acquire important information relevant to the outcome of their dispute. Actor A's most likely reaction is to deny such information to the opponent by using secrecy and deception. A third prototype emerges when Actor B has already acquired the information that may affect outcomes in his favor and Actor A is aware of it. This prototype has two subtracks. In one, Actor B is unaware of the significance the information may have and Actor A tries to prevent his realizing its significance, using both deception and secrecy. Alternatively, Actor B may be fully aware of the significance of the information and how it could be used to his advantage. Actor A may then try to raise false uncertainty about the credibility of the information or confuse or distort its interpretation to encourage the adversary not to use it. Deception and disinformation are the main means to these ends. A different way of influencing the balance of knowledge is through increasing personal knowledge. A less informed actor can invest resources in the collection and interpretation of information on all, or only on a selective range of, issues. This pattern can be used in tandem with the patterns that are directed at manipulating the other side.

Certain attributes may give the advantage to a specific actor in implementing one of these patterns of behavior. For example, closed societies can more easily deny knowledge to rival open societies than open societies can to them. On the other hand, a technologically advanced society can gain easier access to information about its less technologically advanced opponent, even if the adversary's is a closed society, than the opponent can gain about it. The participants are aware of their areas of relative advantage, and the mix of patterns chosen—denial, manipulation, and self-improvement—are likely to be decided accordingly.

As all participants in the game of nations play simultaneously according to these patterns and are usually aware of these facts, they are never sure how successful they have been in manipulating information or denying it to their opponents; as Goffman observes, "Information is the hardest to guard, since it can be stolen without removing it" (1969: 78–79). At the same time they are constantly uncertain how credible the information acquired by themselves is. Hence, actors need not only knowledge about the environment but also knowledge about knowledge; they need to know how much others know, what the quality of their knowledge is, and what these others know about one's knowledge of their knowledge. The acquisition of both knowledge and knowledge about knowledge is critically hampered by the nature of information and the patterns of behavior in international politics, as will be discussed later in this section.[3] The coping strategies designed to deal with the effects of these characteristics of information processing, whether they are latent or manifest, conscious or unconscious, systematic or heuristic, are discussed in the following chapters. Although they may be necessary and unavoidable, they may also impede accurate perception and understanding of the environment and ultimately of successful foreign policy decisionmaking.

The accuracy of perceptions depends on the effectiveness of information processing. But the realm of international politics presents decisionmakers with particular difficulties in carrying out the basic tasks of information processing: search, evaluation, and revision. The difficulties stem from some of the attributes of the environment that is the source of the information, as well as from the nature of the information itself. Here we must examine the possible components of the generic term information (Fig. 1):

Occurrence. Anything happening in the actor's environment, whether it originates in a specific intended decision or from random circumstances

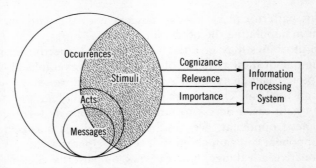

Fig. 1. The components of information.

or from a process (such as a change in the structure of the international system).

Act. A specific behavior (including verbal behavior) stemming from a decision by an actor with the authority and power to commit resources for carrying out the specific behavior. Every act is an occurrence, but not all occurrences are acts. An act is limited in time and space, but an occurrence may not be.

Message. An act or occurrence that results from a decision of the actor and that has a specific, predetermined target. The message may not necessarily reach, or be perceived as a message by, the defined target. Every message is an act, but not all acts are messages.

Stimulus. An occurrence, act, or message that penetrates the cognitive system of a given actor. Every message may become a stimulus, but not all stimuli are messages, though they may be perceived as such.

For an occurrence, act, or message to become a stimulus, that is, to penetrate the decisionmakers' cognitive systems, the decisionmakers must allocate attention and give meaning to the information in question so that it makes sense. To that end decisionmakers involved with information processing face a number of critical questions; these are, in the logical order of their appearance:

1. Is what they are dealing with truly informative?
2. If it is informative, is it relevant to the problems with which they are occupied?
3. If it is relevant, is it important?
4. If it is relevant and important, which of a set of possible alternative interpretations is the correct one?

The answer given to any of these questions may lead to a Type 1 or a Type 2 error. A Type 1 error is made when what should have been

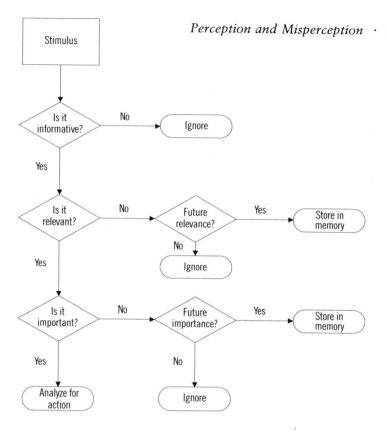

Fig. 2. Information assessment flow.

grasped as information is rejected—that is, it did not penetrate the cognitive system—or when information that should have been considered relevant is rejected as irrelevant, or when information that should have been assessed as important is dismissed as unimportant. A Type 2 error is made when noise and static are perceived as meaningful information (as will be discussed below), or when information that should have been rejected as irrelevant is seen as relevant, or when information that should have been evaluated as unimportant is regarded as important. Making an error when determining the correct interpretation of the information usually implies making both a Type 1 and a Type 2 error simultaneously, as the rejection of a correct interpretation (Type 1) is concurrent with the adoption of an incorrect one (Type 2), except, that is, when the rejection of one interpretation is not followed by the adoption of another because no acute need is felt for a definition of the situation (Fig. 2).

What makes avoiding mistakes of one type or another difficult and potentially bias bound are the following characteristics of the international political environment:

1. *Multiplicity of actors.* The international society is dense with actors. Their multiplicity produces large quantities of stimuli flowing into the information processing systems of the participating actors. The systems have difficulties in allocating attention and in absorbing and systematically decoding information. Decisionmakers are subject to distractions and cannot fully assimilate all information available. At the same time each actor participates simultaneously in a number of games on different issues, which may become intermixed, and receives feedback from several sources, increasing the overload and making the information still more complex. As Simon has pointed out: "In a world where information is relatively scarce, and where problems for decision are few and simple, information is almost always a positive good. In a world where attention is a major scarce resource, information may be an expensive luxury, for it may turn our attention from what is important to what is unimportant" (1978a: 13).

Furthermore, actors—states, international organizations, and nonstate actors—are not unitary but are comprised of a number of subactors or bureaucratic bodies that struggle for influence over policymaking (Allison, 1969, 1971). The subactors contribute to the quantity of information; the multiplicity of interpretations given to specific bits of information as they are made to fit with each subactor's particular goals; and the accumulation of noise and static in the communication system. The final result is an increased probability that those dealing with the gathering and processing of information will be confused.[4]

Actor and subactor density in the environment thus inhibits both effective *horizontal integration* of information, that is, the fusion of information from various sources and on different issues into a coherent and comprehensive picture, and *vertical integration* of information, that is, the fusion of all decision-relevant information in the decision process.

2. *Technological accessibility.* At the same time that the amount of foreign-policy-related information produced by domestic and foreign actors has grown in a quantum leap, the technological revolution in monitoring, surveillance, interception, and communication has made much of that information accessible. In fact, intelligence organizations have an inherent propensity for lack of restraint and indiscrimination in gathering information about foreign actors that is enhanced by the availability of new, sophisticated hardware for collating it (Bracken, 1983: 31–34; Feldman and March, 1981; L. K. Johnson, 1983; Levine, Samet,

and Brahlek, 1975). But the capabilities of intelligence organizations to analyze and interpret information have not kept up with the growth in the quantity of information they are able to gather.

Furthermore, modern communication technology allows the decision-making center to control and monitor, in real time, all activities in the periphery. Consequently the responsibility and accountability of top decisionmakers for activities of local military commanders or diplomats abroad has increased, compared with the past, when the lower echelons had more autonomy and could not be controlled directly. This account-ability contributed significantly to the demand for and supply of infor-mation at the decisionmaking center about activities of domestic actors. The combined effect of multiplying actors and sophisticated technology creates a problem of information overload for decisionmakers that will be discussed in detail in Chapter 2.

3. *Deception.* The use of deception has been tacitly accepted as quasi-legitimate in relations between states, and states have learned to expect it as a way of life. It was Sir Henry Wolton who described an ambassador as "an honest man who is sent abroad to lie for the good of his country." Actors attempt to mislead and manipulate target actors by disseminating incorrect or only partially correct facts and interpretations to create de-sired expectations and conceptions. As a result, it may become difficult to distinguish between and accurately interpret the following stimuli and messages:

a. *Signals.* Statements or acts, the significance of which has been de-cided on by explicit or implicit agreement between actors. Both sender and receiver are aware that their signals may express either true or false facts.

b. *Indices.* Statements or acts that, in contrast to signals, contain in their substance proof that the facts they express cannot be false. An example is an act whose cost is too high to have been carried out just to deceive the opponent. In other words, the action is intrinsically connected to the true intentions and capacities of the actor who performed it (Jervis, 1970: 18).

c. *Noise.* Misleading signals, either deliberately transmitted or gener-ated by random effects, that do not have relevance and significance in the context of the issue at hand but that are interpreted by an actor as containing relevant and significant information (Holst, 1966; Wohlstet-ter, 1962: 3; Wohlstetter, 1965). However, once the target actor identi-fies a signal as an adversary's hoax, it can become an indication of the adversary's actual intentions.

d. *Static.* Stimuli that distract the attention of the decisionmaker from relevant events, signals, and indices or mask their actual meaning or importance. The stimuli causing the distracting effects are not themselves given a meaning associated with the issue in question. The decisionmaker may be unaware of their effects and, even if aware, unable to do much about the masking effects. The sources of static can be domestic events— such as an election campaign that dominates the decisionmaker's time and attention—or dramatic, attention-grabbing events in other parts of the international system. In Austria on September 29, 1973, for example, two Palestinian terrorists hijacked a train carrying Soviet Jewish immigrants on its way from Moscow to Vienna. They took five immigrants and an Austrian customs official hostage and demanded a plane to carry them and their hostages to an Arab country. The Austrian prime minister, Bruno Kreisky, agreed to close down the immigration transfer camp in Schönau, near Vienna, for the release of the hostages. The terrorists accepted. The event and the Austrian surrender to the terrorists dominated the attention of the Israeli government and in particular that of Prime Minister Golda Meir, who went to Vienna to meet Kreisky to persuade him to change his decision—but without succeeding. Whether the hijack, in drawing the Israeli leaders' attention away from the impending Arab military attack, was actually an integral part of the Arab deception plan is not clear (Herzog, 1975: 57; Nakdimon, 1982: 64–66).

e. *Silence.* The transmission of nothing at all on a particular issue, which can serve as a signal or as a means for creating noise. For example, if State A does not respond at all to a declarative behavior of State B on a controversial subject that should have elicited a response, the lack of response could be interpreted as tacit acceptance of State A's declared policy. But it could instead be a signal produced purposefully to deceive State A into thinking that its behavior is acceptable so as not to alert it to future responses planned by State B. Silence could also reflect that B is unaware of A's behavior or that B does not know how to respond or cannot make up its mind how to respond (e.g. because of disagreements within the decisionmaking group). Hence it is neither a signal nor a purposefully generated noise but becomes an unintentionally produced noise when it is interpreted by one of the participants as tacit but meaningful communication.

Thus, the potential multifunctional character of stimuli leads to difficulties in understanding and interpretation, which can result either from the opponent's intentional behavior or from one side's apprehension that the opponent intends to deceive, leading to doubts whether specific information is static, noise, or a signal. Such doubts originate in the recognition that bargaining power and other advantages in international politics are related to the ability to deceive and pretend to influence expectations and, as a result, behavior (Daniel and Herbig, 1982a,b; Schelling, 1970: 23).

The cost of deception as an acceptable norm of behavior is also reflected in the inability of actors to exchange information even when it is in the best interest of both sides. This is the consequence of the lemon principle, a market failure noted by Akerlof (1970). In a nutshell, he argues that dishonest car dealers drive honest car dealers out of the market, even though there may be potential sellers and buyers in the appropriate price range. Prospective buyers know that they cannot reliably determine when a used car is a lemon. They insist on paying less than the real value; the owners may be unwilling to sell; and mutually profitable deals therefore do not take place. Similarly, in the exchange of mutually profitable information between international actors, the actors on one side may fear that they are being misled or deceived and so ask for additional assurance by demanding more definitive or higher quality information. However, the other side may see the demand as unacceptable for fear of risking other goals (e.g. relations with other international and domestic actors). Hence an exchange of information that is in principle mutually necessary and beneficial is avoided, affecting the possibility of reaching agreement and reducing or avoiding tensions or worse.

4. *Secrecy.* Actors on the international scene tend to keep a great deal of information required by other actors under a curtain of secrecy. The result is a shortage of information classified as sensitive, or at least a subjective sense of such a lack. On the other hand, what is defined as mundane, routine, redundant, and not particularly desirable information seems to be relatively abundant. The greater the demand for the first kind and the less its availability, the higher the price consumers are willing to pay for it. A main consequence of the rise in price is the lowering of the threshold for critical appraisal of the information's reliability. In other words, consumers accept desired information as true, even if it does not stand up to all the criteria of reliability and validity. They expose themselves to manipulation by adversaries who will make access to information even more difficult and then plant deceptive information (Goffman, 1969: 62–63). To illustrate: Theodore Shackly, chief of the Central Intelligence Agency (CIA) station in Saigon (1969–72), was unsatisfied with the station's accomplishments and pushed its personnel hard to recruit more agents. In 1974 over a hundred Vietcong "agents" were discovered to be fabricators who knew nothing of Communist plans and who cleverly patched together information from newspaper stories and gossip to look like valid intelligence (Snepp, 1978: 13).

The irony is that secrecy, which is actually directed toward the opponent, has side effects—reduction of the costs of lying to one's own people and confirmation of the need-to-know principle, which inhibits sharing information with associates. To avoid the leaking of secret information, access to it is strictly curtailed even to members of one's own bureaucracy and the organizations that should have it, thus hampering their ability to evaluate the credibility of, effectively deal with, and properly interpret incoming information (Betts, 1980–81: 556; Franck and Weisband, 1974; Kam, 1988: 192–95; Kaiser, 1980; Neubauer, 1977). Furthermore, since not having access usually translates into unawareness of what is actually available, the potential consumers cannot remedy the situation by demanding, bargaining for, or applying pressure to obtain the necessary background information.

This argument does not suggest that secrecy is unnecessary or that the need to know and compartmentalization can be avoided altogether but rather that secrecy has opportunity costs that may turn its gains into a net loss in the overall calculus of information processing quality. Decisionmakers are rarely able to assess or be fully attentive to the net effects of secrecy. Even more disturbing is the fact that top-level decisionmakers do not know exactly how these secrecy-maintaining principles are applied at lower levels, so that even if they mandate adherence to these principles, their ability to control the manner and rationality of their operationalization is limited. A major failure may alert them to the opportunity costs, but by then it is already too late.

Shortage of information about the adversary stemming from secrecy sometimes makes it easier for decisionmakers to justify the adoption of a convenient definition of the situation that serves their political expectations and needs, personal or domestic, even if the definition is not realistic. On the other hand, the shortage of sensitive information increases uncalled-for doubts as to what has already been gathered and processed. And since important information is accepted as secret, increasing its availability may lower its perceived reliability in the eyes of the consumer. Anwar el-Sadat's clear and repeated warnings from 1971, which he described as the "year of decision," that he was preparing for war were ignored and ridiculed, particularly when they were not carried out, in spite of his explanations. When war was indeed launched on October 6, 1973, the Israel Defense Forces (IDF) were caught unprepared.

5. *Nonexistence of information.* Certain kinds of desired information simply do not exist. For example, how is it possible to find information concerning opponents' intentions if they themselves have not yet decided what their intentions are? On the other hand, people tend to assume that important information probably exists. This problem creates difficulties similar to those that result when secrecy gives rise to information short-

age and may lead to the invention of information based mostly on noises or other irrelevant data and to guesswork. The combination of secrecy and uncertainty in issues important to an actor are fertile ground for the creation of rumors (Allport and Postman, [1947] 1972: 33), which are noises that interfere with appropriate attention to and interpretation of relevant information.

6. *Content ambiguity*. Information is likely to have multiple significance and can be given competing interpretations. Even when the information itself is unambivalent, its implications in terms of future results or the reactions it warrants are often not obvious or clear-cut. This ambiguity could be the result either of the content of the specific information or of the actor's awareness that intentional deception by the adversary is an accepted rule of the game. That awareness creates a tendency to look for additional meanings in the information and to attribute ambivalence to it unnecessarily.

Windfalls of accurate information are often rejected as plants, since deception, as all actors are aware, is often based on the supply of seemingly accurate and verifiable data (Daniel and Herbig, 1982a: 17; Handel, 1984: 236) (e.g. Soviet surprise at the German invasion in 1941 in spite of having acquired earlier information warning of German plans). Uncertainty is not necessarily reduced by verification of accuracy. Actors, particularly in adversarial situations, are likely to discount even verified information if they have been deceived before and to prefer reliance on prior beliefs and theories, into which they assimilate the new information or, if that cannot be done, reject or ignore it. To illustrate: information about General Vo Nguyen Giap's overall plan for drawing U.S. and allied forces in Vietnam to the border regions, where they could be pinned down by the North Vietnamese army, freeing the Vietcong and local forces to penetrate, subvert, and attack unprotected populated regions, was available to American intelligence; Giap declared his intentions in September 1967. When Hanoi made no unusual efforts at secrecy with regard to the Tet offensive and an abundance of signals pointed to the forthcoming offensive against the cities, General William C. Westmoreland's staff discounted the evidence as too pat. An American intelligence analyst admitted later: "If we'd gotten the whole battle plan, it would not have been credible to us" (D. R. Palmer, 1978: 169, 179–80). Westmoreland and his staff remained focused on, even obsessed with, the Khe Sanh siege, where they expected a repeat of the 1954 performance at Dien Bien Phu. American forces were pulled out of the cities to face what seemed to be a concentration of North Vietnamese regular forces for an onslaught on the northern provinces. Instead they were surprised by the Tet offensive.

7. *Content inconsistency.* Messages exchanged among nations have several potential audiences: the domestic public, the domestic elite, the opponent's public, the opponent's elite, elites in other countries, and the world public. As a result, even when the content of a particular message is unambivalent, different messages, delivered on the same subject to different potential audiences, may contradict each other. An actor then encounters the difficulty of identifying the message representing the true intentions of the sender.[5] This benefits the sender of the messages by decreasing the costs of cheating; he still can carry out a different behavior than he actually intended, even when the message conveying his true intentions can be pinpointed. If, say, a certain intention, threat, or promise was contained in a message originally meant only for domestic consumption, then, since such a message does exist, he can legitimately carry out the stated behavior, not the originally intended behavior, without losing too much credibility and trustworthiness.

8. *Source ambiguity.* An important criterion for the relevance and salience of a message and its potential to become a stimulus is who initiated it. Is is not always possible to locate the source easily and with certainty, especially when the initiator and the known sender of the message are not one and the same, as when the latter acts as a front or proxy.

9. *Issue linkage.* A main feature of an interdependent world is that issues are arranged horizontally rather than hierarchically, which also means that both causes and outcomes in one issue area are affected by occurrences, acts, and developments in a number of other issue areas, thereby creating "a dense policy space" (Keohane, 1984: 79). The increased variety and quantity of information that becomes relevant to any particular problem requires an increased share of the decisionmaker's attention. The outcome of the combined effects of an increase in complexity and a decrease of hierarchy in information systems is a demand for a step-level rise in the decisionmaker's memory and computational capacities (Simon, 1981). Such a burden is often beyond the cognitive capabilities of a decisionmaker and the organizational and administrative capabilities of the institutional system coping with information processing tasks.

10. *Kinetics.* The picture of the political world must be continuously adjusted and updated as the balance between constants and variables is decisively weighed. Information already processed may change its relevance, importance, or meaning. Thus the search for new information and its interpretation and reinterpretation must be an ongoing process. The kinetic character of information about the political world places heavy

demands on the information processor's attentiveness, absorption, and comprehension capabilities. Ironically, information acquisition and its correct interpretation may lead, in some cases, to losing the advantage of knowing, since knowledge can make what is known useless. For example, accurate intelligence about the location of opponents' military formations, positions, or intentions could lead to their reacting by changing their plans—thus making the knowledge acquired useless.

11. *Modularity.* Information is frequently composed of multiple data items that have to be interpreted as a whole rather than singly. Yet there is rarely a single self-imposing logic that determines the order of the different items. Different organization sequences imposed on the data items by the processor produce different and sometimes contradicting definitions of a situation. Modularity introduces a kaleidoscopic effect into information processing and enhances uncertainty. Proving the superiority of one arrangement and the superior validity of the resultant definition of the situation over another is often difficult. Debates within intelligence communities regarding interpretation of the situation are rooted in this attribute, with the sides to the debate using the same data items but ordering and organizing them differently to support their views.

The result of the barriers to processing difficulties is a state of complex uncertainty.[6] Not only are foreign policy decisionmakers often faced with a lack of information about the probability of occurrence of specific outcomes, which is the first dimension of complex uncertainty, but they may also lack reliable information about three additional dimensions. To start with, what is the range of possible outcomes? Can decisionmakers be imaginative enough to anticipate the unthinkable in a world where the bizarre and unpredictable have become common? Modern social forces and technology have given rise to a growing number of states and non-state actors that have at their disposal the means to do that which strains credulity. Even when the probability of such unanticipated outcomes is low, they cannot be dismissed from decisionmakers' agendas because of their potential, devastating costs (e.g. a successful blowing-up of an active nuclear reactor by a terrorist group). At the same time accurate quantitative assessment of the probabilities of hard-to-model events and of very small probabilities is often extremely difficult (Fairley, 1977; Fischhoff, 1983). In discussing the calculations for a decision to use nuclear weapons, Morgan correctly observes that "The sensible decisionmaker considering attack is inhibited not by the prospect of large costs so much as by his inability to calculate the costs at all. To attack is to step into the unknown where the consequences could be terrible—not just if the worst happens but because it is not clear just what the worst is" (1977: 116). The range of possible outcomes is, then, the second dimension of complex uncertainty.

Coping and preventive actions require information about when the specific outcome will take place or, if the exact timing cannot be pinpointed, at least knowledge about the time range within which it could occur. Temporal uncertainty is enhanced by the possible occurrence of highly unlikely events, because they are the most difficult to place in time. Dangerous possibilities about which one does not have any notion of timing create more stress than those about which one has such a notion (Close, 1979). Timing is the third dimension of complex uncertainty.

Finally, there is uncertainty about the event-outcome sequence. Alternate paths to a specific outcome may pass through different sequences of events. To prevent or facilitate that outcome, the decisionmaker would have to predict correctly the sequence of events leading to it; correct prediction would enable intervention to produce the most preferred outcome or to prevent the least preferred one from occurring (which is not the same). The other side of the coin is that the same sequence may lead to different outcomes and sometimes to unanticipated ones. Event-outcome sequence is then the fourth dimension of complex uncertainty. What complicates things still further is the interdimensional interaction, that is, the interdependence among dimensions. For example, knowledge of the sequence may affect knowledge about timing, probability, and range of outcomes.[7]

Awareness of this wide range of difficulties, the constant need to deal with the problems that they present in connection with the reliability and validity of available information, the high level of uncertainty faced, the resultant complexity, and on the other hand the increasing challenge of making decisions that necessitate at least a minimum of reliable information create a conscious or unconscious need to set standards and criteria, arbitrary or otherwise, of acceptability. Without such criteria decisionmakers will find themselves helpless to perform their functions. Hence, information processing encompasses all the rules, schemata, reference points, heuristics, and other procedures, such as deductive logic, of constructing alternative symbolic formats (W. L. Bennett, 1982: 188), which are applied properly or improperly to the data at hand to establish a coherent, sensible picture of the environment. This need makes decisionmakers' coping behavior more predictable because "greater uncertainty will cause behavioral rules to be more restrictive in eliminating particular actions or response patterns to potential information. This will further constrain behavior to simpler, less sophisticated patterns which are easier for an observer to recognize and predict. Therefore, greater uncertainty will cause rule-governed behavior to exhibit increasingly predictable regularities, so that uncertainty becomes the basic source of predictable behavior" (Heiner, 1983: 570). At the same time the potential for biases that could affect the accuracy of information processing make misperception in the domain of international politics more likely and pervasive than in most other domains. This is the case, not because each of the problems discussed above is in itself unique to international politics, but because their cumulation and severity in that field is acute. Misperception is especially unfortunate here in that it endangers some of the most vital interests of human society.

Some Epistemological Assumptions and Problems

Information processing is the purposeful behavior by which any individual, group, or organization becomes cognizant of, handles, manages, resolves, or controls complexity and uncertainty and their consequences. The outcomes or consequences are manifested in the cognitive-perceptual field, that is, in image formation and its end product—the cognitive, evaluative, and affective consciousness of the environmental stimuli. That being the case, the quality of the process can be evaluated against its product by determining the accuracy of perception or, in other words, the extent of misperception produced. Misperception can then be defined and measured in terms of the discrepancy between the real (objective) world and the mental (subjective) world. In this the current study follows the ecological approach introduced into the study of international relations in the mid-1950s (Sprout and Sprout, 1956, 1962, 1969), which has gained broad acceptance across the social sciences. It contends that the connection between the environment and a decision is not direct but is mediated by subjective perceptual representation (or psychological climate) and the construction of the environment in the decisionmaker's mind.[8] The critical input in the decisionmaking process is thus the perception of the environment rather than the real environment. The outcomes of decision implementation reshape the environment, but at the same time the environment operates as a constraint on the range of decisions that can be taken, on their implementation, and on the possible outcomes of a decision. The intricate interactive process involving the environment, its perception, a decision, its implementation, and outcomes is schematized in Fig. 3.

Often enough, images do not coincide exactly with reality.[9] This bears decisively on the essential nature of relations between states. The image each holds of the other, and of the decisional and behavioral constraints

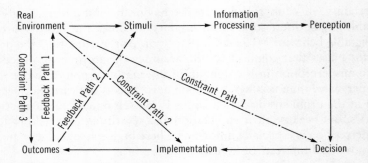

Fig. 3. Environment-decision-outcomes nexus. Constraint Path 1 occurs when the environment affects the type of decision that can be taken; Constraint Path 2 occurs when the environment affects the implementation of the decision and thus indirectly the potential range of outcomes; Constraint Path 3 occurs when the environment determines or affects the range of possible outcomes. Feedback Path 1 occurs when outcomes reshape the environment, so the source of further stimuli is in the reshaped environment; Feedback Path 2 occurs when the outcomes themselves become direct inputs. Various combinations of feedback path patterns, constraint path patterns, and constraint with feedback patterns are possible.

imposed by the environment on the self and others, largely determines the nature of relations between actors on the international scene, their patterns of behavior, and their location on the war-peace continuum. The gap between image and reality is liable to be a major factor in the emergence of an illusory discrepancy between the interests of various actors and their notion of viable reactions and remedies to a situation that may lead to conflict generation. Alternatively, misperceptions may account for failure to discern a real discrepancy among the interests, goals, and options of competing actors, and the perception adopted may be shaped by a basic assumption of harmony between interests and goals that are in fact imcompatible. Thus misperception can facilitate conflict avoidance or cooperation (Boulding, 1969; A. A. Stein, 1982). Under certain conditions, however, such conflict avoidance may in the long run breed instability through the generation of an image of weakness by other potential adversaries, leading to war by miscalculation (J. S. Levy, 1983: 87). An obvious example is provided by Neville Chamberlain's dealings with Hitler in 1938. His misperception was to believe Hitler's assurances that his demands with regard to Czechoslovakia were his last demands. The misperception prevented immediate armed conflict but eventually resulted in further demands by Hitler that led to the outbreak of war. Since the quality of decisions is largely influenced by the effective use of information; other things being equal, it is much more likely that the quality of a decision (in terms of desirable outcomes) will be directly related to the quality of information processing and inversely related to the degree of misperception involved.[10]

What has been asserted thus far poses a number of epistemological dilemmas. The first arises from the implied assumption that two realities exist—one objective and the other, the reality perceived by the decision-maker, subjective. This approach takes the objective reality as the rod against which the accuracy of the policymaker's perception is measured to determine the degree of misperception according to the degree of congruence between the perception and objective reality. The obvious question is what justifies the assumption that the observer is indeed competent to determine and define objective reality. Does not the objective reality defined by the researcher in fact constitute a subjective reality or psychological environment? Are we not comparing the psychological environment of the policymaker with that of the researcher? And is not the measuring rod, then, once more a subjective reality of some kind? Indeed, reality as defined by the researcher cannot represent perfect objectivity. Yet since we are dealing with a soft science, we must rest content with qualified objectivity, that is, the researcher's perception of reality, and not allow this to deter us from dealing with the subject and making the best of it.[11] "Truth is both fragile and subtle. . . . Science at its best is thus like a firm but gentle hand that holds a butterfly without crushing it" (Bowers, 1973: 333).

When applying this comparative criterion of the operational-psychological environment in academic research on historical case studies, two important factors favor researchers' objectivity of judgment. One is their noninvolvement. That is, because of their not being affected by or responsible for the decision they are analyzing, they are able to remain more objective than decisionmakers, who carry the burden of personal responsibility without being disciplined by adherence to scholarly standards. The other is the benefit of time perspective. This has two facets when analyzing an event a posteriori. The first concerns information available, that is, information uncovered and accumulated since the event in question took place that may not have been at the policymaker's disposal at the time. The second facet concerns evaluation. The passage of time permits reappraisal of the information formerly at the policymaker's disposal in light of new information (in the Bayesian sense) and also in light of the known outcomes and their consequences. One may, of course, contend that such reappraisal is nothing more than wisdom by hindsight, but what difference should that make? The intellectual interest in learning the correct lessons from the past is precisely to attain wisdom after the event. The questions to be answered are what the reasons for the event are and whether the wisdom acquired after the event was not also within reach before the event, taking into account the amount and quality of information available to the decisionmaker at the time.[12]

Another implicit assumption—that there tends to be a direct relationship between the quality of the decision and the antecedent degree of accuracy of perception—presents a certain difficulty. Has this assumption any theoretical justification? Perhaps the answer is to be found on two planes of argumentation. On the normative-philosophical level, recognition of the human wish and capacity to influence, control, and direct interstate relations, at least to some degree, both in peaceful times and in crises, has always been important. The core notion of crisis and conflict management stems from the need for and belief in this capacity. The belief depends on the probability—as distinguished from the certainty—that a given decision will be the optimal one under the given circumstances. It is more likely to be so the more closely perception of the environment mirrors objective reality.[13] The term probability implies the possible existence of exceptions, the causes of which may well be disclosed by careful examination.

On the other hand, acceptance of the contrary assumption—that it is possible to consistently reach optimal decisions, optimal, that is, in terms of their consequences, irrespective of the extent to which the perceptions involved in the decisions correspond to reality—has an unacceptable implication for scientific analysis. The implication is that the main explanation of interstate relations is chance. This notion has long been rejected by social scientists and historians alike.[14] If it were true, it would follow that relations between the actors on the international scene are predetermined in some inexplicable, unforeseeable, and uncontrollable way. One would then be obliged to stop trying to adjust and improve the nature of the international political environment or the patterns of actors' interactions and to renounce all attempts to establish a basis for any hypothesis or scientific theory whatsoever regarding this social domain, leaving the individual and the state absolutely helpless under the sway of some "unseen hand." That is not to deny the occasional role of chance in causing specific, even major, historical outcomes (e.g. the fate of the Spanish Armada in 1588), but to deny chance a systematic role in shaping history.

On a practical level, a distinction must be drawn between the terms foreign policy and international relations. Foreign policy relates to the state's conduct of its foreign affairs, with stress on the unilateral, self-regarding aspect. International relations concerns the multilateral, reciprocal interactions among the actors in the international system. The extent to which a given foreign policy decision is the optimal one—in terms of maximizing the utility or minimizing the damage to the actor's interest—is not just the product of the unilateral behavior of the state in question; it is largely a function of the reciprocal relations between the political entities concerned, as they react to each other's actions and as the interactive nature of their relations is recognized (cf. Kaplowitz, 1984; Keohane, 1986). Since the interactions between the actors are both strategic and symbolic, the accuracy of actors' images of each other and of the international system in which they operate can assume one of four possible reciprocal modes.

1. Both actors perceive the interactive situation erroneously.

2. Actor A perceives the interactive situation accurately, and Actor B perceives it erroneously.

3. Actor A perceives the interactive situation erroneously, and Actor B perceives it accurately.

4. Both actors perceive the interactive situation accurately.

If an image that is congruent with reality is to produce optimal decisions in terms of their outcomes, both the actors concerned must simultaneously perceive each other and the international system accurately. If, on the other hand, State A's decisionmakers perceive reality accurately, it is enough if the decisionmakers of State B perceive it erroneously to undermine the quality, as measured by results, of the decision that State A reaches. The decisionmakers of State B are liable to misperceive the correct decision by Actor A or perceive inaccurately Actor A's perceptions of Actor B and consequently react in a way that harms the interests of Actor A, a reaction not called for had they perceived Actor A's behavior or perceptions accurately.[15] On the other hand, the negative effects of a suboptimal decision reached on the basis of misperception may well be offset by a misperception of the decision by the actor on whose account the decision was made—that is, misperceptions may compensate for each other. This, however, is largely an uncontrollable outcome.

The conclusion that emerges is that a necessary, though not sufficient, condition for achieving outcome rationality in a strategic-interaction situation is simultaneous process rationality in all participating actors. Process rationality in one actor does not in any way imply outcome rationality even for that same actor.[16] Actually, outcome optimization of foreign policy decisions, among other things, is a function of the capacity of the actors making the decisions to monitor, perceive, and accurately anticipate misperception on the part of their adversaries and adjust themselves to it by building it into their own calculations. This is a tall order and asks much of the decisionmaking system.[17]

Process rationality is more often than not bounded rationality, rather than perfect rationality, however, because of the limitations of individuals and organizations as information processors and problem solvers (Betts, 1978; Dawes, 1976; Fischhoff, 1983; Nisbett and Ross, 1980; Simon, 1985; Slovic, Fischhoff, and Lichtenstein, 1977).[18] Furthermore, a world of interdependence, in which policy issues are interrelated and affect each other and which is characterized by complexity, poses an additional challenge to rationality, because the rationality of each policy sector (issue-area) does not necessarily imply overall coordinated rationality (cf. Gustafsson and Richardson, 1979). There is, then, a trade-off, which has to be recognized by policymakers, between process efficiency, which necessitates the decomposition of problems, and process rationality.

This suggests a certain level of misperception is inevitable in every decisionmaking system. A normal failure in information processing is distinct from systematic failure; that is, even though the process that produced misperceptions was flawless, it still resulted in failure.[19] Hence, the art of choosing between competing interpretations of information may well not necessarily involve the ability to choose between accurate images and misperceptions of the environment but rather the ability to choose between different potential misperceptions. The choice has to be made according to the criterion of the least damage done, that is, the principle of rationality. For example, if one possible consequence of a state of anxiety and stress is sometimes likely to be, among other things, misperception of the time factor—a sense that the time available for response is shorter than it in fact is (O. R. Holsti, 1972a)—this misperception may, in certain circumstances, be preferable to a lack of anxiety and stress, which is likely to lower the decisionmakers' alertness to important stimuli and lead them to believe they have plenty of time to make up their minds and no need for an immediate decision. Even if no decisionmaking system is immune to misperception, and every such system is liable to be vulnerable to its consequences, such as military and diplomatic surprise (Betts, 1978; Handel, 1977; Kam, 1988), still, a degree of control over its consequences should be aimed at, and may even be secured, by understanding the sources and types of possible misperceptions and then choosing consciously among them according to the minimax principle, that is, by minimizing the maximum loss. Information processing could then become an instrument for hedging and preventive policymaking more than a means to maximize benefits.

Real and Psychological Environments: Constraints and Content

The definition of the dimensions and content of the real and the psychological environments is crucial, as the discrepancy between the two has been posited as an indicator of misperception. The two environments can each be described as containing two circles of components: the outer circle, which marks the limits imposed on the actors' behavioral options, and the inner circle, which includes the specific details of the definition of the situation. Seven dimensions determine the structural constraints on behavior that are imposed by the real environment and that draw the boundaries within which actors' coping must take place (cf. Moos, 1973):

1. *The ecological dimension.* Constraints resulting from geographical, topographical, and climatic elements.

2. *The organizational-structural dimension.* Constraints emanating from the organization and structure of the international system and their consequences, such as, How many poles does the global system have, and what degree of flexibility and freedom does the number of poles imply for the actors? What international organizations exist? What are their areas of activity? What is the degree of their influence?

3. *The reinforcement dimension.* The rewards and punishments that the international society of actors provide for different forms of behavior. For example, is an aggressive state punished? Or is aggression countenanced complacently by nations not directly harmed by it? The existence or nonexistence of sanctions may in itself act as a constraint and affect behavior.

4. *The normative dimension.* The system of values, beliefs, norms, and dominant aspirations that may act as a constraint on behavior contradicting it. This dimension may also contribute to or be related to the reinforcement dimension by encouraging or deterring certain kinds of behavior.

5. *The commitment dimension.* Tacit and explicit self-imposed commitments to other political entities and their determination of actors' behavioral patterns. Thus, partnership in an alliance imposes certain types of behavior toward other partners and a different sort toward those outside the alliance. Membership in an organization such as the United Nations demands, at least nominally, the adoption of specific standards of behavior, and any deviation from them is supposed to require explanation or self-justification.

6. *The domestic-political dimension.* The structure of and balance

between domestic political forces and institutions, as well as the process through which policy is made, which affect the range of decisions that can and are likely to be made in response to any situation that arises.

7. *The capability dimension.* The available resources, tangible and intangible, that determine which types of behavior are feasible and which are not and consequently which decisions can be implemented.

How decisionmakers perceive the overall balance of these constraints is a crucial input to their perceived range of policy options. Once a preference for a particular policy emerges, the judgment of how it fits the set of perceived constraints is the basis of its actual adoption, reevaluation, and adjustment.

The rigidity of the behavioral constraints imposed on actors by the limitations, that is, their ability to break out of their confines and reshape their setting and with it the range of possible behaviors and their outcomes, is dependent on a number of factors. First is the power of the actor in question. For example, superpowers have fewer environmental limitations than smaller states do, and their ability to mold the environment, or parts of it, is greater. Second is the nature of the action taken. The effects of some acts, especially those involving large-scale use of force, are often greater than those of pure persuasion in reshaping the environmental balance of constraints. The third factor is the nature of the targeted attributes constituting the environment. Some elements in the environment are flexible and allow for deviations from the limitations set at a given time. Other more rigid elements dictate unchangeable limitations. For example, in the contemporary global system, the nuclear military balance between the two superpowers dictates rigid limitations on behavior, which cannot be changed in the foreseeable future. For the limitations to change, one of the superpowers would have to achieve a significant technological breakthrough, of a kind that would guarantee it first-strike capacity and the ability to survive any counterattack. On the other hand, an aspect of the nuclear dimension of the global system is flexible, namely, the number of nations having a nuclear military option, which has changed over time.

To summarize, we could say that the implications of the reciprocal relations between the environmental constraints and the actors are a function of the actors' attributes, the attributes of their behavior, and the environmental attributes. The accurate understanding of these factors is crucially important for the actors to accurately assess the extent to which they can change the environment or prevent it from obstructing the implementation of their goals and decisions. However, the interpretation and perception of limitations are influenced by the functional role of perception for the decisionmakers: "Perceiving is goal-directed behavior. The goal of perception, in its broadest sense, is the construction of a meaningful behavioral environment—an environment congruent with 'reality' on the one hand and the needs and dispositions of the organism on the other" (Postman and Bruner, 1948: 314). This gives us a clue to why both the search for and treatment of information about the decisionmaking and the consequent psychological environment may at times have to be oversimplified or even distorted to satisfy the decisionmakers' instrumental needs, producing motivated irrationality (Atkin, 1973; Pears, 1984).

The perception of constraints affects choice. In choosing among options decisionmakers may systematically analyze the content of the issue at hand and the constraints imposed by the environment on choice, the implementation of the chosen alternative, and the possible consequences of any relevant option. Yet the path to choice may not be analytic, so only part of the relevant information may be considered and evaluated. In that case choice is often made by default, that is, through a process of eliminating other available options (Tversky, 1972). Approaching a problem for decision solely through the analysis of constraints may serve as a full or partial substitute for the time- and resource-consuming effort of systematically analyzing all available issue-related information. The analysis of constraints is a process of disposing of particular options or categories of options relatively easily by looking at the balance of constraints on the decisionmaking, implementation, or outcome stage for each option in question. The constraints become the criteria by which options are eliminated, lightening the burden of choice; choice is then made by default. Elimination by constraints holds an additional and inherent attraction: it justifies the chosen option, an important aspect of political choice (P. A. Anderson, 1981).

It could sometimes be rational to use the nonanalytic process of choosing, for example, when time is at a premium or when the price of error in choice is acceptable. But in general, constraints and their impact must be considered in the context of the problem's overall content, rather than exclusively on their own, especially when major change is required. Choice by elimination in the latter case is choice based on inadequate information. The consequences are further aggravated when the balance of constraints is misperceived. Thus the need to justify a particular choice could cause an evaluation error by upgrading the importance of the perceived effects of those constraints that are expected to be useful in the post-decisional justification process.

Apart from the broad constraints that determine the scope and range of possible foreign and domestic policy behaviors and outcomes, an actor's decision environment contains specific contents at any point in time. The elements, which may or may not be perceived accurately, provide the details and color of the definition of the situation. One of the most detailed descriptions of these elements, as applied to foreign policy, is offered by Brecher, Steinberg, and Stein (1969), to which I have made some additions and modifications.[20] The elements include the structure and nature of the global system; the structure and nature of the immediate subsystem; the impact of other subsystems; relations with the superpowers; reciprocal relations with other actors, national and transnational, state and nonstate; geographical influences; military power; economic power; the structure of the actor's political system and institutions; pressure groups; competing elites representing alternative conceptions of the totality of problems and orientations in foreign policy; and the legal status of the specific issue in question. The interaction between perceived constraints and specific content provides the core knowledge for the decision process. The following chapters deal in detail with the question of how the decisionmaker acquires and structures this knowledge and what affects its accuracy.

Information Processing Outcomes and Dynamics: A Typology

As the product of information processing is perceptual, the quality of the process can and should be evaluated by observing its perceptual consequences and their dynamics over time. Two sets of typologies are suggested for this purpose. Misperception is measured by the discrepancy between the real environment and its perception at a given point in time, T_0. Still, perception is a dynamic phenomenon, and the dynamic dimension determines what happens to perception over time, that is, in the period from T_0 to T_1. What happens in this period is likely to determine what the static dimension of the misperception (the discrepancy between the real environment and its perception) will be at T_1. The two dimensions complement each other.[21]

The relationship between the real and psychological environments can take a number of prototypical forms, which have obvious implications for the accuracy of judgment and inference:

1. *Congruence.* A situation in which there is no significant discrepancy between the psychological and real environments. Congruence between perception and reality, once achieved, is not permanent; the ever-changing features of the environment demand continuous attention, updating, and fine-tuning. Adjustment is a heavy burden owing to the

nature of international-politics-related information; the odds favor the demise of congruence and a regression to one of the states of noncongruence between perception and reality, discussed below.

2. *Cognizance gap.* The discrepancy between reality and the perception arising from the decisionmaker's noncognizance of relevant components in the environment. This is a purely qualitative gap. The components in question have no representation whatsoever in the mind of the decisionmaker, who is not aware of their existence.

3. *Relevance gap.* The discrepancy arising from the decisionmaker's failure to perceive certain components of the environment as relevant to a specific issue, even though they are indeed relevant to it, or relevant for interpreting the situation at hand. The decisionmaker is aware of the existence of the components in the environment but attaches zero weight to them. The other side of the coin is the consideration of irrelevant variables as relevant.

4. *Evaluation gap.* The discrepancy arising when the decisionmaker perceives all the components relevant to the issue in question but does not attach due weight to their actual importance in the definition of the situation. This gap is a purely quantitative one.

We should note the following: (1) all cognizance gaps lead by definition to relevance and evaluation gaps, as far as the specific datum about which the actor is not aware is concerned; (2) all relevance gaps lead by definition to evaluation gaps, as far as the specific datum that is considered irrelevant to the issue-area at hand in concerned; and (3) the import for the overall picture of cognizance, relevance, and evaluation gaps concerning a specific datum depends on the relative weight of the specific datum misperceived in the overall definition of the situation. The decisionmaker may fall simultaneously into more than one type of misperception regarding the different elements and constraints within the same issue-area as well as within different issue-areas of decision. The effects of each type of perceptual distortion can be evaluated in relation to three main areas of potential impact: quality of decision, level of aggregation affected, and spillover effects within the perceptual domain. The contribution of each type of misperception to making faulty decisions (in terms of outcomes) is the product of the following:

1. *Weight of the misperceived variables* within the whole set of variables relevant to the decision. The greater their weight, the greater the effect of the misperception on the quality of the decision.

2. *Type of misperception.* Correcting misperceptions is easier when the decisionmaker is aware that a certain variable exists and is relevant, even if he does not give it its due weight, than it will be if the variable is not represented at all in his mind.

3. *Degree of interdependence.* The extent to which the misperception of a given variable necessarily involves misperceptions regarding additional variables—which hinges on the extent to which the different variables are perceived as interdependent. This has to do with covariation (causal and noncausal) judgment (see Chapter 2).

Misperceptions not only take different forms but also take place at different levels. Four levels of aggregation of occurrences represent the range and extent of fallacious information processing:

1. *A single (distinct) occurrence.* The misperception may relate to the interpretation of a single occurrence or even nonoccurrence. In social relations the fact that something did not occur is sometimes no less meaningful than the fact that something did occur. Even the nonoccurrence of any event at all is given an interpretation that is rooted in antedecent perceptions of the individual, although such nonevents could lead to less restructuring of one's perceptions than they should (Fischhoff, 1977: 357).

2. *Sequence of distinct occurrences.* The misperception may relate, not to the misinterpretation of a single event, but to the pattern seen emerging from a set of events; in this case it involves covariation judgment. For example, during the month of September 1973 an accumulation of data from multiple diplomatic and intelligence sources indicated the possibility of a coordinated Syrian-Egyptian attack on Israel's northern and southern fronts sometime in October. At the request of Defense Minister Moshe Dayan the prime minister, Golda Meir, convened a meeting of her top advisers, senior ministers, and the chief of the research division of military intelligence on October 3 to discuss the meaning of the threat. The data presented at this meeting indicate that the Israeli intelligence community had accurate, detailed knowledge of Egyptian and Syrian military preparations. But the emerging pattern was missed. Egyptian military activities were interpreted as part of the annual military exercise; Syrian preparations were interpreted as a defensive alert in response to the shooting down of thirteen MiG fighters by the Israeli air force on September 13. The two occurrences were not seen as related or as establishing an alarming pattern of a coordinated, impending attack (Schiff, 1974: 17–19, 248). Accurate data about distinct events thus do not necessarily lead to their accurate interpretation when they are part of a sequence.

3. *Continuous occurrences.* Sometimes there is misperception of processes that are not bound by specific salient events but are continuous. This can produce what Wohlstetter describes as "slow Pearl Harbors" (1979).

4. *The ecology.* Misperception here concerns the overall environmen-

tal constraints within which the decisionmaker is obliged to operate and within whose context the isolated, sequential, or continuous occurrences are evaluated and interpreted.

The four levels of aggregation are in fact interdependent in the sense that each is a necessary part of a higher level of aggregation. Any set of occurrences is made up of individual occurrences. Any process is at least partly made up of patterns that are the outcome of combinations and interactions of occurrence-sets that are not additive, meaning that the sum is not a simple function of adding up the individual occurrences but is more or different from that sum owing to the interaction effect. And any change of the ecology is, in the long run, an outcome of a combination of the other three. Consequently, misperception at the level of the distinct, isolated event will have an impact—at the sequence or continuous-occurrence levels—to the degree that that particular event was part of those. However, predicting the final degree of misperception is very difficult without specific information about the relative weight of the single misperceived event and its exact relationship with the other components of the set or process.

The process of adjustment comprises four general phases: becoming aware of the need for adjustment; relating a trigger datum to a specific area of misperception and direction of adjustment; weighing the importance of the datum with regard to the area it relates to and the scope of required adjustment; and choosing the specific adjustment to be implemented from among available alternative interpretations. Any failure in one or more of these phases of the process results in one or more type of misperception. The processes of adjustment and revision due to feedback or new available information can thus be classified into three simple, logically exhaustive categories in terms of their outcomes:

1. *Maladaptation.* The discrepancy between reality and perception increases over time.

2. *Nonadaptation.* The discrepancy remains about the same over time.

3. *Positive adaptation.* The discrepancy is reduced over time.

A decisionmaker can be subject to a number of processes at the same time. There can be, for example, maladaptation to certain discrepancies and adaptation to others. That variables relevant at T_0 may not necessarily also be relevant at T_1 is not an obstacle to the analyst, even though the two points in time do not at first glance seem comparable. What is of interest is a more general question, whether the decisionmaker's level of performance, as far as information processing is concerned, improves over time.[22] In other words, what is the role of experience in improving the accuracy of perception? Or to what extent do the decisionmakers

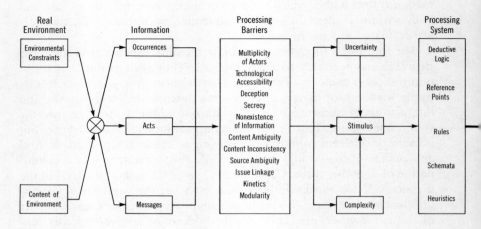

Fig. 4. Information flow and transformation.

succeed, with the passage of time, in improving their performance with regard to information processing as "naive scientists" or as "naive statisticians"?[23] The main arguments about information flow and transformation and its perceptual consequences are presented in Fig. 4.

Conclusions

Actors in the international system deal with a multitude of unknowns and incomprehensibles in addition to stimuli, complexities, and uncertainties. This is reflected in their foreign policies. Their two patterns of response in making decisions generally conform to the choice between fight and flight. The first pattern refers to recognition of the constraints imposed by the environment. A tendency toward this pattern of response leads to what we have defined as positive adaptation. In this case, foreign policy continues to serve its purpose of enabling the actor to make the optimal adjustment to the changing international environment. The second pattern refers to attempted escape from the existing environment to one in which the required characteristics and patterns of behavior are compatible with those the actor finds preferable and convenient. This adjustment pattern constitutes an option that is not open to an actor in the international system; as a substitute, he is liable to perceive the environment as if it were other than it is. His escape takes place in the mind, in misperceiving the environment to conform with personal expectations.

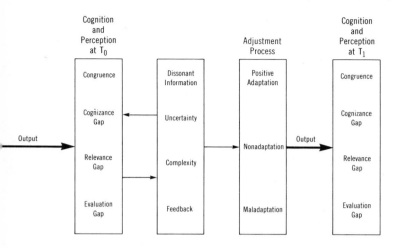

Processing circle reflects the fact that aspects of two or more states or variables are combined in some definable way, resulting in a new state or variable.

This pattern of response is bound to lead to nonadaptation or maladaptation.

The extent to which the decisionmakers' choice is likely to be the optimal one can be affected differently by different types of misperception as a direct consequence of their degree of gravity and the decisionmakers' ability to adjust and adapt. The effects of the type of misperception at T_0 on the adjustment process that occurs in the course of time are worth exploring, for the interaction determines the end product at T_1 and the process repeats itself time and again. In fact, it is a sort of *perpetuum mobile*.

The outcomes and quality of information processing make a web of cognizance, relevance, and evaluation gaps on the one hand and accurate perceptions and shrewd insights into the world on the other. The complex relations of accurate perceptions, errors, and misperceptions are dynamic. Over time the players either show good sense by adjusting and improving the accuracy of their definition of the situation or fail to do so. The end results and their input into decisionmaking reflect the balance among accurate, partly accurate, and erroneous elements in the players' picture of the world, as well as the quality of their adjustment processes, and the balance between the different players (individuals, groups, and organizations), who have a particular view of the world in their individual and collective minds, which they try to convince other players to

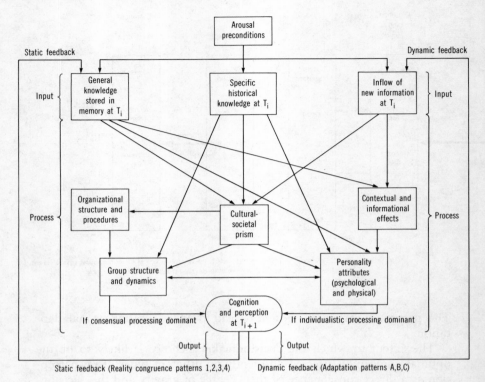

Fig. 5. The sociocognitive model of information processing. The reality congruence patterns are (1) congruence, (2) cognizance gap, (3) relevance gap, and (4) evaluation gap; the adaptation patterns are (A) positive adaptation, (B) nonadaptation, and (C) maladaptation.

accept or even impose on those others. In the following chapters we shall discuss in detail the five variable-sets that affect information processing and determine its dynamics and outcomes: the characteristics of the information and the rules of its processing; the personality and style of the information processor; the organizational setting within which the processor operates; small-group contexts and dynamics; and societal-cultural effects. A scheme of my sociocognitive approach introducing these variable-sets and the pattern of their interactions is presented in Fig. 5.

CHAPTER 2

The Information: Attributes
and Access

....

"It is a great nuisance that knowledge can only be acquired by hard work.
It would be fine if we could swallow the powder of profitable information
made palatable by the jam of fiction." w. SOMERSET MAUGHAM

Clues to a Puzzle

The subject matter of information processing is information. Hence
the nature and properties of the available information presumably significantly affect its processing outcomes. This chapter will deal with the
following questions: What transforms information into stimuli, able to
attract the decisionmaker's attention? Why is some information given
priority over other information in allocating attention resources? How
do the nature and properties of information, and access to and interaction with information, affect judgment and inference? What are the potential errors and biases involved in processing that arise from the characteristics, organization, packaging, and volume of information and the
nature of access channels by which it becomes available? The general
argument is that context and form, as much as and at times even more
than content, determine the outcomes and accuracy of processing, judgment, and inference and produce what seems a paradoxical result but is
not—namely, that the same variables have different, sometimes contradictory effects. For example, the same factors that call attention to information may also be the cause of its neglect. Hence it is important not
only to identify those factors but also to specify the particular forms of
influence they exert and the circumstances in which they exert it.

Information processing can then be viewed as a serial or simultaneous
process of multiple puzzle solving. It depends on cues, rules, and signposts that (1) call attention to the puzzles and bring about their recognition and (2) help decide each puzzle's content and its relation to other

puzzles in terms of priority, order of solution, and outcome interdependence, that is, whether and how a particular solution affects the solution of other puzzles. Decisionmakers have to figure out the shortest, most economical, and most efficient way to crack the puzzles. While taking cognitive and environmental constraints into account, they must calculate and form expectations about how the process of resolution and the solution itself will affect their interests, goals, and accountability for outcomes (Tetlock, 1985a). They must try to balance the most correct manner with the most practical manner—and these are not the same—to exploit available information for this purpose. The outcome is too often at best a satisficing solution to the puzzles and not necessarily an optimal one.

Information processing is multidimensional. It entails different levels of processing along a continuum from direct knowing, or perception-based knowledge, to indirect knowing, or cognition-based knowledge. The acquisition of both direct knowing and indirect knowing is mostly a serial process that depends on limited-capacity, short-term memory and the more comprehensive long-term memory and can be data driven or concept driven. The mix of data-driven and concept-driven information processing depends on the nature of the information and the nature of the task (Baron, 1981; Baron and Harvey, 1980; W. L. Bennett, 1981, 1982; Higgins and Bargh, 1987; Lindsay and Norman, 1977: 489; Simon, 1974, 1978b). Both data-driven and concept-driven information processing entail a mix of *systematic* and *heuristic* information processing.

According to a systematic view, recipients exert considerable cognitive effort in performing this task [information processing]: They actively attempt to comprehend and evaluate the message's arguments as well as to assess their validity in relation to the message's conclusion. In contrast, according to a heuristic view of persuasion, recipients exert comparatively little effort in judging message validity: Rather than processing argumentation, recipients may rely on (typically) more accessible information such as the source's identity or other non-content cues in deciding to accept a message's conclusion. (Chaiken, 1980: 752)

In systematic information processing recipients focus primarily on substantive message content but use source and other non-content cues secondarily as aids in assessment of, for example, validity. Systematic processing involves acceptance and internalization of the message, whereas heuristic processing involves only acceptance or rejection of the message's overall conclusion. Decisionmakers prefer systematic processing for high-involvement issues (Chaiken, 1980), although, as will be elaborated later in the book, such issues often have attributes that make systematic processing difficult. Overreliance on heuristic processing may inflate the chances of both Type 1 and Type 2 errors occurring. The

TABLE 1
Information Processing Modes

	Perception	Cognition
Systematic processing	Data driven	Data driven and/or concept driven
Heuristic processing	Concept driven	Concept driven

choice between heuristic and systematic processing can be made sponta-neously or rationally (for example, What is more cost-effective under the existing constraints in terms of reducing time, involvement and account-ability, complexity, uncertainty, or stress?). Whatever processing pattern is preferred, decisionmakers are not implicitly aware of the systematic, cognitively and motivationally based biases that ensue from either.[1]

Table 1 indicates the possible contingent combinations of various in-teracting dimensions of information processing. The content of each square describes a primary orientation in information processing but does not preclude a secondary role for the other orientation. The follow-ing sections will elaborate and specify the dimensions of information processing and the potential biases and errors related to them in connec-tion with the particular stages and tasks of information processing (e.g. the search for information could be concept driven yet attention could be data driven).

The Search for Information

The active search for politically relevant information by both individ-ual decisionmakers and organizations is mostly guided by defined func-tional and personal goals and expectancies about the self, others, and the milieu in which they interact. Decisionmakers are not, however, will-ing—or, even more important, able—to pay attention to all sources of information available to them and then decide what is relevant. Attention is a scarce resource and is therefore selective. Its allocation is mostly directed by the focus of interest: a specific issue or actor or a specific issue or actor within a specific context. Still, the search for information also has an automatic dimension; information is detected by those "more or less indifferent to context and meaning" (Neisser, 1976: 95).

Problems in the political domain in general and in international politics in particular are frequently ill defined, meaning that they are characterized by open attributes. These attributes "include one or more parameters the values of which are left unspecified as the problem is given to the problem-solving system from outside or transmitted within the system over time" (Reitman, 1964: 292–93; see also Milburn and Billings, 1976). The problem's being ill defined makes highly uncertain and vague exactly which information is relevant and leads to the ignoring of information that could prove relevant and important or to hyperattention and the indiscriminate collecting of quantities of information that will only overburden the information processing system and negatively affect its problem-solving capacity. When ill-defined problems compete for attention with well-defined and structured problems, the latter often distract attention from the former (Turner, 1976: 388). Decisionmakers prefer to deal with what seems manageable rather than with what is ambiguous even if it is possibly more important and potentially dangerous. Yet decisionmakers are not always aware of the differences between well-defined and ill-structured problems. In fact they unconsciously transform ill-structured problems into well-defined ones by ignoring their indistinct attributes. But even when problems are well defined, the problem-solving system's having been given clear systematic criteria by which to decide when a proposed solution is acceptable and the goal is attained, what constitutes relevant information is not necessarily well defined, because the high level of uncertainty about the nature and scope of future outcomes and needs can persist.

The search for information is not always purposeful: it can be triggered by a mere vague awareness of possible future needs for information even when the exact nature of such needs is unclear. Then the search for and accumulation of information loses focus and becomes undiscriminating, producing information overload on the one hand and inattention to relevant information on the other. For example, when expecting to be challenged by adversaries holding different views and possibly to have to defend personal or organizational views, decisionmakers may decide to accumulate and store knowledge even if the exact nature of the challenge and its timing are unknown to them. Information that seems salient to their need is likely to attract attention and be given weight, whereas other information is likely to escape attention even if it warrants it. Since the range and nature of future outcomes are frequently unclear, the question of what constitutes relevant information becomes even more difficult to answer, causing inattention to what could prove to be relevant information ex post facto.

When the structure of authority in the decisionmaking system precludes challenges to established opinions, the motivation to search for and the alertness to information, supportive and dissonant alike, declines, making the updating of views unlikely. The search for information is then routine and mechanical at best. Those in power may feel free of the need to anticipate future criticism, and those not holding positions of power may despair of influencing policy in a different direction, believing that searching for information that cannot be effectively used anyway and may even have adverse effects is pointless, so that even when dissonant information is available, it is ignored. For example, in April 1970 when the White House was considering an invasion of Cambodia, aimed at wiping out North Vietnam's military sanctuaries and buttressing Lon Nol's regime, Director Richard Helms of the Central Intelligence Agency (CIA) received a National Intelligence Estimate on the Cambodian situation drafted by the CIA's Indochina specialists. The estimate made it clear that an invasion would be unwise. It would require large numbers of American and South Vietnamese infantry and heavy and sustained bombing; even if the bombing was successful, "it probably would not prevent them [the North Vietnamese] from continuing the struggle in some form" (quoted in Shawcross, 1979: 137). Helms did not forward the memorandum to the White House but sent it back to the chairman of the CIA's National Estimates Board. He knew what his analysts did not—that Nixon was already planning an invasion. Their lack of awareness in fact freed them of political pressures. The CIA director knew that dissenting information would not be well received by the president, who looked for support, not misgivings. Fear of the White House was such that inconvenient views were ignored or suppressed (Shawcross, 1979: 137).

Satisfaction with the status quo and a high level of self-assurance, with its attendant lack of anticipatory regret, also check attention and inhibit the active search for inconsistent information that may challenge the validity of currently held positions. Valuable information goes unnoticed as the vigilance of information processors declines. After Israel's victory in the Six Day War, for example, its leadership perceived the balance of power and the political-diplomatic initiative in the region to have been decisively tilted in its favor for a long time to come. The new status quo provided a sense of security and self-assurance to the point of arrogance; and the possibility of change in the state of affairs seemed remote and unlikely, particularly after Egypt's failure in the War of Attrition. Information challenging this mind-set was not sought for, and indications of change (e.g. Sadat's warnings) were underestimated or ignored (Brecher with Geist, 1980; Handel, 1976; Perlmutter, 1975).

Information Properties and Contextual
Effects on Attention

The problem of how information becomes a meaningful stimulus has two aspects. The first relates to the actual transformation of the information into a stimulus: What makes information successfully cross the threshold of awareness? What factors operate to raise or lower the threshold of awareness vis-à-vis any given information? The second aspect of the problem is, How does information that has succeeded in becoming a stimulus come to influence existing knowledge and perceptions? In other words, what causes a stimulus to be perceived as relevant to and important for the issues preoccupying the perceiver? Factors besides the specific substantive content of information affect attention to information and the manner in which the information is integrated with prior perceptions and knowledge about any particular issue. The factors are related to the properties of the information and the contextual circumstances in which it becomes available and is used. They may in fact be no less important than the actual content of the information. However, the same factors often have countervailing effects on processing outcomes. We shall see, for example, that the very same factors that illuminate certain information may also diminish its perceived importance or relevance, reducing its impact on the final mental picture.

Attention is not necessarily allocated only, or even mainly, according to the actual quality, importance, and relevance of information. The likelihood that information will be given attention is dependent on two types of effect information could have. One is not conditional on change in the existing attention threshold but only on the properties of the incoming information—the extent to which it meets preset criteria for attracting attention. The second type involves raising or lowering the level of the existing attention threshold. If the level is changed, information that in the past succeeded in penetrating awareness may not be recognized in the present or in the future, and vice versa.

Attention allocation is affected by the properties of the stimulus, or its vividness; the context in which the information is set, or its salience; its perceived relationship to other information; and the timing factor. Attention-attracting properties are pertinent in recognizing information that is not part of goal-directed scanning but are no less important in detecting goal-directed, requested information. Even when the problems, or issues, or actors, or situations, about which information is sought are well defined, the notion of just what constitutes relevant information is frequently fuzzy. Thus the allocation of attention can be determined by non-content properties, as will be elaborated below.

The vividness of a stimulus is composed, in the first place, of its magnitude.[2] For example, an international border incident in which casualties occurred is more difficult to ignore than one with no casualties. Concreteness is another feature of vividness (Nisbett and Ross, 1980: 47–49). An event reported in detail, delimited in time, place, action, and participating actors, is less likely to go unnoticed than an event reported in more abstract and general terms. Pallid information, even highly probative data like summaries and statistics, is more likely to be ignored than vivid, although anecdotal, case-history-type information, which, even if it is much less probative, attracts attention and is highly weighted (Borgida and Nisbett, 1977; Nisbett and Ross, 1980: 55–59; Reyes, Thompson, and Bower, 1980) and consequently could gain undeserved judgmental and diagnostic value. Such was the case with America's pet theory regarding Southeast Asia—the domino theory. Years of political rhetoric were invested in convincing the public that should South Vietnam fall, Cambodia, Laos, Thailand, Malaya, the Philippines, Indonesia, and Australia would more than likely fall soon to the Communists in their proper order. The domino metaphor was effective in conveying the purported risks of Communist victory. It persisted in the face of all contradictory information because it was vivid and provided a simple, clear, and convincing script that submerged all uncertainties and overcame counterfactual evidence, presenting a persuasive strategic logic and justification for American military intervention in the war. It became a guide to selective information processing, focusing and holding the attention of decisionmakers on information supporting it and enabling them to reject or ignore information contradicting its assumptions and predictions.

The less mundane a stimulus, the less likely it is to be ignored. In general, the more extreme or dramatic the content of information, the less likely it is to go unobserved. Yet importance is not necessarily attributed to information. On the contrary, dramatic information is likely to be discounted as exaggeration, even when it should be highly valued. Hitler's future plans as exposed in his *Mein Kampf* were discounted even after he came to power.

The less ambiguous the information, the harder ignoring it, or discounting its relevance when interpreting it, becomes. Unambiguous information, once it has gained attention and is perceived as relevant, can be difficult to adapt to decisionmakers' cognitive and motivational needs. Unambiguous information about an imminent threat or great danger can trigger a search for additional information either about the nature of the threat or about means of coping with it if such information appears to be lacking. However, if the decisionmakers are sure of their ability to deal effectively with the threat, they may not be alert to further information about it. At the same time, the willingness to be exposed to dissonant information grows with decisionmakers' confidence in their ability to deal with the threat; the threshold for the entry of dissonant information is lowered (Janis, 1962; Janis and Mann, 1977: 214–18; Lazarus, 1966: 89; Whithey, 1962: 114).

These effects of ambiguity can be observed in the period from September 30 to October 5, 1973, the day before the Yom Kippur War broke out, when accumulating information indicated the growing probability of war; included was information on preparations for the evacuation of Soviet experts and their families from Syria and Egypt and on an unusual concentration of Egyptian and Syrian forces along the Suez Canal and the cease-fire line on the Golan Heights. This was not enough, however, to convince the chief of military intelligence, Major General Eli Zeira, to revise his assessment of the low probability of war. One reason that neither he nor others, who had more doubts about that assessment, did not act decisively in the face of dissonant information was that the information was ambiguous. It could be interpreted as indicating offensive as well as defensive intentions. If defensive, the preparations were precautions against a possible Israeli attack, taken in response to public warnings by the Israeli defense minister and the chief of staff in the preceding weeks. An important goal of the Arab deception plan was in fact to convince Israeli intelligence that the Arabs feared a preemptive attack. The Israelis explained the large forward deployment of Syrian forces in terms of the growing bilateral tensions attributable to the shooting down of thirteen Syrian MiGs on September 13; a Syrian reprisal operation was considered possible—but not full-scale war. The Egyptian concentration of forces was explained as part of an offensive military exercise to test Egyptian plans to reoccupy the Sinai. The unusually high state of alert declared in the Egyptian army was also attributed to precautions against an impending attack by Israel and seen as an act of solidarity with Syria (Bartov, 1978a: 292–324; Nakdimon, 1982: 81–96). Zeira did not suppress the incoming information that was clearly inconsistent with his own estimates but emphasized his belief that the intelligence community would provide ample time for preparation through early warning and that even if war did break out, every possible combination of Arab armies could be defeated decisively within a few days.

The subject matter of information is highly pertinent in determining its vividness and consequently affects the allocation of attention. The more elitist the organization or personality the information is about, the lower is the threshold for its penetration into cognizance even if its actual validity is not as high or its actual diagnostic value not as significant as the validity and value of information about less elitist objects. Information about elites also tends to be evaluated as more important than it actually is because of the tendency to search for the locus of control and decision and the natural preference for finding it in the elite. Hence information about the elite, especially those personalities who trigger strong emotional interest, is considered worth seeking out and more informative than other types of information. This perception of value is logically related to the predisposition to perceive most actions of other actors as planned—orchestrated by some central guiding authority and reflecting a basic disposition—rather than interpreting the actions as having their causes in particularistic and circumstantial motivations or viewing individuals and organizations as acting according to some narrowly defined interest and not necessarily as part of an overall, coordinated effort.

The salience of a stimulus is relative to its context and hence affects attention and social judgment even when the context is logically irrelevant to the judgment task. Salient events do not necessarily provide diagnostic information. Yet they are likely to attract attention and distract it from the really important contextual processes.[3] Concentrating on the immediate salient occurrences produces insensitivity to the time dimension and a misunderstanding of the impact of long-range processes (Lanir, 1983: 167–68). A number of factors could make a stimulus more salient than other, more informative stimuli.[4] The temporal context is important in drawing attention. When there is a demand for particular information, the awareness threshold for that information is lowered either because an active search is involved or because attention is focused (Janis and Mann, 1977: 212–14; Jervis, 1976: 203–4; Triandis, 1971: 98). Timing not only serves to channel attention but also imbues the information with relevance or importance it does not necessarily have.

National Security Adviser McGeorge Bundy's memo upon returning from Saigon and Pleiku in February 1965 weighed the balance in favor of those supporting bombing North Vietnam as part of a policy of gradual and continuing reprisal; and one reason for the memo's influence was its context and timing. The memo was coupled with the first Vietcong attack on the American barracks in Pleiku, in the Central Highlands, in February 1965, in which eight Americans were killed and sixty wounded. The attack not only had a strong emotional impact on Bundy himself, who was in Vietnam at the time, but created a mind-set among decision-makers in Washington that focused attention on and attributed utmost importance to information about how to deal with the new challenge. The memo, coming at such a time and from someone respected for his intellect who was on the spot when the event occurred, gained high salience (Halberstam, 1972: 524–26).

The contexts of prior knowledge or expectancies also generate salience. Repetitive information is not likely to be ignored. Information that has already gained attention in the past and penetrated the perceiver's cognitive system continues to attract attention, so that information of a similar kind, even if its informative value has declined, is likely to be noticed when it reappears and to easily cross the awareness threshold. Yet upon being recognized, it is not reassessed, just absorbed routinely. The perceiver could consequently be preoccupied with the already known, allocating little attention to the novel and thus encouraging conservatism.

The cognizance threshold for signals that confirm the receiver's view is lower than for signals that contradict it. The higher the degree of confidence in a theory, the higher is the recognition threshold for incongruent information (Heuer, 1982: 51–53; O. R. Holsti, 1967a: 29–33, 70; Shlaim, 1976). Even when incongruence between expectations and reality is recognized, it is likely to be dismissed. Stated more broadly, a stimulus that is consonant with prior expectations, beliefs, or theories is likely to be noticed.[5] Even when it is noticed, a selective process may operate to determine which particular aspects of the stimulus will be attended to. Moreover, information consistent with expectations is better remembered and more accurately rated than inconsistent information (Berman, Read, and Kenny, 1983; De Rivera, 1968: 40–42). Consistent information, once stored in long-term memory, becomes more available in judging future information and therefore more influential over its processing. In particular, information that fits into existing schemata— that is, cognitive structures of organized prior knowledge abstracted from specific experiences (Lau and Sears, 1986; Fiske and Linville, 1980)—is noticed earlier, considered more valid, and processed much faster than information that contradicts or does not fit into any particular schema. The more available the schema, the stronger and more immediate is its impact on the information, producing a primacy effect that blocks dissonant information from being noticed or considered seriously.

Members of the decisionmaking groups and intelligence communities in the United States and Israel shared the supposition that war between Israel and an Egyptian-Syrian coalition was unlikely before 1975. Syria, it was thought, might initiate local military operations, but it was unlikely to initiate a full-scale war without Egyptian participation. The assumptions were based on a broad range of arguments—military, po-

The Information · 61

litical, economic, and historical. The military balance was believed to be heavily tilted in favor of Israel. According to The Conception of Israeli military intelligence, Israel's air superiority was a decisive deterrent as long as Egypt preserved and recognized it. In addition, the lessons of the Six Day War and the War of Attrition seemed to be that Arab soldiers lacked technological skills, sophistication, and motivation. Sadat was thought to believe that Soviet-American détente would lead to a declining Soviet interest in the Middle East, and in the Arab cause in particular, and that consequently Egypt should focus on improving relations with Washington. At the same time Moscow was believed not to desire another Arab-Israeli war. Also, war would presumably increase domestic economic difficulties in the Arab world and so would not be favored. The IDF's General Staff did believe that starting in 1975 the probability of war would increase significantly because of the flow of modern Soviet weaponry to the Arabs, which by then would have increased the Arabs' capabilities and confidence enough for them to initiate a war. Until then, however, a two-front war was thought to be unlikely (Agranat Commission, 1975; Bartov, 1978a; Nakdimon, 1982).

Israel, the deterring actor, thus assumed rationality on the part of the challenger—Egypt. The Arab deception plan encouraged Israel to believe that Egypt's military and civilian decisionmakers were aware of Israel's military, and particularly air, superiority (J. G. Stein, 1985b); hence the conclusion that effective deterrence prevailed did not succumb to dissonant information. Information that supported the Israeli conception was weighted more heavily in the integrative assessment of dissonant and consonant information. Ironically, in the final few days before the war most of the consonant information (e.g. Egypt's fear of an Israeli attack and the pretext that the concentration of Egyptian forces was an army exercise) came from Egyptian sources, whereas most of the dissonant information came from Israeli intelligence (e.g. observations from IDF posts along the Suez Canal and air reconnaissance reports). Yet Israel still had a motivational bias to discount source cues and concentrate on context cues that supported prior expectations.

A corollary to the above hypothesis can also be posited: the more highly inconsistent an unambiguous behavior is with the perceiver's prior image of its performer, the less likely it is to go unnoticed.[6] Yet such information does not necessarily lead to a revision of prior images and judgments. On the contrary, its unconventional nature could cause it to be interpreted as out of line, unrepresentative, deceitful, or merely reflective of special circumstances, thus providing the perceiver with an excuse to avoid updating views already espoused.

The structure of the data-set is another context-produced salience.

Information describing a process (rather than a distinct event) is susceptible to uneven attention; certain parts of it draw the eye. The tendency
is to pay attention only to the beginning or end of the process, either of
which is usually more striking than the bulk of the process itself, which
often eludes attention. To illustrate: a child has its parents' attention
when it is born; then after a certain time they realize that the child has
grown up without their being fully conscious of the process that took
place between those two points in time.

The effects of vividness and salience are particularly prominent when
time is short (e.g. crisis) or when search, evaluation, and judgment are
constrained; the decisionmaker focuses on what is easily available in the
memory and noticeable in the environment. Accessible information
sources are used more frequently and less discriminately than inaccessible
ones. They are attributed higher validity than is deserved even if they are
of low quality and the decisionmaker is aware that they are (O'Reilly,
1982). To illustrate: a principal target of the CIA station in Saigon was
the South Vietnamese military. The main pipeline to the South Vietnamese high command was Charles Timmes, who served as chief of the U.S.
advisory command in Vietnam from 1962 to 1964 and during that period befriended up-and-coming young officers who in later years would
become powerful figures in politics and the military. In 1967 the CIA
asked Timmes to return to Vietnam to reactivate his old ties and report
on the state of affairs within the Vietnamese army. In fact the CIA knew
that his reports from the field were often drafted with the help of the
Vietnamese field commander and reflected what the South Vietnamese
wanted to convey to the U.S. Embassy. At first his reports were treated
accordingly, but as other sources became scarce from 1970 to 1971 with
the reduction and later the removal of American advisory teams in the
countryside, Timmes's reports and findings began to be treated at face
value and used to support the wishful thinking of bureaucrats in Washington about the resilience of the South Vietnamese army. Timmes himself never claimed such validity for his reports; he made it clear that they
relfected only what his Vietnamese friends told him (Snepp, 1978: 15–
17).

After attention to a stimulus comes the weighing of its importance,
interpretation, and integration with preexisting knowledge. Yet the various stages are not independent and have mutually reinforcing effects.
Attention can exaggerate causal judgment in the direction implied by
prior knowledge so that causal attribution follows the focus of attention.
Similarly, salience and vividness enhance the perceived prominence of the
stimulus and exaggerate its evaluation in whichever direction they initially tend (Fiske and Taylor, 1984: 188–89). Attention is thus not only

related to cognizance but also has spillover effects on judgment before the actual judgment process formally begins.

The Judgment of Stimuli

The properties of information and the context in which it becomes available affect not only cognizance and attention but also evaluation, judgment, and consequently the comprehension of information. The last section mentioned some factors that exert such multiple influences; this section will discuss additional properties of information and context that can affect judgment and inference. In the first place, the quantity of information and the amount of detail it contains influence the importance attached to it. The more plentiful and rich in detail the information, the greater the tendency is to perceive it as reliable and attach weight to it. The tendency is particularly strong in international politics, a domain often characterized by the perceived lack of the most desired information and by deception, complexity, and uncertainty. Detail and quantity seem to provide an insurance against errors in judgment and a measure of credibility. When plentiful, detailed information contradicts previously reached judgments and inferences that decisionmakers are unable and unwilling to give up for cognitive or motivational reasons, it imposes on them a search for argumentation that will discredit its validity or its relevance. The information cannot just be ignored or suppressed but has to be explained away convincingly. In the process the validity of these judgments and inferences is elevated.

Information is judged by the context in which it generally appears or in which it appeared and was judged in the past. Intelligence analysts are involved in observing a problem from the early stages, when information is scant and ambiguous. They must rely at first on concept-driven information processing and on forming conceptual frameworks that allow them to draw inferences that go beyond the information given. As they proceed, they become predisposed toward both the preconceptions and their related interpretations, resulting in premature cognitive commitment. New information is then assimilated to early images. That in most cases such information is received incrementally only facilitates the assimilation of new information and the perseverance of initially held interpretations and beliefs. Perseverance is reinforced by people's tendency to be overconfident about how much they know and their difficulty in accurately factoring the absence of evidence into the judgment process. Even when the information that formed a particular impression has been discredited, the initial impression tends to persist. Thoroughly discredited evidence is uncommon, however, particularly in international politics, where an element of uncertainty often survives even when information has been discredited.

In the face of discrediting information, beliefs based on vivid, concrete historical data persist longer than beliefs based on abstract data, mainly because of the increased propensity to engage in causal processing when processing concrete data (C. A. Anderson, 1983). In fact, when detailed base-rate information (distributional information) is available, decision-makers tend to underutilize it in favor of singular or individuating information in explanation and prediction, particularly if the base-rate information is not perceived to have causal significance. Base-rate information is, however, likely to be used when no causal information is available at all or when the base-rate information is given a causal interpretation (Ajzen, 1977; Bar Hillel, 1980; Borgida and Brekke, 1981; Tversky and Kahneman, 1980).

It is also true that when base-rate information's situational applicability is salient, the decisionmakers are likely to prefer utilization of base-rate information over individuating information if they perceive it as relevant to the judgmental task and if they comprehend statistical logic and rules (Kruglanski, Friedland, and Farkash, 1984; Trope and Ginossar, 1988). But very often the case is that average decisionmakers (unlike the sophisticated subjects in typical psychology experiments), even when they are convinced of the relevance of base-rate information, do not know how to apply statistical rules and measurements correctly. In subjective probability estimates they tend to use symbolic ordinal and categorical descriptions of numbers (e.g. low, moderate, greater than) rather than use numbers, which are subject to mathematical operations with measurable errors and biases (Kuipers, Moskowitz, and Kassirer, 1988). Thus, even when decisionmakers realize the relevance and intend to use base-rate information, they operationalize their intention in a way that is normatively incorrect, often using the base-rate information the way they would use individuating information, although they may erroneously believe that they are actually utilizing the available base-rate information and doing it correctly. Furthermore, decisionmakers prefer individuating over base-rate information not only because the latter is more pallid but also because as cognitive misers, they prefer information that calls for less processing before use over information that requires more processing. The use of base-rate information calls for identifying the pattern or patterns, interpreting their significance, and relating them to the problem at hand. Individuating information often seems self-explanatory, and the path from raw data to inference is shorter, easier, and more visible than with base-rate information. This is markedly the case when a decision-maker has little training in how to use base-rate information.

Sometimes a single exposure to information that results in its mindless processing (e.g. because of its perceived irrelevance) may imprint some premature cognitive commitment. If decisionmakers do not have some specific incentive, they are not likely to subject the same information to serious scrutiny when it recurs in the future even if it now has direct relevance. The context of initial exposure may thus result in rigid representation that is not questioned or reconsidered (Chanowitz and Langer, 1981). Decisionmakers who have had little or no prior experience in foreign policy therefore tend not to reconsider and reevaluate their impressionistic knowledge and beliefs about particular foreign policy issues but to assume that the knowledge and beliefs to which they were exposed and that they themselves formed earlier in their careers are in principle accurate and relevant.

When information processors are confident that there will be an opportunity to correct any personal errors before any real harm is done, the perseverance of conservatism in the face of dissonant information is enhanced (Slovic and Lichtenstein, 1971) even if the assumptions of reversibility are optimistic and motivated by the wish to avoid change. Belief in a second chance could support the preference for conservatism in judgment, and a preference for conservatism justifies conservatism by biasing estimates of the availability of second chances. The tendency for conservatism to persist is reinforced by the fact that the uncertainty, deception, and complexity of information common to international politics lead information consumers to expect inconsistencies and information that contradicts their currently held perceptions and evaluations. The actual appearance of such information does not necessarily cause consternation or an urgent drive for reevaluation; it is considered par for the course in the game of nations. At the same time, as already stated, the more out of line discrepant information appears to be, the less influence it has on judgment—after all, the exceptional can be explained away as unusual and therefore as nondiagnostic. Discrepant information, then, has little or no effect on the prevailing definition of the situation.

The low alertness of Israel's military and civilian decisionmakers to warning information before the Yom Kippur War can be traced to overconfidence in their capability to deal with potential threats. In the first place, the chief of military intelligence estimated a high to very high probability that military intelligence would provide a warning 48 hours before an Arab attack. Although the estimate did not preclude the remote possibility that an early warning would not be given, that possibility, despite its potentially grave consequences, did not serve to increase the level of alertness to threatening information because the General Staff and the Northern and Southern commands were overconfident of their ability to deal effectively with an attack, even a surprise attack. This belief, which found expression in war games and operational planning, was shared by the military high command as well as by the political-civilian authorities—particularly by the prime minister and the defense minister. It was based on the assumption that the regular army, supported by the air force, with its unchallenged air superiority, could withstand a combined attack on two fronts and even carry out limited counterattacks, thus allowing ample time (72 hours) to mobilize the reserves, which would then allow for an all-out counterattack that would repel the senseless Arab attack within a few days. Even the worst-case analysis assumed only very minor accomplishments for the adversary, and they were expected to be short-lived. Such beliefs were held despite the growing vividness and salience of information indicating the increasing plausibility of a two-front war. The only effect the information had was to strengthen defenses in the Golan Heights, mainly by deploying there the elite Seventh Armored Brigade at the expense of weakening defenses in the Sinai (Bartov, 1978a: 216–19; Bartov, 1978b: 14, 19; Brecher with Geist, 1980: 53–69; Handel, 1976; Lanir, 1983: 18–30).

When interdependence between or dependence of other information-sets on any particular information-set increases, the particular information-set is perceived as increasingly central, important, and credible. Subsequently a broadening range of what is considered orderly valid knowledge is threatened by dissonant information. The judgment that information-sets are interrelated, that they are not isolated islands of knowledge, thus increases the likelihood of cognitive conservatism and perseverance.

Issues that are uppermost in the information processor's mind at any point have a priming effect and exert disproportionate influence on the interpretation of incoming information, biasing it in terms of these particular concerns even if the bias is not justified. The same information is evaluated and judged differently by decisionmakers preoccupied with different issues (e.g. owing to different roles or areas of interest and responsibility), and not only because the decisionmakers represent different types of bureaucratic parochialism, as the bureaucratic and organizational models claim; there are cognitively based reasons as well.

The probability of distortion in the evaluation and judgment of single-item information is lower than with multiple, complex information-sets. The latter involve additional obstacles to accurate processing. In the first place, not all data items necessarily gain attention, so that part of the data-set may be missing. Second, even if all data items succeed in crossing the awareness threshold, decisionmakers may not discern the relationships among the various items and hence may not interpret the ensemble as a whole. Finally, even if they realize that the data items should be interpreted as part of one picture, they could still miss the appropriate pattern or sequence because of the kinetic and modular properties of information in international politics (discussed in Chapter 1). Commenting on the difficulties of information processing in crisis situations, a senior member of the U.S. National Security Council observed: "There aren't a thousand people in this nation who are good integrators of knowledge" (R. J. Smith, 1984: 908).

The complexity of integrating multiple indicators into a unitary assessment of the situation (e.g. the adversary's intentions) encourages a motivational bias toward deriving a single indicator from one's conceptual framework to infer the adversary's expected behavior. With a single dominant indicator as a decisive input into judgment not only does the whole process of searching for and evaluating information become simplified but the probability that multiple indicators will produce inconsistency and a need for choice between alternative incongruent action orientations, with a resultant value trade-off, is preempted and avoided as well. To illustrate: beginning in 1969 the IDF's intelligence relied on one indicator to assess the probability of attack. It derived from the strategic assumptions of The Conception that Egypt would not attack unless it acquired a capability to strike at Israel in depth and at Israel's airfields in particular; that when Egypt acquired that capability, it would strike across the Sinai; and that only then, in conjunction with Egypt, would Syria be likely to attack. Therefore, the principal indicator of the probability of an Egyptian attack would be a change in Egypt's evaluation of its aerial strike capability; an increase in its capability would have to be accompanied by a change in its own perception of its capability. The resultant behavior would be an operation to reoccupy the Sinai (J. G. Stein, 1985b). This Israeli reliance on a single indicator was largely responsible for the conservatism that dominated the intelligence assessment of the low probability of attack.

By the same reasoning, a multistage inference process, in which the probability estimate for each stage depends on the probabilistic outputs of previous stages, could be insensitive to variation in the distribution of probabilities across all but the most likely events in the subsequent stages of inference (Gettys, Kelly, and Peterson, 1973). Such a bias has a cascading error effect as the number of stages in the process increases. Complex multiple and multistage information processing in general, as well as its related manifestations in the main tasks facing the intelligence analyst—namely, identifying a decision already taken by the adversary, analyzing responsive decisions, and predicting the outcome of a developing situation (S. Gazit, 1980)—depend upon covariation judgment. For the last two tasks, information cues are integrated through covariation judgment to predict responses by another actor or to assess the likelihood of alternative outcomes through the establishment of a causal or predictive link between the information cues and the response or outcome. Yet statistically naive individuals have a tenuous grasp of the concept of covariation and their judgments of covariation are frequently inaccurate or biased.[7]

Predictions of covariation are strongly affected by previously held theories. When covariations between events are unexpected or unpredicted by previously held theories, even those of consequential magnitude may go undetected. Expectations produce a vigilance for weak relationships and predictions of stronger empirical relationships than those that actually exist (Jennings, Amabile, and Ross, 1982). Attention-getting actors may be perceived as co-occurring with attention-getting behavior more often than they really do (McArthur, 1981: 220), thus biasing observers' judgments of actor-behavior covariation and influencing their predictions of other actors' future behavior. Illusory correlations persist in the face of contradictory reality; at the same time the influence of illusory correlations is so unapparent that decisionmakers overlook it (Chapman and Chapman, 1969; Golding and Rorer, 1972; McArthur, 1980). For a long time, for example, judgments of the progress of American military efforts in Vietnam were associated with body count. The more Vietcong and North Vietnamese regulars reported killed, the more successful American strategy was judged to be, and the more optimistic were the estimates, before the 1968 Tet offensive, of how soon an acceptable settlement would be reached (e.g. according to General Westmoreland, in 1967, and according to Assistant Secretary of Defense John McNaughton, possibly in 1968). President Johnson, in an interview in February 1966, referred to a staggering number of casualties that the Vietcong reportedly suffered, and observed: "Think of how terrible it would be if our losses were proportionately as high as theirs. We don't think Hanoi knows how serious it is. . . . They are looking at things through rose-colored glasses" (Graff, 1970: 98). His comment reflected the supposition that once the enemy realized the actual number of their casualties, they would reach the breaking point and relent—a view that overlooked the implications of the extraordinarily high morale of the North Vietnamese army despite its heavy losses, its excellent discipline, its committed and savvy leadership. Whatever the North Vietnamese breaking point was, they could not be beaten at a cost the United States was willing to pay (Mueller, 1980).

The effects of illusory correlations are evident with regard to the judgment of covariation between potential causes and observed outcomes. If a predicted outcome occurs as expected, the observers infer that its occurrence proves that their premises about the cause-effect link hold true and overlook the fact that the same outcome could be the result of another cause as well; one could be wrong in spite of being right. When the original causal theory is now believed wrongly to be true and is used more frequently to predict future events of the same type, the evaluations are biased.[8] To illustrate: in May 1973, notwithstanding the existence of information about an impending Arab attack, Israeli military intelligence considered war to be unlikely because the Arabs did not have the capability or thus the intention. The prediction seemed to be proven correct when war did not break out. Yet according to some analysts, the cause of Arab behavior in May was wrongly evaluated. War did not break out, not because the balance of deterrence held, but because the Soviets refused to support Arab war initiatives, hoping, after the Strategic Arms Limitations Talks (SALT) agreement in 1972, to reach some important accommodations with the United States. The lack of Soviet support together with expectations of additional arms deliveries from the Soviet Union led President Sadat to postpone the planned attack. The Soviets did not, however, think that the Nixon-Brezhnev summit of June 1973 forwarded any of their high-priority goals; and they withdrew their pressure for restraint from their Arab clients. Hence the wrong reasons for the May 1973 success in evaluation carried over to the October 1973 failure in evaluation—that is, the Israelis mistakenly assumed that the Arabs felt they did not have the capability and thus lacked the intention to initiate war (Ben Porat, 1985; J. G. Stein, 1982a).

An important element of the judgment and comprehension of information is the attribution of causality. The propensity for causal processing increases when dealing with concrete (e.g. case history) data (C. A. Anderson, 1983). Salience, which has already been shown to affect attention and judgment, plays an important role in causal attribution as well. In general, perceptually salient information is overrepresented in subsequent causal explanations. Salient causal agents are given weight because they are available (Pryor and Kriss, 1977; Smith and Miller, 1979; Taylor and Fiske, 1978). Higher causal effects are attributed to persons than to objects, which explains the tendency to attribute an enemy state's behavior to the predisposition of its leadership rather than to environmental or accidental factors and explains the concentration of attention on the elite's behavior.[9] Once causal knowledge about an event has been established, it affects not only the comprehension and explanation of the event but also the perception of its likelihood. The perceivers are then more willing to make the leap from possibility to probability (Ross et al., 1977), even though such a leap is frequently not necessarily justified by available information and actually biases probability estimates.

Categorization and Labeling

The categorization stage is essential for decisionmakers to impose some initial order and meaning and assess the usefulness of the confusing array of available information. They look for a quick fix, taking into account the various constraints they are under, among them time, role, and information overload. Thus they must rely on an accessible, simple set of categorization criteria to serve as cognitive reference points or labels, which, when assigned to the information at hand, will give at least an initially satisficing understanding of its significance. If stimuli can be identified as belonging to a certain category, then the necessity to systematically examine and identify new stimuli constantly is reduced. Labeling is important when hard, reliable evaluative standards are absent (Fischhoff et al., 1981; Marks, 1977), which is—as indicated in the first chapter—so often the case with information on international politics. Labeling provides a key for accessing and defining the relevance boundaries of the decisionmakers' metacognitive knowledge, that is, "all the knowledge and beliefs . . . acquired and stored in long-term memory that concern anything pertinent to social cognition," and metacognitive experiences, which are "any conscious cognitive and/or affective experiences or states of awareness that accompany and relate to a social cognitive enterprise" (Flavell, 1981b: 273; see also Flavell, 1981a). Once available information is placed in a particular category, categorization also allows information processors to go beyond the information given because he can add to it all the available knowledge about the category. Hence placing complex problems in familiar, although not always appropriate, categories helps in reducing the stress of dealing with them (Brislin, 1981: 80–81, 86). Finally, categorization provides cues about the potential for personal involvement and, through it, for deciding which information should be systematically processed and which should be heuristically processed. Expected personal involvement disposes decisionmakers toward systematic processing.

Categorization combines *holistic* and *component* analysis operations.

The two dimensions interact with and affect each other. Holistic analysis is issue and object centered and answers the core questions, What is the information about, and who is the information about? Component analysis answers a set of additional questions about pertinent aspects of information attributes, yielding generic knowledge that is helpful in advanced and specific processing and inference operations.

We shall look first at holistic categorization. As a cognitive miser, with limited information processing resources, the processor (individual or organization) attempts to be selective about investing the resources at hand. Hence the information attended to goes first through shallow processing, which requires only minimal cognitive effort. The decisionmaker decides how to proceed by applying two criteria for mapping the information. One focuses on categorizing information content by issue-area. The other focuses on the object of the information—categorization by primary actor description (e.g. enemy or ally). The interaction between the criteria provides the decisionmaker with an immediate first impression of the importance and relevance of the information. For example, if the object is an enemy and the issue-area, security, the information is guaranteed attention and is attributed a high priority in processing. Also by identifying the object of the information as an enemy, the information processor may then make automatic inferences from the categorical definition, such as motives, capability, style, and decision locus, to interpret the information (M. L. Cottam, 1986; R. W. Cottam, 1977: 62–80). In the process the information available becomes richer.[10]

Categorization by issue-area is basic and useful in organizing information and providing a broad and yet simple conceptual basis for judgment and inference. The conceptual categories are the issues to which the information relates.[11] Whatever the analytic, objective definitions of the issue-areas are, what counts is the subjective definition of the information by the decisionmaker. Empirical studies indicate this clearly. "Most striking, the evidence suggests that, while it is valid to define issue-areas objectively, that is, by the content of the decision, the analytically significant dimension of the issue-area concept for understanding the behavior of states is not that *reality* definition but, rather, the way decision-makers *perceive* the issue" (Brecher, 1974: 573).

Issue-area categories are organized hierarchically, that is, in order of their perceived importance for particular individuals or organizations, depending on their goals and interests.[12] Whether or not information is classified into what is considered an important issue category determines if and how much attention is allocated to it. If it is not classified into an issue category that is perceived as having general or specific importance to the decisionmaker's roles and responsibilities, it will gain little or no attention even if objectively it is pertinent to the national interest and the roles and responsibilities of other decisionmakers (cf. Underdal, 1979). Hence the question of which individuals or organizations perceive the information as falling within an issue-area considered their domain of responsibility and accountability is sometimes no less, or even more, important for calling attention to it than the actual content of the information.

The hierarchical organization of issues has an additional effect. The lower the importance attributed to an issue, and the fewer links it is perceived to have with issues of higher importance, the more likely is dissonant information to be given attention. The reason is that the threat posed by the issue to the decisionmakers' core beliefs and attitudes is of little importance to them; thus they can afford to be proven wrong or even to revise initially held views. On the other hand, the more important the issue, the stronger the motivation is to actively scan the environment in search of supportive information and the greater the alertness to information of this kind; discrepant information is more likely to be ignored or to go unnoticed.

The object and issue-area categorizations of information facilitate necessary, instant coping tasks: recognizing events; placing large quantities of complicated, sometimes confusing, inconsistent data in context and perspective; weighing the importance of the information, and consequently the urgency, timing, and order of its analysis compared with other tasks on the agenda that compete for the decisionmaker's limited resources of attention; and establishing a preliminary notion of what strategies are required to deal with it (e.g. ego-defense, assimilation, rejection, procrastination, bolstering). Being able to perform coping tasks reduces the potential for panic, anxiety, and stress by providing the decisionmaker an instant sense of control over what might otherwise seem an overwhelming flow of information. The two core categories also define the relevance of the information to and interdependence with other issues on the decisionmaker's agenda. Not only is judgment of the present value of information affected by holistic categorizations but the future implications of the information for value satisfaction are also inferred and predicted from it. The labeling of information by issue-area and object sets the general framework and parameters for the interpretation and inference of possible implications.[13]

Categories are usually not empty; that is, they contain data that were received, experienced, and stored earlier. By playing an important role in retrieving information already stored in memory (Spyropoulos and Ceraso, 1977), categorization indirectly affects its availability for processing other information. The categories now provide the context for the current interpretation of new information. Yet such second-order effects of categorization are not always obvious to information processors, and they do not take precautions to avoid the unwarranted contextual effects that categorization may produce, such as unjustified covariation judgments that are prompted by the easy availability of related, memory-stored information. At the same time categorization entails inferential leaps that go beyond the information given. All members of a category are assumed to have the perceptible properties the category concept is supposed to imply. Yet having the necessary and sufficient properties for inclusion in the category does not logically imply all the additional information inferred.

Categorization by issue-area can reflect division of labor or determine it. The fact that a given individual or organization has been responsible for particular issue-areas and assigned to gathering information in those areas labels the information from that source from the very outset as relevant mainly to those particular areas—again an unwarranted inferential leap on the part of its consumers. Conversely, information processors decide who the consumers of the information should be. That is, categorizing the information into a particular issue-area, and hence into an area with which certain decisionmakers are associated, determines who gets what and how much of the information—who gets all of it, who gets only part, and who does not get any. This view is in line with the basic principles of the cybernetic paradigm (Steinbruner, 1974: 47–87), which maintains that the decisionmaking requires simplifying information processing by transforming a complicated problem with a considerable element of uncertainty into a set of simple problems. One way to transform a complex problem is to break it down into a series of simple subproblems that can be coped with sequentially or allocated among different policymaking bodies and individuals.

Interfacing with and following the initial stage of the holistic categorization process are a number of more specific, complementary component categorization judgments that are issue and object related but provide further orientation cues before the decisionmaker proceeds with more detailed processing. The labeling factors considered by the information processors are some or all of the following.[14]

1. The spatial factor determines the actor's definition of self, others, and issues in the context of each particular issue. Decisionmakers may apply different spatial categorizations to different issues. For example, the United States may think of itself as an Atlantic or a Pacific nation, depending on the issue in question.

2. The temporal factor determines how each actor sees time and its implications for his behavior in any particular context. Is the passage of

time perceived as neutral, as acting against him, or as acting in his favor? Does he estimate that he has enough time to make a choice, or does he feel pressured for time?

3. The interaction factor determines core beliefs about the subject matter and about the relationship between the actor and his environment, such as to what extent the international environment is perceived as conflict-ridden or harmonious, hostile or friendly, changeable or fixed. It thus determines expectations about the possible results of alternative modes of behavior.[15] The temporal and interaction factors affect the type of bounded rationality each decisionmaker adheres to (George, 1979b: 103).

4. The affective factor determines the feelings of the actor toward the object of perception. Events cause people to respond affectively, and affect has a primary effect on thinking (Heise, 1979: viii; Zajonc, 1980).

5. The core-values factor determines the scale of values applied to categorize any particular object of perception. The scale indicates what is normatively acceptable and what is not.[16]

6. The consensus factor determines the extent to which the actor believes that his views and perceptions are shared by others, that is, that his is consensual knowledge.[17]

7. The self-others factor determines whether certain information is believed to be relevant for and impinge on self-perception or the perception of others and hence whether and what type of ego-defensive mechanism should be used.

8. The knowledge factor determines the degree to which the actor believes that the available information represents all the knowledge necessary to make a sound judgment.

9. The level-of-uncertainty factor determines the degree of faith the actor has in the validity of his judgment, which determines how resistant to change it will prove.

The various factors influence and reinforce one another.[18] Thus, for example, the affective factor, the labeling of certain objects as liked or disliked, may be influenced by the core-values factor. The degree of uncertainty may be influenced by the consensus factor, that is, the extent to which a person assumes particular judgment is supported by the identical perceptions of others. These components also have a bearing on the dynamics of perceptions challenged by dissonant information. For example, the smaller the factor of uncertainty, or the greater the faith that the existing concepts are consensual, the lower is the readiness to consider changing current attitudes in the face of dissonant information.

Component categorization is important not only for direct processing of information but also for the routine of segmentation, which involves "classifying stimuli in terms of similarity on separate dimensions of a stimulus, rather than on its totality" (Graber, 1984: 135). Complex, multifaceted information is broken into several simpler components. Each can be integrated into different preexisting schemata, thus providing an opportunity to tap an array of schema options. Segmentation based on categorization is also useful in making complex value judgments. When information processors find it difficult to make integrated global judgments about people or situations, they use segmentation to provide a sequential series of single-faceted value judgments (Graber, 1984: 135–37).

Finally, decisionmakers need not run systematically through all the components. They are more likely to go through categorization dimensions sequentially and adopt a satisficing strategy. In taking this approach information processors look for the dimension that is most salient to them or that comes most easily to mind. If they are satisfied with the result, they stop there; if not, they apply additional dimensions, one by one, until they reach a satisfactory level of understanding the information or decide how to proceed in processing.

The consequences of holistic and component categorization can be observed in the American approach to the Vietnam issue. Successive American administrations and decisionmakers labeled the war in Vietnam a Communist-bloc-directed act of aggression, an attempt to export the revolution from one state, North Vietnam, to another, South Vietnam, and thereafter to all of Southeast Asia. They rejected the notion that it was a civil war motivated by Vietnamese nationalism even more than by Communist ideology. The initial holistic categorization was complemented by some additional, more detailed and specific characterizations. South Vietnam was perceived to be part of the "free world," which was threatened by Communist aggression that was basically evil and externally dependent. At risk were core values that the United States represented and was committed to uphold as part of its manifest destiny. America was deemed capable of coping with the problems because of the superior resources available to it—political, economic, military, and technological. Time was working in its favor, so that it could contain the threat and at the least be assured of an indefinite stalemate (Kattenburg, 1980: 172–74, 236).

The U.S. conception placed events in Vietnam in the broader context of East-West global relations and provided American decisionmakers with a clear and certain notion of the importance of the issue and the appropriate U.S. policy orientation even if actual policy was sometimes ambiguous. In this sense the Vietnam problem was perceived to be no different from other past and present events that belonged to the same category (e.g. Berlin, Korea). It was not a novelty but a relatively well-structured problem, the details of which—that is, country expertise—were not particularly important; in fact categorization eliminated the need for expertise. It was mainly an issue to be managed by the military once the United States had decided that it had a commitment to South Vietnam. The premises for evaluative and predictive judgments of future events and developments were thus set, fixing the parameters of the interpretations and options to be considered.

Proto-Rules: Orientation-Preference Cues

An important set of signposts, or proto-rules, for attention allocation, judgment, and inference is based on the decisionmaker's preferred orientation: toward source, message, target, audience, or any combination thereof. Proto-rules affect the interest in and attention to information; the level of credibility attributed to information; its importance within the whole ensemble of information; and, finally, the preference for one among competing interpretations. Orientation-preference cues can be applied universally and consistently to actors, issues, and contexts or can be specific to actor, issue, and context. Dependence on judging by orientation cues grows with the increase of uncertainty and complexity, because the judgments follow simple rules that are easy to understand and apply.

Source orientation cues. Attention to and judgment of information is based on the evaluation of the identified source of the message. Herein, then, lies the first obstacle, namely, the difficulties often encountered in international politics in identifying the actual source of a message. Such a high degree of identification with the sender may be created that the content of the message becomes assimilated with the receiver's attitude toward the communicator (Aronson, Turner, and Carlsmith, 1963; Kelman and Eagly, 1974). Thus a reliable message could be rejected purely on the basis of dislike and the low credibility consequently accorded to the source, and the same message arriving from two different sources could be assigned different meanings by the same decoder (Cioffi-Revilla, 1979; Johnson and Scileppi, 1969). Three patterns of orientation toward the source of a message can be discerned:

1. Orientation toward the source resulting from the source's personality, which attracts attention and generates respect, credibility, and trust or their opposites.

2. Orientation toward the source resulting from identification with the source's value system and positions. Strangers whose positions approach

those of the recipient are accepted by the recipient as wiser, more moral, and more knowledgeable than strangers whose positions differ. In general, perceived similarities between the source and the recipient of a message can increase the attractiveness and credibility of the source and thus the persuasiveness and the effect the source has on the recipient's judgment (Byrne, 1961; Hass, 1981).

3. Orientation toward the source resulting from factors that do not inhere in the source itself but in the source's position, status, or power in the social system. For example, engineers appear to be more credible than dishwashers even regarding information unrelated to their expertise as engineers (Aronson and Golden, 1962). Ironically, a message coming from a low-prestige source and containing dissonant information involves a lower probability of distortion and manipulation than such a message from a high-prestige source (Manis, 1961). The source's low prestige prevents the recipient from perceiving the dissonant information as a threat and hence from reacting defensively to protect the self-image or other beliefs.

One difference between the three patterns is that in the first and second cases, the sources benefit from a preferential attitude by virtue of attributes personally inherent in them, not by virtue of extraneous social factors; this is not the case with the source in the third pattern, since the messages of any person occupying the same social position gains the same level of credibility, importance, and persuasiveness.

A second difference concerns the mode of persuasion. In the first case, the attractiveness of the source produces attitude change through a process of identification, where persuasion is not dependent on the existence or validity of evidence for the message. The learned attitudes are not integrated into the decisionmaker's belief system or maintained independent of the continued influence by the source. In the second case, credibility produces attitude change through a process of internalization, in which the learned attitude is integrated into the decisionmaker's belief system and then becomes independent of reinforcement by the source. In the third case, the power of the source persuades through a process of compliance that, as in the first case, does not involve internalization. It is possible, however, that over time, beliefs and attitudes produced by identification or compliance will be internalized or ignored because they will become increasingly difficult to maintain in isolation from the rest of the decisionmaker's beliefs and attitudes (Hass, 1981).

These attributes of source cues have implications for the processing of two categories of information. One category comprises information arriving at the processing system from the environment, from what is defined as an adversary or a foreign actor. The history of deception and surprise in international politics is so rich in examples of how source manipulation by the adversary or even self-inflicted errors in source judgment have led to major intelligence failures that this category needs no further elaboration (e.g. Handel, 1984; Whaley, 1973).

The other category consists of information that comes from within the decisionmaking system and flows to another part of it. The information can either be generated in the actor's own system or, after having arrived from the environment, be processed and interpreted by various bureaucratic and organizational players competing for the ear of high-ranking policymakers. The policymakers' orientation toward an external source could become crucial in their choosing among alternative interpretations of the situation. The source's rank in the bureaucratic and political hierarchy also has an effect: elite sources are more liable to be accepted as dependable and their information as important than lower-ranking sources, even if the latter are in a position to obtain more relevant and accurate information. Moreover, the high-level decisionmakers' orientation encourages those competing for their attention to develop techniques that attract them to a particular source and that arouse confidence in the source rather than in the essence of the information. In those instances the content is downgraded to a secondary importance.

It has been suggested that Lyndon Johnson unconsciously divided those around him into "men" and "boys." The men were the doers, who acted instead of talking and who deserved and received the respect of other men. The boys were the talkers, writers, and intellectuals, who spent their time thinking, criticizing, and doubting instead of doing and thus did not deserve the respect of the men. Johnson considered doubt a feminine quality and did not respect doubters. Thus advocacy of the hawks was taken more seriously than, and their optimism about the outcome of bombing North Vietnam was preferred to, the pessimism and doubt of the boys at the State Department and in the editorial rooms of the press. In early 1965, when Johnson had to decide whether to approve the bombing campaign, stigmatizing the sources of information enabled him to overcome some of his own inner doubts about the effects and utility of bombing, so that the dice were already loaded when the decision had to be made (Halberstam, 1972: 530–33).

Content orientation cues. For an individual preferring this orientation, the judgment and evaluation criteria are mainly of two kinds. One concerns the structural order in which arguments are presented, for example, presentation of the threat and then the promise, or presentation of the areas of agreement before the issues of disagreement. The initial stages of impression formation create a perceptual and cognitive set that predisposes a reader to, say, pay attention to specific elements and thus continue making connections (covariation or causal judgments) similar to the ones made earlier. The second concerns the attributes of the essence of the message, such as the degree of hedonism, the level of concreteness, or the level of implied threat (Perry, 1979: 50; Triandis, 1971: 95, 187–90). Cases involving both kinds of content orientation cues allow for the manipulation of the message by treating its structure and other attributes cosmetically without the receiver's awareness. Advisers or adversaries who know policymakers' orientation preferences can influence their reactions to information by manipulating the manner in which it is organized, phrased, and presented to them. In early 1965, for instance, when General Westmoreland asked for "just" two marine battalions, he was supported by U.S. Admiral Grant Sharp, commander-in-chief, Pacific (CINCPAC). Sharp promoted Westmoreland's request with well-chosen words designed to implant anxiety in civilians in Washington: he urged that the troops be deployed "before the tragedy." Washington, of course, acceded (Halberstam, 1972: 538). No politician would dare to take the risk of being blamed later for what, according to the inference from Sharp's wording, could turn out to be a costly mistake, especially when Westmoreland's request seemed a minor and justified one both in terms of the type of mission (security for the U.S. air base at Danang) and the size of the force requested. That it could become the first step toward an expanded ground presence was overlooked, although many in Washington and Saigon were aware of this.

Similarly, as the administration was edging toward a large-scale commitment of American troops to Vietnam in April 1965, after the Honolulu Conference, at which the figure of 80,000 troops was mentioned as necessary, Under Secretary of State George Ball argued that a threshold was being crossed that could lead to a much larger involvement. His main adversary was Robert S. McNamara, the secretary of defense, who was at the time a forceful advocate of escalation. In the ensuing debates between the two, Ball almost always lost; McNamara was confident, and skillful in using concrete facts and figures on force ratios. Yet some of the figures did not exist; McNamara had invented them. Ball, however, had no opposing figures. He acquired vague doubts and left the meetings feeling depressed and defeated (Halberstam, 1972: 579–81).

In summary, orientation toward content can cause recipients to isolate some properties of content from important elements of the message, making them unable to evaluate the message on its merits and in its full context. This inability can result in their accepting, rejecting, or interpreting a message, not on the basis of its substantive content, but rather according to its less important properties.

Target orientation cues. As already noted, because of the plurality of potential target actors (domestic and foreign) in international politics, messages may be meant for various destinations. The target of a message can be another criterion for attention allocation and judgment. Thus, when the need to evaluate the importance or reliability of a message arises, one possibility is to judge and draw inferences based on who the target of the message is believed to be. The criterion by itself does not fully relate to content or to the message's general background, context, and other properties, so evaluations based on it are likely to bias judgment and cause misperceptions. To illustrate: about the time that the Kennedy administration was coming into office, Khrushchev gave a major speech legitimizing wars of national liberation. The Kennedy administration interpreted the speech as a direct challenge; and its members made learning how to cope with guerrilla warfare a subject of intense interest. Years later high Soviet officials revealed that the speech was actually aimed at the Chinese (Halberstam, 1972: 122), in the context of the growing rift and competition between the Soviet Union and China.

Audience orientation cues. A subsidiary judgment cue for assessing both the credibility and importance of information, one that can be used by itself or can interact with each of the other three orientation cues, is the audience, forum, or, more generally, the social context in which the message becomes available. This variable can work both ways, that is, it can clarify or muddle judgment and inference. Information provided in a public forum (a parliament, an election campaign speech, etc.) could raise the question of who the intended target audience is, which may not be the same as the audience overtly addressed (domestic public, foreign actors, etc.). Moreover, given the conspiratorial character of international politics and the corollary tendency to attribute higher credibility to information that is not in the public domain than to information that is, a dilemma arises as to how credible and important publicly available information is. On the other hand, private forums also raise doubts about the credibility of private messages, since the lack of publicity may affect the level of commitment and accountability the source feels toward promises or threats in the message. Lack of publicity may also affect the source's assessment of the costs of cheating and deceiving, because the private forum makes denial, without the risk of losing future credibility, much easier.

Sadat threatened to resort to force in the early 1970s mostly while addressing domestic audiences. At the same time he used foreign channels to express conciliatory messages, including inquiries about the possibilities of a political settlement in the Middle East (e.g. talks between various Egyptian emissaries and Henry Kissinger; talks with the foreign ministers of Brazil, Italy, and Switzerland and the U.N. secretary-general;

and interviews with journalists like Arnaud de Borchgrave, *Newsweek*'s foreign editor). The conciliatory messages only reinforced views in both Washington and Jerusalem that the public threats were intended mostly for domestic consumption, whereas Sadat actually recognized his inability to carry them out and thus was searching for a diplomatic solution. In fact, one explanation offered for Sadat's ambiguous behavior was that the threats were also intended to prompt the United States to play an active role in encouraging a settlement by applying pressure on Israel, hence the expectation among some in the Israeli establishment of possibly reaching some political settlement with Egypt in 1974. Such interpretations, of course, only reinforced the dominant view prior to October 1973, that the probability of war was low.

Integrated criteria. An orientation for interpretation and judgment more complex, and probably more likely, than any single-criterion orientation, is one that combines two or more criteria; that is, judgment is based on both source and content, or on source and target, or on source, content, audience, and target. Although an integrated approach is optimal, it too poses several problems, for the combination of a number of criteria into an integrative judgment assumes that the decisionmaker has the cognitive capability of performing precise, intuitive, weighted-average calculations. Even the decisionmaker who can calculate, if such calculations are possible, has to be aware of the components of the equation and spell them out. First to be determined is, Should all four criteria be given equal weight in the integrated calculus? If so, where at least three of the four criteria point toward a particular interpretation, then that interpretation should be considered the correct one. The dilemma arises when various criteria support different interpretations. In such ambiguous situations the decisionmaker has an incentive to make an arbitrary, rather than analytic, choice from among alternative interpretations. Second, should any of the four criteria be given more weight, and should any order of priorities be set up? Here there is a danger that an order of preference will be attached arbitrarily or universally according to some fixed rule without regard for contextual variables. The information processor may also be unable to handle adequately the complexity of a process combining four differently weighted dimensions into a single integrated outcome (thereby coming up with a single weighted average) and yet not be aware of personal inadequacy in this matter.[19]

Finally, a caveat must be added. We must not assume from the above discussion that background factors, such as the source, content properties, target, or audience of the message, are unimportant or irrelevant to judging and defining the situation. They could, on the contrary, provide important and useful cues; but whether they were correctly weighted, properly integrated, and assigned appropriate relevance to the information must be carefully examined. Yet sometimes information processors use these extrinsic criteria not as they should, to deal with the actual meaning of information, but mainly to make it easier to absorb, process, and employ information for their own functional and motivational purposes.[20]

Stated more generally, the argument that the heuristic processing of persuasive messages (by attending to extrinsic persuasion cues) and their systematic processing are not mutually exclusive (see also Chaiken, 1987) is congruent with the fact that in international politics extrinsic cues are often informative. In the games nations play, form is often part of the message and in some cases the message itself (e.g. R. Cohen, 1987; Miller and Siegelman, 1978). Moreover, in some cases, for example, when time is at a premium, heuristic processing is much more efficient than systematic processing, which may even be counterproductive. Optimally, decisionmakers should use the heuristic processing of messages selectively, understand its cost and appropriate application, and combine heuristic with systematic processing as required by the task and situation.

Interaction Effects

Thus far we have considered the influence of information properties on the decisionmaker's attitude toward information. But no less significant effects emanate from the interaction between information and its recipient. These have an impact in several areas: the degree of openness to new information, the weight and credibility attributed to it, and the degree of cognitive conservatism in the face of dissonant information. Here we shall briefly discuss the importance of directness of contact and degree of involvement.

Directness of contact has implications for a number of processing aspects. Information obtained or experienced firsthand is more vivid than information received through indirect channels; it is consequently perceived as more reliable and weighted more heavily (Borgida and Nisbett, 1977; Nisbett and Ross, 1980: 50) and is therefore preferred. Direct contact with the object of an attitude is likely to have a bearing on the affective component of the attitude toward it as well, creating tenacious emotional commitments (Triandis, 1971: 67) and thus enhancing the tendency toward cognitive conservatism.

Policymakers who have secured information by direct contact with other people are likely to refuse to admit that they are mistaken, misinformed, or deliberately misled, even if a reliable source tells them so. Such an admission would be damaging to their self-esteem. This issue is particularly important in contacts between people from different cultures, which often occur in international politics. The actual contact influences both self-perception and perception of the adversary because one has reason to compare one's own positive attributes with the negative ones of the rival; therefore, when a conflict of interests arises, a positive auto-stereotype emerges (Triandis and Vassiliou, 1967), producing a sense of self-righteousness, which makes empathy with the other side and an understanding of the other's mind-set difficult. On the other hand, some studies (e.g. Druckman and Ludwig, 1970; Kelman, 1975: 98) indicate that positive, active, direct contacts with members of a different nation can positively affect the perception and evaluation of intentions, though not necessarily in line with the objective content of the specific information. It is no wonder, then, that sometimes summit meetings serve as a source of self-delusion or a means of deception, when friendly and direct interaction becomes the main input for evaluation while at the same time leading to a rejection of discrepant, even if reliable, information. "Trivial and transitory factors may assume an inordinate importance in the eyes of the participants. The policymaker may succumb to more vivid and immediate impressions of a personal nature, displacing or blurring the more important and permanent background factors" (Groth, 1964: 836). An obvious example is Khrushchev's promise to Kennedy at their meeting in Vienna in 1961 that he would not do anything to embarrass the U.S. president before the coming congressional elections. As a result, Kennedy refused to accept the possibility of missiles' being installed in Cuba, hence his intense emotional reaction when it was made clear to him, beyond doubt, that he had been misled.

Decisionmakers often prefer to acquire instant, direct knowledge, which tends to be shallow and tendentious yet gives them an unwarranted sense of confidence in their judgment. Even rational and unemotional decisionmakers get an unwarranted sense of confidence from such information insofar as firsthand impressions can have dramatic consequences. An illustration is the impact on McGeorge Bundy of his critical mission in February 1965 to review the situation in Vietnam prior to a decision on whether to escalate the war by resorting to bombing. Until then, Bundy had not been committed to that option. While he was in Saigon, however, the Vietcong struck the American barracks at Pleiku with mortars; eight Americans were killed and sixty wounded. The next day Bundy flew to Pleiku and visited the wounded; he was strongly affected by the direct contact with the consequences of war and immediately recommended a retaliatory strike. His mind was now made up: he joined the hawks. Indeed, his memo written on the way home from

Pleiku called for, and became a major input to, the decision to launch a sustained bombing campaign. He wrote: "The policy of graduated and continuing reprisal outlined in Annex A is the most promising course available, in my judgment" (Halberstam, 1972: 525).

Just as important, direct contact may increase the sense of personal involvement.[21] The degree of involvement is the degree to which information processors consider themselves accountable for an outcome or personally affected by it. It has a number of important ramifications. First, it determines what type of information is included in the areas of immediate interest and attention, so that the alertness threshold for this type of information is lowered, and the likelihood of its becoming a stimulus is raised. Second, involvement means that actions and behavior of the adversary are regarded as a function of their personal implications for the decisionmakers in question. If behavior is interpreted in the context of its perceived personal implications (Jones and DeCharms, 1957; Petty, Cacioppo, and Goldman, 1981), the actions of Actor A are perceived differently by Actor B if he thinks their results will affect him than if he thinks they will not. Hence the degree of perceived potential involvement could affect the degree to which people consider themselves committed to specific positions and attitudes. The position policymakers take toward warning information that is relevant to their commitments depends on whether they foresee a decisive role for themselves should the threat and danger implied in the warning materialize (Janis, 1962).

Indeed, as involvement increases and the issue becomes more central, decisionmakers become more concerned with veridicality and the costs of errors and hence are more motivated to engage in deeper, systematic processing (Chaiken, 1987; Petty and Cacioppo, 1986). But they are not always able to do so, for example, when an unanticipated, quickly developing international crisis requires instant judgment and response. In that case they may be unable to perform systematic processing; they may be unwilling to appear indecisive and at the same time unable to form an adequate response. Consequently decisionmakers may resort to heuristic processing in spite of their obvious preference for systematic processing and their realization of the cost of error. The judgments and attitudes formed as a result of heuristic processing are not necessarily less persistent than those formed by thoughtful elaboration; public commitment to the policy or to behavior that is congruent with the policy reinforces those judgments and attitudes. The emergent policy and its related attitudes tend to become entrenched and resistant to counterargumentation or dissonant feedback information. Thus involvement not only influences the interpretation of content and the importance attributed to it but relates inversely to the effectiveness of dissonant information. In situations with a high level of personal involvement, the selective search for information intensifies.[22] As a corollary, the tendency toward cognitive conservatism increases (Apsler and Sears, 1968; Frey, 1986; N. Miller, 1974), as does premature cognitive closure.

One obvious effect of a strong sense of involvement and responsibility for the consequences of a policy is its personification. Major foreign policy issues, long-standing ones in particular, are likely to become personalized because of the high cost of failure and the high value of success. In the process the line between state interest and personal interest becomes almost indistinguishable. Decisionmakers increasingly feel that they personify the state, and the other state's behavior is construed as challenging them directly and having grave personal implications. Adversaries' words and actions are judged and interpreted through a self-centered prism without much consideration for their actual motives and interests or the circumstances under which they operate.

Early in his presidency Richard Nixon began to personalize the Vietnam War. By April 1970 he was worried about the coup in Cambodia and the stalemated military situation in Vietnam. It seemed that Kissinger's secret talks with the Vietnamese were leading nowhere and that North Vietnam intended to overthrow the Lon Nol regime and take over Cambodia. In fact, Hanoi showed no sign of being impressed by the administration's repeated warnings, while Moscow's apparent response to explorations of the possibility of a summit was increased involvement in Egypt. Domestically, the doves in the Congress were trying to force the administration into seeking a ban on the MIRV missile, and the House and the Senate had rejected Nixon's nominees to the Supreme Court. The antiwar critics forced him to announce the withdrawal of 150,000 troops from Vietnam by the spring of 1971. Thus Nixon, in the view of some, felt besieged by both foreign and domestic adversaries who defied his authority. He had to prove that he could not be pushed around, and so on April 28, 1970, he issued a secret order that American troops invade Cambodia for a ground assault on the North Vietnamese sanctuaries there in a joint large-scale operation with the South Vietnamese army. He ordered this despite an abundance of analyses and assessments from the Pentagon, the State Department, and the National Security Council suggesting that such a course of action would only provoke the North Vietnamese to overthrow Lon Nol's government to defend their supply lines and troops. Some of Kissinger's aides also warned of tremendous domestic consequences and, in addition, pointed out that an invasion of Cambodia by American troops would leave the defense of South Vietnam exposed and that in general the operational plan was imprecise and vague as well. The policy appeared to many to be irrational, and the intelligence on which it was based, unpersuasive. But evidence and arguments had little importance compared to Nixon's belief that he was being defied by Hanoi and thus had to prove his toughness and resilience. He paid selective attention to argumentation and assessment. Senior cabinet members, like Melvin Laird and William Rogers, who might object and raise counterarguments were avoided and were neither informed nor consulted on the matter. The operation was justified as necessary for salvaging Cambodia as well as the Vietnamization process and for convincing the North Vietnamese to take the Paris talks on a negotiated settlement seriously (Hersh, 1983: 184–93; Shawcross, 1979: 134–35).

To summarize, directness of interaction and the degree of personal involvement affect the allocation of attention, the assessment of the importance of information, and to a lesser degree the potential for cognitive conservatism.

Effects of Volume and Overload

A dimension of information that is vitally important in processing is its volume. Two contingent situations are of interest in this regard: insufficient information and information overload. We shall not discuss in detail the problems that arise from a real or imaginary lack of information. While the problems in the former case are obvious, they can be compounded when the real lack is not conceived as such—when the criteria adopted by information processors as to how much is enough allow them to define the situation with adequate certainty despite the scarcity of information. On the other hand, the information processors can perceive an insufficiency of information when in fact more information would not necessarily add accuracy to the evaluation or the quantity of available information already suffices for reasonably accurate inference and judgment. The perception of a lack might encourage procrastination in decisionmaking or arbitrary decisions built on the assumption that all or most of the alternative interpretations and evaluations are potentially more or less equally valid.

Particularly pertinent, however, is the situation in which an information processor must cope with information overload, owing to the limits on human capacity for processing information (Bobrow, 1972: 60–61; G. A. Miller, 1956). Even when not all of the information is relevant to the decision, it distracts the decisionmaker. This prevalent problem in foreign policy decisionmaking stems not only from the plurality of players, arenas, issues, and issue linkages, which generate increasing quantities of heterogeneous information, but also from the inherent propensity of individuals and organizations to lack selective restraint in gathering and collating the information made available by new sophisticated hardware.

Another reason for information overload is that the cost of error or omission can be so high that foreign policy decisionmakers build organizational redundancy into intelligence collection and interpretation. In other words, the boundaries between areas of responsibility are on purpose not mutually exclusive; allowing jurisdictional overlaps among the various intelligence organizations means that if one misses some vital information by oversight or owing to error in interpretation, another may possibly pick it up. This approach is in principle sensible—it takes into account the nature of foreign-policy-related information—but the cost to the decisionmaking system is that most of the time organizational redundancy contributes to information overload; producing redundant information adds to the burden of information processing without being cost-effective in terms of improved knowledge. Nor does redundancy in information collection result only from premeditated intent; in an interdependent world, where issues are closely interrelated, clear and exclusive boundaries of responsibility for each organization are impossible to determine and maintain, and the implied perfect coordination in information exchange among competitive organizations is practically unattainable. Hence organizational redundancy in information processing and the consequent overload are largely unavoidable.

Moreover, the very nature of international politics necessitates a trade-off in information-processing-related problem solving. For example, the effort to reduce unanticipated crises produces growth in the volume of accumulated information, which results in information overload (Oneal, 1982: 317). At what point the costs and benefits of more information are balanced with the costs and benefits of early anticipation of crises is a question impossible to answer with satisfaction and clarity. The same dilemma pertains in efforts to distinguish between signals and noises when the cost could be the accumulation of additional information, leading to an overload problem.

Information overload cannot be defined absolutely but must be defined specifically with regard to the capacities of each decisionmaking system to absorb and process data.[23] However, the overload phenomenon in itself, the patterns of coping with it, information's diminishing returns to scale (or quantity), and the consequences of all these have properties and forms that can be characterized in broad general terms. Conceptually, information overload is defined as a situation where the needs posed by information management exceed the capacities of the decisionmaking system, be it an individual or an organization, to respond to those needs. In operational terms information overload has two faces that can appear separately or together.

One measure of information load is the ratio between the volume of information and the time available for its processing. Overload in this sense is, then, a situation where the absolute quantity of information surpasses the processor's ability to absorb it within a particular time frame. The overload could be a permanent state of affairs, that is, *structural overload,* or an ad hoc phenomenon due, for example, to a crisis or emergency, that is, *situational overload.* A typical case of structural overload occurs in a system in which decisionmakers at the top carry more roles than they can effectively handle. Role overload produces information overload. Yet even when the usual role allocation does not overburden the decisionmakers, situational role overload could emerge if a crisis brings about the centralization of power, forcing the decisionmakers to assume additional roles and responsibilities. The combination significantly increases information load because of, on the one hand, the properties of the situation (crisis) that generate growing quantities of information and shrinking response time and, on the other, broader areas of responsibility. Moreover, in emergencies, because of the high stakes involved and the much higher level of accountability expected of decisionmakers, they are less inclined to delegate processing responsibilities even to trusted subordinates. All in all, they face a time-poor, information-rich decision environment, while the much higher stakes and accountability levels increase stress and anxiety, possibly further reducing their capacity to cope when they are most needed. With the advent of the Middle East crisis in October 1973, for example, communication in the American decisionmaking system became mostly vertical; increasing quantities of raw data went straight to the top, to Kissinger and a few close aides. Information was not circulated horizontally, so that much of it lacked expert interpretation and analysis and had to be processed at the top, causing a heavy overload (Dowty, 1984: 303–4).

A related problem occurs when the share of information that needs to be processed simultaneously (rather than serially) increases significantly. People's abilities to process simultaneously vary widely. Overload reflects cognitive constraints on simultaneous processing at any one point in time, even when the absolute volume of information over time is not unusually heavy.

The other measure of information load is the ratio between ambiguous, uncertain, inconsistent information and unambiguous, certain, consistent information. Overload occurs when the ratio is heavily weighted in favor of the former. In other words, a limited number of problematic information items occupy a significant share of the decisionmaker's attention and processing capability space, causing a decline in the absolute quantity of information that can be processed. The typical kind of uncertainty, which affects the ratio between time and information and produces overload effects, is response uncertainty. It is characterized by the number of alternatives and by the probability distribution across alternatives. As the number of alternatives increases and the probability distribution approaches equality, so does subjective uncertainty, which entails an increase in required decision time and a decrease in confidence in the decision (Hoge and Lanzetta, 1968).

How does the information processor deal with the various forms of overload? In principle, coping can involve manipulation of any one or a combination of the following: the process of absorbing information from the environment, the channels of information flow, the content of information, and the problem to which information relates. Each strategy for coping is operationalized through particular techniques.[24]

1. Manipulating the absorption process entails either *ignoring* additional information once the load threshold has been reached or *delaying* (queuing) its absorption until the pressure eases off, thus processing the load over an extended period of time. A variation on the delay tactic is to sequentially process information bits that should actually be processed simultaneously, which could lead to a failure to correctly comprehend the integrative meaning of the information. Which information should be delayed might be decided by establishing a hierarchical order of importance among information bits and processing them in that order. But order is more likely to be decided in a less analytic and more myopic manner, for example, by assigning primacy in the temporal order information enters the processing system. An adversary can exploit the delay technique by spewing out large amounts of disinformation before attack to delay the target's response until it is too late, thus gaining by deception the advantage of surprise (Betts, 1982: 110). A different technique is *filtering,* or not processing certain categories of information according to criteria decided upon in advance. Filtering by category—by, for example, the hierarchical ordering of issues (low concern versus high concern) or the source of information—is often nondifferential and rigid. Once a decision has been made as to which data categories are not to be processed, adapting the decision to changing circumstances is not likely. The rule will be applied mindlessly; whole categories of information will not be processed, precluding any discrimination between items or reevaluation of the value of items within such categories. Unpleasant information—information that does not support strongly held preconceptions or is schema-inconsistent—is likely to be ignored, filtered out, or delayed in processing (O. R. Holsti, 1971; Sherman and Corty, 1984: 242).

2. Manipulating information channels usually involves the common technique of *decentralization,* or the division of labor among a number of individuals or organizations, and the resultant substitution of the volume problem with a coordination problem. Adopting this technique entails at least a tacit belief that the coordination problem is more manageable than the volume problem. Even if the coordination problem is overcome, decentralization assumes decomposability, that is, "that relatively independent units or chunks of the problem can be identified well in advance and preserve their boundaries over time" (Bobrow, 1977: 106). As the volume of information increases, decentralization can be further expanded physically by adding layers to the existing processing system. This generates taller processing hierarchies, creates more opportunities for information distortion, and raises the processing costs per unit of information; at the same time it also aggravates the coordination problem. Alternatively, the expansion of decentralization can take the form of allowing lower echelons more latitude for screening out more information before sending it higher. This, however, may reduce the quality of information processing in the system because less information reaches the higher decisionmaking levels (Downs, 1967: 129–30). That increases the chance of errors and misperceptions resulting from insufficient information. It thus becomes a choice between the risk of errors due to information overload and errors due to insufficient information. Striking a balance is an extremely difficult task. One way top-level decisionmakers avoid the dilemma of choice between these risks in crisis situations, when the stakes are high, is by the centralization of authority in their hands. This sometimes leads to ad hoc channels of communication being improvised; for example, heads of governments could bypass inputs from regular communication channels and reduce the information load by communicating directly (O. R. Holsti, 1971).

An alternative technique is *accessibility reduction,* that is, stringent gatekeeping to reduce the number of information processing units that have access to top policymakers. Here, although the system is managing and coping with all the information, in fact only part of the information reaches the top.

These techniques are not very useful in high-threat nuclear crisis situations. Bracken (1983: 56–59) points out the difference, in this sense, between the conventional hierarchical military command and control structure and the command and control structure for nuclear forces. In times of heightened military (which may well mean nuclear) activity, the warning and intelligence networks of the United States bypass much of the military command structure, reporting directly to the top political leadership. At the same time, the tight coupling of the systems of warning and intelligence involves the entire military organization in the management of the threat, so that the information from the systems overwhelms the political decisionmakers. Yet if the decisionmakers attempt to impose a hierarchical centralized order on the systems so that information can be allocated among the various units and subunits that act as gatekeepers, they may lose the capability to cope timely with the threat and to fully control the response.

3. Manipulating the content of information takes place when the decisionmaker is aware of its relevance and usually involves a superficial, perfunctory acquaintance with the information and the avoidance of full-scale, in-depth processing. One possible technique is *routinization*, absorbing and filing without fully processing, that is, operating under the assumption that the information in question is routine and does not add or change the essence of prior interpretations, thus promoting premature cognitive closure. On September 10–15, 1964, a war game code-named Sigma II that simulated the effects of bombing North Vietnam was run. Among the participants were some of the government's top Vietnam policy makers. The results of the game were startling. The game revealed that North Vietnam was invulnerable to U.S. bombing. Yet, it had little effect on those who participated, according to William Bundy, one of the participants. He explains: "I cannot recall that any of the relevant staff members ever invoked the outcome in later discussions. Perhaps this reflects one of the most basic elements in this whole story—how much of planning and policy review came in the middle of days already full, and without chance to stop and reflect" (Gibbons, 1986: 353–54).

Another routinization technique might be to use computers that apply prestructured sequences of interpretation to incoming information. But this solution assumes the ability to conceive of alternative situations and types of information; even if possible, a priori conceptualization involves complex programming for which effective software is probably not currently available (Bobrow, 1977: 106; Knorr, 1979: 84). Progress in developing artificial intelligence computing systems may help resolve this problem in the future.

Routinization can have either primacy or recency effects. In the latter, and more likely, case, once information has been fully processed and policy guidelines based on it have been set, the decisionmakers move on to deal with other, more recent items on the agenda, considering the earlier subjects closed and calling for only a fraction of their attention in the future. Incoming information on the earlier subjects is either dealt with at lower levels or given a perfunctory treatment and then filed. When, on the other hand, the primacy effect operates, the decisionmakers are preoccupied with the subjects that first gained their attention to the extent that they become fixated on them. The decisionmakers now delegate authority to deal with more recent issues to lower-level bureaucrats, attributing less importance to those issues and assuming that concomitant information requires either none of their attention or only a fraction of it and can mostly be dealt with through bureaucratic routines.

A different but related technique is *ritualization,* or performing symbolic acts of processing when avoidance of the information or outright delay in processing is politically or normatively unacceptable. Ritualization entails going through the motions of processing without actually doing it, for example, asking aides to summarize a large and complex volume of information in half a page or in a briefing of a few minutes. Although the act is useless, research has shown that decisionmakers prefer short and oral reports (O'Reilly, 1983: 118). Such summaries give them a sense of control and knowledge that is often unjustified.

As the information overload worsens, intelligence organizations *encapsulate* information, that is, capture its essence through some transformation that bypasses the quantity problem. In principle this is a necessary and sensible approach to organizing information and transmitting it upward through channels easily and effectively. Yet it can become problematic when it is applied habitually and mindlessly. Two related and frequently used encapsulating techniques are quantifying so that the data can be summarized in a table and presenting data graphically. Quantification, when used indiscriminately, translates verbal, complex, and uncertain information into a neat set of numbers in a table, often providing a false sense of clarity and certainty. High-level decisionmakers are consequently prevented from raising doubts because the triggers of such doubts have been eliminated in the quantifying process, which has produced an uncertainty absorption effect (March and Simon, 1958: 164–65). When using the graphic presentation technique, the colorful and visual presentation of the data is even more imposing than their mere quantification. In many cases quantification and graphic presentation go together and are imposed on data that are impossible or very difficult to accurately represent in either way, so that in fact they are misrepresented. The drive to impose these transformations indiscriminately is particularly strong because military and intelligence organizations often adopt these techniques as part of their standard operating procedures of communication and presentation.

With the implementation of the Vietnamization-pacification strategy in 1969, Secretary of Defense Laird instructed the assistant secretary of defense for program analysis and evaluation to devise a monitoring system. This resulted in the Pacification Evaluation System (PACES), which was divided into six subsystems, the most important of which was the Hamlet Evaluation System (HES). The HES was a fully automated procedure for quantitative evaluation of the Vietnamization-pacification program at the hamlet level. The reports were used by the Johnson and Nixon administrations in a much broader context in their conduct of the war. The district senior advisers (DSAs) administered the HES questionnaire, with its 21 variables concerned with hamlet security, political issues, and socioeconomic development. A specific variable could be scored *A, B, C, D, E, N, X,* or *V* to describe the degree of success or failure in pacifying a particular hamlet. The scores were then integrated into an overall evaluation of each hamlet. The summary scores for all hamlets were grouped into the following categories for analysis and decisionmaking: secure (*A, B, C*), contested (*D, E*), not visited (*N*), abandoned (*X*), enemy controled (*V*). However, if one did not consult the detailed distribution of scores on each group of questions, the averaging of the different scores masked the complicated patterns of government and Vietcong influence in the hamlets to the point of being misleading. Nevertheless, the higher the policymaker, up the line to the secretary of defense, the greater the tendency was to look only at overall averages. Top policymakers focused on national and corps summaries, which could be misleading because the insurgency was not countrywide or corpswide but localized. Looking at district-level scores or even lower-level scores would have made more sense.

The HES indicators for measuring socioeconomic development and the establishment of political community further masked realities, especially with regard to areas that the Vietcong and the South Vietnamese government contested. For example, if government medical services were accessible to hamlet residents and a government-sponsored dispensary was located in the village and accessible to residents, the hamlet would be given an *A* score with respect to public health evaluation. As more households participated in government-sponsored economic improvement programs and self-development programs, the hamlet got higher ratings. Households that owned television sets and motorized vehicles boosted a hamlet's economic activity evaluation. However, these indicators did not mean much when a hamlet still had an active Vietcong element because the Vietcong still had access to and influence over the population; nor did these indicators measure trends in population support for the government. At the same time high marks on the variables artificially raised the overall monthly scores, thus concealing the contested nature of the local situation and encouraging undue optimism by decisionmakers in Washington (Colby and Forbath, 1978: 259; Shultz, 1982).

Finally, information content can be manipulated by the *approximation* technique, that is, by being satisfied with a superficial or crude interpretation of the information. In its extreme form approximation risks totally erroneous processing (an outcome of which the policymaker is unaware). For example, after the Yom Kippur War broke out, the U.S. intelligence community did not meet to formally evaluate the situation. Rather the Defense Intelligence Agency (DIA), CIA, and Kissinger himself made quick estimates, which were dysfunctional in terms of quality. In fact, the DIA proved unable to deal effectively with the deluge of reports that soon engulfed it. The Pike report also contends that "randomized" intelligence may have contributed to one overreaction—the worldwide alert of October 24–25 (Dowty, 1984: 304–5).

4. Manipulating the problem to which the information relates can take the form of suspending confrontation with the problem by *defensive procrastination* (George, 1980a: 36; Janis and Mann, 1977: 86–88). This technique involves the ignoring, nonprocessing, or delayed processing of significant quantities of information pertaining to the problem and can be resorted to when a decision is not immediately needed. If a problem cannot be ignored, the information load it imposes can be reduced by *decomposing* the problem into subproblems and dealing with those defined as most crucial while delaying, ignoring, or delegating other subproblems to others. Thies (1982: 299–322) cites numerous instances indicating that when faced with the complex environment in which decisions with regard to Vietnam had to be made, the president and other government leaders dealt with military and diplomatic activities sequentially and not simultaneously, gave sequential attention to different aspects of the same problem, and disaggregated complex problems into their component parts. Once decisions were made, orchestrating their implementation by the various agencies very often failed, and any attempts to keep close control over implementation only increased the overwhelming work load under which government leaders already operated.

Decisionmakers may also turn to coping techniques that are based on *leapfrogging* information processing by relying on general theories and rules, heuristics, belief systems, or historical analogies and on a minimal amount of data. Either they may believe that even a satisficing solution to the problem is enough and that generalities will provide it, or they may convince themselves that such shortcuts are superior to the meticulous but time-consuming analysis of complex, often inconsistent information—an argument that is sometimes but not always rational.[25]

Manipulation of the problem is sometimes a necessary precondition for using other manipulation strategies. For example, depreciating the importance of the problem can be used as an excuse for not processing or delaying the processing of all information categories related to it.

TABLE 2
The Management of Information Overload

Focus of manipulation strategy	Tactics
1. Absorption process	a. Delaying
	b. Ignoring
	c. Filtering
2. Information channels	a. Reduction of accessibility
	b. Decentralization
3. Information content	a. Routinization
	b. Encapsulation
	c. Ritualization
	d. Approximation
4. Problem	a. Defensive procrastination
	b. Decomposition
	c. Leapfrogging

An illuminating case in which the decisionmaker applied most of the strategies and techniques for coping with situational overload, summarized in Table 2, is Richard Nixon's behavior throughout the period of the Watergate debacle. The need to deal with the growing political and emotional burden of public criticism and the emerging threat to his presidency and career captured most of Nixon's attention. High stress and anxiety and their related emotional consequences reduced his overall capability to absorb information and deal with other issues. Their combined effect was to create a serious overload (Dean, 1976: 184; Nixon, 1978: 786, 839, 922). This particularly affected Nixon's management of the main foreign policy issues that dominated the agenda: the Middle East powder keg, the Vietnam War, and to a lesser degree the Cyprus crisis.

Nixon used manipulation of information channels as his primary strategy. His standard operating procedure included using H. R. Haldeman, the White House chief of staff, to limit access to the president; as the Watergate investigations progressed, Nixon employed the technique of reducing his accessibility to an ever-greater extent (Kissinger, 1982: 95–96). Once Haldeman resigned, Nixon chose Alexander Haig to replace Haldeman because "in his growing loneliness, what Nixon needed above all was a keeper of the gate" (Kissinger, 1982: 106). Frequently, Nixon withdrew to one of his retreats—Camp David, Key Biscayne, or San Clemente—and thereby cut off the flow of information to him (Kissinger, 1982: 422, 1191).

In addition, Nixon employed the technique of decentralization to manipulate the White House information channels. Always one to rely on his presidential assistants to carry out the minutiae of policy decisions, during the Watergate period he increasingly delegated decisionmaking authority to his immediate subordinates. In foreign policy matters, this meant a more and more important role for Henry Kissinger, his assistant for national security affairs. To solve the coordination problem between Kissinger and Secretary of State Rogers, Nixon simply relied most heavily on Kissinger as his personal agent and increasingly relegated Rogers to the periphery. The division of labor shielded Nixon from much of the information reaching the White House and was the cause of much confusion (Kissinger, 1982: 125–26, 416–20). Perhaps the best illustration of Nixon's manipulation of information channels is his handling of the Yom Kippur War in 1973. Throughout the war and the ensuing negotiations, Nixon left the day-to-day decisions in the hands of his advisers, being "preoccupied with his domestic scandals" (Kissinger, 1982: 495). More so than at any other time in the Nixon presidency, the Washington Special Actions Group (WSAG) functioned almost independently of any presidential guidance (Kissinger, 1982: 1193; Nixon, 1978: 929–43).

Nixon also manipulated information content. Especially toward the end of his presidency, he used routinization and ritualization to lessen the burdens already on him. Even by early 1973, Kissinger relates,

I found it difficult to get Nixon to focus on foreign policy. . . . In the past, even in calm periods, he had immersed himself in foreign policy. . . . Now it was difficult to get him to address memoranda. They came back without the plethora of marginal comments that indicated they had been carefully read. On at least one occasion Nixon checked every box of an options paper, defeating its purpose. (Kissinger, 1982: 77–78)

As the crisis deepened into the spring of 1973, Nixon was "going through the motions of governing" without his "characteristic" concentration and attention to detail. Kissinger and Nixon "went over the day's foreign policy events in a routine fashion." Most revealingly, Kissinger writes, "he would sign memoranda or accept my recommendations almost absentmindedly now" (Kissinger, 1982: 106, 416, 1193, 415–16).

When confronted with policy decisions relating to Vietnam, Nixon most frequently used the strategy of manipulating the problem, with defensive procrastination his main technique. He frequently equivocated, stalled for time, and changed his mind when decisions concerning bombing, withdrawal, and so on needed to be made. The president was "indecisive," he "temporized," was marked by "the now familiar symptoms of Presidential ambivalence" (Kissinger, 1982: 318–23). He was "a different Nixon in March 1973. He approached the problem of the [North

Vietnamese cease-fire agreement] violations in a curiously desultory fashion. He drifted. He did not home in on the decision in the single-minded, almost possessed, manner that was his hallmark. . . . In retrospect we know that by March Watergate was boiling" (Kissinger, 1982: 318–19). Because of Nixon's inability to concentrate and make detailed analyses, sometimes he made gut decisions based, for example, on the spontaneous need to look tougher than others (leapfrogging) (Kissinger, 1982: 321–22).

On at least one occasion Nixon used a number of coping techniques simultaneously. At the latest stages of the Watergate events, during the Cyprus crisis in the summer of 1974, he ensconced himself in San Clemente (reducing his accessibility) and dealt with Kissinger by phone for summary reporting and consultations (encapsulation) (Kissinger, 1982: 1187–93). In addition, Nixon manipulated his absorption procedures by filtering techniques, refusing even to process foreign-policy-related information, as Kissinger describes:

The preoccupation with Watergate had reached a point where we were losing even the ability to transmit papers bearing on vital foreign policy matters instantaneously between the President and the White House. So many documents relating to Watergate were being moved over the circuits. . . . [that] I had had to ask for special priority for cables bearing on the Cyprus crisis. (Kissinger, 1982: 1191–92)

Nixon can be seen ignoring important foreign policy information, procrastinating or delaying in processing it, and filtering it.

Dealing effectively and appropriately with information overload demands accurate recognition of the overload problem, its causes, and its nature (situational or structural). A mistaken diagnosis of the problem could result in recourse to wrong remedies; for example, identifying a structural overload problem as situational leads to dealing with the problem on an ad hoc basis (e.g. by delaying processing some information) rather than dealing with it comprehensively (e.g. by reevaluating the role burden and reallocating it). A number of points should be noted in this regard.

It can be postulated that the preference for one coping strategy over another is guided by two sets of considerations: (1) what is perceived as possible, taking into account available time, the nature of the issue, the structure of the decisionmaking system, the constraints of accountability, and the nature and properties of the information; and (2) what seems to demand the least effort to implement at the lowest cognitive and organizational-administrative costs. For example, as in the case of Nixon, when decisionmakers already apply a mild version of a particular coping technique regularly, that technique is available when they face an over-load problem. Thus a more extreme version of the technique is used to cope with the overload.

Beyond the functional-practical need that people have to deal with overload is an emotional, psychological aspect as well. An information overload on an already overburdened decisionmaker creates a state of stress and anxiety that might have negative cognitive side effects, such as reduction of the scope of attention, cognitive rigidity, or adoption of a short-term perspective. These make accurate interpretation of the infor-mation even more difficult and less likely than it was (O. R. Holsti, 1971; Holsti and George, 1975: 273; Lazarus, Deese, and Osler, 1952). In a crisis situation of great threat, high stakes, and a limited response time, decisionmakers' recognition of the costs of errors in judgment on the one hand and the limited response time on the other interact with their awareness of information load to increase the perceived possibility of a costly failure, whose implications produce a sense of personal threat and cognitive rigidity (O. R. Holsti, 1972a: 111–14; Pally, 1955). The mag-nitude of the stress effects that information overload causes depends on the degree to which the sudden influx of information was anticipated. If it was anticipated, its stress effects are moderate because the decision-makers could take steps to prepare themselves.[26]

The anticipation and predictability of information overload may also imply a preference for a type of coping technique. They could induce a preference for time-consuming techniques or techniques that require prior preparations, such as making contingency plans for the division of labor, decomposing the problem, or preparing filtering rules. When the situation imposes a very short response time, then defensive procrasti-nation, decomposition of the problem, and division of labor are less likely because they are more time-consuming than other techniques. De-cisionmakers might, for example, resort to leapfrogging, relying on the intuitive use of abstract rules and heuristics with which they had suc-cessful experiences before.

Yet another point worth noting about overload is that the volume of information is dependent on role definition and the number of roles played by the holder of a particular position. Hence a transfer of position due, for example, to a new appointment entails a transfer of roles to the new position holder. But since different people have varying capabilities of processing information, the same position has dissimilar effects on different position holders with regard to how well they manage to cope with the information load it entails. What for one is a manageable load could for another be an overload. As the number of roles taken on by decisionmakers increases and with it the resultant information overload, their ability to deal with the overload decreases. They are then likely to adopt leapfrogging to circumvent the time-consuming information processing, particularly in regard to issues with which they have already had similar experiences in the past and to which acquired beliefs, schemata, heuristics, and other conceptual frameworks can hence be applied. Consequently, information that should serve to update previously acquired beliefs and knowledge structures is likely to be ignored or assimilated into information on existing early experiences, thereby enhancing cognitive conservatism.

Coping with information overload enhances the tendency toward selectivity in information processing, which is "pervasive throughout the cognitive continuum, from input to output" (Erdelyi, 1974: 12; see also Frey, 1986). Overload can be used as a rational-practical justification for selectivity. Yet selectivity is often misused: it can, for example, become an excuse for defensive cognitive measures when disconfirming information that is inconsistent with expectations, preferences, and prior knowledge is ignored, rather than information that is redundant or of lesser importance.

Further, since decisionmakers facing information overload do not always consciously choose the technique of handling it, they may be unaware of the threat it poses to accuracy of information processing and of the efficiency-versus-accuracy trade-offs involved.

Under time pressure and other distractions, when judgment involves a personal investment, commitment, and possible negative outcomes, decisionmakers tend to place greater weight on negative evidence than they would in less stressful conditions (Wright, 1974). Perhaps by focusing on the negative attributes, decisionmakers can use them to choose among alternatives by elimination rather than having to make complex analytic calculations (Tversky, 1972). Consequently, judgment of the adversaries' intentions becomes more pessimistic than it should, and the evaluation of information about their own ability to cope effectively with the potential threat is biased toward underestimation. The dual effect could be to enhance the probability of conflict escalation by eliminating options, like waiting before acting, and to make tempting the premature use of preventive military measures.

A final point is that the ability to cope with information overload, whether it is related to role overload or to the structure of the situation, seems at least partly to be a function of physical-biological constraints on human behavior. Factors such as fatigue, age, or ill health (Wiegele, 1973, 1977) and the use of drugs (stimulants, sedatives, and tranquilizers) (Lubit and Russett, 1984; Park, 1986) affect, to a large degree, the amount of information a person can handle and properly process at any point in time and the rate at which this capacity declines over time. Sometimes the process is self-perpetuating: role and information overload can lead to fatigue, ill health, and the use of drugs (L'Etang, 1980: 56–58; Lipowski, 1974), which in turn may lead to a declining ability to process information properly. If these conditions prevail over long periods of time, they can bring about a general deterioration in the quality of decisionmaking—which might itself cause further stress and anxiety and hence further dependence on drugs and a continuation of the cycle.

A structural and persistent cause of information overload can be traced to the managerial styles adopted by the head of state. Hence, a preference for formal, competitive, or collegial styles (R. T. Johnson, 1974) affects the availability of and preference for particular strategies for coping with information overload. When the leader adopts a formal approach, which stresses order, analysis, and the best solution to national problems rather than politicking and compromise among conflicting views, a structured decisionmaking process can be attained. Such was President Nixon's style in his first term in office. A formal managerial style may result, then, in restricted but well-selected, well-organized, and well-focused information processing in which only the most necessary and relevant information on critical issues and major problems reaches the top decisionmaker. Selectivity here is not accidental but preordained by rational criteria. The disadvantage to this approach is that the rigid hierarchy for screening the information may also distort it sometimes by isolating the head of state from the realities of political pressures and public sentiment.

At the other end of the spectrum is the competitive style, by which the head of state may encourage conflict and competition among organizations and individuals, often leaving jurisdictional boundaries between organizations ill defined; fostering duplication of effort, information redundancy, and multiple channels of communication; and placing the decisionmaker in the center of the information network. Such was Franklin D. Roosevelt's style. The competitive style places heavy demands on decisionmakers' time and increases unnecessarily the amount of information they have to deal with, much of it redundant and often unstructured. The overall effect is an increase in information overload, requiring the decisionmakers to settle for satisficing solutions to their problems. They may have to pay selective attention to information based on political expediency or stress information dealing with the immediate short run while neglecting information dealing with the long run. In the process almost any of the coping techniques that produce selectivity may be applied.

The collegial style, like the competitive style, recognizes the merits of conflict, but it emphasizes teamwork and the fusion of the strongest elements of divergent points of view rather than the promotion of winning as a means to meet objectives. Such tended to be Kennedy's style. The collegial style is mainly based on the division of labor but involves decisionmakers in the information network and requires them to invest much time in coordinating and mediating differences in views and interests to maintain teamwork. This is less demanding in terms of information load than is the centralization of the competitive style.[27]

To conclude, a necessary, although insufficient, condition for rationality is comprehensive information, but comprehensive information can, when it entails information overload, invoke information processing strategies that impair rational decisionmaking. Decisionmakers thus make, usually unconsciously, a choice between two evils—potential errors due to the use of less than all the relevant information or potential errors due to the attempt to use all or most of the relevant information—either of which results in deficient processing because of the inherent constraints on cognitive capabilities.

Message Encoding, Decoding, and Manipulation

International politics without the transmission of messages, even between sworn enemies, is unthinkable. Exchanges are meant to influence the expectations and behavior of the other side and are useful in avoiding misunderstandings; yet at the same time messages are a main avenue for deception through the manipulation of (1) data and (2) their interpretation. In the first case, the purpose of one or both of the actors is deception by transmitting messages containing false data or from which vital data are missing. In the second case, an actor assumes that he cannot manipulate the raw data acquired by the other side and uses the message exchange system to manipulate the interpretation the other actor gives to the available data. Deception usually involves a combination of both manipulation and interpretation, and unraveling the effects of each requires radically different approaches by the analyst of the message (Epstein, 1980). Thus the question of what the message within or behind the message is, if it exists at all, is highly pertinent in assessing the sender's intentions and in revising and updating the receiver's expectations.

The nature of the signaling system may, however, lead a target to form misperceptions even when the sender does not mean to mislead.[28] Two categories of failure that could arise from the signaling system are (1) failures to send suitable signals of one's intentions—encoding errors[29]—and (2) failures to interpret suitable signals correctly—decoding errors.[30] In the second case the blame for the perceptual fallacies must rest with the target.[31]

Countries that wish to maintain efficient signaling systems must be aware of encoding and decoding errors and their various combinational possibilities in interactions between any pair of actors. There are four patterns of possible combinations.

1. Both actors commit encoding errors. If, say, each actor is unable to understand the other's perspective and thought processes, the result is a lack of efficient communication between the two sides.

2. Actor A performs encoding errors, that is, misunderstands the opponent's thought patterns. Actor B commits decoding errors because of weakness in absorbing or interpreting information or because Actor A is making intentional attempts to deceive Actor B[32] or is employing new signals (or has changed the meanings of the old signals) without managing to inform the adversary.

3. Actor A makes errors of decoding and Actor B makes errors of encoding, the reverse of the second pattern.

4. Both actors make errors in decoding. Either each is attempting to mislead the other or both have changed the meaning of their signals or added new signals to the code without informing the opponent and without being aware themselves that the opponent is unaware of the changes.[33]

Errors of encoding and decoding, as noted earlier, may lead to the misperception of signals and their meanings.[34] The main fallacies caused by encoding errors are as follows:

1. The sender is often unaware that a signal may express information different from or even contradictory to what he is trying to convey. The transmitter of the signal assumes that its meaning is clear and that the recipient will understand the message.[35] The recipient, however, may not have the necessary antecedent information, or contextual or cultural knowledge, to do so.[36] Since signals can so easily be overlooked or misinterpreted, it is sometimes counterproductive to use ambiguous, intricate, sophisticated diplomatic language, which may become just another source of encoding errors for the target. The target will thus misinterpret or be unaware of the intended message, and the sender may then interpret the target's behavior as a response to the message contained in the signal, thus attributing irrelevant meanings to the opponent's acts.

Operation Plan 34A was a three-phase program of covert operations in February 1964 and Barrel Roll, a covert program of air strikes by U.S. planes against infiltration targets in Laos that began in December 1964. Both were supposed to signal clearly to North Vietnam that the United States was willing to raise the stakes. Yet in neither case were there indications that the Democratic Republic of Vietnam (DRV) felt itself under new or heavier pressure, or got the message that the United States was prepared to escalate should North Vietnam not end its involvement in the insurgency in the South. In fact, North Vietnam viewed Operation Plan 34A as an extension of a CIA activity since 1961—airdropping sabotage teams into North Vietnam. It did not see the air strikes of Barrel Roll as separate from the reconnaissance flights and escort missions that the U.S. air force had started in May 1964 (Yankee Team) or from Laotian air force T-28 strikes (Thies, 1982: 23–24, 66–67). American decisionmakers, however, interpreted North Vietnamese behavior as further evidence of their intransigence.

2. When Actor A changes the mutually accepted meaning of a signal or introduces new signals into the communication system with Actor B, and Actor B is unaware of this, Actor A may not be aware that Actor B is unaware of the changes. Actor A therefore assumes that Actor B's reactions or failure to react express B's response to the information conveyed by the signal as B currently interprets it, when in fact Actor B is reacting to a completely different meaning. What follows is a dialogue of the deaf.

3. The signaling party assumes that he is capable of signaling in a way that will isolate the signal from other environmental noises that might affect its decoding.[37] In particular, the signaling party believes that he can act as a unitary actor. This, however, is not the case. While the decision to signal is being implemented, bureaucratic and organizational processes come into operation, coordination fails, and the decisionmakers in the system do not act in concert. The decisionmaker sending the signal is not even aware that the lack of coordination produces no one signal, but a set of signals and noises. The adversary reacts in fact to a set of signals and noises that may convey a completely different meaning than was originally intended. The signaler, however, interprets the response of the target as a reaction to his initial message and deals with it within that frame of reference, which necessarily results in miscommunication.

For example, in December 1966, at the same time that the United States was making attempts (code-named Marigold) to open direct talks with North Vietnam in Warsaw, the military command in charge of the air war made strikes not far from the center of Hanoi that had been authorized in early November. The strikes had been delayed for three weeks owing to bad weather over the target area. The air attack strengthened the position of those North Vietnamese leaders who were skeptical about negotiations, and jeopardized the chances of the Warsaw talks to materialize. Not only was the declared policy—orchestrating military moves with diplomatic initiatives—a failure, but to justify, or at least belittle the impact of, the failure, high-level officials, including President Johnson, denied the relationship between the bombing raids on Hanoi and the failure of diplomatic efforts (Thies, 1982: 143–47).

4. When an actor is not trying to conceal, or even tries to actively expose, his interests, intentions, or capabilities, the actor assumes that the other side perceives them accurately (Jervis, 1969). The sender in such a case does not distinguish between likelihood and certainty. The receiver of the message may distrust the sender because of the tradition of secrecy and deception in foreign policy and interpret the lack of an attempt at disguise as an attempt to mislead and deceive.

5. Signaling to warn an adversary against a possible reaction to one's possible behavior is particularly complicated when the signaler has a range of behavior options. To tailor and fine-tune the signal for each possible option individually and yet avoid confusing the target is extremely difficult (cf. George and Smoke, 1974: 561–65). Moreover, in some such cases the signaling party, if not sure that the adversary is aware of all the options, uses vague signals to avoid giving the adversary any new ideas.

6. Even if the signaling actor is sure that he is able to convey the general thrust of the message, the tone and intensity are a different matter. They are much more difficult to encode at his end and more susceptible to error at the decoding end. Hence when the tone and intensity are pertinent components of a message, the probability of miscommunication increases. In cases where the signal must not be intercepted or overheard by other actors, it is even more difficult to encode it to ensure the target's attention and accurate awareness of tone and intensity, hidden as they may be under the layers of defenses against other actors' eavesdropping.

7. Using time as an indicator poses a special problem. When Actor A sends a signal meant to test how Actor B will respond to a particular move (to decide whether it is safe or worthwhile to proceed with the policy hinted at in the signal), Actor A may determine in advance that Actor B probably does not object to the policy suggested if it does not respond at all, or at least not negatively, within the expected time span. The more the sender perceives the signal to be clear and unambiguous, the more the sender expects a response; hence a nonresponse, silence, is perceived as acquiescence. But response time is often estimated incorrectly for various reasons: for example, the signal's content may allow for reactions unforeseen by the signaler, in which case the target actor may need more time than anticipated to choose among alternative reactions. A response's not being received in the time allotted may create a false impression related to the sender's time calculations, which are projected onto the receiver.

In February 1967 Prime Minister Harold Wilson of Britain attempted to arrange an extension of the Tet bombing pause in exchange for a halt in the movement south of some North Vietnamese divisions that were deployed north of the demilitarized zone. His proposal reached Washington just a few hours before the bombing was to resume. Wilson asked for a delay in the bombing to allow the North Vietnamese leadership time to respond. President Johnson agreed to a 10-hour extension only on the ground that "it does not take all that long to cable 'yes' or 'no' or 'We are giving it serious study.'" He assumed that the DRV was a unitary actor following a coherent policy and could respond quickly, not taking into account, for example, debates within the North Vietnamese leadership on the interpretation of the message and the best response to it (Thies, 1982: 367).

8. Since the international scene is fraught with a multiplicity of actors, each involved simultaneously in a number of games, actors often cannot transmit their messages explicitly and clearly to other specific actors for fear that the messages will be intercepted or overheard by actors for whom they are not intended—which would have a negative impact on other games in which they take part.

The following are the main fallacies that can be caused by decoding errors:

1. The distinction between signals and indices (see Chapter 1) can pose a number of difficulties. For one, an action that in the past had a high price attached to it, such that it could be regarded as an index, might attain a new, lower value after a reevaluation of the cost-benefit relationship. Thus at present it may serve only as a signal (Jervis, 1970: 52). Another difficulty occurs when actors notice that an opponent perceives a certain action of theirs as an index. The index then becomes a candidate for manipulation and a means for misleading the opponent. The cost-benefit ratio of the action has changed: to the benefits has now been added that of misleading the enemy. As a rule, how other actors assess risk is difficult to estimate. Taking a high-risk action could be considered cost-effective if the adversary is likely to believe that the action will not be taken because of its cost, making a successful strategic surprise highly likely. Surprise is a force multiplier; what seemed a high-cost operation could actually become a much lower cost one and hence more likely and rational. This rationale contributed at least in part to Egypt's and Syria's risk taking in 1973.

Standard operating procedures can be used to deceive and surprise the adversary that observes them and draws inferences from the pattern of behavior. Sudden unanticipated changes in the standard operating procedures cause surprise. But there are costs. If standard operating procedures are going to be used for deception later, they must be maintained in the meantime by allowing the adversary to make valid inferences about one's behavior in the interim period. That is the cost of building credibility for the sake of deception at some later time when the stakes will be higher. Actors should be aware that rules of inference based upon observation of their adversaries' standard operating procedures, which worked when stakes were low, may not work when the stakes become higher (Axelrod, 1979). Yet information processors tend to neglect the volatility of the stakes when assessing the relevance and validity of their information about their adversaries' past performance and instead focus their attention exclusively on noncontextual criteria as valid predictive indicators.

2. Evaluating an opponent's move as an index because its price seems too high to be used only for deception presupposes one or more of the following, none of which is necessarily true: (a) that the opponent's modus operandi is based upon the use of cost-benefit analysis, in other words, that he is rational;[38] (b) that if he applies cost-benefit calculations, they must be correct;[39] and (c) that the adversary's notion of rationality is correctly understood. To illustrate: in 1964–65 the Johnson administration saw the DRV incorrectly as a unitary-rational actor capable of calculating costs and gains and backing off or seeking accommodation when the cost of pursuing a losing cause became excessive. Thus, for example, the administration believed that the North Vietnamese would choose to negotiate rather than face the risk of losing their industrial infrastructure. In fact, General Maxwell Taylor admits: "One likes to feel able to count on the rationality and good sense of a dangerous opponent" (M. D. Taylor, 1972: 319; Thies, 1982: 35, 220–22).

3. Noises, self-generated, adversary generated, and system generated, in particular when signals must compete for attention with dramatic events, interfere with the reception of and attention to signals (Handel, 1976, 1977; Lebow, 1985: 206). However, what for a long time were noises may become signals or even indices without anyone's noticing when the information-gathering system has not updated its interpretations. For instance, a military maneuver that takes place regularly may be perceived as a noise. At a certain point in time, however, it could change into a signal. Yet, because the same behavior was considered a noise for so long without that image's being made conditional on, say, contextual circumstances, the image becomes a perceptual fallacy, what should be evaluated as a noise with conditional probability is perceived as a noise with an unconditional probability.

Israel's intelligence was accustomed to and expected biannual, seasonal exercises by the Egyptian army along the Suez Canal. A large-scale movement of Egyptian forces in the canal area during September–October 1973, although it was closely monitored, was not considered unusual and did not unduly alarm the Intelligence Branch of the Southern Command in spite of dissenting views voiced by Lieutenant General Yisrael Tal, the deputy chief of staff, and by a young intelligence officer, Lieutenant Binyamin Siman-Tov, the desk officer for Egypt in the Southern Command Intelligence Branch and the navy's intelligence officer, who both argued that the exercise might only be a façade for the real thing. To reinforce an unalarming interpretation by Israel's intelligence, Egyptian and Syrian forces were sent to the front in the preceding months and then withdrawn so that the movement of forces came to be perceived as practically routine (Herzog, 1975: 55–56; Schiff, 1974: 15, 18, 35).

4. The tendency to regard actions as indices and words as signals ignores the committing power of words.[40] Thus both the American and North Vietnamese officials preferred to rely on their adversaries' actions as clues to their intentions and motives rather than pay attention to verbal explanations (Thies, 1982: 364).

5. In conflict situations where the time perspective is not similar for the two sides, distortions in signal perceptions may result. One actor's behavior may be considered an index because of its perceived high cost for the actor who has the shorter time perspective, although the behavior might actually have a low cost to the actor who has a longer time perspective on the conflict—given that what is too costly in the short term may certainly be worthwhile in the long.[41] For example, escalating military pressures on North Vietnam had no chance of convincing Hanoi to halt its support for the Vietcong and its intervention in the South; because the United States judged the costs to the DRV in a short-term perspective, it assumed that the escalation would force the DRV to a negotiated settlement. Whereas the United States viewed the war as only a limited one whose purpose was to deny a Communist victory, the North Vietnamese were fighting a total war, a protracted struggle with no rigid timetable, with the ultimate goal of winning decisively. Thus their cost-benefit calculus was completely different from the one attributed to them by American decisionmakers (L. Berman, 1982: 144).

6. When antecedent steps are necessary in the sequence leading to a particular action, taking the steps creates an opening for that action to take place—but does not mean that it will necessarily take place. There is, however, a tendency to perceive such steps as if they predicted the inevitable occurrence of the action. In more general terms, signals can be part of a specific script or independent of it. Interpreting a signal entails deciding whether it is part of a script—which gives rise to expectations

about the unfolding of the rest of the script—or whether it is independent of the script—which gives rise to a completely different interpretation.[42]

7. The tendency to exaggerate the degree of coordination in the opponent's decisionmaking system (Jervis, 1969) may lead to a perception that every adversary bureaucrat's every step is an expression of the adversary's overall policy even if the domestic actors are not in fact major policymakers. The result is, again, that noises are interpreted as signals.

8. To distinguish between caution and fear on the part of the opponent is difficult since the external signs of both may be identical. A display of caution might be regarded as fear by an opponent, who may then be emboldened to take the very steps that the other side was trying to avoid by means of the cautious actions.

9. The repeated use of a signal containing a threat or promise or its indiscriminate use with a great many actors might create the perception that the signal should not be taken seriously. (a) A signal repeated many times without its content being materialized may point to a lack of seriousness of intention. But precisely because the move hinted at has still not been executed, the sender might also be compelled to finally carry it out to regain credibility. (b) The target actors may well assume that the signaling actor cannot possibly carry out the content of the signal. And even if they assume that the signaling actor can and will carry it out, each recipient tends to believe that some other recipient will be the actual target or at least that his risk of being the target is low. Thus the estimate of the likelihood that the move will be made diminishes as a function of the number of actors toward whom the same signal is directed. In any case such thinking may be valid in terms of objective probability but is not necessarily valid in terms of subjective probability, which is more relevant in assessing the potential behavior of the signaling actor. Moreover, when the costs to a target actor could be high, even low probabilities must be taken seriously.

For instance, Sadat's repeated public threats since 1970 to use force to liberate the Israeli-occupied territories, and his express preparedness to sacrifice up to a million soldiers in the "sacred cause," were empty—until October 1973. He was not taken seriously by either the American or the Israeli decisionmakers; some even assumed that he would not survive in power. Thus, in the face of a complete lack of progress on the diplomatic front, he had to act to save his reputation precisely because he had not carried out his repeated threats in the past and his credibility had reached a low point. That is, the costs of not acting were perceived as much higher than the possible costs of failing to act.

Conclusions

The main thrust of this discussion is that factors that are exogenous to the substantive content of information may, frequently without justification, intervene and have significant influence on the perception of information content; the definition of the importance of the information; and the question of its gaining the attention of, and penetrating, the policymaker's cognitive system in the first place. The need to develop a set of exogeneous evaluation and judgment criteria stems from the characteristics of information in international politics (Chapter 1), which make its processing on a content basis alone problematic and difficult. Decisionmakers' awareness of the difficulties, their constant need to cope with the processing problems that arise in connection with the reliability of available information and its actual meaning, and the increasing challenge of making decisions in an adversarial environment of high complexity and uncertainty that requires at least a minimum amount of valid information produce (not necessarily consciously) a motivation to establish necessary criteria of validity and acceptability. Policymakers find themselves helpless to carry out their tasks without such criteria, which actually determine the margin of error policymakers are prepared to risk in making judgments and inferences about information, which often involves a high level of complexity, uncertainty, and unreliability. Hence these criteria constitute an important link in the series of evaluative and judgmental measures that serve to control and make manageable a complex and confusing inflow of information about the surrounding world. They transform the treatment of information and its decoding into an economical, dependable, rapid, and simple procedure that, in addition, minimizes the psychological stress of coping. Yet at the same time the criteria sometimes cost information consumers vital information that, having been disregarded, fails to become a stimulus or lead to biased, inaccurate judgments and interpretations of stimuli, as well as to unwarranted inferences.

This view of information processing is congruent both with the cognitive paradigm and its related schemata theory and with important components of the cybernetic paradigm (e.g. Axelrod, 1972, 1973; Reed, 1973: 26–32; J. L. Snyder, 1978; Stein and Tanter, 1980; Steinbruner, 1974). These paradigms differ from the analytic paradigm, which assumes that when new information arrives, it is integrated into the recipient's causal models of reality and that a process of adaptation, updating, and refinement of the models takes place on the basis of this information. The analytic paradigm further assumes that there is a process of perfect learning, in which all information is examined and relevant conclusions are drawn, then immediately integrated into the existing perceptual system and utilized as the basis of any future analysis. Actually, as this and the following chapters show, perfect learning does not, or only rarely, takes place. The information processor acts as a cognitive miser, frequently preferring abstracted organizing frames that link the highest number of disparate items of information in the most tightly connected (e.g. any order is preferable to a mere combination), simplest, and most conventional manner. Under the conditions the information processor faces, the nonrational approach is often more practical, logical, and cost-effective than the analytic one, but it can also be costly in terms of the accuracy of information processing and the quality of decisions dependent on it. This trade-off between efficiency and accuracy is not always performed consciously by the information processor.

CHAPTER 3

The Decisionmaker: Personality
and Cognition

....

"Man is a riddle solving riddles."   NATHAN ALTERMAN

Human Nature

The core of any decisionmaking and information processing operation is the human being, whose personality structure, attributes, and style have a decisive, sometimes dominant effect on the manner and outcomes of information processing. The term personality is used here in its broadest sense to include the structure and content of the belief system, values, and attitudes, as well as the unique personality traits, of a person. Personality variables have both direct and indirect effects. The direct effects are those that link individual cognitive and personality structure and style directly to information processing behavior. The indirect ones are those that affect the person's social interactions within the group or organizational contexts and through them the final information processing outputs. We shall also look at biophysiological effects on cognitive processes.

This study takes the view that ostensibly competitive cognitive and personality theories are actually complementary. Attempts to explain cognitive operations by a single theory are parsimonious but also reductionist. They fail to grasp the multidimensionality of the personality or the variable contingencies and circumstances in which information processing takes place, thus missing the integrative character of human behavior. It is no coincidence that each single theory finds it difficult to explain inconsistencies between theory and actual behavior. Society contains far more than one type of person—not one prototypical decisionmaker but many, who have dissimilar cognitive structures and who are driven by different motives and affected by different personality traits. Nor is there a single prototypical situation but many dissimilar situations, which call for different types of cognitive operation and allow for different expressions of individual cognitive structures, motives, and personality traits (cf. Bem and Allen, 1974; Mischel, 1968, 1977). People can reveal one type of personality on one occasion (e.g. act as consistency seekers; see Abelson et al., 1968) and a different one on others (e.g. act as intuitive scientists; see Ross, 1981). Some people are more sophisticated and cognitively complex than others, and to them being rational means acting as intuitive scientists. To others rationality is identified with simple consistency.

The model of the individual as an intuitive scientist captures important aspects of a person's approach to interpreting and understanding the environment, but it is not the only relevant perspective nor is it the full portrayal of such behavior, because people acting both individually and collectively are much more complex than any single model can capture. The attribution process is not always cognitively guided but is also affected by motivational factors, such as personal-identity and social-identity maintenance. One reflects ego-defensive needs and the other reflects social-esteem needs (Bradley, 1978; Pyszczynski and Greenberg, 1987; M. Rosenberg, 1969; Shaver, 1975: 89; Tetlock and Levi, 1982). This image of people is captured by the metaphor of the individual as an intuitive politician. "Whereas the central motive for intuitive scientists is the quest to achieve causal understanding and reduce uncertainty, the central motive for intuitive politicians is the quest to convince both themselves and others that they possess desired traits or characteristics" (Tetlock, 1985b: 208; see also Higgins and Bargh, 1987). Like the intuitive scientist, the intuitive politician also suffers the consequences of biases and errors; but the two types may be linked. "Indeed many of our shortcomings as intuitive politicians may directly derive from our shortcomings as intuitive scientists" (Tetlock, 1985b: 221).

Moreover, people have the capability, although it is differential, to apply a variety of cognitive mechanisms sequentially or simultaneously, consciously or thoughtlessly, in dealing with their environment. Hence in some cases the cognitive processes are "hot" and in others "cold." Sometimes people are given information by others and have to decide whether the messages they have received are persuasive and should lead to attitude change or should be rejected. In other cases they initiate their own search for information about their milieu, attempting to explore the causes of other actors' behavior.

People are not always sure what their own attitudes and beliefs on particular issues are, and in seeking that information, they try to make inferences from their own behavior. But people are not ideal scientists in search only of truth. Often, like real-life scientists, they prefer a particular truth over other, more accurate truths because, for example, it does not cause cognitive dissonance and inconsistency or because it is simpler to deal with and thus satisfies the cognitive miser's need for parsimony. People strive to lighten the burden of information processing by avoiding comprehensive expenditures of thought and energy, by using heuristics, and by structuring their experiences into cognitive schemata that provide shortcuts to judgment, even at the cost of accuracy, and that store information in memory in a form that is economical, accessible, and resistant to decay. Cognitive structure and substance, once formed, tend to persevere, although change is not impossible.[1] This chapter will seek to portray this human complexity.

The Core Cognitive Constructs

The most elementary cognitive tools with which the decisionmaker approaches, and attempts to clarify and impose meaning on, the complex and uncertain environment are beliefs, values, and stereotypes. They serve as guides to information processing and become a baseline for interpretations, expectations, and predictions of others' behavior. For example, a value orientation toward cooperation causes people to over-emphasize the aspects of their attitudes that are similar to those of other actors, while a competitive orientation toward conflict resolution leads them to focus attention on the dissimilarities (Judd, 1978). As a result, the search for and attention to information is biased toward information that is congruent with a priori expectations and predictions, and the interpretation of ambiguous events, toward their being consistent with expectations (Berman, Read, and Kenny, 1983). At the same time beliefs, values, and stereotypes provide a means for confirming or disconfirming the validity of information, in particular where no other validating cues are contained in the information itself.

Beliefs, values, and stereotypes are also the building blocks of more elaborate cognitive constructs, to be discussed later, such as attitudes and schemata, which are applied to information processing tasks. These constructs can take various forms, simple or complex, and contain additional elements, such as emotions and motives. The emergent knowledge structures, based on perceptions of accumulated experience, are schemata of different types and levels of generality. Beliefs are the building materials for experience-based scripts; values are the bases for normative scripts, which are a key to expectations about norm-based behavior; stereotypes are the source of persona-type scripts. Once these cognitive structures become established and well practiced, they become cognitive habits, easily available and thoughtlessly used for making inferences that a person not sharing the same cognitive components and structure would not make (S. E. Taylor, 1982).

Beliefs. The individual's belief-set represents all the hypotheses and theories that he is convinced are valid at a given moment in time. Parallel to the belief-set is the disbelief-set, which includes all the hypotheses and theories that he believes to be invalid at a given point in time (Rokeach, 1960: 33). A person locates available information on a spectrum between belief and disbelief, and thus the belief system takes on a central role in the processing of information, given that

in order to function, every individual acquires during the course of his development a set of beliefs and personal constructs about the physical and social environment. These beliefs provide him with a relatively coherent way of organizing and making sense of what would otherwise be a confusing and overwhelming array of signals and cues picked up from the environment by his senses. (George, 1980a: 57; see also Cobb, 1973; Lazarus, 1966)

Beliefs, as opposed to attitudes, are more general in content and usually include principles and general ideas on the nature of the social and physical environment that constitutes the policymaker's field of action. Within the entire set of beliefs, the subset of operational code beliefs (especially its philosophical part) plays a major role in political information processing (George, 1969, 1979b; O. R. Holsti, 1977). The beliefs in the subset deal with the most basic images about the nature of the political world and the place and role of the person in it and with the most effective means by which to realize goals. The operational code therefore has "diagnostic propensities, which extend or restrict the scope of search and evaluation and influence his diagnosis of the situation in certain directions" (George, 1979b: 103). Its role as a diagnostic and prescriptive framework is particularly important under one or more of the following conditions: novel situations; highly uncertain situations in which information may be scarce, contradictory, unreliable, or abundant; and stressful situations involving surprise and emotional strain (O. R. Holsti, 1977: 16–18).

Operational code beliefs were particularly important for Lyndon Johnson. The new president had no experience in the foreign policy field and felt insecure in dealing with what were for him overwhelming international problems, the complex problem of Vietnam in particular. He had to make sense of available information concerning the very nature of the problem: Was it a domestic war or a case of external aggression?

Lyndon Johnson's world view was one of a "universal conflict of values between freedom and unfreedom."

Thus every conflict in which one of the warring parties fought under the ideological banner of Communism was part of the continuing battle for domination of the future. This outlook made it possible to view wars among the people within a single nation as, in reality, an aspect of international aggression. In every such war, Johnson believed, the enemy is an agent of an alien force that is invading the home of an ally. (Kearns, 1976: 257)

An example of this is Johnson's 3-hour tirade in response to his biographer Doris Kearns's questioning U.S. goals in Vietnam, during which he said,

It's just perverted history to claim that it's civil war, just pure bad history manufactured by the Harvards and the Galbraiths. No understanding of the thirty years before. There was no insurrection before the Communists decided to take part. Ho [Chi Minh] was a Communist all his life. He was trained in Moscow Communist Headquarters. He was the founding father of the Communist Party in Indochina. (Kearns, 1976: 328)

The operational code of each decisionmaker contains a set of philosophical and instrumental core beliefs, which are grouped into two, usually coherent clusters, each containing a combination of general and specific philosophical beliefs and their counterpart instrumental beliefs. The first cluster of beliefs deals with the essence of the political world and political actors. It includes philosophical beliefs about the essentials of politics, the nature of the political universe—whether it is harmonious or conflictual—and the nature of political conflict. Their instrumental counterparts concern beliefs about the best approach for selecting political goals. Other philosophical beliefs in the cluster deal with the fundamental character of one's allies and opponents, and their instrumental counterparts prescribe how best to deal with allies and enemies.

The second cluster of beliefs in the operational code focuses on the controllability and predictability of historical-political developments. It contains philosophical beliefs regarding how much control one can exert over historical-political developments. Their instrumental counterparts concern beliefs about how risk should be calculated and controlled and how much risk should be taken. Other philosophical beliefs in the cluster refer to the question of whether the future is predictable. Their instrumental counterparts deal with the correct timing for action. Arising from the above-mentioned beliefs is the issue of optimism, in other words, whether one should be optimistic about the prospects for achieving one's ends, and the related instrumental beliefs about what the best and most efficient means for achieving those ends are (George, 1969; L. K. Johnson, 1977). The first cluster of operational-code beliefs provides decisionmakers with guiding insights into the environment in which they operate, while the second cluster of operational-code beliefs provides understanding of the odds they face and how best to cope with them.

The specific content of beliefs about control over events and outcomes can show a number of alternative patterns: a generalized belief or disbelief in control over the unfolding of events and outcomes or more restricted and sophisticated beliefs dealing with the controllability of specific issues or actors, that is, beliefs that one has control over events and/or outcomes in specific domains but not in other domains, or that one can affect the behavior of particular actors (e.g. allies) but not other actors (e.g. the enemy), or, finally, that one has control over particular events and their outcomes. Beliefs about control are personal constructs, although they may sometimes be commonly shared when they are culturally affected.[2]

Locus-of-control beliefs have important information processing implications. In the first place, to the degree that people believe in an external locus of control, whether in general or in a specific context, they place a lower value on information in general or in that specific context because it is not estimated to be highly instrumental in allowing control over events or other actors' behavior (Davis and Phares, 1967; Rotter, 1966). The search for information, then, is focused only on information relevant to coping behavior, if it is available. The signals and communications of the adversary are likely to go mostly unnoticed or unattended and to be attributed low relevance and importance at best. Comprehension of the motives of the other side is considered merely of academic value and hence of marginal utility. Information about one's capabilities to deal with the situation are the focus of attention and interest. When threatening situations or events materialize, information processors with beliefs in lack of controllability experience increased stress and possibly even a defensive avoidance of information about the threat, unless it is accompanied by information about how to effectively cope with it and manage it at a reasonable cost.

Because foreign policy, unlike domestic politics, was an issue-area about which President Johnson had scant knowledge and with which he had little experience, he was unsure whether he could recognize, manipulate, and control possibilities so that goals could be reached and disruptions avoided. The problem took on serious dimensions given his general Hobbesian view of international politics and his more specific beliefs that U.S. failure in Indochina would have dire consequences for him personally, for the U.S. position in world affairs, and as a result for world peace and order—possibly leading to World War III. To avoid these consequences, it was imperative that the president somehow establish control over domestic response and external developments.

What was called for was a policy that would prevent a deep cleavage in the American polity between doves and hawks over the question, Who lost Vietnam? Hence a retreat from the U.S. commitment to Vietnam was unthinkable (L. B. Johnson, 1971: 151–52). The policy would have to satisfy hawks and doves equally by dissatisfying both equally. It would then assure domestic support for the president's approach—and this the Tonkin Gulf Resolution seemed to confirm. Next he had to establish control over the external arena. Once Johnson rejected the option of withdrawal and became committed to some form of bombing, he decided to reject the option of large-scale strategic bombing because that risked China's or Russia's being brought in and thus the danger of uncontrolled escalation on a global scale. The obvious choice was the gradual escalation of bombing in North Vietnam. Not only was it the middle ground between the two extremes but it also afforded careful monitoring of the other two powers' reactions, thus allowing more control over the developments. No less important, gradual escalation could be construed as a political bargaining game between Johnson and Ho Chi Minh. For Johnson, the use of force as a means of bargaining was familiar ground. He was confident that he had the skills to control the situation even if he remained aware of his inadequacy in the foreign policy domain. Moreover, he would retain the final say over when and where to bomb, making sure he controlled the situation so that it would not get out of hand (Kearns, 1976: 260–70). Thus Johnson's Vietnam strategy was based on the need to produce a controllable domestic and external environment.

The attributes and role of beliefs as a whole, and especially the interdependence of those core beliefs that form the operational code, make them a possible source of biased information processing. First, the importance and relevance attached to information is largely determined by its location on the belief-disbelief continuum. The closer to the disbelief pole that the decisionmaker perceives information to be, the less its perceived relevance and importance, and vice versa.[3] Second, when the core beliefs of another person or actor are in line with one's own, one tends to see them as even closer than they actually are; conversely, when they are divergent, one tends to conceive of them as much more dissimilar and incongruent than they actually are (Atkins, Deaux, and Bieri, 1967; Sherif and Sherif, 1967), leading to a spurious perception of agreement where there is only discord and of zero-sum conflict where there is only disagreement. Evaluation or relevance gaps might develop because of misunderstanding the behavior and goals of the adversary, possibly culminating in illusory beliefs of compatibility between incongruent interests or incompatibility between essentially common interests.

Third, as personal involvement increases, the latitude of acceptance narrows and the latitude of rejection broadens.[4] At high levels of personal involvement the latitude of noncommitment (that is to say, the amount of information with regard to which the policymaker does not have any position) narrows significantly. Thus, and in particular when personification takes place (see Chapter 2), personal involvement is likely to reduce the readiness for adjustment, and available information is likely to be perceived and analyzed as relevant to the acute situation and to be interpreted in terms of the situation and its implications for oneself. Consequently, out-of-context attribution and interpretation of information may occur. President Johnson, for example, perceived his commitment to the Vietnam War in personal terms (e.g. "my Security Council," "my State Department," "my troops"). It was his war, and when the Vietcong attacked they were attacking him (Barber, 1977: 51–53). Events relating to the war were personalized, and the interpretations made and inferences drawn by the president reflected this.

Similarly, the more Nixon and Kissinger moved away from their pre-election promises to bring the war to a speedy end, and made the war theirs, particularly after the invasion of Cambodia, "the more they were compelled to assert illusory achievements and unreachable goals" (Isaacs, 1983: 490). Nixon's need to justify his decisions by showing success led him to overestimate the Saigon government's effectiveness, the probability that Hanoi would prove flexible or could be pressured into an agreement acceptable to the United States (Isaacs, 1983: 490-93), and the willingness of China and the Soviet Union to deliver such a settlement in return for American concessions on other matters.

Fourth, the greater the differentiation between, and insulation of, different beliefs, the greater the possibility for inconsistent beliefs to coexist simultaneously (Rokeach, 1956). In other words, the less systemically beliefs are organized, the higher the probability that internal contradictions go undetected—providing the basis for processing contradictory pieces of data without proper attention to logical coherence. On the positive side, the greater the differentiation among beliefs, the less the drive toward imposing unwarranted consistency on belief-sets.

Fifth, the centrality of any single belief, as measured by the dependence of other beliefs on it, influences its degree of resistance to change in the sense that change in the belief necessarily requires changes in some or all other beliefs belonging to that belief subset (Converse, 1964; Rokeach, 1968b: 5). The greater the centrality, the greater the rigidity. Hence, information concerning beliefs that constitute the operational code and indicating the need for significant adjustments to and the introduction of changes in it is likely to be manipulated and distorted because of the centrality of the beliefs.[5]

Central beliefs about the self and the adversary underlie major strategic assumptions that guide political-military thinking. Consequently, the strategic assumptions of possibilities are resistant to tactical indicators of actualities, and that is one cause of surprise in spite of available warning. The suggestion that the evaluation of tactical actualities be separated from strategic assumptions (Ben-Zvi, 1976) is cognitively impractical and unlikely to succeed in preventing surprise. For separation to be effective requires the prior existence of conditions that will make the information processor receptive to competing beliefs. Kissinger's attitudes concerning the role of negotiations were tied to his operational code beliefs that decisionmakers have no control over history and hence negotiations play a pivotal role in the least risky path to goal attainment (Walker, 1977: 139; Walker, 1986: 19). This view was reinforced by his realpolitik view of the world. "He believed that the United States, through a series of shrewd trade-offs and concessions to the Soviet Union and China, could settle all outstanding world issues, including the Vietnam War and the Middle East dispute, on favorable terms" (Hersh, 1983: 509; see also Shawcross, 1979: 306). Kissinger's strong belief in the power of negotiations, combined with his personal stakes in Vietnam as a test of the validity of his beliefs and consequently of his credibility, led to his personalizing the war and his role in it. Even when it became obvious that South Vietnam was lost, "Kissinger persisted in trying to justify the fruits of his 1972 negotiations" (Mazlish, 1976: 242) as confirming his beliefs that the other side also realized the benefits of self-imposed limitations.

Sixth, every belief is capable of activating other beliefs by functioning as a cue. A belief is embedded in several other belief clusters, and its activation makes the related beliefs available. They are then likely to be brought to bear on information processing. A number of mechanisms can bring about the evocation of other beliefs. The first is representativeness; that is, beliefs that are representative of the cuing belief are likely to be activated. The second is inferential generation; that is, some beliefs can be inferred from the cuing belief. The third mechanism is hierarchical substitution; that is, people form many belief hierarchies along various dimensions, such as personal preference, importance, and relevance. Inadequacy of one belief in coping and giving meaning to information is likely to invoke the next highest in the hierarchy (Kreitler and Kreitler, 1976: 97–100). Thus the search for meaning is directive and hierarchically organized, with people bringing their beliefs to bear in a hierarchical order until they are satisfied with the interpretation. At that point the search for interpretation ceases even if better interpretations can be generated by continued search.

Finally, beliefs may activate deep motivations, because of the interactive relationship between basic needs for affiliation and for achievement and power on the one hand and operational code beliefs on the other. People tend to adopt beliefs that are compatible with their core needs (Walker, 1983), which are acquired in childhood. When environmental stimuli activate the beliefs, they may also activate the needs embedded in the belief system, contributing to the cognitive rigidity of the belief system and reinforcing its stability against dissonant information.

No less important than the content of beliefs is the confidence with which beliefs are held and their susceptibility to discrepant information that invalidates information on which they are based. Believers show overconfidence in their knowledge and reasoning; they do not inquire into inferences, treating them as though no uncertainty were associated with earlier stages of the inference process. They tend to believe that knowledge has been drawn directly from memory, not inferred, and perceive memories as copied exactly from original experiences, rather than restructured from the components of experience. Hence believers do not ask relevant validity questions (Einhorn and Hogarth, 1978; Fischhoff, Slovic, and Lichtenstein, 1977; Koriat, Lichtenstein, and Fischhoff, 1980). Consequently, people tend to exaggerate their information processing sophistication (Fischhoff, 1976: 432). They have unwarranted confidence in their judgment processes, the underlying theories directing those processes, and further reason to ignore incongruent information or to neglect the search for additional information to validate their judgment. They are unaware of the impact their current beliefs and overconfidence have on their inferences and their interpretation of information. They tend to think that information has only a single, self-evident interpretation, which cannot be reconciled with other, totally different beliefs. People thus perceive their interpretation as compelling and see it as an independent confirmation of their beliefs and, by definition, a disconfirmation of other beliefs (Jervis, 1976: 181–87; Jervis, 1982–83). Their beliefs become powerful incentives for suppressing doubts or even contemplation of their view of the world.

People also tend to encounter new, discrepant information without revising their confidence in their theories as normative dictates would require. If they later discover that the initial evidence on which their beliefs are based is false, even then the theory survives. Its not being discredited is partly owing to their emotional investment in their beliefs. But even when no such emotional investment exists, people tend to seek out, recall, and interpret incoming evidence so that it sustains their beliefs (Nisbett and Ross, 1980: 167–92; Oskamp, 1965).[6] Perseverance of beliefs is particularly enhanced when they have already generated an explanatory causal script or theory that continues to support the existence of the relationship postulated by the beliefs, even when data that led to its postulation were subsequently invalidated (Anderson, Lepper, and Ross, 1980). The emergent causal schema induces a search for confirmation of the explanation, rather than for information that will disconfirm alternative hypotheses, for reasons of cognitive economy (Hansen, 1980). In the search the perseverance of beliefs is further enhanced.

A blatant case of ignoring clearly disconfirming evidence of beliefs by misinterpreting it is supplied by Nixon's and Kissinger's reactions to the defeat of South Vietnam. They found no fault with their earlier policies and perceptions, and they did not acknowledge "Vietnamese causes for Vietnamese events." Their views remained unchanged; they explained the evidence that disconfirmed their beliefs and policies as actually consistent with Nixon's long-ago assertion that only Americans can defeat the United States. The blame for losing the war was put on the Congress that refused to allow U.S. bombing to enforce the Paris Agreement and weakened South Vietnam's forces by reducing U.S. material support (Isaacs, 1983: 500).

What also helps in generating confidence in one's beliefs and theories is the degree of consensus that they arouse. Yet in judging the level of consensus, people tend to see their positions as more accepted by others than they actually are, and minorities in particular tend to overestimate consensus (Mullen, 1983; Ross, Greene, and House, 1977). The phenomenon of false consensus has both motivational and cognitive sources.

Feedback thus has in many cases little debiasing effect, because people have little direct introspective access to their high-order cognitive processes (Nisbett and Wilson, 1977a). Nevertheless, people believe that they actually do have the introspective power to trace their cognitive processes. They are unaware of stimuli that importantly influence responses, unaware of the actual motives for their responses or of stimulus-response covariations—and unaware that they are unaware. As a result, their judgments of high-order cognitive processes are based on a priori, implicit causal theories or on the belief in the plausibility of a particular stimulus's being the cause of a specific response. Subjective introspective certainty is greater when causal candidates are salient and highly plausible even if they are not actually influential. Subjective certainties are difficult to disconfirm because the relevant information is difficult to come by. In addition, there is a motivational ground for people's belief in their introspective powers: namely, the need to feel in control, which requires a belief in one's knowledge of the working of one's own mind.

Decisionmakers tend, systematically and actively, to solicit feedbacks that verify and confirm their self-conceptions. Self-confirmatory feedbacks are considered especially informative and more diagnostic and compelling than disconfirmatory ones (Swann and Read, 1981). Feedbacks that confirm the positive self-images of decisionmakers in group contexts decrease the likelihood of policy adjustment. Flattery and positive evaluations of the leader's performance by other group members are likely to be more heavily weighted than in-group and out-group criticisms when the leader has a self-image of power and competence. These negative effects are potent when the leader is charismatic and narcissistic. President Johnson himself was noted for the seriousness and sacrosanctity that he accorded to presidential beliefs: "As American participation in the Vietnam War heightened, it was becoming clear how reluctant President Johnson was to approve the right of dissent against Presidential decisions in foreign policy" (E. F. Goldman, 1974: 490). Similarly, Tuchman notes that for Nixon "the point of the war had now been transformed into a test of the prestige and reputation of the United States—and, as he was bound to see it, of the President personally. Nixon too had no wish to preside over defeat" (1984: 359).

Prior commitments to particular beliefs shape sensitivity to cues, define areas of meaning, and guide people into and away from challenging or threatening situations. The strength of a commitment determines vulnerability to psychological stress in the area of the commitment. In this sense public commitments present a particularly sensitive area of vulnerability when they are challenged, because of the potential consequences to self-image and self-esteem in the eyes of significant others (Lazarus and Folkman, 1984: 56–63).[7] Decisionmakers attribute a high value to projecting an image of themselves as subtle, persistent, and credible (though sometimes it can be advantageous to project the opposite image). Changing publicly known beliefs, even if justified in the light of new information, is difficult to explain because the public is rarely fully aware of the informational basis of the currently held beliefs and goals and consequently cannot properly appreciate how new information should affect them. Furthermore, in the field of foreign policy, it is often impossible to expose new information to the public to explain a change in commitment because of various secrecy imperatives (e.g. defending intelligence sources). Thus reappraisal and revision of commitment may be perceived by the public as erratic responses; they affect the credibility of the decisionmaker, who may thus avoid information that can lead to reappraisal or explain it away to avoid revising commitments.

Another source of confidence in beliefs and theories lies in people's acting in a manner that produces self-fulfilling prophecies, people make theories self-confirmatory. Consequently, a kind of feedback data that is often neglected is information about "what happened or would have happened to the alternatives that were not selected and the outcomes therefore omitted from consideration" (Brown and Agnew, 1986: 34; Fischhoff, 1977; Hogarth, 1980: 104). Information about rejected alternatives and their potential outcomes is often missing, but even when it is available, people tend to ignore it. When selected alternatives are judged as successful or tolerable, confidence in the selection criteria increases and improvement of the selection process is unlikely for lack of a control group, so that a broad comparative analysis that includes rejected alternatives is not executed. Even an apparently successful choice can be misleading because in some situations one failure may be more important than a large number of successes, whereas in other situations the converse is true. This is particularly true in international politics, for example, when uncompromising brinksmanship strategy leads the adversary to repeatedly and cautiously yield until the stakes are so high that the same strategy leads the adversary to take an unanticipated, unyielding stand that is likely to be misinterpreted and may trigger violent responses, the cost of which may be higher than all past gains.

To summarize, decisionmakers' belief systems are a critical link in the scanning for, attention to, and interpretation of information. Specific beliefs and belief-sets have varied levels of complexity and importance. Within the network of beliefs the core beliefs relevant for political analysis and action are the operational code beliefs, the philosophical and instrumental ones, that have decisive diagnostic and prognostic roles. Even though beliefs are necessary constructs for making sense of the information picked up from the environment, they are also a source of bias and nonadaptation. The belief system sets bounds within which interpretations are accepted or rejected. The more central the beliefs, the less adaptive they are to dissonant information. They encourage decisionmakers to feel an overweening sense of confidence, which produces an immunity to critical review and analysis of knowledge and theories and generates automatic, rather than systematic, inferences. This confidence may lead to the ignoring and nonconsideration of alternative interpretations and to unjustified perseverance of theories even when the data on which the theories were originally based are invalidated. Feedback may thus be of little use in modifying inaccurate beliefs because the attention to it is selective, biased toward verification and confirmation, and neglectful of counterfactual argumentation.

Values. Values and ideologies determine what is desirable. Values are beliefs about desirable behavior, objects, and situations along a continuum of relative importance (Rokeach, 1973: 5).[8] Decision-oriented information processing is necessarily value bound and is unlikely to be value neutral. The information processor does not only want to know what the objective truth and knowledge contained in the information is but also assesses its value implications—more specifically, its significance for enhancing value realization. Thus the value system becomes an important factor in allocating attention and in judging the relevance and importance of information.[9] It follows that the importance of value systems and ideologies lies in their function as criteria for the evaluation of information and the classification of behavior, objects, and situations into desirable and undesirable categories. An object defined as negative according to ideological-ethical criteria tends to be evaluated, along with all the information associated with it, not objectively in terms of its content, but negatively as a matter of course.[10]

The relative permanence of the value system and the commitment to it often cause rigidity, which increases in proportion to the centrality of the values in question, as change would necessitate a restructuring of related values (Ostorm and Brock, 1969). Thus information that is incongruent with such values must be either ignored or manipulated in some other way to avoid a comprehensive value adjustment.

Prime Minister Golda Meir's insensitivity since 1971 to information indicating opportunities for negotiations with Egypt can be partly explained by its relation to two of her core values, the existence of the Israeli state and its security in a basically hostile world. Major concessions would, she thought, surrender the state to Palestine Liberation Organization (PLO) leader Yasir Arafat and Sadat by weakening Israel and overlooking the bitter lessons of Jewish history (Meir, 1975: 293). Hence Egyptian signals were unattended to or their validity and good faith doubted. Her responses to the signals reflected this distrust, which produced similar distrust and frustration on the Egyptian side.

The extent to which a particular value or value system is brought to bear on the judgment and evaluation of particular information bits depends on a number of factors. The most obvious is the extent to which decisionmakers perceive available information to be associated with their values. The association may, however, be unwarranted on either of two counts. Information may be linked to, and evaluated in terms of, irrelevant values—here the misperception lies in attributing nonexistent relevance to a particular value—or information that should have been associated with a particular value and judged in that context is not.

When decisionmakers have sufficient interest in the subject of the information, they relate their values to the information. Because of the importance that individuals tend to attach to their core values, they do not superimpose them on information or objects unless they consider them important. The other side of the same coin is that the values in question must be sufficiently important to decisionmakers for them to utilize the values in judging and evaluating information. To illustrate: President Johnson often invoked the values of national honor and of defending freedom against Communist aggression to explain the necessity for remaining in Indochina and bombing North Vietnam, in spite of the attendant human misery (Kearns, 1976: 327–31). Both Nixon and Kissinger valued a "strong" America, and for them "the Vietnamese war was a test of our strength and character as a people" (Mazlish, 1976: 219). All three associated a particular value (strength of will and purpose) with the U.S. effort in Vietnam. The values applied make all the difference in judging the same information, and thus dissenters spoke of the dishonor of bombing and napalming the people of Vietnam. "Even when the facts were not in dispute, their implications were. As the body count of enemies multiplied, Johnson took comfort from this sign of progress, while his opponents condemned the mounting toll in human life" (Kearns, 1976: 327).

Value-bound judgment has a number of implications. There is an increased sensitivity to stimuli that are compatible with one's values at the expense of attention to other stimuli; in other words, the threshold of penetration for compatible information is lower, and for information that threatens or questions important values, it is higher. In some cases the inclination is to produce information artificially to justify the adoption or maintenance of important values. Hence people holding the value of cooperation in the management of conflicts tend to judge their and their adversaries' positions as closer than they actually are (Judd, 1978). Finally, because ideology and praxis are not always congruent—because the values people hold are inconsistent with their actual behavior—they may perceive their behavior in a way that distorts its true meaning to avoid cognitive dissonance. This point will be elaborated later in the chapter.

Stereotypes. A stereotype is a simplistic, unsophisticated belief about an individual or group that can be either descriptive or normative. Normative stereotypes, those sanctioned by social institutions (e.g. school, church, state), determine the proper way to think about groups or individuals. They are rich in content and detail compared with descriptive stereotypes and are held with a greater degree of certainty than is normatively justified even when their holder has never had any direct contact with the subject of the stereotypes (Triandis, 1971: 105–6). Autostereotypes have an important role in building self-esteem and the self-image generally and ego-defense, a role that makes them inflexible and resistant to change. Stereotypes enable decisionmakers to fit a broad range of events into well-defined, narrow categories and thereby contribute to the speed and economy of mental effort, at the cost of nuance.[11]

Stereotypes are used as judgmental heuristics in interpreting the behavior of other actors despite the availability of other judgment-relevant information. "People, in general, seem to have implicit theories of personality, theories about what characteristics or behaviors are likely to be related, and they use these implicit theories to fill in gaps in their knowledge of others" (R. A. Jones, 1977: 3). Decisionmakers search for alternative interpretations only if stereotype-based interpretations are inapplicable, because stereotypes are usually readily available. Dependence on stereotypes increases when information processing is complex and the correct judgment is not implied directly by the information but built on inference (Bodenhausen and Wyer, 1985). Hence, when information is meager or ambiguous, stereotypes are used to go beyond it and play an active role in constructing reality (Stewart, Powell, and Chetwynd, 1979: 5). This process can produce the halo effect, defined as the influence of a global evaluation on the evaluation of individual attributes. For example, liking a person may lead to the assumption that those attributes of the person about which one knows little are also favorable (Nisbett and Wilson, 1977b). The halo effect gives stereotypes a judgmental spillover effect far beyond the immediate object on which the stereotype is focused.

An important influence in judging one's capability to attain a foreign policy goal is the view of the balance of power between allies, adversaries, and one's own country. People tend to overvalue allies and disparage adversaries (Bass and Dunteman, 1963). Such assessments are often based, not on a realistic evaluation, but on a stereotypic view of oneself and others. Where an adversary is racially different, the assessments may involve bigotry; the stereotype becomes more vivid by the use of derogatory language, which reinforces a tendency to underestimate the enemy. Johnson referred to North Vietnam as "that raggedy-ass little fourth-rate country" (Tuchman, 1984: 321). Both Nixon and Kissinger used a similar stereotype of North Vietnam as a "fourth-rate power," and Kissinger concluded from it: "I refuse to believe that a little fourth-rate power like North Vietnam does not have a breaking point" (Hersh, 1983: 126). The absolutism of their image blinded them to the fact that being an underdeveloped society was a blessing in disguise. Vietnam could withstand, without relenting, the heavy punishment of strategic bombing. Referring in general to the influence of racial prejudices and stereotypes prevailing among Nixon and his advisers, one of the participants concludes:

There is no documentary evidence—save perhaps the inaccessible White House tapes on national security subjects—that this racism was the decisive influence in Kissinger-Nixon policies in Africa, Vietnam, or elsewhere. . . . But it is impossible to pretend that the cast of mind that harbors such casual bigotry did not have some effect on American foreign policy toward the overwhelming majority of the world which is nonwhite. (R. Morris, 1977: 131–32)

A number of the characteristics of stereotypes make them an acute threat to the accuracy of perception. Stereotypes have a large degree of absolutism. Once a particular trait is attributed to a collective as a whole, the tendency is to attribute the same trait to every member of the collective without exception or to make unitary-actor assumptions (Child and Doob, 1943). For example, if a certain nation is perceived as aggressive, then the expectation is that all its decisionmakers will possess the same quality—hence the tendency to explain and perceive the verbal and actual behavior of all decisionmakers in the same terms without making objectively justified distinctions between people.

Stereotypes are often symptoms of deep hostile or friendly attitudes and thus determine and justify particular patterns of behavior and thinking, making those patterns even more resistant to change. Images based on stereotypes emphasize the discreteness in motives and behavior of the holders and objects of the stereotypes. As a result, self-perceptions and perceptions of others' behavior serve to justify the distinctions actors draw between themselves and others, for better or worse: they judge the behavior of others in less benign terms than they judge their own, attributing to it causes that diverge sharply from causes attributed to their own, same, behavior, and so on. Such causal attributions are simplistic and unrealistic. Unsuitable explanations may consequently be given to events, and unrealistic expectations may be formed. Those expectations shape behavior and may become self-fulfilling prophecies (Hamilton, 1979). Finally, stereotypes initiate and guide the process of remembering and interpretation in ways that provide the individual with stereotype-confirming evidence more readily than with stereotype-disconfirming evidence (Hamilton, 1981: M. Snyder, 1981). Hence stereotypes are rigid cognitive constructs that are extremely difficult to disconfirm.

Attitudes and Their Function

At the meeting ground between decisionmakers' beliefs, values, stereotypes, affect, and behavioral dispositions regarding objects and situations are attitudes.[12] The term attitude is defined for our purposes as an ideational formation having affective and cognitive dimensions that create a disposition for a particular pattern of behavior toward specific objects or categories of objects and social situations or some combination thereof (e.g. an object in a social situation). An attitude, then, is the result of a judgmental-evaluative process, which includes three elements: the cognitive, the affective, and the conative.[13]

Attitudes play a crucial role in easing a person's adjustment to a complex environment by guiding the selection of the appropriate coping behavior for the situations and objects. Metaphorically speaking, the decisionmaker's choice of response to situations and objects becomes a standard operating procedure; or, to put it differently, choosing is similar to activating a stored computer program. Once an object or situation is classified in a particular category, the choice of response pattern calls for little further search for information or thoughtful consideration of available information and becomes relatively effortless. However, this behavioral predisposition does not necessarily determine how people will actually behave but only what their behavioral intentions are. Behavioral intentions and actions are not always correlated. The significance of this fact and its contribution to possible biases, errors, and perceptual distortions will be discussed in detail later in this chapter.

A particular attitude is not an isolated cognitive component but part of a network of interrelated subsets forming the person's overall cognitive map. It is part of a subset of attitudes on the specific subject with which it deals, it is part of a subset of attitudes relating to the issue-area under discussion (e.g. foreign policy), and it is part of the set of general attitudes about social life; it is also connected to the person's values, beliefs, and stereotypes and reflects at least part of them. Any specific attitude influences and is influenced by broad attitude-sets concerning the same subject, issue-area, aspect of social life, and other relevant cognitive elements, such as beliefs and values. Unrealistic attitudes have potentially wide spillover effects. At the same time any attitude is potentially the conveyer of biases, errors, and misperceptions originating in the other components of the decisionmaker's cognitive system.

Inclusive judgment on an issue involves the integration of attitude-toward-situation and attitude-toward-object (Rokeach, 1966, 1968a). The problem is to continuously adjust the attitude-toward-object to situational circumstances and combine both attitudes in an integrative judgment, which is especially difficult when the two have contradictory implications. The interaction between the two components is what, in the final account, determines behavioral preference. The interaction may have several implications: (1) when decisionmakers determine their overall attitude by their attitude toward a situation, they risk overpragmatization and judgments that are merely circumstantial; (2) when decisionmakers determine their overall attitude mainly on the basis of the traits of the object, they tend toward conservatism and rigid nonadjustment to new situations and changes in the environment; (3) when decisionmakers accord equal weight to attitude-toward-object and attitude-toward-situation, they may be deficient in two areas. Their approach is mechanical: the equal-weight equation is a highly available rule but a doubtful reflection of reality, which is not so easily and smoothly divisible. Moreover, it is doubtful that decisionmakers can consistently produce integrated computations that correctly reflect the equal weights of object and situation, because of the limited ability of human beings to act as intuitive statisticians.[14]

A striking case in which attitude-toward-situation and attitude-toward-object had contradictory implications can be found in the positions of Israel's decisionmakers prior to the Yom Kippur War. Central figures in the decisionmaking elite, such as Defense Minister Dayan and Foreign Minister Eban, realized that the status quo and the continued diplomatic freeze were dangerous (attitude-toward-situation). They realized that it was unlikely that Egypt would resign itself and accept Israel's presence along the Suez Canal and the occupation of the Sinai indefinitely or that the Syrians would accept Israel's long-term control of the Golan Heights. The question, according to Dayan himself, was, not whether war would break out, but when. At the same time, attitude-toward-object (Egypt and Syria) saw the two Arab states as inherently too weak to initiate general war. Their dependence on the Soviets for arms supplies and the Soviets' refusal to supply certain items considered necessary for an offensive, the perceived weakness of Sadat's domestic position, Arab inferiority in the air, the perceived lack of competence of Egypt's and Syria's high commands, and détente between the two superpowers, who were believed to be uninterested in a destabilizing war, were all considered causes of Arab political-military weakness that would dispose their leadership toward a policy of risk avoidance (Dayan, 1976; Eban, 1978: 470–73, 480–81; Herzog, 1975: 18–19). The contradictory implications of attitude-toward-situation and attitude-toward-object were conveniently resolved in favor of the latter by adopting the position that war was unlikely.

One explanation of the insensitivity to situational implications, of which the decisionmakers were aware, has to do with the tendency to prefer dispositional explanations of the other actors' behavior (e.g. inherent weakness). This tendency is further reinforced by the tendency of active perceivers, who are immersed in the social interactions that they interpret, to be insensitive to those aspects of the targets' behavior that cannot be explained in terms of the perceivers' inducing behavior (Gilbert, Jones, and Pelham, 1987). In international politics inherent ambiguities allow active perceivers to focus on the one source of influence that is unambiguous to them—their own; all competing sources of explanation are ambiguous enough to be ignored or underevaluated. For example, Israeli decisionmakers focused on deterrence; they assumed they could independently use military power to influence their Arab counterparts' behavior, an assumption supported by a simplistic view of a hostile world where self-reliance was the only viable policy. Given this political-strategic world view, they interpreted the Arab leaders' behavior as a reaction to the success of Israel's military deterrence that in their view compounded the inherent weaknesses of the Arab adversary. This dispositional explanation created an insensitivity to other factors that affected the Arab nonuse of large-scale military power to change the status quo from 1971 to 1973. Hence the surprise when deterrence—although all its ingredients were unchanged—failed to prevent the outbreak of a war initiated by the "weaker" side.

The interaction between attitude-toward-situation and attitude-toward-object is particularly important for understanding turning-point decisions. Turning-point decisions, that is, decisions that deviate significantly from the pattern of prior decisions, leading to major policy shifts on a particular issue, depend on resolving the contradiction between attitude-toward-object and attitude-toward-situation in favor of the latter. This results in the next stage, after reducing dissonance, in a modification of the attitude-toward-object. The stronger the post-decisional dissonance, the greater is the change in attitude-toward-object (Auerbach, 1986).

The cognitive system has teleological and structural attributes that decisively affect information processing. In the first place, because a person's cognitive map is functional and has purpose, it may display a tendency toward self-serving biases and distortion of information or toward the ignoring of feedbacks that would require changes in attitudes that would render those attitudes dysfunctional in serving one or more of their purposes (Herek, 1986; Katz, 1960; McGuire, 1969: 157–60). Information interpretation may thus become subservient to the preservation and enhancement of the functional needs served by existing attitudes. To elaborate, we shall look at the various functions attitudes fulfill and the related biases and errors in information processing that these functions may cause.

Instrumental-utilitarian functions. Preference for a particular attitude may be predicated on the extent to which that attitude is believed to have an instrumental-utilitarian value. Thus foreign policy decisionmakers who believe that a particular attitude is not in line with attitudes held by other, more powerful personalities, even though it may better reflect the dictates of reality, adopt attitudes that may be less appropriate but more functional and serve their interests better. The Johnson administration "publicly endowed the struggle in Vietnam with enormous importance," with a great emphasis on "how the United States looked"; yet in fact

> both the President and his advisors often seemed to have difficulty in distinguishing between their personal prestige and that of the United States. These advisors clearly believed that further American military escalation might work. In any case it was consistent with the primarily military approach with which they and their careers had already become so closely identified, and consistency is usually a prerequisite for protecting a public career. (Kahin, 1986: 312–13)

Knowledge functions. Attitudes can express people's need to impose order and structure on a complex social reality, improve their understanding, reduce ambiguity, and guide their behavior toward objects. Knowledge is associated with order and simple, parsimonious structures that include an internally consistent organization of cognition, affect, and behavioral disposition; with consistency within the attitude-set; and with consistency within the broader cognitive system, that is, among attitudes, values, beliefs, and expectations. Thus no matter how complex the cognitive system is, its components are liable to form simpler structures; consistency is maintained within the system even if feedbacks to the contrary have to be ignored (Axelrod, 1976: 248). The desire to extend and improve knowledge, the consequent alertness to new, updated information, and the readiness to process it and assimilate it into existing complex cognitive maps are liable to create distortion because of the tendency to seek consistency, which is associated with rationality. Reality, however, is not necessarily consistent; hence an attempt to fit information about reality into a consistent framework may entail imposing consistency where it does not exist—which in practice means giving a distorted interpretation to the information.

President Johnson viewed the Vietnam conflict as just another bargaining situation, of the type with which he had had so much experience in domestic politics, where the contenders on both sides were reasonable people, who could recognize when the balance of power had tilted against them and act accordingly (Kearns, 1976: 264–66). This attitude provided Johnson with a readily available understanding of the intricacies of a domain that was new to him—foreign policy—and of a region and culture he did not know much about. "Although Johnson recognized the 'foreignness' of the Vietnamese, he simply could not accept the possibility that they might not share important qualities with Americans. Otherwise, how could Johnson hope to deal with them?" (Kearns, 1976: 265).

Value-expressive functions. People adopt attitudes that seem to them congruent with their values, particularly their core values, which are tied to self-expression and self-identity. The expression of attitudes provides an opportunity for acting out inner tensions. Even more important, the attitude-set is a means of self-realization; through it people create distinctive identities and bolster or justify their own behavior. The danger is that attitudes expressing values reflect wishful thinking rather than reality. Another problem involves the lack of adjustment likely to result when attitudes are anchored in core values that are bound to self-identity. Attitude change depends on change in these core values, which are, however, among the cognitive components most resistant to change. For Johnson, for example, the bombing of North Vietnam was not a campaign of vengeance and destruction but a means of bargaining without words—the stick in the negotiations. The carrot was a billion-dollar program—the Mekong River Basin Development Project—for the social and economic betterment of North and South Vietnam, as well as the rest of Southeast Asia. Paradoxically, then, his attitude toward the struggle in Vietnam reflected the core American values of rationality and compromise. He did not realize that the North Vietnamese interpreted the situation in a completely different way because they were guided by different values and assumptions (Kearns, 1976: 266–69).

Ego-defensive functions. A vital psychological drive is the need for ego-defense and the preservation of self-esteem (M. Rosenberg, 1969: 54–57, 260–78; Sarnoff and Katz, 1954). Attitudes are supposed to help people deal with their intrapsychic conflicts; for example, attitudes expressing aggression may actually be a protective projection of the lack of self-confidence. Attitudes defend psychological integrity by preventing or resolving inner conflicts that people are not prepared to face. Ego-defensive attitudes are likely to emerge when particular issues and situations evoke such needs and touch the deeper layers of the decisionmaker's personality (Greenstein, 1975: 57–61). Johnson's attitudes on Vietnam were heavily influenced by his fear of projecting an image of "a coward," "an unmanly man," "a man without a spine" (Kearns, 1976: 253, 263).

The price paid for ego-defense is liable to be the distortion of reality or a refusal to recognize the need for attitude change called for by environmental transformation. Ego-defensive attitudes are impervious to change by informational inputs, adamantly so in the face of dissonant information,[15] partly because "motives which have been eliminated from consciousness by an ego defense are not readily amenable to recall, even after lengthy and deliberate efforts to remember them" (Sarnoff, 1960: 256). Ego-defensive needs are a source of motivational biases in judgments related to uncertain outcomes that may pose threats to self-esteem or have high affective significance. In situations in which avoiding failure is very important but the desire for success is strong—situations typical of politics—people may employ defensive pessimism, that is, lowered expectations of the likelihood of the desired outcome. Pessimists may alternatively derogate the value of the desired but uncertain outcome. Optimists believe in their success and cope with failure post hoc: their preferred strategy is denying that they had control over the situation (R. A. Jones, 1977: 126–65; Norem and Cantor, 1986; Pyszczynski, 1982). Pessimists' strategies result in estimates of the probabilities of success that are biased downward and estimates of the probabilities of failure that are biased upward, or, instead, in a new rank order of options, the value of alternative outcomes having been reassessed to avoid negative affect. When pessimists simultaneously use both strategies, they distort the information maximally. Optimists, on the other hand, cannot enjoy the benefits of feedback to improve their future performance because they attribute negative outcomes to factors beyond their control.

A person's attitudes fill all those functions.[16] Any attitude may perform several functions simultaneously. The more functions an attitude performs, the more central it is and the less likely it is to change even when its validity is challenged by new information. Attitudes that have no function are peripheral and easily changed. The balance between the various attitudes is predicated on a person's most acute needs and preferences, which reflect personality traits, issues of concern, and situational circumstances (e.g. the analysis of Kennedy's decisionmaking in Mongar, 1969). For example, a considerable part of an insecure person's attitudes are focused on the task of ego-defense. On the other hand, an individual who is in the midst of a power struggle is far more inclined to adopt attitudes useful in the struggle.

Cognitive Style

"The term cognitive style refers to the characteristic way in which individuals conceptually organize the environment" (Goldstein and Blackman, 1979: 2). It is a generic construct that emphasizes the structure (the organization of cognition) rather than the content of thought (e.g. motivation or emotion). It is also stable across situations, and its behavioral output, here the main information processing effects, shows consistent characteristics. First, attention to information is related to the openness or closedness of the decisionmaker's cognitive system. Systems are closed when decisionmakers believe that the knowledge in their system fully covers the subject matter (W. A. Scott, 1965). The more closed the cognitive system is, and the more decisionmakers are convinced that they do not need additional information, the less intensive is the search for additional information and the less likely is attention to new information and attitude change to occur. Thus perceived completeness of available knowledge becomes a determining criterion that guides the search for, attention to, and perception of the relevance of new information.

Second, cognitive systems have variable levels of complexity, that is, the number and combination of dimensions applied to characterize objects or situations, or, more generally stated, the complexity of the cognitive rules used to process information. The more complex the cognitive system, the more capable the individual decisionmaker is of dealing with information that demands new or more subtle distinctions (Bieri, 1966; W. A. Scott, 1963; W. A. Scott, 1965: 87; Suedfeld and Rank, 1976; Suedfeld and Tetlock, 1977).[17] Complexity is not the number of dimensions in itself: "Given complex combinatory rules, the potential for generating new attributes of information is higher, and the degree to which one stimulus can be discriminated from another is increased as the number of perceived dimensions increases" (Schroder, Driver, and Streufert, 1967: 14–15). Decisionmakers who possess multiple judgment dimensions also tend to possess some rules of abstraction that facilitate the integration and comparison of information. They tend to produce alternative interpretations of stimuli but, by using their capacity for abstraction and integration, are able to resolve ambiguities, leading to stable attitudes and judgments. Lack of such rules for abstraction is bound to culminate in confusion and inefficient information processing, as is the case with people of intermediate cognitive complexity. They produce ambiguous judgments that tend to be unstable because they take multiple dimensions of the issue into account without having some integration and abstraction rule as a guide. As for decisionmakers, with low cognitive complexity they tend to produce absolute, fixed, unyielding judgments about events (W. L. Bennett, 1975: 33–35).

Decisionmakers with a more abstract cognitive structure are also better prepared to deal with information overload, and their awareness threshold is lower, so that they are alerted earlier to relevant information (Nydegger, 1975; Schroder, Driver, and Streufert, 1967: 155–57). Decisionmakers who are high in cognitive complexity are also more likely to be high in the need for cognition, giving them a stronger motivation for preferring systematic processing over heuristic processing. Cognitive complexity may also have a spillover effect on actual behavior. Cognitively complex decisionmakers prefer more cooperation in conflict situations because of their ability to see disputes from the adversary's point of view as well as their own (Tetlock, 1985c).

As vice president and then as president, Johnson had a mixed bag of characteristic American ideas. "The battle against Communism must be joined in Southeast Asia with the strength and determination to achieve success there—or the United States must inevitably surrender the Pacific . . . and pull back our defenses to San Francisco'" (Tuchman, 1984: 293). His views on American foreign policy in general and the Vietnam issue in particular reflect the degree to which his central beliefs and attitudes were closed and simplistic. Johnson felt strongly that for too long America had been seen as weak-willed, or, in his words, "'fat and fifty, like the country-club set.'" This perception led to the development of a closed attitude about his administration's foreign policy. "Consequently, he was sure that the United States should move promptly and vigorously to counter anything which was significantly harmful to American interests" (E. F. Goldman, 1974: 449)—an extremely simplistic point of view. Yet these were central and focal attitudes that, precisely because of their lack of sophistication, afforded little room for the recognition of discrepant information and the opponent's position.

The level of cognitive complexity is not unchanging but is responsive to situational and socializing factors. Crisis-produced stress decreases cognitive complexity (Levi and Tetlock, 1980). Similarly, values predispose cognitive style and shape typical thinking about issues. Pluralistic ideologies, with room for conflicting values, may socialize and sensitize adherents to the need to balance competing goals and objectives, in different ways in different situations (Tetlock, 1983b, 1984), thus increasing cognitive complexity.

Third, the higher the interrelatedness of the components of the cognitive system—defined as "(a) mutual dependence of elements within the system on one another; (b) 'boundedness' of the system in the sense that the rate or intensity of interaction of the component elements with each other is greater than their interaction with outside elements; (c) tendency towards self-maintenance and resistance to incursion or alteration by outside forces" (W. A. Scott, 1958: 10), the less likely is dissonant information to cause attitude change. This is the case because dissonant information is likely to require complex considerations of trade-offs among values, a situation that people preferably avoid (Deutsch and Merritt, 1965: 174–79; Jervis, 1976: 128–42; J. L. Snyder, 1978), or a comprehensive reorganization and adjustment of the cognitive system.

Fourth, organization of the different judgment dimensions of an issue in covariation relationships allows effortless inferences, whenever one of the dimensions is observed in a situation or object, that go beyond the information given about the existence of the covaried dimension. When the covariation relationship is causal, going beyond the information given entails higher-order cognitive processes of attribution. For example, assumptions about the interrelatedness of economic and political dimensions in situations of instability leads political instability to be inferred from information about economic instability.

The fifth attribute of cognitive style is category width. A category is defined as broader in direct relationship to the amount of discrepancy tolerated among category members still labeled with the same name.[18] Differences between people with regard to category width are likely to yield differences in the categorization of the same stimulus, and differences in categorization yield differences in interpretation (Detweiler, 1978). The broader the category, the less likely contradictory information is to require the consideration of attitude change; the narrower the category, the greater is the pressure for such a change (Eagly, 1969). For example, if a category for what a particular decisionmaker defines as hostile actions relates to both hostile statements and acts, then information about a friendly verbal expression by a hostile adversary does not cause a change of attitude toward that actor, for it can be argued that as long as the adversary does not actually perform a friendly act, there is no room for attitude change. The tendency in fact is to attribute a Machiavellian motive to friendly verbal behavior.

In addition to the structural attributes of the cognitive system as a whole, three characteristics of individual beliefs and attitudes have important implications for information processing, namely, centrality, generality, and affective intensity. Both generality and affective intensity appear to covary with centrality. Central beliefs and attitudes are the core around which interdependent clusters of attitudes and beliefs are transformed into belief and attitude systems. Centrality, as already mentioned, means that change in the perceived validity, desirability, or content of the central belief or attitude results in compensating changes in all or some of the beliefs or attitudes in the cluster. Any change is necessarily compounded by and cannot be undergone without its causing a great deal of psychological inconvenience. Central beliefs and attitudes tend to be stable over time (Converse, 1964); centrality thus becomes a cause of bias toward conservatism and premature cognitive closure. Central beliefs and attitudes, especially when they cause many other beliefs and attitudes to be organized around them, serve as a means of cognitive economizing by providing actors with an easily available guide for judging novel information and behavioral disposition. Knowledge of the core beliefs and attitudes of other actors is particularly helpful in evaluative judgments and predictions of their behavior, because decisionmakers are likely to anticipate a linear relationship between the central beliefs and attitudes of adversaries and their behavior. This point will be further elaborated later.

Closely related to centrality is the notion of generality. The more general an attitude or belief is, the more difficult it is to change, because it is more central. At the same time generality facilitates the manipulation of dissonant information by applying a readily justifiable assimilation process to it. For example, almost from the very beginning of U.S. intervention in Vietnam, maintaining credibility, or "the impression that the United States was tough enough and effective enough to meet its responsibilities in the world," was one of the main general goals the Vietnam policy was supposed to uphold. The exact nature of credibility was never defined because its reality could never be proven. By the time Nixon came to power, credibility became the dominant value pursued. All the other goals of intervention were vanishing. The centrality of credibility was further increased by Nixon and Kissinger, who implied that failure in Vietnam would have a domino effect not only in Asia but globally, a sort of "super-domino theory." The stakes involved in upholding credibility were almost unlimited and affected every region and subject in which U.S. foreign policy was involved (Isaacs, 1983: 494–97; Kissinger, 1979: 292; Ward, 1974: 333).

Finally, the greater the emotional intensity of a belief or attitude, the greater is its resistance to change by disconfirming information or reasoning. Centrality and emotional intensity are likely to covary; that is, centrality may cause emotional intensity, or emotional intensity may reinforce centrality.[19]

The Decisionmaker as a Consistency Seeker

Individuals have a strong need to maintain a consistent cognitive system that produces stable and simplified cognitive structures.[20] This consistency operates on three levels. First, there is consistency within attitudes among the cognitive, affective, and conative components; "the individual will tend to act so as to balance the maximum number of triads [components of attitudes]" (Insko and Schopler, 1971: 32). Second, there is consistency among attitudes, mainly an attempt to avoid cognitive dissonance (Festinger, 1957, 1964). Finally, on the most general level, there is the attempt to prevent the emergence of imbalance in the cognitive entirety, that is, among attitudes, beliefs, and values. The need for consistency produces the tendency of a consistent cognitive system to remain stable (Burnstein, 1967; Jervis, 1976; W. A. Scott,

1959, 1969), either by ignoring information that threatens consistency or by attending to and manipulating it. Most of the strategies people use to protect themselves from the results of inconsistency are connected in some way to increasing rigidity of attitudes and beliefs. A state of consistency creates a sense of satisfaction, psychological well-being, and harmony that a person would like to preserve.

The need for consistency makes itself felt only when the stimulus for it is present (J. E. Singer, 1968; Wicklund and Brehm, 1976), in other words, when the issue with which the imbalance is concerned becomes personally important and preoccupying. A perceived inconsistency may well go unattended so long as the decisionmaker is not preoccupied with the issue in question. Inconsistencies evoke corrective processes only when a certain threshold of inconsistency is crossed. Similarly, imbalances concerning peripheral beliefs do not necessarily call for correction at all even if the decisionmaker is aware of them. Not all people have the same need for balance. The higher the complexity of the decisionmaker's cognitive system, the smaller is the need for balance and the greater the readiness to come to terms with inconsistencies in the system (Heradstveit and Narvesen, 1978; Kelman and Baron, 1968; M. J. Rosenberg, 1960b).

The drive for consistency also depends on how much freedom of choice decisionmakers believe they have. The less free they perceive themselves to be, the less annoyed they are with inconsistency. When decisionmakers believe that an irresistible extrinsic pressure is causing behavior that is not in line with one or more of the cognitive components, the dissonance thus engendered is mild and the need for consistency is considerably reduced (A. R. Cohen, 1960; Wicklund and Brehm, 1976). The counterattitudinal behavior of leaders under pressure from public opinion creates a reduced drive for attitude-behavior consistency so long as they do not come to believe that they behaved as they did on their own accord. Thus decisionmakers who have changed their public attitude because of public pressure do not feel a strong sense of inconvenience and in due time may even internalize the new beliefs and attitudes by using one or more of the techniques described below.

From the need for consistency, several conclusions as to possible distortions in information processing may be drawn. First, people attempt to create and preserve a consistent and balanced cognitive system, and "because many of the structures in the world are balanced, the tendency to perceive balance will often serve people well" (Jervis, 1976: 125). Yet in many instances social reality is neither consistent nor balanced. Because people see the social environment as consistent and balanced, they believe that a policy that serves one value is also likely to contribute to other values, thus avoiding consideration of value trade-offs. If decision-makers believe that a particular policy has an advantage over all alternative policy options on all relevant dimensions, they are not open to reconsider their choice, even in the light of new information that the policy is failing to achieve some important goals, because they believe that it is still best on other dimensions. In general, value trade-offs are least likely to be found where they are easily avoided or where they are painful (e.g. where they involve intensely held values) (Jervis, 1976: 128–41).

In the process of avoiding value trade-offs and attempting to make a particular option consistently attractive over all value dimensions, even salient internal contradictions are sometimes blatantly ignored. The option of a preemptive strike by the air force, which was already fully mobilized, was suggested by Israel's chief of staff on the morning of October 6, 1973, when the outbreak of war later that day had become a certainty. Yet this option was rejected by the defense minister and the prime minister, who argued that such an act would create an adverse U.S. reaction, causing the loss of U.S. political support and, more important, the forfeiture of necessary American military aid (Nakdimon, 1982: 108–16). Their argument clearly contradicted the view prevailing among most of the country's political and military elite: that Israel was a regional power that could defy, and had defied, the United States on important issues (such as rejecting American peace initiatives involving concessions concerning the occupied territories) and that it was an invaluable U.S. ally and partner and not a client. Meir and Dayan's argument was, however, consistent with the also-prevalent view that Israel's military superiority would allow it to absorb a first strike and then counterattack. The contradiction pointed out was at the time completely overlooked, but its unsettling latent effect can be discerned in the post-war recollections of Meir and to a lesser degree in those of Dayan, who fluctuated between justifying the decision not to preempt on the one hand and regretting and even feeling guilt over it on the other (e.g. Meir, 1975: 313; Nakdimon, 1982: 114–15).

A second conclusion is that causal connections are fabricated when they do not necessarily exist,[21] such as the assumption that actors described by negative character traits therefore have hostile intentions and pose a threat. Such a conclusion is often unrealistic, as the actors' traits do not necessarily imply their actual intentions, capabilities to cause damage, or their actual behavior.

Third, there is also the danger of a chain reaction of distortion when the cognitive system's components are logically and integrally interconnected (McGuire, 1960). Consistency-motivated adjustment or rigidity causes adjustments that are normatively unjustified across a broad range of attitudes, beliefs, and values, and thus cognitive distortion has a comprehensive spillover effect, especially when it is related to central beliefs or attitudes. If the cognitive system is already in balance, the resultant sense of psychological comfort produces cognitive conservatism, so that attention and receptivity to information likely to undermine the balanced structure are reduced, regardless of whether the information is valid. The basic trend is to conserve existing attitudes unchanged (M. J. Rosenberg, 1960a) and to retain the existing pattern of causal connections.[22] In a nutshell, inconsistency produces pressures for consistency, but consistency produces cognitive rigidity and closure. The distortions created to reach consistency from inconsistency are hard to correct, as the existing state of affairs is psychologically convenient and reassuring.

Fourth, an internally consistent belief system encourages decisionmakers to construct a view of a stable, regularized, and orderly environment in their minds. It gives them a sense of confidence in their understanding of the world and of unjustified assurance that their policies are likely to achieve their ends, leaving a much smaller margin for error and surprise than reality demands (Kinder and Weiss, 1978). Commitment to specific behavioral dispositions, particularly when they formerly acted in line with those dispositions and when the cognitive-affective-conative components of the relevant attitudes are consistent, reinforces the rigidity of attitudes (Kiesler, 1971). That is the case because change in the cognitive or affective components is liable to trigger a need for change in the behavioral disposition to which a person is already committed. Defensive coping with dissonant information may even precede the actual encounter with the information when a forewarning of discrepant communication on topics of high involvement activate cognitive defenses, increasing resistance to persuasion (Petty and Cacioppo, 1977). For example, knowing that a particular source may provide dissonant information, the decisionmaker can describe the source as biased or unreliable even before the information becomes available, avoiding the need to process the information and confront its implications for attitude change.

Inconsistency-handling mechanisms can be divided into two modes. The first contains those reactions that involve the refusal to tolerate inconsistency and are intended to reduce it by ignoring or eliminating the incompatible element. One path to follow is denial of the existence of the incompatible element—rejecting its validity, distorting its meaning, derogating its source, or rationalizing it. All of these contribute to the capability to record discrepant information but avoid coming to terms with its implications. For example, confronted with the choice between the competing values of war avoidance and credibility maintenance, the decisionmaker may sidestep potential dissonance by rationalization, reconceptualizing the dilemma as a choice between "risk war now or incur destruction later"; that is, only by running some risk of war over the current disputed issue can the decisionmaker demonstrate a credible resolve to adversaries and thus avoid war in the future (J. L. Snyder, 1978). The second path to follow in refusing to tolerate inconsistency is confrontation with the inconsistency through, for example, attitude change or change of behavior.

The other mode of dealing with inconsistency is to maintain inconsistency while reducing the consequent discomforts. Again there are two paths. The first is manipulation of the social situation to reduce the salience of the inconsistent relationship. People may, for example, compartmentalize, keeping different areas of their lives separate, and thus secure the ability to maintain inconsistent beliefs; or they may institutionalize, insulating the inconsistent behavior from the rest of their attitudes, beliefs, and values (e.g. soldiers as members of a military organization are expected to kill the enemy even if killing is inconsistent with their values); or they may engage in symbolic ritualism that hides inconsistency without removing it (e.g. by pretending to consider change in an inconsistent cognitive element) (Kelman and Baron, 1968). The second path entails confronting inconsistency through bolstering, differentiation, transcendence, or delinking (Abelson, 1959).

In *bolstering*, a challenged cognitive object is strengthened by being attached to a more highly valued object by seeking new information and developing new arguments so that the effect of imbalance is reduced. For example, Kearns, in describing the development of Lyndon Johnson's continued magnification of the stakes as the war escalated beyond initial intentions, pinpoints five stages. From "just a test case for wars of national liberation" and a "lesson for aggressors," through a necessity to "prevent the fall of Southeast Asia" and a part of the "containment of China," Johnson arrived at the ultimate justification: "America fought in Vietnam to prevent the otherwise inevitable onset of World War III" (1976: 270). Reducing the malaise created by an unbalanced cognitive structure by bolstering the attitudes in question, through linking them in turn to important values that are not actually relevant to the issue at hand, distorts judgment. Moreover, repeated bolstering increases the intensity of existing attitudes toward the object and at the same time links them with other important attitudes and values, so that their centrality is enhanced. The use of this technique makes the bolstered attitudes still more rigid.

In *differentiation*, one of the unbalanced cognitive components is split into two distinct parts so that each part can be treated in isolation. When

U.S. decisionmakers support nondemocratic regimes and prefer them over democratic regimes in accordance with their degree of alliance with the Western bloc—an attitude that clashes with U.S. core values—they resolve the dissonance by explaining that there are two kinds of totalitarian or non-democratic regime: those maintaining links with the West, which could possibly change their character through being exposed to American influence and values, and those maintaining close links with the Soviet Union, which are enemies of the West and therefore offer no prospect of liberalization. We can see another example in the way Kissinger approached criticism on the use of military power in Cambodia. "For Kissinger, the use of American power in Cambodia was not a moral question. It was only a logical extension of his doctrine that force—a deliberately shocking use of force—was required on occasion to advance the cause of diplomacy—in this case, the negotiation of a dignified American withdrawal from Indochina" (Kalb and Kalb, 1974: 172).

In *transcendence*, the unbalanced cognitive objects are built up and elevated to a higher, superordinate level. The resolution of the inconvenience produced by unbalanced cognitive objects is achieved not by changing them but by elevating and conserving them. The use of this means is liable to constrain the capacity for adjusting attitudes. Robert McNamara, once he had lost faith in the war effort, solved his own cognitive dilemma by a form of transcendence. As Tuchman describes it, McNamara remained "loyal to the government game" and continued to preside over a strategy he believed futile and wrong. To do otherwise, [he] would have said, would be to show disbelief, giving comfort to the enemy" (1984: 346; see also Kinnard, 1980: 101). Thus McNamara repressed what must have been for him an extremely bothersome cognitive imbalance—between the emotional intensity of his now-altered attitude toward the war and his strong belief in the value of loyalty to the president—by elevating the latter to a transcendent position. McNamara considered loyalty a higher goal.

In *delinking*, the cognitive links between the incongruent cognitive components are severed and the components are considered irrelevant to each other. An acute case of delinking is the divorce of adversaries' capabilities from their intentions when the capabilities are incongruent with one's beliefs that their intentions are nonviolent. For example, by April 1973 Israeli intelligence already had detailed information on the main components of Egypt's war plans. But Zeira, the director of military intelligence, refused to change his basic assessment that war was highly unlikely. To account for the dissonant information, he delinked it from the immediate military-strategic intentions of Egypt and linked it instead to diplomatic maneuvers, particularly National Security Adviser Hafez Ismail's forthcoming talks with Kissinger in Washington, which were intended to improve Arab bargaining positions. To sound the alarm, Zeira believed, would be playing Sadat's game and inviting new American initiatives unacceptable to Israel (Bartov, 1978a: 241–42).

To summarize, the manipulation of information to reduce cognitive inconsistency has three potential targets: information regarding the object of the attitude; information regarding the situation; and information regarding the motives for the object's behavior. In choosing a strategy to overcome inconsistency, decisionmakers are guided by a number of general principles. The basic urge is conservatism—to abstain as far as possible from introducing changes in values, beliefs, and attitudes. Conservatism does not operate with the same intensity for every cognitive component—the more marginal the attitude, the weaker is the urge to preserve it unchanged. If consistency-reducing techniques have to be applied, the dominant preference is for balance-restoring techniques that are not intellectually demanding and require little cognitive labor.[23] Techniques such as differentiation and transcendence demand greater intellectual effort and sophistication than do denial and bolstering (Abelson, 1959: 348). If change is unavoidable, only the minimum changes needed for the purpose are made, rather than a general reorganization and reconsideration of the related cognitive components (Abelson and Rosenberg, 1958; Bonham, Shapiro, and Trumble, 1979; Triandis, 1971: 74). Changing isolated cognitions rather than central cognitions is preferred because altering a central cognition to reduce imbalance is likely to cause more imbalance than it eliminates. Another criterion for choice is whether or not the solution is challenged by present events and information. Decisionmakers attempt to avoid future dissonance by preferring a stable solution that is unlikely to be challenged by future information, which might cause embarrassment should others discover that they indulge in distortion (Walster, Berscheid, and Barclay, 1967).

These principles reflect the fact that human beings are not only consistency seekers but also cognitive misers. Thus the need for cognitive balance, the means by which it is achieved, and the balance itself once it is achieved can all become obstacles to accurate information processing. Although people are usually slow and inflexible in changing their convictions even when confronted with disconfirming information, they demonstrate surprising agility and initiative in defending the consistent structure of their convictions. They are nimble in applying various defensive strategies sequentially or simultaneously and then abandoning one strategy for the next when they sense that it has become ineffective.

Shortcuts to Judgment and Prediction:
Heuristics and Biases

Beliefs, values, and attitudes provide signposts for policymakers, who grope in a maze of uncertainty as to the meaning of the past, the nature of the present, and the shape of the future, who search for manageable formulas for attributing causality and predicting outcomes.[24] But faced with highly complex information, the ramifications of whose potentially relevant aspects all need to be considered integratively, decisionmakers often prefer to apply heuristics (nonoptimal rules of thumb) over algorithms (optimal procedures based on systematic consideration of all relevant aspects of the information available),[25] especially when time is limited because of the requirements of the task to which the information pertains or the need to attend to other tasks. Heuristics are general principles for reducing complex judgment tasks to simpler mental operations by emphasizing some properties of the data and ignoring others. They are informal intuitive procedures that are applied both consciously and thoughtlessly. Heuristics are not necessarily applied consistently, even by the same person to the same type of problem and circumstances. Since their application involves selectivity in the use of information, they are a source of typical biases—deviations in judgment that are consistent and predictable. These biases are nonmotivational.

There are a number of widely used heuristics. One is *representativeness*, which is applied in assessing the probability that Object A belongs to Class B, or that Event A originates from Process B. It is based on matching the essential feature of the sample events or sample statistics to the parent population or the generating process. Decisionmakers look for causes that resemble the explained effect when applying it in its primitive form to the search for causal explanation. With its sophisticated form, people search for a general theory on effects of the type for which explanation is sought. Once they have hit upon a theory and located in it a causal factor similar to the one presumed to be present in the current case, they attribute the causal influence in the case at hand to that factor (Kahneman and Tversky, 1972; Nisbett and Ross, 1980; Tversky and Kahneman, 1974).

To illustrate: as protests against the Nixon administration mounted after the Cambodian invasion, Kissinger feared that the very institutions of government were threatened. He defined the situation as potentially destabilizing for American society and identified in the situation the ingredients similar to ones found where societies drifted toward Fascism. He saw a beleaguered head of state—the president—trying to do what was right, deserted by the establishment, attacked by intellectuals and liberals, and a looming danger that the locus of decision might move into the streets. The authority of the regime was being undermined, and the country could not afford it. What illuminated the representativeness of the current situation as a member of the general category of destabilized societies controlled by mobs and street thugs was the Weimar Republic analogy, which Kissinger knew from personal experience (Kalb and Kalb, 1974: 169; Kissinger, 1979: 228; Ward, 1974: 334).

Representativeness is used because it is accessible; it is often correlated with probability, but people tend to overestimate the correlation. Although similarity is sometimes a useful and valid cue in judging likelihood, other features that are not related to similarity also affect likelihood. An example is the belief that State A's giving economic aid to State B will render State B dependent on State A, since the receiving is perceived as a necessary and sufficient condition for dependence on the aid donor. Such expectations may lead to the operational conclusion that a fully reliable way to acquire political influence is by giving economic aid. Another example is the prevailing belief in the covariation between radical regimes and identification with the Soviet Union, which has led to the conclusion that radical regimes voluntarily serve Soviet interests and thus automatically are threats to U.S. interests.

Judgment by representativeness does not consider sample size and tends in general to ignore base-rate information; that is, the prior probability based upon past occurrences of the outcome is not taken into account (Kahneman and Tversky, 1973; Tversky and Kahneman, 1982). President Johnson, for example, was sure that the Mekong River Basin Development Project would be a great success, bringing with it prosperity and a higher standard of living for the population. In optimistically assessing the program's chances for success, he was aware of, but ignored, base-rate information about past failures of American foreign aid programs, especially of large programs with economic, social, and political complexity. However, he saw the project as belonging in the same category as his Great Society program—it came at the height of the Great Society program at home—only the Mekong River Basin project was a matter of implementating social engineering in a foreign country (Kearns, 1976: 268).

Foreign policy decisionmakers do indeed neglect the appropriate use of base-rate information in the process of using representativeness, though not always the reliance on base rates as such. In foreign policy the use of the base rate and its identification by the observer are highly problematic. Few formal data banks contain readily accessible, detailed (distributional) base-rate information because decisionmaking systems are not interested in accumulating this type of information, nor are they trained to use it even when it is somehow available.[26] For that matter, available base-rate information is usually not objective or provided by an authority. Hence, when foreign policy decisionmakers use the equivalent of base-rate information, it is often based on a very small unrepresentative sample of cases or even on a sample of one. In many instances

past analyses, which cannot be independently assessed as "right" or "wrong" are a misleading basis for predicting the likelihood of a single event in the future, a task which is extraordinarily difficult even under the best of circumstances. To predict a military attack, an intelligence expert has recourse to "hard" evidence of military capability, from which limited inference can be drawn, to "soft" evidence of intentions, from which important inferences must be drawn, and to past experience, which is a poor guide to the future. (J. G. Stein, 1982b: 53)

Yet past events become base-rate information in which predictions of future behavior are anchored. When the base-rate data-set contains a single sample case, the adjustment of present judgment can be only guess-work rather than systematic updating in the Bayesian sense.

To illustrate: in early October 1973, Israel's Chief of Staff David Elazar had to judge the probability that mobilizing the reserves would be to react to a false alarm, as suggested by the director of military intelligence, compared with the probability that it would turn out to be a necessary precaution. The most-available information was not systematically accumulated base-rate information about false alarms in the past, or cost-benefit calculations of the risks of not mobilizing compared with the risks of mobilizing, or even an in-depth analysis of Arab leaders' intentions. The main inputs were the costs of mobilizing and then having the mobilization turn out to be unnecessary. The vivid recent memory of the May 1973 mobilization reminded Elazar that he had decided on mobilization against the advice of the military intelligence and been proven wrong. Thus he was convinced in October to concur with the assessment of the director of military intelligence that the probability of war was very low (Bartov, 1978a: 307–8; Herzog, 1975: 40).

When base rates are used, their choice depends on the decisionmakers' a priori beliefs and theories about international politics; therefore the answer to the question of which base-rate populations are relevant is subjective. The theories, which take the form of well-rehearsed schemata for dealing with certain types of abstract data-summary information, are the reason that base-rate information is sometimes used rather than ig-nored (Nisbett and Borgida, 1975: 943). Because of the nature of base-rate information, it is more likely to be used, even if incorrectly, and to be applied even more often in foreign policy than in other social domains and to play a considerable role in judgment and inference. Hence beliefs about relevant base rates may influence the interpretation of information about specific instances of other actors' behavior.

In other cases base-rate information is already incorporated into the decisionmakers' beliefs and theories about foreign states and into their expectations of how the states are likely to behave in specific situations. Furthermore, because base-rate information is sometimes built through direct experience with the environment and is salient, decisionmakers have reason to be confident that their estimates are correct. The base rates are not pallid statistical summaries of data but historical cases, that is, individuating information, or, in other words, a sample of very few cases. Their retrieval from memory is triggered by a concrete example (cf. von Winterfeldt and Edwards, 1986: 537). Because this base-rate information is perceived as highly relevant and is easily available, it is often used in familiar instances (cf. Borgida and Brekke, 1981). But when decisionmakers encounter a novel situation, judgment is more likely to entail representativeness—to involve comparing the specific instance to some prototype and stressing the importance of individuating information that bears directly on the case examined, particularly when other information is ambiguous. Given a novel situation, policymakers tend to ignore base-rate information about how international actors are likely to behave in general and to perceive others as having intentions that are actually rare and unlikely. They base their judgment on dramatic bits of individuating information about the other nation's behavior and treat those data as if they were completely diagnostic (Jervis, 1985b: 24; Jervis, 1986).

Because people believe that the predicted outcome should be highly representative of the initial input, they feel that the better estimates of later scores are earlier scores, no matter how extreme they were. Consequently, regression to the mean is interpreted as a significant change that requires explanation. The diametrically opposite error, the gambler's fallacy, is also recurrent; it involves the belief that deviating outcomes balance out. Hence people predict future outcomes by determining what they should be in their view in order to balance out any present deviations from expected values (Tversky and Kahneman, 1971).

The gambler's fallacy as well as other effects of representativeness in biasing causal analysis can be seen in the pressure that the U.S. military exerted to escalate bombing in North Vietnam even when it became clear that the strategy did not work. The military, in particular the air force, had strongly held beliefs in the efficacy of bombing to break the enemy's will that were based on their view of the rational relationship between severe damage to property, land, and population and modifications in one's position. This relationship was never validated in the case of North Vietnam and was indeed proven wrong. Yet negative feedback information (i.e. that North Vietnam's commitment to the support of the insurgency in the South was unswerving) was not used to reverse the reasoning based on outcomes. The discrepancy between the predicted outcomes of bombing and the actual outcomes of bombing were dealt with in a manner resembling the gambler's fallacy.

A high degree of representativeness induces a tendency to neglect close scrutiny of the reliability and validity of the evidence. Hence, even where representativeness is in principle a normatively legitimate rule of judgment, it can lead to errors in likelihood estimates; and neglecting to take the reliability of the information into account leads to overconfidence in one's judgment (Slovic, Fischhoff, and Lichtenstein, 1977) and thus to premature cognitive closure. A high degree of representativeness leads to a high level of faith in predictions, even when there is an awareness of factors limiting the accuracy of the prediction. Representativeness becomes so central in the thought process that factors limiting accuracy, such as the lack of sufficient information, the inaccuracy of information, or the unique aspects of the specific situation, are discounted, seen as marginal, and underestimated.

The use of representativeness eliminates complexity because in spite of the actual complexity of the environment, an environmental aspect may be perceived as so representative of a particular class of outcomes that judgment of the likelihood of alternative outcomes is based on that single dimension. For example, when a certain state or type of regime is defined in favorable terms, the subjective probability attributed to positive outcomes of its behavior and policies increases—and when defined in unfavorable terms, it decreases—while other aspects are neglected. Similarly, when actors define events in positive terms, they are also likely to evaluate positively the way the consequences will affect them.

Representativeness also affects causal judgment. Attributers exaggerate the role of representative causes in accounting for outcomes or the behavior of other actors. Furthermore, the implicit theories people have point to particular features of the situation, which thus become representative and are consequently detected easily to the extent that they fit a priori theories of causality. The effects of implicit theories on judgments of covariance explain why people see what they want to see: they are primed to see particular relationships. Representativeness is thus more influential than normative considerations in causal judgment. This influence spills over into probability judgments because people tend to reason from causes to consequences, not the other way around, and are more confident in their judgment when they reason forward than when they reason backward. Outcomes are attributed to the success or failure of a specific behavior that preceded them on the assumption that if Event A preceded Event B, then A caused B. Here the representativeness is expressed in the linear time sequence between the events. The fallacy lies in perceiving a temporal order as identical with a causal one, which has no necessary objective justification.

Reasoning from causes to consequences may seriously distort the inference of intention. Decisionmakers tend to attribute greater coherence to their adversaries than the evidence warrants, to overestimate the control their adversaries have over their machinery of government, and to attribute intent to most of their actions and premeditation to the outcomes of actions. Consequently they are likely to be vulnerable to the proportionality bias. They correlate the cost of the adversaries' actions with the initial intentions and the importance attributed to the objectives at stake (Stein, 1988), rather than considering the possibility of spuriousness—that the costs may have resulted from unanticipated, unplanned outcomes. Their reactions reflect the error in their inference of the opponents' intentions and often have the effect of a self-fulfilling prophecy by actually raising the stakes for the adversaries and forcing them to respond by escalating their own behavior.

A second common heuristic is *availability*. In judging the frequency of a category, the likelihood of an event, or the frequency of the co-occurrence of events, people often use as a criterion the ease with which they can bring specific instances to mind (Tversky and Kahneman, 1973, 1974). Thus, for example, an estimate that a certain policy is doomed to fail may depend on the ease and speed with which the decisionmaker can imagine the various difficulties to be encountered. Although availability can be useful for taking shortcuts to reasonable judgments of frequency and probability, it can also be highly misleading in many cases because frequency and probability are predicated on other factors than availability. I shall mention them here only briefly since they were already discussed in Chapter 2.

In many instances the sample of available cases is not necessarily random and unbiased. The salience and vividness of data make them available, especially in judgments involving ambiguous events, even where salience and vividness have nothing to do with frequency or likelihood. Nonsalient events are less available even if they are highly diagnostic. Thus nonoccurrences are used less in judgments than occurrences because they are not salient, although they may have diagnostic value. Similarly, because people are prone to search for positive, confirming instances of hypotheses that they hold, they fail to use disconfirming evidence sufficiently when they encounter it (Einhorn and Hogarth,

1978; Nisbett and Ross, 1980: 113–38; Reyes, Thompson, and Bower, 1980; S. E. Taylor, 1982). Thus disconfirming information is less available even if decisionmakers are aware of its existence.

Easily available theories or causes are likely to be considered in attributing causes, and the availability produced by associating events can produce illusory correlation judgments (Chapman and Chapman, 1969; Tversky and Kahneman, 1973). Yet the theories on which associative correlations rely are rarely scientifically tested. They are often primitive theories that have little or no factual basis and may have their sources in superficial impressions. An available associative covariation between two events leads to the conclusion that they covaried more often than they actually did and from there to the inference that the two events do indeed have a basic substantive connection. This misperception withstands even contradictory evidence; for example, the association between Suez and the route to India remained entwined in the British mind long after the British Empire had ceased to exist.

The choice of a particular theory for a particular case is strongly influenced by its availability rather than by a meticulous comparison with the explanatory power of alternatively relevant theories. A decisionmaker's search terminates with a satisficing theory rather than continuing until the best-founded, most valid theory is discovered. Nevertheless, people are overconfident in the explanations they generate in this questionable manner. They bring to bear theories that are often founded on culture-based stereotypes of other nations; on knowledge that has not passed validity tests; on hearsay, movies, newspaper stories, novels, or their own limited and unsystematic acquaintance with history (see Chapter 6). From these dubious sources decisionmakers draw a repertoire of readily available general theories as well as issue- and situation-specific hypotheses. For example, early in April 1970, shortly before the invasion of Cambodia, when Nixon was faced with congressional opposition to expanding the war, Nixon viewed the film *Patton*, about the unconventional general who defied authority, risked everything, and achieved success in the Battle of the Bulge. "The film appealed to Nixon's self-image, and he had a second showing as the Cambodian crisis deepened. [Secretary of State] William Rogers was dismayed to hear the President repeatedly citing *Patton* in this context" (Shawcross, 1979: 135).

Even if the decisionmakers have never visited the respective countries, they know, with a certainty, derived from popular culture, everything about French women, English food, or the American life-style. In other cases decisionmakers extrapolate from interpersonal relations with which they had direct experience to international relations with which they yet have had little or no experience. For example, a disagreement with allies may be interpreted from the perspective of domestic husband-and-wife disagreement episodes; a conflict with adversarial nations may be viewed as equivalent to disputes with unfriendly neighbors. The complexity of international politics is thus reduced to the banality of everyday life. Describing the dangers of appeasement, Lyndon Johnson used this colorful metaphor: "If you let a bully come into your front yard one day, the next day he'll be up on your porch and the day after that he'll rape your wife in your own bed." Drawing on his experience in the Congress, he expected that "if Ho Chi Minh was a reasonable man, then he, too, would recognize superior resources. . . . The war, Johnson said, would be 'like a filibuster—enormous resistance at first, then a steady whittling away, then Ho hurrying to get it over with'" (Kearns, 1976: 258, 266).

Lack of empathy for other states and viewing their behavior through the perspective of one's own culture is also related to the availability heuristic, since it is easier to think of others in terms that are available than to try to adopt someone else's perspective. That is one reason that rational actors think about other actors in rational terms, as though their behavior were guided by the same principles that guide them.

Overconfidence sometimes appears because problems that are not mentioned explicitly may not be thought of; not realizing what is missing, the analyst may overestimate the completeness of the analysis (Fischhoff, Slovic, and Lichtenstein, 1978; Slovic, Fischhoff, and Lichtenstein, 1976, 1982; Mehle et al., 1981). In other words, availability biases judgments of the completeness of an analysis and reduces the motivation to search for additional information.

But availability may also bias judgments of the likelihood of particular dangers. It highlights certain risky outcomes, so that they are easier to imagine or recall and are therefore given more weight in the overall calculus of a decision than they actually deserve. Thus U.S. decisionmakers tended to evaluate the uncertain outcome of their intervention in Vietnam by using quantitative indicators, such as firepower and body count, and to ignore factors that were harder to measure, such as morale, determination, and quality of leadership. The availability of causes or reasons for a predicted outcome is influential in inclining decisionmakers to increase the estimate of that event's probability (Levi and Pryor, 1987). For example, most American military and civilian decisionmakers could easily come up with arguments why the U.S. could not possibly lose the war in Vietnam once it got fully militarily involved, given its decisive technological superiority. Similarly Israel's military and civilian decisionmakers could easily think in 1973 about reasons, inferred from their preconception of the Arab states, for the Arabs' not being likely to initiate war.

The availability heuristic probably accounts for the "unsqueaky-wheel trap" (Janis, 1985: 189–92), according to which decisionmakers may focus their information search, evaluation, and emergency planning entirely on the elements known from the outset to be fraught with dangers and may totally overlook subtle risks in what they consider the routine steps of the plan. The error is not in paying more attention to riskier steps, which is logical, but in disregarding risks that should have been considered even if their probability is lower. For example, in the foiled rescue of American hostages in Iran in 1980, the top policymakers in the Carter administration completely failed to consider the possibility that the mission might have to be aborted because several of the helicopters might malfunction.

The ease with which it is possible to get information in many cases merely reflects bureaucratic and organizational interests in making certain information more available than other information. Policymakers tend to overlook that fact, whereas they find it difficult to systematically factor in what they do not know and should have known, because it is very difficult to factor the impact of missing data into judgments of abstract intelligence or foreign policy problems, the structure of those problems being as indistinct as it is (Heuer, 1982). This was the case, for instance, in late September 1973, when Israeli intelligence on Egyptian and Syrian military activities clearly indicated that their armed forces were deployed and capable of launching an attack on very short notice; Soviet preparations for evacuating Soviet personnel and their families further signified that war was likely; and other intelligence sources also warned of an outbreak of war. Yet the director of military intelligence stuck with his original evaluation that the probability of war was low. On October 5, however, he had to admit that there were many question marks and that he did not fully comprehend why the Soviet personnel were being withdrawn. Nevertheless, he did not adjust his overall assessment (Nakdimon, 1982: 81, 93; J. G. Stein, 1985b: 74). Major General Zeira was unable to factor what he did not know into his definition of the situation, preferring conservatism instead, although he obviously understood that his assessment should have taken the unknown into account.

Lack of an ability to imagine certain threats may decrease the subjective probability attributed to their occurrence, even when the outcomes deserve higher probability judgments. Moreover, since it is easier to envisage the future one wants than unwanted futures, the tendency is to forecast the desired future even if there are no objective grounds for doing so. No wonder decisionmakers seem to be more sensitive to the risks of change than they are to the risks of prevailing policies. New policies bring easily to mind a host of images of what might go wrong, not images of how things might improve, and produce uncertainty about how to deal with things that may go wrong. Existing policies bring easily to mind their beneficial effects or useful means of coping with what might go wrong because they have already been experienced or elaborated.

The choice between availability or representativeness is affected by a number of factors. People use individual instances, that is, exemplars (availability heuristic) rather than abstracted prototypes (representativeness heuristic) when the exemplars are salient in some way. Put differently, this means people use the availability heuristic to decide which heuristic to use. When examplars come more easily to mind, then availability is used; and when abstracted prototypes are more easily accessible, then representativeness is used. Representativeness is also used when specific exemplars are unavailable for judgment, for example, when information is encoded and organized in memory only in an abstracted, prototypical form. However, when a prototype cannot easily be abstracted from an information-set, exemplar matching is used. There may also be individual differences in the ability to abstract prototypes; people whose ability to do so is limited are likely to use the availability heuristic more often than the representativeness heuristic.

A third often-used heuristic is *simulation*. When people have to predict a future event, assess the probability of a specific event, make counterfactual judgments, or assess the causality of an instance, they run a mental simulation of the event in question. The ease of the simulation of any outcome is a basis for judging its likelihood (Kahneman and Tversky, 1982c). Lyndon Johnson knew the political consequences of the loss of China but they "were chickenshit compared with what might happen if we lost Vietnam." He could imagine what would happen to him.

For this time there would be Robert Kennedy out in front leading the fight against me, telling everyone that I had betrayed John Kennedy's commitment to South Vietnam. That I had let a democracy fall into the hands of the Communists. That I was a coward. An unmanly man. A man without a spine. Oh, I could see it coming all right. Every night when I fell asleep I would see myself tied to the ground in the middle of a long, open space. In the distance, I could hear the voices of thousands of people. They were all shouting at me and running toward me: 'Coward! Traitor! Weakling!' They kept coming closer. They began throwing stones. At exactly that moment I would generally wake up . . . terribly shaken. But there was more. You see, I was as sure as any man could be that once we showed how weak we were, Moscow and Peking would move in a flash to exploit our weakness. They might move independently or they might move together. But move they would—whether through nuclear blackmail, through subversion, with regular armed forces or in some other manner. As nearly as anyone can be certain of anything, I knew they couldn't resist the opportunity to expand their control over the vacuum of power we would leave behind us. And so would begin World War III. So you see, I was bound to be crucified either way I moved. (Kearns, 1976: 253)

As with the more general heuristic of availability, the reliance on the simulation heuristic produces biases because the ease of constructing particular scenarios or paths to an outcome does not necessarily indicate that it is the most likely outcome. Plausible scenarios survive and continue to affect judgment even when their information base has been invalidated. Scenarios explaining events that have already occurred are perceived as highly plausible and inevitable (Fischhoff, 1975; Fischhoff and Beyth, 1975); hence people assume that the events could have been foreseen and judge harshly those who did not predict them. On the other hand, potential future events for which no elaborate simulated scenario is easily available appear highly improbable.

The fourth heuristic is *anchoring and adjustment*. Estimates are made by beginning with some base value and then adjusting it as more information becomes available (Tversky and Kahneman, 1974). The point of departure can be an ideology that dictates anticipations, rules of behavior, and a world view. The degree to which the point of departure is suitable depends on its continuous updating with changing circumstances. Since 1961, for example, the U.S. military had been encouraged by President John Kennedy to emphasize the counterinsurgency doctrine. Guerrilla wars were considered the main type of military engagement for the army in the future. America's growing involvement in Vietnam seemed to confirm this view about the new nature of war. The adversary's propaganda emphasizing the importance of "a people's war" helped reinforce and entrench the belief among the American field commanders, in particular General Westmoreland, that the Communists in Vietnam were waging a classical revolutionary war. Actually, the North Vietnamese leadership, especially after the Tet offensive in 1968, when the Vietcong suffered very heavy casualties and failed to rouse the people in the cities to support the attack forces, used the Vietcong to harass and distract U.S. and South Vietnamese military forces so that North Vietnamese regular forces could decide the war's outcome in conventional battles. The definition of the Vietnam War as a revolutionary war and the prominence of the counterinsurgency doctrine lasted until 1975 without its being appropriately adjusted to reality (Summer, 1984: 107–18).

The mere existence of a master plan, or of an ideology that presents such a plan, causes policymakers' subjective evaluations of the plan's chances of success to increase. For example, during the early months of 1969, Nixon and Kissinger believed they could reach a speedy negotiated settlement of the war in Vietnam. Kissinger was sure that he would succeed where the Johnson administration had failed "because he had a plan. He had worked it out even before he moved into his White House office" (Kalb and Kalb, 1974: 120–21). He was, of course, proven wrong. A plan gives a feeling, often not justified, of power and control over a situation. Moreover, the plan's likelihood of success, which depends on the execution of a series of sequential actions, is seen as higher than is warranted because of the continuous nature of the plan. Decisionmakers are likely to overestimate the probability of the occurrence of conjunctive events; even though the first one or two events in the chain may indeed have a high probability of success, people do not adjust the end-state probability to the fact that as one moves along the chain of conditional links the probability of occurrence declines. Small probabilities are especially difficult to judge and are prone to being anchored (Sjöberg, 1979). Anchoring also explains the tendency to ignore information that requires changes in previously held theories and hypotheses: new information and feedbacks are assimilated with existing beliefs and theories (Chan, 1982; Lord, Ross, and Lepper, 1979; Sherman and Corty, 1984: 197–226).

The use of heuristics is most likely to take place when decisions are of low importance and errors are not costly or incorrectable. Decisions with an element of high personal involvement are likely to be approached in a formal and analytic manner. When time is at a premium and when decisionmakers are faced with information overload, they use heuristics as a shortcut to judgment. Their level of expertise and cognitive sophistication is another factor; at both extremes there is a tendency to use heuristics. When decisionmakers are unsophisticated and untrained, they prefer to simplify coping with a complex world by relying on heuristics to avoid cognitive strain; but when decisionmakers are highly experienced and sophisticated, they may also use heuristics that are based on expertise and experience. In both cases, the heuristics are then applied thoughtlessly (Sherman and Corty, 1984). Even when the use of heuristics and the heuristic chosen are normatively justified, the fact that judgment was based on heuristics tends to be forgotten, and resultant judgments and inferences become inputs for judging new information. The fact that new information becomes available to validate and reassess prior judgments without resorting to heuristics does not have any effect. Previous perceptions are accepted as reality and are not reexamined.

Why do decisionmakers use heuristics in spite of the costs of biases and errors? A number of reasons are suggested by Sherman and Corty (1984: 270–76). In the first place, in many cases heuristics are reasonable rules of thumb that produce reasonably accurate judgments. Furthermore, they are useful devices for overcoming cognitive constraints under adverse situations of strain and overload. Second, the use of heuristics helps users to maintain confidence in their judgments. They overestimate, for example, the correlation between frequency and representativeness or between frequency and availability. At the same time they use those same heuristics to judge their own judgments, so that the quality of judgment appears to be better than it actually was. Hence they do not encounter negative feedbacks that could deter decisionmakers from repeatedly using the same heuristics. They focus their attention on instances where judgments were correct and ignore instances where they were wrong or where they were correct without using heuristics. Correct judgments become salient and more available than incorrect judgments, and in many instances corrective feedback is unavailable or costly to come by in terms of time and effort. Third, which rule led to a particular error is not always obvious, because judgments involve more than one heuristic simultaneously. Moreover, biases caused by different heuristics may cancel each other out, producing a reasonably correct judgment. Fourth, decisionmakers may be unaware that a better judgment or solution is available because the heuristic provides a satisficing solution. Fifth, once a judgment is made, inconsistent information about outcomes is manipulated to make the prediction look better by discounting it or even ignoring it. Alternatively, through a dissonance reduction process people may convince themselves that the outcome is not all that bad. Finally, a judgment, even if incorrect, can affect outcomes through a process of self-fulfilling prophecy. Judgments based on simplifying heuristic principles lead to strongly held expectations that can fulfill themselves; thus people are misled to think that their judgment principles are adequate.

Constructing and Using Schemata

Schemata are the result of an active reconstruction of experience into a general, abstracted representation, as opposed to a mere photographic representation. The process of reconstruction depends and draws on existing beliefs, values, stereotypes, and attitudes that, when applied to raw data about one's experience, either produce new schemata of various types and levels of complexity or provide for the development and change of existing ones. "A schema is a cognitive structure that represents organized knowledge about a given concept or type of stimulus. A schema contains both the attributes of the concept and the relationships among the attributes" (Fiske and Taylor, 1984: 140). A schema fulfills a number of cognitive functions. First, it lends structure to experience: the ordering of relations among the components of a schema is imposed on the elements of the stimulus. Second, imposing a schema on a stimulus increases recall, especially of schema-relevant information. Third, a schema reduces processing time. Fourth, it enables the perceiver to go beyond the information given and fill in missing gaps in the data. Finally, a schema enables decisionmakers to predict the future but biases them to perceive schema-relevant events or behavior as more likely to occur than irrelevant ones.

The use of schemata involves an element of cognitive gambling, because it entails selective attention, encoding, representation, and retrieval that result in information loss. A number of typical errors are involved in schematic processing. The most common is the use of the wrong schema. Second, schematic processing may produce illusory data—assumptions, inferences, and bits of information—that are not part of the original data-set but are contributed by the schema, information that comes to be perceived as indistinguishable from the original data. Third, data may be interpreted as consistent with a schema when they are actually neutral or inconsistent with that or any schema. And, fourth, the magnitude of schema-consistent covariations tends to be overestimated; the magnitude of schema-inconsistent covariation, to be underestimated. This happens because schema-consistent evidence is readily available and is consequently likely to be brought to bear on covariation judgments (Taylor and Crocker, 1981).

Schemata are flexible cognitive structures and come in various forms that reflect the type and organization of knowledge the schemata represent. Foreign policy decisionmakers possess two types of general knowledge schema. One represents standard general knowledge, which enables them to make sense of, understand, and interpret the behavior of any other state, simply because it is a sovereign actor operating in the international environment and as such is believed to have standard imperatives and patterns of behavior. The assumption that all states have, broadly put, similar motives and interests and pursue them in a similar manner leads to projective judgments of other states' intentions and behavior, based on the policymakers' introspective views of their own motives and behavior (cf. Jervis, 1985b: 23). Attributions to others are consequently biased by self-based attributions. Beliefs of similarity simplify the task of attribution considerably and hence are attractive. The knowledge can be independent of direct experience. The second type of structured knowledge is knowledge that enables decisionmakers to interpret and participate in events of a kind with which they have had direct prior experience, allowing them to understand similar situations with little processing of information. This more specific knowledge is a representation of the sequential flow of events, which becomes the referent script (Schank and Abelson, 1977: 36–42).

Scripts are knowledge structures that represent appropriate sequences of events in well-known situations. Abelson (1976b) suggests three types of script. The *episodic* script stores a single experience. At a higher level of abstraction is the *categorical* script, which groups single experiences according to the one or more similar features that they share. The third is the *hypothetical* script, which not only groups similar experiences but also differentiates contrasting experiences and includes conditional and inferential concepts and abstract rules that distinguish different possible categorical scripts. This type of script is more abstract, flexible, and complex than the other two. All three are ways to organize generic expectations about objects or situations and thus reduce ambiguity and uncertainty. They offer probability judgments of outcomes and can become a basis for a decisionmaker's choice of which attitude to activate toward the object or situation in question.

Analyzing threats is a particularly important area where decisionmakers' scripts can take each of these three forms. A script provides a sense of certainty about what future threats will be like and how they will develop, which is a precondition for feelings of control. When decisionmakers consider a range of alternative threats, rarely is more than a single scenario—the most threatening—elaborated in detail. "Threat perception, this suggests, is associated with the inability of the observer to look beyond one particular, obsessive image of disaster. . . . Certain dangers are selected by experience as especial objects of concern, and even before any crisis develops these dangers have been imaginatively rehearsed and planned for" (R. Cohen, 1979: 160). That image of disaster becomes the evoked-set script, which is easily imposed on ambiguous information while other, less available threat scripts are neglected.

When different people have different situational scripts based on dissimilarities in specific knowledge-based beliefs, their expectations may diverge and lead to misperceptions; for people are not fully aware that other actors' scripts are different, at least in some elements, from their own. This is especially true when each participant in a decisionmaking group has a latent personal script that differs from the situational script that they collectively share (Schank and Abelson, 1977: 61–64).

Another type of schema besides the general-knowledge types is the self-schema. "Self-schemata are cognitive generalizations about the self, derived from past experience, that organize and guide the processing of self-related information contained in the individual's social experiences" (Markus, 1977: 64). Self-schemata are useful in providing guidelines for quick and effortless judgments and decisions about the best way to deal with a situation. They are highly resistant to information that is counterschematic. Under stress and information overload, self-schemata are particularly useful in providing shortcuts to decisions that leapfrog a systematic analysis of information. For example, during the Watergate scandal, when President Nixon was under heavy stress, he decided military issues by referring to his self-schema—his image as a tough leader—and his beliefs about how tough leaders behave rather than by systematically considering available information.

We shall look briefly at only two more types of schema. One is the persona—a cognitive structure representing the personal traits and characteristic behavior of particular human types. When evoked, personas guide subsequent expectations about their objects as well as preferences for particular interpretations of their objects' behavior. At the same time, judgments about appropriate responses to the objects are at least partly dictated by their persona-based characterizations (Nisbett and Ross, 1980: 35). Finally, there is the content-free schema, which does not refer to content-specific knowledge structures but specifies links among items of information (e.g. consistency, linear ordering) as a processing rule does (Fiske and Taylor, 1984: 169–70). How schemata develop and change, how they are activated and used, will be further discussed in Chapter 6, because many of the schemata used by foreign policy decisionmakers are based on historical experience.[27]

Israeli decisionmakers' information processing behavior in 1973 was decisively affected by a set of various schema types. The Conception, described in Chapter 2, can be explained in script terms. The Conception was in fact a sequence of events that were conceived as the only plausible path to an Arab-initiated war. The script ran as follows: The Soviets supply modern weapon systems in large quantities to Syria and Egypt; Syria and Egypt believe that they have achieved air superiority or at least equivalence with the Israeli air force; they coordinate their military and diplomatic strategies and initiate war. This script is based on a number of beliefs, values, and attitudes: that war, as a rule, is not initiated if there is no clear chance of winning; that air superiority is a precondition for winning; that military superiority is equivalent to deterrence; that sacrificing lives in an initiated war that is not likely to be won, just to gain political advantages, is immoral.

Similarly, Meir's decision not to have a preemptive strike can be traced to two complementary patron-client scripts. The first ran as follows: Israel mobilizes and attacks, which the superpower patron, the United States, interprets as an aggression that damages its vital interest in the Middle East; the patron cooperates with the Soviets in applying pressure on Israel to give up all military spoils gained by preemption by threatening or taking actions against Israel (i.e. withdraws military and economic support). The alternative script ran: Israel takes a defensive posture (e.g. deploys regular army troops, partially mobilizes, warns Egypt through the United States); Egypt and Syria irrationally, despite warnings, attack and gain some military advantages; the IDF mobilizes and counterattacks within 48 hours; it defeats any combination of Arab armies; Israel wins the support of the United States and of world public opinion; the Arabs recognize the futility of any attempt to change the status quo by force or even agree to negotiate a nonaggression pact. The two scripts accept that Israel cannot allow itself to be perceived as an aggressor; that the IDF will get an early warning that will allow for timely mobilization; that after mobilization the IDF has decisive superiority over any combination of Arab forces; that Arab soldiers and command are highly incompetent. The last two scripts drew on lessons from the past, namely, the period following the Sinai Campaign of 1956, when Israel did not have U.S. support and was forced to withdraw and give up its military achievements, and the aftermath of the Six Day War, when Israel had U.S. support for its policy or at least faced no serious, active pressure or threats from the Americans to withdraw from all occupied territories.

These scripts were supported by a persona-type schema of Sadat as the prototypical Arab leader: a man of words and not action, boastful and unrealistic; driven by the need to satisfy and inflame the public's imagination with words and fictitious promises (e.g. "year of decision"), not trustworthy or credible, and not to be taken too seriously.

Dispositional and Situational Attribution of Causality

International politics, like all other social situations, involves interactions between actors. People spontaneously engage in attributional activities. The activities occur undirected when expectations are disconfirmed or a goal is unattained. Events that are stressful, novel, or personally important are also effective antecedents for attributional activities. The primary focus of these activities is the locus of the control (internal versus external) dimensions of causality (Wong and Weiner, 1981). In general, effective interpretations of others' behavior and inferences of their intentions require that participants be aware of the causes of their own as well as the others' behavior. Comprehending the causes of others' behavior is a prerequisite for choosing among alternative interpretations of their behavior and correctly inferring their intentions. For example, a military alert by an adversary has one meaning to the observer if attributed to inherently aggressive intentions and a completely different one if attributed to a reaction to a real or imagined external threat.

For similar reasons, people's awareness of their own causes of behavior affects the way they think observers should interpret their behavior and, as a result, influences their expectations of how the observers should or might react to it—which in turn affects how they interpret the actual response. This is true even when people intend to deceive others about the causes of their behavior: an awareness of the goals of deception shapes expectations of others' reactions. People's beliefs about the causes of their own and others' behavior are, then, important factors in information processing, and to the degree that they reflect systematic biases, the accuracy of information processing declines.

In assessing the causes of other people's behavior or in attempting to predict their future behavior or their response to the perceiver's own behavior, the perceiver has to know what the target knows. Knowledge about others' knowledge is one of the most important and difficult domains of intelligence work. If intelligence organizations do not know what their targets know, they tend to attribute to them knowledge they themselves have, because people overestimate the commonality of knowledge and are more likely to assume that other people have a particular item of information if they themselves have it than if they do not (Nickerson, Baddeley, and Freeman, 1987). People do not invariably impute their own knowledge to other people; if they can find a persuasive reason to assume the opposite—that their knowledge is somehow unique (e.g. expert knowledge, achieved through special access)—they may refrain from projecting their knowledge onto others.

People not only assume the commonality of their knowledge but are also biased toward incorrectly assuming knowledge-inference unity, that is, that only a single inference can be plausibly made from a particular bit of knowledge, often not realizing that the same bit of knowledge may legitimately give rise to different inferences. As a result, even where people's assumption about the commonality of their knowledge is correct, the next step—inferring from it the commonality of their inferences with inferences made by the adversary—is often incorrect. Israel's decisionmakers assumed correctly that Sadat was aware of the IDF's overall military superiority over the Egyptian military or even the combined military capabilities of Syria and Egypt and that, notwithstanding the multiplier effect of a successful Arab surprise, the risk of military defeat was immense. Yet they were incorrect in assuming that Sadat would infer from that knowledge, as they did, that the risk was not worth taking and that the costs of failure would outweigh the benefits (Stein, 1985a). The assumption of the commonality of knowledge can be attributed to the unconscious use of the availability heuristic, while the assumption of knowledge-inference unity can be attributed to the unconscious use of the representativeness heuristic.

To be effective in imposing meaning on ambiguity in social interactions, people follow simple rules about when to attribute the behavior of others and themselves to dispositional factors (internal locus of control) and when to attribute it to situational factors (external locus of control). Dispositional attributions have the clear advantage that they impose regularity and predictability and thus enhance the feeling of control (Miller, Norman, and Wright, 1978). Yet it does not make sense to believe that all behavior has dispositional causes. People would question such a blatant departure from logical reasoning and from, in some cases, their own reality-testing experience. The advantage of feeling in control, provided by dispositional causal explanations, has to be balanced against other needs, such as the need for veridicality. These other needs may result, however, in self-serving situational explanations of others' behavior.

The use of simple dispositional and situational causal attribution models is mitigated by mediating variables determining when the consistent use of one or the other type of causal attribution is preferred. In general, people attribute the behavior of others to their inherent nature, whereas their own behavior is likely to be perceived as affected almost exclusively by situational causes (Heuer, 1980; E. E. Jones, 1979; Jones and Nisbett, 1971; L. Ross, 1977). The occurrence of this bias, the fundamental attribution bias, is mediated by the level of ambiguity or ignorance about the true causes of an adversary's behavior or about the nature of the situation to which the adversary responds and by the level of dislike for or empathy with other actors. Ambiguous information is likely to be interpreted as consistent with prior hypotheses about an actor's motivations and hence used to support a dispositional attribution involving the other actor: the actor is assumed to have a choice even when the observer is aware of possible situational constraints (Ajzen, Dalto, and Blyth, 1979; Jones and Davis, 1965). This was the case when Israel's military and political leadership attempted to infer intentions from Egyptian military deployment behavior, and although they were aware of the domestic and external pressures on Sadat to resume large-scale military operations, they underestimated the probability of such behavior occurring and interpreted ambiguous information as consistent with prior strategic assumptions about the inherent incapability of the Egyptian army to launch a war.

Dislike tends to evoke dispositional explanations for undesirable actions by others, while empathy biases explanations of such behavior toward situational attribution. Success or failure can also have a mediating effect on this bias. People tend to attribute success to their own efforts and inherent attributes and thus to overestimate the influence of their own behavior on other actors' responses rather than attributing the responses to situational factors. Decisionmakers' tendency to attribute success to their policies, even where it should be ascribed to external factors over which they have no control (Oneal, 1982: 326–27), can be explained by their use of the representativeness heuristic, which assumes causality between their policies and the outcomes when the latter are congruent with their initial intentions. Conversely, the failure of efforts to influence others to behave as desired is attributed to factors beyond the decisionmakers' control, usually the dispositional attributes of the adversary. People also tend to assume that the undesirable outcomes were actually intended by the adversary; they do not consider the possibility that the adversary's behavior has causes that have little or nothing to do with themselves. This tendency is prominent when outcomes are personally important (Greenwald, 1980; Heuer, 1982; Kuiper, 1978). Failure to perceive a sufficient salient stimulus that is correlated with the behavior of others may also lead people to attribute it to dispositional factors (Wells, 1981) rather than investing resources in an intensive search for environmental and situational causes that are not salient.[28]

Decisionmakers' biases in detecting the correct causes of adversaries' as well as of their own behavior lead to serious failures to understand and to properly adapt responses to the actual requirements of the situation, and hinder learning from feedback, thus perpetuating behavior based on misperceptions. Behavior that is congruent with the prior conception of an observer is considered dispositional, but when it is incongruent, it is likely to be explained in situational terms (Kulik, 1983). Thus subsequent conceptions of other actors become self-confirmatory and are not as sensitive to disconfirmatory feedback as they should be. Attributional distortions lead decisionmakers to overestimate their own country's capacity to act successfully, creating an exaggerated confidence and a propensity for risk taking. The enemy's failures are attributed to dispositional factors of ineptitude; successes, to situational factors, producing an unrealistic assessment of the balance of power and possibly encouraging a challenge to a stronger rival even if a similar challenge failed in the past. Positive actions and signals by the adversary are interpreted as situational, not as reflective of truly peaceful motives (Rosenberg and Wolfsfeld, 1977). Some dispositional explanations of personal influence on others' behavior (e.g. cultural superiority) tend to be deterministic in that they are assumed to operate under all circumstances and stay constant over time,[29] leading to inattention to change as well as conservatism and premature cognitive closure in the definition of the situation.

The effects of learning from policy failures or successes are also seriously constrained by the relationship between initial positions on the policy and the explanations the position holders provide for the outcomes of the policy. The ex post facto analysis of decisionmakers does not objectively assess the reasons for policy outcomes, a step that is a necessary condition for learning correct lessons from those outcomes; their explanations are strongly influenced by whether they subsequently supported or criticized the policy in question. Holsti and Rosenau (1984: 29–48) show that American leaders clearly disagree on why U.S. policies toward Vietnam failed, depending on what their prior positions toward those policies were. To take the two extremes: supporters of the policies attribute failure to America's "no win" approach; the restricted use of air power; Soviet and Chinese aid to North Vietnam; the media's intervention; the failure to heed military advice; the dissidents, who hurt U.S. credibility; North Vietnam's peace-treaty violations; congressional interference; and the absence of clear-cut U.S. goals. Critics, on the other hand, attribute the failure to Saigon's lack of popular support; North Vietnamese dedication; a misunderstanding of Third World nationalism; U.S. ignorance of Vietnam; the absence of realistic, clear-cut U.S. goals; and the opposition of world opinion. The differences are obvious and profound. According to the first set of explanations, the war was winnable and the Americans can blame only themselves for losing it: they mishandled it and the domestic opposition undermined the national war effort. According to the second set of explanations, the war was unwinnable from the very beginning, and the policy a blunder: for Americans had little or no influence over events and hence should not have been drawn into it.

The Attitude-Behavior Nexus

In inferring and predicting others' behavior, decisionmakers develop theories and expectations about attitude-behavior covariation as a cue for anticipating their behavior. Thus the problem in international politics is not only to judge the relationship between intentions and capabilities but also to estimate the degree to which the other side's intentions predict their actual future behavior (assuming no unexpected, external environmental interferences). Decisionmakers find it difficult to identify the factors actually controlling behavioral outputs. People's behavior is sometimes guided by motives and information that are not consciously represented. But because people feel uneasy with behavior they cannot explain, they attribute causality in overt behavior to consciously represented factors. They learn from what they can observe. At the same time some factors influence the conscious experience and explanation of behavior but not necessarily the observed behavior itself. In many cases the understanding of a phenomenon must precede its observation if the observers want to comprehend it accurately, because observation can be misleading. Moreover, even when people are able to observe a relationship, they look for information that confirms existing hypotheses and neglect to observe disconfirming evidence. Positive feedback is thus weighted more heavily than negative feedback (Bowers, 1981; Hogarth, 1980: 75–92).

Decisionmakers are biased against randomness as an explanation and tend to impose consistent, causal explanations that are not always justified by the information. They overestimate the extent to which other countries are pursuing coherent, rational, goal-maximizing policies. Thus, in making inferences about relations between variables (e.g. attitudes and behavior), people prefer to assume that there is a rule rather than that there is no rule, that the rule is a positive linear function, and that it is deterministic rather than probabilistic because they lack statistical schemata that allow them to detect the probabilistic nature of reality (Brehmer, 1980; Heuer, 1982: 56–57; Hogarth, 1980: 90). In principle, decisionmakers act as intuitive scientists when they attempt to establish a causal model representing the relationship between attitudes and behavior. They look for a model that is consistent, consensual, and distinctive (Kelley, 1967). In other words, its accuracy is judged by the degree to which the behavior occurs primarily in the presence of one attitude instead of another (distinctiveness), the extent to which a particular behavior is observed whenever a particular known attitude is present (consistency), and the degree to which other people respond in the same way whenever they hold the same attitude (consensus). Three ideal types represent the range of alternative causal models decisionmakers apply to comprehend, infer, and anticipate other actors' behavior or attitudes.

The first theory is based on a rule that is deterministic and reflects a positive linear relationship: the assumption of complete congruence between attitude and behavior. It assumes that one can confidently infer and anticipate behavior from knowledge of other people's attitudes. Where attitudes of others are not known, it is thought to be possible, through reverse behavioral engineering, to infer attitudes from past behavior. Those attitudes then become the basis for anticipating future behavior.

The second alternative theory is a reverse of the first and assumes complete lack of congruence. The decisionmaker assumes that it is impossible to infer other actors' behavior from their known, especially stated attitudes, that the benefits of deception are too great and tempting. If no a priori information is available about other actors' attitudes, their attitudes cannot be inferred from their past behavior. The theory expresses lack of confidence in the sincerity or the ability of others, particularly adversaries, to realize their attitudes. Thus the theory is deterministic and linear. For example, from 1971 to 1973 Israeli decisionmakers applied the incongruence model in judging Anwar el-Sadat's intentions. They assumed that his expressed attitudes, whether on a peaceful settlement or threats of war, did not reflect his actual behavioral intentions and should be viewed with a great deal of suspicion. This does not mean that such suspicions had no reasonable basis, only that they were systematically applied and prevented full pursuit of Egyptian proposals for a settlement. Similarly, influential decisionmakers assumed that such behavioral indicators as the growing capability of Egypt's military forces should not be interpreted as indicators of strongly held attitudes reflecting acute aggressive intentions posing an immediate threat but rather as indicators of Egypt's long-range intentions. These intentions, it was believed, would be carried out only in the particular circumstances specified in The Conception (Bartov, 1978a; M. Gazit, 1984).

The third theory assumes selectivity—that to infer and predict the behavior of other actors from their known attitudes is sometimes possible, and at other times it is not. The problem decisionmakers face, then, is deciding when attitude and behavior are linked and what the mediating factors are. Certain subjective influences come into play here. For example, when attitudes predict a behavior that decisionmakers hope will occur, they may well tend toward wishful thinking—in this case they are likely to assume that attitudes predict behavior. Past experience can determine when positive covariation of this kind exists and in which spheres of activity it exists. Alternatively, observers may use their assessments of the capabilities of attitude holders to predict whether their intentions can and will be put into practice. In other cases judgment of the attitude-behavior nexus is value based; for example, the nature of the regime is used as a cue to determine the nature of the attitude-behavior nexus (e.g. a democratic regime acts in accordance with its expressed attitudes, but not a totalitarian regime).

Some qualifications are necessary at this point. First, people prefer a deterministic, linear-relationship mode; that is, they believe that there is consistent attitude-behavior congruence or consistent incongruence. They more readily recognize cases where attitude and behavior are congruent than cases where attitude and behavior are incongruent, especially if they already believe in the congruence mode. "It may be that the training in our society leads the layman to expect attitude-behavior consistency. This expectation is particularly strong as it applies to public officials" (Wicker, 1971: 141). Once such a belief is entrenched, decisionmakers tend to perceive behavior as reflecting prior attitudinal dispositions, refusing to accept that some behavior is a random outcome (e.g. due to coincidence or to bureaucratic-political compromises). If people adopt the alternative model of incongruence, they anticipate actions that are totally out of line with known attitudes. Hence, behavior that is compatible with known attitudes is left out of their expectations. When congruent behavior occurs and is observed, it has to be explained away (e.g. coincidence or duress—that the behavior was forced on the performing actor).

Second, although decisionmakers prefer simple causal theories, they do not necessarily apply the same theory to all the actors and issues they deal with. Only paranoid decisionmakers apply the incongruence mode theory without discrimination, and only completely naive ones adopt the congruence mode without qualifications. They are, however, likely to apply the congruence or the incongruence mode consistently to a particular state or group of states, for example, allies, enemies, states with a common political culture, or within a particular issue-area, for example, by taking an overcautious position in matters of national security and deciding that the intentions of other states should not be inferred from their expressed attitudes but only from judgments of their actual capabilities. They may thus avoid the trap of deception by others at the cost of trapping themselves. Adversaries, for instance, may act in a way that judgments of their resources do not anticipate if they are willing to take the risk of incurring heavy losses, as was the case with Israel's 1973 intelligence misjudgment of the probability of a war initiated by Egypt and Syria. Or adversaries may decide not to utilize their resources to the limit.

Third, the congruence and incongruence modes are based on decisionmakers' assumptions that give an unequivocal preference to their attitudes-toward-object over attitudes-toward-situation.

Fourth, it can be argued that decisionmakers whose philosophical code reflects a Hobbesian view prefer the incongruence mode, whereas those with a Kantian outlook are likely to prefer the congruence mode. In both cases, however, the decisionmakers are likely to have low cognitive complexity, while decisionmakers with high cognitive complexity are likely to prefer the third mode—selectivity.

Fifth, when decisionmakers' perceptions of the content of the other side's attitudes are inaccurate, then even where their theory of the attitude-behavior nexus is accurate, their expectations of the other side's behavior may be unrealistic.

Sixth, even if the basic attitude-behavior model reflects reality and the other actors' attitudes are correctly perceived, a particular attitude may still operatively justify dissimilar behavior. General attitudes toward objects or situations predict only the overall pattern of behavior and are of little value in predicting a particular action with respect to the specific object or situation. To predict a single action, decisionmakers have to assess the person's attitude toward the action in question (Ajzen, 1982). By the same token, when the attitudes of another actor are accurately perceived, different perceptions about what behavior should result from those attitudes may still be possible, and can lead to inaccurate expectations. Consequently, "statesmen tend to define legitimacy in terms of their own experience; they fail to realize that their actions are inconsistent with other conceptions of legitimacy and often appear threatening to others" (Lockhart, 1973: 7).[30]

Decisionmakers fail to see that policies they perceive as defensive are seen by rivals as aggressive. Even when they perceive their own policies as aggressive, they attribute legitimacy to their behavior and illegitimacy to the behavior of others even if it is defensive. Judgments of their and the adversaries' behavior are thus biased by knowledge and the interpretation of motivations. One side assumes that its motives are good and that the other side's motives, especially in cases of acute conflict, are bad, so that the interactions between adversaries result in mirror-image misperceptions (Bronfenbrenner, 1961; Snyder and Diesing, 1977: 293–95). Decisionmakers expect adversaries to "correctly" perceive their motives as they do. Yet they do not demand the same of their own interpretation of the adversaries' behavior. These types of judgment are obvious in the Vietnam conflict. The American leadership perceived its policies as defensive—protecting the free world; they saw bombing as a legitimate means of bargaining, troop deployment as self-defense and as a legitimate act of fulfilling their treaty obligations, North Vietnamese intervention using their regular army as an act of external aggression. Similarly, North Vietnam perceived intervention as a legitimate expression of Vietnamese nationalism facing a foreign aggressor, bombing as a war crime, American troop deployment as a blatant act of foreign aggression inspired by imperialistic motives (cf. R. K. White, 1970).

The impression that may have been formed so far, that action always follows cognition, is unrealistic. Decisionmakers do not always postpone action until they have fully comprehended the situation (Lazarus and Folkman, 1984: 272; Starbuck, 1985: 339), either because they think the situation requires immediate response or because they believe they already know enough. Premature decisions and actions may constrain objective treatment of information acquired after the decision and action were taken, inducing selective attention that focuses on supportive information, especially when behavior is repetitive or its consequences are irreversible (Frey and Rosch, 1984).

When behavior precedes cognition, the reverse link, from behavior to attitude, becomes important. Sometimes behavior leads to the development of attitudes because people infer from their own behavior what their beliefs, attitudes, and values are. For people to infer their attitudes from information they have about their behavior, the information has to be sufficiently relevant and consistent to allow clear inferences (Salanick and Conway, 1975; Zanna, Olson, and Fazio, 1980). Once they are convinced that their behavior was guided by a priori beliefs, they are likely to let their convictions direct future behavior. Attitude change follows change in behavior rather than the other way around. This is a dominant cognitive mechanism in the early stages of development of attitudes and beliefs (Bem, 1967, 1972; Fazio, Zanna, and Cooper, 1977; Jervis, 1980; Nisbett and Valins, 1971). Particularly those decisionmakers who lack an integrated, well-defined, internally consistent belief structure readily change attitudes in response to events (Bem and Funder, 1978). Thus decisionmakers who have had no past experience in the foreign policy field learn their attitudes on the job, and their attitudes change as their behavior changes.

Inferring attitudes from behavior poses problems of validity. For instance, for behavior to reflect attitudes, the context of action has to be individuated so that it sharpens awareness of the relevance of essential self-orientations. But in many cases behavior is governed by scripts; it is not triggered by an awareness of self-orientations but learned well and activated automatically without the person's considering first what the relevant attitudes are. Such behavior can actually be counterattitudinal. Also, deindividuating contexts (e.g. group contexts) may result in behavior that does not reflect personal attitudes but reflects conformity with social pressure (Abelson, 1982; M. Snyder, 1979). Inferring attitudes from behavior in those two instances may have negative implications for the observers' accuracy in explaining or predicting the future behavior of the observed actors. Observers assume that attitudes are stable over time and that similar situations evoke the same attitudes, therefore leading to the same behavior. They are not aware when behavior is scripted or deindividuated and hence does not reflect self-orientations and has no diagnostic value for situations that do not evoke the same scripted or deindividuated behavior.

An important facet of attitude-behavior linkage is the decisionmakers' judgment of the congruence between their own attitudes and behavior. This judgment is linked with self-esteem, requires self-monitoring, and is related to impression management. The clear preference is for a self-image that fits the congruence model. In general, decisionmakers need to perceive their behavior as reflective of and compatible with their attitudes,[31] whether their need results from the public's expectations, from prevailing social values and norms, or from other psychological motives, such as the need for consistency (Carter, 1959). In one problematic area of international politics—the conflict between moral values and the pragmatic behavior required by realpolitik and national interest—that need poses an acute dilemma for leaders who have a declared commitment to morality in politics (e.g. Woodrow Wilson, Jawaharlal Nehru, Jimmy Carter). Moral dissonance produces a threat to people's self-esteem, prompting a need to explain their behavior in a way that prevents the emergence of such dissonance,[32] to defensively ignore information that poses moral-dissonance threats, or to adjust the interpretation of information in a way that allows them to avoid behavior that is incongruent with their attitudes.

Another possibility is to attribute to adversaries the very same undesirable behavior that the actors cannot admit that they themselves are guilty of (Gladstone, 1959). Attributing a deviation to an adversary provides legitimacy for a similar reaction on the part of the actor—now the injured party, as it were—or at least reduces the malaise resulting from the dissonance. Decisionmakers making judgments based on ambiguous information and incomplete knowledge resort to projective intuitions of this sort. For example, ambitious, competitive decisionmakers who are inclined to use force perceive their opponents as expansionists against whom hard-line policies are justified (Etheredge, 1978). President Johnson's Hobbesian presuppositions about the standing of the United States in a belligerent world made manipulation, coercion, and the use of military force permissible means. His presuppositions posed a problem.

The desire for moral approbation (internal and external) led him, however, to deny the existence of the aggressive tendency in his character. . . . [But] given Johnson's proclivity to see the world in the light of projected hostility, it is not surprising that he was involved in fighting two wars. With respect to Vietnam, the incident in the Gulf of Tonkin was the perfect trigger for Johnson's aggressive tendency; it proved that the D.R.V. was willing to attack U.S. forces, and thus justified retaliation. . . . By starting from his conception of the event, Johnson was able to view the D.R.V. as the aggressor. Accordingly, the war was a just one. (Wolfenstein, 1974: 384, 385)

Decisionmakers' need to find consistency between their attitudes and behavior may cause discrepancies between their image of their behavior and other actors' perceptions of their behavior. When decisionmakers cannot behave in a manner compatible with their attitudes, they may perform a substitute symbolic act that they perceive as a congruent act, whereas others may see it for what it is. For example, with the intensive bombing of Christmas 1972, Nixon seemed to signal to Hanoi: "OK now, I'm leaving, but before I finally do I want you to see how strong I still am and what dastardly deeds I can do. . . . Don't try anything funny; you can never tell, I'm unreliable, I'm mean, and I might return" (Kattenburg, 1980: 148). The North Vietnamese leadership was not deterred. They knew that the Congress would not allow new American intervention.

Another possibility open to decisionmakers is to perform referent acts—behavior that relates to the attitude in question but is not congruent with it.[33] Thus, for example, an attitude favoring the reduction of dependence on foreign powers can find expression in sponsoring academic research on the possibility of self-reliance. When such acts are a necessary but not sufficient condition for congruent acts to be performed, some may expect that a given referent act is an antecedent in the sequence, leading to the anticipated act, rather than being just a substitute act, although the substitute act is all that the actor has the power to perform.

Do people actually know what their beliefs and attitudes are? Not necessarily—and not only because they do not have introspective access to their high cognitive processes but also because, as we have seen, when their behavior antedates the formation of beliefs or attitudes or is inconsistent with them, they restore the consistency or rationalize the behavior by attributing the behavior to an appropriate attitude. Once they believe that they hold a particular belief or attitude, they actually acquire it (Pears, 1984: 42–48, 59), and the acquisition can cause both conservatism and attitude change. The first occurs when information at their disposal indicates that they should adopt new beliefs and yet they continue to behave as they did before. The latter may occur when people refuse to change their views despite informational inputs requiring it but are then forced by circumstances to behave in a counterattitudinal manner; they may consequently change the relevant beliefs and attitudes while at the same time believing that they have always held them and retrospectively interpreting their behavior as stemming from them. This process is consistent with people's view of themselves as rational, because rational behavior is linked in their minds with the sequence belief-behavior rather than with the opposite one, behavior-belief. And it is particularly common with regard to important foreign and defense policy decisions, which are normatively required to be premeditated and based on well-considered and valid beliefs and attitudes.

The Cognitive and Motivational Consequences of Personality Traits

So far we have looked at distinctive patterns of motives, needs, cognitive styles, and processes that have potential implications for information processing. However, a number of personality traits are, more than others, associated with the development of specific cognitive styles and motivational patterns. Some or all of these personality traits are either causes of the above-described phenomena—biases, conservatism, overconfidence, and so forth—or at least symptoms of their existence.[34]

Authoritarianism. A number of the symptoms connected with this central personality trait[35] are directly related to the manner in which decisionmakers cope with information processing tasks. First, stereotyping is directly related. Second, low tolerance of ambivalence (Budner, 1962; Sidanius, 1978) and the need for unequivocal interpretations even if the information itself does not readily lend itself to them—for example, in cases where contradictory information exists—may lead people to ignore information that may cause ambiguity or to manipulate information to impose on it an unambiguous meaning. Disregard and manipulation may also occur when the new information is in itself unambiguous but threatens to create ambiguity in information already stored in memory. A third symptom, rigidity, involves differentiating between various cognitive bits (W. A. Scott, 1960a). This produces a tendency to consider information through a narrow perspective, relating it only to a particular issue-area without perceiving its implications for other areas, thus enabling the decisionmaker to hold contradictory beliefs and expectations at the same time without feeling inconvenienced. Fourth is ethnocentrism, which leads to a biased negative judgment of other actors and their behavior and a positive judgment of the self. Related to ethnocentrism is the difficulty in differentiating between reality and wishful thinking (Saenger and Flowerman, 1954; I. D. Steiner, 1964). Fifth, respect for authority, means that sources of information are judged according to their authority rather than their reliability (Johnson, Toncivia, and Poprick, 1968). People with authoritarian personalities attempt to impose their views on others but when faced with higher authority are willing to comply and conform (Steiner and Johnson, 1963). The implications for group decisionmaking are obvious. The authoritarian personality is likely to generate group conformity whether the decisionmaker is a group leader or a group member (see also Chapter 4).

Dogmatism. This trait affects the organization of beliefs and ideas into a closed system (Rokeach, McGovney, and Denny, 1955). A number of symptoms accompany the increase of dogmatism. The need to differentiate sharply between the belief system and the disbelief system strengthens; issues are viewed and judged in black-and-white terms and points of congruence are ignored. The tendency to ignore information that threatens the existing closed belief system also increases, and the possibility that beliefs will adjust to new information declines (Rokeach, 1954). Also enhanced is the inclination to retrieve belief-confirming and congruent information from memory rather than information that disconfirms beliefs (Kleck and Wheaton, 1967).[36]

Preference for concreteness. This trait is closely related to the development of a simple cognitive structure in which information is characterized by a limited number of categories. Such a cognitive system is also associated with a pronounced need for cognitive consistency and the adoption of stereotypes (Harvey, 1967).

Introversion and extraversion. Introverted types tend to assimilate reality to their subjective psychological needs (Eysenck, 1954: 267). Their attitudes are resistant to change. Extraverts are more attuned to cues from the social system in which they operate (McClintock, 1958; L. W. Morris, 1979: 69). They are more vulnerable to the conformism resulting from social pressure and adapt their views accordingly. As a result, extraverts are more vulnerable to misperceptions collectively shared by the society or group. When the leader of a decisionmaking group is an extravert and group members support and reinforce his views, the likelihood that dissonant information will be noticed or attributed relevance and importance is low.[37]

Self-esteem. Self-esteem leads, on the one hand, to openness in the absorption of new information because people feel confident enough of their ability to deal with it. On the other hand, high self-esteem leads to overconfidence in the beliefs and theories people hold even in the face of dissonant information; those with a lower opinion of themselves are more open to be persuaded and changed by new information (Block and Petersen, 1955; Janis, 1954; McClosky, 1967).

An important case of a decisionmaker with high self-esteem is the charismatic leader. People viewed in their social environment as charismatic have special, almost supernatural traits attributed to them and tend to have very high self-esteem. They invariably show low readiness to change their beliefs and attitudes when confronted with dissonant information, particularly since their attitudes are supported by their social group. As one study contends in distinguishing between charisma and credibility: "Credibility demands above-average capacity to perceive changes, while charisma is based mainly on stronger than average opposition to doing so" (Hirschman, 1968: 934). Charisma usually involves the identification of the leader with existing social norms and views, even if they do not fit reality. In fact, charismatic decisionmakers draw their strength from their identification with those norms and perceptions; whether the leader dictated them to the masses or adopted existing ones makes no difference.[38]

Closely related to charismatic leaders are those with narcissistic personalities, who regard themselves as endowed with great power, physical appeal, and the right to assert their will. "Not all charismatic leaders necessarily have the narcissistic personality organization described here, but the converse may be true: the individual who becomes a powerful leader in response to a national crisis and who has a narcissistic personality organization may be perceived as charismatic" (Volkan, 1980: 138). Narcissistic personalities are characterized by the simultaneous existence in the mind of two different and unintegrated subjective experiences of the self. One is an insecure self characterized by low self-esteem, feelings of inadequacy, insecurity, and shame. The other is a grandiose self driven by the need for achievement and recognition, by fantasies of self-confidence and control. Narcissists are continually seeking public approbation. They assume a Hobbesian world, where pursuing self-interest is everyone's guiding concern, and hence they are suspicious of others' intentions. Narcissists have an authoritarian style that leads them to present their views with more self-confidence than available information warrants. When they are the ranking members of decisionmaking groups whose other members have no independent power base, they give their fellows little autonomy, demanding total loyalty and conformism and abhorring challenge, which is interpreted as betrayal, thus making the emergence of groupthink likely (Etheredge, 1979; Volkan, 1980).

It is probably no coincidence that central members of Israeli decisionmaking group in 1973, both political and military, had all or most of these personality traits. Meir has often been described as authoritarian and dogmatic, a woman with high self-esteem as well as a strong preference for concreteness. Dayan was authoritarian and introverted, a man with very high self-esteem and charisma and a narcissistic personality. He was acutely aware of the effects of his charisma on his peers and exploited it effectively. Major General Zeira, director of military intelligence, was also authoritarian and had very high self-esteem (Bartov, 1978a: 211, 313, 323; Dayan, 1976: 576; Eban, 1978: 488; Falk, 1984,

1985; Herzog, 1975: 21–22, 23–24, 51). Not only did the combination of these personality characteristics raise the probability of biased information processing for each person,[39] but that consequence was reinforced by the social interactions among the three. Their agreement over the low probability of war produced conformity and reduced the motivation of dissenters to express their views (as we shall see in some detail in the next chapter). The shared confidence of these decisionmakers in their evaluation of the situation, their imposing personalities, and their lack of openness to information challenging their strongly held views discouraged the emergence of real debate, questioning, and doubt about the underlying assumptions of their evaluations until the very last moment in the early morning of October 6. Consequently, even obvious indications of the increasing probablity of war were underestimated or ignored.

Similarly, President Johnson possessed most of these personality traits. He was described, for example, as "forceful and domineering, a man infatuated with himself, Johnson was affected in his conduct of Vietnam policy by three elements in his character: an ego that was insatiable and never secure; a bottomless capacity to use and impose the powers of office without inhibition; a profound aversion, once fixed upon a course of action, to any contra-indications" (Tuchman, 1984: 311). Lyndon Johnson relied, in various periods in his public career, on men like Dean Acheson, John Foster Dulles, Dean Rusk, McGeorge Bundy, and Robert McNamara as men of authority in an area—international relations—in which he was insecure. As long as his policies were approved by those men, who represented the established wisdom, he did not worry about the accuracy of either their information or their conclusions (Kearns, 1976: 256). His need to avoid ambivalence and to perceive issues in black-and-white terms, to ignore information that threatened his closed belief system regarding the essence of international politics, the role of the United States, and the meaning of the Vietnam conflict, was amply demonstrated earlier in this chapter. Johnson was an extravert.

So strong was Johnson's need for affection, and so vital his need for public gratitude, that he experienced . . . rejection of his "good works" as an absolute rejection of himself. Denied the appreciation which not only empowered but sustained his self, the love which validated his identity, the anatomy which gave Lyndon Johnson's ego its shape was dissolved. His energy and capacity to direct that energy outward abandoned him. Every presidential responsibility . . . took inordinate effort. (Kearns, 1976: 341)

Finally, he was not a charismatic president but showed the symptoms of a narcissistic personality. As president, he planned to be " 'the greatest of them all, the whole bunch of them'" (E. F. Goldman, 1974: 21). Yet underlying this show of ebullient confidence was a deep sense of insecurity and inadequacy.

Moods, Emotional States, and Minor Psychological Disturbances

The analysis of information processing behavior has to take into account not only stable traits, motives, needs, and unmotivational cognitive factors but also circumstantial mediating factors that are common in everyday life. The effects of circumstantial factors are accentuated in the highly uncertain, ambiguous, and high-stakes environment of foreign policy decisionmaking and are more pronounced the higher the position held.

High office has high psychic costs because of the workload, strain induced by responsibility and position, and fatigue. They may lead to a retreat from the real world into a private world and may sometimes produce chronic or nonchronic paranoid suspicion (e.g. Woodrow Wilson, James Forrestal, Richard Nixon). Paranoia increases feelings of insecurity, from which aggressive action may offer an illusory security (Kantor and Herron, 1968). A paranoid mentality also causes an inability to alter fixed ideas. Paranoid decisionmakers find it difficult to consult with others (e.g. advisers, members of the decisionmaking group), because they do not trust others with their doubts, so misinterpretations accumulate. Dealing with the symptoms is difficult because paranoics are always resistant to suggestions that they are mentally ill and hence do not recognize the possible need to step down from their position.

Emotions are another influence on cognition. They may cause cognition, or conversely cognition may cause emotions. They cause cognition where a prior experience triggers instant affective reactions before cold cognitive processes take place. Patterned knowledge and expectations (schemata) cue at least the valence of emotion (Fiske, 1981). "An emotional state may influence the interpretation of ambiguous stimuli because the emotion primes into readiness congruent concepts and categories" (Gilligan and Bower, 1984: 567).

Closely related to emotions are moods, especially intense moods (e.g. depression, anxiety) that are difficult to control. They may result in both subtle and pervasive deleterious effects on social cognition. Nonchronic depression is a minor psychological disturbance. The term refers to the

lesser pathologies of behavior observed in common daily life. In contrast to major psychiatric disorders, the nature of the psychopathology of such behavior is mild and less disturbing; it is seldom dealt with as a psychiatric problem in a clinical setting and, therefore, may be referred to as "subclinical"; the nature of such behavior is more or less psychological in nature and occurs as a reaction to stress rather than as a disease process with biological/endogenous predisposition; and finally, such phenomena may occur so commonly in daily life, and may involve so many people, that they may be viewed as normal individuals' suboptimal reactions to stresses and frustrations. (Tseng and Hsu, 1980: 62)

Depression produces rigid, narrowly focused information processing (Showers and Cantor, 1985). Depression at all levels, from the mildly neurotic to the severely psychotic, especially when it affects decision-makers continually for a long period, has serious cognitive distortion effects. For example, when the psychological pressures of the Watergate investigations began to have their effect, "Nixon was a distracted man. On March 6, for instance, he ordered a bombing strike of one day's duration on the Ho Chi Minh trail. . . . The next day, March 7, he cancelled the order. Again he said he did not want to give the North Vietnamese a pretext for delaying the release of the next batch of American prisoners. I doubt whether this was a considered reason" (Kissinger, 1982: 319).

Depression may lead to the arbitrary interpretation of information, particularly ambiguous information, which is not based on factual evidence or is even counterfactual. Alternative interpretations are almost automatically rejected as implausible. In the process decisionmakers focus and base their interpretations on details taken out of context, ignoring other, more salient features. Conclusions manifest overgeneralizations and extreme assessments, often abetted by inexact labeling of the event or situation in extreme terms that magnify it. The extreme assessments tend to be overpessimistic and based on a selective memory for events that had real or illusory consequences. Depressed people exhibit pessimism in predicting the likelihood of future outcomes for themselves and others, probably based on a belief in universal helplessness (Alloy and Ahrens, 1987; Rogow, 1969). Their judgment tends to be based on short-term considerations and can be further impaired by physiological symptoms of depression, such as loss of appetite, disturbed sleep, and fatigability (discussed in the next section). They find depressive thoughts to be highly valid, especially when accompanied by strong affective reactions (e.g. anger, anxiety, sadness) (Alloy and Ahrens, 1987; Beck, 1963; Shaw, 1979). Consequently, their cognitions are highly unadaptive and unresponsive to disconfirming information.

Depression also affects the attribution of causality. Unlike nondepressives who attribute failure to external causes, depressives attribute it to dispositional causes. Blaming themselves enhances their feelings of unworthiness, guilt, and loss of self-esteem (Kuiper, 1978). President Johnson was at times "glum and irritable at this foreign mess [Vietnam]." At other moments making decisions about Vietnam "brought a shoulder-back sense of command, a feeling of the Churchillian role" (E. F. Goldman, 1974: 491). These moods affected the policymaking process.

The content of the [Tuesday lunch] meetings varied substantially with Johnson's shifting moods. If he felt momentarily good about something—some article of praise or some news from the field—he could focus well and hard on the decisions that had to be made. But during periods of depression he would spend hours in rambling talk, turning listlessly from one extraneous subject to another. (Kearns, 1976: 322)

Treatment sometimes produces hypomania, found in many patients relieved of manic or depressive episodes. Hypomanics are constantly and exaggeratedly active and energetic. They convey an air of confidence and courage and look optimistically toward the future. They are perceptive and imaginative. Since hypomanics need others to confirm their sense of omnipotence and omniscience, they try to impress and please them. They do not tolerate criticism well. Their needs as well as their qualities create the potential for leadership; but when hypomania is recurrently interrupted by episodes of mania or depression or both, serious problems result. Manic states produce illusions and delusions that are utterly unrealistic, while depressive states produce passivity and pessimism and their related symptoms (Ostow, 1980).

Psychological disturbances are often caused by stress, yet stress has variable effects on different people because people have different stress disruption thresholds. Research findings indicate a curvilinear, inverted-U-shaped relationship between stress and the quality of problem solving by individuals and groups (George, 1980a: 48–49; Lanzetta, 1965; Oneal, 1988; Pruitt, 1965: 395). Mild levels of stress often facilitate improved performance, but as stress becomes intense and protracted tolerance for ambiguity weakens, the ability to discriminate the dangerous from the trivial is reduced and cognitive complexity diminishes. The ability to judge time is impaired, so that there is a significant overestimation of how quickly time is passing, which further increases stress and produces a tendency to narrow down the number of options considered. More specifically, stress fosters a tendency to seize on solutions before all alternatives have been considered and to scan the alternatives in a disorganized and unsystematic fashion (Keinan, Friedland, and Ben-Porath, 1987). The alternatives are considered in order of their availability, so less available ones are given scant attention or none at all. Decisionmakers concentrate on a single approach to problem solving with little or no adaptation. There is also a growing propensity to rely on stereotypes, narrow the focus of attention, and concentrate on the present and the immediate future (O. R. Holsti, 1971; Smock, 1955; Weldon and Stagner, 1956).

As the attention span narrows, fewer cues are attended to and the cue-filtering procedures (discussed in Chapter 2) decline in accuracy, so that pertinent dimensions of the situation are not considered. Stress also increases intolerance to ambiguity. Intense stress produces cognitive rigidity, which leads to a decreased capability to deal with complexity, diminished creativity, and a failure to adjust existing beliefs and theories to new information. There is increased reliance on random rules and simplistic, single criteria rather than multiple criteria in interpreting information, eliminating the possibility of complex multidimensional processing, which would produce competing interpretations and the need to choose from among them. Decisionmakers are likely not to be aware of side effects and unintended consequences, but they magnify the benefits of the preferred option and the deficiencies of other options, thus making choice a clear-cut operation. They tend to believe that a single option satisfies all or most value dimensions without requiring value trade-offs. After a decision is made, attention to negative feedback is limited. Low tolerance for stress produces fatigue and a tendency to consult with like-minded others, which also reduces the scope of alternatives considered (M. G. Hermann, 1979a; Holsti and George, 1975: 275–84; Kilpatrick, 1969; Milburn, 1972).

The need for control and predictability is accentuated under conditions of novelty and high threat. Novel situations, in which decisionmakers are not clear about the meaning of the event, require inferences, thus increasing the probability of error in interpretation. Awareness of this risk in turn increases stress, particularly when the situation itself is inherently stressful. Stress is bound to be even more pronounced when novelty implies the lack of coping skills and hence increases the anxiety posed by the situation. Attempts to impose structure on the environment so as to reduce anxiety are more pronounced as threat-induced stress increases. The wish to avoid stress and anxiety explains bureaucratic and individual inertia even in the face of information that should have raised doubts about the existing levels of threat perception (Knorr, 1976: 113; Pervin, 1963). Doubts and ambiguity reduce predictability and the sense of being in control. Inertia assures the individual or organization of both control and predictability.

Chronic, persistent stressors over a long time tend to wear people down.[40] Decisionmakers who have to endure acute stress often succumb to the pressures they face and develop severe behavioral pathologies or physical illness, which has serious implications for their ability to perform their role (L'Etang, 1970). Decisionmakers may, however, get used to the situation and learn to deal with its demands or learn how to avoid them (e.g. learn to keep calm and not lose sleep in spite of high stress) (Lazarus and Folkman, 1984: 98–101). Although the reactions to some disturbances occurring in everyday life, reactions such as excessive consumption of alcohol or drugs, may only modestly impair everyday cognitive operations, their consequences at the national decisionmaking level, especially in periods of crisis and high stress, when the stakes are high, can be significantly negative for the quality of information processing and decisionmaking (e.g. Nixon's drinking habits). They may affect coping capabilities by slowing reactions and producing confusion, delusions, detachment from reality, and the impairment of sociopersonal functions. Another consideration is the threshold-crossing effect of these minor psychological disturbances. When added to other obstructions to effective information processing, the disturbances, even when they are in themselves marginal, could have the effect of the straw that breaks the camel's back in affecting the quality of cognitive performance.

Some Physiological Influences on Cognition

Not enough systematic attention has been given to physiological effects on the nature and quality of cognitive processes in general, particularly in the domain of political decisionmaking, and most of the literature is descriptive rather than analytic or prescriptive (e.g. Torre, 1964; L'Etang, 1980). A number of reasons can be suggested for this state of affairs. First, people tend to think of those making decisions, especially the top national leadership, as some abstract entity—"decisionmakers"—and not as flesh-and-blood human beings. People expect them to rise above their physical vulnerabilities and not be affected by them. Second, decisionmakers jealously guard their physical deficiencies from exposure; they do not want to risk losing the demigod image they consciously and unconsciously attempt to build among their followers. At the same time there is probably a sense among political scientists that issues relating to physiology-bound behavior are more in the nature of gossip than a legitimate and possible area of research. These two sources of reluctance, on both the scholars' and the decisionmakers' parts, are complementary and reinforcing. Finally, detailed research into these issues requires a broad education and knowledge in biology and medicine that social scientists lack, and a comprehensive knowledge in the social sciences that life scientists lack. Alternatively, such research could involve close cooperation between social scientists and scholars from the life sciences, which is difficult to achieve because of the vast divergence of the disciplines.

Yet the subject of physiological influences on cognition is important for a realistic assessment of information processing, in extended periods of crisis with high stakes, stress, and ambiguity in particular. I shall not attempt here a detailed analysis of the problem, for there is not yet a coherent, comprehensive body of accumulated scientific findings. Instead this section will only briefly highlight the main problem areas in three core issues: physical fitness, aging, and psychopharmacology.

Physical fitness. Ill health and pain, especially chronic pain, increase a person's preoccupation with somatic symptoms, disrupt interpersonal relationships, and disturb sleep, appetite, and libido. They probably affect the attention, concentration, and overall cognitive resources available for information processing. They act as distractions from task-related information and affect the attention span, since they reduce the capability to concentrate on the information even when it has caught a decisionmaker's attention, making its processing likely to be superficial. Distracted, inattentive decisionmakers prefer to deal with encapsulated information, since preprocessing reduces their burden of processing. Consequently, they are likely to lose control of information processing tasks, be dependent on others (aides, assistants), and become passive consumers. They are also unlikely to be creative because the motivation to persist in intellectual efforts is constrained by their physical condition. Hence new information is likely to be assimilated to existing conceptions and beliefs, rather than trigger a process of reevaluation involving an extensive investment of time and effort. Information on situations for which there are available schemata, which reduce effort without necessarily reducing quality of processing, is better attended to and processed than information that cannot be fitted into a schema. To the degree that pain, particularly chronic states of pain, generates periods of depression in decisionmakers (e.g. Dayan; see Falk, 1985), it causes cognitive impairment in the areas of abstraction, associative tightness (i.e. being able or unable to make correct associations), and speed of information processing (Skevington, 1983; Sprock et al., 1983), in addition to the other effects of depression discussed earlier.

Overburdened top-level decisionmakers often suffer the effects of fatigue, which can be chronic or situational. When chronic, fatigue reflects structural problems related to an inefficient allocation of role loads; when situational, it reflects ad hoc circumstances, such as an acute crisis or jet lag produced by extensive traveling (Wiegele, 1973). In both cases the cause is lack of appropriate rest or actual deprivation of sleep. Decisionmakers who continually deprive themselves of sleep believe that they can develop compensatory or coping capacities that will offset performance decrement. They cannot. Sleep deprivation may increase cognitive operation decrements, especially vigilance and reaction time (Tharp, 1978; Webb and Levy, 1984). Sleep loss reduces the ability to attend to stimuli for extended periods, leading to possible misperceptions owing to the decreased capacity to distinguish relevant from irrelevant information. These lapses are accompanied by memory decrements (Elkin and Murray, 1974; Meddis, 1982; Polzella, 1975). There are, however, substantial individual differences in response to sleep deprivation.

Since fatigue influences attention span and search, decisionmakers succumb to using shortcuts to interpretation, making their dependence on applying heuristics likely to increase. When decisionmakers are depleted of physical energy, they are likely to be reluctant to deal with information by a time-consuming reevaluation of existing conceptions. They are likely to depend to a growing extent on availability and representativeness to judge complex situations, pay less attention to base-rate information, and focus on salient individuating information. Fatigue also causes narrow-mindedness, lack of stamina for thinking afresh and perceiving opportunities, and a preference for inertia rather than the uncertainties of adjustment and new initiatives. Decisionmakers probably do not notice missing elements when assessing risks and are consequently overconfident in the completeness of their analyses. Fatigued decisionmakers become irritable, impatient, and often bad-tempered. Their disposition has negative effects on their coworkers, who become reluctant to raise doubts and suggest new approaches out of fear of their possible responses, thus bolstering cognitive conservatism (Wiegele, 1973). Fatigue has a long-range, cumulative effect: during the period in which a decisionmaker is in power, the ongoing process of coping with each stressful situation leaves a residue of fatigue. For example,

[by 1968] daily contact with the real world—with the evidence of a deepening inflation, with the results of the Tet offensive, and with the challenge of the primaries—was forcing Johnson back to reality.... No good works, no love, no self-esteem. Only the endless repetition of sordid, unhappy days. Johnson's enthusiasm and vitality steadily receded. He was really tired, and he knew it. (Kearns, 1976: 341–42)

Politicians are highly sensitive to their public image, and they try to conceal, even from those close to them, evidence of mental or physical weakness (Wiegele, 1977; L'Etang, 1970) and attempt to project a vigorous and energetic image. Thus coping by consulting a doctor, psychiatrist, or friend is unlikely; not consulting perpetuates the state of physical or mental impairment. With aging the effects have even more severe consequences, because physical fitness and stamina decrease, lowering the threshold for dysfunctional fatigue. It is true that "whereas health and energy certainly facilitate coping—it is easier to cope when one is feeling well than when one is not—people who are ill and enervated can usually mobilize sufficiently to cope when the stakes are high enough" (Lazarus and Folkman, 1984: 159) (e.g. Harry Hopkins, President Roosevelt's foreign policy adviser). It can be safely argued, however, that decisionmakers are more likely to pursue a satisficing pattern in information processing, as in other tasks, when they are not healthy and lack physical stamina.

Aging. Foreign policy decisionmakers at the highest level often belong to the over-60 age-group. The amount of mental energy or attentional resources available for performing unpracticed and novel cognitive tasks declines with age, causing impairment of cognitive efficiency in the elderly. Particularly affected are the deep and elaborate memory encoding and retrieval processes (Craik and Byrd, 1982). More specifically, aging tends to produce rigidity, overconfidence and a preference for extreme choices, weakness in short-term memory, and difficulty in dealing with complex situations and decoding problems, which are manifested in slowness in the early phases of the problem-solving process (Wiegele, 1973).

Older people, even the well-educated and the well-preserved, have difficulty in making inferences, that is, in extracting information that is not stated but implied. The difficulty is increased when the rate of input exceeds processing capacity (C. Cohen, 1981). That is, older people cope less effectively with information overload in terms of the quality of information processing. Their reactions are slower than younger people's. They take longer to learn information and respond to it owing to the decline of central nervous system functioning, a decline that bears on perception and cognition. Reaction time is particularly slow when the situation is novel and the task complex. Performing intelligence tasks, such as reasoning and perceptual integration, also declines with age. Problem-solving capacities are impaired too. Older people prefer concrete tasks over abstract tasks and are not so flexible in their thinking. Older problem solvers tend to obtain more redundant information than younger ones, which wastes time and obstructs processing. They find it difficult to take into account and make proper use of information about hypothetical events, but they are more alert to, and handle better, personally meaningful information. At the same time their efficiency in organizing information is reduced (Botwinick, 1984). It stands to reason, however, that older people who were trained and accustomed to make inferences effectively earlier in life are less affected by aging than those whose inference skills are basically intuitive. One possible reason is that the reduction in processing efficiency in old age can be at least partly compensated for by training in choosing the most economic processing strategy (Cohen and Faulkner, 1983; Staudinger, Cornelius, and Baltes, 1989).

Elderly leaders sometimes suffer hearing and/or vision impairments. In some cases their impairments may seriously affect the quality of their information processing by significantly diminishing the amount of information they can effectively deal with. Even more important, such impairments can easily lead to serious problems in judging, assimilating, and comprehending information because of missed visual and auditory cues. Very often decisionmakers neglect to do anything about their incapacitation because of a reluctance to call attention to it or a subliminal refusal to recognize unacceptable handicaps (L'Etang, 1980: 133–42).

In some cases aging involves cerebral degenerative disease, such as arteriosclerosis (e.g. Gamal Abdel Nasser). In its incipient stages the sick people suffer impairment in their abstract thinking capacity. Response becomes inflexible and stereotypic. Intellectual capabilities generally decline. The sick people are irritable and susceptible to being easily provoked to euphoric or depressive reactions. Their attitudes tend to be expressed in an exaggerated way; for example, a distrustful person may become paranoid (Post, 1973, 1980). These symptoms significantly reduce their information processing capabilities. The search for information declines, as does the capacity to continually adjust positions and judgments to new information, leading to premature cognitive closure. What makes situations in which leaders are cerebrally diseased particularly dangerous is their tendency to deny the extent of the disability (e.g. Woodrow Wilson). When the denial behavior is supported by intimate associates, it hides the problem from the public and allows the impaired leader to stay in office.

The historical record shows that acts of duplicity by national leaders' physicians (e.g. Cary Grayson and Ross McIntire, the physicians of Wilson and Franklin Roosevelt respectively) are not uncommon and have to do with the special relationship that the physicians develop with their famous, sometimes awe-inspiring patients. In some cases not only are they misleading the public about their patients' physical and cognitive state of health but they do not have the courage or will to inform their patients of their disability either. Such was the case with Ross McIntire, who in 1944 assured the president, already desperately sick, that his illness was only a case of sinuses and bronchitis (Park, 1986: 244). Even when cognitive disabilities are not permanent but intermittent, keeping them secret is analogous to playing Russian roulette with the national interest, for the physician does not know when and under what circumstances the cognitive impairment will be activated and dominate the decisionmaker's behavior. In fact, *"the chances are good that the real emergency will come in the area of presidential neurologic disability, either temporary or permanent.* It has arisen on at least three occasions already in the twentieth century" (Park, 1986: 317–18).

Aging can also influence motivational biases toward overconservatism and risk avoidance as well as toward hyperactivism and risk taking. Elderly decisionmakers who feel that they are reaching the end of their career may become extremely risk averse in the interest of ending their career with dignity. They consequently ignore or even distort the interpretation of information indicating the need for major policy changes. At the other end of the spectrum are the decisionmakers who have a strong sense that time is running out and with it an enhanced drive to leave their imprint on history. Their risk estimates are biased downward to make risk taking rational and justifiable both to themselves and to the public.

On the positive side it should be remembered that elderly leaders are able to rely and draw on accumulated experience, which decreases the time required for response as well as the anxiety of dealing with novel problems. With age, few problems are novel. Some studies argue that age in itself is not a main explanatory variable of impairment in social cognition and that age is mediated by the extent and quality of social interactions (Dolen and Bearison, 1982).[41] This hypothesis implies that elderly people who are highly involved in social interactions experience less decline in cognitive functioning than those who are solitary. This might also explain their reluctance to retire, which reflects a reflexive intuitive-defensive fear of cognitive functioning decline.

Finally, aging has differential effects on the capacities of leaders. Hence "it is impossible to generalize about the capacities of aging leaders, for some may be severely influenced, while others may maintain a high degree of creativity and intellectual acuity in their later years" (Post, 1973: 116).[42]

Psychopharmacology. People in the top-level foreign policy decisionmakers' age-group are more likely than younger people to use depressant and stimulant drugs that are either prescribed or acquired over the counter. Although extreme cases of psychosis among decisionmakers are not unheard of (e.g. Stalin, Nkrumah), more common are the less severe cases of neurosis, where the symptoms are related to situational stress circumstances (crisis, success, failure) or physical illness combined with treatment by drugs that have psychoactive effects. Alcohol and drug abuse in high-stress circumstances is not unheard of. Psychoactive drugs and other agents have a variable effect on different individuals. Depending on emotional and physical state, effects vary, even with the same person (L'Etang, 1980: 80–98; Lubit and Russett, 1984; Park, 1986).

Psychoactive drugs have a number of cognitive impairment effects on vigilance, memory, and the speed of cognitive processes. Minor tranquilizers and other drugs can affect decisionmakers' behavior as social actors, that is, their group interactions, or their behavior as individuals. In fact all psychopharmacologicals are sociogenic. Whether in the sphere of social or individual behavior, they affect the quality of decisions without the decisionmaker's being aware of it. Yet there is no inventory of accumulated, comprehensively organized knowledge that can help society in coping with the risks involved (Kleinknecht and Donaldson, 1975; Lennard, Epstein, and Katzung, 1967; Somit, 1968; Stix, 1974). To illustrate the potential severity of the problem, I shall mention the effects of some widely prescribed and used drugs.

Long-term memory is strongly affected by the use of diazepam or scopalamine. They impede the permanent acquisition of new information, although learning, short-term memory, and retrieval capacities from long-term memory are unaffected (Frith et al., 1984; Ghoneim, Mewaldt, and Hinrichs, 1984; Kleinknecht and Donaldson, 1975; Mewaldt, Hinrichs, and Ghoneim, 1983). Diazepines depress mental functioning, causing sedation, drowsiness, and confusion and possibly also short-term euphoria (Jäättelä et al., 1971; Lubit and Russett, 1984). Amnesic effects were also observed for porazepam (Healey et al., 1983). Barbiturates, although short-term in effect, cause the processing and encoding of stimuli to slow. Alcohol, on the other hand, impairs both the speed and accuracy of the cognitive processes (Rundell, William, and Lester, 1978). Benzodiazepines (valium and librium) that are widely prescribed for providing symptomatic relief of insomnia also possess amnesic properties (Roth et al., 1980). This effect, however, wears off after a critical period of wakefulness. Stimulants, such as dextroamphetamine, cause euphoria (Rapoport et al., 1980). Chlordiazepoxide (librium) reduces anxiety but brings on irritability and overreaction to minor annoyances (Stix, 1974). Subordinates may be reluctant to interfere with their chlordiazepoxide-ingesting leader's peace of mind by presenting information that might undermine consistency or the leader's strongly held beliefs.[43]

Amphetamines, drugs prescribed for raising the energy level and stimulating the appetite, can cause insomnia, paranoia, wakefulness, alertness, elation, and euphoria (e.g. Anthony Eden). After prolonged use or in large doses they can cause depression, fatigue, confusion, and delirium. Amphetamines induce a significantly favorable self-appraisal of performance (Hurst, Weidner, and Radlow, 1967; Lubit and Russett, 1984), causing self-criticism and accurate monitoring of one's performance to decrease.

Some drugs used for treating chronic illness have strong effects on mood. Cortisone, for example, produces a euphoric outlook (e.g. John Kennedy received the drug as treatment for Addison's disease). Other drugs produce feelings of fatigue (e.g. antibiotics), depression, and other psychological and physiological negative effects (L'Etang, 1970; Wiegele, 1973).

Although social drinking is an everyday phenomenon, current knowledge about the cognitive aftereffects of drinking is limited. Drinking problems are not unknown among decisionmakers at the highest level. Nixon had a low capacity for alcohol and seemed to have developed a drinking problem. He drank at night, and in particular at his retreats in Key Biscayne and Camp David. Kissinger's aide Roger Morris remembers that "there were many times when a cable would come in late and Henry would say, 'There's no sense in waking him up—he'd be incoherent.'" Morris "often wondered what would happen if the Soviet Union attacked at night" (Hersh, 1983: 108). Yet this side of Nixon went unexposed. Those who knew about it shielded the president—out of patriotism, admiration for his potential greatness, or the desire to protect their position in the White House (R. Morris, 1977: 146–48). The drinking problem became even more serious during the Watergate crisis.

There is evidence that a nonalcoholic who uses alcohol in socially normative ways suffers decrements in adaptive abilities, concept formation, and the capacity to shift from one idea to another. The cognitive decrements are subtle and graded but may have functional significance for decisionmakers engaged in cognitively demanding activities (MacVane et al., 1982; Parker, 1982; Parker and Noble, 1977). Alcohol probably worsens performance in information processing, especially when stimulus-response conditions are novel (Huntley, 1974).

Jaros (1972) suggests a number of influences alcohol and other depressants may have, influences that have significant implications for cognitive processes. Depressants impair cognitive operations; people who use them are unlikely to notice subtle differences among alternatives and likely to find meaningful only the grossest and most extreme stimuli. Alcohol not only dulls the capacity to make fine distinctions and to concentrate. It also leads to increased confidence, mood swings, depression, hallucinations, and paranoia (Lubit and Russett, 1984). Alcohol and other depressants reduce anxiety and fear and in general suppress the effect of inhibitory mechanisms. Under the influence of alcohol and depressant drugs, then, decisionmakers make risk assessments that are unrealistically low; they may even be completely blind to the costs and dangers of failure and overestimate the probabilities of success. Depressants also affect social relations by inducing dependency, which may lead people to take positions contrary to their own previously expressed opinions, thus producing a higher probability of conformism and groupthink in group decisionmaking.

The discussion so far is only a preliminary indication of the importance of this domain—the physiological influences on cognition—for further research to establish a body of policy-relevant information. Even at this point past and contemporary examples show that society and its decisionmaking organizations must establish a carefully thought out backup system not only for major contingencies, such as assassinations of leaders, but also for lesser problems that may not incapacitate the chief executives or decisionmakers but nonetheless call into question their ability to carry out their duties effectively.

In many cases the highest-ranking policymakers reach their position at an advanced age and have to cope with serious health problems that can significantly affect their performance. Top-level incumbents should therefore be required to pass an annual medical examination by an independent board of doctors that would decide their physical and mental competence and effectiveness. At present the personal doctors of policymakers protect them from having their competence evaluated; the doctors feel more committed to their patients and to the ethics of the doctor-patient relationship than to the national interest.[44] By making the results of the suggested periodic medical examination open to public scrutiny it is likely that the negative effects of the doctor-patient relationship can be controlled.

It may be advisable too to impose a compulsory retirement age on top elected political decisionmakers like the one imposed on all civil servants. Rarely do active politicians recognize their infirmities and the effects their infirmities have on their capacity to carry out their roles effectively. Rarely do they retire of their own free will. When they are forced out, the damage due to physical and intellectual incapacitation has often already been done. The common wisdom that old age is associated with ripeness and wisdom does not always hold true, and the risks of incapacitation in office more than outweigh the benefits to be gained from the accumulated experience brought to office. A compulsory retirement age would prevent some of the excesses associated with elderly politicians holding office and still allow them to play a useful consultancy role.[45]

Finally, to establish fitness guidelines, it is necessary to have a valid body of data and accumulated experience on the interaction of health and cognitive performance in the high-level decisionmaking environment. It is advisable that medical files of policymakers be opened to researchers upon their passing away rather than indiscriminately and indefinitely applying the code of medical secrecy. Opening confidential files poses ethical problems, yet it is the only way to learn how illness and drugs affect decisionmakers in real-life situations. Re-creating a realistic decisionmaking environment in the laboratory is almost impossible. After all,

> great men are different from you and me. When a great man fails it is difficult to decide when incapacity begins; difficult to assess the degree of incapacity; and even more difficult to tell him that he is incapacitated. The role of the doctor in regard to this small and select group of patients is unique and most practitioners have neither personal experience, nor second-hand knowledge from experienced colleagues, of the correct approach and of the special problems that are involved. (L'Etang, 1970: 211)

The costs of not improving society's knowledge in this domain are much higher than the costs of not preserving the individual's basic right to medical privacy. Politicians should recognize as a professional hazard that their complete medical files will become public knowledge after their death.

Conclusions

Personality affects information processing, the generic term personality being interpreted in the broadest sense. Human beings as information processing organisms are highly complex creatures who are driven by variable, sometimes contradictory needs; who can act to avoid recognizing their psychological and physiological vulnerabilities; and who may at the same time preserve at least a semblance of rationality. The quality of their information processing reflects the balance among these factors; the weight of each in the final outcome may change in different environments and situations. Any attempt to label human beings exclusively as one thing or another (e.g. consistency seekers, intuitive scientists) is misleading.

In an ambiguous and uncertain world, information tends to be extremely fuzzy. Its fuzziness legitimizes the use of nonrational means to deal with it; indeed, at times the only rational way to deal with problems that have important nonrationalistic elements may be to subject the rational elements to the domination of intuitive, nonrationalistic procedures (M. Steiner, 1983).[46] Whether nonrationalistic procedures (e.g. intuition, heuristics) are the rational choice depends, however, on whether the decisionmaker in question is trained in applying them to such problems. Decisionmakers do not cope equally well with the complex international environment; some are better skilled and prepared than others in using available cues, particularly in inferring the causal structure of the situation or event, in their attempts to impose meaning on their environment. Among the cues utilized are covariations between variables; temporal order, which indicates which is the cause and which is the effect; contiguity in time and space, which directs attention to contingent variables; and similarity between variables, which serves as a cue for judging probable cause (Einhorn and Hogarth, 1986).

Participants in the decisionmaking group may become locked into one position with little data to support them, though the data may nonetheless provide preliminary cues. Consequently, new data are likely to be assimilated with initial impressions, unless this new information is overwhelmingly incongruent with them. The initial impressions are in most cases concept driven rather than data driven; that is, they are guided by beliefs and theories the decisionmakers hold. Yet being unaware of their internal cognitive processes, decisionmakers believe that their inferences and conclusions are data based.[47] Moreover, in judging the validity of their inferences and conclusions decisionmakers overestimate the complexity of their thought processes—assuming that they have taken most of the relevant variables and information into account when in fact they have used simple models that ignore value trade-offs and believing that their policy choice is better than each alternative on many logical independent dimensions. Consequently, they become overconfident in the validity of their views, pay little attention to negative feedbacks, and overestimate the likelihood that they can successfully implement intricate policies that require complex coordination and continuous fine-tuning.

Information processing is, then, a combination of cold and hot, conscious and unconscious, intuitive and rule driven, introspective and thoughtless operations. It may result in numerous biases in judgment, inference, and prediction. Unmotivational biases are the products of the complexity of the environment, the inherent limitations on cognitive capabilities, and the strategies used to overcome them. Motivational biases arise from emotions, personal motives, and needs and have ego-defensive functions. Awareness of unmotivational biases may lead to attempts to avoid them; however, because they are embedded in objective cognitive limitations, such attempts are likely to fail. On the other hand, even when aware of the second type of bias, people are not likely to attempt to correct them because of the psychological discomforts correction may entail—although if they attempt to avoid them, they might be successful since motivational biases are not grounded in inherent, objective limitations on cognitive capabilities. When motivational biases affect decisionmakers' behavior, the observer cannot easily predict the state's behavior because such obvious causal factors as the situation, state interests, or past behavior are modified by psychological needs and personality traits, which are difficult to observe directly or infer indirectly and about which information is almost impossible to validate.

CHAPTER 4

The Social Milieu: Small-Group and
Organizational Effects

....

"Truth, far from being a solemn and severe master, is a docile and
obedient servant." NELSON GOODMAN

The Significance of the Organization
and the Small Group

Information processing and decisionmaking in foreign policy are usually not the affairs of one person only but are a collective enterprise. The
activities are sometimes undertaken by professional organizations and
sometimes by small groups composed of politicians and top bureaucrats
(e.g. cabinet members and their advisers). Collective decisionmaking is
therefore a social act unlike the task facing the solitary decisionmaker.
The questions of import in this context are how organizational processes,
and the interactions among individuals in the small decisionmaking
group, as well as the interactions between that group and other information-processing organizations and individuals, affect (1) the search for
and selection and evaluation of information, (2) the degree of openness
to discrepant information, and (3) the processes of adaptation to new
incoming information. These questions have particular significance for
the quality of information processing in the context of foreign policymaking because of the complexity, ambiguity, and uncertainty of the
information and the high stakes involved.

This chapter deals with the small groups, institutionalized or ad hoc,
and the organizations with which decisionmakers are associated. In a
nutshell, the difference between a small group and an organization is that
a group has no required fixed number of members but is small enough to
be manageable and that each member interacts directly with every other
member. In contrast, the key to an organization is dependence on pro-

cedures. An organization is a collection of people and machines for which explicit procedures for coordination and task enactment have been established to achieve specified objectives. Unlike a small group, an organization has no necessary requirement that the members directly interact with each other.

Whereas belonging to a nation is usually determined from birth, belonging to an organization and a group is a matter of individual choice that is sometimes an unconscious externalization of the individual's psychological needs (Diamond, 1984, 1985; Diamond and Allcorn, 1986; Dixon, 1976; LaBier, 1983). Since national belonging, like familial belonging, is usually determined from birth, exposure to the modes of thinking and perception these settings represent begins when one has not yet been exposed to strong competing modes of thinking and perception. In contrast, joining the other, more restricted social setting—the organization and the group—takes place in adulthood, when a set of core perceptions, beliefs, and mental processes has already been shaped by earlier familial, national, and cultural processes of socialization. Yet the influence of the social milieu of the organization and the group on the decisionmaker is highly significant, often pervasive; and although the two are social structures, they can be treated as sets of thinking practices and collective cognitive attributes (Lerner, 1982; Weick, 1979). At the same time small-group and organizational operation and behavior reflect at least in part societal-cultural style and values (see Chapter 5).

Although the group and the organization are two separate variable-sets, the dividing line between the two can be very fine or blurred, for the small group is often the top decisionmaking body of the organization, with the chiefs of the organization's subunits as participants. An additional methodological problem is that of distinguishing collective impact from individual impacts. There are parallels between individual and organizational behavior because individuals and organizations face the same problems of complexity, ambiguity, and uncertainty and have the same need to impose structure on the environment and also because organizations are populated by individuals whose patterns of behavior are manifested in organizational behavior. Organizational and group behavior may, for instance, reflect the dominant personality's pathologies (Kets de Vries and Miller, 1984). The difference is that organizational action, unlike small-group action, is not necessarily a direct by-product of individual preferences and behavior but may be their indirect by-product, after they are mediated by politicking, coalition formation, and hierarchical structures. I shall attempt therefore to isolate the effects of groups and organizations as collective entities.

The Organization and the Small Group as Subcultures

Broadly speaking, every organization or group embodies a more or less coherent set of explicit or tacit beliefs and values, a behavioral ethos, and myths that develop in response to its functional tasks and past experience, which endow it with and shape its particular style and character. The older the group or organization, the more explicit and extensive the beliefs, values, ethos, and myths become. Together they form the decisionmaking subculture of the group or organization and provide a shared frame of reference that organizes and channels the cognitive process of each individual member, reduces conceptual variety among members, serves as a source of the inventory of routine behavior, determines relations with the broader social environment, and gives the group or organization a distinct identity (Albert and Whetten, 1985; Brunsson, 1985: 9; Gordon, 1973; Schein, 1983; Selznick, [1957] 1984; Simon, 1976; Thompson and McEwen, 1969).

More specifically, the subculture is a combination of formal and informal constructs, which cannot always be depicted with precision, that varies in complexity and transparence from one group and organization to another. It is obviously influenced by the formal organizational and group structure in which it is embedded and in turn shapes the mode, quality, and consequences of organizational and group performance and affects recruiting predispositions, which will indirectly influence organizational and group decisions in the future. The subculture contains beliefs and norms shared by most members about the goals, stakes, and commitments of the group and organization, their modi operandi, and the modes of legitimate behavior that should prevail among members and toward out-groups. The beliefs and norms have direct implications for the style and quality of information processing. For example, a belief that each problem is unique and hence must be dealt with ad hoc would mean that the organization does not accumulate information about past experiences as a basis for making judgments and inferences about present and future problems, regarding it as useless. Or the don't-make-waves norm would imply that to present interpretations of information that sharply contradict the conventional wisdom could trigger sanctions against the dissident—thus prescribing modes of behavior that stress accommodation, conformity, caution, and probably cognitive rigidity, consequently enhancing the inherent organizational bias toward control and stability (Destler, 1974: 75–78; Sederberg, 1984; Turner, 1976), which is at least partly based on noncognizance of the need for change and adjustment. "Members of the subculture are often remarkably untroubled by the gaps in their knowledge and understanding. The explanation is that they are unaware of them. They don't know how much they don't know because it never occurs to them that they might know more than they now know" (A. M. Scott, 1969: 13). Similarly, the subculture influences the preference for the time perspective in which information is judged and interpreted by fostering beliefs about the relevance and usefulness—or, alternatively, the impracticality—of long-term thinking and planning and by allocating responsibilities that may or may not allow the decisionmaker time to make long-term calculations rather than deal only with the acute and immediate. Finally, the subculture is also instrumental in stratification and status attribution, which goes beyond the formal status-through-position allocation. Similar positions, formally considered equal, are attributed different status ranks by organization and group members by prevailing beliefs that are not anchored in formal procedures or rules. Thus equal formal positions may have differential consequences in terms of the capacity of position holders to influence group and organizational judgments and evaluation of information.

Two small-group situations should be distinguished. In one, the small group is part of a larger organization and includes the ranking individuals within it (e.g. State Department, Defense Department). In the other, group membership is interorganizational (e.g. Lyndon Johnson's Tuesday lunch cabinet or a committee of chiefs of intelligence organizations). Although the two types of group demonstrate the same general structural attributes, the cohesiveness, the commonality and detail of the subculture, and the intensity of affective relationships within the group show important differences. A shared and detailed subculture is more likely to emerge in a group within an organization, where it largely reflects attributes of the already established organizational culture. An interorganizational group has to establish its own subculture, which emerges and is consolidated over time as group members interact. Moreover, the rules of power and status allocation are bound to be much fuzzier in the interorganizational group than in the other type, in which status is often defined by the hierarchy of positions in the organization. In the interorganizational group, status allocation is more likely to be the outcome of the jockeying for influence and status; the representatives of the different organizations use the power of their respective organizations and their own skills as resources in this competition. In both types of group, however, the more cohesive groups generally develop a more complex and detailed subculture (Ridgeway, 1983: 106–7).

The subculture of the group and the organization plays a cognitive mediation role by providing members with a benchmark and a sense of direction for coping with and understanding their complex environment and determines the framework within which incoming information is treated, in particular the causal connection between the information and group and organizational goals (Lerner, 1982). More specifically, when an organization or group evaluates incoming information, the members ask, To what extent does the information or its interpretation point to an increase or decrease in the likelihood that our organization or group will succeed in achieving its objectives? If the answer is negative, the next question is, Can anything be done with this information in order to eliminate the negative effect? But if the answer is positive, the next question is, What can be done to utilize the positive potential of the information and increase its effect? The information, especially under conditions of ambiguity, becomes instrumental in working out the relations between the organization or group and its environment so that the maximum benefit accrues or at least so that a minimum amount of damage is done to the organization or its members. The treatment of information can thus become parochially self-serving rather than substance oriented. Particularly susceptible to such instrumental treatment is information suggesting that an organization and its decisionmakers are not effective—especially if it concerns long-standing policies toward which a strong commitment exists in the subculture of either the information-providing organization or the information consumers higher up. When an organization provides information to a decisionmaking group, especially if some of its senior members are also members of the decisionmaking group, it is well placed to prevent the dissemination of information that could require adjusting judgments and evaluations if the adjusted ones would conflict with its own concepts, motives, and interests.

These problems are magnified by the difficulties the adaptation process may encounter, given (1) the abstruseness of—even the impossibility of verbally defining—some of the cultural characteristics of an organization and (2) the intolerable cost of admitting the existence and impact of such factors as parochialism in the organizational culture. Regarding the first, Katz and Kahn note: "Though the subculture of the organization provides the frame of reference within which its members interpret activities and events, the members will not be able to verbalise in any precise fashion this frame of reference. They will be clear about the judgments they make, but not about the basic standards or frames they employ in reaching a judgment" (1966: 66). When the criteria for judging and evaluating information are not clearly defined and recognized, the motivation for reevaluating judgments is reduced. And even when such motivation exists, a proper reappraisal is made difficult when the sources of the mistaken evaluation are hard to locate. In an opaque subculture the rules according to which judgments, inferences, and evaluations are made are hard to trace and define precisely.

As for the intolerable cost of a clear and definite statement of vested organizational interest, an organization or its members will not admit that their information processing behavior is motivated by parochial thinking, that is, by their own narrow interests—in part, certainly, out of fear that the organization, upon such an admission, might be penalized by a reduction in its authority, resources, or, in extreme cases, by dissolution. There are also moral reasons, reflected in the norms that form part of the subculture and prevent such an admission, for social norms declare that the purpose of a social organization is to serve society at large and not itself. This is particularly true for organizations dealing with national security and foreign policy, the topmost national interests.[1] Under such conditions, when neither the organization nor its individual members will admit even to themselves the motives that underlie their interpretations of incoming information, a process of adjustment and adaptation is not highly likely to occur, even when information is clearly at odds with important components of the subculture.

The more fundamental and long-standing the views and attitudes in question and the more firmly they are embedded in the collective mind of the organization, and the more they are closely identified with the organization, so that it cannot evade or share with other organizations the burden of responsibility for fundamental errors stemming from them, the higher the cost of admitting such errors becomes. The cost in terms of organizational prestige, an important element of the culture, may be particularly high, given the implications it has for the social status of each member. For example, the stakes of the organizations involved in the formulation and implementation of the Vietnam policy were varied. Among the U.S. military services, the air force and the marines had the most at stake. For the marines, unlike the army, failure could possibly mean absorption into the army and a loss of autonomy. The air force's existence was not in question because it had important roles that could not be affected by the war, but what the air force perceived to be at stake was its core missions, the achievement of which had important implications for budget allocation and morale. These missions were strategic bombing, tactical interdiction, and air-to-air combat (Gallucci, 1975: 71–73).

The missions were largely independent of outside intervention and assured the service's autonomy, unlike close air support to ground forces, which was guided by the ground forces. They were the more glamorous missions, which provided the building blocks for the organization's myths and identity, more than even the most important logistic tasks. It is not surprising, then, that the air force became a strong proponent of strategic bombing, based on very optimistic projections that it would affect the outcome of the war by diminishing North Vietnam's capability and determination to continue supporting the insurgency in the South; the air force even presented air power as an effective substitute for large-scale ground forces. This view ignored the lessons of World War II and, later, the accumulating evidence of North Vietnam's ability to adapt to the bombing by dispersing potential targets or by falling back on their allies, the Soviet Union and China; and it also ignored the clear indications that not only was strategic bombing ineffective in reducing North Vietnam's capability but it had also failed to affect North Vietnam's will to continue the struggle in spite of the costs to its industrial complex (Lewy, 1978: 389–96).

The air force continued to press for the release of strategic targets and received most of what it wanted despite little success in delivering the promised effects on the outcome of the war. If the air force had admitted that strategic bombing was not viable and given it up, an essential component of the air force's raison d'être—its autonomous position and its capability to decide military outcomes significantly—would have been negatively affected. The more immediate consequences might have been cuts in the budget for acquiring more-advanced aircraft for the mission.

Similarly, the air force embarked on the mission of tactical interdiction against lines of communication in North Vietnam's panhandle and against the trail system in Laos and Cambodia despite evidence of the high possibility of failure. Past experience in Korea, coupled with the even worse conditions prevailing in Southeast Asia—the deadlier anti-aircraft fire, the greater redundancy of routes, the denser cover, the less favorable weather—should have served as warning cues. But again the air force needed to preserve the mission and convince civilian decision-makers that such missions were vital and could be carried out successfully. It was unthinkable to the members of the organization that a major war effort could be undertaken without the air force's playing a role of tactical interdiction.

In the case of both strategic and tactical interdiction, pressure from the Joint Chiefs of Staff (JCS) bore fruit when most of the items on their target list were authorized. In particular, the very large number of tactical interdiction sorties approved served to compensate the air force for some constraints on strategic targets (Gallucci, 1975: 73–80, 89–93; Littauer and Uphoff, 1972). With so much of the organization's prestige invested in strategic and tactical interdiction, members of the organization tended to grossly exaggerate the effects of bombing. And when the reality that the air war was not achieving its goals had to be faced, the air force blamed the failure on the civilians at the Department of Defense, arguing that they did not permit the air force to bomb important targets. In fact most of the targets suggested by 1967 had been authorized and bombed. The air force also argued that the piecemeal manner in which the targets were approved did not allow it to effectively exploit the shock effects of a sharp blow to North Vietnam's military and war-supporting facilities.

The term subculture applies to both formal and informal organizations and groups and cuts across national boundaries. In this sense, it is possible to speak of world elites, such as the subculture of foreign ministers. Being a member of such a subculture generates a sense of solidarity and identity that influences cognitive and affective processes (Clarke, 1974; Modelski, 1970).[2]

Diplomats are infatuated with language. They meet, or bypass, the confrontations of the real world through various forms of semantic compromise. The international fellowship of diplomats has a common stake in these professional techniques so that psychologically and culturally it often happens that diplomats worldwide have more in common with one another than they do with their domestic counterparts. (Hughes, 1967: 675)

This camaraderie influences expectations about other nations' behavior; more specifically it encourages members of the world elite to feel confident of their ability to settle disagreements between their respective nations through mutual understanding, common values, and shared membership in a group of enlightened people who can achieve conflict resolution through face-to-face interactions with one another. This naive sentiment was well elaborated by a former foreign minister of Australia, Paul Hasluck: "Personal diplomacy has caused a lot of mischief and harm. . . . It leads to the almost pathetic belief of some Foreign Ministers that if they have had lunch with someone and called him by his Christian name they have changed the fundamental facts of relationship between nations" (quoted in Modelski, 1970: 158). It comes as no surprise, then, that the use of personal diplomacy by ranking diplomats has become one of the most efficient instruments of international deception. The traducement is the direct outcome of their naive belief that the principles of action shared in the subculture are stronger than differences of national interest.

Thus foreign policy decisionmakers can be members of a number of subcultures simultaneously, but the situation might be a source of inner conflict for them, requiring adjustment. Participation in the international subculture can in some cases become participation in a counterculture[3] if subcultural beliefs and attitudes stand in contradiction to national ones. The extent to which the belief and value system of the subculture (e.g. of the world elite) is preferred to the national value and belief system is a function of each foreign minister's personal ranking of beliefs and values. The more international the decisionmakers are in their world view, the more importance they attach to values that pertain to and affect their membership in the world elite, rather than to values and beliefs arising from their membership in the national elite (Lutzker, 1960; Modelski, 1970: 166–68).[4] (One can compare, for example, Jawaharlal Nehru or Cordell Hull to John Foster Dulles or Dean Acheson.) The need to choose between the two sets of values poses a dilemma, which they tend to resolve by selective information processing that avoids information and interpretations that point to contradictions or allows the explaining away of contradictions.[5]

The tendency to use this coping strategy is pervasive when the organization collecting and processing information serves a number of masters who have different goals, attitudes, and beliefs. In this case the organization may either become attuned only to information that confirms the beliefs of all its masters or prefer to interpret the information in a manner that satisfies all and avoids organizational stress related to conflicting roles (Kahn et al., 1964). Moreover, the motivational bias toward a definition of the situation that will not create role-based conflict among the various subcultures in which the information processing organization simultaneously participates or between the organization and the different masters it simultaneously serves is highly like to survive negative feedback and new information that should have undermined its validity. In other words, the organization is prone to premature cognitive closure.

An illustration of the consequences of serving more than one master can be found during the early days of bombing North Vietnam, in 1965, when the U.S. Defense Intelligence Agency had to deal with counterpressures from the army and the air force. The army wanted to prove that the bombing policy had failed and that North Vietnamese forces were pouring into the South, because it wanted to introduce American ground forces on a large scale. The air force, on the other hand, wanted to show that the bombings were effective and that only a few North Vietnamese troops were infiltrating the South (McGarvey, 1973). The DIA chose a compromise that refuted none of the contradictory claims, stating: "Enemy infiltration continued at a rate higher than last month. However, the cumulative effect of U.S. bombing has seriously degraded his ability to mount a large-scale offensive" (McGarvey, 1973: 320).

General Problems in Organizational
Information Processing

Organizations are putatively neutral but in actuality have only a limited ability to achieve rationality. The quality of their information processing suffers from serious constraints, and their learning capability is poor. These attributes are pronounced under conditions of high ambiguity regarding means-ends or cause-effect relationships and regarding the criteria for evaluating the quality of outcomes. Consequently, organizational structure, missions, and processes bias the quality of information processing.

Access and avoidance. In the sprawling foreign policy and defense bureaucracies, the question of access to information is critical. Because of the importance attached to secrecy and deception, access is much more constrained than in other decision domains. The combination of secrecy, ambiguity, uncertainty, and complexity, together with the large quantity of information, make understanding the structure of information flow critical to the comprehension of information processing outcomes. I shall outline here only the broad framework and its implications.

The core questions are, Who gets access to or sees what, when, and in what form (e.g. raw data, brief summaries, inferences)? In principle, information can flow in three directions: from the top of the decision-making hierarchy down, from the lower levels of the bureaucracy up, and between subunits within the same organization or between various organizations at the same level. The three patterns differ significantly.

Information flowing from the top down deals with the decision-makers' areas of acute interest and with goals and plans about which the lower echelons are to provide information. It supplies the guidelines for the information search. But as knowledge moves down the hierarchy, it goes through transformations that make it less detailed and more general. In the process the security declassification of the information declines, making it more accessible but at the same time less useful.

Information flowing from the lower levels up is either a direct response to the demands from the top or an offering based on the collectors' guesses, intuitions, and inferences from past experience of what is of interest at the top—whether as a cue for reevaluation of current policies and goals, a basis for new initiatives, or a bolster for the parochial goals of the organization. As the information moves up, however, it loses its original form, acquiring the form of interpretations and inferences as it is screened and categorized. It becomes accessible to a decreasing number of individuals and organizations as it becomes more highly classified, and it is seen less by area experts and more by foreign policy generalists. In some cases limiting the lower echelons' access to information creates a paradox: those who have access are so preoccupied with other tasks and issues that they have little time to deal in depth with all the information available on each issue, whereas those who have time and competence do not have access. This was seen in the Vietnam case. Referring to the State Department's Research and Policy Planning staffs, Chester Cooper, a senior member of the Johnson administration, observes: "These folk saw so few important communications on Vietnam that their assistance to policymakers was minimal. This was especially unfortunate, since those who had the necessary access tended to be so imprisoned in day-to-day operations and chronic crises that they had little time themselves for contemplative or innovative analysis" (1970: 415).

Information that flows horizontally between subunits and organizations involves interactions between equals reflecting the efficient exchange of benefits from a division of labor based on competence and specialization. The information exchanged can take various forms (e.g. all available data, some of them encapsulated data), depending on the existing terms of reciprocity among the subunits and organizations, which mirror either the formal rules of exchange or, where no such rules exist, the results of tacit and explicit bargaining.

The scope of access to information thus has two dimensions: (1) access regarding a particular issue and (2) access across issues. The higher one is in the hierarchy, the more access one has on both dimensions, and vice versa. The dimensions reflect the need-to-know principle and the specialization-and-compartmentalization principle. The degree of access indirectly becomes a measure of status within the organization and the decisionmaking structure as a whole.[6] Stated more generally, the direction of information flow and access to and dissemination of information are the result of dependencies between the providers and the consumers of the information, the competencies of the organizations involved, and the distribution of resources, particularly power.

Access to information may reflect not the actual need to know, based on such rational, functional considerations as position, role, and responsibility for relevant decisions, but the quality of personal relationships, including trust and distrust, among members of the decisionmaking group. Access and the prevention of access are used as a resource in power plays, so that some are rewarded with the privilege of knowing what they do not necessarily need to know and others are punished by being denied information that they need to carry out their tasks. The practice of manipulating information flow is common in the foreign policy and national security domains, where the norms of secrecy provide a façade of legitimacy for its use. This motivated intervention by high political echelons introduces ambiguity and uncertainty into decisions made at lower levels in the bureaucracy regarding who should see what because such functional rules as the need to know do not prevail anymore. The resulting confusion is likely to disrupt the flow and the rational distribution of information and thus affect negatively the overall quality of information processing. For example, when, in the summer of 1968, President Johnson was displeased with Secretary of Defense Clark Clifford's strong support for a complete halt of the bombing in order to break the stalemate in the Paris talks, he struck Clifford's name from the distribution list for sensitive telegrams and restricted all other Defense Department officials from receiving telegrams about the Paris negotiations. Access to this information was given again five weeks later after the policy was changed to favor a unilateral cessation of bombing in North Vietnam. There was a general atmosphere of confusion in the administration regarding who had access to what confidential information; even senior members of the administration, such as the director of the State Department's Bureau of Intelligence and Research, were kept in the dark about sensitive developments. Access to telegrams was frequently based on whether a particular official was "on the team" or close enough to the highest echelons to be trusted. Consequently, unpopular ideas could be easily rejected on the ground that their advocates were not privy to what was actually going on (Cooper, 1970: 402–5, 415–16).

Intelligence organizations face two main information processing situations. In the first, the parameters of the problem are framed deductively by the top decisionmakers, and the organization's task is to collect and provide information relating to those parameters as initially defined. In the second, the organization identifies a real or imagined problem in its undirected scanning of the environment for information, defines the parameters of the problem incrementally, based on available information, and presents the problem to top decisionmakers in a structured form that includes its definition, possible options, and an evaluation of the implications of each.

The latitude for manipulating information to serve the organization's preferences and goals is much broader in the second situation. In fact, the organization can use such situations to capture the attention of the top decisionmakers and divert them from, or even prevent them from dealing with, other subjects that are of less interest to the organization or that it considers damaging to itself. Thus the organization avoids anticipated crises and the resulting stress for individual members.[7] Organizations may prefer the status quo even when available information indicates the possibility that change will lead to important opportunities for gain, because opportunities, too, can trigger a crisis and produce excitement and anxiety that the leading members of the organization may wish to avoid. They may ignore information that will mean an additional work load, stress, adaptation of the standard operating procedures, reallocation of the division of labor within the organization, and probable organizational infighting.[8] Whether the impending crisis is one of threat or opportunity, the more uncertain the consequences of coping, the more severe the crisis will be, and the more likely the organization is to ignore problem-related cues in available information, unless dealing with the problem is imposed by some higher authority. But that authority may not be aware of the impending problem and thus may not get involved.

Access is also affected by the fact that organizations cherish their autonomy. Information management becomes a means of safeguarding that autonomy: they do not provide all the information to the external decisionmakers. Military organizations in particular are unwilling to provide civilian decisionmakers with the full information about their doctrines and operational tactics. Or they may introduce a high level of unnecessary complexity in a deliberate attempt to limit the understanding and consequently the influence of civilian decisionmakers (J. S. Levy, 1986: 207). Decisionmakers are therefore not always able to analyze the operational and strategic arguments raised by the military critically and place them in the broader political-military context. Ignorance helps to promote the options preferred by the military without the decisionmakers' fully realizing the constraints it imposes on the rationality of the political process.

Access to information is thus differential within and between organizations, so that the image of the world within and between organizations also differs. Each viewpoint takes in different parts of the picture, perhaps even dissimilar pictures. Feedback, which is an important element of learning, can thus have different meanings for the various subunits of the same organization. Not only is the feedback viewed within different contexts but uncertainty and ambiguity also obscure what the outcomes of past behavior were and whether they should be regarded as successes or failures—thus enhancing the tendency of the organization and its subunits to learn what they want to learn rather than what they should learn. Because experience has such a segmented, uneven effect, the retrieval of information from the organization's recorded history produces dissimilar sets of experiences and lessons, depending on who retrieves it and for what purposes.

Feedback, feedwithin, and feedforward. An organization must be attuned to three different types of feed. *Feedback* from the external environment regards the results of the organization's past behavior and *feed-*

forward entails scanning the environment for indications of future trends and anticipated changes. Unlike the individual decisionmaker, groups and organizations also attend closely to *feedwithin*, which involves monitoring the quality of administrative performance (e.g. coordination, information flow) and the internal social interactions of members and units and their impact on the future nature and needs of the group and organization (Bogart, 1980). This three-tiered attention span increases the burden of search, collection, and interpretation both quantitatively and qualitatively. Moreover, because feedback, feedforward, and feedwithin information can have mutual interaction effects, not only does the amount of information to be processed grow but the assessment of its actual and potential social influences adds ambiguity and uncertainty about the substance of the information as well. Consequently, there are also perpetual dilemmas of choice between manipulating information for personal benefit or using it to advance the interests of the organization as a whole even at a cost to personal interests and parochial subunit interests that may not be congruent with the overall interests. Coping with these dilemmas consumes time and energy and diverts attention from feedback and feedforward information. It may reduce the quality of the search for and the processing of information in these two categories, particularly when the feedwithin information dominates attention. All other types of information may then come to be viewed in terms of and subjected to the needs deriving from the preoccupation with feedwithin, that is, the concentration on system control and coordination. Feedback and feedforward information may not have the positive adaptation effects they are supposed to have unless they are viewed as contributing to the control and coordination of the system as a whole in a way that benefits the decisionmaking group or organization in question. The preoccupation with feedwithin is likely, then, to have negative effects on the quality of information processing and can lead to all sorts of perceptual gaps of cognizance, relevance, and evaluation.

Even when feedback is attended to and the organization attempts to learn lessons from its experience, the learning is often lopsided and selective, directed by the organization's subculture, so that two different organizations or even two subunits within the same organization learn different lessons from the same experience. Moreover, selectivity is sensitive to salient cues, particularly the preferences of main actors in the organizations' task environment (e.g. the president) that control the allocation of vital organizational resources.

As task ambiguity and elusiveness grow, so does the tendency to rely on quantifiable and visible feedback and ignore other feedback (Lovell, 1984). But unlike market organizations, with their profit orientation, nonmarket organizations do not have clearly defined goals that provide an obvious consensual focal point. Judging the quality of performance of nonmarket organizations is difficult because if objectives are not clearly and consensually defined, constructing agreed-upon measures of success or failure at each stage of program implementation is difficult. In other words, information about the quality of performance is ambiguous for lack of consensual judgment criteria for interpreting performance. Failure or success has to be dramatic to become obvious. Routine feedback from performance is likely to cause little or no adjustment of performance because of its ambiguity on the one hand and the organization's preference for inertia on the other hand. As a consequence, feedback is manipulated to serve this inertia. The nature of feedback information about foreign policy performance makes it particularly susceptible to manipulation, so that failure is often recognized when the time to adjust effectively or without great cost is already past.

Ambiguity, the elusiveness of the definition of objectives, and the lack of clear measures of success and failure have significant implications for interactions within and between organizations. Interorganizational and intraorganizational disagreements over what specifically should be done to achieve general agreed-upon goals and how the general goals should be translated into specific subgoals are common. Measuring how policies have been functioning poses a severe problem because each organizational unit has its own measurements of performance according to what it believes to be important. Often these measurements are not integrated into a uniform system that evaluates the overall effectiveness of the policy. Feedback is thus fragmented and manipulable, and the actual failure to achieve goals goes unobserved.

Ambiguity was a predominant attribute of information about most aspects of the Vietnam conflict. It significantly increased the complexity of evaluating the impact of programs (feedback) as well as organizational effectiveness in their execution (feedwithin). To overcome this problem, a heavy emphasis was placed on the use of quantitative indicators for measuring success and monitoring the implementation of programs. For instance, although in 1965 there was a broad consensus over the need to increase military pressure on North Vietnam, there was no agreement over what the pressure was to accomplish. Operation Rolling Thunder (the bombing of North Vietnam from February 1965 to March 1968) was attributed at least six different goals: to reduce the flow of supplies and troops being infiltrated by North Vietnam; to limit the combat capacity of the Vietcong; to raise morale in South Vietnam; to demonstrate U.S. commitment and resolve; to bring North Vietnam to the negotiating table; and to reduce criticism of the administration. The measurement of progress in achieving each of these objectives required different indicators. Particularly problematic in this regard were the last three objectives, partly because data that could have measured them directly could not be obtained. For example, infiltration had to be measured indirectly by air surveillance, electronic sensors, the monitoring of enemy communications, and, to a much lesser degree, patrols. These methods could produce only rudimentary data because of redundancy, double-counting, the impossibility of fully and consistently covering all infiltration routes, and other technical problems. Alternative indicators, such as assessing bomb damage, relied on pilots' reports, which tended to be exaggerated and often unsubstantiated. Using the number of tons of bombs dropped as an indicator was also misleading because when aircraft carrying bombs were engaged by enemy fighters, they sometimes had to jettison their bombs to increase maneuverability; the bombs fell on unauthorized targets and into swamps, jungles, and fields. Moreover, North Vietnam was not an industrialized country, so the damage it incurred from bombing was limited, no matter how may tons of bombs were dropped. At the same time this monitoring technique had feedback and feedwithin effects on organizational behavior. On the one hand, the air force's and the navy's operational activities were oriented toward flying more sorties and dropping more bombs. On the other hand, the technique encouraged interservice competition for a larger share of the number of sorties flown and the number of tons of bombs dropped (Thompson, 1980: 85–92).

Types of decisionmaker. Organizations view information as instrumental and manipulative and use it to advance their self-interest. Their self-interest is not necessarily congruent with the formal goals set for the organization; the information may also be manipulated to advance the parochial goals of individuals within the organization. Whether and which of these happens depends on the type of chief decisionmaker involved. Five basic types are suggested by Downs (1967); climbers, conservers, zealots, advocates, and statesmen. All use their position and the standard operating procedures of the organization as tools to manipulate information to serve their goals.

Climbers are completely self-centered. They use their position and manipulate information to advance their major interests: power, prestige, and self-aggrandizement. Their relation to authority is submissive: they search for, analyze, and adapt information to please their superiors. Consequently, they tend to assert their own authority over subordinates to ensure that they will not get out of line and that they will be attentive and supply facts and judgments to serve their superiors' interests. Climbers make certain to neglect or actively subdue all information that is harmful to their interests. They submit to what they consider to be the dominant views, yet they are flexible if they sense that the dominant views have changed.

The *conservers* are also self-centered, but their interests are convenience and security. Unlike climbers, they do not care much for hyperactivity and try to avoid involvement and active search activities if they do not sense a threat to their security. They tend to be submissive toward superiors and benign toward subordinates so long as the subordinates do not seem to threaten their own secure position. Conservers are extremely cautious, self-effacing, risk aversive, and cognitively conservative. They follow rules rigidly so that if things go wrong they can easily protect themselves. Conservers thus avoid innovations and reassessments, which may undermine the stable environment they have constructed for themselves. They search selectively for information that assures that their current definition of the situation is still valid and avoid discrepant information or try to underplay its importance.

Zealots are fervently devoted to a limited number of goals that they consider sacrosanct—whether for selfish or altruistic motives or, often, a combination of both. Regarding those goals, they tend to be almost single-minded and completely inflexible, and they are particularly attentive to goal-advancing information; in fact, all information is assessed in terms of its implications for their goals. On the other hand, they compromise on other matters if they can thereby gain the support of others for their own sacrosanct commitments. For these they will risk nonconformity and even confrontation with superiors. At the same time zealots demonstrate strong, assertive leadership toward subordinates and do not allow them to express views that might undermine the all-important goals.

Advocates are loyal to a broader set of policies than zealots. They are willing to promote views that will help their organization and its policies even at a personal cost to themselves and will even go so far as to antagonize their superiors. Yet in general, since they are other-directed, advocates are susceptible to influence by superiors, equals, and even subordinates. They are likely to promote issues that are under their own jurisdiction and thus tend to be sensitive to information that impinges on those issues and to underestimate the value or relevance of other information. Yet within the range of issues that are under their jurisdiction they can show considerable flexibility and open-mindedness. Advocates are prepared to compromise and to make trade-offs so long as they do not cause damage to the organization, in order to gain the future support of others for evaluations and policies that they feel will increase the power and prestige of their organization. In fact, advocates often identify the national interest with the interest of the organization they lead or are a member of.

The *statesmen* (and stateswomen) are a relatively rare breed. They are loyal to society as a whole, and their goals are mostly altruistic. They take a broad view and are inner-directed, so that they persist in maintaining their outlook and do not succumb to pressures to conform. Statesmen are open-minded, willing to consider new information and judgments even at a cost to their personal and organizational interests because they can see the broader societal picture. They tend to be academic and philosophical in style and to seek to reconcile conflicting points of view whenever possible, especially when their responsibilities clash with those views. However, when the contradiction between the two is brought to a head by particular information, they may use their intellectual skills to square the circle—to apply sophisticated cognitive techniques that distort the interpretation of the information. Their values usually do not allow them to avoid or neglect the bothersome information altogether, but they find other ways to deal with inconsistencies (see also Chapter 3).

At the various levels of decisionmaking and in the various agencies involved in the Vietnam War, managers representing these types can be readily identified. For example, the advocate is typified by General Earle Wheeler, and the other Joint Chiefs of Staff, who gave military-inclined analyses to incoming information. The Joint Chiefs saw themselves as supporters of the commander in the field; they used available information for this purpose and did not attempt to organize data to systematically assess strategy (Komer, 1986: 77; Krepinevich, 1986: 165–68). The zealot is best typified by Admiral Grant Sharp, commander of U.S. armed forces in the Pacific. The climber is perhaps represented by Henry Kissinger as well as by both Presidents Johnson and Nixon. Secretary of State Dean Rusk represents the conserver (Halberstam, 1972: 343–46, 634–35), while Clark Clifford (in 1968) and Robert McNamara (especially as of 1967) are closer to the statesman type than to any other.

Standard operating procedures. Information processing organizations, like organizations in general, are active rather than reflective. The search for information and its processing often follow action rather than precede it in order to justify the actions taken or choices made. Thus organizations fantasize threats and opportunities that justify action. They are bound to programs and standard operating procedures (SOPs) that reflect crystallized learning experiences and that are applied consistently and often mindlessly across situations (Allison, 1971; Halperin, 1974; O'Reilly, 1983; Starbuck, 1983, 1985). As a consequence, organizations can react quickly to environmental challenges by activating previously learned programs; these encompass role allocations among members. Since changes in programs and SOPs could threaten the established role allocations and the power structure, the environment has to be a stable one, where established routines can deal with the level of change. Organizations are slow to adapt cognitively and operationally to environmental cues and demonstrate defensive conservatism in the belief that the future is only marginally different from the past and present. Information that indicates a need for nonroutinized change and reorientation is ignored, belittled, or explained away. Preset programs and SOPs construct reality to fit their assumptions through their impact on the processing of information.

SOPs not only are guides to action but are also constraints on and shapers of cognitive operations. In fact, they are a source of anchoring heuristics; they provide ready-made responses to internal or external stimuli, so the stimuli can be interpreted with little reflection. In this sense they are rational only if the responses to stimuli are flexible enough to adapt to changing circumstances; but SOPs are usually inflexible. Paradoxically, the more complex and uncertain the environment, the less likely SOPs are to be flexible—first, because such environments foster complex SOPs that represent a large investment of time and intraorganizational bargaining. Once a SOP is established and accepted, the organization becomes committed to it and avoids making necessary adjustments. Second, the more complex and ambiguous the environment, the higher the perceived probability of failure is; and since exchanging an established and familiar routine, which has already gained acceptance and probably has some record of past success, for an untested alternative looks like a risky gamble, conservatism prevails instead.

SOPS have been blamed for a number of inadequacies in the U.S. intelligence community's performance in Vietnam.

The kinds of intelligence most needed in Vietnam were simply alien to the standard institutional repertoires of most US and GVN [Government of Vietnam] intelligence services involved. [They] . . . were focused in classic style mostly on military order of battle. Identifying and locating enemy main force units and movements (or targets) was the order of the day, to the neglect of such elements of a highly unconventional enemy establishment as local self-defense groups or the Viet Cong infrastructure.

Many military intelligence officers . . . seemed to have closed minds to such other facets of the war. It was not their job, after all. (Komer, 1986: 61)

In information processing, deadlines are important; beyond the deadline the information loses relevance or becomes completely useless. Some SOPs deal with deadlines—for example, reports have to be submitted periodically on a particular day and hour. To meet deadlines requires that information processing activities, which involve interorganizational and intraorganizational cooperation be tightly synchronized and that projects be precisely scheduled. In this way participants know how, when, and for how long to play their roles, and the overall amount of time is allocated rationally—scheduling is especially important when the work is sequential (McGrath and Rotchford, 1983). Thus uncertainty, conflicting organizational interests, and scarcity of time are managed efficiently. A highly competitive or conflictory organizational environment enhances the need for coordination norms; but at the same time it makes coordination less feasible insofar as it affects actors' ability to carry out their operations as scheduled, increasing the probability of bottlenecks in information processing, which lead in turn to decisions based on incomplete, low-quality, or outdated information about the definition of the problem, options, and outcomes.

Organizations deal with ambiguity by avoiding it. Consequently information dealing with general or long-term developments receives little attention compared to information dealing with the specific and current. Information about long-term developments that does not suggest clear, immediate deadlines is easier to ignore or postpone dealing with. SOPs are structured to deal with the immediate, providing an unambiguous, albeit satisficing, response in an otherwise ambiguous, uncertain, complex environment (Etheredge, 1981: 128–29; March and Olsen, 1980: 50; March and Simon, 1958: 169–71).

Operational imperatives. Organizations like to be, or at least look, busy. If they do not, their budget may be cut, their personnel reduced, their status diminished, and the like. Thus an underburdened organization collects information nobody needs, just to keep busy; and to prove how busy it is, it transmits unnecessary information upward. Information of marginal value is artificially overvalued by attributing to it meaning it does not have.

This tendency can be exacerbated when organizations that collect and process information, such as intelligence organizations, scan the environment for information, not always knowing if and for what decisions it is or will be needed. Either the organization is not told of the purpose by the decisionmakers or the decisionmakers themselves are unable to anticipate future contingencies and hence to guide intelligence gathering. The easiest rule to apply is to collect, store, or disseminate anything that has or may have a vague or remote relationship to security and foreign policy—which means almost everything—to cover all possible future requests for information. Second, and related to the above, since information gathering is separated from evaluation and implementation, the organization that collects information is able to transfer the costs of redundancy to other organizations and at the same time enjoy the benefits of covering all contingencies, ensuring that in the future the charge that too little information was provided cannot be leveled at it. Finally, the cultural commitment to reason and rational discourse means that "the gathering of information provides a ritualistic assurance that appropriate attitudes about decision making exist. . . . The belief that more information characterizes better decisions engenders a belief that having information, in itself, is good and that a person or organization with more information is better than a person or organization with less" (Feldman and March, 1981: 177–78).

This symbolic value of information leads to the gathering of more information than is actually justified and to a belief in its instrumental value even when unfounded. In turn, the quantity of information increases the decisionmaker's confidence, even though redundant information in fact produces an overload that impairs judgment (O'Reilly, 1983: 127). Chester Cooper, a member of McGeorge Bundy's staff, comments about the information flow in Saigon and Washington:

Critical statistics on priority programs in key provinces, graphs, slides and charts, regression curves [were requested]. Numbers! There was a number mill in every military and AID [Agency for International Development] installation in Vietnam. Numbers flowed into Saigon and from there into Washington like the Mekong River during the flood season. Sometimes the numbers were plucked out of the air, sometimes the numbers were not accurate. Sometimes they were accurate but not relevant. Sometimes they were relevant but misinterpreted. (1970: 422)

Situational effects: crisis and stress. In crisis situations scanning for information intensifies, which in turn tends to overload communication channels. Yet information received is likely to be similar to information of the past because of the heavy reliance on SOPs and previous ways of processing and interpreting information and the low complexity of communication. As the threat grows, so does the centralization of authority (C. F. Hermann, 1963; Paige, 1972; Smart and Vertinsky, 1977; Staw, Sandelands, and Dutton, 1981).[9] Much more information flows up to the top, and less is screened at earlier stages. At the same time, in situations of high threat, complexity, and uncertainty the lower echelons attempt to avoid responsibility out of fear of failure, thus inadvertently enhancing the tendency toward centralization.

In crisis situations the total number of communication channels and screening checkpoints that are used for the exchange and dissemination of information is reduced. Yet, as noted, the overall amount of information increases because of objective circumstances that lead to an intensified search for information. The combined effect of the reduced number of communication channels and screening checkpoints, the increased amount of information, and the increased centralization of authority is that the information flows through fewer channels, causing transmission bottlenecks and an increase in information processing tasks per time unit, subunit, and individual. The augmented work load reinforces the stress and anxiety already inherent in the threat to values posed by the crisis situation and decreases the effectiveness of screening routines, further reducing decisionmakers' capability to deal efficiently with available information.

Moreover, as time pressure increases and interactions and exchanges of information within decisionmaking units decrease, the efficiency of the organization as an information processing unit declines because efforts to coordinate processes and responses among members and among organizations are limited (Bronner, 1982). Compartmentalization is a formidable obstacle to the necessary coordination, exchange, and flow of information and ideas, and the division of labor becomes counterproductive. The result may be that a single individual or a few individuals monopolize policymaking.

An analyst of American information processing observed these symptoms during the Yom Kippur crisis:

There was a flood of "raw" data to the top, and a significant acceleration of the entire information processing system. . . . Communication became mostly "vertical," with little or no time for the "horizontal" circulation and analysis of information . . . [T]his led to complaints that only Kissinger and a few select NSC [National Security Council] aides knew the whole picture, and that they were in fact overloaded with a mass of information, much of it lacking the expert interpretation needed to put it into focus. . . .

Though the amount of information required and generated was substantially greater than under non-crisis conditions, much of it was personally collected, analyzed, and used by Kissinger and his closest aides alone. By centralizing American diplomacy around his personal contacts with foreign leaders, Kissinger guaranteed to himself a near monopoly on the information regarding the crucial diplomatic issues and the positions of the negotiating parties. (Dowty, 1984: 303–4, 305–6)

Crisis and stress also increase the weight and probability of intuitive and emotional responses compared to analytic ones, with adverse, stress-bound physiological responses further impairing analytic capabilities. Stress can induce leading figures in the decisionmaking hierarchy to withdraw (C. F. Hermann, 1963). Withdrawal behavior can take a number of forms, such as a nervous breakdown, resignation and apathy, or, alternatively, hyperactivity that reflects a need to get rid of the problem by doing something drastic.[10] Hyperactive decisionmakers may abandon the SOPs used for carefully monitoring and anticipating the adversary's moves, which were originally introduced to avoid an unwanted escalation to hostilities, and may show less reluctance to use force with less prior deliberation than they did before. Stress also reduces the number of communication channels used between the top leadership and the lower levels in the hierarchy, and thus the knowledge gap between the center and the periphery increases, adversely affecting the inward and outward flow of relevant information.

Stress mounting beyond a certain functional level, stress that is often enhanced by surprise and uncertainty, increases interorganizational factionalism and conflict and intensifies parochialism, which in its turn leads to a further decrease in the sharing of information within the organization (C. F. Hermann, 1963; Smart and Vertinsky, 1977). Reduced communication and the sharing of information produce redundancy in information processing activities, inefficient synchronization and an ineffective division of labor, and a wasteful allocation of time. A likely consequence is an information overload within some subunits while others have unused time resources.

As the war in Vietnam went on without victory and an acceptable resolution became more elusive, criticism by the public and the Congress became more hostile and the Johnson administration felt more and more isolated and anxious. Those feelings were accompanied by a tendency toward greater centralization of authority and an increasing appetite for information at the top. Washington wanted to know everything and take charge, circumventing lower levels, like the commander of American forces in the Pacific. At the highest decisionmaking levels the officials' fatigued minds had been so long under siege that they had lost the ability to think innovatively and imaginatively or, even worse, to distinguish reality from unreality. President Johnson became extremely secretive, and his secretiveness influenced people in other layers of the administration to behave similarly, causing more disruption of the information flow and further centralization of decisionmaking in the president and the inner group. The information processing style showed the stress of a heavy work load—everyday duties included coping with Vietnam as well as other emerging crises—and a psychological sense of threat that led to a concentration on tactics and immediate problems as opposed to longer-range planning (Cooper, 1970: 413–27; Hoopes, 1969: 117, 150).

Stressful situations do, however, have positive side effects. Some of the negative effects of bureauorganizational politics are mitigated in situations where the stakes are high. Information that is usually distorted in the course of many transformations while going up through all levels of the hierarchy now enters the organization at a higher level and, against established rules, can bypass some of the levels between the entry point and the users. Thus the probability of errors is reduced. Since time is scarce, opportunities for bureaucratic politicking are also reduced. More of the information processing is done by top-level decisionmakers, who apply a broader view to the analysis than those lower down can. Consequently the information is less affected at this final stage by parochial interests, and such interests become less legitimate because of the high stakes involved, making it much more difficult, though not impossible, to justify a preference for a narrow parochial view. Decisionmakers are less reluctant to use informal channels and extraorganizational advice and to deviate from SOPs (Brecher with Geist, 1980; Downs, 1967; George, 1974; Holsti and George, 1975; Wilensky, 1967) because the organization's leadership realizes that with the high stakes involved, low-quality information processing may be very costly to them personally as well as to their organization. The evidence for such effects supports the view that stress is functional up to a certain point.

Yet circumventing regular procedures also results in the suspension of the usual screening process, which leads to an information overload that can be highly dysfunctional (see Chapter 2). Moreover, because stressful situations are expected to occur at one point or another, organizations prepare for them; they rely on contingency plans, applying them thoughtlessly and thus canceling some of the useful functional effects of stress while reintroducing organizational inertia. The final outcome in terms of the quality of information processing depends in each case on the balance between functional and dysfunctional effects.

In sum, the restriction on the effectiveness of information processing, the decrease of control and autonomy at the lower levels, and the ensuing burden at the top decisionmaking levels increase centralization at the cost of growing inefficiency and a rising probability of error in analyzing the problem, the options, and the implications because the repertoire of past knowledge is emphasized and the important and novel aspects of the problem are neglected and underestimated. In addition, the combination of the centralization of control, information overload, and overburdened channels of communication increases the probability of error in transmission, which may be critical for the accurate evaluation of threat.

In organizations that deal continually with potentially disruptive and threatening situations that involve a high degree of uncertainty, ambiguity, and complexity, such as organizations dealing with national security and foreign affairs, the top-level officials and decisionmakers may adopt a wait-and-see attitude toward information about threats. First, experience has taught them that lower-level officials and subunits exaggerate threats either to project an image of their own importance or to cover themselves in case some far-fetched threat really does materialize. Second, in their experience most potential threats fail to materialize. Third, not enough resources are available to respond to all alleged threats simultaneously. And finally, the ambivalence inherent in most international political situations makes available at least some reassuring evidence that can support more optimistic expectations. Sometimes such information is actually provided by the adversary as a deception (Betts, 1982: 108; Downs, 1967: 189–90).

The wait-and-see attitude has a number of corollaries. Information is compiled and is assessed repetitively as additional information is added, thus contributing to information overload. What is more, a real threat may finally be recognized as such quite late in the game, when the situation has become difficult to contain or resolve, even though signals regarding its existence were available much earlier. Yet it must be emphasized that delay sometimes makes sense in spite of its possible negative consequences.

The slow process of learning and adjusting to negative feedback creates a self-defeating momentum. As time passes and the old policies lead top political decisionmakers to invest more and more political and material resources, the decisionmakers may find it preferable to ignore suggestions to adjust. By then the cost of admitting ultimate responsibility for expensive mistakes has become high both practically and psychologically.

During the spring of 1967 those civilian officials who had supported the "graduated pressures" approach to Hanoi since 1964 reappraised and repudiated it. This strategy assumed that the prospects of mounting destruction would eventually erode the will of North Vietnam to continue the war in the South. But by February 1967 most civilian officials had come to the conclusion that increasing pressures only strengthened North Vietnam's determination to fight, a point that was made by both William Bundy and John McNaughton. The Systems Analysis Office in the Pentagon made a similar point about enlarging the number of troops for the ground war in the South. Yet President Johnson ordered more bombings and authorized an increase in the number of troops up to 525,000, although he was aware that that approach had so far not contributed to progress toward a settlement of the conflict (Thies, 1982: 171–79).

The Effects of Bureauorganizational Politics

Attention to information and its assessment, judgment, and interpretation are strongly affected by the structure of relationships within the bureaucratic organization, but they are also affected by the relationship between the organization and the political environment in which it operates. What is the relationship between organizational and national goals, and where do group processes come in? In the foreign affairs and security domains, national goals, beyond the most basic ones, such as survival, are rarely specifically and operationally defined. Because it is difficult to predict and anticipate the numerous contingencies that may arise, it is preferable to define national goals in terms that encompass as broad a range of contingencies as possible and still preserve maximum flexibility for decisionmakers to react.

Compared to national goals, organizational goals and the standard operating procedures to realize them are, formally or informally, well defined and specified. The relevant organizations collect and interpret information on specific issues and use it to specify the acute national goals as they perceive them. The goals are then translated into operative and specific details, and ways to reach the goals must be set by relevant organizations (Freedman, 1976; Oneal, 1982), though they do not necessarily agree on the definitions of the goals or on the ways to implement them. Bridges must then be built to link various, sometimes competing organizational goals and procedures with the national goals and policies. The high level of ambiguity and uncertainty makes this task more difficult in the foreign policy and security domains than in other domains because agreement is more difficult to reach. The small group is the arena in which these bridges are constructed through a social process involving argumentation and politicking among proponents of competing views. Appropriate goals and policies emerge sequentially and are then used to focus attention on particular constraints, imperatives, and alternatives. The first priority for each participant is to avoid failure, since the costs inhibit organizational interests. It is not unusual for an unattractive alternative to be chosen if it promises a high probability of not making things worse (P. A. Anderson, 1983a). Justification becomes a vital element of organizational behavior. It serves to convince the members that the organization knows what it is doing and to resolve ambiguities in order to create shared attitudes among the members. At the same time justification serves to convince outsiders of the organization's rationality and efficiency (Staw, 1980), which ensures its continued existence and the continued or even increased allocation of resources to it. In argumentation and justification, information is the main tool of each participant, including those who are powerful enough to impose their views on others. Information is transformed to fit the needs of the participants, often with little consideration for its actual meaning.

In the security and foreign policy issue-areas, the tasks of searching for collecting, sorting, interpreting, and disseminating information are allocated among a number of organizations according to both functional and need-to-know principles. These organizations then pass the product on to the political decisionmakers, either as raw data, a summary, or a full or partial interpretation. Attention to information at the lower echelon is therefore affected by prior knowledge, inferences, or expectations about the overall goals, plans, and interests that the information is supposed to serve, that is, the broader policy context. But these are often inaccurate.

In the first place, the bureaucratic echelon, by its very nature and composition, has a narrowly defined role, which focuses it on information that is of clear and immediate significance for the issue-areas it is responsible for. Amid the great volume of inflowing information, each subunit has to pay attention to what is recognized as relevant, and relevance is defined in narrow terms. Information that may be of great value for the interpretation of the broader picture is therefore lost. When customers for information distributed from the center of the decisionmaking system are located at the periphery (e.g. an ambassador in a foreign country), the loss may be acute. The periphery could, on the one hand, provide essential feedback that might lead to a complete reevaluation of the situation, but on the other hand, as mentioned earlier, the periphery could—for reasons of rank, status, distance, and secrecy—be unaware of the details of the center's perceptions, evaluations, and goals (Betts, 1980–81, 1982). That is, the periphery, even when it has access to relevant information, is not always aware of its significance and may decide not to process and transmit information that seems to it, based on its limited perspective, to be at best marginal but that could in fact be vital. As a result, relevant feedback from the periphery, capable of providing decisionmakers at the center with critical knowledge that would prompt them to correct and adjust their definition of the situation or their action orientation, is missing.

Second, the lower-level bureaucratic echelon that is responsible for collecting, sorting, collating, and disseminating information is often not let in on the overall picture because of concern over secrecy, and consequently it may be unaware of the full scope and true nature of the information needs of the higher political echelon. Thus the bureaucratic echelon does not always pay attention to information that could be important to the political echelon; even if it does, it may not accord the information sufficient importance or relevance to justify passing it on to the political authorities. Secrecy, a major characteristic of foreign policy making, constitutes an obstacle to the flow of vital information, not only between international actors but also between organizations and people within a single information processing system. Secrecy often prevents the efficient utilization of available information. The House Select Committee on Intelligence (the Pike Committee), which was organized in July 1975 to investigate the intelligence activities by U.S. government agencies, was told by high U.S. intelligence officials that Kissinger's oversecretive approach was partly to blame for the U.S. intelligence community's failure to monitor events and foresee the outbreak of the Yom Kippur War. Kissinger had been in close diplomatic contact with the Soviets and Arabs in the prewar period and could have provided valuable indicators of Arab capabilities and intentions, yet he denied intelligence officials access to his notes of the talks (Lathem, 1976: 78).

Even when bureaucrats acquire information that is clearly essential, they may fear recrimination if the information is unpleasant to their superiors; and hence unpalatable or embarrassing information is withheld altogether or intentionally misreported (Lebow, 1981: 153–69).[11] For example, the "loss of China" shaded Vietnam reporting by career officers in the State Department. They remembered the fate of their colleagues who wrote frankly from China in the 1940s criticizing the Chinese Nationalists, and the memory inhibited honest reporting of the strength of the Vietcong and the weakness of the Ngo Dinh Diem regime (Thomson, 1973: 101). This type of behavior prevailed at all levels. Thus the army staff intuitively protected the commander from what they felt he would not like to know. When, in April 1965, the military arm of the Military Assistance Command, Vietnam, was asked to do an estimate of the North Vietnamese capacity for reinforcement, the intelligence officer preparing it came up with a staggering number. When he brought it to one of Westmoreland's generals, he was told: "If we tell this to the people in Washington we'll be out of the war tomorrow. We'll have to revise it downward." And the revision was duly made (Halberstam, 1972: 545). Similarly, according to one of the participants in the decisionmaking process, in the early years of Johnson's Vietnam intervention policy Johnson believed that the war was going to be over soon, a belief shared by most members of his inner group. There were reports questioning this belief, but they were unlikely to be included in the president's "night reading" list (Cooper, 1970: 424).

The lower bureaucratic echelon is aware and apprehensive of the high potential for and costs of committing errors in evaluation. The dilemma is more acute the higher the prospective penalty for a failure of judgment is, and hence intelligence organizations may decide to avoid disseminating uncertain forecasts because of the possibility of being proven wrong and losing their credibility, preferring instead to preserve their reputation for a day when they may need it more (Chan, 1979: 172). A stronger temptation is to produce evaluations that are conservative and as close as possible to the views known to be held by the higher echelon. The assumption is that in case of an error the producer of the faulty judgment will, by sharing the errors of higher-level, more powerful decisionmakers, be protected under their umbrella. This phenomenon is especially typical of closed societies (Farrell, 1966). Following the Tet offensive in January 1968, for example, General Westmoreland's position was that the enemy had suffered a total military defeat. The Defense Intelligence Agency's position was different, yet it watered down all of its papers on the subject so that its views could not be determined. But soon after General Wheeler returned from Saigon with Westmoreland's request for an additional 206,000 troops to "clean up" the "defeated enemy," it became legitimate to argue that the Tet offensive had set the United States back, and the DIA became a chief proponent of gloomy estimates (McGarvey, 1973: 325).

Still, one risk cannot be completely avoided: that the lower bureaucratic levels (e.g. intelligence organizations) become scapegoats for the higher political echelon, for failure can be attributed to a lack of or lacunae in the knowledge dimension of a decision. To reduce the chances of being held responsible for possible policy failures, bureaucrats find that it pays to provide general, vague, or ambiguous evaluations of information precisely in those instances when uncertainty and risk are greatest and when policymakers are most in need of as unambiguous a definition of the situation as possible. They create vague and ambiguous assessments by hedging and overwriting, which later allow for a degree of responsibility denial. At the same time such assessments encourage the decisionmakers using them to seize on those parts that support their predispositions (Betts, 1982: 103–4; L. K. Johnson, 1984).

Another strategy used by intelligence and other organizations is to submit large quantities of reports unselectively, covering everything in them to ensure themselves against accusations of not providing the proper information (Harkabi, 1984); they thus contribute to information overload and its negative consequences (discussed in Chapter 2). In the debate over troop withdrawal within the framework of the Vietnamization policy that emerged in mid-1970, agencies were divided about the possible implications of and hence the management of troop withdrawal. Secretary of State William Rogers favored the largest possible withdrawal in the shortest time. Secretary of Defense Melvin Laird, shrewd and politically subtle, favored leaving a residual force of a few hundred thousand; he wanted to reach that number rapidly and yet make the withdrawal look as inexorable as possible. Kissinger was more skeptical about Vietnamization and believed that South Vietnam should be given enough time to adjust to the withdrawal of U.S. troops and that the president should be allowed the discretion to accelerate or slow down withdrawal so that he would have leverage in his negotiations with North Vietnam. The participants were aware of the political credit and, alternatively, the strategic risk of defeat that the policy entailed. Memoranda proliferated, the participants intending them to be available for future reference. Laird "produced a blizzard of memoranda that would make it next to impossible to determine either his real intentions or—what was more important to him—his precise recommendation" (Kissinger, 1979: 477).

A prevailing problem is that verbal probability expressions, such as "not likely," "reasonable chance," and "possible," are used despite the high variability in their interpretations. A decisionmaker receiving a forecast may interpret the event's probability differently from the way the producer of the forecast intended. Not even the context in which the probability forecast appears helps reduce the incongruence between interpretations. Though incongruence can lead decisionmakers to propagate serious errors, verbal probability expressions are very common. People are not always aware of the ambiguity inherent in them and tend to resist numerical probabilities anyway (Beyth-Marom, 1982). Basing decisions on verbal probabilities affords them a means of reducing responsibility in case of failure, especially in situations of high risk and uncertainty.

Competition between organizations over positions, roles, and status has the result, inter alia, that the organizations transmit selective information and interpretations to serve their own parochial interests, their definition of the situation, and the line of action they recommend (Allison, 1971; Allison and Halperin, 1972; Downs, 1967; Halperin, 1974; Kissinger, 1969). To illustrate: The U.S. air force's reports on the results of bombing North Vietnamese targets were at worst false and at best greatly exaggerated. Pilots consistently claimed far greater destruction than the much more accurate photointelligence reflected, but the air force stuck with the exaggerated claims. For the air force the choice was to bomb, which carried prestige and publicity, or do nothing and thus be the loser in the interservice rivalry. At the same time the promotion system created strong incentives for conformity, so that for air force intelligence officers the penalty of criticizing the claims of the organization was very high in terms of advancement. Few dared to take a step that might put their career on the line (Blachman, 1973).

The larger and more complex the organizational network and the greater the urgency of taking action, the greater is the tendency to compromise to obtain concurrence, since action can more easily be taken after members have reached an agreed-upon, collective definition of the situation than before. A larger bureaucracy, however, also means longer lines of communication between the top officials and lower-level ones, creating more opportunities for misunderstanding or the possibility that needed information will not reach its consumers. Furthermore, because large organizations are hierarchical, when the amount of available information increases, subordinates do not pass all of it up the line. Instead they synthesize and summarize the facts, transforming them into synthesized inferences and judgments at an earlier stage, before the information reaches the top. "If the chain of communications is very long, each link must take the judgments of lower echelons and use them as facts" (Destler, 1974: 79). In the process, the higher decisionmaking echelon loses the opportunity to make its own judgments and apply its own perspectives to the information. Thus it is unable to detect, control, and correct the lower echelon's mistakes in information processing.

Compromise and politicking are not necessarily dirty words, however; they do not always cause distortions in information processing but can also contribute to making it more accurate, if correctly channeled. For example, when two organizations are at cross-purposes, each uses available information to promote its goals by biasing the interpretation of the information in its own preferred direction as far as it dares. The final compromise definition of the situation that emerges during interorganizational politicking can be closer to reality than any of the interpretations suggested initially by either organization. Furthermore, because each organization pays selective attention to information in a manner that serves its parochial interests, the overall combined range of attention to information is broader than either one's alone and is thus closer to what it should be, at least partly canceling out the effects of selectivity. Hence the benefits of compromise and politicking have to be weighed against their costs in each case.[12] In other words, the modi operandi of organizations and groups contain inbuilt antinomies in terms of their contribution to the quality of information processing.

Small-Group Structure, Stratification, and Dynamics

Small groups are of different sizes, importance, and functions in the decisionmaking process. Yet they all have a number of attributes in common: members interact continually; members share a basic set of shared values, attitudes, and beliefs and some affective links; and members divide formal and informal roles among themselves (DeLamater, 1974: 39). These attributes generate the core context for the behavior of decisionmakers acting as information processors within a small-group setting.

Attention to information, judgment of its relevance and importance, and preference for one among alternative interpretations are affected by the perceived implications for the group's internal needs, structure, and cohesiveness. For instance, who in the group will benefit and who will lose by focusing the group's attention on particular information or an interpretation thereof? Where a group consensus already exists, is it worthwhile to raise an issue that might cause the disintegration of that convenient consensual framework or to confront powerful members of the group who may have an interest in maintaining it? As for the leaders of the group, should they put their leadership to the test if their suggested interpretations conflict with the interests and concepts of other members? What is the significance of each alternative interpretation for the group's issue-area of main concern, and what amount of group energy and time will it take to consider it?[13]

All of these matters have a bearing on the emotional relations among group members. Being part of the group enhances the desire to be accepted or at least not to be rejected by the other members. The presentation of information and interpretations that might harm the delicate tissue of common precepts is risky in this sense. Generally, the social tissue is woven with much effort over an extended period, and it forms the affective basis of the relations among group members as well as of the members' sense of their acceptance by the others. Hence a tendency to avoid offense is common, even at the price of a conformity that involves distorted perceptions of reality.

Small-group effects on the quality of information processing are complex and antinomic. Decisionmakers operating in a group are likely to be exposed to new information and interpretations more rapidly than if they were operating alone and to arguments they might not have been aware of as independent decisionmakers; both exposure and arguments improve the quality of group members' problem solving and learning. Groups potentially provide individuals a larger scope for learning and a chance for a broader and more complex approach to the analysis of information. Argumentation in the process of group decisionmaking clarifies ambiguities and inconsistencies by disseminating information and alternative perspectives and can illuminate weaknesses in the logical structure of accumulated knowledge and beliefs, particularly with regard to complex problems and for group members who show a moderate to high cognitive complexity (Davis, 1978; Stein and Tanter, 1980: 51). In fact group decisionmaking can have a debiasing effect of forcing individual members to rethink and reconsider their judgments by exposing their biases, particularly their motivational biases, in the process of group discussion. This potential, however, often remains unfulfilled because other attributes and pathologies of the group act to narrow the scope and complexity of information processing operations and encourage parochialism and conformity,[14] which reinforce existing biases. For a group to work cooperatively and effectively it must have a diversity of viewpoints, accompanied by a tolerance for differences of opinion (L. R. Hoffman, 1978a: 82). On the other hand, a large number of alternative interpretations can cause information overload, increasing ambiguity and thereby making errors, or the avoidance of decisions altogether, more likely. Groups develop procedural norms for information processing that reflect their experience. Groups successful in processing large amounts of information are later prepared to attend to most available information; those that fail foster procedures to avoid information. In both cases, if a problem is perceived as having an obvious solution, group members tend to avoid investing resources in collecting and analyzing information and risking intragroup dissent by in-depth discussion (Burnstein and Berbaum, 1983).

Group leaders who depend on the emergence of consensus among members may become biased on several counts at the stages of both consensus formation and consensus change, in particular if the latter involves a reallocation of resources and power. Information that suggests complexity and uncertainty is ignored or at least underestimated, since the higher the level of complexity and uncertainty, the more difficult it is to reach a consensus or change the existing consensus. In the security area, strategic warning forecasts are often ignored if acceptance could upset existing bureaucratic routines (Chan, 1979: 172). Information about alternatives and their effects tends to ignore or exclude the effects considered marginal in order to reduce the amount of opposition that needs to be overcome. Thus, on the whole, information processing and other decisionmaking tasks performed by a group show a mixed quality when compared with the tasks performed by the individual, and in almost all circumstances groups are likely to use significantly more resources than individuals (Holsti and George, 1975: 288).

The size of a group is an important element affecting performance and intragroup interactions. The larger the group, the more inhibited the introverted members become, and thus the influence of the self-confident members who are willing to speak up increases, as does the likelihood of groupthink. The overbearing influence of self-confident members is common where the group has no formal leader who can prevent it (L. R. Hoffman, 1978a: 76–77; Swap, 1984a: 55; Swap, 1984b). The size of the group can be set or can change with functional and situational needs. A fixed number is mostly the case in formal groups; a flexible number, in informal groups. But even when the size is set, the effective group can be either smaller or larger than the formal number. The effective, or inner, group (e.g. minicabinet, or kitchen cabinet), comprises those members who are actually involved and most influential in all stages of decision-making, either because the top decisionmaker values their advice or because the situation demands a small forum for consultation (e.g. the response time is short). Nevertheless, the final decision may have to be formally approved by the plenum if that is required by the formal rules of decision.[15]

Informal groups that do not have well-structured rules of exchange and argumentation or an orderly record of decisions become a source of ambiguous products. The informal atmosphere of exchange may encourage the expression of dissident views, but the drifting style of argumentation may produce fuzzy judgments, evaluations, and decisions. Participants in the discussion have dissimilar perceptions of what was agreed on and what form the consensus took. Yet they often come away with a false sense that some consensual knowledge has emerged and that their views of what transpired are shared by others. This misperception encourages rigidity of judgment, which is stiffened further when they discover that others have different interpretations of what the group's judgments and choices were and they insist that theirs is the only correct version. A main criticism leveled against President Johnson's Tuesday lunch cabinet is that its informal procedures of discussion and decision generated confusion among organizations that had to implement the decisions: they found themselves facing a Rashomon-style situation, in which all the participants had their own version (Humphrey, 1984).

Small-group dynamics breed two main complementary effects, compromise and conformity, which reflect not only the structure of power within the group but also members' skill and capacity to exploit the group's structural attributes to promote their own preferences. The nature of shared perceptions, the manner in which they are formed, and the degree to which they reflect groups' needs and wishes rather than the essence of information determine the degree of reality versus the motivational instrumentality of group concepts. The greater the role of shared perceptions in bolstering group cohesion and group-directed goal attainment, the greater is the risk of faulty information processing and of perceptual distortions of all three kinds—cognizance, relevance, and evaluation.

Group stratification reflects both the functional division of labor, which is actually an expression of formal power, and informal status, which arises from personal relations within the group, such as close personal relations with and easy access to the chief policymaker. Stratification determines the ability of each member to deviate from basic shared perceptions if the available information so indicates.[16] On the other hand, high status in the group, manifested as an ability to gain the maximum attention of other members, brings an acceptance of the conventional wisdom, both because status enhances self-confidence and cognitive conservatism and because other group members are apprehensive of contradicting the status holder. Status thus has a mixed impact on the effects of attention to dissonant information regarding the revision of the common wisdom by the status holder.

The effect of status is partly responsible for the failure of the Israeli intelligence community on the eve of the Yom Kippur War. On the one hand, the exaggerated self-confidence of the director of military intelligence, Major General Eli Zeira, which stemmed from his special status as the top authority on intelligence, head of one of the most prestigious intelligence organizations in the world, candidate next in line for the position of chief of staff, and from his reputation among peers and underlings as both brilliant and arrogant, prevented him from fully reappraising information that challenged his initial evaluation that the likelihood of war was minimal. At the same time, because of Zeira's status, another member of the intelligence community, the Mossad director, Major General Zvi Zamir, hesitated to take a firm stand on his own, although he presented his views that war was likely to the prime minister and the defense minister. Zeira's status was further reinforced by his accurate prediction in May 1973, in a similar situation, that Egypt would not go to war. The Mossad's failure in the Ahmed Bushiki affair, in which an Arab waiter in Lillehammer, Norway, was wrongly identified as one of the commanders of Black September and executed by Mossad agents, who were subsequently caught and tried, along with Zamir's more pessimistic position in May, which was proven wrong, reduced Zamir's credibility and his taste for forcefully challenging the evaluation by military intelligence (Nakdimon, 1982: 29–30, 79–80).

Members' status and roles are related, and the group is composed of individuals who have different roles within it. As a consequence of the distribution of status and roles, members differ in access to, and have unequal sensitivities to, information arriving from the external environment. They perceive information chiefly in terms of its discernible connections with those issues with which they are mostly preoccupied (Jervis, 1976: 206–11; Simon, 1976: 210–12).[17] To illustrate: By the end of 1964 a consensus had been reached among President Johnson's advisers regarding the need to increase military pressure on North Vietnam. Yet there was no agreement on the precise strategy to be used nor on commonly held expectations about the outcomes of military pressure. The military people, as we have seen, favored strong and forceful action that would interdict the supply routes into South Vietnam, destroy North Vietnam's capacity to support the Vietcong, raise the morale of the people in the South, and at the same time punish North Vietnam for its involvement in the South. State Department officials (and some civilians in the Defense Department) favored a gradual, restrained approach, one taking into account the international ramifications of escalation, and stressed less the damage inflicted and more the signaling effect that using force would have on North Vietnam and other Communist countries as well as on U.S. allies. An escalation, they felt, would serve both as an indication of resolve and an invitation to negotiate. When the question of bombing North Vietnam was discussed in early 1965, these decision-makers supported a flexible program of reprisals that would be sensitive to the level of Vietcong activity in the South. The military, however, suggested a forceful program of graduated pressure to convince North Vietnam of the prohibitive cost of subversion and aggression in Southeast Asia (Schandler, 1977: 9–10, 14).

When a decisionmaker has several roles that require different emphases and attention spans, he is liable to internal conflict, as "when the role expectations placed upon him are incompatible, making it impossible to confirm both sets of expectations" (Thomas, 1968: 709). This is a frequent problem for national decisionmakers in foreign policy, whose roles in the national arena (e.g. protecting national interests) sometimes contradict their roles in the international arena (e.g. preserving world peace). Or a role at the partisan domestic level (e.g. party leader) may impose on the decisionmaker a parochial perspective that does not necessarily coincide with the broader national interests. Moreover, the decisionmaker with a number of roles may face the problem of role overload, which means that information processing demands are in excess of his cognitive capacity. The information overload produces cognizance gaps and unsystematic judgment and interpretation processes, leading to errors and thence to relevance and evaluation gaps, as discussed in Chapter 2.

Role by itself cannot explain positions taken by individual decisionmakers (S. Smith, 1984–85), especially when they approach their roles with an already well defined world view. Both role and world view leave a decisionmaker a certain latitude regarding how to apply them in any particular situation, although both have a predisposing effect. The relationship between role and world view can be of two types: adjustment and transformation. In adjustment, either the role interpretation or the the decisionmaker's world view adjusts to the other to eliminate incompatibility. In transformation, when the possibility of a contradiction between role-based mind-sets and initial world view arises, the troublesome information is transformed to eliminate incompatibility.

The implications of role playing can prove even more complex when the decisionmaker's perception of the role requirements is incongruent with others' expectations (Levinson, 1959). Colleagues in the decision-making group or fellow citizens might, for example, have a different concept of what agenda and priorities the job entails or a different notion of how contradictions between roles on the national and international scenes should be resolved. The differing notions tend to engender diverse views of events and the behavior of external actors. Situations where role expectations are incongruent are sources of individual and organizational stress (Kahn et al., 1964) that might have adverse effects on the ability to deal effectively with information. The individual or organization may find it easier to ignore information highlighting role contradictions and their implications, than to deal with it or to attribute less importance to it than it actually has, or to interpret it to avoid the conflict of expectations even if this calls for distortion.[18]

Stress is another factor affecting group performance negatively by encouraging cohesion and conformity in face of a common threat, with deviation declining in legitimacy as the frequency and intensity of inter-actions among group members increase. Stress tends to reduce both the receptivity to discrepant information and the propensity to search for it. Consequently the likelihood of premature cognitive closure increases, while the effectiveness of information about negative feedback decreases. More particularly, when the stress-generating threat is external to the group and the group believes it can successfully meet it, cohesiveness, the pressure toward uniformity, and support for the leader increase as each individual searches for social support. The likely outcome is consensus seeking and support for the policies of the leadership, with a declining likelihood of dissent. Leadership then becomes more directive because it encounters much less opposition (Holsti and George, 1975: 285–93; Janis, 1982: 250–54; Madsen, 1982: 105; Staw, Sandelands, and Dutton, 1981). When, on the other hand, a group's level of aspiration is low, that is, when it perceives itself to be unable to meet the threat effectively, the pressure toward uniformity can decrease, cohesiveness and support for the leader can decline, and the likelihood that dissenting views will be expressed more forcefully than before can grow. The same applies in cases where, although the group believes in its ability to cope with the threat successfully, its initial responses prove a failure, thus intensifying the perception of the threat and inducing anxiety. Nevertheless, group rigidities in threat situations have their sources not only in group dynamics but also in the constraining cognitive effects threat has on group members as individuals (see Chapter 3), which members bring into the group.

The Resolution of Disagreements

When incoming information is perceived to lack significance for the issues particular group members carry responsibility for, they tend to accept the interpretation offered by the majority of the group or dictated by the chief policymaker. When, however, the information is conceived as pertinent to the issues preoccupying the group members and is controversial as well; they may come into conflict with other policymakers who have differing interpretations embedded in different realms of interest or world views. Yet even when there is disagreement in the group, if differing perceptions lead to similar operative conclusions, the group members are not likely to face the need to reach a perceptual consensus; they are likely to contain their conflicting perceptions as long as an *operative consensus*, which is what counts, can be maintained. Moreover, positive feedback from operational decisions in this case paradoxically serves to verify essentially differing definitions of the situation—in part because bureaucracies are action oriented rather than knowledge and reasoning oriented. Information and knowledge are only secondary to "getting the job done" and are important and relevant to the degree that they are perceived to be linearly related to that primary objective. Hence an operative consensus tends to subdue the cognitive and intellectual dimensions of policy so long as the participants agree over what to do; the why is relegated backstage and appears front and center only if the policy fails or the operative consensus is eroded.

A good example of an operative consensus at work is the emergence of the policy of bombing North Vietnam in early 1965. As already discussed in some detail, the air force believed bombing was a function of its organizational identity. The other services had less faith in the effectiveness of bombing the North but perceived bombing as a way to commit the United States to a large-scale use of force that would ultimately require their participation and result in the military's obtaining the resources it requested to win the war on the ground. Maxwell Taylor, the U.S. ambassador to South Vietnam, supported bombing as a means of weakening the will of the North Vietnamese leadership, improving the morale of the South Vietnamese government, and reducing the North's ability to support the insurgency. McGeorge Bundy, the national security adviser, and his deputy Walt Rostow held similar views; they believed that bombing was efficient and that bombing key industrial targets could coerce the North into ending its support for the insurgency in the South. Under Secretary of State George Ball, on the other hand, was skeptical of and even hostile toward the bombing policy but went along with it. First, he was not yet prepared to resign, hoping to influence policy from within while not diverging too much from the values and objectives of the mainstream. Second, he believed that bombing would be a substitute for the use of ground forces, which he wanted to avoid even more. Rusk and McNamara, as well as Johnson, hoped that bombing would be sufficient to bend the will of a fourth-rate Asian power. They had in mind the U.S. success in coercing the Soviet Union in the Cuban missile crisis. They also hoped that if bombing worked, they could avoid committing ground forces to Vietnam. Yet they did not fully expect it to suffice. The president, however, also believed that if he did not take this course, he would lose public support by showing himself to be "soft on Communism." Moreover, if ground troops were to be introduced, the president believed he had to demonstrate first that bombing on its own could not work.

Although there was an operative consensus over the policy of bombing per se, it did not extend to the objectives of the policy. As soon as the policy was adopted, a debate erupted over how to implement it. A compromise over the conduct of the bombing policy—rather than a critical reevaluation of the policy assumptions and expectations as a whole—was thus necessary to preserve the consensus. Ironically, the compromise resulted in a failure to achieve any of the objectives, which led to the erosion of the consensus the compromise was supposed to save (Gallucci, 1975: 47–56).

On the other hand, when an incongruence between perceptions leads to different operational conclusions, several different outcomes may occur. First, the chief policymakers, if they have the power, may impose their preference. Second, a majority in favor of one of the interpretations may form, imposing the decision on the minority. The decision is then accepted and sometimes internalized by the deviating members because loyalty to the group legitimizes the acceptance of majority rule and because recognition of the necessity to make sacrifices (such as conformity) is an important part of the group ethos (Schwartz, 1980: 158).[19] Acceptance can be preceded or followed by internalization, based on a process of rationalizing that the majority is actually right, not only because it has both the moral authority and practical power of imposing its view but also because, conversely, its holding a particular view presumably proves that the view is the correct one.

Internalization is fostered by one or a number of conditions (Deutsch and Gerard, 1955: 629–30) relating to the attributes of the information, the group, and the individual processor. The more ambiguous and uncertain the information, the less confident is any single person in his ability to cope with it accurately and thus interpret it correctly; consequently he is more willing to conform and accept the group judgment as correct (Hochbaum, 1954; W. A. Scott, 1960a). An important element in internalizing the group's position is the attributes of the group itself. The important ones are the distribution of power, roles, and status within the group and the affective links of the individual to the group. The larger the majority who seem to support a particular interpretation, or the more powerful the personalities who back it, the stronger the tendency is to convince oneself of its accuracy. Allison (1969, 1971) points out that at the time of the Cuban missile crisis, members of the U.S. decisionmaking group found the alternative of a blockade more attractive than other alternatives as soon as it became clear that the blockade was supported by Robert Kennedy (who was perceived to be expressing the inclinations of his brother President Kennedy) and by Theodore Sorensen, special counsel to the president, and McNamara (who were known to be close to the president).

The distribution of roles and the stratification of status in the group determine the extent of each decisionmaker's responsibility for any success or failure that might flow from the judgment, interpretation, and evaluation of the situation reached by the group. The greater the decisionmaker's need to prepare a safety net against possible personal failure, the stronger the tendency is to accept and internalize the group's judgment. Conformity also reduces the chance of future cognitive dissonance, because the individual can rationalize that the group imposed its judgment (cf. Brehm, 1960) or that the majority is generally right and its opinion has to be respected from the normative point of view.

Some people's personality traits dispose them more than others toward being persuaded to prefer group judgments to their own. They tend toward conformity and search for consensus and harmony in their social environment (Asch, 1958), giving those values more worth than their own independent judgment. As we shall see in the next section, compliance can take a number of forms.

The third possible outcome of incongruence between group members' definitions of the situation is that the balance of power in the group makes adjudication impossible. In that case, if there is a pressing need to reach a decision, a compromise is reached because a decision demands some mutually accepted perceptual basis for its formation. Information processing is an iterative interaction of social exchanges motivated by both egotistic instrumentality and prevailing norms of obligation. These are embedded in the nature of the social structure and the subculture of the small group and find operative expression in both specific and diffused reciprocity. In specific reciprocity, items of equivalent value are exchanged in a strictly delimited sequence. In diffused reciprocity the sequence of events is less narrowly bound and the definition of equivalence is less precise (Keohane, 1986: 4); that is, one partner to the exchange accumulates an obligation toward the other to be repaid at some future time in the sequence of their continuous interaction. Reciprocity, whether specific or diffused, is, then, the core of compromise, which may take several forms.

In *content compromise*, the most common form, a third evaluation is adopted as a substitute for the conflicting evaluations. It may be formulated to contain elements from the original incongruent evaluations or, alternatively, be completely different from either. Of course, the compromise does not reflect the substance of the information but is the product of the balance of power in the decisionmaking group.[20] Reciprocity in this case is specific.

In *temporal compromise*, one side in the dispute may be willing to yield and accept the other's perception with the tacit understanding that, should a similar situation arise in the future, the other side will forfeit its stand in return. In such a case both present and future perceptions are determined on the basis of some mutually acceptable rate of exchange and not on the basis of the substantive content of the information. Reciprocity in this case can be either specific or diffused.[21]

Interissue compromise can occur when the disagreement simultaneously involves more than one information set regarding two or more different issue-areas. In such a case each side may relinquish what seems to it the less important definition of the situation and on that issue adopt the other side's interpretation. Again, the end result is determined not on the basis of the information's substantive content but on the basis of some exchange-ratio trade-off. Here reciprocity is specific.

Two illustrations will clarify some of these points. In February 1968 General Wheeler, chairman of the Joint Chiefs of Staff, visited Vietnam to assess the situation after the Tet offensive. The report he submitted upon returning to the United States included support for a request by General Westmoreland for an additional 206,000 troops. The request was justified by the need to maintain security in the cities and in the government as well as in the countryside; to defend the borders, the demilitarized zone, and the northern provinces of the South; and to provide forces for offensive operations. The president then asked Clark Clifford, the incoming secretary of defense, to study the problems involved. Paul Warnke, assistant secretary of defense for international security affairs, was given the task of preparing a detailed study of the additional troop request, its implications, and policy options. His conclusion was, in a nutshell, that no level of additional American forces alone could achieve an early end to the war, unless the South Vietnamese government provided effective military and political leadership. The memorandum proposed a drastic change of strategy without increasing U.S. forces in Vietnam substantially; instead the United States would limit its objectives and concentrate on population security to give the government of South Vietnam and its army time to develop democratic institutions and to grow in effectiveness.

Clifford found Warnke's draft "quite persuasive," but General Wheeler objected vehemently on military grounds, arguing that the new strategy would mean increased fighting in or close to population centers, which would result in increased civilian casualties. He held that a static defense posture would also allow the enemy to mass its forces near population centers. Nor could he accept the implied criticism of past strategy; he did not think that civilians in the Defense Department should be involved in issuing specific military guidance to the field commander (Westmoreland) and felt that it was his obligation to support the requests of his field commander. Consequently Clifford's report to the president was a compromise. In substance it was in many ways similar to all the other studies that had been produced in the past in response to requests for enlarged troop deployment; but at the same time it contained incremental, though important, differences. Specifically, it recommended that additional troops be furnished only to a level that would not disrupt normal political and economic life in the United States. It recognized the need for new strategic guidance but suggested that an actual decision on such guidance be deferred pending a further complete reassessment of U.S. strategy (Krepinevich, 1986: 240–47; Schandler, 1977: 121–76).

A second example can be seen in McNamara's opposition to the deployment of an antiballistic missile (ABM) system because of his reservations about its utility. The president felt that some ABM deployment was necessary. Thus McNamara, to preserve his effectiveness on other issues, agreed to yield to the president and support the deployment of a "thin" ABM system to offset an irrational Chinese attack (Hoopes, 1969: 84). Chief among the other issues that concerned McNamara was the question of curtailing the bombing of North Vietnam.

Once a definition of the situation has been accepted by the group, it acquires a life of its own. Those policymakers who were not party to the judgment-formation process tend to assume that definitions of the situation that are the outcomes of compromise have a firm objective basis, that they originated from information and not, as is actually the case, from irrelevant social influences. Their perceptions then form the basis for the evaluation of new information and for new decisions. Perceptual dynamics like these, which result in long-range contaminating effects, are what makes basing a perceptual consensus on compromise so costly. A firsthand account by anonymous Defense Department analysts illustrates the process.

In the late fall of 1964, President Johnson made a tentative decision in favor of limited military pressures against North Vietnam. He acted on the consensus recommendation of his principal advisors, a consensus achieved by a process of compromising alternatives into a lowest-common-denominator proposal at the sub-cabinet and cabinet level, thereby precluding any real Presidential choice among viable options. The choices he was given all included greater pressures against North Vietnam. (*Pentagon Papers*, 1971: 111)

Group-inspired Compliance

As ambiguity, complexity, and uncertainty increase, the more exposed, and receptive, decisionmakers are likely to be to social pressures. In such cases they need to validate their judgment by comparing it with the consensual judgment of the group; and if the two are incongruent, they find security and reassurance, especially when the costs of error can be high, in conforming and adapting their views to those of the majority. This option becomes even more tempting when in addition to external uncertainty people face internal doubts about their capabilities that reflect low self-esteem owing, for example, to recent failures, the risk and complexity of decisions, or moral dilemmas that the issue raises (Moscovici, 1976: 25–31).

The dynamics of group membership involve a process by which commitment to the group increases the more members invest or sacrifice for the sake of membership. They can, for example, invest time, put their personal prestige on the line, or sacrifice opportunities to take different positions in other groups. In other cases the group provides opportunities that force members to choose between group interests and personal interests, such as old friendships and loyalties; a choice in favor of group interests, combined with the impact of the feelings of group togetherness and the sense of mission (prevalent in foreign and defense bureaucracies), intensifies their commitment to the group and its norms, values, and beliefs. Thus cohesiveness increases, and group membership becomes bound up with the sense of self (Ridgeway, 1983: 110). Such values as intragroup solidarity and defense of the group's parochial interests can then become more important than accurate information processing.

Furthermore, although conformity in small groups is not automatic but comes about when members are aware of other members' expectations that they conform (Wilson, 1978: 108), the awareness is quasi-automatic in groups with high solidarity because their atmosphere engenders a state of mind that encourages such expectations. But it should be noted that pressure toward conformity does not necessarily imply uniformity of opinions on all policy positions (George, 1980a: 92).

Group membership entails frequent interactions among members that further enhance the desire to be accepted by the other members, which not only reinforces conformity but has two additional negative side effects. In the first place, members adopt attitudes that they believe to enhance a desirable image of themselves in the minds of the other members. Sorensen (1964), describing decisionmaking in the White House, contends that it was not unusual for military solutions to be supported by doves, who wanted to present a tough and uncompromising image of themselves in order not to be accused of being appeasers, whereas the same military solutions were rejected by military people, who did not want to appear trigger-happy. Second, and related, decisionmakers neglect or cover up information when they fear that their bringing it to the attention of the other group members would show them in a bad light. When the suppression of information produces cognitive dissonance because of its being contradictory to the moral ethos, the suppression is legitimized when the information is discounted as unimportant or irrelevant—a biased judgment of the relevance and importance of the information in question. Suppressors further rationalize that not bringing the information to light avoids burdening group members or the leader with additional information processing. Such a rationalization works best when group members are actually overburdened, so that the need to sift and selectively process information is acute, as in crisis situations.

A more general consequence of group interactions is polarization. It has been suggested that intragroup interactions enhance already existing individual predispositions. The interactive process tends to activate similar and related associations regarding information that members share. Consequently, members reinforce (unconsciously) each other's inferences and end up sharing the same, often questionable, collective inferences. Similarly, in cases where group members, in the interest of efficiency, each have specialized knowledge an inference error made by the expert is likely to be passively accepted by other group members, who defer to the group expert in his area of expertise (Gouran, 1986; Minix, 1982; Myers and Lamm, 1976; Semmel, 1982). The accentuation of individual predispositions is significant in maintaining a higher threshold of resistance to the penetration of dissonant information and a higher level of cognitive conservatism than would characterize the individuals if they were not members of the group. Thus the search for information is selectively directed toward confirming already existing interpretations and diverted away from disconfirming them, giving leverage to assertive members.

Small groups are sometimes inclined to take more risks than individuals under the same circumstances (e.g. Dion, Baron, and Miller, 1978; Golembiewski and Miller, 1981: 5–7). This is known as the risky-shift phenomenon—a case of polarization with special relevance to foreign policy. A risky shift could involve the underestimation of warning information and the overestimation of one's coping and risk management capabilities,[22] both of which justify the risk taken.

Group membership might too, as argued, encourage self-imposed compliance. Four patterns of self-imposed conformity can be distinguished, depending on the motives behind each.[23]

In *instrumental conformity*, the most common case, the group members conform for the instrumental value of compliance—to be rewarded or to avoid punishment or rejection by the group leader or other members. Conforming with the leader's views and declining to express dissenting views can take place even when individuals are sure of their position and influence in the decisionmaking group; yet they may fear a rude, abusive response by the leader that would humiliate them and cause them to lose face in front of their peers. President Johnson, for example, bullied those who worked for him, so that "[they] lived in mortal fear of him" (Halberstam, 1972: 436–37). Witnessing others being tongue-lashed generates a negative learning process within the decisionmaking group, creating an atmosphere permeated by the I-wouldn't-want-to-be-in-their-shoes feeling, which produces self-censorship and a preference for pleasing the leader or at least avoiding open disagreement and deviation from the leader's views.

The probable outcome of instrumental conformity is an increased alertness to information or interpretations that support the prevalent views of the group and its leader and decreased attention to dissonant information and interpretations. At the extreme, the individual may be involved knowingly in distorting either information or its interpretation in order to please. Conscious distortion can be expected to occur in a decisionmaking group with a rigid hierarchical structure and a highly authoritarian leader.

Identification conformity arises when the attractiveness or charisma of the chief policymaker is the main basis of the group members' willingness to accept his concepts and situation evaluations. Here the pleasure is in the actual act of conforming and not necessarily in the reward (or avoidance of punishment) that follows. The act of conforming gives the member a sense of identification with an admirable person—the leader.[24] Even General Elazar, in 1973 the much respected IDF chief of staff, who had a close relationship with, and the support of, three of the most influential members of the Israeli cabinet (Golda Meir, Yigal Allon, and Yisrael Galili), treated then Defense Minister Moshe Dayan with reverence. Thus from May to early October Elazar suppressed his earlier political assessment that Sadat could not accept the status quo much longer and that war could be expected that year and adapted his views to Dayan's forecast, made in late June, that no major war was to be expected in the next few years (Bartov, 1978a: 313).

Identification conformity carries with it dangers similar to those associated with instrumental conformity. In both situations the chief policymaker is the source of information and guidelines for interpreting it, so that any change in perception must come from him. And yet a change in his concepts can come about only as a result of suitable information and feedback, of which he might be deprived because of the other group members' conformity. Moreover, when individuals conform to the opinions of people they admire, they also tend to judge those people to be more proficient than they are themselves (L. R. Hoffman, 1978a: 71), which, even though not necessarily the case, further reinforces their tendency toward conformity.

In *internalization conformity*, group members adopt the group's concepts because they are in line with their own value system or beliefs or because they regard conformity to the dominant majority view as a value in itself. The attitude could originate in personal values—supporting the majority is important—or in cultural values—harmony is more important than confrontation.

Finally, *integrative conformity* is a combination of two or all three of the above types. For example, certain group members could conform to the group's definition of a situation because it suits their values and beliefs, causes them pleasure as they identify with the group's leader, and at the same time provides them with instrumental benefits. Integrative conformity is more difficult to avoid than unidimensional conformity.

Indeed, the conformity encountered in groups is not usually homogeneous. The nature and patterns of conformity are influenced by and reflect the method of recruiting the members of the decisionmaking group. Thus, for example, people brought into the group on a functional basis—because of their roles in relevant organizations (e.g. foreign ministry or ministry of defense), their professional knowledge of a particular subject, or their political status (e.g. a powerful position in the ruling party)—are likely to tend toward instrumental conformity. The type of conformity might also be influenced by the functions that relevant attitudes fulfill for individuals. For example, instrumental conformity may well serve the function of ego-defense by ensuring the avoidance of rejection by the group.

Decisionmakers do not necessarily succumb cynically to pressure for conformity without realizing the consequences. They are often acutely aware of their duty to take a stand and make judgments based on merit on the one hand and on the convenience of conforming on the other, and they have to cope with the resultant moral dissonance. This awareness of duty is particularly true for those involved in defense and foreign policy decisionmaking, where the repercussions of errors and biases in judgment can be most serious. If, however, decisionmakers can convince themselves that even if conforming requires them to support the wrong decision, the costs of error are manageable, then self- and other-generated pressures toward conformity are likely to gain the upper hand over reluctance to conform.

Another important factor is the personality of the policymaker. The intensity of the need for conformity may depend on personal traits, such as extraversion, submissiveness, or intolerance of ambivalence. Extraverts who are affectively dependent on the reactions of other people are likely to adjust their views and judgments to those of their social environment. Submissive people tend to yield to the pressures for conformity. Finally, intolerance of ambivalence and ambiguity can take one of two diametrically opposed forms: either decisionmakers try to impose their attitudes and evaluations on the group or, alternatively, if they do not have the capacity to impose conformity on others they impose it on themselves, adopting attitudes and perceptions acceptable to other group members and thus avoiding ambivalent evaluations and helping to build consensus.

Many of the factors inducing compliance and many of the symptoms of the different types of conformity can be observed in the Israeli decisionmaking group in 1973.[25] Golda Meir's kitchen cabinet was a cohesive group. Basically, members shared the core values regarding national security affairs, although they diverged on a number of tactical issues. Most of them had a military-security background. All shared confidence in the deterrent posture of the IDF and underestimated the adversaries' capabilities. Meir, the very popular prime minister, was the person who held the group together and bridged personal rivalries and the cleavage between doves and hawks. She also wielded over her party and the government the threat that she might resign and that the ruling Labor Party would then face a devastating struggle for leadership. In spite of latent personal rivalries, members of two age-groups within the cabinet, the older generation (e.g. Meir, Galili) and the younger one (e.g. Allon, Dayan), had much in common in terms of background and a long working acquaintance with each other, going back to the prestate years. In important matters pertaining to national security it was unlikely that a joint Meir-Dayan view would be assertively contested by other members, though doubts might be expressed. Meir herself tended to rely on Dayan, her independent-minded and charismatic defense minister, for estimates and judgments in security and defense matters.

The core of the enlarged decisionmaking group for security and defense policy comprised the prime minister, the defense minister, Director of Military Intelligence Zeira, and IDF Chief of Staff Elazar. But all members of the group, not only the prime minister, deferred to Dayan and to a lesser degree to Zeira and Elazar. Dayan and Zeira stood out for their analytic intellectual capabilities, self-confidence, and charisma; all three military men had a heroic military record, and they formed what one observer described as a "hierarchy of heroes" (Hareven, 1978), bold and risk inclined. Zeira also had the advantage of being entrusted with providing the integrated national intelligence estimate to the government because of his position as director of military intelligence, the most powerful and resource-rich intelligence organization in the nation, and because of his being personally associated with, and enjoying the full support of, Dayan. Dayan and Zeira's relationship went back many years, to Dayan's days of active service, and they shared views about Israel's national goals and how they should be achieved.

In the context of the decisionmaking group's cohesiveness and intragroup dynamics, Dayan's optimism became the predominant input into the group's judgments. Even though some members, including Meir herself, sustained doubts about the estimated low likelihood of war, they did not express them assertively; in fact they censored their doubts themselves. That Dayan's views were supported by the chief of staff and the director of military intelligence, making it even less likely that they would be challenged in the cabinet or the military. And even those who had doubts about the low probability of war did not doubt the military's assessment that should war become imminent, the intelligence community would be able to provide a warning 48 hours in advance, and all agreed with the estimate that any Arab coalition would be decisively defeated within days. This belief, in fact, tacitly legitimized a nonassertive expression of doubts, eventually culminating in an acceptance of the low probability of war because the cost of error seemed acceptable (Bartov, 1978a: 241, 276–79, 306–10, 313–14; Brecher with Geist, 1980: 57–69; Hareven, 1978: 12–17; Herzog, 1975: 51; Nakdimon, 1982: 29–33, 61–62, 79–80, 135; Salpeter and Elitzur, 1973: 33–77).

Pressure to conform can also spill across national borders when information processors from different countries interact on a regular basis. It is now obvious that the close working relationship between the Israeli and American intelligence communities was an important factor in influencing the latter to dismiss, in September 1973, an impressive array of information indicating Arab war intentions. The information from the

American regional and satellite monitoring systems supported an earlier, May 1973, estimate by the CIA and the Intelligence and Research Bureau of the State Department that war in the Middle East was coming "sometime soon" (Insight Team, 1974: 71). Yet the American intelligence community, impressed with the reputation of the Israeli intelligence organizations, opted for the Israeli interpretation (Kissinger, 1982: 463–67; Shlaim, 1976: 360–61; Insight Team, 1974: 70–71, 102–4), and decisionmakers on both sides received unanimous estimates of the low probability of war. For both sides, the ally's intelligence estimate seemed to independently support, and thus reinforce their confidence in, their own intelligence estimate, in turn providing a further incentive for conformity with the prevailing view in the decisionmaking group in each country. Hence the cross-border conformity reinforced intragroup conformity.

A different pattern of self-imposed compliance is the minority effect. The majority does not always prevail. If it did, societies would rarely change, and we know that historically, minorities were on many occasions able to change existing trends and convert the majority to their views. Yet the minority, at least at the beginning of the process, usually lacks the power resources to achieve this transformation. It does not have the numbers, the broad consensus, the informational resources, or the normative leverage of withdrawing approval. Thus to be effective, it has to have a distinctive behavioral style that will first attract the majority's attention and then raise doubts within the majority regarding the validity of its position. The minority must project consistency, certainty, confidence, and credibility; it thereby focuses attention on its position both when the majority already has a fixed, well-defined position and when it does not. The minority's willingness to face conflict rather than avoid it is what makes it effective.[26]

A minority is able to project the attributes mentioned because its members respond to the perceived external threat to their unpopular position with loyalty (in-group cohesiveness) and commitment, which is reinforced by self-bolstering. For this reason disagreement within a minority group tends to be more rapidly resolved than in a majority group. In some cases membership may carry the sense of exclusivity and of moral or intellectual elitism, further bolstering unity (Gerard, 1985; Moscovici, 1976: 68–93; Moscovici and Nemeth, 1974; Nemeth, 1982). Thus factions, as I shall discuss later, can be powerful in forming and transforming judgments and assessments within the decisionmaking group even when they constitute only a minority of the group membership.

The minority's influence should not be measured simply by whether its position is eventually adopted. A broader view of minority influence would include the indirect effects of the minority's demonstration of confidence and persistence in the position it advocates, which raises enough doubts in the majority to foster active consideration and careful examination of the stimuli and an expanded range of alternatives (Nemeth, 1987). In short, the minority's influence could produce deeper processing and reduce the chances of heuristic processing.

Groupthink and Its Counterpart

Frequent interactions among group members, along with the drive for conformity that interaction brings about, increases the cognitive similarity of members over time, which in turn encourages further interactions, thus creating a closed circle. The most extreme case of group conformity, which arises from concurrence seeking and reflects the collective defensive avoidance of dissonant information, is what Janis has termed groupthink, in which all the group members think as one (Janis, 1982, 1985; Janis and Mann, 1977: 129–33; Moorhead, 1982; von Bergen and Kirk, 1978).

The occurrence of groupthink depends on a number of antecedent conditions (Hensley and Griffin, 1986; Janis, 1982: 242–56; I. D. Steiner, 1982). To start with, the group must be highly cohesive, or at least group members must desire personal acceptance and approval by others. Cohesiveness can be caused or reinforced by the homogeneity of members' social background and ideology. Cohesiveness reinforces group unity and introduces an illusion of invulnerability, but is not by itself enough to produce groupthink. In some cases, in groups that have a tradition of working together, cohesiveness can actually have positive effects on information processing by encouraging vigilance in the information-gathering stage (Leana, 1985). Hence, whether cohesiveness will have detrimental effects depends on the distribution of group members' personalities and on the situational context. Dependence on the group will be particularly strong among members with a low sense of security, who are also the ones most prone to self-censorship in the face of other members' views. Thus in cohesive groups in which members' sense of security is distributed unevenly—that is, some of the members feel confident and others feel insecure—groupthink is not likely to result. It is considerably more probable where most members of a cohesive group feel insecure (Dittes and Kelley, 1956; Flowers, 1977; Longley and Pruitt, 1980)—and still more probable if, in addition, group members are low-dominance personalities and have a low level of integrative complexity (Callaway, Marriott, and Esser, 1985; Tetlock, 1979). The effect of these personality attributes on the defective performance of a cohesive group will be most pronounced in a situation of high stress from external or internal sources where there is little hope of finding a better solution than the one advocated; such a situation will increase members' dependence on the group and the likelihood of groupthink. Another condition is insulation from outside influences, which works to downgrade the value and credibility of information coming from external sources, especially when the group lacks explicit norms requiring methodical procedures for search and assessment. But the most potent condition is leadership practices that are directive-assertive and not modified by a tradition of impartiality. This may sometimes be disguised in the form of encouraging the voicing of dissonant views but only to shoot them down, thus providing a façade of false openness.

Groupthink has a number of symptoms (Janis, 1982: 174–77, 256–59).

1. Overoptimism prevails, thus encouraging the taking of unwarranted risks.

2. The group collectively attempts to rationalize its evaluations in order to ignore those items of information that threaten the evaluations.

3. Some group members appoint themselves responsible for the protection of the group from dissonant information.

4. The group profoundly believes in its own righteousness.

5. The opponent is conceived in stereotypic terms and regarded as extremely evil and stupid (the supposed stupidity of the opponent also serves to justify overoptimism).

6. Group members censor their own doubts about the accuracy of the judgments and evaluations shared by the group.

7. Direct pressure is brought to bear on deviating group members.

8. A shared perception about the existence of group consensus emerges.[27]

The negative implications of these symptoms, in terms of both the accuracy of the definition of the situation adopted by the group and the possibility of its adjustment to reality, are self-evident.[28] The symptoms of groupthink can also cause deindividuation, which leads the group not only to avoid carefully weighing alternatives and risks and seeking outside opinions but also to draw its attention away from moral and ethical norms (Swap, 1984b: 74–75). Nevertheless, the ingredients of groupthink are necessary ingredients of collective decisionmaking, which requires the forming of a consensus within the group around a focused collective view. Problems arise, not from concurrence seeking as such, but from premature concurrence seeking (Longley and Pruitt, 1980: 76; Walsh, Henderson, and Deighton, 1988). Counter to Janis's claim, however, it can be argued that groupthink does not necessarily enhance undue optimism or unquestioning belief in the group's inherent morality. On the contrary, in some cases it may produce collective agonizing, magnify doubt by sharing it out, and thus generate excessive pessimism, which may result in procrastination and inactivity when action is called for. Groupthink may cause failure to cope and adjust.

The symptoms of groupthink and their corollaries were evident in Johnson's inner group. The group that included McGeorge Bundy (replaced in 1966 by Walt Rostow), Robert McNamara (replaced in 1968 by Clark Clifford), Dean Rusk, Earl Wheeler, Richard Helms (after 1966), and to a lesser degree Bill Moyers (replaced as press secretary by George Christian in 1967) and George Ball, was characterized by mutual support, cordiality among its members, and a strong feeling of commitment and loyalty toward its leader, President Johnson. These attributes were reinforced as the members came to feel themselves increasingly beleaguered by outsiders' sharp criticism of their Vietnam policy, which only heightened their felt need for affiliation and for a collective overriding of doubts and second thoughts. From the start the members shared similar orientations to such basic issues as Communism and its threat, the U.S. role in world affairs, and the consequences if it did not carry out this role (i.e. the domino theory). Over time the members came even closer in their attitudes because of the polarization effect of ongoing, daily, intensive interactions with one other. They came to adopt a black-and-white view of the Indochina conflict, which contrasted a diabolical image of the opponent with the image of an invariably moral and virile American government. This view was instrumental in generating a detached, dehumanized attitude toward the war and its human victims, which strengthened support for the escalation option even in the face of growing criticism and costs. Similarly, domestic "enemies," that is, the administration's critics, were described in stereotypic terms as "simpletons," "cut-and-run people" with "no guts."

Members tended to collectively rationalize the Vietnam policy with deductive, rational arguments (e.g. the effect of bombing on North Vietnam's capabilities), reinterpretations of feedback information indicating possible policy failure, or the use of dubious analogies (e.g. Vietnam as an Asian Berlin, a Munich-type sellout). The group tended to isolate itself from outside experts' dissenting views by avoiding their reports as much as possible, by adopting extreme measures of secretiveness (this was one of the purposes of the Tuesday lunch meetings), and by using information gatekeepers, who played the role of mindguarding (e.g. Rostow). Isolation helped in promoting and safeguarding a strong sense of optimism that the policies applied would work and that the war would be over soon, and supported the continued underestimation of the risks of failure. When members raised doubts, they were quickly subdued by being subjected to strong social pressures orchestrated by the president. In other cases doubters were domesticated, as occurred with Moyers and Ball (e.g. "Mr. Stop-the-Bombing," "our favorite dove"). Finally, when these measures did not work, the dissenters were made to resign (Cooper, 1970: 413, 424; Gelb, 1972; Gelb with Betts, 1979: 116–20; Graff, 1970: 3, 6; Hoopes, 1969: 116, 181, 218; Humphrey, 1984; Janis, 1982: 97–130; Oberdorfer, 1984: 99; R. K. White, 1970: 182–215).

The symptoms of groupthink reflect two types of motive for concurrence seeking. The people involved may become either overoptimistic, and thus lack the motivation to search for or attend to all available information, or overpessimistic, and assume that suggesting views that deviate from the consensus makes no sense. Overpessimistic members believe that deviationists pay the price of their nonconformity and stand only a slight chance of improving the accuracy of the group's consensual conceptions. Overpessimism, combined with the perceived material and emotional benefits of not making waves, produces over time a tendency to rationalize the group consensus as accurately reflecting reality.[29] When the group feels beforehand that a particular individual is likely to cause problems by deviating from the group consensus, it excludes them from participation in discussion. Or if exclusion is impossible, an alternative solution can be domestication (Janis, 1982: 119–20), which misleadingly gives the illusion of open-mindedness. Dissenters are allowed to express their views so long as they are not too deviant and do not provide ammunition to the group's external rivals and critics (e.g. by allowing dissenting views to leak beyond the group boundaries).

It would be incorrect to assume that groupthink is necessarily a structural attribute of a particular decisionmaking group, that is, that a particular group is disposed toward groupthink under all circumstances. For example, Kennedy's foreign policy advisers exhibited groupthink behavior in the Bay of Pigs affair but not in the Cuban missile crisis. It can be argued that in different stages in the group's formation, different tendencies toward groupthink emerge. In the early stages of the group's existence,

group members are uncertain about their roles and status and thus are concerned about the possibility of being made a scapegoat or even excluded from the group. Hence they are likely to avoid expressing opinions that are different from those proposed by the leader or other powerful persons in the group, to avoid conflict by failing to criticize one another's ideas, and even to agree overtly with other people's suggestions while disagreeing covertly. (Longley and Pruitt, 1980: 87)

Once the pattern of intragroup relationships has been settled, members may feel secure about criticizing others and venturing their own independent ideas.

However, in some groups the pattern of relations that emerges is such that groupthink becomes a structural attribute, dominating discussions of significant issues. It can become a structured attribute in a dynamic transformation process in which even nonhomogeneous small groups become homogeneous ones, which increase the likelihood of groupthink's emergence. When dissenters are not listened to and are losing access to the top policymakers, they often decide to resign out of frustration and a sense of declining effectiveness. The group then becomes more homogeneous, dissenting views are fewer in number and assertiveness, and groupthink becomes much more likely most of the time on almost every issue. The process is incremental and self-perpetuating. It actually occurred in the Johnson administration during 1966 and 1967, when both hawks and doves who tried to reason with the president and affect his Vietnam policy were frustrated by their lack of success in reaching him and by his antagonistic response. He came to view the critics as enemies and traitors, and their influence and accessibility to him declined and finally disappeared. The president became more and more isolated from dissent and nonconforming views; at the same time those who had tried to voice their doubts about the direction the Vietnam policy was taking began their exodus from the White House.

At the other end of the conformity spectrum is a less discussed but no less potent type of group dynamic. Here intragroup interactions are characterized by an extreme tendency toward confrontation with and opposition to the leader; members are not yea-sayers but nay-sayers. The consequences are negative, as with groupthink. In an extreme case the top decisionmakers' energies are wasted in struggling for political survival or in pushing through decisions. Even minor decisions cause a major contest of wills; this further raises the level of the chief decisionmakers' stress and anxiety, thus further reducing their will, ability, and available time for appropriately processing new information. Their attention is also diverted toward information that is potentially useful in the ongoing intragroup contest, not toward the truly important issues that they must deal with. Moreover, a tendency toward cognitive closure is highly likely, because any change of prior beliefs and assessments may be interpreted as an admission of error, which would further weaken the decisionmakers' position. Beleaguered and overstrained leaders acting in a permanently hostile and competitive social environment face growing difficulties in objectively considering incoming information. They may not even notice the extent to which information processing is diverted from the substance of matters because of their preoccupation with the intragroup struggle.

Such a situation may emerge when the decisionmaking group is a coalition of more or less evenly balanced factions divided by unbridgeable differences in ideologies, motives, and interests or when the group is leaderless because its leader has lost authority—owing for example, to declining health, a chain of policy failures, or both—and when for constitutional and political reasons it is either impossible, impractical, or inconvenient to remove and replace the leader. In this case, especially when group members were accustomed in the past to taking their cues from the leader, they must now learn to react independently to information, which could cause some confusion in the interim period until they form their own rules for judgment and inference; and they must develop new patterns of self-imposed discipline that allow for at least a minimum of cooperation in a competitive group context.

Thus, a decisionmaking group should be composed of both people who say yes and people who say no. The role of the former is to provide a supportive social environment, offer quiet advice, and shield the top decisionmaker from unrelenting aggressive criticism. The latter can prevent cognitive stagnation, approach the dominant common wisdom critically, and prevent group conformity from setting in.

Factional Politics

The faction, a distinctive type of small group, is usually a temporary alignment of individuals that constitutes a fragment of a larger group. A coalition serves the participants' interests or their values and beliefs, and within the coalition they think and act collectively. Unlike the organization, the faction usually does not have a formally structured hierarchy and a set of rules and procedures; rules are often fuzzy and tacit, although they may become formalized de facto over time (Table 3).

Four factors affect the emergence of factions. First, when some members in the decisionmaking group conform to a shared set of beliefs and values that differ from those of the other members, their beliefs and values create a common frame of reference for viewing and interpreting information inputs and responding to them. Second, one or more of the emergent faction's members must provide strong leadership that binds the differing personal interests together by providing payoffs, such as material resources, power, prestige, positions, and security, to all the faction members. Third, memberships as well as interactions must be continual in order to maintain cohesion in the relationships between the

TABLE 3
The Attributes of Organizations, Small Groups, and Factions

Attribute	Organization	Small group	Faction
1. Number of members	Many	Limited	Small
2. Structure	a. Formal	a. Formal or informal	a. Informal
	b. Rigid	b. More flexible	b. Fuzzy
3. Relations within the unit	a. Based on formal procedures	a. Based on quasi-formal procedures	a. Informal
	b. Functional	b. Functional	b. Functional
	c. Division of labor	c. More flexible division of labor	c. No strict division of labor
	d. Impersonal	d. Mixed	d. Intimate
4. Power structure	Formal power and status allocations	Formal or quasi-formal power and status allocations	Mostly informal power and status allocations, often fuzzy
5. Commitment	To organizational goals and interests	To group and personal goals and interests	To factional, personal, and other members' goals and interests
6. Affect	Low to medium	Medium to high	High
7. Leadership	Formal	Formal or informal	Informal
8. Degree of openness to new members	a. Open	a. Constrained	a. Closed
	b. Depends on formal procedures	b. Depends on formal or informal procedures	b. Depends on informal or fuzzy procedures
9. View of other units	Competitors	Competitors	Threats

members and the core leadership on the one hand and among the members themselves on the other. Finally, members' perceptions of a real or imagined external threat to their position or power must be met successfully by recourse to the collective power resources of the faction and its leader. Success provides a sense of security to the members and thus compounds loyalties to the faction, which in turn dampens intrafactional dislikes and rivalries (Bailey, 1969: 51–55; Belloni and Beller, 1976; Golembiewski and Miller, 1981: 32–34; Lasswell, 1931; Nicholas, 1965, 1966; Pye, 1981: 6–21; Rastogi, 1975: 3–15).

The *New York Times* edition of *The Pentagon Papers* relates that beginning in 1966 a number of factions existed in the Johnson administration. Three identifiable camps are described: the McNamara group or the "disillusioned doves," who tried to set limits on the war and then curtail it; the military faction, led by the Joint Chiefs of Staff and General Westmoreland, who pressed for an expanded war; and President Johnson as well as senior civilian officials at the White House and State Department, who took a middle position (Sheehan et al., 1971: 511). Factional politics took on a new meaning when factions of separate bureaucracies ended up joining together because of their similar positions. When the bombing halt was in place and its extent and duration were being debated, the bickering factions of the Pentagon (Secretary of Defense Clifford versus the Joint Chiefs) aligned with those of the State Department (Ambassadors Maxwell Taylor and Ellsworth Bunker versus Ambassador Averell Harriman and Cyrus Vance) to press their various cases (Hoopes, 1969: 227).[30]

What factions are and why they exist affects decisively what they do. A faction is less structured than an organization but more uniform and cohesive than the original group and thus has more unity of interests and action and a pervasive influence on group affairs. Factional interests overshadow the interests of the various organizations or units that are represented by faction members. Although their preeminence may seem a blessing because it diminishes parochial organizational or suborganizational interests, these types of parochialism may be replaced by factional parochialism.

Furthermore, because of the unique relationship of the faction to the small group, the effect of factionalism is to reduce debate and discussion within the group. First, some individual views that might have been expressed tend to be absorbed into the collective views of the faction. Second, because the faction operates as a collective, it has power resources that enable it to impose its views on group members without the give-and-take that goes on in a group, where power is distributed more evenly. Third, that a number of group members are able to share the task of searching out, pooling, and communicating information in support of the faction's positions enhances the likelihood that supportive information will submerge dissonant information (Stasser, Kerr, and Davis, 1980: 436). On the whole, the faction, in that it exists, disrupts the free flow and sharing of information by potential users who are not faction members. Thus factions promote conformity in the evaluation of information, raise the level of instrumentality used in interpreting it, and accentuate conservatism in the approach to dissonant information.

In addition, two group phenomena, polarization and groupthink, are more likely to occur in the faction than in the larger group. Polarization is more likely because faction members' beliefs and attitudes are closer than in the group as a whole; they reinforce one another, leading to polarization. Groupthink is more likely because the valence and initial proximity of beliefs and attitudes create the climate for the emergence of all the other symptoms of groupthink. When faction members perceive themselves to be facing a hostile external world of competing factions, and their membership is perceived to be a common shield against it, their information processing is likely to be biased toward maintaining and accentuating the psychological distance between in-group and out-group. In the process they move psychologically closer to other in-group members, thus enhancing the possibility of factional groupthink (Vertzberger, 1984b; Wilder and Allen, 1978).

Factional polarization and groupthink have a spillover effect on the group as a whole because of the power a faction wields, which can be counterbalanced only by a rival faction. The emergence of an effective rival faction depends primarily on the availability of leadership resources, the absence of which precludes its formation. Without a rival, the group or organizational arena is dominated by a single powerful faction whose conceptions go unchallenged, producing selective information processing and premature cognitive closure.

The Impact of Peer and Reference Groups

A member of a political decisionmaking group, such as the cabinet, is usually at the same time a high-ranking member of some formal organization or informal social group (with, for example, a ministerial portfolio, senior military rank, or membership in an ethnic, cultural, or professional group). Here the *peer group* and the *reference group* must be distinguished. The former is the group to which a person physically and formally belongs at a given moment, whereas the latter is the group to which he looks as a source of norms, rules for making judgments and evaluation, and basic conceptions. The reference group partially determines the criteria that the person applies to the evaluation of incoming information, as well as the degree of acceptance that alternative interpretations enjoy (Kelley, 1965; Shibutani, 1967).[31] Even anticipating participation in a group can affect the range of alternatives considered through the latent effects of mental group dynamics, which are similar to the effects of the simulation heuristic (Kahneman and Tversky, 1982c; McWhirter, 1978). Using this heuristic, the individual performs a mental simulation to predict the responses and expectations of his future peer group, which in the process becomes his reference group.

No problem arises so long as the peer and reference groups are congruent—either physically, by being one and the same group, or cognitively, by having the same values, beliefs, and judgmental criteria. The problems emerge when there is no such congruence, that is, when the reference group employs criteria for judgment and evaluation different from those of the peer group, resulting in different interpretations of the same information. Incongruence occurs, for example, when interorganizational think tanks are formed. On the surface, setting up such a team has the advantage of overcoming organizational parochialism and facilitating multidimensional thinking by detaching the team's members from the imposing environment of their original organization and its standard operating procedures and creating an environment where cognitive flexibility will be greater. But team members in fact go on being influenced by the ways of thinking dominant in their original organization—to which, after all, they will return once they have completed their work on the team. Thus their evaluation of information and their definition of the situation are affected by their anticipation of how the members of their respective reference groups would have judged the information and by the instrumental implications of any particular evaluation for the goals of their original organization.

Yet decisionmakers who are members of a group that is supraorganizational are not always cognizant that their judgment continues to be affected by their original organizational parochialism and that consequently their definition of the situation is affected by considerations not always strictly material to available information. Outsiders, persons and groups that are not physically present, become shadow participants either because group members tacitly take their views into account or because group members informally consult them. Thus, for example, when academicians enter political life, one of their considerations—at least in the early stages[32]—is how the academic community will react to their judgments. That was Kissinger's concern with his Indochina policies (Kalb and Kalb, 1974: 164–70, 301). In sum, to try and counter organizational parochialism by establishing coordination committees with interorganizational representation may create a situation where the solution becomes the problem, while a false belief in the broad-minded, nonparochial treatment of the information may take root, making it difficult to see what the problem is.

The following conditions, among others, affect the influence of the reference group. For one, the closer the beliefs of the reference group and everything it represents are to the personal values and beliefs of policymakers, the greater its importance is to them. Their tendency to respond to what is represented by the reference group and to conceive their environment in those terms increases too. As noted, the time span during which someone belongs to the peer group is also of great importance. The longer the time spent in the peer group, the smaller the influence of the reference group is. Another important factor is how permanent membership is expected to be. If people expect their presence in the peer group to be permanent, then they pay reduced attention to the reference group, and its significance as a source of norms declines. On the other hand, if policymakers assume that their presence in the peer group is temporary or ad hoc, the reference group plays a considerable part in their judgments and their definitions of the situation. Finally, the balance of power (not necessarily the formal one) between the reference and peer groups must be taken into account. When the peer group has more real power than the reference group and can, as a result, impose a hierarchy of loyalties, the importance of the reference group diminishes.

The interaction among these conditions determines the ability of the peer group to generate conformity to its own perspectives despite differing reference-group-rooted perspectives among its members. Decisionmakers may not always feel comfortable with the conformity imposed on them and may even feel guilty for not properly representing the views and values they are, at least tacitly, expected to uphold. To prevent these feelings, they may take one of two courses of action: either to try and reach an agreement with the peer group about a perceptual compromise that is normatively acceptable to them and practically acceptable to both the peer and reference groups or, if unsuccessful in reaching a compromise, to attempt to search for information and interpretations of that information that will support the peer-group evaluation they have adopted. The decisionmakers can then rationalize that their conformity is in fact a move toward overcoming parochialism, which again reduces the discomfort they may feel and helps resolve their cognitive dissonance.

Having to take the differing considerations of peer and reference groups into account can cause role conflict. The perceived need to reinterpret role enactment in a manner that will avoid conflict produces role ambiguity, since a role enactment that will satisfy both the peer and the reference groups is difficult if not impossible to achieve. Role conflict and role ambiguity result in stress, which can have adverse effects on the quality of a decisionmaker's information processing; such effects as procrastination, inaction, agonizing, and withdrawal were discussed earlier. To illustrate: the Defense Intelligence Agency was one of the two principal sources of intelligence during the Vietnam War, the other being the CIA. The DIA was largely staffed by military personnel at the upper levels, and its director reported to the Joint Chiefs of Staff and to the secretary of defense through the Joint Chiefs. This organizational structure provided incentives to distort intelligence. Members' career advancement was linked to a particular military service, although the organization to which they were assigned was designed to serve two masters (the Joint Chiefs and the Office of the Secretary of Defense), who often disagreed, and one of them (the Joint Chiefs) was at times internally divided. DIA personnel sometimes found themselves in a position where they had responsibility for evaluating policy but were also originally members of an organization with operational responsibility for implementing that same policy. Hence they were tempted to manipulate information to satisfy multiple masters. The information processor's original service expected him to prove himself useful by influencing certain decisions to suit its interests, but he could best prove his objectivity in his current position by pointing out the flaws in arguments advanced by his own service. An air force officer assigned to the DIA sometimes found his report at odds with the interests of his parent organization, giving him an incentive either to completely reverse his position or, more often, to adopt a compromise evaluation in order not to endanger his air force career. Such alterations were one of the reasons for the ambiguous nature of some DIA analyses (Gallucci, 1975: 66–69).

Of particular relevance to the relationship between the decisionmaking group and the auxiliary organizations that supply information and interpretations (e.g. intelligence organizations and research institutes) is the mediating role of gatekeepers. The gatekeeping function is performed at two levels. The first is between an auxiliary organization and the decisionmaking group. Here the role of gatekeeper is sometimes performed by senior members of the auxiliary organization (e.g. the chief of intelligence). Their task is to decide which data should be presented to whom and how; and their decisions are affected by their roles—that is, they may function as gatekeepers pure and simple, or they may simultaneously be members of the auxiliary organization, gatekeepers, and members of the decisionmaking group. Major General Zeira, director of military intelligence and the man responsible for preparing the national intelligence assessment, was also one of the main gatekeepers for intelligence information. He made it a rule not to present raw intelligence data to the chief of staff and other senior officers. He explained this as necessary so the chief of staff would not get a distorted picture because of partial and unprocessed information (Nakdimon, 1982: 80). But as a result, General Elazar was not aware of the full range of data available. After the war the chief of staff commented bitterly that he would have been much more alert to the possibility of war had he been shown that raw data and that he would probably have rejected the inference of the low probability of war (Bartov, 1978a: 312).

Sometimes there is also a second-level gatekeeper, or "intelligence waiter" (Harkabi, 1984), who is not a member of the auxiliary organization but of the decisionmaker's staff and whose role is to choose what reaches the decisionmaker's attention and in what form (e.g. raw material in full or an encapsulated version). This type of gatekeeper may be tempted to transform the information to meet his own or the decisionmaker's needs as the gatekeeper understands them. This was, for example, the case with the Rostow-Johnson relationship. "Shielded by Rostow, [Johnson] was probably unaware that his subcabinet group and an influential segment of the foreign-military bureaucracy were increasingly disenchanted with his leadership" (Hoopes, 1969: 116).

First-level gatekeepers, when they have multiple roles to play, face the problem of contradictory peer-group and reference-group values and interests and may be tempted to use their control over the flow of information to protect their position in the decisionmaking group. Their task is even more complicated when they have to balance their role playing between the competing groups in the context of bureaucratic politics. For example, the director of military intelligence of the Israeli army in 1973 was a member of the General Staff and at the same time a participant in Prime Minister Meir's decisionmaking group.

Knowing who the gatekeepers are, how they operate, and at which junction of the information flow they are located is extremely useful to adversaries planning deception (Sherwin, 1982). Similarly useful is understanding how the bureauorganizational game is played and what goals motivate the players. With this knowledge at hand adversaries can effectively manipulate information at the different processing stages because they know with some certainty which information will be attended to when and by whom and which is likely to be attributed the meaning that best serves the deceivers' purposes. Furthermore, they can increase and decrease the level of ambiguity and information overload, making a correct evaluation of the situation by the decisionmakers on the other side much more difficult and affecting their confidence in their inferences and judgments so that their responses to information are much slower than they should be.

Group and Organizational Levels of Aspiration

Foreign policy and national security decisionmakers take great pride in their appointments to and positions in the relevant decisionmaking organization or group and develop a sense of elitism that gives special meaning to their roles. They tend to see the future of the nation as in the hands of their group or organization and to identify the successful performance of the state with the performance of their group or themselves. Their level of aspiration in relation to their group, or that of the group in toto, is therefore important.

The level of aspiration, defined as the quality of performance expected of the group or organization in the future (Zander, 1971: 180),[33] is measured in terms of the perceived success of the group's decisions and actions. The more individuals identify themselves with their group or organization, the more the level of aspiration increases in importance to them. Group and organizational success thus becomes more closely connected with positive self-perception, and people become more motivated to assess past performance retrospectively in position terms when self-esteem is high—even when the success of their actions is questionable.[34] The overestimation of past success then becomes the anchoring value by which members form their own expectations of self-efficacy, which are therefore overoptimistic (Cervone and Peake, 1986); and their optimism in turn increases their tendency to take risks and reduces their propensity to pay attention to information questioning or contradicting their optimism. As a result, the impact of negative feedback, which is meant to allow the recognition of past mistakes and bring about adjustments in present perceptions and future expectations, is reduced.[35] Furthermore, because of the egocentric bias in the perception of success, people tend to increase their perceived personal association with positive outcomes and decrease their personal association with negative outcomes (Ross and Sicoly, 1979; Schlenker and Miller, 1977). Group successes thus become more closely linked with members' self-perception than they should be for effective decisionmaking. The opposite is true for failures, which become less associated with self-perception. In cases of success individuals consider themselves to be personally responsible for the group's quality of performance, and in cases of failure, less so.

The lack of appropriate feedback encourages mutual backslapping, which further enhances overconfidence and raises the threshold for the entry of dissonant information that might question and disturb it. The more exaggerated the positive perception of past performance, the greater is the optimism about the group's ability to succeed in the future.

This often baseless optimism encourage the dismissal of information indicating potential danger, sometimes with disastrous consequences. Prime Minister Meir's decisionmaking group, for example, had a high level of aspiration based on its achievements, mainly in the security and foreign policy fields—in particular, ending the War of Attrition with no gains for Egypt and continuing to increase the favorable military balance vis-à-vis the Arab states. This feeling was best expressed by Dayan when he said: "We have never had it so good. I think that our situation is good militarily and politically" (quoted in Schiff, 1974: 63). Meir, the group leader, felt strongly that the policies followed by her government were not only highly effective but also morally correct. The mutual back-slapping was reinforced by the public's admiration for both Dayan and Meir. In early October 1973, when the writing was on the wall, the group could not admit that their judgment had been so completely wrong on such a critical issue as military preparedness, especially with a national election about to take place at the end of the month (Nak-dimon, 1982: 84). Both the politicians and the military thus preferred to rationalize or ignore damning information. The director of military intelligence went on believing that war would not break out even on the morning of October 6, when information from a highly reliable source confirmed that Egypt and Syria would jointly attack later in the day (Nakdimon, 1982: 109).

The level of aspiration is not only a quality that individuals attribute to their group or organization. It works both ways: because it becomes a distinctive part of the organizational climate or subculture, it is also imposed by the group or organization on each of its members or on particular people who play specific roles. Performing at the expected level becomes for those people a condition for safeguarding their position and status. Organizations expect their leaders to achieve certain levels of performance in the interorganizational competition for resources. Achievement is measured, for example, by the relative or absolute size of the budget the leaders are able to obtain for their organization. Knowing that failure to perform accordingly will be costly in terms of their social, informal position even if they retain their formal position, they are bound to search selectively for information and prefer definitions of the situation that enhance their ability to perform at the expected level or help explain away the failure to perform as expected. For example, when the military establishment expects the minister of defense to obtain an increase in the defense budget, he tends to amass information selectively and to add up threat assessments and perceptions that justify that funding level. Alternatively, if the "chief" cannot deliver what the "Indians" expect of him, to use Allison's metaphor (1971: 164), he is attuned to information, interpretations, and assessments justifying a low threat perception.

Conclusions

A keen observer of organizational behavior remarks: "The very structure of organizations—the units, the levels, the hierarchy—is designed to reduce data to manageable and manipulatable proportions" (Wildavsky, 1983: 29). Taken at face value, this statement may be somewhat exaggerated; still, it is indubitably true that the essence of organizational behavior is managing and transforming information to influence choice. Indeed, organizations and small groups are necessary and unavoidable social constructs for information processing, choice, and implementation. Yet inherent in their structural attributes are the factors that undermine their quality of performance, leading to selective attention to information, parochial and self-serving judgments and interpretations, and premature closure to new information. The goals of the organization and group, the affective links among individuals, the climate or subculture, the effects of both group-imposed and self-imposed conformism and compromise—all these combine to make information processing instrumental, biased, and more sensitive to constraints in the social environment than to the actual objective substance of the information. Thus knowledge becomes subservient to personal and social needs and motives, even though the social institutions that generate needs and motives were established to overcome cognitive parochialism and provide a broader and more accurate understanding of reality. Once a given collective image is secured within a group or organization, it becomes so important for the preservation of solidarity, and the forging of a new consensus appears so difficult to achieve, especially when the information is ambivalent, that the result is the entrenchment of existing perceptions in preferences to the prospectively difficult and unpleasant process of forging a new consensual definition of the situation.

These observations have a number of implications for the paradigms that underlie this chapter. Few systematic approaches to the analysis of foreign policy behavior gained more attention in the last decade than the paradigms of bureaucratic and organizational politics (Allison, 1969, 1971; Allison and Halperin, 1972; Halperin, 1974; Williamson, 1979). Yet questions have been raised about their external validity and, in particular, their applicability to developing countries (e.g. Caldwell, 1977: 94; Hill, 1978: 2–3; Migdal, 1974: 515–16; S. Smith, 1980: 31–32)—

questions on which at least some of the arguments raised in this chapter have a bearing.

Some conclusions regarding bureaucratic and organizational politics, in a Third World context in particular, can now be drawn. In the first place, the paradigms are indeed applicable in explaining information processing and foreign policy behavior not only in developed countries but also at least in a certain group of Third World countries (Vertzberger, 1984b). Moreover, it can be inferred that once the elements of bureau-organizational politics are introduced into non-Western societies, their influence on information processing and policy outcomes will be accentuated by particular qualities in the societies. Some qualities are (1) the lack of a sharp distinction between political relations and social and personal relations, (2) the prevalence of cliques, and (3) the absence of a consensus about the legitimate ends and means of political action (Pye, 1961). These qualities offer a wide latitude for successfully delimiting and defending organizational and bureaucratic turf because the actors involved are not inhibited by strong, restricting social norms. In certain cases there is little or no distinction between the interests of the state and those of a particular organization (e.g. when the military fully or partly controls the state and state organs). In such instances the organization in question is perfectly situated to act as a protective association for its collective interests and the interests of individual members. Biased information processing, including highly selective attention to information, is very likely.

Second, the distinction between "action games," "decision games," and "policy games" (Allison and Halperin, 1972) is of particular relevance to an underdeveloped country. The ineffectiveness of the central authority structure in many developing societies allows organizations and individuals freedom of maneuver in action games. The outcomes of the games then influence the outcomes of future decision games by changing the environment. Changes in the environment change the attributes of future contexts and occasions for decisionmaking and thus affect policy, that is, aspirations about outcomes.

Third, because of the characteristics of the political process in non-Western societies, and organizational networks less complex than those in Western societies, it can be stipulated that the bureauorganizational paradigm, when applicable in a Third World context, is dominated by the bureaucratic dimension, with a special emphasis on small-group dynamics and factional politics.

Fourth, it is a common and simplistic fallacy that the only possible outcome of an information processing and decisionmaking process dominated by bureauorganizational politics is a compromise between competing alternatives (e.g. Migdal, 1974). In fact, although the name of the game is indeed bargaining (Allison, 1969: 708), the outcome is not necessarily compromise; the range of possible outcomes is actually much richer and depends on the nature of the bureaucratic milieu. It is possible to foresee situations in which bureauorganizational politics lead to a stalemated decision process with the result that no decision is made. It is also possible that one of the competing options will gain the upper hand with just minor modifications or, in still other cases, that minority effects will occur.

Once the acceptance of a certain option is assured, the logic of bureauorganizational politics may dictate a change of attitude even to non-supporters. The cautious, pragmatic actors cut their losses and draw the proper conclusions with regard to the significance that acceptance of the winning option has for the balance of power among the players. Organizations and individuals go out of their way to demonstrate support for the winning option in a specific subgame and are likely to add their efforts to a selective search for supportive information because they simultaneously participate in other subgames as well; such behavior is necessary to defend their stakes in other subgames where the bargaining still goes on and coalitions with or support of the other winning players may be called for.

Fifth, the proponents of the paradigms have neglected to consider that a main battlefield of competing perceptions and interests is the small-group setting (Kellerman, 1983), where the participating bureaucratic and organizational actors actually play out their roles. This chapter, however, has shown the crucial importance of small-group-based dynamics in some detail.

An interesting, related aspect, one neglected in the literature, is that once a certain group perceives another one as a coherent group with specific, well-defined interests, the makings of bureaufactional behavior exist on both sides as part of an almost reactive defense mechanism. Whether coherent groups of adversaries actually exist or are the creatures of the perceivers' imagination may then become an academic question. In the bureauorganizational battlefield the defensive impulse dictates the countergrouping of available forces and the intensification of factional behavior, which is self-reinforcing.

Finally, it has been argued that the effects of bureauorganizational politics seem to be more dominant in decisions primarily about institutionally grounded issues—those that have direct predictable results for the structure of institutions and for their long-term prosperity and competitive position—than in decisions about major policy shifts, interventions with military force or decisions in times of crisis (Art, 1973; Oneal,

1988). But even regarding the latter, the probability of bureauorganizational politics is high at the information processing stage, when the various players try to bias the direction of the top-level decisionmakers' definition of the problem in a manner that will best serve the players' own understanding of the national interest and can be reconciled with their institutional preferences. It is not in fact correct that decisionmakers have a shared image of high-priority national interests. They may agree on the general definition of the national interest but not on the specifics and even less on the means-ends relationships that best serve the national interest. Disagreement is typical when the information is ambiguous and complex and the situation is uncertain. These attributes on the one hand allow room for legitimate alternative interpretations and on the other produce an even higher level of uncertainty about the ramifications that major policy shifts and military intervention will have, whether favorable or adverse, for the long-term prosperity and the competitive position of the organization or group in question.

CHAPTER 5

The Societal-Cultural Prism

....

"The job of achieving understanding and insight into the mental process of others is much more serious than most of us care to admit."

EDWARD T. HALL

Societal Context and Information Processing

Societal-level effects on judgment, inference, and perception have received little attention in the theoretical literature on international relations, which has focused instead on subsocietal-level variables, namely, the individual, small group, and organization.[1] Nor do decisionmakers realize and take into account the important implications of societal diversity factors. To an extent this neglect is understandable, since ultimately the subsocietal units are the bodies actually carrying out decisionmaking tasks, whereas societal factors are less apparent to the observer.

Decisionmaking by individuals and groups cannot be fully understood apart from the broader societal background. Individuals', organizations', and groups' information processing and definitions of the situation are affected and sometimes actually dictated by their being part of a distinct societal-national environment, culture, and experience (Bradburn, 1963; Crozier and Friedberg, 1980: 97–112; Knorr, 1964: 461; Lebow, 1981: 192–228; M. J. Levy, 1966: 725–29; Sampson and Walker, 1987). Societal-cultural attributes are important sources of beliefs, expectations, role perceptions, values, mind-sets, time perspectives, and cognitive and operational styles, and in general they provide the decisionmaker with the needed "symbolic sources of illumination to find his bearings in the world" (Geertz, 1973: 45). Thus any encounter of decisionmakers from different nations is a meeting of differing cultural and conceptual systems.

Societal attributes affect the nation's image of self and of other actors in the international system. They act as a guiding constraint on what policymakers perceive as a possible, accountable, and legitimate range of interpretations and judgments. The attributes, which are formed in a process of socialization that policymakers are exposed to in the various stages of their life cycle and career, exist as generic frames of reference stored in memory and easily retrievable. They are well anchored, sometimes being unchallengeable and even unchangeable. Significant deviations from these collectively shared conceptual frames of reference may be penalized in democratic regimes through the electoral process or in nondemocratic regimes by the decline of public support for policies and possibly by the loss of power.

As will be explained later in the chapter, societal attributes can be expected to affect information processing at various stages and levels. First, they affect the weight attached to foreign policy issues compared to other issues on the decisionmakers' agenda and hence affect the allocation of attention to and cognizance of foreign-policy-related information. Second, once information has been recognized and has gained attention, societal factors may impinge on the assessment of the importance of a particular datum and its diagnostic value. Third, societal attributes may influence the open-mindedness of decisionmakers to dissonant information and their preparedness to readjust existing definitions of the situation in the light of new information. Finally, these attributes affect the interpretation of available information and the choice among competing interpretations.

Societal attributes have both indirect and direct effects. The former are those effects on the final output—that is, on the definition of the situation—made through the impact of societal-cultural factors on the individual's, organization's, or group's style of information processing. Direct effects, however, serve as direct societal-cultural inputs into that final definition-of-the-situation output. Here I shall not assess the importance of direct versus indirect inputs, nor is it ultimately a matter of consequence. Instead, I shall suggest the scope and range of societal-cultural impacts on information processing, taking into account that these variables cut across all three levels of analysis: individual, state, and systemic.

It is extremely difficult to positively prove the causal links, direct and indirect, between societal-cultural variables and foreign-policy-related information processing. The difficulty in directly observing societal-cultural effects, however, does not prove the opposite, that is, that societal-cultural influences are minor or negligible. I believe that the influences are important, even though they are not always tangible and easily observable. My purpose is to postulate a set of society- and culture-bound structures and processes concerning the essence of societal-cultural effects on information—a set that has an internal logic, is consistent with empirical historical data, and has deductive explanatory power.

Effects of Societal-Structural Attributes

Structural attributes of the national society impose constraints on cognition and perception. I shall discuss the effects of three of these attributes: level of development, the age of the nation, and national style and character.

Level of development. In underdeveloped countries, where domestic problems often seem insoluble and are perceived as an uncertain source for gaining political credit, decisionmakers tend to turn their attention to foreign policy. International politics is perceived to be a more structured domain than domestic politics, with more manipulable players; thus the chances of projecting an image of success are better there (e.g. Tito, Sukarno), especially since the criteria for success in foreign policy are often vague in the minds of the general public. Moreover, since the domestic political process is perceived as less structured and the domestic public as relatively indifferent to the day-to-day management of foreign affairs, decisionmakers in underdeveloped countries are less reluctant than their peers elsewhere to take more clearly defined positions on international as compared with domestic issues and intentionally tilt the allocation of attention in favor of foreign-policy-related information.

The lower the level of political and economic development and the less institutionalized and bureaucratized a country's political system, the greater are the opportunities for externalizing personal preferences and related psychological needs and the more likely are the personality characteristics of the head of state to affect information processing (M. G. Hermann, 1976). These tendencies are reinforced by the fact that in political systems of this type there is little public interest in acquiring knowledge about mundane foreign policy matters; this allows a comprehensive freedom of maneuver to decisionmakers. Perceptions of the external environment thus flow from the top down, that is, from decisionmakers to the society at large, especially for issues not arousing strong public sentiment.

In less developed countries there is also less differentiation between public-political and personal-social relationships than in highly developed countries. Thus there is a greater tendency to subordinate judgments of and inferences from information to their perceived implications for personal or social relations. The potential effect of the information and the degree of preference for alternative assessments is more likely to depend on who will support the various assessments, rather than on the actual content of the information. Moreover, the practice of not differentiating personal from political relations is projected to the international arena when decisionmakers identify their personal relationships with leaders of other states with the objective interests of those states. More particularly, the tendency to identify friendly personal relations with compatible national interests, and hostile personal relations with conflicting national interests, goes far beyond whatever supportive or disruptive effects the personal relationship may actually have.

To avoid errors in interpreting collective behavior, it is important to be able to distinguish cases where nondifferentiation of the public-political domain from the personal-social domain is not an indicator of underdevelopment but rather an attribute of the national culture. American decisionmakers never fully grasped the depth of the differences between the Vietnamese way of life, culture, and patterns of thinking and their own or the way those differences affected Vietnamese perceptions of American policies and, consequently, the policies' effectiveness in winning the hearts and minds of the Vietnamese people. Nor did they judge correctly the likely reactions of both the North Vietnamese people and their leaders to the use of force. Their judgments and evaluations were based on Western philosophical and intellectual premises, while those of both North and South Vietnamese were rooted in traditional Confucian intellectual premises, which are totally different (Fitzgerald, 1973). Thus American officials dealing with the South Vietnamese government occupied themselves with the development of policies and programs and with organization and reorganization. In part this reflected the traditional Western view of government as an instrument for attaining desired goals—a view in which personalities, although important, are in the final analysis replaceable. The South Vietnamese, on the other hand, showed more concern with personalities than with the programs associated with them; in large part this emphasis had to do with their notion that government is tied closely to the personal life and private morality of those who govern. "Vietnamese do not differentiate between a man's style and his 'principles,' between his private and public 'roles': they look at the whole man" (Fitzgerald, 1973: 38). Ho Chi Minh understood this and made a conscious, successful effort to present a picture of "correct behavior" to signal the difference between his regime and the Saigon regime. The Americans, of course, interpreted the Vietnamese conception as an indication of the society's underdevelopment and tried unsuccessfully to overcome the deeply rooted cultural attitude the Vietnamese had toward government.

A related aspect of underdevelopment and little political institutionalization is the fuzzier distinction between the various roles played by decisionmakers (Pye, 1961). Role ambiguity may pose a dilemma: choosing between the different, sometimes conflicting perspectives that originate in the different roles one decisionmaker carries out simultaneously. The need to either avoid or resolve role conflict leads to the adoption of interpretations that involve either compromising between conflictory role-dependent perceptions, ignoring problematic information, or preferring an interpretation that does not raise such a dilemma. Each of these choices affects the quality of information processing negatively, since the interpretation is subservient to its significance for avoiding inconsistencies within the individual's cognitive system.

The level of economic development has been found to be correlated with conceptions of the national role that pertain to perceptions of influence and dominance in the international system (Wish, 1987). These areas of concern consequently gain importance in the allocation of attention to information. Furthermore, M. G. Hermann (1979a: 39) found that lower levels of modernization are correlated with stronger nationalism and distrust of others by heads of state. Nationalism and distrust have obvious implications for information processing, for they act to channel judgments and inferences of other nations' intentions and behavior, so that others are perceived as more hostile and threatening than they actually are. The guiding beliefs about the environment are based on a bad faith model.

The breadth of the social stratum from which decisionmakers are recruited partially determines the degree of homogeneity of the decisionmaking group. In developing countries, where this stratum is rather narrow because of traditional social structures, the decisionmaking group is often highly homogeneous. When homogeneity is added to the aforementioned lack of differentiation between the political and personal spheres, the likelihood that groupthink will develop in the decisionmaking group increases.

Certain societal-cultural conditions provide a favorable context for the emergence of charismatic leaders. It has been suggested that in non-Western societies that are going through a phase of social change, in which the communication of emotions is much less difficult than the communication of subtle or abstract points of view, and that sanction the emergence of such leaders, the likelihood that they will emerge increases (Pye, 1961; Willner, 1968). Charismatic leaders' beliefs and perceptions are rigid and closed to dissonant information because of their high self-esteem and their wish to be identified with beliefs and perceptions prevailing in the society regardless of their congruence with reality.

Age. Another important characteristic of a state and society is its age.

In the first place, age affects national attributes. Older societies usually have greater institutionalization of the political system and greater differentiation between public and private domains and between roles. Decisionmakers are recruited from a broader social stratum, so that there is less homogeneity in their decisionmaking groups. All of these combine to increase the constraints on the decisionmakers' freedom to externalize their personal needs in foreign policy. In addition, the age of core national beliefs and conceptions determines their degree of embeddedness in the collective national consciousness and in the mind of each policymaker. The more rooted the images, beliefs, and conceptions, the more difficult it is to eradicate them even if they no longer fit new realities; and consequently it is also more difficult to change other images and beliefs associated with and conditioned by them. For example, even when China was weak and divided, its leaders clung to traditional Sinocentric views of their country as the center of the world and a dominant power. Another effect of age is that more mature states are less susceptible to acquiring a persecution complex. Younger states are more inclined to take shadows for realities, to see threats to their independence where no such threats exist, to imagine and even uncover international conspiracies against them and plotters supposedly intent on robbing them of their newly won independence.

The age of a state also determines the content and richness of its historical heritage. Older states have a richer history, so collectively shared memories are available to provide analogies and lessons in many issue-areas. As a result, there are more issues on which the national leadership's freedom of choice among alternative interpretations is constrained, for the historical heritage to some extent imposes a general frame of reference, within which information is analyzed rather than interpreted exclusively in terms of its current, actual content. In younger states the leadership is likely to impose its images and judgments of reality on the public, whereas in older states, with their highly institutionalized political systems, the leaders tend to "share the mass image rather than impose it" (Boulding, 1969: 424).

The importance of the historical heritage in shaping cognition and perception increases in proportion to the historical consciousness of a society. When two nations have different views of history and its relevance for the present, the possibility of misinterpreting current beliefs, expectations, and time perspectives, as well as the meaning of behavior, increases sharply. The American and the Vietnamese views of history were diametrically opposed. To the Americans history was marginal; everything was new and solvable, and goals could be achieved by the power of will, science, and competition. Indeed, the American experience has been one of rapid change, growth, and improvement both in the nation's position as a whole and in the lot of the individuals composing it. The Vietnamese, on the other hand, were oriented toward the past by their whole tradition. At the family level they practiced ancestor worship, and at the broader state level Confucianism served as a "sacralization of the past." The bureaucratic elite, the mandarins, directed their scholarship toward repetition of the past rather than toward innovation and progress (Fitzgerald, 1973: 9–16). In the Vietnamese time perspective, history moves in cycles and repeats itself. They already had a long history of survival in the face of superior foreign power, so that the North Vietnamese perceived the American intervention as no different from earlier Chinese suzerainty.

The more ambiguous the information environment in which policymakers operate, the greater is the role played by national history in providing cues for judgment, evaluation, and choice. But since the use and abuse of history are discussed in detail in the next chapter, I shall make at this point just a few brief comments on the subject. History is used as a source for metaphors, analogies, and extrapolations, and that is often a cause for very serious biases and errors in information processing. Historical events unimportant in themselves (such as the victory of David over Goliath) may become, when viewed from a macrohistorical perspective, symbols loaded with emotional meaning and hence powerful and imposing tools of judgment. Furthermore, history is rich in analogies that can be attributed conflictory meanings, providing the opportunity to justify different and even contradictory evaluations and inferences. Finally, perceptions and expectations based on historical analogies are more rigid in the face of disconfirming information than those based on deductive logic and analysis.

National character. A fuzzier societal attribute, but one that has a number of effects on various aspects of judgment and inference in social and information-processing contexts, is national character.[2] The national character represents a modal personality, a characteristic sociopsychological structure within a given society, particularly among its elite (Inkeles and Levinson, 1969; Terhune, 1970b). The structure is enduring and stable, although some of the components can change over time, and is determinant of behavior potentials. It tends to dispose members of the society toward given behavioral patterns in specific domains and contexts and thus sets the boundaries within which the foreign and domestic environments are analyzed and interpreted and decisions formulated. Consequently national character has both direct and indirect implications for information processing at the individual and group levels. For instance, basic needs, such as achievement, approval, or dependence, have implications for the manner in which disagreements over the interpretation of information are expressed, managed, and resolved within the decisionmaking group. Tendencies toward self-examination, high or low self-esteem, consistency, and inner balance have an indirect significance for attention and for the preferred treatment of dissonant information, which impinge on self-perception and the maintenance of inner equilibrium.

Related to the effects of national character on information processing are its effects on coping strategies, which find expression, for example, in the treatment of forced compliance and cognitive dissonance (Hiniker 1969), in the ways of explaining causality in social behavior (Bond, 1983), and in national differences in motivational effects. The need to master the situation or win competitions leads to the manipulation and management of information about the self, others, and the international environment so that those objectives can be achieved.

An important dimension of national character is attitude toward authority, authority-subordinate relations, and conformity and its opposite, encouragement of intellectual independence and a readiness to challenge the evaluations and judgments made by higher authority and present alternative interpretations. Herein lie significant implications for the likelihood of the emergence of conformity and groupthink in group decisionmaking.

To conclude, some core societal attributes—the level of development, which determines the degree to which the political system is institutionalized, the degree of differentiation between the social sphere and the personal one, the degree of role differentiation, and the homogeneity or heterogeneity of the decisionmaking group; the age of the state; and national character—affect attention to information and the preference for certain types of information, the framework within which interpretations and evaluations are formed, and the degree to which information processing reflects an externalization of the personal psychological needs and biases of decisionmakers.

Effects of Cultural Attributes

Culture represents a unified set of ideas that are shared by the members of a society and that establish a set of shared premises, values, expectations, and action predispositions among the members of the nation that as a whole constitute the national style.[3] Culture is disseminated either through direct participation or indirectly by the transfer of the national-societal heritage of experience and consensual knowledge through the education and socialization systems. The shared premises and values are translated at the individual level into learned attitudes and beliefs that reflect the individual's life experience within a certain political and social environment (Davidson and Thomson, 1980; Gudykunst and Kim, 1984 10–12; Spradley, 1972).

To illustrate: throughout the war American officials could not comprehend why Vietnamese non-Communist political groups were never able to reach some agreement and a modicum of cooperation even about the common cause of opposing the Communists. The Americans had been brought up in a pluralistic culture, where almost all social relations were managed by compromise, but not so the Vietnamese. They had been socialized since childhood in a hierarchical society where the patriarch governed the life of everybody in his family. Historically, the emperor held similar power over his subjects and presided over the one correct way of life. Correct conduct resulted in peace, and peace meant not a compromise between various interest groups and organizations but unanimity. Thus Western-style intellectual freedom was not as highly valued as American decisionmakers, who depicted it as a cherished core value that was threatened by the Communists, tried to convince the American public was the case. In fact, in Vietnam the non-Communist leaders did not believe in intellectual freedom any more than did their Communist counterparts, for Vietnamese culture perceived the intellectual world as uniform and absolute (Fitzgerald, 1973: 20–23).

At the core of a culture, in most cases, are broad and general beliefs and attitudes about one's own nation, about other nations, and about the relationships that actually obtain or that should obtain between the self and other actors in the international arena. Very often the beliefs and attitudes take the form of nationally shared stereotypes, which can be modified in the individual over time by particularistic experiences and lessons. However, the original beliefs and attitudes, having been acquired at an early age, have a primacy effect that may well sensitize the person to confirming information that reinforces them. That the cognitive set has been socially sanctioned adds to its primacy effect. These assumptions, expectations, beliefs, and attitudes also affect the judgment of new information because the information processor is already committed to them.

When a decisionmaker or group of decisionmakers are culture-bound, that is, unable to see the world through the eyes of a different national or ethnic group, ethnocentrism prevails. Ethnocentrism involves strong feelings of self-group centrality and superiority, often based on myths embedded in the national culture and history that are extremely difficult to refute and have a number of impacts.

Myths, which frequently manipulate fear and superstition, may also assure in-vulnerable security—even give dangerous illusions of false security. Myths evoke the shared emotions of nationalism. Myths create social cohesion and stimulate the social consciousness of group politics. . . .

Notorious for their echnocentricity, myths frequently provide cultural defense mechanisms. They provide a psychological insulation which enforces cultural solidarity. Some peoples maintain myths pertinaciously even in the face of ex-ternal attack. As systems of belief, myths tend to be extremely antipragmatic. Myth systems in conflict are punctuated by fanaticism and violence. (Cuthbert-son, 1975: 157)

Ethnocentrism breeds stereotyping, which leads to the misjudgment of other nations' motives, intentions, and capabilities. Ethnocentrism thus becomes a powerful mechanism for screening and interpreting informa-tion, producing rigidity of perception and cognitive closure and finding expression in overconfidence and a misplaced suspicion of others' inten-tions (Booth, 1979). In part, Israeli decisionmakers' confidence, after the Six Day War, in Israel's invincibility, their belief in the capability of the intelligence community to provide an early warning, their underestima-tion of the Arab states' ability to mislead and surprise the IDF, and their certainty of a decisive and rapid victory in case of an attack by any combination of Arab forces can be attributed to their stereotype of Arabs as incompetent, cowardly, primitive, and stupid, which was contraposed to the stereotype of the Israeli as competent, decisive, clever, heroic, and efficient. Stereotyping bred overconfidence in October 1973 and led to Israeli surprise at the Egyptian and Syrian orchestrated attack on Yom Kippur.

Kissinger experienced the effect stereotyping can have on negotiations between two nations with the North Vietnamese after 1968. The clash of two different culture-bound cognitive sets and diplomatic styles provides an illuminating illustration. He observes that a history in which survival depended on skill in manipulating powerful foreign adversaries im-pressed upon the Vietnamese the compelling notion that an appearance of weakness must be avoided at almost all costs; compromise might appear to implicitly grant some validity to the adversary's point of view. Communist ideology combined with Vietnamese historical experience produced a deep suspicion and a sense of what Kissinger calls "ferocious self-righteousness" (1979: 259). To this was added the legacy of Carte-sian logic, acquired by the Vietnamese elite under French colonial rule, which bred a doctrinaire approach: North Vietnam saw its own propos-als as the sole logical truth and stated each of its demands in the imper-ative.

American history was different. The United States became great by assimilating immigrants from different cultures, and assimilation fostered an ethic of tolerance, a belief in the efficacy of goodwill, and a perception that compromise was central to bridging schisms and resolving disagreements. An approach founded on such beliefs was bound to be despised by dedicated Leninists who perceived themselves as bearers of an absolute truth and a superior moral system. They interpreted the American proposals as frivolous and as indicating that the Americans took them lightly. Kissinger concludes: "It would have been impossible to find two societies less intended by fate to understand each other than the Vietnamese and the American" (1979: 259).

Culture shapes the decisionmaker's style of thinking, mode of judgment, and attitude toward information. The norms of rationality are culture-bound; that is, the same behavior may be interpreted differently in different cultures.[4] Similar stereotypes have different connotations in different cultures, and consequently affective reactions to the stereotypes can be different.[5] Evaluations of the same behavior, objects, and issues differ in cultures representing different systems of values and beliefs.[6] The categorization of information, as well as the perceived connections between categories, is different from one culture to another (Bond, 1983; Brislin, 1981: 72–108; Triandis, 1964)—a function of historical experience and cultural dispositions. Hence a degree of cross-cultural compatibility or similarity of values, beliefs, and attitudes is a necessary condition for the establishment of some stable order in international politics in an interdependent world (Vincent, 1980). A good example is provided by the response of a high-level Korean official in an interview to a question about the Koreagate scandal, which involved the illegal spending of huge sums of money by the Korean government, often at the American taxpayers' expense, to win friends in Congress.

Q. Why has there been such a lack of response by Korean officials to Koreagate?

A. In Confucian societies, if someone fights back really hard, then there is a natural presumption there must be something wrong. If someone is really confident that he has done nothing wrong, then he knows the truth in the end will prevail. The art of waiting is a very fine Oriental art; you cannot understand our diplomacy unless you have a feel for this art of waiting. (*Newsweek*, Aug. 21, 1978, p. 48)

Yet "culture does not impose a cognitive map upon persons but provides them with a set of principles for map-making and navigation" (Ehrenhaus, 1983: 263). In particular, culture may influence the attribution process and the predisposition toward contextual, situationally based causal explanations or dispositionally based causal explanations. Consequently, culture influences the decision about what the most relevant type of information for judgments and inferences about other actors' behavior is (Ehrenhaus, 1983), so that attention, the directed search for information, and decisions about what information is important and relevant, are also affected. This culture-bound effect is likely to prove even more influential in information-overload contexts, such as crisis situations, when the order in which information is processed and decisions about which information to delay processing can be affected by cultural predispositions. Culturally based knowledge is, however, most often utilized in unfamiliar situations. Confronted by an incomprehensible situation, the decisionmaker imposes meaning by applying culturally based knowledge and interpreting the situation accordingly.[7]

In high-context cultures most of the information communicated is either part of the physical context or internalized in the communicator; in other cultures most of the information is vested in the coded, explicit portion of the message (Gudykunst and Kim, 1984: 12–13; Hall, 1976). Thus decisionmakers from high-context cultures are more aware of cultural screening processes than are those from low-context cultures. This distinction may be a source of Type 1 and Type 2 errors (see Chapter 1). A decisionmaker from a low-context culture is more likely to miss information contained in the contextual part of the communication process (Type 1 error), whereas a decisionmaker from a high-context culture is more likely to perceive meaning where none exists, that is, by unjustifiably going beyond the information given (Type 2 error).

The national cultural context sometimes provides opportunities for effective deception and makes the unmasking of deception a very difficult task. For example, in the Arab cultures the verbal articulation of imagery is as important as the underlying meaning. Many political acts, verbal and other, are performed more for their symbolic value and emotive effect than for any substantive reason—making it very difficult to distinguish true meaning and intentions from mere noise and providing a built-in cover for deception. In 1973 information about Egypt's and Syria's preparation for war and their threats to that effect were in part discounted as traditional saber rattling and usual Arab-style exaggerations, perpetrated for domestic purposes. Ironically this same cultural attribute can cut both ways. In 1967 the hyperbolic assertions of Egyptian leaders and the media convinced most Israelis of the Arab's genocidal intentions, despite President Nasser's disclaimers and gratifications. The Israeli interpretation eventually led to war and a humiliating defeat for Egypt and its allies (Amos, 1982; R. Cohen, 1988). The fact that Egypt is a high-context culture and Israel is a low-context culture exacerbated the misunderstandings.

Attention to danger and assessment of risk are also affected by cultural biases. "People who adhere to different forms of social organizations are disposed to take (and avoid) different kinds of risks. To alter risk selection and risk perception, then, would depend on changing the social organization" (Douglas and Wildavsky, 1982: 9). Each culture has its own set of social values and a hierarchy among them. The measurement of costs and benefits, the notion of what constitute unacceptable costs, and the perception of risk (the threat to values) differ from one culture to another. Hence the search for information is biased accordingly—toward information that promises knowledge about threats to high-priority values and particular dimensions of cost.

Not only is risk assessment culture-bound but the strategy of coping with risk and the assessment of its outcomes depend on attitudes encouraged by cultural norms about risk taking and risk aversion (e.g. Hong, 1978), which affect perceptions of the costs of adopting one approach or another. When cultural norms encourage risk taking, the costs of risk taking compared with the costs of risk aversion are perceived to be lower, and vice versa. For example, preference for a high-risk versus a low-risk military strategy and the estimate of the probability of success each depend on the value attributed to risk taking and risk aversion. When risk taking is the dominant value, the probability of success and the payoffs of a high-risk strategy are estimated to be higher than the probability and payoffs of a low-risk strategy. The probabilities and payoffs are inferred from culturally based norms when available information about them is ambiguous or lacking.[8]

That cultural norms shape risk assessment does not imply, however, that one person's beliefs and values cannot in some cases hold sway. Strong personalities with strongly held countercultural beliefs and values based on idiosyncratic experiences or knowledge sometimes override cultural norms when the situation and the information are ambiguous. But people seldom diverge from cultural values, because they fear doing so would prove difficult to justify, particularly in case of failure. "In risk perception, humans act less as individuals and more as social beings who have internalized social pressures" (Douglas and Wildavsky, 1982: 80). This internalization is built into the judgment process and is not easily given to self-monitoring, especially in the foreign and defense policy domains, which, even more than other issue-areas, are supposed to involve shared national beliefs and values rather than particularistic interests.

The accumulated historical experience, the political culture, as well as geopolitics, provide enduring perspectives, attitudes and beliefs, within which defense and security policy predispositions emerge. Taken as a whole, these perspectives and predispositions form the national strategic culture or style (Booth, 1979; Gray, 1981, 1986; R. G. Lord, 1985;

Segal, 1985). This then becomes the prism through which all information pertaining to national security and defense is seen when it is interpreted, judged, and evaluated. The strategic culture mirrors the national style and is an integral part of it.

American core values affected U.S. decisionmakers' approach to the problems they faced in Vietnam. The rejection of authority and the elevation of competition and equality to a cultural imperative were major influences on policymakers' thinking. Competition produced a functional approach to problems that created a predisposition toward technical solutions. The combination of competition and equality produced an atomized, present-oriented approach; policymakers rejected or were uninterested in the broad lessons of the past. Interest in the past was self-centered, and its use, mechanical and self-serving. These attributes were related to a cultural distaste for intellectual pursuits and a self-righteousness and ethnocentrism mainfested in the belief that the American way is the rational and only way and cannot fail, as American achievements prove. The combined effect of these cultural traits on the military was an almost complete ignorance of low-intensity conflicts like the ones expressed in the historical experiences of Rome, Spain, France, Britain, and Russia; and even the American experiences in the Revolutionary War, the Mexican War, and the wars in Cuba and the Philippines were mostly disregarded. American decisionmakers, the military in particular, did not understand that they were engaged first and foremost in a war for the hearts and minds of the Vietnamese people but focused their attention on the conventional, technical-military aspects, which were divorced from the political dimension of building grass-roots support (at least until 1968), and manifested their bias in the use of indicators like firepower and body count. A concomitant ignorance of Vietnamese history led to an overemphasis on the ramifications of the imbalance in sheer military power between the United States and its adversary and a misgauging of the cost of destruction that North Vietnam could bear. But a long history of fighting foreign invaders showed that the Vietnamese were willing to die for their national identity and suffer hardships to a degree Americans could not conceive of. Americans could not imagine that individuals and a society as a whole could absorb such costs and suffering without giving in. In other words, American decisionmakers were never able to think like Vietnamese.

The gap between the type of war actually fought in Vietnam and the type of war the American military knew how to fight was further enlarged when combat units were introduced in 1965. The unsuitability of this strategy again involved a misunderstanding due to ignorance of the actual problem, and not to a lack of information about the Vietcong's modus operandi. The American army was designed for high-technology conventional warfare, with massed battles, clearly identifiable enemies, and simple, sharply discernible objectives. Operations were assumed to take place where the climate was temperate, the population friendly, and material resources unlimited (Gibson, 1988; Vought, 1982). Almost none of these conditions obtained in Vietnam except for the availability of material resources. Much of the population was unfriendly, the enemy almost always avoided large-scale battles, the climate was extremely difficult for the recruits to adjust to, with the flora and fauna posing additional hazards for everyday life in the field; by the time soldiers became somewhat acclimatized, their twelve-month tour of duty was over and new recruits were taking their place and going through the same adjustment cycle all over again.

The national culture disposes national decisionmakers toward particular modes of cognitive operation across situations, expressed in *abstractive* versus *associative* thinking or in a *universalistic* versus *case-particularistic* response to information (E. S. Glenn, 1966; Glenn et al., 1970; Hoffmann, 1968b). Associative and abstractive modes of thinking are mechanisms for the selection, acquisition, and organization of knowledge. Associative thinking, because of its dependence on past habits and established structures, has a low capability to integrate novel information; consequently it is rigid and incapable of transforming existing knowledge structures in an orderly way. Also, because of the ill-defined relationships between its components, associative thinkers may absorb new associations without detecting inner contradictions. As information overload grows, associative thinkers may face growing difficulties in coping with it because coping requires imposing hierarchical structure and organization on the information in ways that may diverge sharply from the regular patterns of cognitive processes. Abstractive thinking, on the other hand, is much more capable of assimilating novel knowledge. It is flexible, more dependent on reason and logic than experience, and because it is hierarchical, better adapted structurally to dealing with a growing information load. It is situation-independent and marked by the search for clear boundaries between information categories. Associative cultures emphasize holistic-intuitive modes of thinking, including emotion-based evaluations and simplistic and highly available historical analogies, whereas abstractive cultures tend to minimize the importance of emotional factors and to favor linear-logical modes of thinking, which emphasize judgment and evaluation in rational-analytic terms.

Universalistic cultures tend to look at issues through broad frames of reference (e.g. theories and principles) and emphasize deductive logic and verbal reasoning. There is more interest in general ideas than in details, and compromise is not readily acceptable. In case-particularistic cultures, on the other hand, frames of reference are narrow, and situation-specific problems are targeted; inductive reasoning is preferred, and compromise is sought in negotiations (E. S. Glenn, 1966; Glenn et al., 1970; Glenn with Glenn, 1981; Hoffmann, 1968b). The tendency toward compromise is reflected not only in the international relations of the state but also in the preference for compromise in settling disagreements within the decisionmaking group (see Chapter 4).

Vietnamese language and socialization through formal and informal education produced an organization of mind that was associative and case particularistic. Until the mid-nineteenth century, writing was based on the Chinese system of characters. Ideograms were composed of pictures of concrete events, so that writing was without abstractions. "Each word was a thing into itself." Education at home emphasized imitating the father rather than learning principles; and at school education was based on memorizing an inventory of unsystematized stories and precepts. The study of Confucian texts involved the acquisition of Confucian logic, which is inductive; that is, the child did not learn an abstract theory of behavior but "a series of cues to the one true way of life" (Fitzgerald, 1973: 24–26). Confucian logic is completely different from Western deductive logic, where thinking depends on abstractions expressed in theories and principles. To the Western mind the dichotomy between objective truth and other social realities, such as morality and politics, is clear. For the Vietnamese, morality, politics, and knowledge were all one unified field that was utilized for the sake of, and judged by its effect on, society. In other words, knowledge and truth were subject to social needs.

An encounter in the international arena between representatives of such different cultures and styles of thinking can easily lead to mutual misunderstandings. Participants on one side perceive each event in its broad context and relate to it in terms of principles, rejecting the possibility of concessions based on pragmatic considerations. Participants on the other side see the same event as merely a detail and their adversaries' principled bargaining stand as an expression of bad faith and inherent hostility. Or decisionmakers from one culture may respond to an event and evaluate it in affective terms and possibly by means of historical analogy, which reinforces the affective element. Decisionmakers from the other culture may evaluate it in cost-benefit, rational-analytic terms. The outcome is contradictory evaluations of the situation, which may be perceived as a conflict of national interests but are actually culturally based misunderstandings. It should be noted, however, that thinking monopolized by one mode or another is rare; cognitive processes often contain elements of both, with cultural socialization predisposing decisionmakers toward one or the other. For example, primitive societies evidently socialize their members mainly toward the associative mode of thinking, whereas modern societies socialize their members more toward the abstractive mode.

Another area where cultural values have an indirect effect on cognition is decisionmaking style. The impact of culture is particularly marked in ill-defined, ambiguous situations (Gaenslen, 1986). In political systems where the dominant cultural values demand that decisions be made by consensus, the openness to dissonant information, which entails deviation from the current consensus, is likely to be low because participants are usually not prepared to undertake a time-consuming reformulation of the consensus. Moreover, decisions are likely to be phrased in vague terms that reflect the consensual common denominator, thus allowing a broad latitude to the bureaucracy in interpreting the decision during implementation. On the other hand, where a dominant cultural value emphasizes strong authoritarian control, it impedes decisional input and feedback from subordinates (Jensen, 1982: 48–49), for they are reluctant to question, or introduce information that questions, the quality of decisions made at higher levels. At the same time authoritarian cultural values provide a broad latitude to top decisionmakers who wish to change policies, since they know that they can count on the compliance of subordinates.

In bargaining situations the national culture influences perceptions of what the most acceptable means for conflict resolution are (e.g. compromise, adjudication) and determine negotiation style (i.e. formal, informal). Unawareness of these factors can lead to misperceptions of how and when agreement is likely or unlikely to be reached and to the making of hopeless proposals that cannot pave the way to common ground, the rejection of which is incorrectly interpreted in bad faith terms. Similarly, body language, which plays a signaling role in interpersonal communication, is also partly culture-bound (Argyle, 1975; R. Cohen, 1987; Gudykunst and Kim, 1984: 156–61). For example, Japanese smile when they are reprimanded, and the uninitiated may consider smiling impertinent. Hence it is important to be aware of cultural factors in international bargaining and negotiation situations; participants should understand not only the other side's verbal behavior but also their physical behavior to avoid misperceptions.

Whereas some societal and cultural attributes are unique to specific societies, others cut across cultures. For example, the American and French societies and cultures have some basic attributes in common that stem from their both being Western and modernized; yet at the same time they have different historical heritages. Whereas Americans tend toward inductive thinking, French tend more toward deductive and abstract thinking. Thus they interpret and judge occurrences in the international system from a perspective whose duality produces a mixture of similarities and dissimilarities in perceptions. In general the thinking style of people in the United States is distinguishable from that of Europeans by its heavier stress on empirical facts, induction, and operationalism (abstractive and case-particularistic thinking). Europeans, on the other hand, stress ideas and theories that give priority to the conceptual world. They attach less importance to the amassing of facts and statistics and more to deductive thinking (abstractive and universalistic thinking). In spite of these differences both cultural groups emphasize cognitive patterns that are logical, categorical, linear, and analytic (Gudykunst and Kim, 1984: 123).

Intelligence and other information processing organizations nevertheless tend either to be only partially attuned to important cultural differences or to assume that the perspectives of the other side and the prism through which it analyzes world affairs are the reverse of their own, so that they decouple the unique attributes of the national culture from their political relevance and significance for statecraft. Misunderstanding and not knowing the original norms and values prevailing in a society's domestic order lead to misjudgments of its foreign policy views and behavior because the inner order tends to be externalized in its relations with the outside world. Intelligence agencies misinterpret façades, the use of commonly shared vocabularies, and forms of organizations for dealing with foreign affairs that were adopted for convenience or imposed by former colonial powers as reflecting the actual substance of the other's world view, goals, intentions, and policy preferences (Bozeman, 1960, 1985); they therefore fail to understand and anticipate change or forecast future developments.

Language as a Conceptual Framework

One of the most prominent and unique expressions of national culture is language. In contact between members of different cultures the preferred basis for judgment and evaluation is verbal interaction, although the nature of the relationship between verbal and nonverbal messages differs in Western and Eastern cultures (Gudykunst and Kim, 1984: 136–44; Jacobson, Kumata, and Gullahorn, 1960). The preference for verbal communication might become a source of misconceptions resulting from the nature of language itself. The meaning of the same words is similar only when the parties using them share the same cultural and historical background, which imbues words with their full symbolic value, as is embedded in a "tacit agreement" between members of the same linguistic culture (Katz, 1974; Ogden and Richards, 1972: 209–42). Language is the verbal expression of a particular world view, representing cultural patterns that are different from those underlying other languages and serving as the means by which occurrences are examined and interpreted, their importance assessed, and decisions made about what should and should not be noticed and attended to. In other words, language is not only an instrument of communication but an integral part of cognition, which shapes and organizes the way people perceive reality. "Thinking is always thinking in some language" (Schaff, 1973: 82, 121–39; see also Brown and Lennenberg, 1954; Whorf, 1956). Comparing Chinese with English, Bloom (1981: 52–60) argues that languages lead their speakers to become the bearers of distinctive cognitive worlds. In this case Chinese speakers, unlike English speakers, are disinclined to engage in purely theoretical thinking.

These two uses of language—as a framework for thinking and as a means of communication—are what makes language problematic in relation to perception and cognition. Fine distinctions in one language that may seem a masterpiece of diplomatic skill are not always readily and fully transferable to another, either through translation or through the medium of a third common language.[9] In certain languages (e.g. Chinese, Japanese) the language structure itself promotes ambiguity. The use of a shared language, when it is not a native tongue, does not change the tendency to think along lines and cognitive habits established by the native tongue. A superficial illusion of mutual understanding may be created by the use of a third shared language, in which terms may have different connotations than they have in the native languages. When reality belies that illusion, a mutual feeling of deception sets in, opening the way to mistrust. The cognitive effects of language differences are more pronounced the more abstract the subject of perception (Fisher, 1972: 99). Therefore, when issues are seen through some abstract cognitive prism (e.g. ideology) or from some world view, language barriers are likely to have strong negative effects on the accuracy of mutual understanding.

The episode in which Khrushchev remarked, "We will bury you," is well known. His words are usually interpreted in their active sense to mean "We will destroy you" or "We will conquer you." The translation is literally correct but in a different sense; it means "We will outlive you," expressing the conviction that Communism will outlast capitalism and not necessarily that the Communists will destroy the West (Klineberg, 1964: 153).

One of the most likely types of misunderstanding may occur when parties discuss concrete subjects without being aware of their broader meanings and deeper implications for each party and thus misinterpret each other's position. An interesting case is the conflict since the 1950's between China and India over Tibet, in which the mutual misunderstanding over the meaning of terms such as autonomy, sovereignty, and suzerainty with regard to Tibet was exacerbated by the differences in the cultural-ideological connotations of the words. The misunderstanding arose over the issue of whether China had sovereignty (the Chinese version) or suzerainty (the Indian version) over Tibet. In fact, the Western concept of sovereignty was alien to the traditional Chinese approach to foreign policy. It gained acceptance only during the last decade of the Ch'ing dynasty, which saw the rise of nationalism; thus the two concepts—sovereignty and nationalism—were emotionally and cognitively tied. The new approach to foreign policy was extremely broad, opposing not only imperialistic acts that threatened to introduce foreign control but all those that infringed, even theoretically, on China's sovereignty. Hence, for the nationalistic Chinese leadership the sovereignty-suzerainty question regarding Tibet was no minor verbal or legal matter but one of major affective and ideological importance, especially in the light of the different connotations the two words have in Chinese. Suzerainty (*tsung chu ch'üan*) has imperialistic connotations (the ideograms describe tribute relations) that sovereignty (*chu ch'üan*) does not have. The Communist leaders rejected defining modern China's relationship with Tibet by the concept of suzerainty, which, for them, contained an unacceptable hidden connotation.

The misunderstanding was made worse by a problem relating to Communist China's unique political terminology, the comprehension of which required a broad acquaintance with its political culture and the nature of Maoist ideology. Thus, when the leaders of India and China spoke of autonomy for Tibet, the term meant different things to each side. The term autonomy in Chinese Communist terminology expresses mainly the fact that in a certain area an ethnic minority makes up most of the population, whereas in Western terminology the term implies an amount of independence (Vertzberger, 1984a: 214).

Important value-loaded connotations often get lost in the transposition of core terms and concepts from one language to another. Thus, for example, in the traditional Vietnamese culture the village has a central and autonomous role both socially and spiritually. The Vietnamese word that carries the full load of traditional connotations of the term village is *xa.* The Vietnamese word for socialism, which appeared in the National Liberation Front's action program, is *xa hoi*. Using it indicated to the Vietnamese peasantry that the revolution would entail no traumatic break with the past but would extend and express their traditional village-based culture—a connotation that contributed considerably to the popularity of the program. In translation, however, the term *xa hoi* loses all its implicit meanings. CIA analysts failed to understand its significance and underestimated the prospect of the program's appealing to the people and gaining their support (A. M. Lewis, 1976).

Words also carry different affective loads in different cultures, and consequently they arouse the expectations bound up with those different affective loads, expectations that fail to be fulfilled in the circumstances we are discussing, especially when the words have symbolic connotations and evoke metaphors carrying an affective load of which the user is not aware. Thus one state may describe another as a sister state or their relationship as brotherly solidarity to convey friendship, whereas to the target state, where the family role may be a central social imperative, the same word may carry a much stronger affective load and arouse expectations of a much deeper commitment than the user intended. As a result, the opening of a cycle of mistrust becomes a real possibility. In a "Black Book" on Vietnamese aspiration for domination in Southwest Asia, the Pol Pot government of Cambodia criticized Vietnam's insistence on calling Ho Chi Minh uncle and argued that "this appellation is closely linked with their ambition to be father of Indo-China" (Chanda, 1979: 20).

Language in a less conventional sense refers also to the terminology of the political culture, which is ingrained in the national ideology and world view but has unique political connotations. Even common words like peace, war, progress, and democracy acquire different connotations in different ideological and cultural contexts and have different meanings for the user and the audience. When President Diem talked about democracy in the 1950's, his American audience understood the word in its Jeffersonian sense, even though he was using it with the nineteenth-century Vietnamese emperor Minh Mang in mind. Minh Mang had proposed the creation of a consultative assembly of mandarins to provide advice and collective approval for the royal decrees. Obviously, Diem was not thinking of a pluralistic political system, nor would such a system have been in line with the Confucian tradition of government, which demanded obedience and unanimity from the people (Fitzgerald, 1973: 116–18). Policymakers who are unaware of alternative connotations misinterpret what they hear from their counterparts in other countries; since they also misjudge how well they themselves are understood by the other side, they end up adopting baseless expectations. The problem is intensified when the ongoing national experience introduces changes in the connotations of the terminologies used and when one of the participants is not aware of the changes.

Another type of linguistic fallacy involves the abuse of meaning through the undisciplined use of language—what Moynihan (1978, 1979) calls semantic infiltration. He points out how the most brutal totalitarian regimes and movements in the world label themselves liberation movements or people's democracies. These terms are then adopted by the United States and other Western democracies, which in the long run may help to distort reality by continually using them.

Semantic infiltration can also be self-inflicted. A catchphrase from the decisionmakers' own political culture can come to dominate their thinking to such a degree that it becomes a reality immune to contradictory evidence. Some American decisionmakers said "defense of the free world" so often with regard to Vietnam that they actually came to believe that the United States was defending the free world there. Growing American involvement became a value-laden necessity, although the hope for a South Vietnamese democratic government that would comply with the most basic moral and political principles being part of the free world entailed became less and less realistic. American decisionmakers spoke about non-Communist Southeast Asia as a coherent political system that faced a common enemy, not realizing the long historical record of fear, animosity, and war among these allies. For example, the Cambodians and Laos feared and distrusted the (South and North) Vietnamese and Thais no less, and maybe even more, than the Communist Chinese. Nor did the Thais see a common cause with the South Vietnamese that obligated them to help them. In fact, the language used by the Americans obliterated the acute national and cultural differences among the non-Communist countries of Southeast Asia but highlighted the national differences between North and South Vietnam that justified the permanent division of the country (Fitzgerald, 1973: 54–56).

A close relative of semantic infiltration is the habitual and thoughtless use of labels like liberal and conservative that are often simplistic or misleading (Laqueur, 1981). The corruption of political language leads to wrong inferences and expectations about other regimes' intentions and behavior. What is particularly dangerous is the misguided sense, stemming from the frequent use of these words, of clarity and unambiguity when the opposite is true. Thus a vicious circle is created in which the more the terms are used, the more unambiguous they seem to be and the less reluctant and less careful the users are to use them again; they use them without being sufficiently aware of the cognitive fallacies that may be entailed.

The powerful impact of these linguistic biases is not in the influence of any one of them separately but in their cumulative effect in definitions of the situation. Minor biases are mutually reinforcing and have other, noncultural sources, so that they are difficult to detect, isolate, and eliminate. They simply slip in, unconsciously affect thinking and information processing, and become rooted in decisionmakers' minds.

National Concepts of Belonging, Role, and Status

The national self-image is focused on three concepts that provide the state with a sense of identity and impinge, directly and indirectly, on its international behavior: (1) the concept of belonging, that is, To which group of nations does the state see itself belonging? (2) the concept of role, that is, What role does it perceive for itself in the international arena? and (3) the concept of status, that is, What status does it believe it has or deserves? Belonging, role, and status conceptions form an integral part of the national style.

Information about role and status allocations in the international system, as well as in regional and functional (e.g., Islamic, nonaligned) subsystems, and the categorization of actors by their belonging to subsystems, geographical or otherwise, provide a source of knowledge based on script and persona-type schemata (e.g. regional leader, mediator) that enable decisionmakers to go beyond the information given. The knowledge facilitates the inferring and predicting of the expectations, world views, and behavior of other actors in general, as well as providing insights about how others view the decisionmakers' state. Consequently the decisionmakers can make what they consider educated guesses about the possible reactions of allies and adversaries to particular situations and events, especially when inside information about those actors is scant or missing altogether. At the same time the knowledge provides the actors with guidelines regarding what are and what are not appropriate action orientations in response to environmental challenges.

Belonging conceptions. The conception of being part of a particular group of states determines the expectations that any specific state entertains about its group members as well as the expectations the other members in the group have toward it. Most states belong to several subsystems at one and the same time. For example, a nation can simultaneously be a developing, Asian, and socialist country. State A's simultaneous membership in several groups sometimes gives the other actors conflicting expectations about its behavior. One of the main strategies for State A in avoiding conflicting expectations is to explain them away as noncontradictory or to ignore the contradictions. Other actors may regard them as serious enough to warrant resolution, a concern that finds expression in their behavior toward the state in question, which the target state may misunderstand. India, for example, has been at the same time a member of the nonaligned movement and of the British Commonwealth. When some countries contended that the two memberships were incompatible, since membership in the British Commonwealth meant tacit alignment with the West, Nehru preferred to ignore the contradiction inherent in the situation and took trouble to explain why it did not exist.

Sometimes, however, the expectations of the state belonging to a particular group of states and the expectations and conceptions of other group members about the commitments arising from that membership are uncorrelated. Pakistan thought its joining the Southeast Asia Treaty Organization (SEATO) would be at least partly instrumental in giving it an edge in its conflict with India and expected some support from other SEATO members. They, however, saw the SEATO alliance solely as an instrument for containing Communist expansion and did not intend to get involved in Indo-Pakistani rivalries. The price of frustrated expectations—unfulfilled in this case because they were altogether misplaced from the outset—is disappointment and a cycle of hypermistrust on both sides.

Finally, incongruent conceptions of belonging may reflect disagreements over the definition of subsystem boundaries. A state that perceives itself as belonging to a certain bloc or subsystem develops expectations about the appropriate attitudes and behavior of other member states toward it. But other actors may have different ideas about the attributes that define the subsystem boundaries and how the traits of that particular state relate to them and may thus not consider it to belong to the subsystem at all. Their ensuing behavior then causes the state in question to feel deceived or mistreated. It does not correctly anticipate the reactions of other member states toward it, whereas the others may not understand why that particular state expects a different treatment.

One case in which conceptions of belonging are fuzzy occurs when a state's bloc membership is unclear. For example, for geographical and historical reasons, the Soviet Union feels that Yugoslavia is within its sphere of influence. But in 1968 Secretary Rusk announced that Yugoslavia and Austria fell within the Western sphere of security interests. Such ambiguity could have important and even dangerous policy implications because it could lead the competing superpowers to apply incongruent rules of behavior to the same situation. One power may perceive an act of intrabloc intervention where its adversary sees an act of inter-bloc intervention. Consequently, even when the rules of the game that are applicable for each situation (e.g. intervention) are clear and shared by the adversaries, a disagreement over the definition of the situation based on different perceptions of belonging may cause a confrontation that the very same shared rules are supposed to prevent.

Role conceptions. The concept of the national role is defined thus: "A national role conception includes the policymakers' own definitions of the general kinds of decisions, commitments, rules and actions suitable to their state, and of the functions, if any, their state should perform on a continuing basis in the international system or in subordinate regional systems" (K. J. Holsti, 1970: 245–46).[10] It follows that any actor's role conception and its expression depend to some degree on the role player's conception of the roles of other actors and those actors' preparedness to play their assigned parts. The cluster of main role and complementary roles among a group of nations is the role-set.

A number of problems may arise. Are all participants in the role-set indeed aware that they are part of it? If so, do they know how to play their assigned roles to conform to the expectations of the main role holder as well as to those of other participants? Those expectations pertain not only to what acts should be performed in particular circumstances but also to how they should be performed (Sarbin and Allen, 1968: 497–98). For example, the role of regional leader would be associated not only with general expectations about playing a leadership role in regional crises but also with specific expectations about how to do it, for example, by forming a regional consensus or by imposing a specific solution to a particular problem. Nor are all role expectations explicit or formally expressed; some are latent, and for them, reaching a convergence of expectations is most difficult, especially when different cultures are involved.

Before further analyzing the complex effects role playing has on information processing about self-images and images of other actors, an illustration of some of the problems will be useful. Let us look at the effects of role conception in the escalation of the Sino-Indian conflict from 1959 to 1962, which culminated in a war between the two powers.

The role conceptions Nehru adopted for India were based on a number of factors that I shall mention only briefly: (1) ancient Indian history, in which India played a central role in Asia and also served as a cultural, political, and economic focus for regions beyond Asia; (2) later Indian history, in which India was subjugated to imperialistic and colonial powers from beyond the subcontinent; (3) Gandhian values and ideology, which rejected power plays and violence among individuals and nations; and (4) the location of the subcontinent at geopolitical and geostrategic crossroads. These factors naturally produced certain role conceptions. First, they qualified India for a position of leadership on two levels: a regional leadership in Asia and a broader leadership position among the nonaligned and developing countries of the world. Second, its colonial history committed India to a central role in the struggle against imperialism. Third, for ideological as well as practical reasons India conceived of two additional roles for itself: one as an international mediator and the other as a bridge between cultures and ideologies, that is, a link between East and West and between the socialist and capitalist worlds. All of these conceptions necessitated India's taking on the role of active neutralism in international politics. Fourth, India saw itself as a political and economic model for other Third World nations. All in all, Nehru conceived of six roles for India in the regional and global arenas that indicated a perception of senior status for India on the international scene; this perception in turn implied a high degree of power, from which India incorrectly inferred a low vulnerability.

Like India, China saw itself as a regional leader in Asia; in addition, it saw a future role for itself as a global leader. On the regional level were the role as bastion of the world revolution, which called for supporting change and the destabilization of anti-Communist regimes, and the role as vanguard of the anti-imperialist and antirevisionist forces. Finally, China saw itself as a social, economic, and political model for all developing countries. China, then, conceived of five roles for itself, which likewise indicated a perceived senior status in the regional and global arenas.

A number of conflicts between these two sets of role conceptions were inevitable. Both countries saw themselves as having leadership roles in the same region. A zero-sum game emerged, for a division of leadership was not possible, especially given the traditional Sinocentric view of the world order as rigidly hierarchical. So long as the relations between the two countries remained friendly because they shared other interests, the effect of the struggle for regional leadership could be subdued; but once relations deteriorated, the struggle became part and parcel of the border dispute between the two states and contributed to the conclusion of the Chinese cost-benefit analysis: that military force would be of use in putting India in its proper place.

Both countries also saw themselves as models for other developing countries. The Indian leadership did not fully realize the significance of the struggle in relation to the differences between the Indian and Chinese cultures. According to the Hindu world view, several truths can coexist, one complementing another. Thus, according to India, different socioeconomic models can coexist without incurring a confrontation. However, according to both the traditional Chinese world view and Maoist doctrine, there is only one truth, which, at some point, when the opposing forces reach an irrevocable polarization, necessarily imposes itself and proves its superiority, by force if necessary. Once the behavior of the Indian leadership, by its treatment of the border dispute, established beyond doubt that the conflicts could not be settled amicably, the basic contradiction between the Indian and Chinese models became an incentive for resolving the border conflict by the use of force. For China to use force fit in with its other role conceptions: with its frontline position in the struggle against imperialism and revisionism, where it saw India as allied to both, and with its support for revolutionary change in the political status quo in countries defined as reactionary, as India now was.

For Nehru the problem was complex. First, he found it intolerable to acknowledge that there was an irreconcilable regional leadership struggle between India and China. The notion completely contradicted his view of Asian solidarity, which applied especially to the two largest countries in Asia. Furthermore, an admission of a Sino-Indian confrontation would contradict the concept of India as a bridge between East and West, North and South, socialism and capitalism; it would also damage Nehru's ability to act as a mediator and peacekeeper. At the same time an admission that the Indian army was incapable of meeting the Chinese challenge would require that India give up its role as an independent nation since massive foreign military aid would be required to cope with the situation. The problem was resolved simply by understating the discrepancies and conflict between India's and China's role conceptions (Vertzberger, 1984a: 221–22).

Several points pertain to role conceptions. First, any actor can play more than one role. Thus, during the Nasser regime Egypt attributed a number of roles to itself, such as regional leader, bastion of the revolution, unifier of the Arab world, and leader of the Third World. The role player's perception of the legitimacy of playing a particular combination of roles can be incongruent with the perceptions of other actors in the system, who may regard the roles as incompatible and taking them on as illegitimate. Yet since the role player does not perceive the contradiction, it may have difficulty becoming cognizant of the negative light in which other actors in the system regard its role playing.[11] In the post–World War II period, the United States did not perceive any contradiction between its role as flag bearer of the lofty ideals of self-determination and democracy and its role as leader of the Western world, a role that committed it to support its allies in holding on to their colonies. Third World nations saw the contradiction, however, as proof of American hypocrisy and responded by displaying a hostile attitude toward the United States.

Second, role conception and enactment both shape and test the reality of beliefs and attitudes about other actors and about the structure of the international system or a regional subsystem. They provide a prism through which incoming information about the self, other actors, and the relationship between the self and others can be seen, then judged and interpreted. The United States, for example, perceived its commitment to and role in Vietnam as a test of its national will. All that was needed to prevail, it believed, was will. This belief was closely related to the fascination with power and the knowledge that no other nation had ever before wielded such power (Thomson, 1973: 107). America believed that it was morally obligated to take on the defense of non-Communist Vietnam as part of its responsibility for shaping and preserving a just and free world, assuming that the combination of morality, power, and the will to apply power could not but lead to final victory. The sense of omnipotence had become more pronounced after the 1962 Cuban missile crisis and matched the world's view of the United States as the arbiter of human affairs. These circumstances supported American ethnocentrism, which expressed itself in the belief that the American way was the only way and that those who were not aware of or denied the American way had to be taught a lesson.

Third, even before a state actually fills a desired role, it may adopt beliefs and attitudes that seem to it appropriate to playing the role in order to convince other actors that it could or should be allowed to play it. For example, an actor that wants the role of intermediary in the international arena tends to adopt attitudes and behavior patterns indicating neutrality or impartiality.

Fourth, a country may refuse to assume a role to which it is entitled or which others expect it to play because of circumstances, such as its level of power or its geostrategic position. An outstanding example is the refusal of Japan until recently to take an active leadership role in Asia. However, in the long run the expectations of other actors may finally impose a role on the actor, along with all the obligations that go with it. Thus pressure from other actors has finally obliged Japan to assume a growing position of active leadership in Asia and to extend it to the international system at large.

When a country refuses to take on a specific role or when other countries try to impose a certain role conception on it, the target's self-conception could be incongruent with others' conceptions of it—but without its being aware of the incongruence since according to its self-conception, the role is not its to play. Nevertheless, the other actors may interpret its behavior in terms of the role they attribute to it. For example, given Japan's history, Southeast Asian states did not accept its refusal to take the position of Asian leader as an expression of its genuine motivations and interests. Whereas Japan perceived its large-scale investments in and foreign assistance to Asian states as having benign economic motivations, the elite in countries such as Malaysia, the Philippines, and Indonesia suspiciously perceived its aid and investments as expressing some form of Japanese neocolonialism.

Two types of misperception may result from role playing. First, a putative main role player may make erroneous judgments about the willingness of other actors to play the roles assigned to them (e.g. if it plays regional leader, others must play followers). Second, even if other actors are ready to accept one actor's role conception, the actor's expectations of what that role entails might still be incompatible with others'. For example, when an actor takes the role of intermediary with the consent of the parties to a conflict, the fact that the parties are ready to accept it as an intermediary creates the illusion that the substance of that role is also agreed upon by all concerned, something that does not always hold true.

These attributes of role playing and role allocation in the international system have implications for role enactment at both the practical and perceptual levels. Role enactment in a complex international environment involves multiple judgment processes with regard to the following issues: What role should be enacted? Are the time and circumstances appropriate for a particular role enactment? How should it be enacted? Does it involve simultaneous role enactments by other members of the role-set, and are they likely to comply? Misjudgment with regard to any one of these questions could lead to negative or unexpected outcomes in the relationship with other members of the role-set (e.g. decline in credibility, weakening of an alliance relationship), with adversaries, or with other actors—the audience that observes role performances for future reference.

A particular role does not necessarily involve a single specific behavior pattern in a particular situation but rather an action orientation that can be translated into various action clusters. Thus it is not unusual even when agreeing on the role a particular state should play for different actors to hold incompatible views about what that role entails in any specific situation. However, since actors may misjudge the degree to which a role is given to different operational interpretations, they are also bound to be surprised when the role holder's behavior does not conform to their expectations because of its own interpretation of what type of behavior is implied.

Walker (1979: 189–90) raises another possibility: that Actor A may be induced to enact a different role behavior toward Actor B than its role conception calls for if Actor B's behavior calls for such a departure. For example, if the enactment of a role calls for conflictory behavior and Actor B, contrary to expectations, acts in a consistently cooperative manner, then Actor A may be forced to adopt cooperative behavior itself. It may either reevaluate its role conception or manipulate information to explain away Actor B's behavior as guile or deception. Or Actor A may perceive and explain Actor B's role enactment as fitting the traditional role conception even though it does not. Dulles chose the first alternative when having to enact the U.S. role as container of Communism and Soviet expansion. He interpreted the Soviet display of tension-reduction overtures as intended to mislead, as reflective of tactical needs based on a current weakness that would change as soon as the correlation of forces shifted in favor of the Soviet Union (O. R. Holsti, 1969).

The deviation of actual behavior from role expectations may lead to a change in other actors' subsequent expectations or to the effective removal of the role holder from its role through the refusal of role-set members to cooperate and play their roles in the future. Such was the case with Egypt's leadership role in the Arab world following its peace treaty with Israel. To the degree that an incongruence between role expectations and behavior stems from misjudgments, inferences about future behavior as well as role reallocations are misplaced, leading to change in the existing international (global or regional) order, which is based on the current role allocations, without necessarily introducing an alternative, clearly structured order. Consequently, changes in the international order may lead to a period in which roles and rules are vague, given to a variety of competing interpretations and views, and likely to breed faulty inferences and mutual misperceptions.

Change poses a particularly difficult problem for the information processor. System change always involves a reallocation of roles within the role-sets and among actors and consequently requires the adjustment of expectations about and interpretations of other actors' behavior. At the same time correctly understanding other actors' expectations and behavior toward oneself depends on being aware of the changes in roles and role-sets. Yet detecting change as it occurs is difficult because it rarely happens in an immediately observable manner; it is often an incremental process with observation lagging behind. It is even more difficult to detect concurrently the two less dramatic types of change: systemic and interaction changes.[12] The first entails changes within the system or subsystem without involving a structural change of the system itself, which entails change in the overall hierarchy of power and prestige and the replacement of declining powers with rising powers. But even such limited changes involve role and status redefinitions for at least some of the actors in the system or subsystem. When not attended to, the cognitive consequences of such changes are not observed, with inaccurate interpretations of information and faulty definitions of the situation as a result. Similarly, interaction changes, that is, modifications in political, economic, and other interactions among the actors, can also encompass redefinitions of role enactments, that is, others' redefined expectations about how the roles an actor plays should be enacted. Noncognizance of interaction change leads to wrong predictions of other actors' behavior and incorrect interpretations of others' expectations of and reactions to one's own acts and messages. In more general terms, system, systemic, or interaction change is likely to produce either role and status change, or changes in role-sets and role enactments, or all of these. To the degree that role and status conceptions are integral to information-processing schemata, their accurate and timely observation is necessary for effective information processing.

Any given international order, then, like a domestic one, is built around tacit or explicit role allocations and the consequent expectations. Some of the roles are institutionalized (e.g. permanent members of the U.N. Security Council), and others are informal (e.g. leaders of regional blocs). The balance between formal and informal, institutionalized and noninstitutionalized roles and the related expectations are differential across issue-areas and may change over time.

When and under what circumstances are national roles likely to be a cause of cognitive conflict?

1. When an actor perceives itself to be committed to multiple roles.

2. When the structure of situational attributes is perceived to require simultaneous multiple role enactments.

3. When environmental constraints or other circumstances produce oblique conceptions of roles and role enactments.

These circumstances indicate the following specific situational contexts in which role-based cognitive conflicts are likely:

1. When a country is deeply involved in international politics.

2. When multiple crisis situations that demand simultaneous treatment require the enactment of more than one role.

3. When a new role enactment with which the actor-state has had little or no prior experience is called for, meaning it is not fully aware of what is expected of it.

4. When system change involves structural change, so that major and secondary actors take on novel roles because they are new to the international system; the roles are new to the actors, which had different roles in the old system; or the roles did not exist in the old system because its structure did not require them.

5. When a change in domestic leadership brings to power decision-makers with no skill in managing role conflict because of lack of experience or lack of creativity.

When any of these conditions apply, role playing, which is an important component of coping, can be inappropriately or improperly done, increasing the probability of the occurrence and mismanagement of international conflict and crisis, including the outbreak of violence. Faulty role playing occurs because learning in the international arena is often a matter of trial and error, with problems considered to be either ad hoc and novel, or because valid knowledge answering to some of the core questions and issues is lacking, given the inadequate education of decisionmakers in the intricacies of international politics. Their insufficient education is partly rooted in the belief that international relations is not an issue-area that calls for specific learning and skills but one in which any skillful amateur with the right intuition can perform effectively.

Status conceptions. The concept of state status is related to the concept of role conception (K. J. Holsti, 1970; Jönsson and Westerlund, 1982; Wish, 1980), since status conception determines what roles the state believes it should play. On the other hand, some roles, more than others, confer high status and prestige on those playing them. A state's status conception and its level of aspiration are important sources of foreign-policy-related opinions, beliefs, and images (Hveem, 1972), as well as sources of misperceptions. Like role conception, status conception has two facets. One is self-conception, the status the state believes it deserves, or achieved status. The other is the status other states in the international system believe that the state deserves, or ascribed status. Status conception is one of the prisms through which the behavior of the self and others is filtered, then evaluated and judged. Different status positions produce different perspectives on the environment (Reychler, 1979: 19), which can pose a number of perceptual problems.

The status accorded a state in the international system, its ascribed status, is not necessarily identical with the status it believes it is due. Studies (East, 1972; Galtung, 1968; Midlarsky, 1975; Wallace, 1973) dealing with the gap between achieved and ascribed status indicate that if a country believes that its status is lower than its due, it tends to react to its frustration by externalizing conflictory behavior. The discrepancy between achieved and ascribed status is necessarily a perceptual phenomenon; hence a nation unaware of an existing discrepancy will not act to correct it. On the other hand, the false cognizance of a discrepancy leads to attempts to correct it if it reaches a certain threshold of annoyance, even at high risks and costs to the state in question.

States are ranked on various dimensions for status: military, political, economic, technological, cultural, and so on. When a state ranks high on one or some but low on other dimensions, the status discrepancy may lead to an incongruence between ascribed and achieved status. A state may differ from others in its judgments about which dimensions decide status or what status combining all the dimensions confers. For the state in question status discrepancy can also be a source of confusion: What should its status be, and how should it be treated by other states in the system? Confusion raises the level of uncertainty in predicting and interpreting other states' expected behavior, as well as in anticipating others' expectations of its own behavior. At the same time status discrepancy raises the level of threat the other states in the system experience vis-à-vis the disequilibrated state (Doran, Hill, and Mladenka, 1979).

The great importance that nations attach to their status makes their leaders ignore or repress information that points to a possibility that their self-attributed status is higher than that accorded them by other nations in the international system. As a result, they may attribute unrealistic roles to themselves. An illuminating example can be found in Polish history. Recognizing, in the sixteenth century, the material superiority of West European civilization and having to reconcile it with their self-ascribed status as the central state in Europe, the Polish leadership stressed the superiority of Polish moral values (chivalry, piety, honesty). Later, in the seventeenth century, Polish superiority and uniqueness were attributed to Poland's national role as the bastion of Christianity and as the shield and granary of Europe. During that time Poland's actual role and status in Europe became increasingly peripheral, yet because it could not recognize that fact, national pride was transformed over time into megalomania (Jasińska-Kania, 1982: 102–3). The historical heritage of a nation, then, bequeaths to it a fixed status conception that does not flexibly correspond to a decline in the state's power over time, so that the state cannot adjust its policies accordingly. Britain, for example, after 1900, should have given more attention than it did to revitalizing its domestic economy, but it continued to follow policies "appropriate for a rising hegemony long after Britain's star had begun to fall" (Krasner, 1976: 342). The historical record confirms that intelligence and other relevant bureaucratic organizations dealing with foreign policy are unable to coordinate their assessments so as to provide a comprehensive integrated appreciation of the nation's position. Instead assessments tend to be fragmented and compartmentalized. Such assessments reflect over-reliance on simple, easily available numerical indicators of capability. What further complicates the making of a long-range realistic assessment of a nation's position in times of change is the fact that a nation's relative economic and military power do not rise and decline in parallel (Friedberg, 1988: 290–91; Kennedy, 1987: xxiii). That makes an accurate multidimensional assessment less likely to be offered because it requires observations based on an abstract understanding of the processes underlying the rise and decline of nations, rather than an observable quantitative indicator at a particular point in time.

When attributed status is higher than deserved status, the state tends to adopt the unrealistic attributed status and to adjust expectations and aspirations to it as if it reflected the state's real power; nations, in general, rarely suffer from excess modesty. The Six Day War of 1967 secured for Israel a status that exceeded its real long-range capabilities, and after the war it adopted that status as expressing its real power and rightful position. The resulting exaggerated sense of security and self-assurance had very serious consequences in 1973. Even when status self-ascription is realistic, nations may perceive status allocations differently, since different cultures set different values as indicators of status. This phenomenon finds clear expression in the age-old struggle over status—between nations that perceive it to arise solely from tangible power resources and those that regard it as at least partially arising from spiritual and moral power. The problem of accurate and consensual role and status conceptions is particularly acute in an international system of complex interdependence. The importance of sheer military power as the main ordering criterion, determining hierarchy and thus dictating role and status conceptions, has diminished significantly. Moreover, in a system of complex interdependence issues are linked and arranged horizontally in terms of importance.[13] Hence another ordering criterion—that of an actor's dominance and high status with respect to what used to be recognized in the past as the most important issue-areas—becomes less useful as a measuring rod for status judgment of states in the current international system.

Furthermore, the current international system is a two-level system. On the nuclear-military level the power structure is clearly bipolar. But at the economic-political level the system is multipolar because nuclear power is not fungible and cannot be transferred and translated effectively to dominate and dictate the outcomes of nonmilitary issues and transactions. Thus the different expectations that arise from different evaluations of what systemic rules apply to any particular issue may cause misunderstandings even between allies. Any given issue below the nuclear-power level can potentially raise the problem of which rules apply to the issue at hand, those of a bipolar or those of a multipolar system. Different answers by the different actors may cause mutually frustrated expectations about the behavior of allies and adversaries alike. Expectations are also frustrated because different role and status conceptions follow the actors' perceptions of which system applies to the situation and issue at hand. Coexisting simultaneously, in fact, are two different systemic structures, which have different distributions of capabilities, different ordering and organizational principles, and different specifications of the functions, roles, and status of units.[14]

Conclusions

Societal attributes have notable psychocultural and sociocultural effects. They shape cognitive style, prime the decisionmaker to use particular patterns of information processing, and become a prism through which information is filtered. The most important attributes are the level of development, national style and culture, the national language, and the historical heritage, which provides historical analogies and lessons and stamps its imprint on national style and character. The shaping process is sometimes a conscious one; but much more frequently it is unconscious, an unawareness that makes feedback ineffective in contributing to learning.

National self-images, which draw on societal attributes, are expressed in conceptions of belonging, status, and role in the international system. The range of roles that a country perceives itself as able and deserving to play is liable to be inconsonant with the range perceived by the other actors in the system. Even when a basic consonance about what roles it should play has already been established, the state's interpretation of what its role, belonging, and status commit it to are liable to be discrepant with the views of other states. These discrepancies create the potential for biased information processing, as do the interactions and mutual influences of conceptions of belonging, status, and role. What emerges is an instrumental relationship of the conceptions to the information as a verification that the country was fulfilling its designated role in the regional and international arenas and at the same time a tendency toward rigidity and self-censorship of, or selective attention to, information indicating the impossibility of realizing the desired role. The importance of these conceptions of role, belonging, and status for the national self-identity, and consequently their rigidity and stability over time, make them resistant to dissonant information.

Although the conceptions of belonging, role, and status are state-level variables, they obviously affect the individual level of analysis. State leaders are often exposed to the consequences of others' role and status conceptions about their state, and it is they who interpret, operationalize, and enact these concepts in foreign policy.[15] While consensus among the decisionmaking elite regarding what belonging, role, and status conceptions are appropriate for their state is possible, it is not always necessarily the case. Decisionmakers may disagree, for example, over which are the relevant roles their state should play, which role to emphasize at any particular point in time or occasion, or how to operationalize agreed-upon role and status conceptions.[16] If a disagreement cannot be resolved, it will result in inaction, policy inconsistencies, or policy compromises attempting to simultaneously satisfy incongruent role conceptions. On the other hand, when predominant national leaders impose uniform role and status conceptions and perceive the state as an extension of themselves and their expectations of personal status and respect are frustrated (cf. Dore, 1975)—as was the case, for example, with de Gaulle's attitude toward other world powers and leaders—foreign policy is bound to mirror their personal needs.

CHAPTER 6

Decisionmakers as Practical-Intuitive Historians: The Use and Abuse of History

···

"Historia magistra vitae."   CICERO

"History is not a cookbook which gives recipes."   HENRY KISSINGER

The Practical-Intuitive Historian

The use of history by foreign policy decisionmakers is a common phenomenon. Instead of approaching history in a scientific manner, however, decisionmakers act as practical-intuitive historians. They are practical in the sense suggested by Oakeshott, who distinguishes the "practical past" from the "historical past." The first consists of "artefacts and utterances alleged to have survived from the past recognized in terms of their worth to us in our current practical engagements. . . . And they become available to us, not in a procedure of critical enquiry but merely in being recalled from where they lie, scattered or collected, in the present" (1983: 35, 38). And decisionmakers are intuitive in the sense suggested by the layperson-scientist analogy, which has become an important focus of research in cognitive psychology and, more particularly, attribution theory (e.g. Nisbett and Ross, 1980). That is, the same analogy applies to the decisionmaker playing the historian.

Practical-intuitive historians are a mixed breed. They range from the more naive ones (e.g. Harry Truman, Lyndon Johnson) to self-educated, aspiring analytic historians (e.g. Winston Churchill, David Ben-Gurion, Jawaharlal Nehru) to academic professional historians turned politicians (e.g. Woodrow Wilson, Henry Kissinger). Their cumulation of knowledge, sophistication, and breadth of historical vision vary widely. In a word, they operate from significantly different data bases, which range from sketchy information to detailed, in-depth knowledge. Yet even those with an academic historical background are not acquainted in equal depth with all historical aspects, periods, and events; they too have only selective knowledge. In both cases the images of particular past events or situations are often based to some degree on a mélange of fact and fiction not always clearly distinguished from each other. There are historical facts, mass media reports, national mythologies, artistic impressions in writing, painting, or artifacts—all reinforced by the person's own imagination and selective memory. The images can be grossly inaccurate with regard to detail and yet accurate enough in their general outline not to be completely misleading and still be relevant, depending on the purpose for which they are used.

Although the people who apply historical knowledge to current tasks have differences among them, they have a number of characteristics in common. First, they show great confidence and a lack of inhibition in using the past in various forms. Second, intuitive historians, much like professional historians, rely on historical facts and transform them by summarizing, evaluating, analyzing, inferring, judging, and interpreting. All depend on conscious or unconscious techniques for coding, storing, and retrieving data. These activities do not strictly follow rules of scientific historical epistemology, even for professional historians who have become decisionmakers. Once removed from their academic milieu, they act as intuitive historians, albeit knowledgeable and sophisticated ones.

History in this context is phenomenological history, that is, the subjective perception and comprehension of past events, near or more distant, and their meaning. History to practical-intuitive historians comprises all those past human activities and situations of societal significance that they perceive, accurately or not (cf. Dray, 1964: 4). Their subject matter is similar to that of professional historians, yet their motives, goals, and treatment of that subject matter are not. The purpose of this chapter is to suggest a theoretical approach to a descriptive, explanatory, and prescriptive analysis of their use of history by focusing on the following issues. What policymaking functions are served by the use of history? How and under what circumstances are the past and the present compared? What are the possible motivations behind the widespread use of history? And what typical shortcomings, biases, and errors are potentially inherent in the use of historically based knowledge structures and heuristics? Thus the chapter deals with a range of contingencies in terms of tasks, processes, motives, and outcomes. The discussion cuts across factors considered in all the previous chapters.

Throughout the chapter the term "use" with reference to history denotes a reliance on, or the employment of, knowledge about past occurrences in performing or contributing to any task related to information processing and decisionmaking in their most comprehensive sense. The "abuse" of history denotes a use of past events that is faulty in that it violates the rules of logical and/or statistical judgment and inference.

Functions of the Use of History

History may serve as four building blocks of information processing and decisionmaking.

1. *Defining the situation.* The structuring and interpretation of information to construct a consistent, valid, and meaningful body of knowledge about the nature of the international environment and the actors perceived to impinge on the definer-actor's achievement of goals and preservation of values.

2. *Circumscribing roles.* The recognition of roles and status appropriate for the actor in the international system.

3. *Determining strategy.* The search for ideas and orientations about, and the choice among, the most effective range of policies for coping with acute problems that face the actor.

4. *Justifying strategy.* The process of convincing other participants, domestic or foreign, that a particular policy is the most logical, practical, and normatively acceptable.

Defining the situation. A situation is defined through the following cognitive operations, employing knowledge of the past in various forms and at varying levels of sophistication.

1. *Association.* Images of historical events feed the individual's or the collective's associative systems. Even though the images may have no specific effect, or at least none that can be pinpointed, they can either appear in the contextual background against which present events are viewed or become a prism through which they are viewed and their interpretation shaped as has been the case with the Holocaust syndrome in Israel's foreign policy (Brecher, 1974: 333–34). History may also serve as a source of associative metaphors or similes, which come to the fore in verbal expressions and are "useful and ornamental in the articulation of ideas" (Fischer, 1970: 224), mostly affecting the manner of argumentation and the argument's emotive content rather than its substance. To determine the exact input of history for any specific behavior output is difficult in such cases, but history probably fulfills a descriptive function by helping to relate and characterize present events or highlight certain features of them.[1] For example, an Israeli policymaker who thinks of Israel's situation in terms of the David and Goliath metaphor adopts an optimistic attitude toward current and future situations; a policymaker who thinks in terms of the Masada metaphor makes a more pessimistic

evaluation. Thus two events of mainly symbolic importance, not central to national history, become important inputs for perceptions and expectations. A more specific effect can be found in the first days of the Yom Kippur War, when the Israeli chief of staff, wanting to impress on his officers that the Egyptian army must not be allowed, at any cost, to cross the Gidi and Mitla passes into the Sinai, used the following metaphor: "This is our Masada, this must not fall to the Egyptian army" (Bartov, 1978b: 156).

Historical association may reinforce, introduce, or remove psychological barriers, thus determining the intensity of the motivational input, or inhibition, for a particular action. Prime Minister Golda Meir, at the meeting in her office on October 5, shortly before the Yom Kippur War broke out, was troubled in spite of assurances by the chief of staff, defense minister, and chief of military intelligence that the probability of war was low. She said at the time: "I have a terrible feeling that all this has already happened before. It reminds me of 1967, when we were accused of concentrating military forces against Syria. That is exactly what the Arab press says now. I think it means something" (Meir, 1975: 308). The association was not enough to overrule the dominating assessment but caused her to support taking some preparatory precautions.

2. *Reality testing.* History can be used for reality testing by searching for consistency between the knowledge and beliefs the decisionmaker holds and the knowledge and beliefs based on the lessons of history (Skemp, 1979: 28). In an environment where information is a legitimate target of manipulation by opponents and, as such, suspect or at best ambiguous, history seems to provide an anchor of validity and truth. History, it seems, cannot be manipulated (or at least attempts to do so can be detected and averted), for the facts and outcomes are known and the true meaning of the past is there for everybody to see. History becomes a safety net, and it becomes a measuring rod against which other sources and the information they provide are compared and checked for credibility and validity. Such a view is romantic, of course, and may have little real value for a decisionmaker seeking veridicality and certainty amid ambiguity and potential deception.

Such was the case with Zbigniew Brzezinski, President Carter's national security adviser. He believed that "it is a well-established Soviet practice to quickly take the measure of a new U.S. President by pressuring him strongly on some issue. Carter was no exception." Shortly after assuming office, Carter approached the Soviet leadership with a broad proposal on arms control and Soviet-American collaboration. The letter Brezhnev sent in response was described by Cyrus Vance, the secretary of state, as "good, hard hitting, to the point." But Brzezinski's diagnosis was quite different. He viewed the letter as a recapitulation of the first encounter between Khrushchev and Kennedy, when the Soviet leader tried to browbeat Kennedy into making concessions, and as further confirmation of his belief about Soviet patterns of behavior (Brzezinski, 1983: 153–56).[2]

3. *Causal inference.* Past events serve to uncover the causes of present events. The multiplicity of actors, as well as the kinetic and modular characteristics of information, produces a large number of candidate causes as explanations for occurrences in the domain of international politics. Identifying actual cause-effect links becomes a complex and difficult task that calls for measures to simplify the choice among competing explanations. The use of historical knowledge is just one such measure. That solution also pertains to cases where the problem is not to choose among competing explanations but where the occurrence defies causal explanation.

Two process modes may be involved here: analogy and extrapolation. In analogizing, the decisionmaker locates a historical event whose causes are perceived to be known and then defines it as equivalent to the present event; an analogy between the causes of both events follows. A two-stage process is entailed: (1) establishing an analogy between the two events and another analogy between their causes and (2) inferring that similar outcomes have similar causes. When seeking to explain Giap's reasons for investing and risking so many resources in an attempt to seize Khe Sanh, Westmoreland analogized from Dien Bien Phu. According to his line of reasoning, Khe Sanh was the key to controlling the northern provinces of South Vietnam before negotiations started, just as the battle for Dien Bien Phu was intended to buttress the North Vietnamese bargaining posture at the Geneva Conference of 1954 (Karnow, 1983: 540). On the other hand, extrapolating involves perceiving the present event as an organic extension of a past event whose causes are known. The assumed continuity is also applied to the causes of the present situation which, by definition, are then the same as those of the earlier event.

4. *Judgment of motives and intentions.* Much of a decisionmaker's time and effort are consumed by trying to uncover the intentions of other actors within his own decisionmaking system, as well as those beyond his national borders. As with causal inferences, history can be used in this context in two ways. In analogizing, the decisionmaker compares a past event in which intentions are known with the current event and infers the actor's intentions in the current event accordingly. For example, in May 1967, when the Egyptian army moved troops across the Suez Canal into the Sinai, Egypt's motives defied explanation by Israeli intelligence. The problem was then defined by analogy to the 1960 precedent, when Egyp-

tian troops had advanced across the Sinai to the Israeli border to demonstrate solidarity with Syria, only to withdraw a few weeks later. The Israeli military assumed that, given the tensions on the Israeli-Syrian border in 1967, Egyptian motives were the same as in 1960 (Eban, 1978: 323). When the decisionmaker extrapolates, however, knowledge of the actor's past intentions provides an understanding of present intentions through the assumption of continuity in intentions. An example, which involves a metaphor as well, can be found in a comment on Soviet policy toward Afghanistan that appeared in Beijing's *People's Daily:* "Afghanistan is strategically very important. The old tsars drooled over it long ago. The new Soviet tsars have assumed the mantle from the old tsars" . (U.S. Foreign Broadcast Information Service, 1979).

5. *Pattern recognition.* Viewing current events in a historical perspective may help highlight continuity and change in the patterns of behavior of the self and others. Consequently a single, specific event acquires meaning far beyond its immediate implications (see also Shieder, 1978: 6). It becomes not an isolated event but part of a pattern and sometimes a law of history, and what is merely descriptive information is given diagnostic qualities. This tendency is encouraged by the human need for pattern and structure in the environment. In analyzing the Vietnam issue within an overall historical framework, for example, Deputy Under Secretary of State Alexis Johnson argued that Vietnam was another stage in a Communist master plan, antedating World War II, to take over all of Southeast Asia. This view was shared by others in the administration as well (May, 1973: 100–101). Vietnam not just became another place in crisis, then, but acquired major strategic and political importance.

6. *Predictive inference.* Not only is history useful in identifying continuity and change after they have occurred, but past events are also used to predict future events or the pattern of evolution of a present event. The analogical inference employed here is one of the following: "In the past, General Category of Events X led to General Category of Outcomes Y, or alternatively, Specific Event A led to Specific Outcome B; the same holds true for the current situation." The analogy involves identifying a past event with a present event and then accepting the premise that the same past outcomes will repeat themselves in the future.[3] To illustrate: President Johnson was, according to his memoirs, preoccupied with the failure of American policy to take an interventionist position prior to World War II, an era that he witnessed when he served in the House. He was sure that noninterventionism had encouraged the enemies of freedom and potential aggressors and would likely do so again if the United States neglected to defend Vietman (L. B. Johnson, 1971: 46–47).

Historical analogies can also be used interactively with deductive logic to produce predictive outputs regarding the relative probability of outcomes, such as when deductive logic generates the range of possible outcomes (e.g. X and Y) and then the more probable outcome is inferred by historical analogy (e.g. "History proves that Outcome X is more probable than Outcome Y"). The American administration, for example, knew almost nothing about the Hanoi leaders and their intentions. Thus when it had to choose from among the possible reactions that they might make to American attempts at coercion, it tended to perceive the leadership as a unitary, rational actor calculating costs and risks and ready to back off whenever the cost-benefit calculus showed costs decisively outnumbering gains. This assumption rested to a certain degree on the lessons of the Korean War: "We were inclined to assume, however, that they [the North Vietnamese] would behave like the North Koreans and the Red Chinese a decade before: that is, they would seek an accommodation with us when the cost of pursuing a losing course became excessive" (M. D. Taylor, 1972: 15; see also Thies, 1982: 218–20).

7. *Dissonance reduction.* When threatened by potential post-decisional cognitive dissonance, decisionmakers may use history to relocate the burden of responsibility from their shoulders to metaphysical ones, to the "course of history." They thus overcome their reluctance to make a decision, especially common in high-risk choice situations, and avoid post-decisional regret and the related urge to reverse the decision (Festinger, 1964). To illustrate: Wilhelm Jordan, a member of the Frankfurt National Assembly in his July 24, 1848, speech in the Frankfurt National Assembly on Poland's partition, explained away the injustice of the partition by including it in an all-embracing metaphysical chain of cause and effect, calling it "nothing more than the proclamation of a death that had been died long since" and at the same time an act that had to be carried out to overcome feudalism (Faber, 1978: 56–57).

Circumscribing roles. The second function served by the use of history is the circumscription of actors' roles, at the individual and national levels, through history's impact on the shaping of self-perception. History provides important inputs for the definition of self and for self-esteem (Thorne, 1983: 125–27). But decisionmakers who are concerned with their place in history are motivated not only by their perception of the past but also by their expectation of being judged by future historians, so they attempt to project the image they hope will go on record. How they perceive themselves can indirectly prompt a preference for, or avoidance of, specific types of international behavior that seem to them to be congruent, or incongruent, with important components of a desired self-perception. General Westmoreland, for example, wanted to fight the battle for Khe Sanh. He was sure that General Giap was looking for a

Dien Bien Phu–style victory but also sure that he could turn Khe Sanh into Giap's Dien Bien Phu by luring the enemy to deploy its forces and then destroying them beneath a Niagara of bombs (Pisor, 1983: 60–61). Khe Sanh was to become Dien Bien Phu in reverse; hence Dien Bien Phu was, to Westmoreland, more of a metaphor than an analogy. Khe Sanh would be held, necessary or not, because he had committed himself to win against the genius of General Giap; winning there became essential to the self-perception of a soldier with an almost perfect military career. Westmoreland would do what no one else had managed to do—defeat Giap.

Judging events in the broad and speculative context of how a person or behavior will be portrayed by future historians may radically affect the interpretation of events—and not necessarily for the better as far as the accuracy of perception is concerned. Yet such judgments do not necessarily preclude decisionmakers' holding unpopular views if they value future glory over present popularity, which means succumbing to public sentiment. Presidents Kennedy, Johnson, and Nixon were each intensely concerned with the need not to become the first president who lost a war. The hope for a positive judgment by history was a major input into their Vietnam policies (Ellsberg, 1971; Gelb with Betts, 1979).

Furthermore, nations learn from history their role, their status, and their prescribed aspirations and how they differ from the aspirations of other nations. The past they rely on is not necessarily actual history but a glorified version of it, which is either wrought from remembered history or fabricated (B. Lewis, 1975). A sense of elitism or a sense of mission may become the source of a preference for specific behavioral patterns, as demonstrated, for example, by Jewish, Japanese, German, or French history. History becomes a source of some of the core national beliefs, shared by both leaders and followers, about the nature of the world and the nation's role and status in it (Bar-Tal, 1983). The role of the Masada complex in Israel's view of itself compared with the rest of the world (Alter, 1973; Gonen, 1975: 215–36) clearly demonstrates these points. In the year 73 C.E. the last stand of the Jewish rebellion against the Roman legions took place at the fortress of Masada. The defenders, realizing they stood no chance, decided to kill themselves and their families to avoid surrender. The legend of Masada supports a view of a hostile world facing a nation with its back to the wall, which must never allow itself to be again in a position where the choice is between death or surrender.

Determining strategy. By circumscribing an actor's role, the use of history has indirect effects on the choice of strategy, but it can also serve as a direct input.

1. *Problem recognition and formulation.* Coping requires recognizing problems and then solving them. Problems, real or imagined, are not detected and recognized only by observation or logical deduction but are frequently inferred from analogical reasoning as well. An awareness of past problems focuses attention on current problems of a similar type. When an analogy is missing, the alertness for problems may decline until their consequences call attention to their existence. At that point it may be too late to adjust and cope effectively.

When problem recognition is stimulated by historical knowledge, the knowledge is bound to become an input in deciding what options and outcomes are to be considered when the problem is formulated and how the terms of the problem are to be operationalized. Kahneman and Tversky's (1979b) "prospect theory" suggests, however, that the way in which problems are formulated can have strong effects of the attractiveness of related options. The implication is that historical knowledge, which is instrumental in the recognition and formulation of problems, indirectly affects the attractiveness of and hence the ranking of preferences for alternative solutions, even when the considered solutions or options in themselves are derived logically and not analogically. The Korean analogy, for example, was on the minds of most decisionmakers in Washington from the early days of American intervention in Vietnam. During the Kennedy administration the military's reluctance to get involved rested heavily on their defining the problem in terms of Korea: they pointed to the costs of a war in Asia and the domestic reaction if the war dragged on. To counter these arguments, Kennedy had to use another analogy, and he came up with the experience of success in defeating Communist insurgencies in Malaya and the Philippines. Kennedy and his intimates demanded that the military make preparations for a Malayan-style counterinsurgency campaign rather than Korean-style conventional land warfare (May, 1973: 97–99).

The Germans' "Copenhagen complex" further illuminates this point. In the autumn of 1807 the British navy launched a surprise attack on Copenhagen, leading to the seizure of the Danish fleet and the bombardment of the city. During the years before 1914, Kaiser Wilhelm II and his military and political advisers feared a repeat performance that would destroy the imperial navy and with it Germany's world position. Thus the memory of Copenhagen "seeped into men's perceptions and became part of the vocabulary of political life. By becoming a fixed point in the German picture of the outside world, the 'Copenhagen complex' in its turn helped to shape the events themselves and played a part often as crucial in the formulation of German policy as the more tangible 'facts' of traditional diplomacy and military strategy" (Steinberg, 1966: 23–24).

German military planning and, in particular, the expansion and role assigned to its naval power were heavily affected by the Copenhagen complex. Diplomatically the Copenhagen complex acted to limit the range of options open to German foreign policy by providing assurance of England's inherent bad faith and its intention to "Copenhagen" (surprise) Germany at the first convenient occasion; it thereby contributed to occasional panics and the deterioration of relations with England (although the effect of the Copenhagen complex declined after 1907, when other, more comprehensive fears of encirclement displaced the specific fear of a British attack) (Steinberg, 1966).

2. *Prescription.* The past provides prescriptions for what should or should not be done. The prescriptions may be simple rules of thumb but may also be more complex guidelines for behavior, say at different levels of generality and abstraction. One abstract and philosophical prescription is Kissinger's assertion that "if history teaches anything it is that there can be no peace without equilibrium and no justice without restraint" (1979: 55). A less abstract but still general foreign policy orientation is "no more Vietnams," which, because it does not suggest a case-specific policy, might cause policymakers to dispute its operational meaning (Ravenal, 1980). But the past can also be a source of more specific policy directions for certain issue-areas or toward specific actors; it could contain cues for friendliness, trust, or alliance or a very specific policy recommendation for a particular situation.

An interesting illustration of a prescriptive strategy for the world revolution through analogy can be found in Lin Piao's famous essay "Long Live the Victory of People's War!" Deriving a lesson from the Chinese revolution, whose success was attained by encircling the cities from the countryside, he makes a suggestion.

Taking the entire globe, if North America and Western Europe can be called 'the cities of the world,' then Asia, Africa and Latin America constitute 'the rural areas of the world.' Since World War II, the proletarian revolutionary movement has for various reasons been temporarily held back in the North American and West European capitalist countries, while the people's revolutionary movement in Asia, Africa and Latin America has been growing vigorously. In a sense, the contemporary world revolution also presents a picture of the encirclement of cities by the rural areas. In the final analysis, the whole cause of world revolution hinges on the revolutionary struggles of the Asian, African and Latin American peoples who make up the overwhelming majority of the world's population. (1972: 396)

In this case the metaphor serves the analogy. Indeed, without the metaphor there is no analogy and hence no relevant lesson.

3. *Consideration and choice of options.* In complex choice situations, decisionmakers, to eliminate some of the available alternatives, may se-

lect particular criteria and apply them to the alternatives at hand, eliminating those not possessing the specified attributes. They repeat this process until they are left with the one alternative meeting all the requisite criteria. According to Tversky (1972), people prefer this approach when faced with an important decision that stimulates the search for a principle of choice more compelling than cost-benefit estimation or similar computations. Historical experience can be a source of benchmarks, the question posed being whether Alternative X has Characteristic Y, which was present in a similar choice situation in the past (e.g. whether support by a superpower, Characteristic Y, is found in Alternative X).

The existence of a historical precedent might in itself be an aspect of choice, so that all alternatives not having a historical precedent are eliminated without being seriously considered. Options, then, are colored by presumptions built upon perceptions of past events. Johnson's options in 1965 were based upon what seemed to him a body of hard-to-refute evidence. Bombing was assumed to be an effective option for inducing North Vietnam to stop aiding the Vietcong because Johnson believed, incorrectly, that strategic bombing in the past (e.g. of Germany, Italy, Japan) had been successful in achieving its coercive objectives. The slow-squeeze option, or gradualism in applying pressure, was inferred at least partly from the success of the same procedure in the Cuban missile crisis. It seemed reasonable that a minor Asian power would capitulate as the Soviet Union, a superpower, had been forced to do. Similarly, when Johnson considered committing American ground forces in Vietnam, he remembered in support of that option that the United States had always won and never lost a war (Gallucci, 1975: 51; Neustadt and May, 1986: 137).

Justifying strategy. Once a preference for a specific strategy emerges, its proponents can also use history to justify it logically or normatively. This process may occur either before the actual choice is made or after the strategy is chosen or implemented.

1. *Argumentation.* When information about the environment is complex and poses a high level of uncertainty and where power is shared (Axelrod, 1977), argumentation by reference to history is a vital component of policy formulation and serves as a means of persuading both the self and others. This form of argumentation is essential in clarifying the causal structure of the situation and the inherent logic of a cause-effect or means-end sequence. It helps in highlighting trends or in narrating events, that is, in revealing meaning and coherence in a complex set of events. In 1969 Nixon attempted to bring the Vietnam War to an end by emulating Eisenhower's method of extracting America from an-

other unpopular conflict, the Korean War. Responding as a presidential candidate to a question in August 1968, he said:

How do you bring a war to a conclusion? I'll tell you how Korea was ended. We got in there and had this messy war on our hands. Eisenhower let the word go out—let the word go out diplomatically—to the Chinese and the North Koreans that we should not tolerate this continual ground war of attrition. And within a matter of months, they negotiated. Well, as far as negotiation [in Vietnam] is concerned that should be our position. (Hersh, 1983: 52)

He was referring to the use of a nuclear threat, which in 1953, in his view, had brought the war to an end.

2. *Acquisition of accountability and legitimacy*. History is used to legitimize policies, rules of behavior, or demands made of other actors. In that regard, history may be the source of the two types of legitimacy, normative and cognitive, that a political leadership requires for its policies in the estimation of its domestic public and the international community. Normative legitimacy establishes the desirability of a policy in terms of its being consistent with fundamental national or international values. History, however, may also be a source of cognitive legitimacy, which depends on a leadership's ability to prove the feasibility of its policies.[4] The proven effectiveness of the nuclear threat in the Korean context was considered to provide both cognitive and normative legitimacy for such a policy in Vietnam. Normative legitimacy arose from the mere fact that there was a precedent to the "madman strategy"; cognitive legitimacy arose from the recognition that the policy had worked in the past by leading to the termination of the Korean War. In the same vein, when explaining to journalist David Frost in 1977 why it was necessary to give false reports in connection with the bombings in Cambodia in 1970, former President Nixon said that "in war there are times when you have to, in dealing with the enemy; in order to mislead them, you may not be able to level with your friends, or even with your own people." He then cited the way the Allies attempted to mislead German intelligence about the site of the Normandy landing (Shawcross, 1979: 290).

Another manner of justifying a policy is through extrapolation: If X was legitimate in the past, the same X is taken to be legitimate in the present. An example is the "prescription" method of acquiring territory: "*Prescription* means that a foreign state occupies a portion of territory claimed by a state, encounters no protest on the part of the 'owner,' and exercises rights of sovereignty over a long period of time. Eventually the original title lapses and the 'squatter state' acquires legal title to the territory" (von Glahn, 1981: 319).

At a more general level, history is used to promote the legitimacy of a social order by proving that its policies are analogical to policies that achieved desired results in the past or by proving that the same leadership has had a record of past successes. In the latter case, the analogy between events is replaced by an extrapolation from the abilities or quality of performance of the leadership in the past and into the present. When Hitler decided to repudiate the Locarno Treaty and reoccupy the Rhineland in 1936, he did so despite strong protests and dire warnings from the German high command. That he emerged from that affair with his first major victory increased his faith in what he described as his *schlafwandlerische Sicherheit* (sleepwalker's assurance) in foreign affairs. This was to cause him to reject all warnings about his daring ventures after the Rhineland affair. After the Munich crisis of 1938, most of the general staff was convinced that the führer was invincible and that there was no choice but to go along with his grandiose schemes (Craig, 1964: 486–89, 500).

Alternatively, a social order and political regime or leadership can be endowed with legitimacy by their association, through analogy, simile, or metaphor, with a historically revered order or regime, venerated historical figures, or legendary cultural heroes. This strategy is typical of charismatic-authoritarian leaders (e.g. Sukarno, Castro, Hitler) (Willner, 1984: 62–84, 172–74). By implication these definitions of the situation and these policies are above criticsm.

History can also be used for rejecting or delegitimizing a policy (e.g. comparing American intervention in Central America with the Vietnam involvement). Withdrawing legitimacy from particular policies could, of course, also act indirectly to support different views and policies by the process of elimination; eliminating some policies makes others predominant.

We have looked at the different functions related to information processing and decisionmaking that are served by the application of historical experience and knowledge. History, we have seen, is used to diagnose the problem, search for information, evaluate alternatives, revise estimates, make choices, and set postdecisional behavior. It is now imperative to understand the mental operation of applying history in order to comprehend the range of contingent outcomes and consequences.

Comparing Past, Present, and Future

Practical-intuitive historians apply their knowledge of history to current problems and tasks in three different but related ways: as metaphor (or simile), analogy, and extrapolation. There are a number of differences among the three strategies. Metaphor is an expression used to stimulate and manipulate the imagination of the audience. Metaphors are particularly important for comprehending political reality, which cannot usually be directly observed. Metaphors make manifest the intelligible structure of political reality and provide economical knowledge about the world, which is characterized in terms of a more familiar world (Fraser, 1979; Landau, 1961; E. F. Miller, 1979; Sederberg, 1984; Turbayne, 1970). Analogy is used in the more abstract and deliberate phase of thought and communication. "In analogies, abstract categories and relationships are transferred from one domain to another in order to organize the latter. In metaphors, new images of one subject or domain are evoked by juxtaposing it with another which is both similar and different; the connotations associated with both subjects play an important role in evoking the images" (Zashin and Chapman, 1974: 311). Both analogy and metaphor rest on a premise of transfer, which assumes discontinuity between the past and the present or future but at least some correspondence between events or processes at two different points in time. Extrapolation, on the other hand, assumes continuity between the past and the present or future.

These strategies of using historical information are reflected at one level in common judgmental heuristics: anchoring, availability, and representativeness, which are shortcuts to performing inferential tasks (see Chapter 3). The use of heuristics is predicated by some of the circumstances under which history is most likely to be used (to be elaborated in the next section): short response time and ambiguity. At a different and more sophisticated level, historical data provide knowledge structures that have multiple purposes and forms of representation with different kinds of structure, levels of abstraction, and propositional content. The store of knowledge can be represented as abstract general beliefs or theories, a practice characteristic of professional historians entering politics. For example, Kissinger observes: "When I entered office, I brought with me a philosophy formed by two decades of the study of history" (1979: 54; see also Walker, 1977). Another type of representation has a schemalike and less propositional structure that anchors generic expectations about people, objects, situations, and event sequences (processes) (see also Chapter 3). Historical schemata have two main forms. Personas are cognitive structures representing the personal characteristics and typical behavior of particular "stock characters" (Cantor and Mischel, 1979; Nisbett and Ross, 1980: 35). Examples are Hitler, Chamberlain, Genghis Khan. A script is a hypothesized cognitive structure which when activated organizes comprehension of event-based situations. In its 'weak' sense, it is a bundle of inferences about the potential occurrence of a set of events, and may be structurally similar to other schemas which do not deal with events. In its 'strong' sense, expectations are present about the order as well as the occurrence of events. (Abelson, 1980b: 8)

Examples of scripts are Balkanization and the Trojan horse. Both personas and scripts provide an interpretive framework—which resolves ambiguity—and fill gaps by supplementing the available information with much assumed information (Gilovich, 1981; Nisbett and Ross, 1980: 29). With both types of schema the decisionmaker overcomes anticipatory regret and is less hesitant to venture beyond the most immediate implications of the information at hand and more prepared to confront rather than avoid complex, uncertain situations.

To demonstrate these effects of using scripts and personas, let us look at two examples. For twenty years Indochina had been the "Asian Berlin" to U.S. decisionmakers, and although they recognized the differences between Berlin and Indochina, they focused on the similarities. Securing Berlin meant the reunification of Germany, which could be achieved only through war with the Soviet Union. Yet abandoning Berlin was seen as inviting the erosion of the North Atlantic Treaty Organization, which would also lead inevitably to war with the Soviet Union. Likewise, security for South Vietnam required destroying the North Vietnamese regime, which would probably lead to war with the Soviet Union and China. Abandoning South Vietnam would lead to its occupation by North Vietnam, which would eventually trigger a general Asian collapse and lead to war with the Soviet Union and China (Gelb with Betts, 1979: 30–32). Thus comparing Vietnam to a salient and permanent foreign policy concern involved applying expectations about how the same script would unfold, given the very low likelihood of winning and the belief that disengagement was not possible except at a high cost. This in turn led to a willingness to take high risks and to accord the Vietnam issue high priority and importance. The other example is similar. By thinking about Stalin as a Tom Pendergast, the Missouri party boss who was Truman's mentor in earlier years, Truman made unwarranted assumptions about Stalin's personality characteristics, his trustworthiness in keeping his word, and his understanding of American public opinion (Larson, 1982: 261, 281).

The storage and representation of past events, could, however, take the form of an available knowledge kit—that is, disjointed bits of concrete information about a single historical event or a number of events stored in memory—to be assembled when circumstances trigger the recall of the data in question. A structure is then imposed on the components of the kit. The particular immediate needs serve to guide the assembly of the knowledge kit into a picture or pattern of the past, which may be accurate or false but nonetheless has diagnostic value. Once it has served its purpose, the assembled kit is restored to memory, either in its assembled form, to be used again in the future, or disassembled, with the different components stored separately.

Learning from the past by analogy involves two basic phases of choice: the choice of analogizing as the preferred coping strategy for the situation at hand and the choice of the content of the analogy, which requires activating specific memory nodes, choosing attributes for comparison, defining acceptable thresholds of similarity, and so on. Here it is useful to distinguish between two modes of analogy. In the first mode, while the decisionmaker is struggling with a problem, an analogy may suggest itself as a way of coping. The choice process is intuitive and unconscious.[5] However, once the choice of strategy is made, the actual preference for a specific analogy may then be reached either deliberately or intuitively. In the second mode, analogizing is chosen as the most cost-effective or appropriate coping strategy after a process of deliberation and comparison of coping strategies. The former mode involves a short search process or perhaps no conscious search and selection process at all. The latter involves careful and time-consuming search and selection processes, the outcome of which is a coping strategy considered likely to be suited to the problem at hand.

Three ideal types of analogizer can be discerned among decisionmakers: the perfectionist, who consistently demands nothing less than a perfect analogy before using it to perform any decisionmaking function; the satisficer, who consistently makes do with a satisficing analogy as a coping strategy; and the pragmatist, who selectively adopts either a satisficing or perfectionist approach. The criteria the progmatist uses to select an approach could be based on one or more of the following: (1) the task or function for which analogizing is used, where the more demanding, committing, and risky the task, the stronger the preference for perfection is; (2) situational effects, such as stress and a short time to react, which produce a preference for satisficing; and (3) the vividness and salience of the analogy under consideration, where the more salient and emotionally loaded the analogical event is, the more easily it is evoked and, once retrieved from long-term memory, the greater the tendency is to see it as relevant to the current issue or problem and to perceive similitude between the current case and the analogical event. With a vivid, salient event, less severe and less comprehensive criteria are required to justify using it as an analogy than with a pallid or nonsalient

TABLE 4
Intuition and Deliberation in the Phases of Choosing an Analogy

	Deliberation		Intuition	
Intuition	Phase 1 Choice of coping strategy		Phase 1 Choice of coping strategy	
		Phase 2 Choice of specific analogy		Phase 2 Choice of specific analogy
Deliberation	Phase 1 Choice of coping strategy		Phase 1 Choice of coping strategy	
		Phase 2 Choice of specific analogy		Phase 2 Choice of specific analogy

one;[6] in other words, a satisficing approach rather than a perfectionist one is adopted. Task and situational attributes affect mainly the decision to choose analogizing as a strategy (Phase 1). The vividness and salience of a particular historical event affect its choice as an analogy (Phase 2). Hence it is possible to have a deliberative process at the first phase and an intuitive process at the second phase, and vice versa (Table 4).

The lessons of history are located along the spectrum from macrohistorical to microhistorical. The macrohistorical lessons are generalized and declarative, such as "History proves that the strong destroy the weak" or "Because there is historical justice, aggression does not pay." A lesson of this type is usually based on a philosophical-historical personal or national sentiment, which is not always grounded in fact; rather, it is formed by the collective impression of the national history or other national histories that bear indirectly but strongly on that history. Macrohistorical lessons give a general orientation to foreign policy. The broader the generalization, the more difficult it is to refute because supportive analogies are more readily available. Microhistorical analogies relate to specific situations. Thus, for example, a state that was never attacked from the north tends to regard that direction as an unlikely one for attack. Such analogies are based only on events from the national history and serve mainly to handle tactical problems. It is not unusual for a combination of microhistorical and macrohistorical analogies to be used for coping with the same problem, for example by using the macrohistorical analogies for defining the problem and the microhistorical analogies for choosing specific tactical guidelines for dealing with it.

Historical knowledge is stored in long-term memory;[7] thus its use involves recall and retrieval. Access to it depends on the triggering event and on the ease of retrieval, which entails the use of heuristics, such as availability or representativeness. During retrieval the superficial properties of the analogical event tend to have a greater impact on the selection of the analogy than the structural properties do. Once the analogical event has been retrieved, the relative effect of its surface properties declines if a meticulous mapping process follows (Holyoak, 1985). After retrieval comes the organization of the components of knowledge about the relevant historical events in a form that makes them usable for current tasks and circumstances. When a historical event has been transformed and stored at a high level of abstract representation, it could cause the analogy to be perceived, perhaps unjustifiably, as highly complete because the mismatching details have been deleted. In other cases historical events are stored as highly generalized schemata facilitating the future availability of the analogy (Gick and Holyoak, 1983; Holyoak, 1984).

The effects of historical experience, as Table 5 indicates, are mediated by the attributes and the learning contexts of the historical knowledge used. The analogizer asks such questions as, Who is the national actor in the analogical historical event? How was the decisionmaker using the analogy involved with the event? What was the timing of the analogical event? What was the range of its impact? The analogies of Korea and Dien Bien Phu were easily available to Presidents Johnson and Nixon, for example. During the Dien Bien Phu siege in 1954 Johnson was a key member of the Armed Services Committee, which discussed possible American intervention, and he came to learn of Vo Nguyen Giap's ruthless but successful tactic and the high price paid by the defenders. Johnson was aware of the details of the battle and saw the terrible pictures of the dead and wounded, and he argued strongly against American intervention: "Dienbienphu had already burned a place in Lyndon Johnson's mind" (Pisor, 1983: 103). Nixon, as Eisenhower's vice president, had had a chance to watch at close quarters the successful use of a nuclear threat: it had worked without having it be implemented.

The degree to which a nation's historical experience is perceived to be universal and generalizable reflects the role for which a nation aspires and the degree to which it believes it provides ideological or political leadership and guidance to others, but it also reflects to some degree the actor's reference to the history of other nations (Table 5). Decisionmakers who learn from the history of others are likely to perceive their

TABLE 5
Attributes of Historical Events and Effects on Task Performance

National actor	Attributes of historical events			Effects of current cognitive processes			
	Timing of event	Degree of personal involvement	Gravity of outcomes	Availability	Perceived potential relevance for current tasks	Perceived importance for tasks at hand	Type of cognitive process
1. Own nation	Own lifetime	High	Even if low or medium	High	High	High	Hot
2. Own nation	Own lifetime	Low or none	High	High	High	Medium	Hot
3. Own nation	Before own lifetime	Low or none	High	Medium	Medium	Medium	Hot or cold
4. Foreign nation	Own lifetime	None	High	Medium	Low	Low	Cold
5. Foreign nation	Own lifetime	Significant effect on own nation	High for other nations	High	Medium	Low or medium	Cold
6. Foreign nation	Before own lifetime	Some effect on own nation	High for other nations	Medium	Low	Low	Cold
7. Foreign nation	Before own lifetime	None	Even if high for other nations	Low	Low	None	Cold

NOTE: (1) Only the most typical and useful cases are presented; the table is not logically exhaustive. (2) Degree of personal involvement refers either to the individual's role in the decisionmaking process or to the effect the outcomes had on the individual; however, when the actor in the historical event is a foreign nation, effects refer to the impact of its outcomes on one's own nation (not necessarily at the individual level). (3) In most instances, especially when other dimensions generally do not contribute much to availability, the gravity of the outcomes was presumed to be high so the events would be available. (4) With regard to effects on the cognitive processes, the underlying assumption was that availability is a precondition for relevance and relevance a precondition for any level of importance for the task at hand.

own national history as providing relevant lessons for others, and the lessons others learn are expected to be the same as those they learned themselves. An example is America's unsuccessful effort to make the Russians think of Afghanistan as their Vietnam (Zimmerman and Axelrod, 1981).

History both produces generational effects and reinforces generational differences (Jervis, 1976: 253–61). People who come of age politically during the same years are exposed to the same formative political experiences because they pay attention to the same salient events. Being marked by the same experiences predisposes their perceptions and is expressed years later as they move up the power ladder. They are likely, for example, to use similar historical analogies. But because different generations are marked by different formative experiences, a polarization effect is likely to occur over time, one that accentuates the generational differences. Events following the formative period of each generation are interpreted in terms of and assimilated with the formative experiences and lessons learned. Hence people belonging to different generations but later going through the same events together experience those shared events differently. The members of each generation are bound to explain current events in terms of their particular formative experiences and to use current events to reinforce and confirm their earlier lessons. This practice accentuates existing generational differences. Thus, paradoxically, the recurrent shared experiences of decision-makers belonging to different generations may deepen the initial generation gap.

Even within the same generation only some of the knowledge about historical events is shared by the individuals within the same social group as part of the common national heritage; other knowledge about history is stored in people's memories in forms that are unique to each of them depending on the way in which each experienced the events in question. People thus have dissimilar interpretations of current events.[8] Four of the principal participants in the Vietnam decisionmaking process in 1965 can be considered to illustrate this point. Dean Rusk, the secretary of state, had been assistant secretary for the Far East in 1950. At that time he had underestimated the Chinese; consequently in the 1960s he became preoccupied with the Chinese threat, stressing the risk of Chinese expansion and intervention. George Ball, under secretary of state, contrasted South Vietnam with South Korea and focused on the former's relative lack of viability in terms of politics, armed forces, climate, terrain, international support, and especially the unhappy legacy of French colonialism. His emphasis, which was related to his European orientation and his close observation of the French political scene, was based on his long acquaintance with Jean Monnet, the father of postwar French economic planning, and his Washington law firm's work for the European Economic Community. Secretary of Defense Robert McNamara was mostly concerned with advancing his corporate career at Ford Motor Company during the Korean War. He did not refer to Korea in the context of Vietnam; what concerned him was providing the president with the military means to avoid the loss of South Vietnam. In contrast, Clark Clifford, Truman's special counsel and his strategist during his first term in office, was well aware of what the protracted war in Korea had done to Truman's and the Democratic party's public standing; so he warned Johnson that Vietnam could become a political quagmire if he were to allow U.S. military intervention to escalate into war (Neustadt and May, 1986: 162–64).

Thus knowledge about public and private history can be helpful in the placement of participants in the decisionmaking group (Neustadt and May, 1986: 186–95, 275). This observation is important for understanding the individual-specific mechanisms that trigger the retrieval and use of the same past events by different members of the decisionmaking elite.[9] It also has implications for the impact of shared historical knowledge on the likelihood of the emergence of groupthink symptoms in the dynamics of small decisionmaking groups. The appearance of groupthink symptoms in small groups depends on a number of necessary preconditions: (1) a situation that triggers associations with the same historical events in the minds of the group's members; (2) a similar interpretation of these historical data by group members; and (3) a felt need for consensus within the group. History can then provide the common denominator for the emergence of consensus, which may also cause a more-than-warranted shift in the choice of an alternative. The analogy offers a simple decision rule, which produces a premature choice that overlooks nonobvious negative consequences (Minix, 1982: 133–38). In the period preceding U.S. intervention in the Dominican Republic in 1965, decisionmaking forums in Washington were preoccupied with avoiding a "second Cuba." Events and personalities related to the Dominican crisis were interpreted with Cuba in mind, leading to a widely shared diagnostic, prognostic, and prescriptive consensus that was actually based on distortion and misperception (Lowenthal, 1972: 153–54).

The search for and retrieval of what is perceived to be currently relevant knowledge about the past must be followed by the critical stage of testing and defining the perceived similitude between the compared events. The outcome largely determines if and how the decisionmaker will proceed in applying the historical knowledge to current needs and tasks. The comparison could result in one of the following contingent conclusions, along the spectrum from identity to irrelevance.

1. *Identity*. The compared events are considered to resemble one another in virtually every respect. In April–May 1945, when Tito's partisans took over Venezia Giulia and later Trieste, a crisis emerged between Tito and the Allies over the control of both places. Under Secretary of State Joseph Grew analyzed the situation: "The parallels are precise with what Hitler did before, during and after Munich." The parallels impressed Truman. He was ready to reverse his earlier firm resolve not to involve the United States in Balkan politics and to use force if necessary because what seemed to be an exact analogy led him to overestimate the probability that Tito's territorial demands would expand like Hitler's (Larson, 1982: 238–39).

2. *Similarity*. The more common case occurs when the main attributes of the compared events are perceived to be identical and other attributes are seen to differ, though the differences are not allowed to interfere with learning lessons from the analogy. An assessment of the probabilities of German collapse prepared by the British Joint Intelligence Subcommittee in September–October 1943 predicted that Germany's will to continue fighting would collapse early owing to the steady deterioration in that country's political, military, and economic situation. This conclusion was partly based on a detailed analogy pointing out the striking similarities between Germany's position in 1943 and its position in the late summer of 1918. The writers of the document recognized that "there are, it is true, big differences between the Germany of 1918 and the Germany of 1943, but we do not think that these differences are so fundamental as to invalidate the comparison and the conclusions that flow from it" (Joint Intelligence Subcommittee, 1943).[10]

3. *Familiarity*. A category may be created around a prototypical historical event or personality (exemplar) to which a current event or personality is compared. It is a fuzzy category whose components are not necessarily similar in any sense and may have only a family resemblance. In Wittgenstein's words:

We see a complicated network of similarities overlapping and criss-crossing: sometimes overall similarities, sometimes similarities of detail. I can think of no better expression to characterize these similarities than "family resemblances"; for the various resemblances between the members of a family: build, features, color of eyes, gait, temperament, etc. overlap and criss-cross in the same way. (1953: 32; see also Smith and Medin, 1981: 143–61)

Reflecting on Vietnam, President Johnson came to the conclusion that the conflict there "included elements of the Korean War, of the Huk

Rebellion in the Philippines, of the Greek Civil War, yet it was unlike any of them" (L. B. Johnson, 1971: 241).

4. *Contradiction.* Compared events that are perceived to be the mirror images of each other carry a lesson learned by counteranalogy. General Westmoreland was aware of the Khe Sanh–Dien Bien Phu analogy, which dominated the thinking in Washington and among his own staff. He, however, pointed out that although the terrain, the weather, and the enemy had superficial resemblances Khe Sanh was very different from Dien Bien Phu. The latter was in a deep valley; Khe Sanh, on a plateau. The Americans held four key terrain features; the French had held none. Finally, the Americans could give artillery support to the defenders from the outside and had immense air power and superior aerial supply capability, which the French had lacked (Westmoreland, 1976: 337–38). Hence Westmoreland expected the outcome to be a Dien Bien Phu in reverse, that is, a decisive defeat for General Giap.

Analogies of the contradiction type can act as guides in eliminating certain alternatives as inappropriate to the event at hand, thus reducing the number of alternative explanations, predictions, or prescriptions to be chosen among and easing the trade-off calculations and cost-benefit analyses facing the decisionmaker.

5. *Irrelevance.* The compared events are perceived to be neither similar nor dissimilar but incomparable and therefore irrelevant to each other. Rejecting an analogy can serve as a reason or justification for inferring that the present event or situation is novel and hence legitimize the adoption of innovative but deviant policies or interpretations.

The degree to which any analogy is perceived to be closer to one or the other side of the identity-irrelevance continuum has a number of general implications. First, different decisionmaking tasks call for different levels of trust in the validity of the lessons learned from historical analogies. Validity is perceived to be related to the level of fit or similitude between the compared events; the decisionmaker sets the minimal level for making valid inferences from analogies. The more demanding, committing, and risky the task before him, the higher that threshold is, even for a satisficer. When the decisionmaker carries the responsibility for policy outcomes, he tends to avoid taking action unless he is as sure as possible (1) that the analogy is valid (he therefore sets strict standards of validity); (2) that no other, better, easier, or more reassuring path to a conclusion exists; and (3) that the need to arrive at an operative conclusion is pressing and that procrastination and delay are impossible.

When Conditions 2 and 3 are present, the strict standards of validity are sometimes relaxed, despite the high-risk personal commitment by the decisionmaker. This is the case, for example, in recurring international crises that are analogous with preceding crises that were met successfully. The circumstances give an impetus to employing the same successful strategies, leading the decisionmaker to neglect the particular circumstances to which the strategies owed their success. Thus, on the eve of World War I Edward Grey, who expected Germany to again restrain Austria as in 1912–13, was preparing to "restrain allies and hold a conference," the strategy that had worked so well in the 1909 Morocco crisis and at the 1912–13 Balkan Conference that he had chaired (Snyder and Diesing, 1977: 370–71).

The question, Is the strategy perceived to have been a success or a failure? has further significance (Jervis, 1976: 232–33, 275–79; Leng, 1983). If a success, the same strategy is repeated and the decisionmaker positively knows what to do, just as Nixon knew the nuclear threat had worked in Korea and was confident that it would work in Vietnam. A past failure, on the other hand, is used as a guide to what should not be done, as in Johnson's reference to the Dien Bien Phu analogy. Thus it eliminates certain policy alternatives but does not serve as a guide to what should be done (unless there are only two policy options). The history of perceived failures serves only to limit the number of alternatives that have to be considered, thereby lightening the burden of choice. To illustrate: Kennedy perceived the possible loss of South Vietnam as analogous to the loss of China by another Democratic administration. He could not allow that to happen again; the loss of China had harmed the Democratic party for a decade and deeply divided the American public (May, 1973: 99–100). In choosing between abandoning South Vietnam and continuing to support it, he therefore preferred the latter alternative. Rejecting abandonment did not, however, give the administration any guidelines on what particular policy would be most effective for reaching its goals.

The logic of analogical reasoning dictates that the greater the perceived correspondence between the past and the present or future, the greater the credibility of the analogy and the appropriateness of analogical reasoning are perceived to be. Consequently the weight given to inferences and definitions of the situation based on lessons from history is higher than the weight given to competing inferences and definitions of the situation based on other knowledge structures, such as deductive logic. In the same vein, the greater the perceived correspondence, the more likely is high credibility and trust in the validity of the analogy; the predispositions and inferences drawn by analogy hence become more resistant to disconfirmation by dissonant information.

Motivations to Use History

Why is the use of history so tempting and widespread among decisionmakers? Because it is functional, convenient, habitual, and socially acceptable. The past, as has been argued, can be exploited to cope with a wide variety of information processing and decisionmaking tasks, and the mental procedures involved are familiar and accessible to political leaders. Foreign policy decisionmakers are not, in most cases, specifically trained and prepared to cope with the complexities of international politics. When beset by the realities of foreign policy problems, by the complexities and uncertainties in the international political arena, they bring to bear those coping mechanisms with which they have had past experience. By transferring skills acquired in other professions and issue-areas to the political field, they avoid the stress and sense of inadequacy that may result from having to search for and apply new and, for them, untested coping strategies.

Reasoning by analogy, simile, and metaphor is pervasive in everyday experience (Lakoff and Johnson, 1980), and applying those methods to foreign policy problems thus comes naturally and seems appropriate, especially since analogizing is a flexible strategy and does not preclude and could fit with the use of other strategies—hence the extensive use of historical analogies in performing foreign policymaking tasks. That familiarity has its drawbacks, however. It prevents or delays the recognition of the limits on the validity that the lessons of history have for current decisionmaking tasks and the recognition of the difference between the realm of politics and other issue-areas because "subjects are remarkably consistent in their approaches to analogy problems, even with problems differing widely in content, format and difficulty" (Sternberg, 1977: 376).

Familiarity with information processing and decisionmaking by analogy consequently enhances a preference for it, as well as an exaggerated perception of similitude between past events and present problems and information.

The tendency to lean on history is further promoted by the nature of human cognitive style, needs, and limits. International politics is one of the more complex and uncertain domains of human involvement. Coping with it is, accordingly, demanding and stressful. Decisionmakers thus frequently, consciously or unconsciously, opt for nonrational and irrational decisionmaking procedures over analytic ones. To define and reach consensus on what is good, rational, or successful policy, even post facto, is troublesome or even impossible when outcomes are already known, not to mention the difficulties of establishing the best alternative before decisions are taken and implemented. As the stakes get higher and the environment less predictable and more complex, failure becomes both more probable and more costly. It becomes tempting to define good policy as that which is easy to explain and justify to the self and others (P. A. Anderson, 1981; Slovic, 1975; Tversky, 1972). The use of history provides, then, a precedent and a key to choice that meets the criterion of accountability rather than the usual normative rational criterion of cost-effectiveness. The need to account for decisions does not necessarily lead to more complex information processing when the decisionmakers do not know the positions of those to whom they have to explain or defend their own position (Tetlock, 1983a). A seemingly convincing historical precedent could be perceived as an effective, simple explanation in generating persuasion, especially for cognitive misers. Decisionmakers who prefer little deliberation and swift, reflexive, intuitive decisions are particularly prone to use simplistic historical analogies to support the predicted outcomes of their decisionmaking process even when faced with complex problems. The decisionmaking style of President Harry Truman demonstrates this point clearly (Bastick, 1982; Larson, 1982: 216).

Another motive is inherent in the social environment. Current foreign policy problems are often grounded in past national history. Decisionmakers are forced to take cognizance of that history and be attuned to it. It becomes part of their evoked set and an immediate input into task performance. At the same time the role of national leadership focuses the attention of role occupants on the common denominators of the national entity, one of the most important of which is the shared heritage of national experience. Moreover, being in a national leadership role requires an awareness of national missions, aspirations, and identity, which draw on the history of the nation, its past glories, defeats, achievements, and performance.

And, finally, the use of history as a guide might be part of a personal or organizational-institutional world view and philosophy,[11] or an attribute of the national culture, or both. Some individuals show a déjà vu syndrome. They have a strong sense of history and see the past as a living reality to be almost always consulted, a rod against which present and future realities are measured. Some nations, especially those with a history reaching back to ancient times, are strongly history-minded and pass that orientation on to their individual members as part of the socialization process. Hence Chinese and Israeli political leaders may show a stronger inclination toward using past experiences than American decisionmakers (cf. Glenn et al., 1970; Hoffmann, 1968b).

All except for the last motive are universal in their application, hence

TABLE 6
Situational Trigger–Motivation Nexus

Situational trigger	Motivation
1. Short response time	a. Transfer b. Cognitive limits c. Justification
2. Ambiguity	a. Cognitive limits b. Justification
3. High risk/uncertainty	a. Cognitive limits b. Justification c. Evoked set
4. Issue-area	a. Evoked set b. World view (individual or cultural)
5. Societal climate	a. Evoked set b. World view (individual or cultural)

the cross-cultural character of the phenomenon we are dealing with. Yet different people call upon knowledge about past experiences in decision-making tasks differently in comparable situations, even in the rare case when their reservoir of historical knowledge is similar. As discussed earlier, the formats in which historical data are stored in memory differ from person to person, and recalling and retrieving past experiences is dependent for each individual on a particular stimulus, which then triggers the proper search mechanism to decide what information will be recalled and in what format; the differences between people affect how historical knowledge is applied to current needs.

The motivations now having been specified, the next step is to stipulate the situational circumstances that interact with those motivations and that are liable to trigger the use of history, either by itself or in conjunction with other coping strategies and knowledge structures. The nexus of motivations and circumstances is summarized in Table 6 and elaborated below.

First, when response time is too short for following formal rules of judgment and systematic inferential procedures to give meaning, to predict, or to prescribe, the retreat to the classroom of history, if an appropriate lesson seems available, is a tempting and even logical shortcut. Past experience then becomes a standard operating procedure and part of a cybernetic path to choice. Second, those situations where information is ambiguous or where evidence seems equally given to contradictory interpretations provide an impetus to search for a decisive input to resolve the ambiguity. A historical precedent would serve this end.

Third, in situations of high risk and uncertainty, when decisionmakers cannot rely on their immediate social circle for reinforcement—because, for example, they are considered too superior to require others to approve their conduct—they fall back on a higher authority: history. Thus it is not coincidental that charismatic leaders often use historical analogies. Ironically, the same approach can be adopted by weak, indecisive leaders who cannot mobilize support and assurance from their immediate social group, which may itself be unsure and unwilling to make risky decisions. They then tend to look for support in the past, where they might find both cognitive and normative legitimacy for their diagnoses and prognoses and gain a sense of control over their environment. Looking backward is especially likely in high-threat and high-stress situations, such as international crises (cf. Paige, 1972: 48), where the risks involved in a mistaken interpretation of the situation and the costs of choosing an inappropriate course of action are high. Support from history, or from historical personalities who are used as authorities and "crown witnesses" becomes a source of assurance and comfort in the face of possible failure and the excessive cost it might entail.

Fourth, certain issue-areas, such as national security, seem more prone than others to invite the use of past national experience as a means of coping, perhaps because past events in this issue-area are more vivid and therefore more available, being easier to recall. Furthermore, nations tend to perceive their historical continuity in a security-political frame of reference and hence are more likely to extrapolate from the past into the present in this issue-area.

Finally, political leaders operate in social-emotional climates, and societies pass through periods in which the reversion to past glories or suffering becomes a pronounced aspect of their mood. In such times it is to be expected that national leaders feel tempted to manipulate and make intensive use of the past in performing their tasks. Special attention is given to those historical events on which the societal climate is already fixated and that best reflect the prevailing national mood.

Shortcomings: Potential Errors and Biases

Using knowledge about the past in decisionmaking tasks may involve abuses that result in biases and fallacies. The abuses can be grouped into four categories: *contextual, transformational, epistemological,* and *subconscious.*

Contextual errors. Contextual abuses are related to the social or learning contexts. Einhorn (1980) contends that rules learned inductively are context oriented to an extreme. Decisionmakers cannot directly transfer rules learned from prior events to current events because contexts always differ at least somewhat. To overcome this problem, they can manipulate either the attributes of the context from which the rules were deduced or the current context. In the first case, they redefine the past context in the most basic, simplistic manner to make it more similar and therefore relevant to present and future occurrences than it actually is. In the latter case, they assimilate the current event, distorting it to make it look as analogous as possible to a similar past event.

What determines when one or the other of these processes will take place? One concerns an ex ante facto situation; the other, an ex post facto situation. When people deal with an episode in the past, they may wish to draw a general rule from it and store the rule in their minds to be used sometime in the future. Realizing that social events do not repeat themselves exactly, they file it in their long-term memory according to some rudimentary dimensions that are certain to be found in some future event (cf. Schank, 1979). When people face a present situation for which they are seeking an analogy, they may find it easy to bend the dimensions of the current event to make it appear more like some easily available past event, disregarding important contextual differences in the process, to justify the use of information about the past as relevant to the present and thus solve the dilemma of coping. This kind of distortion is particularly evident in high-threat, high-stress situations as one of the symptoms of rigidity in the face of threat because it makes the stressful situation much easier to deal with (M. G. Hermann, 1979b: 40–41; Staw, Sandelands, and Dutton, 1981).

For example, the similarities between Korea and Vietnam seemed obvious and striking on the surface. Both were divided Asian countries where the Communists, supported by China and the Soviet Union, were the enemy and where the United States supported the non-Communist regimes. The wars were entered into and managed initially by administrations controlled by Democratic presidents that were unable to bring them to an end and then inherited by an incoming Republican administration. Hence there was a temptation to draw prescriptive lessons from Korea for Vietnam and overlook the contextual dissimilarities that overshadowed the basic structural similarities. During the Korean War the United States had nuclear dominance, whereas by the mid-1960's the two superpowers had reached nuclear parity—and a countervailing power made all the difference. Additional dissimilarities were indicated in a letter from George Ball to Dean Rusk, Robert McNamara, and Mc-

George Bundy. Ball pointed out the inappropriateness of the Korean analogy and the uniqueness of the South Vietnamese problems: intervention was not expressly sanctioned by the international community; the United States was going it alone; unlike South Korea, South Vietnam did not have a stable government; the South Vietnamese were tired after twenty years of war and had no commitment to fighting for their independence; finally, no internationally accepted justification for U.S. intervention, like the one given by North Korea's invasion of the South existed in the case of South Vietnam (Ball, 1972).

Further, past events with which decisionmakers were personally associated or which were observed firsthand are stored in a context-dependent form, though not necessarily with the full and appropriate context, whereas historical events that are learned secondhand are stored in a relatively context-free form, especially if the decisionmakers are not trained historians. Hence, although firsthand knowledge comes more easily to a person's mind, that knowledge will seem analogous in fewer cases than similar knowledge that is stored in a context-free form.

The context of learning also defines how much is learned and with what effects. Historical events involving the nation that the decisionmaker participated in or observed firsthand have much stronger and more lasting effects than other types of historical data. They are consequently more likely to become sources of hot cognitions (Janis and Mann, 1977), to be more available, to be recognized early as candidates for analogy, and to be used by the decisionmaker more often for that purpose—and frequent use in turn increases their availability. The events are a source of more concrete information for the decisionmaker than other historical events and, being more vivid, are likely to call up additional information and organized schemata from memory (Borgida and Nisbett, 1977; Nisbett and Ross, 1980: 54). They dominate the decisionmaker's mental procedures, they are disproportionately used, and they teach more than can be learned in other contexts (Jervis, 1976: 232–42; Reyes, Thompson, and Bower, 1980). At the extreme such events are overlearned and used mindlessly, leading to premature cognitive commitment and low creativity in task enactment.[12]

The U.S. intelligence community's assessment of Arab intentions in 1973 was closely related to its estimate of Arab capabilities, which were judged by the humiliating Arab defeat in 1967 and the lack of military success in the War of Attrition in 1969–70. U.S. intelligence assumed that the Arabs, being aware of their military inadequacies, would not dare to attack Israel. Similarly, it ignored signals warning of an Arab oil embargo, available since early 1973, partly because the lessons of the failures in 1956 and 1967 to effectively use the oil weapon seemed to indicate that an oil embargo would not work (Dowty, 1984: 205–8). The estimates neglected to take into account the significant differences in the circumstances in 1973: that the power of the oil majors had been declining since the late 1960s, compared with the power of the oil-producing states, and that their willingness to cooperate with the Arab states was growing, in contrast to the situation in 1956 and 1967.

U.S. intelligence also misjudged the purpose of a potential Arab military initiative, seeing it in the framework of American values—that is, one fights a war to achieve victory. In fact, the Arabs hoped for a limited military achievement at best. Their main goal was political, namely, to upset the status quo in the Middle East, which benefited Israel, and involve the superpowers. Their capabilities were practically irrelevant to the inference of intentions. On these two points—an Arab attack and an oil embargo—overlearned historical experiences supported wrong conceptions reached inductively and deductively,[13] fortifying them with additional validity. U.S. intelligence consistently misread signals and warnings; even after Egypt and Syria struck first and its estimates were proven wrong, those responsible made only minimal cognitive adjustments for about a week (Dowty, 1984: 210–12). They believed that the whole thing would soon be over and that the Arabs would be defeated by the superior Israeli army.

And yet experiencing or even participating in a historical event does not necessarily make it always available when a current relevant situation or problem arises. Past experiences can be suppressed, though not unlearned or destroyed (Bjork, 1978), in the same way and for the same reasons that other cognitive components are suppressed. Lessons of history are suppressed rather than unlearned owing to their resistance to complete disconfirmation; history provides the practical-intuitive historian with generic knowledge, hypotheses, and theories about the nature of the world and the actors in it. Suppression is functional in serving such needs as ego-defense or preserving cognitive consistency. Moreover, research has shown that there is a general preference for attempting to confirm initially held hypotheses rather than disconfirm them or thoroughly check alternative hypotheses (Anderson, Lepper, and Ross, 1980: 1045–47; Hansen, 1980: 1009; Wason and Johnson-Laird, 1972: 241). This research would also seem to suggest that theories, conclusions, and lessons drawn from historical knowledge tend to bias one's acquisition and use of further information toward confirmation and away from disconfirmation. But even when discrediting information becomes available, beliefs based on case histories tend to persist to a much greater extent than beliefs based on statistical summaries or other abstract data (C. A. Anderson, 1983). In particular, knowledge that is embedded in traumatic historical events, that contains a strong affective element, and that becomes a source of central beliefs is immensely difficult to refute or falsify. It encourages a continuing search for validating evidence and has stereotypic effects with regard to the expected behavior of other actors (Snyder and Swann, 1978).

Some analogies that seem to disconfirm strongly held beliefs are so salient that they cannot be either suppressed or ignored and decision-makers have to deal with them head on. They cope with the challenge to their beliefs by overemphasizing the dissimilarities between the past and present. Although this coping strategy is intended to convince others that their beliefs are accurate and need no adjustment, it is mainly intended to convince the decisionmakers themselves and erase their own doubts. Elevating the differences between the analogical case history and the current event and ignoring or deemphasizing the similarities bolsters currently held beliefs. Their future disconfirmation now becomes even less likely than it was for two reasons. First, the rejection of the analogy is conceived as positive evidence that the beliefs are irrefutable. Second, to account for refuting the analogy requires processing in depth, which ensures that the related arguments and the conclusions confirming the beliefs in question are better remembered and more available than less thoroughly processed ones (Bobrow and Norman, 1975: 144–45).

American decisionmakers at all levels, from presidents down, were aware to one degree or another of the dramatic failure of the French in Indochina and could not ignore the obvious analogy. But the French experience was explained away as basically irrelevant. They believed that the U.S. was militarily much more powerful, would use force in a more sophisticated manner both militarily and politically, and would in general show broader vision. Most important, being unencumbered by a colonial legacy and fighting not a colonial but a popular war against Communism were likely to win the support of the local population. The battle at Dien Bien Phu was regarded as a curiosity, where weak and weary French forces, lacking a determined commander and facing superior Vietnamese firepower, were defeated with relative ease. In a word, the "French had been French" and their experience dramatic but unique (Kattenburg, 1980: 174–75; see also Ball, 1982: 376).

A biased sensitivity to confirming evidence leads to a decreasing awareness or even a complete disregard for disconfirming evidence, which provides a false sense that the belief in question is valid and reliable. The tendency to have a superior recall for data confirming previously held expectancies and beliefs sets a self-perpetuating process in train (Koriat, Lichtenstein, and Fischhoff, 1980; Rothbart, Evans, and Fulero, 1979). The beliefs become too readily accessible, leading to premature cognitive closure and snowballing errors. Applying scripts based on historical events produces conclusions and interpretations that are even less amenable to logical or evidential challenges than are deductive, abstract theories (L. Ross, 1978). The sequence of historical events is perceived as closed, indubitable, based on irrefutable fact, whereas theories can at least be questioned until proven valid. Furthermore, the decisionmaker's data base of historical knowledge is in most cases too limited and superficial for further validation or disconfirmation of initial conclusions. Feis describes President Truman's knowledge of history as "sketchy" (1967: 101). Nevertheless, Truman did not hesitate to use spontaneous historical analogies to define the problem of and U.S. reaction to the North Korean attack on South Korea with little premeditation and a great deal of confidence that was based on his firsthand experience.

In my generation this was not the first occasion when the strong had attacked the weak. I recalled some earlier instances: Manchuria, Ethiopia, Austria. I remembered how each time that the democracies failed to act it had encouraged the aggressors to keep going ahead. Communism was acting in Korea just as Hitler, Mussolini, and the Japanese had acted ten, fifteen, and twenty years earlier. I felt certain that if South Korea was allowed to fall Communist leaders would be emboldened to override nations closer to our own shores. If the Communists were permitted to force their way into the Republic of Korea without opposition from the free world, no small nation would have the courage to resist threats and aggression by stronger Communist neighbors. If this was allowed to go unchallenged it would mean a third world war, just as similar incidents had brought on the second world war. (Truman, 1956: 332–33)

The sense of certainty that the lessons of history instill affect negatively decisionmakers' open-mindedness and attention to discrepant information. All too often they fail to treat new information in a Bayesian manner to update the initial lessons and their policy implications.

Another learning context fallacy is associated with a critical learning function found in every organism, that is, to observe and assess change in its environment and adapt its reactions to the change to assure optimal adjustment at a minimal cost. Detecting and observing abrupt revolutionary change is simple because it attracts attention. However, gradual, continuous, incremental change is much more difficult to detect and learning from it is limited and selective. Slowly evolving change, spread over long periods of time, is elusive and does not attract attention until the observer is faced with the final transformation. In international politics decisionmakers are often unaware of change until shocked by war or some other major crisis into recognizing it.

Change is the transformation of an object or situation between two points in time. Hence observing change implies that an object or situation is memorized as it was at T_0 and its state compared to its state at T_1. Observing and defining the nature of change depend on the quality of historical memory. We have already noted that historical memory is prone to manipulation, whereby the past is transformed to look more like the present (M. Snyder, 1981) or knowledge is selectively learned and memorized. Consequently the observation of change and the accuracy of its perception depend on the extent to which the past was manipulated by memory-encoding processes.

Social context provides a different opportunity for context-related biases in judgment. Decisionmaking within a small-group environment involves commonly shared knowledge and feelings about preeminent historical events and can lead to groupthink even in the face of reliable disconfirming information. What keeps group members in line and prevents deviation is the authority of history, which plays the role usually ascribed in groupthink theory to one of the group members—the whip. One can sometimes argue with an authoritative human being; it is more difficult to argue with a metaphysical entity, like history. When historical analogies generate a strong sense of external threat, intragroup dissent is even less likely than before and conformity comes to dominate group discussions.

Transformation errors. A second category of errors and biases is related to the consequences of transformation, or the insidious elevation effects that historical analogies, similes, and metaphors may have on information. In extreme cases certain historical events are elevated to the status of myths. When this transformation occurs, the affective power of the event involves hot cognitive processes whenever that event comes up in decisionmaking tasks. A myth cannot be disconfirmed even when no evidence bears it out or even when evidence actually disproves it. Yet myths control the minds of generations as conclusive reality. The double effect of, on the one hand, a myth's being both easily available and vivid in the minds of the decisionmakers and, on the other, its persistence, makes it a factor continuously affecting cognitive tasks, consciously and unconsciously, and a powerful barrier to adjusting to new and dissonant information.[14]

Another problem is what Fischer (1970: 244) has termed the use of "insidious analogy," which relates to the use of metaphor in everyday speech. Metaphor is sometimes a form of analogy,[15] but users may be unaware that they are using an analogy. Artificial or insidious analogies (e.g. the use of terms like quisling, renaissance, Spartan) have a strong directive impact upon conceptualization through the spillover of analogous connotations and thus bring unconscious biases to the interpretation of information. The insidious analogies direct attention to some aspects of the subject at the expense of others (Landau, 1961; E. F. Miller, 1979; Verbrugge and McCarrell, 1977) and not always to the most important and relevant aspects. Thus metaphorical expressions that are used only for literal articulation become, inadvertently and unbeknownst to the user, an input into the channeling and allocation of attention. Similarly, the power of analogies that are used only for clarification, improved understanding, and vivid argument is such that they are sometimes mistaken for proof; the plausibility that an analogy adds to the argument is confused with validity.

Furthermore, when concrete historical analogies compete with pallid but highly probative information presented in statistical form, their effect is stronger than that of the statistical information (cf. Nisbett and Ross, 1980: 55–59). Historical metaphors add vividness to a data-set, and nondiagnostic data thereby gain a diagnostic impact they do not deserve. Diagnostic data that do not lend themselves to effective metaphorical representation may be ignored or undervalued. That is, for example, the case with statistical as opposed to anecdotal information.

In the same vein, given a vivid perception of threat, triggered or interpreted in the context of an analogical historical situation, the threat seems real, is pervasive, and dominates the attention and the affective and cognitive processes. It is not an abstract source of anxiety but becomes a specific, detailed mental picture. The historical analogy transforms the threat by injecting into it a false sense of reality, which may go beyond its actual reality—just like watching a movie seems to have more reality than participating in a theoretical discussion. The reality of the analogy is particularly intense when it is a historical event that is already the object of literary and artistic attention. President Johnson, who was aware of the gruesome details of Dien Bien Phu, began dreaming and having nightmares about it during the battle of Khe Sanh. He began to spend his wakeful nights in the White House basement reading cables and demanding detailed information, photographs, and maps, but the image of Dien Bien Phu was always with him (Pisor, 1983: 105, 114).

Epistemological errors. The third category of biases and errors resulting from the misuse of knowledge about the past concerns epistemological abuses, that is, those biases and errors resulting from the misuse of legitimate rules and heuristics, such as representativeness, availability, and anchoring heuristics, treatment of samples, and comparative analysis. Extrapolation of the past into the present (continuity) is tempting for two reasons: it is simple, and it conforms to the widely used anchoring heuristic (Tversky and Kahneman, 1974: 1128). Yet the present may not be an extrapolation of the past for human affairs are often discontinuous. And even when there is a basic continuity, some important elements of discontinuity might also be present. Hence the past can serve as an anchor for knowledge about the present, but adjustments need to be made. For adjustments to occur decisionmakers must be aware of the information requiring adjustment, but if they are biased in favor of hypothesis confirmation rather than disconfirmation, they are unlikely to make adjustments because their assumption that the present is a replication of the past will be immune to revision.

Use of the representativeness heuristic might be triggered by anecdotally similar features of compared situations, increasing the availability of certain past events; available but irrelevant schemata may come to seem representative of a current situation. In the early months of World War I, for example, President Woodrow Wilson found himself in dispute with the British over American rights on the seas; the British were searching American ships illegally as they had done before the War of 1812. The diary of Colonel Edward House records the president as saying; "Madison and I are the only two Princeton men that have become President. The circumstances of the war of 1812 and now run parallel. I sincerely hope they will not go further" (May, 1973: ix). The anecdotal information that both he and Madison, the incumbent presidents, were Princeton men led President Wilson to draw an analogy between the two Anglo-American disputes, fret about the possibility of war with England, and behave cautiously.

That a state of affairs is characterized as similar to an event in the past hardly makes it identical with that event. However, people tend to use the representativeness heuristic to find identity where the similarities relevant to the problem at hand are limited. The result may be a tendency to belittle the significance of unique circumstances and to make misplaced generalizations (Jervis, 1976: 230). The tendency is accentuated by the preference people have for attributing the behavior of others to dispositional human factors—an integral part of the Protestant ethic of Western culture. They abandon their careful search for situation-specific features and instead overgeneralize and neglect the relevance of context to outcome.

When the historical events required for analogical reasoning are either rare in human history or rare in the decisionmaker's store of knowledge, the decisionmaker may indulge in assimilation, that is, interpreting available but dissimilar events in a way that increases their similarity to the current problem, to increase the number of cases in the sample and enhance the validity of inferences. In the same vein, scripts based on historical knowledge structures are activated when an evoking context is present and the decisionmaker decides to apply them to situations at hand. Once the decisionmaker recognizes a central component of a known script in a current problem, that component cues the script even if it is a false script that is actually irrelevant to the current event. The evoked script triggers a gap-filling process that relates all the components of the false script, including the irrelevant ones, to the current event. The perceiver thus constructs a fictitious reality and has related misguided expectations about how events will unfold. Two fallacies inherent in the logic of script-based information processing explain this series of errors. First, since different scripts can share scenes, more evidence is needed before identifying the relevant script. Some decisionmakers neglect to consider the commonality of certain central components of scripts. Second, the existence of some script components does not necessarily mean that the rest of the script will unfold, as the representativeness heuristic inclines the perceiver to expect. Hence certainty about the evolution of events is sometimes unwarranted.

A damaging manifestation of the use of false scripts occurs because of the predisposition to invoke an action script derived from a past success indiscriminately when some of the script's components are recognized in the present situation and the perceiver infers identity. Highly available, salient successes of the recent past are influential in affecting policy—particularly when the past event seems clearly and simply structured and the cause-outcome relationship seems clear—and provide obvious operative lessons that can be replayed. Practical-intuitive historians are always searching for useful successes. They do not search for failures, nor do they attempt to compare failures with successes and use the first as a control group. They take the shortcut of looking for easily recognized instances of success and eliminating cases with fuzzy or unsuccessful outcomes. The analogies are then applied with little scrutiny or attention to the question of whether the similarity is not superficially misleading. Hard-pressed decisionmakers grab at the solution the analogy offers; they feel confident of success, not realizing that the dissimilarities can turn the repeat performance of the same strategy into a disaster.

An instructive example is provided by the Strategic Hamlet Program, which was the centerpiece of American strategy in Vietnam in the early 1960's. The idea, which had its origins in the successful strategy the British used against the Communist insurgency in Malaya, was suggested by Sir Robert Thomson, who masterminded the success of the policy in Malaya. The program was supposed to cut the Vietcong off from the villages by building up a system of fortified villages, which could be easily defended by the armed forces. The major difficulty was that the planners did not pay attention to the ethnic aspect that made for success in Malaya. There the British fortified Malay villages against Chinese insurgents; in Vietnam the Vietnamese would have to fortify Vietnamese hamlets against other Vietnamese who grew up in the same villages and whose families and friends still lived there. Nor did the program consider the economic and cultural differences between Malay villages and Vietnamese villages. Villagers in the Mekong delta did not live in concentrated settlements but in farmhouses scattered among the paddies and along the edges of the dikes. Many of the peasants who moved into the hamlets practically lost their land because they now lived too far away to walk to their fields and back each day. The distance from home to field became a source of resentment. Peasants who were relocated to entirely new hamlets were infuriated by having to leave the graves of the ancestors they worshiped, seeing their houses torn down or burned, and then being forced to build new ones, inferior to their former homes, with their own labor and at their own expense. Those peasants who were permitted to keep their original homes found in many cases that neighbors were squatting in houses built on their land. They were also angry at being forced into compulsory labor to fortify the hamlets. All of these played into the hands of the Vietcong by further alienating the peasants from the regime. So at best the hamlet program gave the South Vietnamese government a short-term military advantage, but politically it was a disaster (Fitzgerald, 1973: 165–68; Sheehan, 1988: 309–11). It was a case of activating a general lesson on managing an Asian rural-based Communist insurgency and applying it to Vietnam without realizing some of the important dissimilarities between Vietnam and Malaya. Instead it was assumed that all Asian Communist insurgencies are uniform in nature and differ only in location.

The availability heuristic gives rise to another fallacy because policymakers are satisfied to rely on a small set of examples of past events perceived to be similar. They tend to believe that if a certain political process or outcome occurs a few times, it will recur, although the sample may be too small to justify the inference. The tendency to assume a similitude between the past and the present or future may be attributed to the preference for consistency. Assumptions about similarity or continuity serve this preference. At the same time perceived consistency increases confidence in the validity of evidence adduced intuitively (Bastick, 1982: 334–36; Kahneman and Tversky, 1979a). The smallness of an available, consistent sample notwithstanding, decisionmakers have more confidence in it than in a larger body of evidence that contains inconsistencies. In fact, they avoid looking at all relevant historical analogies because as the number of cases observed grows, so does the probability that inconsistencies will emerge and muddle what looks like a clear-cut and consistent lesson.

An extreme manifestation of the phenomenon occurs when decisionmakers rely on a sample of one (Jervis, 1976; Read, 1983). The complexity of an abstract propositional rule can induce them to avoid learning it. Instead, reasoning from a single available exemplar may simultaneously satisfy the availability heuristic and the desire for consistency and simplicity. An application of the satisficing principle can also be observed when decisionmakers use a single instance as their sample for lack of better support for their judgment, inference, or choice. In fact, in some cases judgment that seems random is actually based on a one-item sample (Lewicki, 1985) that is considered satisfactory.

The tendency to rely on a single analogical past case to draw unwarranted conclusions is reinforced when observing another actor's (e.g. ally, adversary) decisionmakers where the very same decisonmakers are in similar roles in the two observed and compared situations. The combined effects of the representativeness and availability heuristics on the one hand and the search for consistency and dispositional attributions of other people's behavior (see Chapter 3) on the other produce the assumption that the same decisionmakers have the same motivations and the same patterns of behavior in what the perceiver believes to be similar context. Consequently, in cases where the element of comparability between two situations at two different points in time is that the decisionmakers in both cases are the same people, the coincidence triggers a search for information about their past behavior; the superficial similarity of behavior in the past then becomes an input into the perceiver's inference that contextually dissimilar situations in the past and present are similar, which is followed by further inferences about the consistency of the observed decisionmakers' motivations in the present or expectations about their behavior in the future. There is, of course, no objective unconditional truth in any of the links of this reasonsing chain; and inferences drawn from it are unjustified.

The use of a small or single-case sample in learning from history may cause practical-intuitive historians to engage in a comparative analysis of the "structured focused comparison" type (George, 1979a) but not follow the appropriate methodology. When a single historical case is used, decisionmakers do not check whether it meets the criteria of a "crucial case study" suggested by Eckstein (1975). When more than one case history is used, they usually behave as satisficers rather than as maximizers; that is, they do not look for more cases to test and further shore up their conclusions and hypotheses. They find meaning even in randomly produced data (Fischhoff, 1982: 344), interpreting history, even when it is primarily a product of chaos, as if it were the outcome of conspiracy. The problem in learning from history is thus not only that the samples are small and biased but also that the procedures used in utilizing it are often faulty, undermining the validity of the conclusions.

It is ironical, but not completely surprising, that those decisionmakers with the most limited historical data bases and the least understanding of the methodology and epistemology of history are also the least hesitant to use history and the most confident in the lessons they have supposedly learned from it. Their poor historical data bases provides clear-cut lessons that are unlikely to contain contradictions; they just do not know enough to realize that history can prove almost everything. Their epistemological ignorance blinds them to validity problems and ambiguities and hence reinforces their confidence in the linearity and clarity of the "lessons of history." Consequently they are more likely not only to find their limited repertoire of historical knowledge applicable to a great number of issues and events but also to find their historical knowledge has specific applicability and meaning rather than just constitutes a source of general lessons.

The use of faulty epistemology is not limited to laypeople who have no experience in using scientifically valid procedures but is shared even by people who enter the political arena from a distinguished academic background. Such was the case, for example, with "the best and the brightest" who served as advisers to Presidents Kennedy and Johnson. The temptation to use historical knowledge carelessly sometimes overpowers the motivation to use acquired epistemological and methodological skills. Once people are removed from the academic environment, with its exacting standards and the critical review of their peers, they adapt to the less vigorous standards and to the pressures for conformity found in the political environment.

In the final analysis the available historical knowledge is not necessarily that most appropriate to the event or case with which it is compared. Some of the factors accounting for the availability of knowledge have little to do with its relevance to the matter at hand. These factors are the following:

1. The range and scope of the policymaker's knowledge of history may well be limited to inappropriate analogies, which, however, constitute the sole reservoir of intellectual capital he has to draw on.[16]

2. Those past historical events in which the policymaker was personally involved are salient and available for being compared to current tasks. Thus Anthony Eden compared concessions to Nasser in the matter of the 1956 seizure of the Suez Canal to Neville Chamberlain's concessions to Hitler in Munich in 1938. He did so in large measure because he had been personally involved in the latter; as a matter of fact, he left the

government because of his distrustful views of Hitler's intentions and goals, which were later proven to have been correct (Björkman, 1984: Jervis, 1969: 249).

3. The nearer in time the past event is to the present information, the more accessible it is. Hence great importance is attached to events that occurred during the policymakers' lifetime and that become part of their inventory of firsthand knowledge, especially if the events took place during the formative stage of the development of their political awareness or after they started their political careers (Jervis, 1969; 1976). However, the analogy nearest in time is not always the most relevant.[17] McNamara seldom referred to any event that took place prior to 1961, when he was preoccupied with his business career. The Bundy brothers, McNamara, McNaughton, and Rusk were not in public life in the 1930's, which May (1973: 113) sees as one reason they did not refer to the events of that decade for analogies.

4. The more vivid and salient the event, the more available it becomes and the more often events of the same type are believed to have taken place, that is, much more often than they actually did. Assertions like "Small countries have always involved the powers in major wars" are usually not anchored in systematic historical research but in an acquaintance with a striking event in modern history, such as the outbreak of World War I. This analogy is available not because it is the most relevant but because it comes most easily to mind.[18] In some cases, events that are unimportant in themselves in the national history (e.g. David's victory over Goliath or the fall of Masada) become symbols loaded with strong affective significance that are used frequently as analogies, similes, and metaphors—gaining further availability in the process.

Thus availability is predicated upon a series of chance variables producing inappropriate analogies. Yet practical-intuitive historians are either unaware of this fact or neglect to take it fully into account in assessing the validity of their inferences. The availability effect, compounded by the consistency motive, makes it easy and simple to think of the future as a replication of the past. Hence there is a strong tendency to forecast the future by analogy; to do so requires little effort, little imagination, and little creativity. Yet the inability to envisage new types of threats are liable to produce zero or low probability estimates of risks that have no available precedent, even when an objective evaluation would assign higher probabilities to those contingencies. India's policymakers, for example, shut their eyes to the danger of a full-scale Chinese attack partly because India had never been invaded by land from the north, only from the northwest. An attack finally took place in October 1962 (Vertzberger, 1984a).

Even when the past could provide valid, relevant, probabilistic, diagnostic information about future outcomes, intuitive human judgment may have difficulties in accurately utilizing such information (Sniezek, 1980). Knowing that a certain outcome has happened in the past increases the belief in the inevitability of its occurrence (Fischhoff, 1975; Fischhoff and Beyth, 1975; Wood, 1978), so the outcomes of historical events seem more inevitable than they actually were. With hindsight the past is often reconstructed as a set of coherent, unfolding events that had a consistent internal logic, that could have been predicted with a great deal of confidence, and that should have held little surprise. The real uncertainty involved in the unfolding of those events is absorbed in the process of reconstruction. The lesson learned is that the present and future have more structure and deterministic logic and less uncertainty and ambiguity than meets the eye—a lesson that leads its learner to underestimate uncertainties in predicting the likelihood of future events. In addition, when analogies are made to a current situation, the potential outcomes analogical to the ones that have already occurred are given higher probabilities of recurring than they should be given. On the other hand, potential outcomes analogical to nonoccurrences are given lower probabilities than they warrant. Focusing attention on events and outcomes that did occur distracts attention from the lessons of events that might have happened but did not, although those, too, are informative (see also Fischhoff, 1977: 357; L. Ross, 1977: 196–97).

In general both analogical reasoning and extrapolation involve, to some degree or another, covariation-based judgments and inferences. But the tenuous grasp of the concept of covariation by the statistically naive decisionmaker has already been observed (see Chapter 2 and Crocker, 1981). Thus it is to be expected that historically based data will be abused when they are applied to the present or future by someone with faulty covariation judgment.

A damaging and mindless use of history is what could be termed the impressionistic-history fallacy, which is based on fictitious sampling. This occurs when no specific past events are used but a lesson of history is drawn nonetheless. Decisionmakers employ history in the service of any task, for example, justifying a strategy, by making general assertions like "The same policy has been used successfully many times before." They make such statements without citing any specific examples and they truly believe that a sample of cases is easily available should they care to search for it. Their impressions could be valid but might also be false on two accounts: either the decisionmakers' inventory of historical knowledge it too limited to provide even one valid analogy, or there are in general no historical analogies to validate the assertions made. When no concrete data base (sample) is presented, neither the decisionmakers themselves nor their peers and adversaries can refute the lesson presented. By implication, assertions based on impressionistic statements cannot be falsified. And since the statements cannot be challenged, people persist in believing that history supports the statements and the inferred assertions, which become knowledge stored to use when interpreting and processing new information in the future.

An interesting question, which goes beyond the scope of this study, is how such false impressions about the existence of historical precedents are formed in the first place. One possible answer is societal-cultural, referring to central beliefs common to all members of a particular society. That is, the centrality of a belief encourages the impression that it is based on a rich variety of previous experiences. Another explanation would be motivational: people in search of evidence to support assertions that seem obvious to them may infer that history surely must support something that is so obvious and that such evidence can be easily uncovered.

Subconscious errors. Finally, a layperson learning from history runs the risk of overlooking an important but unobservable factor that may be inherent in past events. This is the hidden plane of historical reality—the motives rooted in the unconscious minds of the actors. The fallacy is highly probable; even trained historians tend to overlook the subsurface motives of individuals and collectives in history. The reasons for this neglect are twofold: (1) even with hindsight, the subsurface factors remain nonsalient, ambiguous, and difficult to prove; and (2) "man remains ill at ease about this kind of history, partly because (as in his daily life) he has troweled over what he senses to be an illogical world. The mysterious forces that govern his unmanageable subworld constitute a jungle which he neither likes nor understands" (Rolle, 1980: 410). The other side of the same coin is the negative consequences of the intuitive historians' lack of awareness of and inability to monitor the subconscious motives that drive them to rely on the past for guidance; they often fixate on it for psychopathological reasons rather than make a balanced evaluation of the relevance of particular historical events to current tasks.

To illustrate: Binion (1969) argues that one of the main motives of King Leopold III of Belgium in continuing a policy of neutrality, even when it ceased to serve Belgian security interests, is to be found in his need to imitate his father, Albert, whom he admired and who had died in a car accident. Binion suggests that Leopold suffered from unconscious Oedipal guilt over a childhood death wish against his father. He was unaware that to compensate, he committed himself to follow in his father's footsteps and carry out what he considered his father's will, expressed in the latter's World War I policy. That policy was inappropriate to the circumstances of Leopold's era.

In summary, these sets of shortcomings could have considerable negative effects on the allocation of attention, judgment of relevance, evaluation of importance, interpretation of content, predisposition toward particular behavior patterns, and reaction to discrepant information.

Conclusions

Students of the past assume that history repeats or replicates itself. Does it, or is history copied? In the light of the above discussion, it seems that both propositions capture only part of the truth. Those who believe that history repeats itself repeat the past by learning history's lessons and reliving them. By reliving the past they make it look as though history does indeed repeat itself, encouraging more people to act as though it does. To paraphrase Santayana: those who cannot remember the past are condemned to repeat it, but those who remember it are tempted to replay it.

In fact, history rarely provides exact analogies, yet historical analogies, similes, metaphors, and extrapolations are functional. They help in cognitive economization, provide illustrations and a sense of direction, structure argumentation, and amplify ideas. However, their main contribution to decisionmaking tasks lies in their power to stimulate thought by pointing to potentially relevant variables for the diagnosis and prognosis of current events, drawn from the same types and categories of occurrence that have taken place in the past. When used critically, history provides creative analogies at a low cost, encourages the search for additional information, and indicates interpretations and options that the decisionmakers might otherwise overlook.

However, as we have noted, history can also be a source of misleading or irrelevant analogies, similes, metaphors, and extrapolations. Learning from history can negatively affect information processing and decisionmaking. It can divert attention from available relevant information; detract from the weight, value, and validity attributed to alternative knowledge structures based on deductive logic or ahistorical inductive reasoning; or add to the diagnostic and prognostic importance attributed to information that does not deserve it. Should policymakers avoid using history because of such risks? History should be used, but with caution and a full awareness of the pitfalls pointed out in this chapter. Learning from history is not a worse approach to the performance of decisionmaking tasks than other shortcuts, which are also prone to biases and fallacies of the same or a different nature. In general, the use of shortcuts is rational and even unavoidable owing both to the limits on human cognitive capabilities and to the environmental and situational constraints on rationality.[19]

Nor is anything deterministic in the abuse of history. Errors and biases can at least be controlled and limited, if not always averted, if the practical-intuitive historian is alerted to them. Yet a passive awareness of the pitfalls in using history is not enough to avoid them because the temptation to apply lessons perceived in salient historical situations is so powerful. The following active measures can and should be taken as well to minimize the chance of abusing history and to override biases:

1. Decisionmakers should clarify to themselves the structure of the situation in which they intend to use history by carefully separating the known, the unclear, and the presumed, thus reducing vagueness; doing so will decrease the likelihood of misusing history by nailing down what the situation involves. Next, they should look at potential analogies, especially the irresistible and captivating ones, and carefully compare likenesses and differences (Neustadt and May, 1986).

2. They should be suspicious of analogies that pop up. The past that is remembered spontaneously, even by those who experienced the remembered event, is not necessarily the past that actually happened. There is reason to believe that the reconstruction bears little resemblance to the actual past experience and is likely be distorted by secondary resources and popular accounts (Loftus and Loftus, 1980). Instant analogies involving the spontaneous recall and recognition of similarity between past and present problems are highly suspect, and their validity deserves special scrutiny.

3. They should look for the equivalents of a control group. They can, among other things, search for additional events of a similar type and check whether they too lead to the conclusions originally reached. Or they can apply completely different strategies, such as deductive logic, to the same problem to check whether different strategies lead to the same or different conclusions.

4. If time and circumstances allow, decisionmakers can let others, professional historians if possible, scrutinize the same analogies to see whether they reach the same conclusions.[20] Even better, the decisionmakers should not reveal their preferred analogical historical events but let the historians suggest an analogical event or events and see if they produce the same events and the same lessons; the same events with different lessons; different events that lead to the same lessons; or different analogical events that lead to different lessons. Such an approach is

valuable in a small-group context to avoid the groupthink symptoms that lead to the premature bolstering of shared beliefs.

Where does the use of history belong in terms of the three decision-making paradigms: the rational-analytic, the cybernetic, and the cognitive? The decisionmaking task and the role enactment of the practical-intuitive historian best fit the cognitive paradigm. The use of historical knowledge structures and heuristics reflects the main goal of the decisionmaker—the management and resolution of complexity and uncertainty—achieved by acting as a believer, perceiver, information processor, strategist, or learner. The management process reflects the effects of the main principles of the cognitive paradigm: reality recording, inferential memory, consistency, simplicity, stability, and coherence (O. R. Holsti, 1976; Stein and Tanter 1980: 38–43; Steinbruner, 1974: 88–124). The theories and beliefs the decisionmaker holds are maintained and reinforced by historical knowledge, despite sample size and apart from the logicality of the connections deduced. However, the use of history can still be a component, albeit a secondary one, of a cybernetic process, for example, as a source of a predetermined repertoire of responses to contingent situations. Nor is the use of history precluded from playing a role in an analytic-rational process. After all, "analogy is not a relatively poor use of logic; rather logic is a relatively good use of analogy" (Sacksteder, 1974: 234).

History does not contain an inherent truth that necessarily reveals itself to the scholar or practitioner. It retains many faces even when studied with great care and through the application of scientific methodology. History teaches by analogy, enlightens by metaphor, and educates by extrapolation; but analogy can mislead, metaphor be misplaced, and extrapolation misguided. Practical-intuitive historians must take these risks when entering the treasure house of human experience.

CHAPTER 7

Conclusions and Policy Implications

....

"This is the excellent foppery of the world; that, when we are sick in fortune—often the surfeit of our own behaviour—we make guilty of our disasters the sun, the moon, and the stars, as if we were villians on necessity,
fools by heavenly compulsion." SHAKESPEARE

Information Processing: The Sociocognitive Approach

In this study I have attempted an integral, holistic view of people as
information processors, with special reference to foreign policy decisionmakers. I have analyzed information processing behavior across contingent circumstances, the attributes of information, the immediate social
environment, and the broad societal-cultural environment; and I have
taken into account the multitude of personality facets, including psychological needs, cognitive constraints, and physiological capacities. This,
the sociocognitive approach, in spite of its complexity, seems to be a
realistic reflection of the nature and context of social information processing.

I believe that the search for a single key that will open all the doors to
the understanding of human information processing is as futile and unrealistic as the search for El Dorado. Observers of the complex phenomenon of information processing must realize that it is not unlike orchestra
conducting. The same instruments in different combinations, in different
sequences, and under different conductors can produce an immensely
broad range of completely different types of music, and even when playing the same composition they can achieve a variety of different nuances.
Hence the approach taken here rejects any single parsimonious model of
the human being and instead sees people as agile, ingenious operators
whose behavior can only be described by a number of complementary
interactive theoretical models, depending on social and situational circumstances. The cost of realism is a much more complex explanation of

information processing behavior and the rejection of more parsimonious explanations that, as analyzed in Chapter 1, are methodologically deficient.[1]

Information processing in general is not primarily a rational-analytic process. It is wide open to irrational, nonrational intuitive, and affective influences, biases, and errors, especially in environments and issue-areas like international politics where uncertainty and complexity prevail. The nature of the process raises serious doubts about the ability of foreign policy makers to realistically cope with and adjust to changes occurring in the external and internal environments, for such an ability is conditional on accurate information processing and the accurate judgment of changes in the environment. If information processing is biased, foreign policy, rather than optimally serving the purposes it aims at, serves subjective and other individual and collective parochial needs that are not necessarily in tune with reality. It is therefore unrealistic to rely on the magical power of feedback, learning, and adaptation, the chain that is supposed to eventually lead to the correction of errors and their future avoidance. Corrective processes are unlikely to occur automatically, for self-monitoring is biased and currently held perceptions serve as important factual and interpretative inputs in the formation of present and future perceptions.[2] The result is a vicious circle in which misperceptions form the basis of additional misperceptions, thus increasing their own centrality in the cognitive system and becoming even more resistant to change.[3]

Three sources of cognitive channeling have been identified: the technical, the psychological, and the social. But the influence of these channeling factors depends on arousal. The first preconditions for arousal are ambiguity and uncertainty,[4] which are the extent to which decisionmakers are confident in their understanding of the situation and the environment, in their capacity to accurately determine the probability of the occurrence of particular events or of their development along certain lines, and in the extent of their capacity to foresee all relevant results and outcomes. Ambiguity is one of the main reasons decisionmakers may ignore threats that develop gradually rather than precipitately. The former do not trigger focused attention and are likely, even if noticed, to be relegated to the category of routine situation (Janis, 1989: 145–47). Whenever ambiguity and uncertainty are high, the definition of the situation is more likely to be a function of the person than of the objective stimulus. When ambiguity and uncertainty increase, the information becomes more open to competitive interpretations and choosing among them becomes more complicated.

Decisionmaking requires uncertainty and ambiguity to be reduced to an acceptable level and at least one alternative to be identified as acceptable. Unless these conditions are met, decisionmakers avoid choosing from among available alternatives. The avoidance of making a decision is not necessarily final; it is just a delay to consider additional alternatives. As the alternatives are processed the decisionmakers seek to extract information from their inspection. They may also delay searching for further information in order to first identify criteria for choosing among the interpretations. But even when all the information required is available, the decisionmakers may not rush to decide, if not forced to, but may spend additional time on deliberation in order to decrease uncertainty and ambiguity and find ways to produce cognitive simplification (Corbin, 1980; Hogarth, 1975).

The second precondition for arousal concerns the perceived importance and complexity of the decision being considered, which concern the range of values and issues that are perceived to be affected by the decision. The third precondition is personal responsibility and involvement, determined by the degree to which policymakers envisage their significant values to be affected by the decision. The fourth precondition is the stress and anxiety caused by the high stakes involved, the limited time available for evaluating the situation and reaching the decision, and the limited freedom to reverse a decision based on particular judgments, inferences and predictions.

When a problem or another stimulus activates the arousal preconditions, it triggers an active search for information. The searchers scan the environment and the personal and organizational stores of memory. If a problem has an obvious solution, no search for information ensues. Similarly, when a problem does not pose any sense of urgency or psychological discomfort or any threat to significant values, it is likely to go unobserved or be ignored and to generate little or no search for information. Furthermore, if decisionmakers believe that they already have all the necessary information or can simply rely on direct historical analogy, they stop actively scanning the environment. Otherwise, the search for relevant information proceeds until the decisionmakers are satisfied. In the search process the attention to information is affected by the inherent attributes of the information and by the contextual attributes that make it vivid and salient.

For reasons intrinsic to the international system and to the attributes of foreign-policy-related information, decisionmakers often find themselves burdened with information overload. Having bounded cognitive capabilities, they have to cope with the overload before processing more deeply. Coping takes in a range of strategies that can be used individually or in a cluster. They involve the manipulation of absorption procedures, information channels, information content, and the problem the information is meant to resolve. These strategies require making trade-offs between efficiency and accuracy in information processing.

Faced with ambiguous and complex information that can be combined and interpreted in various ways, sensible cognitive misers first categorize and label the information to decide whether to invest resources in deeper processing and, if so, how many to invest. The next step is to use available extrinsic cues (e.g. source orientation cues, target orientation cues) to make sense of the information and to assess its relevance, validity, and importance.

After the initial, shallow processing, the cognitive and motivational constructs that are activated by the nature of the issue, the specific content of the information, and the attributes of the situation are consciously and unconsciously brought to bear on the information. The basic cognitive constructs, which include beliefs, values, stereotypes, and attitudes, have diagnostic and prognostic functions and are applied to impose structure and meaning on information that seems to lack coherent meaning and certain validity. Information that is inconsistent with or disconfirms the validity of central cognitive elements is likely to be ignored and discounted. However, the problem and the related information may activate not only cognitive elements but also innate or ad hoc needs and fears. Information is then used and abused to serve these needs, resulting in motivational biases; a potent and basic need is the need for an orderly and consistent world. New information may pose a threat to the existing consistency within attitudes, between attitudes or beliefs or values, or among different elements in the cognitive structure (e.g. beliefs and values). The threat has to be met by either imposing consistency or reducing the inconvenience that inconsistency causes. The various modes of coping with inconsistency may be another source of motivational biases.

Decisionmakers also approach uncertainty, ambiguity, and complexity by applying schemata that are abstract, structured encapsulations of past experience or are based on historical knowledge. Alternatively, they may apply any one or a combination of heuristics (representativeness, availability, anchoring, and simulation) or other rules of thumb that provide shortcuts to interpreting the available information. Moreover, by using them, they can go beyond the given information with minimum effort, but they risk unmotivational biases, which may lead to errors in the definition of the situation. The preference for particular beliefs or values, the dependence on sterotypes, and the dominance of some needs over others are heavily influenced by some key personality traits that are stable over time and across situations. These traits are in some cases generated by the process of cultural-societal socialization and are likely to be activated when cultural norms make them salient and acceptable. Cognitive processes are sometimes more, sometimes less, adequate over the course of time. They can be influenced by the amount of stress and anxiety, which is related to the gravity of the problems and issues that the decisionmaker has to cope with and to the decisionmaker's personal problems, state of health, level of fatigue, and age and in some cases to the ingestion of prescribed and over-the-counter drugs that are taken because of age and illness. In that these factors can increase stress and anxiety and affect mental competence all of them may cause a significant decline in intellectual and cognitive capabilities and may affect the quality of information processing.

But people operate within a social context. They are either members of an organization or a small group. Organizations are particularly important in the early stages of collecting information, which in the foreign policy domain is an institutional operation more than an individual one. Organizational missions and goals channel attention and affect the selection of information as well as the preference for interpretations that are parochial and self-serving in the process of bureauorganizational politics. Structure, hierarchy, and procedures within an organization decide to whom and at what stage access to information is given. Standard operating procedures are particularly important in directing attention and in preserving existing views by avoiding, ignoring, or misinterpreting information that may indicate the need for a comprehensive change in missions and pattern of operation. The effectiveness of SOPs for information processing may be adversely affected by situational factors, such as crises, threats, and stress, that cause a reduced exchange of information among units and a general decline in processing efficiency. As a result, organizational collection and interpretation of information may provide the individual or the small decisionmaking group with an input of selected raw information as well as with information that is fully processed, synthesized, and transformed into inferences and judgments that already reflect organizational biases.

Representatives of the competing policymaking organs of the state coordinate and carry out decisionmaking activities in a small-group context, where the participants interact directly. The interactive processes can involve different levels of intensity and duration and different types of hierarchical relationships and can have important implications for the quality of information processing. Intragroup interaction provides an opportunity for learning and acquiring new information and perspectives on the subjects under review, and intragroup argumentation provides a chance to clarify ambiguities and inconsistencies and discover blind spots. The small-group context also provides opportunities for generating serious pathologies that negatively affect the quality of information processing. Individual members of the group may be in a position to impose conformity on others or may find themselves conforming with the dominating views of others; conformity leads in extreme cases to groupthink or to compromises on the meaning of the information made against an individual's best judgment. Here, again, cultural norms, situational factors, and the personality attributes of the members may significantly influence what pattern of group interactive processes emerges and whether conformity, dissent, or compromise dominates group proceedings.

The nature of the political power structure and the power-sharing arrangement decide whether the emerging definition of the situation is dominated mostly by group processes or by individual processing. In either case the end results of information processing may represent an improvement in accuracy over the prior definition of the situation, or no change or adjustment compared with the past, or even a deterioration of the accuracy of perception (cf. J. P. Bennett, 1975; Rosenau, 1970). The specific images of reality that are the output of information processing can be congruent with reality, or they can be inaccurate because they contain cognizance, relevance, or evaluation gaps. The images become informational inputs stored in the memory and used eventually in processing new information (see Fig. 5, Chapter 1).

Time acts as a misperception multiplier. The longer misperceptions remain uncorrected, the more difficult they are to adjust because of their cumulative effect. Cumulation increases dependence on existing judgments and perceptions, compounding their centrality and, as a result, their rigidity. This proposition is counterintuitive. One might expect that the longer people hold misperceptions, the greater the probability is that they will be exposed to a feedback that will call their attention to the need to correct their perceptual fallacies. But feedback does not necessarily affect misperceptions in this way; the factors mentioned in this study, such as overconfidence, premature cognitive closure, and the need to preserve consistency, often counter the corrective impact of feedback. Thus the opposite often occurs: the longer misperceptions persist, the more difficult they become to correct and to adjust; in fact they become self-perpetuating. Their centrality often associates them with the decisionmaker's self-perception, so that admitting errors arouses ego-defensive reactions that support conservatism and cognitive closure.

Which variable-sets are the most dominant? At the early stages of information processing—that is, during search and the allocation of attention—the contextual and inherent attributes of the information and the cultural-societal variable-sets are dominant, and the same is true during the initial, shallow-processing stage. As people move toward deeper processing, the social (group and organization) and personality variable-sets become dominant. The organizational variables become salient, particularly when the issue is familiar and not unusually important and can be dealt with through standard organizational procedures. But when the stakes are high and the issue is central, personality and small-group variables become salient in interpreting and providing the final definition of the situation. However, at the stage of deep processing, when the information is characterized by high ambiguity and uncertainty, societal and cultural rules of judgment become salient; historical analogies and national conceptions of self-identity (e.g. role, status, belonging) and the appropriate relationships with other nations that they imply are often used in making judgments. Personality-related variables that provide deductive rules and heuristics for resolving ambiguity are of similar import at the deep-processing stage. The importance of group interaction may decline when the emphasis is on resolving ambiguity and uncertainty in the most cognitively economic manner because group interaction, which raises competing interpretations, is likely to be a source of increased ambiguity and uncertainty.

The analysis in the preceding chapters inevitably leads to pessimistic conclusions regarding the average quality of information processing by foreign policy decisionmakers.[5]

Policy Implications

This pessimistic view of human beings as information processors raises the question, What prevented the consequences of indifferent information processing, as reflected in the history of the society of states, from being much worse? There are a number of possible answers, which are in fact complementary. First, history is indeed a sad-enough tale of the march of human folly that cannot be made light of by the counterfactual argument that things could have been much worse. The avoidable errors and the consequent suffering reflect the less-than-adequate human capability to respond appropriately and cope optimally with the international environment.

Second, not all biases are translated into errors, although they raise significantly the propensity to err in a given direction. Biases can also lead to the avoidance of errors by canceling out the effects of other biases. If a large number of independent biases operate, the net error may be less than the sum of their individual effects (Nisbett and Ross, 1980: 254–55, 266–68). Sometimes biased assessments based on strong gut feelings can even prove to be more accurate than objective evaluations of the situation (Laqueur, 1985: 278–79). On other occasions, however, mutually reinforcing feedbacks compound errors, as the case histories of the Vietnam and Yom Kippur wars amply illustrate.

Third, heuristics and other intuitive knowledge structures serve decisionmakers well in many cases (cf. Thorngate, 1980), especially in dealing with simple, everyday problems, or at least produce judgments that, although not strictly appropriate in normative terms, may nevertheless yield answers not too far away from those produced by normatively appropriate strategies.

Fourth, some of the measures taken to avoid error-bound biases work, at least some of the time. Hence the actual number of errors is smaller than the potential for error would suggest. In addition, some errors in cognition are not translated into behavior because, for example, environmental or situational constraints prevent their translation.

Fifth, although learning may be far from perfect, it sometimes occurs, especially when the costs of initial error are high and vivid. In those cases the costs provide an immediate negative feedback that may allow for a change of course before the full costs are incurred.

Sixth, the lessons of past costs and the awareness of the high potential for future errors tend in many cases to encourage risk-averse and conservative policies with a large safety margin. Thus the probability of the occurrence of major errors carrying high costs declines. Even revisionist states often prefer a careful, incremental policy rather than an adventurous one. With step-by-step change, smaller-scale errors accumulate than with sweeping change. Yet conservatism, too, has its costs. Erring on the side of overcautiousness leads to missed opportunities, which can mean raised costs in the future. For example, had the Western powers intervened resolutely after the 1917 revolution in Russia, what would the nature of international politics be at present? Had France and Britain taken a decisive stand toward Hitler and Germany in the 1930's would not World War II have been prevented and the whole structure of the current international system have been different?

But these constraining effects, which may have worked in the past to limit the potential effects of biases, may not work in the future. Although the worst errors in the past had expensive consequences (e.g. World Wars I and II), and the dramatically negative feedbacks encouraged and allowed for some learning and adjustment in the course of history, technology in the nuclear age is more likely to cause irreversible outcomes and make it impossible to fully or even partially correct past errors and regain missed opportunities, even when feedbacks produce learning.[6]

There is an element of determinism in the formation and preservation of misperceptions. Beyond a certain stage there is a point of no return—where misperceptions become inevitable. At least some of the discussed variables are by nature stable and relatively unchangeable. National style and culture, which cannot be changed or manipulated in the short or even the long run, have a direct impact on thinking processes and an indirect impact on other variables, such as group and organizational behavior. The personality of any given decisionmaker at any given point in time cannot be transformed, only nullified through a change of leadership, which often cannot be effected, even in cases of discernible incompetence, at least in the short run.[7] But even changes in personnel could hardly guarantee that the next incumbent leadership would process information any more appropriately than its predecessor.

The qualifications for effective and accurate information processing are not necessarily identical to those needed to achieve a leadership position, although a leadership position demands continuous involvement in information processing. Yet good judgment cannot be expected from people with bad judgment habits, hence, strict competence tests for top government decisionmaking positions are more critical than ever before. First of all, as indicated in Chapter 1, the complexity and uncertainty involved in any major decisionmaking situation have dramatically increased in the twentieth century. Second, the direct costs as well as the indirect costs of errors have multiplied. Third, some decisions have irreversible consequences; others cannot be reversed at a reasonable cost, although they may be reversible at an unreasonable cost. Fourth, and related, in a technological society decisions are implemented so fast that the time and the opportunities for reversing and adjusting behavior are significantly curtailed and doing so becomes very costly.

Society is careful in restricting access to positions where the role holders can endanger a few of its members (such as commercial airline pilots) but at the same time liberally unrestrictive in allowing access to positions of political power where the role holders can by their doings and undoings threaten the lives and welfare of vast numbers of people or even the existence of human society itself. Such heedlessness is justified in the name of noble democratic ideas about the equal right of every citizen to be elected to high office. To argue that constraints on this right would open the way for further infringements on individual rights is irresponsible. Society must exercise its own right to allow only selective access to power without being apprehensive that the erosion of liberal democracy will inevitably ensue. Ironically, constraints on participation already exist, but they are based on technical grounds—for example, to be a candidate for the U.S. presidency, a person must have been born in the United States. Yet candidates do not have to prove that they are competent and qualified physically, intellectually, and emotionally for the most influential office in the Western world (except in the extreme case, when they have a history of mental illness). Citizens are told to trust in the electoral process—in an age when the mass media sell candidates and manipulate candidates' images and election outcomes in the same way they market toothpaste and cookies.

I am not suggesting that clear criteria can be applied immediately. They do not exist, not least because restricting access to top political positions has been considered illiberal or undemocratic, and little thought, if any, has been given the matter. Yet various professional occupations have tests that check psychological competence for making high-risk decisions. These tests can and should be adapted and applied to politics. Another criterion that could be easily applied relates to the level of education needed to become a candidate for any given post. The requirements should reflect the complexity of the area in which the office holders operate. The myth that policymakers can rely on professional advice is unsupported; to get relevant advice one has to be able to ask relevant questions and have the intellectual tools to judge and question the quality of the advice one gets.

In current political systems, both democratic and nondemocratic, the survivors in the long marathon to the top of the political decisionmaking hierarchy are not necessarily the most competent and most knowledgeable. Reaching the top calls for skills that are very different from the skills required to make the best decisions about substantive tasks. Moreover, decisionmakers at the top tend to be less exposed to the critical evaluation of their performance by peers and subordinates because they can deflect or ignore criticism by using their resources to allocate rewards and punishment or restrict access to information that will serve critics. This divide between the skills required for reaching the top positions and the skills required to perform top leadership tasks effectively sharpens in domains where performance evaluation criteria are fuzzy and where social norms, such as equal opportunity for all, prevail to such a degree that they overrule functional norms of competence, so that even proven incompetence often becomes a remote secondary consideration in promotion. This situation is more likely to occur in politics than in, for example, business or academia.[8]

One way, and probably the most effective, to limit the consequences of the division of skills is through strengthening and institutionalizing the duality of the decisionmaking apparatus that separates the bureaucratic echelon from the political echelon. The allocation of bureaucratic positions should be guided primarily by functional norms of professional competence; the qualification for political positions may also have to take nonfunctional norms into account. To safeguard the effectiveness of the decisionmaking system, it is imperative that the power of the political echelon to intervene in bureaucratic appointments be strictly controlled by explicit laws and rules that cannot be manipulated; the number of bureaucratic appointments that can be made by the political echelon without reference to criteria of professional competence should be limited to a bare minimum. Although most states claim to follow some rules or others of this sort, the reality is that political appointments are common and extensive.

Moreover, it seems that the main organizations dealing with foreign-policy-related information, those of the intelligence community, are poorly prepared and trained to deal systematically and scientifically with the inference, interpretation, and prediction stages of information processing. The reason has to do with outdated but established beliefs and with the concomitant, self-reinforcing SOPs, concerning what information processing is and which skills it requires, especially for the high-level cognitive processes, where the complexity and uncertainty of information are the greatest.

If intelligence is a craft, it is not one that is easy to master. Apprenticeship in medicine today takes, at the very least, seven years, and not much less time in many other professions. A discipline such as intelligence involves competence not only in current affairs, in history and geography, in psychology and sociology, in economics, science, and technology, but it should include firsthand experience of at least some foreign countries and at least a working knowledge of a foreign language. Much thought has been given in recent decades to improving medical education, but very little to the acquisition of the skills and the knowledge needed in intelligence. Yet the quality of analysts will remain the decisive factor in intelligence in the future as it has been in the past. (Laqueur, 1985: 308)

Nevertheless, the emphasis of intelligence organizations is on (1) the collection of data, under the assumption that once one has enough data the picture will be clear because the facts will speak for themselves; (2) the information processor's experience and intuition, under the assumption that information processing is an art for which the most relevant skills cannot be learned but are acquired with time and experience; (3) expertise about a specific country, under the assumption that such knowledge is the most important prerequisite for correctly evaluating information about that country and that firsthand experience practically overshadows all other requirements; and (4) accumulated experience and intuition, under the assumption that theoretical knowledge provided by the social sciences, as well as research methodology, are of no or minor importance in comparison. In fact, investing in improving methodological skills and theoretical knowledge is basically seen as a waste of resources.

Thus intelligence organizations, great believers in the power of data, busy themselves collecting facts; rarely are those responsible for the evaluation of information well trained to understand the methodology and epistemology of research and knowledge, nor do they feel that this understanding is necessary. They also tend not to be trained to understand the psychological, sociological, and cultural processes and factors that may bias judgment, and yet they often feel confident in their judgment. Many of them arrive at their positions in intelligence organizations on the regular road to promotion without their having analytic proficiency in the fields for which they are responsible. Yet after a few months they consider themselves regional or country experts on a par, for example, with people in research institutes or universities who have spent a lifetime dealing with the same subjects. Doubt is something they brush away and express mainly to cover their flanks in case they turn out to be wrong. Self-criticism is rare. After all, admitting errors, or performing a critical self-analysis of one's own work, can only harm one's chances of promotion.

These characteristics of intelligence organizations and analysts are enhanced by the bureaucratic procedures for promotion. People move up the career ladder because of their success and experience as country experts, skillful at the collection of data; their tendency to view situations narrowly is strongly ingrained after years of narrowly focused experience. The pervasive emphasis on country expertise results in gross deficiencies in the intellectual capabilities of career intelligence officers for integrating large quantities of complex information that possesses a high degree of uncertainty and viewing it from a broad perspective, not to mention understanding the opportunities for bias and error and their effect on the validity of the available information and consequently on the quality of alternative inferences that can be drawn from it. These tendencies are operationally reflected in the training programs of intelligence communities, which deal very little with theory and methodology, and instead teach the technical skills of collecting, storing, and retrieving information; the structure and organization of intelligence communities; and the forms and procedures for organizing information and intelligence reports (Lanir, 1983: 107–16).

At the consumer end of their estimates and judgments the intelligence analysts meet decisionmakers, who are rarely any better educated or better qualified to judge critically the product submitted to them and who are usually too burdened with work to do so even if they are. Even worse, the decisionmakers are generally not even conscious of their inadequacies. To the degree that they are willing to recognize them, they have easy cures that justify confidence in their judgment: reliance on intuition, experience, and expert subordinates. Supposedly, their superior intuition and lifelong experience more than compensate for what they lack in intellectual faculties. This belief is perpetuated by mutual reinforcement. Most of the participants in the process have similar inadequacies, so that they have a mutual interest in assuring each other that in fact their lack of education is not important and in certain cases is even advantageous. Their approach, according to them, is hardheaded rather than egg-headed. Thus ignorance is elevated to a merit or at least a necessity.

Notably, attempts to deal with information processing shortcomings often focus on organizational change, and some of the proposals indeed demonstrate a great deal of ingenuity (e.g. George, 1972, 1980a). People believe that organizational change involves manipulable variables and suggest increasing the number of organizations that deal with information processing to provide a variety of inputs and a plurality of analyses, or they suggest improving intraorganizational communication and objectivity. There is, however, general agreement that such reforms can have at best only limited effects because, to take an example, in establishing a multiple-advocacy system, it is impossible to reallocate all types of resource evenly, as is required for such a system to be effective (George, 1972, 1980a; Handel, 1984: 266–70; Smart and Vertinsky, 1977). To multiply intelligence organizations does not ipso facto pluralize estimates. Because none recruit intellectual or ideological deviants, all continue to try to ingratiate themselves with the same consumer (the decisionmaking elite). Competition and the necessity of coordination is highly likely to produce compromises that obfuscate alternative viewpoints and the hoarding and manipulation of information; and even when alternative viewpoints are presented, decisionmakers may still simply choose the most congenial one. Finally, even pluralism within a government cannot guarantee that the effects of psychological, cultural, and sociological predispositions will be neutralized (cf. Berkowitz, 1985; Betts, 1982: 288–90; Morgan, 1983: 231).

In fact historical evidence demonstrates that organizational change is not a sufficient remedy for failure and is sometimes a cause of it; organizational structure does not seem to matter (May, 1984: 534). Organizational change is effective only when it accompanies individual improvement in both the political and bureaucratic echelons. Improvement in turn requires the careful selection of personnel as well as high-quality training for enhanced creativity and the management of biases. These arguments explain the empirical finding, based on studies of the performance of intelligence organizations between the two world wars, that the record "does not . . . supply confidence that more data, more analysts, or more investment in intelligence collection and analysis will yield shrewder assessments" (May, 1984: 531–32) and the finding that most intelligence organizations performed poorly then in making long-term projections and made more significant contributions in assessing short-term developments (May 1984: 534–35, 541).

One should not conclude that being aware of and avoiding obstacles in information processing is a substitute for in-depth knowledge of the actors and issues about which information is collected. On the other hand, even the best available information and knowledge do not guarantee an accurate definition of the situation for reasons that have been elaborated in the preceding chapters. Hence an awareness of factors that may interfere with accurate judgment and inference is essential for optimal information processing. It would thus be useful to establish a two-tier processing system, one tier to deal with current information on a daily basis, the other to deal with information patterns and processes that emerge over time. The second tier of the system would refrain from concerning itself with current information and instead work solely on an aggregative, periodical basis; being cut off from daily detail would enable it to acquire the necessary perspective to discern major trends. Those working in the second tier should have a broad social science education rather than a narrow area expertise.

A two-tier system is also needed because of the effects of incrementalism and preconceptions that cause discrepant information to be assimilated into existing images; after a while, information on any particular issue must be looked at afresh. To overcome the effects of both incrementalism and preconceptions, a new team of analysts (in addition to those permanently on the job) should be given the task of reevaluating the cumulative information. This team should be inexperienced in the specific issue-area because experience can be counterproductive due to preconceptions.

Intelligence organizations are naturally oriented toward acquiring information about the adversary. They are much less concerned about the nature of their own society. They assume that their self-knowledge is full, valid, and accurate because it is easily available. Hence they lack a sense that their knowledge about their own side urgently needs critical reassessment. Shared views about what is true and correct that are prevalent in the decisionmaking environment are likely to be adopted with little or no critical consideration. Insofar as the knowledge produced is perceived to be inadequate, the sense of inadequacy relates mainly to the validity and accuracy of knowledge about the adversary. This perception on the part of intelligence organizations reflects their perception of what their main objectives are and where their vulnerability in carrying them out lies. Yet policy-relevant information is inextricably linked to both types of knowledge. The correct meaning and relevance of the adversary's behavior, capabilities, and intentions must be coupled with one's own behavior, capabilities, and intentions; the information makes sense only when viewed interactively.

In traditional societies the role of alerting decisionmakers to lacunae in perceptions of one's own society was played by prophets. In modern societies this role is practically absent and exists only to the degree that the political opposition to the incumbent elite fills it. But its criticism is usually discounted as reflecting parochial and self-serving political interests, and anyway a responsible opposition is not supposed to criticize core beliefs shared by most of the members of the society.[9] Paradoxically, intelligence organizations may have more valid and accurate knowledge about the adversary than they have about their own side, yet they believe that the opposite is true.

Despite being prone to bias and error, information processing organizations do not systematically monitor their own success rate as measured by the accuracy of their predictions. They do not, in other words, accumulate base-rate information that would allow them to learn from their pattern of successes and failures. There are a number of reasons for their not doing so. First, the potentially high costs of admitting to failure and having it documented deters them from institutionalizing the monitoring of their performance. Second, in many cases the organizations make predictions without being aware that they are actually doing so. Third, where long-range predictions are involved, those who originally made them are not around any more when the accuracy or inaccuracy of their predictions can be verified, so that nobody is accountable for being wrong. Thus long-range predictions are safer to make than short-range ones and are likely to be made in a less responsible and thoughtful manner. Fourth, to decide at what point the accuracy of predictions should be evaluated is often difficult. For example, a prediction that is accurate at a particular point in time may be inaccurate in an earlier or later point in time. Finally, critical observers may disagree over what constitutes a successful prediction and what constitutes failure.

The complete avoidance of faulty information processing is practically impossible because its sources are so diverse and numerous, inherent in human nature and social institutions and often unknown. Yet a great deal can be done and measures can and should be taken to limit the extent of faulty information processing because of the disastrous consequences it can have on the quality of decisionmaking in general and critical high-stakes decisionmaking in particular. The most elementary and obvious measure is learning to be aware of and recognize the main pitfalls of information processing. To be aware is to be warned. It is impossible to avoid biases and errors if one is not cognizant of them. Decisionmakers should be trained formally or informally to recognize the processes that underlie bias-bound, error-prone, and self-serving information processing. Raising their awareness of possible fallacies will increase their ability to monitor the quality of their own information processing and appraise the information processing products of others (e.g. aides, peers). At the same time it may make them open to the relevance and importance of the external monitoring of information processing, suggested below.

Avoiding information processing errors and biases is an uphill struggle for decisionmakers. They must keep constantly in mind the factors that may bias their information processing and must monitor their own cognitive operations. Continually searching soul and mind while trying to monitor the motives of other relevant actors costs time and intellectual and emotional effort. In addition, role overload, which most political leaders find themselves contending with either by choice or otherwise, is likely to keep them from going through the process no matter how willing they may be to do so.

Awareness of the obstacles to unbiased information processing may not only stimulate decisionmakers to avoid biases but may also encourage them to institute basic training to improve information processing. For example, group leaders may become cognizant that what they consider as their natural right and duty—that is, to propose solutions, to evaluate their own and others' solutions, and to control discussions—is counterproductive, and as a result they may realize the need to acquire techniques for effective group problem-solving (Hoffman, 1978b).

Creativity and imagination have major impacts on the quality of information processing, particularly in domains where complexity, uncertainty, and ambiguity prevail. "Creativity occurs when ideas, 'things' or associations are produced in some new combination that is either useful or appropriate for a particular problem or purpose, and/or is aesthetically pleasing" (Hogarth, 1980: 111). Creativity is reflected in the ability to handle complexity without reducing it through avoidance; to visualize the full scope of outcomes, contingencies, and their consequences; to perceive the ambiguities inherent in information, not miss and ignore them; and at the same time to translate and combine incomplete, fuzzy information into definitive, detail-rich alternative interpretations.[10] These cognitive operations require a great deal of originality, especially when dealing with contingencies and situations never experienced before personally or by the society in which the information processor operates.

In fact, creativity and imagination play a key role in information processing, whenever going beyond the information given is required. They are obviously relevant to foreign-policy-related information processing. Both are qualities most people have, but in varying degrees. Although their effects can sometimes be counterproductive—when they are inappropriate and lead to unwarranted associations and combinations of ideas, such as imagining nonexistent threats and enemies—the risks are acceptable, considering cases where decisionmakers are low in imagination and creativity.

A number of techniques encourage and improve creative thinking (see Hogarth, 1980: 121–28). That people involved in information processing be periodically exposed to training in these techniques, supervised by experts, is recommended over allowing creativity to emerge "naturally," as most individuals and organizations prefer.[11] Generating creative ideas in the judgment process is not enough, however, to guarantee their acceptance. Decisionmakers must also be capable of withstanding ridicule, fear of failure, and social pressure to conform so that creative ideas stand a chance of being seriously considered and accepted by others rather than rejected out of hand when they represent a divergence from common wisdom.

It would be naive to assume that senior decisionmakers are prepared or able to indulge in long awareness-raising or creativity-development training programs or able to attain a degree of objectivity that would fully allow detached and extensive self-criticism. Still, they may recognize the necessity of, and accept the external monitoring of, the information processing system and of individuals, including themselves, for the sake of utilitarian self-interest—namely, the avoidance of costly policy errors. What I suggest is the establishment of information processing quality-control units. The members of the units would act as watchdogs over the quality of both the process and product of the search, evaluation, and analysis of information by individuals and organizations. They would be trained to recognize the whole range of possible sources of biases and errors in information processing presented in this study. They would submit periodic assessments of the quality of judgments and predictions by consistently monitoring them, and they would point to the soft spots in the process. The units would also monitor the capabilities of individuals and organizations to learn from past mistakes and criticism in order to improve the quality of information processing performance. In a word, the quality-control units would become the mirror in which the quality of information processing is clearly and continuously reflected. Obviously, they should be completely independent both administratively and financially from the government personnel and institutions they are monitoring.

The role of these units should not be confused with that of devil's advocate. Devil's advocates suggest options and ideas that nobody else considered or that are unpopular; in the process they may themselves be prone to the same biases and errors in information processing to which others succumb. Quality-control units are not responsible for raising alternative interpretations, although they may occasionally do so, but rather for assessing the process and product of the evaluations and interpretations raised—including those of devil's advocates.

Another important area of training is acquiring intellectual tools for statistical reasoning about everyday events. The tools should be attainable, since some of the intuitive reasoning skills include strategies similar to formal statistical rules. The training, particularly if adapted to and emphasizing ways to use statistical principles in everyday life, may be effective in improving reasoning in the following ways: facilitating recognition of the distribution of events and their statistical parameters; encouraging more frequent and effective use of base-rate information; clarifying the role of chance in producing outcomes; expanding the available repertoire of statistical heuristics and improving the comprehension of how they should be used (Hogarth, 1975; Holland et al., 1986; Nisbett et al., 1983; Slovic and Fischhoff, 1977; von Winterfeldt and Edwards, 1986).

When people are made aware, through an explicit theoretical account, of the processes that cause their beliefs to persist, they are much less influenced by discredited information (Nisbett and Ross, 1980: 191; Ross, Lepper, and Hubbard, 1975). "Knowledge of inferential principles and failings, and skill in applying that knowledge, does not guarantee correct inferences. But it can greatly reduce the likelihood of error in at least some domains of judgment and can reduce the likelihood at least marginally in a great many more" (Nisbett and Ross, 1980: 280). The suggested training program should have two purposes: to improve the quality of information processing through self-monitoring and to improve the ability to critically appraise theories, arguments, inferences, and predictions made by others, recognize their faults, and critically assess their validity. This type of training is important because people are unaware of their inner cognitive processes (Taylor and Fiske, 1978) and are consequently unable to monitor them and ask relevant validity questions. Their confidence in their judgment is unjustified.

Reliance on expert advice is imperative. There is evidence that novices differ from experts not only in the content and structure of their knowledge but also in strategies of information processing. "[Experts] can control the trade-off between efficiency and accuracy that comes with schematic processing" (Showers and Cantor, 1985: 292). One reason is that experts have more tightly organized knowledge, which allows them to handle greater quantities of information more efficiently. "Studies have shown that in various fields amateurs have predicted as well as professionals. International politics, however, is not one of these fields" (Laqueur, 1985: 307). Because of their extensive knowledge and higher efficiency, experts are more likely to attend to inconsistent information, assimilate it, and creatively take it into consideration when making inferences. Novices, on the other hand, are relatively inefficient in organizing information; they are more likely to concentrate on information consistent with prior expectations because doing so requires less effort and resources than dealing with inconsistent information. Their interpretations are therefore less accurate (Fiske, Kinder, and Larter, 1983; Lau and Sears, 1986; Shanteau, 1988).

Training does not remove the motives that lead people to distort information; hence the remedy for motivational, self-serving biases, if there is any, requires treating motives. Motivational biases should be differentiated from unmotivational ones, however. With the latter, the awareness of bias is a necessary, although not sufficient, condition for recognizing biased information processing, and training in how to monitor the use of heuristics as well as specific knowledge-oriented training (e.g. learning the use of statistical rules in everyday life) can improve the trainee's control over heuristically-based information processing. In the case of motivational biases, awareness of their existence does not guarantee an interest in avoiding or correcting them because of the costs this entails in terms of the decisionmaker's needs.

If this gloomy prognosis about the high probability of faulty information processing and its unavoidability is correct, then much more effort than is now expended should be devoted to preparing decisionmaking systems to expect and manage the potential negative consequences of misperceptions; meanwhile, concentrating solely on the almost impossible task of completely preventing misperceptions should be avoided. More specifically, decisionmakers must concentrate on dealing with the outcomes of misperception—for example, planning for emergencies by making extreme assumptions, namely, that all or most core beliefs and expectations may prove to be wrong. Although decisionmaking systems often plan for alternative futures as a matter of course, the possibility of being completely wrong is often overlooked. Even pessimists among decisionmakers find it difficult to admit that they could be involved in and responsible for fiascos in matters of momentous importance to the national interest and, by implication, to their own personal interests and values. Few ranking decisionmakers have the courage to admit the possibility of major blunders. People who might doubt their future performance do not usually aspire to leadership positions in the first place.

It is true that planning and preparing for the worst case might plant the seeds of self-fulfilling prophecies. However, the chance of sowing those seeds seems a small price to pay compared with the advantages of being ready for emergencies and avoiding the consequences, both physical and psychological, of being caught unprepared amid the collapse of disconfirmed beliefs and expectations and with the related consequences of confusion, fear, and anxiety that further undermine appropriate reaction, taking their toll especially when no remedy is on hand. An abundance of historical evidence describes the complete disruption of command, control, and communications; the cost in human life and resources; and the long-term political consequences caused at critical junctures by the failure to prepare reactions in advance. It should also be noted that planning for extreme cases may include planning for positive developments, such as peace proposals by an enemy. Positive developments are sometimes overlooked because of the disbelief they engender. Such was almost the case with Sadat's offer to travel to Jerusalem, which met with the distrust of those in the Israeli intelligence community, who feared it to be part of a deception plan.

A responsible national leadership has a duty, then, to take all necessary steps to reduce the probability of a failure in information processing and at the same time prepare for failure. To do so requires a critical view of human competence and capabilities. Also required is that decisionmakers recognize their cognitive limits and demonstrate their willingness to improve their capabilities through training and expert advice. Finally, they may want to reconsider the question of setting strict, comprehensive rules of qualification for the topmost political positions, rather than leaving the selection of leaders to the hidden hand of fate when so much, up to and including the survival of humankind, is at stake.

To recognize that decisionmakers cannot always be optimally rational (J. G. Stein, 1977) does not preclude judging their responsibility. First, from a pragmatic standpoint the question of responsibility is not conditional on the objective, uncontrollable constraints on rationality. The price of power and authority is responsibility, no matter what. The role of leader entails bearing the cost of failure. Second, even if one accepts that accountability is determined by objective constraints on rationality, accountability still pertains even if rationality is bounded; the question should be whether everything within the recognized limits of bounded rationality was done. Thus accountability, like rationality, is relative—if interdependence between the two is assumed.

There is also a lesson from this study on what future research programs on the subject of information processing should take into account. The methodology of laboratory experiments that has dominated much of the research cannot re-create the full complexity of personality-situation interactions and the effect of continuous interaction over long periods of time. They can capture the essence of isolated paths of behavior over very limited time periods. On the one hand, laboratory experimentation is necessary to identify, isolate, and characterize each cognitive and motivational pattern, but on the other hand, it also biases the researcher to believe that a particular pattern of behavior is the only or the dominating one. This bias in favor of parsimony is part of the reason for the slow pace at which researchers have come to recognize the complementarity of cognitive theories. In fact, the only source of observable human behavior that is not distorted by the laboratory experimental environment and that has both the complexity and time dimension of real life is analytic history (e.g. Brecher with Geist, 1980; Dixon, 1976; George, 1980a; Janis, 1982; Jervis, 1976; Larson, 1985; Vertzberger, 1984a). Yet psychologists have as a rule avoided this source because it is not given to controlled, manipulable laboratory experimentation. They prefer the more "scientific" internal validity of laboratory experimentation over the external validity provided by case histories.

In this context, the need for interdisciplinary cooperation is urgent. Although there is a great deal of interdisciplinary research within disciplines, the instances of actual cooperation between researchers across disciplines are few indeed. Scholars prefer to cooperate with members of the same discipline because they speak the same language and have a shared experience and research culture. Yet the improvement and advancement of socially relevant knowledge requires that scholars make an effort to overcome their biases. What social scientists ask of decision-makers applies to social scientists first.

Reference Matter

Notes

....

Complete authors' names, titles, and publication data are given in the Bibliography.

Introduction

1. Israel's intelligence community was surprised and twice wrong in 1967. It was completely unprepared for the entry of Egyptian troops into the Sinai on May 15; it believed that Egypt would not be ready for war before 1970. That assessment was revised on May 23, and military intelligence warned of a pre-emptive Egyptian offensive on May 26 that did not materialize (Granot, 1987; see also Ben-Porat, 1983: 38).

2. The term crucial case history is used here in the sense given it by Eckstein (1975: 118; see also Vertzberger, 1984a: 287).

Chapter 1

1. See also A. A. Stein, 1982: 505. The terms integrative and additive accumulation are suggested by Zinnes (1976) in another context.

2. For criticism of unidimensional explanations in the social sciences in general and on the importance of a multidisciplinary approach and the reasons it is lacking in many studies, see Laszlo, 1975; Mead, 1970; Pennings, 1985: 28–30. For criticism along the same lines but with special reference to political decision-making, see, for example, Kirkpatrick, Davis, and Robertson, 1976; J. G. Stein, 1988. In fact, research on the causes of disasters and other failures of foresight (Turner, 1976) indicates that the failures cannot be attributed to single factors but are embedded in complex chains of interacting factors: informational, institutional, cultural, and psychological. For a sample of studies emphasizing the relevance of findings from the behavioral sciences to the analysis of international politics, see Etzioni, 1969; Kelman, 1965b, 1970; J. D. Singer, 1961a; Tetlock and McGuire, 1984.

3. The need to conceal from one's adversaries the knowledge one has acquired about them often poses a dilemma. The information has to be checked for

validity and reliability, for example, whether it is a plant by an adversary or a third party. But checking the information can alert adversaries to one's own possession of it and lead to a change in their plans that will render it useless. On the other hand, unverified information is less credible and less likely to be properly utilized. The adversaries for their part may take steps to raise doubts about the information's validity in the mind of its possessor if they become aware that an adversary has acquired it; the latter would then avoid using it. A good example is the treatment of defectors and turned agents. See also Goffman's (1969: 19–28, 50–51) discussion of what he terms counter-covering moves.

4. The growth of government has made it more difficult to assess ambiguous information. More domestic bureauorganizational actors' competing views and interests operate in the adversary's system, which hampers the foreign assessor in both collecting information and providing an integrated interpretation of its meaning regarding the adversary's intentions and likely future behavior. The growth of the assessor's own bureaucracy causes the perspective of the international environment to be increasingly fractured by competing parochial interests and information overload. Competing intelligence analyses also give decisionmakers more opportunities to select facts and analyses fitting their preconceptions (cf. May, 1984: 527–28).

5. Miller and Siegelman phrased the difficulty aptly in arguing that "to some extent the audience *is* the message" (1978: 79; also in Siegelman and Miller, 1978).

6. A. M. Scott (1982) defines uncertainty as the ratio of anticipated to unanticipated consequences and discusses in some detail the reasons for the increase of unanticipated consequences in the current international system. The behavior of crazy states (actors) is one major potential source of uncertainty (Dror, 1971), but uncertainty is embedded in the nature and attributes of international politics in general, as shall be argued later in the chapter. For a general discussion of judgmental and behavioral consequences of uncertainty, see Fischoff, 1983; Jenkins, 1975. For a discussion of the implications of uncertainty for risk taking, see Adomeit, 1982; Brunsson, 1985.

7. The kinetic nature of international politics makes any estimate of probabilities unstable. Changes in either the event-outcome sequence, the probability of occurrence of any single event, or the possibility of the occurrence of new unanticipated outcomes immediately affect some or all of the probabilistic estimates. Yet decisionmakers are often insensitive to the unstable nature of their probabilistic estimates, thus avoiding revisions of their estimates. However, not all changes in probabilities require a change of policy. Probabilities of events and outcomes can fluctuate within a given limit without necessarily calling for a policy adjustment. But this does not absolve decisionmakers of closely monitoring changes in probabilities so they will know immediately when a change reaches a threshold at which policy adaptation is required.

8. This is what has been defined in the classical approach to the mind-body problem as the dualist-interactionist position, where dualist refers to the existence of two realms of reality and interactionist to a two-way causal influence (Holt, 1972: 6). For a sample of cross-disciplinary literature, see Billings, Milburn, and Schaalman, 1980; Boulding, 1956, 1965; Brecher, Steinberg, and Stein, 1969; Brecher, 1972; O. R. Holsti, 1965a,b; Holzner and Marx, 1979; James et al., 1978; James and Sells, 1981; Jervis, 1976; Lazarus and Folkman, 1984; Zinnes, North, and Koch, 1961.

9. For an evaluation of the ecological approach, see Zinnes, 1972; Gold, 1978. It must be stressed, however, that perceptions will not necessarily fail to coincide with reality (Zinnes, Zinnes, and McClure, 1972); misperceptions are avoidable.

10. For a definition of quality in decisionmaking and criteria to evaluate quality, see George, 1980a, 1984; Janis, 1989; Janis and Mann, 1977: 10–14, 367–404; J. G. Stein, 1978.

11. Thus we must differentiate, on the one hand, and relate, on the other, the notions of objective and subjective probability. See Abelson, 1976a: 62–63; Raiffa, 1968. On making the best of it, see also Holt, 1972: 9.

12. One must differentiate between recognizing the existence of a misperception and recognizing its causes. The analyst's now having information that was not available to the involved actor at the time should not cause any difficulty. Although the lack of information can be used as a possible explanation for the actor's misperception, the a posteriori information enables the researcher to establish for descriptive purposes the existence (or nonexistence) and nature of the misperception in any particular case and draw policy-relevant conclusions.

13. For empirical confirmation of this assertion, see Herek, Janis, and Huth, 1987; Janis, 1989: 119–35.

14. See Carr (1973: 87–108) for the arguments against the "Cleopatra's nose" theory, which posits chance as a variable that explains historical events.

15. Misperception is irrelevant to the decisionmaker with a dominant strategy because a misperceiving actor can choose a course of action that maximizes returns, one that provides a preferred outcome no matter what the other actor does (A. A. Stein, 1982; McClintock et al., 1963). On the relationship among misperceptions, preferences, and outcomes, see also Sexton and Young, 1985.

16. The gap between process rationality and outcome rationality is discussed by observers of organizational behavior who argue that process rationality does not necessarily produce action rationality and that the two are not always identical (Brunsson, 1985; Gladstein and Quinn, 1985). It follows, then, that a necessary condition for outcome rationality is simultaneous process rationality in both actors. But some cases also require action rationality in each actor as a mediating variable between process rationality and outcome rationality. For example, outcome rationality in a case of surprise depends to a large degree on the decisionmaker's acting on the available information. Implementation of an active response to a threat may fail, not because of a misperception of the threat, but because of the problems experienced by the target in deciding whether and how to respond and in implementing the decided-upon response (Levite, 1987).

17. This does not imply that irrationality does not sometimes have its uses. In fact, under particular circumstances it is rational to behave irrationally. Still, "the utility of irrationality is mainly for the irrational state alone, when irrationality is used only intermittently over time and the rest of the world is composed largely of nations which think and act rationally most of the time" (Mandel, 1987: 121).

18. For a different definition of irrationality, one that does not differentiate between nonrationality and irrationality, see Mandel, 1987. According to this approach, irrationality can be of two heuristic types (daredevil and stick-in-the-mud), has potentially one or more of four dimensions (incompatibility with goals, consensus, or outcomes; noncomprehensive search-and-evaluation; inconsistency of statements or actions; and a non-dispassionate style of decisionmaking), and can take place at all or any one of the decisionmaking stages (problem

identification, information gathering, information processing, decision formulation, action implementation, and feedback responsivensss). According to this definition, bounded rationality is irrationality.

19. The terms normal failure and systematic failure are borrowed from P. A. Anderson, 1983b.

20. Alternatives to Brecher's framework can also be found in Snyder, Bruck, and Sapin (1962) and Rosenau (1966).

21. Psychologists are thinking along similar lines when they distinguish between learning as a process and learning as an achievement or acquisition, where the latter is new knowledge being acquired in the learning process (Helson, 1964: 392–93).

22. This is compatible with the distinction made by various studies (e.g. Kilpatrick, 1970) between two kinds of learning: (1) learning as a result of feedback, which is viewed by the cybernetic school as the dominant kind and which is more frequent when the variables are identical at the two points in time, and (2) learning that takes in novel phenomena, which is more frequent when the relevant variables in the later period are substantially different from those in the preceding period.

23. For a detailed treatment of these terms and their implications for human judgment and inference, see Fischhoff, 1976; Nisbett and Ross, 1980; Peterson and Beach, 1967.

Chapter 2

1. For an argument that there are no systematic biases, either motivational or cognitive, even though people's judgment may deviate from normative expectations, see Ajzen and Fishbein (1983). They argue that people are Bayesian in making reasonable systematic use of the information available to them in arriving at their attribution judgments even if they do not take all objectively relevant and available information into account.

2. For a review of experimental studies testing the vividness effect and its elusiveness, see Taylor and Thompson (1982). They argue that the vividness effect is elusive in experimental research because it may occur mainly when vivid and pallid information compete for attention—a condition not created in most experiments.

3. Some aspects of vividness and salience are very similar to the characteristics that affect the amount of attention attracted by foreign news (Galtung and Ruge, 1965; Graber, 1984; S. Peterson, 1979).

4. Current research suggests a number of reasons for the effects of salience: (1) information about salient stimuli may be more apt to be recalled and thus has more impact upon all social judgments than information about nonsalient stimuli; (2) information may be perceptually organized in a manner that highlights the causal role of salient stimuli; (3) information about salient stimuli may be encoded to be more cognitively available to the perceiver and thus has more impact upon all social judgments; (4) information about salient stimuli may be encoded to be more linked to the perceiver's affective responses and thus has more impact upon evaluative judgments. The available research does not provide a sound basis for choosing among these four possible mediations, although there is some evidence against the first one (McArthur, 1981: 240).

5. Active and passive expectations differ. Active expectations draw on limited resources of attention, and hence active preparation for one target of attention

slows response to another anticipated target. On the other hand, passive expectations are automatic and effortless, forming a disposition that yields a faster response when they are confirmed, but at the same time they do not impede the response to targets that have not been primed (Kahneman and Tversky, 1982b).

6. On the other hand, when the behavior of others is ambiguous, the perceiver selectively attends to the aspects that fit expectations, and those aspects exert a disproportionate influence upon impression formation (McArthur, 1981: 226).

7. Crocker (1981) has identified six steps involved in covariation judgments and the potential errors at each stage. Since naive scientists must engage in covariation judgments at each step, a potential for biases exists. Errors at earlier stages carry over to later ones or produce inappropriate methods of combining data. First, decisionmakers must decide what data are relevant; confirming cases are likely to be regarded as relevant. Second, they must decide on the sample. Easily available cases are likely to be included in the sample even if they are not representative. Moreover, decisionmakers may make confident estimates of covariations on the basis of very few observations. Third, the observed cases must be assigned values or classified; initial expectations are likely to determine whether ambiguous events are interpreted as confirming or disconfirming, making it difficult to disconfirm expected covariations. Fourth, the decisionmakers have to estimate the frequency of confirming and disconfirming cases. Expected instances have an advantage in that the frequency of the co-occurrence of the two events is overestimated. Fifth, the decisionmakers have to assess the degree of covariation in the sample of instances. Naive estimates of covariation might be biased owing to prior expectations, schemata, or superior recall for the covariation in question. Sixth, the decisionmakers use their estimates to make judgments and decisions. Some factors, however, operate against normatively appropriate use of covariation estimates, including the tendency for anecdotal case histories to exert a disproportionate influence compared to detailed base-rate information (Bar-Hillel, 1980), the tendency for prediction not to regress toward the mean, and the tendency to infer a causal relationship from information about covariation (Crocker, 1981; McArthur, 1980).

8. Using causal theories gives them further ascendance; they become even more available and, thus, likely to be used more often (Pyszczynski and Greenberg, 1987).

9. Concentrating on the elite and perceiving the adversary's behavior as fully controlled by the top centralized decisionmaking leadership has to do with the elite's salience as a causal factor; the adversary can use that perception for deception purposes. The tendency to concentrate on the elite dominates perception of the adversary's behavior in a crisis, when time constraints foster dependence on cues, such as salience, because of the lack of time for elaborate thinking (Ross et al., 1977; Strack and Erber, 1982).

10. Decisionmakers classify a state or nonstate actor into one of seven categories: the hegemonist, the puppet, the enemy, the dependent of the enemy, the ally, the neutral, and the dependent of the decisionmakers' state. In the classification process decisionmakers first make a nominal judgment about the particular category an object belongs to and then an ordinal judgment to decide how typical a member of the category the object is (M. L. Cottam, 1986). A slightly different classification of actors is suggested by R. W. Cottam, 1977.

11. For various approaches to the categorization of issue-areas, see Brecher,

Steinberg, and Stein, 1969; Brewer, 1973; Mansbach and Vasquez, 1981; W. C. Potter, 1980; Rosenau, 1966; Vasquez, 1983; Zimmerman, 1973.

12. Preferences for information about particular issue-areas and the hierarchical organization of issue-areas can be affected by a number of considerations, such as the level of threat that the issue poses to important values; the level of uncertainty; the tangibility of the issue; the scope of its possible impacts (i.e. domestic, external, or both); the degree of interdependence with other issues; the degree of control over outcomes; and the perceived probability of success in goal attainment.

13. In inference construction the overall theme of the material plays an important directive role (Harris, 1981: 92–94). Labeling information by issue-area is equivalent to identifying the overall theme. It supplies the issue context, thus reducing the burden of calculation and the costs of decisionmaking (Wildavsky, 1962). In fact information processing is governed by rules, and categorization is essential for rule-governed behavior (Segal and Stacy, 1975).

14. This part of the discussion was influenced by the pioneering work of Boulding (1956: 47–48).

15. This factor is linked to a large extent to the "philosophic code" (George, 1969; O. R. Holsti, 1977), explained in Chapter 3.

16. "Value, whether positive or negative, leads to perceptual accentuation" (Bruner and Postman, 1948: 206; see also Postman, Bruner, and McGinnies, 1948).

17. This factor could play an important role in connection with the social pressures exerted on the decisionmaker, both in small-group decisionmaking processes and in the search for public legitimacy for policies.

18. The mutual influences and reinforcement effects sometimes encourage the rigidity of existing images and make adjustment difficult; see Pruitt (1965).

19. This inadequacy has been indicated in studies on choice among multiattribute alternatives (Shephard, 1964). See also Hogarth (1980: 29–52) for a discussion of the general problem of combining information from several sources in making judgments.

20. When the need for information is pressing and no better sources are available, those available are elevated in the decisionmaker's evaluation and attributed more credibility than an objective evaluation would suggest (Daniel and Herbig, 1982a: 19). Additional judgment criteria could be useful here in providing a control effect.

21. For a review of various definitions for, and types of personal involvement and their implications for, dealing with information, see Chaiken and Stangor, 1987.

22. This statement may not be equally true for all cases. The phenomenon is particularly noticeable in people with low self-esteem (Clarke and James, 1967).

23. The question of limits on the capacity of processing has inspired a debate on the stage at which processing is no longer effortless (i.e. requires processing capacity)—whether before or after the encoding stage (Egeth, 1977). Dretske (1981: 148–50) argues that although the cognitive capacity for information processing has a limit, the capacity for sensory processing does not. Others claim that information in short-term storage that fails to be encoded into more permanent memory is lost to the perceiver though it is registered fleetingly in iconic memory, which has a vast perceptual capacity (Erdelyi, 1974: 20).

24. Some of these techniques are also discussed by J. G. Miller (1965).

25. Preference for leapfrogging is probably associated with a cognitive style of theoretical thinking defined as one "in which the decision maker adopts very abstract and extensive belief patterns, patterns which are internally consistent and stable over time and to which he displays a great deal of commitment" (Steinbruner, 1974: 131).

26. For a review of the impact of predictability, see Mineka and Hendersen (1985).

27. Management style can either foster a particular organizational culture or be the product of the organizational culture. Each of the presidential styles suggested by R. T. Johnson (1974) obviously correlates with the organizational cultures suggested by Thompson and Wildavsky (1985). More specifically, a formal managerial style is closely associated with a hierarchical organizational culture, which features institutionalized authority, specialization, and a division of labor. A competitive managerial style is closely associated with the social ideal of market cultures, which favor self-regulation, bidding, and bargaining. A collegial managerial style is likely to be related to a sectarian (egalitarian) culture, which stresses voluntary association and status equalization for individuals and organizational units.

28. The outstanding studies on signaling systems, their manipulation, and their contribution to deception and interpretation failures are Wohlstetter (1962) and Jervis (1970). See also Speier, 1980.

29. An interesting encoding error ensues when Actor A transmits a signal meant to mislead Actor B, but Actor B makes a mistake other than the one Actor A intended.

30. Encoding errors are possible only for initiated signals, whose existence the senders are fully aware of and which they intend to serve as messages. Decoding errors, on the other hand, may occur even when the signals are not intentional; their sources may not be aware that their signals are being interpreted as signals. This distinction is inherent in the definitions of the two types of error.

31. Allocating the blame for the error is problematic given the question of whether the decoding error stemmed from an encoding error or whether it was independent of the encoding process.

32. For a deception to succeed, its initiator must generate and design signals that will be perceived by the target, be accepted as valid, be competitive with other signals and messages from sources not controlled by the deceiver, and be interpreted in the manner originally planned by the deceiver. For a fuller discussion of these points, see Reese (1982).

33. For an extensive analysis of the problems related to changing meaning and introducing new signals and indices, see Jervis (1970: 142–45, 179–90).

34. In a sample of signals and indices exchanged in international crises that is analyzed by Snyder and Diesing (1977: 316) most of the errors (51 percent) in the transmission of messages were in decoding, whereas encoding errors constituted only 9 percent of the total sample.

35. For a discussion of the tendency of intelligence communities to believe that information (insofar as it is clear) has only one categorical meaning and to assume that facts have an inner truth, see Hilsman (1956, 1961) and Wasserman (1960).

36. For a discussion of the implications of this signaling problem for deterrence failure, see Jervis, 1982–83; Lebow, 1985; J. G. Stein, 1988.

37. When implicit signaling (e.g. facial expression, atmosphere) of attitude is inconsistent with an explicit content communication of attitude, the contribution of the implicit component may be disproportionately greater than its independent effect (Mehrabian and Wiener, 1967: 114). This is of particular importance in understanding miscommunication between decisionmakers from two adversary countries in meetings where the atmosphere is inconsistent with the essence of explicitly exchanged messages. A danger lies in disregarding or discounting the actual content of the message and basing judgment mainly on some other, less tangible component (e.g. atmosphere) rather than on the actual message or, alternatively, in assimilating the content component to the message implied in the contextual component and misreading the other side. Decisionmakers are advised to match implicit signaling with the actual message they want to convey.

38. Not only is assuming that people act to optimize costs and benefits logical but it also reduces the complexity of anticipating the adversary's behavior. Irrationality can take many different forms, while rational behavior is perceived as consisting of a single, open option. Thus although decisionmakers do not necessarily act rationally, the observer assumes that they do in the interest of reducing complexity and uncertainty.

39. See also Knorr, 1964: 464. Intuitive cost-benefit calculations do not necessarily lead to objectively rational outcomes in terms of maximizing expected utility or in terms of the subjective preferences and values of the decisionmakers themselves (Slovic and Lichtenstein, 1971).

40. For a discussion of the power of words in international politics, see Franck and Weisband (1971).

41. In their analysis of deterrence failures, George and Smoke (1974: 583–86) and Jervis (1982–83) emphasize that misjudging adversaries' utility calculations could lead to miscalculating their intentions.

42. People show systematic biases and errors in judging relationships between events and their responses to events and between events and outcomes because both cognitive and motivational factors affect the organization of information rather than its perception. The factors may operate synergistically; that is, people may resort to errors in reasoning, such as confusing the inference of necessity with concept-based propositions of sufficiency, to attain motivational goals, such as enhancement of self-esteem (Abramson and Alloy, 1980).

Chapter 3

1. For a concise review of the main approaches to attitude change with reference to foreign policy, see Larson (1985).

2. For discussions of the importance and broad range of effects that locus-of-control beliefs have, see Fiske and Taylor, 1984: 100–138; Langer, 1975; Lazarus and Folkman, 1984: 65–77; Lefcourt, 1976; Rotter, 1966.

3. Terms equivalent to belief and disbelief are latitude of acceptance (the range of positions on an issue that are acceptable to a particular person) and latitude of rejection (the range of positions on the issue that the person finds objectionable). A third concept, latitude of noncommitment, includes those positions that are neither acceptable nor objectionable (Powell, 1966).

4. Researchers are divided: some think that the latitude of acceptance is a personality trait (e.g. N. Miller, 1974), whereas others do not think so (e.g. Eagly and Telaak, 1974). The difference of opinion is of some importance since ac-

cording to the former, the latitude of acceptance is a global phenomenon pertaining to every issue of concern to a person, but according to the latter, it is a local phenomenon bearing on certain issues and not on others. In determining policy, this means that if a decisionmaker has a broad latitude of acceptance with regard to one issue in foreign policy, those holding the first view can infer that the same will pertain to every issue, whereas those holding the latter view cannot draw conclusions with regard to other fields or other issues.

5. Belief systems are not equivalent to knowledge systems. For an analysis of the differences, see Abelson (1980a).

6. People pay more attention to information that confirms beliefs if it is difficult to refute than if it is easy to refute. When information is not supportive, easy-to-refute information is attended to more than difficult-to-refute information (Kleinhesselink and Edwards, 1975).

7. Having to justify judgments is likely to lead to a more analytic judgmental process, which means more consistent procedures owing to better recognition and awareness of the rules that guide judgment (Hagafors and Brehmer, 1983). Hence information processing in a hierarchically organized environment is vulnerable to influence by nonanalytic considerations when those at the top do not feel compelled to justify their judgments.

8. The difference between an attitude and a value is that an attitude relates to a specific object or situation, whereas a value relates to categories of objects and situations.

9. There seems to be a connection between personal values in everyday life and those values a person applies to relations among nations (Christiansen, 1959: 97–128; W. A. Scott, 1960b). For example, someone who regards personal status as important emphasizes the importance of national prestige, whereas someone who sees loyalty as important tends toward chauvinism.

10. Ideology should not, however, be considered a cognitive component only. Every ideology, even rational ones, also includes a strong affective component (Ashford, 1972: 109). The affective component gives ideologies an accrued ridigity, which explains their low capability to adjust to disconfirming information.

11. For example, a person who is not a spendthrift can be described as either frugal (positive) or miserly (negative). The same stereotype often has different meanings and connotations in different contexts, so that the same phenomenon can easily receive contradictory explanations.

12. For two competing views of the utility of the attitude construct, compare Abelson (1972) and Kelman (1974).

13. This definition represents an attempt to combine multidimensional dynamic and static aspects, in contrast to definitions that are unidimensional and have either a dominant static aspect (e.g. Fishbein, 1966; Triandis, 1971: 2) or a dominant dynamic aspect that relates chiefly to the judgmental-evaluative process (e.g. Lee, 1966: 88).

14. This limitation poses a number of problems even if the decisionmaker is capable of the mental computation exercise. Where attitude-toward-object and attitude-toward-situation are positively or negatively congruent, the direction of the overall attitude is easy to determine. But when they are incongruent, that is, when attitude-toward-situation is positive and attitude-toward-object is negative, or vice versa, a decisionmaker has serious difficulties in judging correctly the integrative effects of combining the contradictory elements if the valences of both

are more or less equal in magnitude. In this case the overall attitude may well be arbitrary. When the valences are widely divergent, the element with the larger valence has the decisive impact.

15. Contact with members of other cultures is thus most likely to change previously held attitudes about those cultures if the attitudes serve the instrumental function or the knowledge function, but is unlikely to affect the attitudes performing the function of ego-defense.

16. The knowledge and value-expressive functions are likely to produce rational attitudes, based on the object's and situation's relations to one's values. The instrumental and ego-defensive functions are likely to produce irrational and nonrational attitudes, resulting from influences external to the cognitive system (the reward structure of the environment or deep unconscious needs; see W. A. Scott, 1959).

17. On the other hand, the more sophisticated the cognitive structure, the more sophisticated are the ways used to ignore stimuli; the more simplistic it is, however, the more use is made of simpler means, such as denial and repression (Witkin, 1974: 101).

18. It appears that the tendency to form broad or narrow categories is not issue specific but is a general attribute of cognitive style (Pettigrew, 1958). Category width is influenced by culture. Narrow categorizers are more likely than broad categorizers to make inappropriate categorizations based on their own cultural values and therefore to form negative inferences about others and inaccurate expectations of their behavior (Detweiler, 1975, 1978, 1980).

19. In extreme cases, where people hold specific beliefs with deep conviction, have social support for them, and have committed themselves by taking action that is difficult to undo, disconfirmatory information may leave them not only unshaken but even more convinced of the truth of their beliefs. They may even fervently attempt to convert other people to their view (Festinger, Riecker, and Schachter, 1956). See also the discussion of self-deception in Audi, 1988.

20. The literature on the need to attain or preserve consistency, balance, or congruence is rich, and although the three theoretical constructs differ somewhat, I shall treat them as equivalent, because they convey the same general idea. Only a sample of the literature discussing the constructs can be mentioned here: Abelson et al., 1968; Abelson and Rosenberg, 1958; Glass, 1968; Heider, 1958; Osgood, 1960a; M. J. Rosenberg, 1960a; Zajonc, 1960. For some applications of consistency theories to foreign policy analysis, see, for example, Adelman, 1973; M. G. Hermann, 1984; Jervis, 1976.

21. When manipulating causal connections as a means of protecting consistency is not possible, the alternative may be to manipulate the interpretation of the motives for action or behavior as a means of protecting consistency (Rosenberg and Wolfsfeld, 1977).

22. Axelrod (1976: 230) points out that studies on the structure of a person's cognitive map show the stability of causal patterns over long periods of time.

23. R. L. Miller (1978) asserts that the preference for modes of inconsistency reduction does not generally follow a pattern of least resistance but is culture bound.

24. The term causality in this context implies both essence, that is, the determination of the independent and the dependent variables, and order, that is, the ordering of the events in time. Naturally the two are interrelated, as the

independent variable, whether event or behavior, occurs before the dependent variable.

25. Parts of the discussion in this section draw on the excellent review and analysis of Sherman and Corty (1984).

26. Normative knowledge, such as base-rate information, is more likely to be used the more it is available, accessible, salient, apparently applicabe and motivationally significant for the user (Higgins and Bargh, 1987: 407–9). Hence "in domains in which event variability and the random aspects of event production are relatively easy to assess, people would be expected to reason more statistically—to generalize less strongly from extreme events, to be less inclined toward causal explanations when outcomes are different on superficially similar occasions, and so on. In domains in which assessment of the above factors is more difficult, people would be expected to reason less statistically" (Holland et al., 1986: 249). Historical and political events obviously fall more often into the second category, and the neglect of base-rate information reflects at least in part the effect of the difficulties in coding, assessing, and constructing the data base in a manner that will facilitate problem solving.

27. People sometimes ignore their schemata and prefer piecemeal processing, which "individuates or particularizes the person, event, or issue, instead of treating it as merely another example of an already familiar category. Piecemeal processing relies only on the information given and combines the available features without reference to an overall organizing structure" (Fiske, 1986: 43). People are likely to ignore their schemata when they fail to associate a stimulus with a particular schema, when the stimulus is blatantly inconsistent with available schemata, when specific instance-oriented judgments are required, when they have a complex view of the judged object, and when judgments can be made at a leisurely pace, reducing the drive to apply a schema (Fiske, 1986: 51).

28. Actors' attributions tend to be more dispositional than situational when the situational context is chosen or constructed by the actors themselves, when situational cues are neutral or inhibit behavior, when an act is associated with subjective choice, when an outcome is perceived as intended, when behavior is consistent with prior experience, when behavior has prior dispositional causes known to them, and when behavior is considered socially desirable. In the same circumstances observers' attributions tend to be more situational than the actors'. Observers also tend to attribute the desired behavior of "good" actors to dispositional factors, while explaining their undesired behavior in terms of situational factors (Heradstveit and Bonham, 1986: 345–48).

29. Deterministic explanations can be attributed to a combination of causes: a reluctance to revise what seems to be a coherent causal model, the decision-makers' skills in explaining away evidence that is incompatible with the model (Tversky and Kahneman, 1980: 60–61), and the preference for minimum causality, that is, interpreting the known presence of one cause as sufficiently explaining the outcome (Schustack, 1988).

30. Whatever decisionmakers' views of the attitude-behavior nexus are, current research points to the conclusion that the actual connection between attitude and behavior is not a direct one but depends on mediating variables, such as other attitudes, intellectual capabilities, social constraints, norms, and the availability of alternative possibilities for behavior. (For a short review of the literature dealing with the variables that mediate between attitude and behavior, see, for

example, Gross and Niman, 1975; Liska, 1974). Insofar as a direct causal connection does exist between attitudes and behavior, the causal connection between a change of behavior and a change of attitude is both stronger and more direct than the reverse connection—that between a change of attitude and a change of behavior—but even when change of attitude is the dependent variable, it lags behind change of behavior (e.g. Fishbein, 1966: 210; Insko and Schapler, 1971: 33). Others have argued that "a person's attitude has a consistently strong relation with his or her behavior when it is directed at the same target and when it involves the same action" (Ajzen and Fishbein, 1977: 912). A similar argument was made earlier by DeFleur and Westie, 1971. In any case people must be aware of their attitudes before they can use them as a guide to action. Any circumstances (e.g. introspection before action) that increase salience and the availability of knowledge about one's attitudes and their specific behavioral implications are likely to promote a correspondence between attitude and behavior, especially for people who are low self-monitoring. Those who are high self-monitoring tend to be sensitive to situational cues, and thus high self-monitoring leads to attitude-behavior inconsistency. Low self-monitoring means a tendency to rely on inner disposition, which increases attitude-behavior consistency. Yet contextual cues sensitize people to the relevant attitudes, and that sensitivity increases the behavioral relevance of attitudes that accentuate the likelihood of attitude-behavior correspondence among both high and low self-monitors. Perceived relevance increases the availability of attitudes, as does their acquisition through direct experience; hence these two factors also increase the likelihood of attitude-behavior correspondence (Cooper and Croyle, 1984; Salanick, 1982; M. Snyder, 1979, 1982).

31. This is particularly true for expressed attitudes known to the public, which should be distinguished from other attitudes. For the committing power of public attitudes, see Graber, 1976: 195–98; Jellison and Mills, 1969.

32. For a discussion of self-justifying excuses and how they work, see C. R. Snyder 1985; Snyder and Higgins, 1988. A common excuse stresses that the deviation was an exceptional case (Festinger, 1964: 151). Although actors might be willing to accept an exceptional-case (i.e. situational) explanation for themselves, they are not necessarily ready to do so for others and indeed are likely to see such an explanation as an attempt at deception. As a result, the significance each side attributes to attitude-behavior incongruence can be quite different and lead to misperception. As a rule, excuses shift attribution of responsibility for negative outcomes to sources that are not central to a person's sense of self.

33. For a discussion of symbolic and referent acts, see Himmelstrand (1960).

34. An important category of explanation in the literature on the development of personality traits traces them to early life experiences, focusing on the family environment, the relationship between the parents and the child's relationship with its parents, its attitudes toward them and its treatment by them (e.g. Dixon, 1976; Erickson, 1963; Friedlander and Cohen, 1975; George and George, 1964; Harvey, 1966, 1967; Henderson, 1976; Rokeach, 1960). For discussions of the intervening variable that affects the potential importance of personality trait variables in determining the definition of a situation, see Berrington (1989); M. G. Hermann (1974, 1976, 1978, 1984); Greenstein (1967, 1975: 46–57); Mongar (1969); Terhune (1970a); Verba (1969). For an empirical exploration of some relationships between personality traits and foreign policy attitudes, see Christiansen, 1959; Etheredge, 1978; Shepard, 1988.

35. The symptoms related to authoritarianism are discussed in the classic study by Adorno et al. (1950).

36. Yet when the need to maintain social status involves accepting dissonant information that is in conflict with beliefs, even dogmatic people tend to accept the information. Maintaining status is closely associated with self-esteem, which is generally even more important than maintaining consonance (Clarke and James, 1967).

37. For a comprehensive discussion of extraversion and introversion, see L. W. Morris (1979). For competing views on the effects of these attributes on the preference for cooperative policies, see Etheredge, 1978; Shepard, 1988.

38. For further discussion on the nature of charisma, see Tucker (1968), Willner and Willner (1965), Willner (1968, 1984).

39. Personality is an integrated collection of traits that interact to produce the whole personality structure. Hence two people who have the same score on any single trait do not necessarily behave in the same way (Bem and Allen, 1974). Moreover, to affect behavior, the relevant personality traits have to be activated by appropriate contextual priming (Beer et al., 1987).

40. For a discussion of the implications of life crises for the quality of decisionmaking, see Kessler, Price, and Wortman, 1985. For an example of the effects, see the discussion on Calvin Coolidge, an astute president, who suffered a major depression and lost interest in the presidency after his son's death in 1924, during his first year in the White House (Gilbert, 1988).

41. For a review of studies indicating that the cognitive effects of aging are mediated by noncognitive variables (e.g. health, education, socioeconomic status), see Okun (1980). Such a mediation implies the reason for the variable effect aging has on the cognitive and intellectual performance of decisionmakers in the same age-group (cf. Botwinick, 1984: 289–90; Staudinger, Cornelius, and Baltes, 1989).

42. Compare, for example, Mao Tse-tung with Chou En-lai.

43. Murray argues that "neither Valium nor Librium in normal doses has strongly deleterious effects on human psychomotor or cognitive functioning" (1984: 182).

44. The special problems that treating the "sick and famous" pose for the doctor-patient relationship and their implications for public disclosure, government legitimacy, and the quality of treatment are discussed by Kucharski, 1978, 1984.

45. For a different view, that a vigorous and free press would provide a better insurance against cases where decisionmakers are too physically or mentally ill to carry out their tasks, see Marmor, 1982.

46. Most theories of intuitive judgment assume the existence of a recognized criterion of validity against which it is possible to compare intuitive judgments; they also assume that people rely on a broad repertoire of information processing modes that are employed selectively, although not always consciously, in different situations. An alternative view sees the process of creating knowledge as having two stages: hypothesis generation and validation. Human beings are perceived as subjectively logical, that is, as operating deductively. The process of hypothesis generating is continuous as long as a person has the capacity (e.g. background knowledge) and motivation, including the need to impose structure on an ambiguous environment or ambiguous issues; the fear of invalidity due to the cost of mistakes; and the preference for desirable conclusions that are con-

gruent with personal wishes. Lack of capacity or motivation may halt hypothesis generation, resulting in cognitive closure. According to this view, all knowledge is subjective and inevitably biased in that it depends on subjective factors in the epistemic process. No objective criterion for comparing a particular judgment technique to objective norms or models of judgment exists, and not all biases, whether motivational or cognitive, result in error. A reliance on statistical reasoning is not more valid than a reliance on heuristics. There is no a priori reason to assume that statistical concepts are superior to other concepts (Kruglanski and Ajzen, 1983; Kruglanski et al., 1983). L. J. Cohen argues along similar lines; he asserts that "the reasoning of adults who have not been systematically educated in any branch of logic or probability theory—cannot be held to be faultily programmed: it sets its own standards. . . . Our fellow humans have to be attributed a competence for reasoning validly" (1981: 317). For a response to Kruglanski and his associates, see Markus and Zajonc, 1985: 196–97; and for peers' commentary on Cohen's arguments, see *Behavioral and Brain Sciences*, 4: 331–70; see also A. I. Goldman, 1986: 311–18.

47. Some researchers believe otherwise—that people are able to attain insight into the causal structures on which their behavior is based and report on them (Heckhausen, Schmalt, and Schneider, 1985: 180).

Chapter 4

1. For a discussion of the conditions under which organizational politics is most likely to occur, see Vredenburgh and Maurer (1984).

2. Additional confirmation of Modelski's findings can be found in a study by Cummins (1973) indicating cross-cultural value identity among decisionmakers from different cultures on the basis of professional identity and in spite of cultural differences among them.

3. On the concept of counterculture, see Yinger (1973).

4. The preference for internationalism can be attributed to a more basic value of trust in other people; see also M. Rosenberg, 1957; M. B. Smith, 1949.

5. See, for example, the detailed discussion of Nehru's dilemma regarding the Sino-Indian conflict in Vertzberger (1984a).

6. This discussion was inspired in part by March and Olsen's (1980: 38–53) analysis of attention structures in organizations.

7. For a discussion of the notion of organizational crisis and its implications, see Milburn, Schuler, and Watman (1983a,b). For an analysis of members' defensive responses to anxiety generated by organizational crisis, see Diamond and Allcorn, 1985.

8. It is not necessarily correct to assume that organizations are by nature predisposed toward imperialism, as argued by Allison (1971). Organizational conservatism may counteract imperialistic tendencies.

9. Brecher and Geist (1980: 376–77) did not find support for this observation in their comparative analysis of Israel's crisis decisionmaking in 1967 and 1973. The seeming contradiction is not difficult to explain. Although the basic tendency is toward centralization of authority, for obvious reasons it may be modified by political and contextual constraints, such as the existence of a broad coalition government (e.g. the National Unity government in Israel), that necessitates broad consultation rather than centralization of authority.

10. The withdrawal behavior of central personalities in the organization can

be manifested in serious organizational pathologies, as discussed by Kets de Vries and Miller (1984).

11. For a discussion of problems concerning the relationship between the intelligence producer and the policy consumer, see Hulnick (1986).

12. Similarly, in some cases the loyalty of members of different organizations to the diverse goals of their subunits within the organization may lead to improved organizational search (M. D. Cohen, 1984).

13. The acuteness of these problems varies from one decisionmaking group to another and is a function of the leader's assertiveness and style, the mutual relations among the group members and their tolerance for each other, the mutual relations between the leader and the group members, and the resulting atmosphere (Gibb, 1974; White and Lippit, 1968).

14. Even when group leaders attempt to allow free discussion, they may implicitly or unconsciously provide cues about their preferred definition of the situation, thus exerting undue influence and encouraging the neglect or cursory treatment of alternative definitions of the situation (L. R. Hoffman, 1978b: 110). In a leaderless group, providing arguments in favor of a particular interpretation and eliciting support for it from other members can become a vehicle for establishing leadership claims. To support the claims, more valid interpretations may be ignored or treated in a cursory manner.

15. Formal groups can be compared with informal groups along six dimensions: the frequency and distribution of interactions; the complexity of existing norms and the degree of group consensus regarding them; consensus on and formalization of the status and role structure; the clarity of the definition of goals and the consensus regarding them; cohesiveness; and the participants' awareness of their group membership (Wilson, 1978: 25–60). The combination of these dimensions affects the level of solidarity and the limits of deviation from group beliefs, values, and attitudes and thus the possibility of avoiding selective exposure to information and premature closure owing to group-inspired conformity.

16. Status is expressed in terms of the ability to deviate from group norms and expectations (Hollander, 1960, 1965).

17. "A given role-definition is influenced by, and has influence upon, the *psyche* as well as the *socius*" (Levinson, 1959: 178). The connection between role and attitude formation is so strong that a change of role might cause a change in attitude (Culbertson, 1957; Greenwald, 1969; Lieberman, 1956).

18. A further complication arises from an inconsistency between how role holders sees their roles and how they actually act. For a discussion of various role-related problems in organizations and the manner in which they are handled, see Gross, McEachern, and Mason, 1965; Kahn et al., 1964; Naylor, Pritchard, and Ilgen, 1980: 115–58.

19. In some societies, such as Japan, the search for consensus is an important sociocultural norm.

20. For a discussion of the implications of negotiated beliefs for strategic decisionmaking, see Walsh and Fahey, 1986. Research on the causes of disasters (Turner, 1976) proves that ambiguities in information and the watering-down of information produced by compromise are at least partly responsible for their occurrence.

21. Multiple incongruent interests in the decision environment cannot all be satisfied at once, so goals are attended to sequentially (Cyert and March, 1963), facilitating temporal compromise.

22. Various explanations have been suggested for the risky-shift phenomenon, ranging from the diffusion of responsibility, which reduces fear of failure; to the persuasiveness of group leaders, who are perceived to prefer riskier decisions; to increased familiarity and decreased uncertainty regarding risk-related items due to group deliberations; to the role of cultural values that encourage risk taking and are stressed in group discussions, bringing the pressure of compliance to bear on the participants (Dion, Baron, and Miller, 1978).

23. These first three types of conformity discussed are adapted from Kelman (1958) and adjusted to the context of this study.

24. This type of conformity when shared by most group members, forms the basis for what is defined by Kets de Vries and Miller (1984: 47–71) as a dependency-group culture.

25. I agree with J. G. Stein (1982b: 47) that this is not a case of groupthink but of conformity, and thus only some symptoms of groupthink are evident.

26. A minority does not have to convert every member or even most members of the majority to its point of view; in some cases converting a small number of the majority is enough to tip the balance and make the minority the majority. The rest may then conform to the new majority. Alternatively, in a group whose members tend to conform with the views of one or two powerful members it is enough to convert the majority's opinion leaders.

27. A group's decision is more likely to be carried out once shared perception about group consensus to act have been formed (E. B. Bennett, 1955). In the context of groupthink such perceptions about consensus encourage the use of information to justify the decision taken or to avoid a reassessment of the decision in the light of new information, so the decision is implemented with little procrastination and few second thoughts.

28. The negative effects include the incomplete survey of alternatives and objectives; the failure to examine risks, extend the time period for reaching a decision, or reappraise initially rejected alternatives; the inadequate search for information and selective bias in processing it; the failure to work out contingency plans; and the failure to regard the potential for using third-party mediators to achieve cooperation (Hensley and Griffin, 1986; Janis, 1982).

29. This rationalization is less likely to occur, however, when group cohesiveness is based on members' attraction to group tasks rather than to other group members or group prestige (Back, 1951). When attraction to the group is based on friendship, disagreements are likely to be ignored or resolved too quickly (Burnstein and Berbaum, 1983: 555).

30. For a description and analysis of factional behavior and its groupthink consequences in the Nixon administration, see Raven (1974).

31. Reference groups may be imaginary or abstract constructs, used when people judge their behavior through the perspective of "future generations," "humanity," or "the world community" (Shibutani, 1967: 164).

32. Siegel and Siegel (1957) assert that the impact of peer-group values and judgments becomes more dominant over time.

33. Care should be taken to distinguish between goals and level of aspiration. The latter refers to expectations about the quality of organizational or group performance, whereas the former is the purpose toward which the common efforts of group members are directed. The group interprets the achievement of goals, or the perception and belief that they have been achieved even if in fact

they have not been, as proof that it did reach its level of aspiration. This then becomes an input for setting the future level of aspiration.

34. The degree to which individuals identify with the decisionmaking group is dependent to a large extent on their status within it. The more central their role, the more they tend to identify the quality of its performance with their own efficiency (Zander, 1971: 196). The more individuals feel integrated into and like being part of the organization or group, the more they are inclined to see what they like and to conform with consensual judgments about what events mean. The converse is true if they feel alienated (Kelley and Volkart, 1952; March and Olsen, 1980: 64–66).

35. The level of aspiration is higher than the average level of performance, meaning that people tend to make unrealistic positive assessments of group and organizational performance (Zander, 1971: 181–83).

Chapter 5

1. Among the few exceptions are Bozeman, 1960, 1985; R. Cohen, 1988; Hoffmann, 1968a; Kelman, 1955; Mead, 1968; Niebuhr, 1968; Northrop, 1953; J. D. Singer, 1968; Spiro, 1966; Wedge, 1966; R. K. White, 1970. But even these studies did not claim to present a comprehensive theoretical effort. Instead they called attention to the importance of societal factors in general or to some specific aspects and particular case studies that demonstrated the salient effects of the societal factors.

2. This discussion was influenced in part by Inkeles, Hanfmann, and Beier, 1958; Inkeles and Levinson, 1969. For a critical overview of the different problems and approaches to the use of national character as an explanatory variable, see Duijker and Frijda, 1960; Platt, 1961; Peabody, 1985: 5–19; D. M. Potter, 1954; Terhune, 1970b.

3. "National style in foreign policy or diplomacy . . . may be understood as a nation's basic assumptions and beliefs about the world and its own role or place in it" (Krakau, 1984: 255).

4. The mere fact that the person with whom one interacts is from a different culture affects the attribution process. If certain behavior would be unexpected in one's own culture and if the source of the behavior belongs to another culture, the behavior is likely to be attributed to some inherent quality in all members of that culture (Jaspars and Hewstone, 1982: 137–41). In other words, the in-group–out-group distinction affects the judgment of attribution.

5. The national culture tends toward stereotyped, generalized conceptions because the general public requires conceptions to be simple and unsophisticated to assimilate them easily. The degree to which stereotypes are dominant varies with the societal level of intellectual sophistication. The less developed the society, the greater the dependence on stereotypes in addressing the masses to gain support and legitimacy for the leadership's definition of the situation.

6. It would be one thing to refer to a policeman in Chicago as a pig and something completely different with much stronger affective connotations in Muslim Jeddah.

7. The impact of culture is uneven over time. Nations go through periods when cultural values assert themselves over considerations of power and other periods when the preoccupation with power relegates culture to a minor role in

their external affairs (Iriye, 1979). In the first case culture affects information processing more profoundly.

8. There is evidence that probabilistic thinking varies among decisionmakers from different cultures. More specifically, decisionmakers from fate-oriented cultures are less likely to think in probabilistic terms. This finding has obvious implications for communication of uncertainty across cultures (Phillips and Wright, 1977; Wright and Phillips, 1980).

9. See, for example, the comparative discussion of the different connotations and emphases of the common word peace in five different cultures (Ishida, 1969).

10. K. J. Holsti (1970) suggests sixteen main role conceptions that are common in the international system. Another list of fifteen role conceptions is suggested by Jönsson and Westerlund (1982). For an attempt to relate role conceptions to specific patterns of foreign policy behavior, see Wish, 1980.

11. Inconsistent role conceptions do not necessarily bother foreign policy decisionmakers so long as the inconsistency does not have operative implications. It takes on operative implications when it presents a choice between clearly conflicting policies that have to be carried out simultaneously and thus highlights the contradiction between the role perceptions. To avoid recognizing the incongruence between role conceptions is much easier if conflicting policies can be carried out sequentially.

12. The differentiation between system, systemic, and interaction changes is made by Gilpin (1981: 39–44). For a discussion of crisis as a trigger of systemic change and its implications for process and structure, see Brecher and Ben Yehuda, 1985.

13. For a discussion of the attributes of complex interdependence, see K. J. Holsti, 1978; Keohane and Nye, 1977: 23–37.

14. For a detailed discussion of these attributes insofar as they describe the structure of the international system, see Waltz, 1979: 79–101.

15. For an innovative set of hypotheses relating leaders' personality attributes, their preference for particular role orientations, and their effect on the quality of decisionmaking, see M. G. Hermann, 1987.

16. Such disagreement may be rooted in the fact that domestic cultural norms do not have to be totally consistent and uniform, so that different members of the decisionmaking elite may apply dissimilar cultural norms in their management of foreign policy (Shih, 1988).

Chapter 6

1. This, in fact, is the typical function of analogies, metaphors, and similes (Ortony, 1975). Metaphors are closely connected to myths; "myths are 'dramatic stories' that provide for the interpretation of events, while the structurally less complicated metaphors more clearly reflect the actual decision-premise" (Kratochwil, 1978: 133). For a general review of theoretical and empirical research on the nature and function of metaphors, see Ortony, Reynolds, and Arter, 1978.

2. For a historical-data-based refutation of the validity of Brzezinski's belief, see Breslauer, 1983–84.

3. See, for example, the interesting attempt to predict the outcomes of the space program by an analogy to the impact of the appearance of the railroads (Mazlish, 1965).

4. The distinction between these two types of legitimacy is discussed in George, 1980b.

5. In some cases, where intuition is synchronous with perception, historical analogies and their implications for current problems are immediate. In other cases intuition may take a short or long incubation period, during which the problem is mentally shelved (Bastick, 1982: 301–5).

6. Salience might lead to a biased search for similarity, with the decision-maker attending more to common than to distinctive features of the analogical and current events (Tversky, 1977: 339). The salience of an analogical event is also in itself an incentive to search for similarity between it and the immediate concerns of the decisionmaker.

7. The accessibility and retrieval of historical information from memory is dependent on its storage. Two types of storage may be distinguished. The first is context associated; that is, storage is in the form "Item I occurred in Context J." To stimulate recognition and comparison, a stimulus that will simultaneously trigger the retrieval of both the context and the item is needed (Lachman, Lachman, and Butterfield, 1979: 280; Spear, 1978: 106). Information may also be stored as an absolute (context-free) memory item, which means that "a chunk node has been formed for the attributes of item 'i' at some time in the past" (Wickelgren, 1979: 254).

8. Those events having an agreed-upon meaning can be used only within the bounds of that shared interpretation (e.g. for the legitimacy function). Other events having no such agreed-upon meaning can be used to serve users' needs according to the particular meaning they attribute to the events. For a detailed discussion of the utility and technique of the placement of individuals, see Neustadt and May, 1986: 157–211.

9. At the organizational level, different organizations in the same country learn dissimilar and selective lessons from the same historical experience and assimilate varied facets of the same experience in response to the prevailing task orientations and performance indicators, which are defined by the organizational subculture or by the administration in power (Lovell, 1984).

10. I am grateful to Tuvia Ben Moshe for bringing the document to my attention.

11. See, for example, the discussion of the uses of history in the military sciences (Beaumont, 1985; Gooch, 1980). It has been suggested that the hunger for lessons based on experience is especially marked in military institutions because of the rarity of war and because of the cost of failure (Beaumont, 1985: 245).

12. When learning by analogy is intuitive, it is accompanied by a sense of satisfaction, certainty, and a lack of self-criticism. These positive feelings reduce anxiety and doubt and cause premature cognitive closure (Bastick, 1982: 150–66, 306–7, 334–36).

13. Conclusions and interpretations with an analytic basis and supported, in addition, by a historical analogy, become extremely rigid even when challenged by strong disconfirming information because "decisionmakers tend to rely on explanations supported by several logically independent reasons" (Shapiro and Bonham, 1973: 167–68).

14. See, for example, the effects of what Harkabi (1983) describes as the Bar Kokhba syndrome in Israel's foreign policy. For a general discussion of the power and function of myth, see Bozeman, 1960: 10–14; Cuthbertson, 1975.

15. The comparison theory of metaphors states that a metaphor is "essen-

tially a comparison between or juxtaposition of objects which are literally disparate" (Ortony, Reynolds, and Arter, 1978: 921).

16. According to Mayer (1968), the most appropriate analogy to the Vietnam situation was none of those analogies so often used but the situation in Greece after World War II.

17. See also the discussion of the "last war's" impact by Jervis (1976: 266–70). However, as pointed out earlier in the chapter, the lessons of the last war may be suppressed and ignored for a variety of reasons, as with European decisionmakers in the years prior to World War I. They overlooked the lessons of the American Civil War, the Russo-Turkish War of 1877–78, the Boer War, and the Russo-Japanese War, which had demonstrated the advantage of the defensive over the offensive. The failure to learn, however, applies mainly to lessons about abstract issues. Lessons about concrete issues, such as weaponry and tactics, were learned fairly accurately (J. Snyder, 1984).

18. The pressure to apply lessons from past salient situations is so powerful that it may overcome the caution even of those who are aware of the pitfalls (Jervis, 1976: 221).

19. Mazlish suggests three criteria for the use of historical analogies: "(1) they shoud be based on detailed, informed empirical studies; (2) they should preferably be concerned with the complex relationships obtaining in a large system, rather than with the simple comparison of two isolated elements; and (3) they should appeal to as large a 'fair sampling' as possible" (1965: 18). These criteria apply to the use of historical analogies not only by scholars but also by decisionmakers. But as we have seen, one or more of the criteria are usually neglected even by scholars when they are involved in decisionmaking.

20. Experts perform better than novices in analogical problem solving, both when problems share structural features but not superficial features and when problems share only superficial but not structural features; see Novick, 1988.

Chapter 7

1. Being human, scientists, like laypeople, are tempted to be consistency seekers; hence they are likely to prefer explanations that hold for all people under all circumstances. They are prone to behave as cognitive misers and thus attempt to avoid complex explanations, instead searching for a single model that holds across various contingencies. They avoid complexity in the name of parsimony. The cases of Vietnam and the Yom Kippur War clearly illustrate that faulty information processing and the ensuing errors and biases have multiple causes that often reinforce each other (cf. Burke and Greenstein, 1989).

2. Biases and misperceptions are deterministic outcomes of cognitive processes if "human cognitive processes are shaped by underlying physiological structures. The end result, simply, is that people think as they do because of their very nature. That is, there is no easy 'escape' from distorted information processing and heuristic decision-making" (S. A. Peterson, 1985: 509).

3. See also Moxlery, 1974; Schoen, 1973: 14. Attempts to change images and attitudes to which a person is committed may boomerang and reinforce them instead (Keisler, 1971: 81), and negative feedback from implementing a decision may instigate an increased rather than a decreased commitment of resources (Staw, 1976).

4. Ambiguity means lack of situational clarity, and uncertainty means con-

fusion about the meaning of environmental configurations. Even when information is unambiguous, someone can experience uncertainty. The reverse is also true; that is, ambiguity does not necessarily lead to uncertainty. The decisionmaker may feel confident about the meaning of information and arbitrarily resolve ambiguity. Ambiguity has a dual effect: it can be a source of anxiety, which the decisionmaker seeks to reduce; at other times ambiguity is advantageous in permitting the maintenance of optimism and hope or preventing the premature closure of options (Lazarus and Folkman, 1984: 105–8).

5. For a discussion of the implications of motivational and unmotivational biases for the failure of deterrence and nuclear crisis management, see Lebow, 1987; Lebow and Stein, 1987.

6. Janis is apparently right in asserting that "fellow executives are often inhibited about bringing charges of incompetence because they know that it could disrupt the organization and adversely affect their own careers. Whistle-blowers rarely are rewarded and most often are severely punished. Consequently it is probably much easier to prevent incompetence in the first place by recruiting and promoting executives who are capable of sound policymaking than it is to get rid of incompetent policymakers after they have reached top-level positions" (1989: 211).

7. Decisionmakers, being human, can simply err without anyone's needing to attach complex explanations to each error. When operating under conditions of high ambiguity and uncertainty, occasional errors and misjudgments are normal. It becomes a matter of scholarly interest when errors occur where available information was more than adequate to warn the decisionmaker against error. It becomes even more important when prior judgments are not adjusted and feedback information is ignored despite postdecisional feedback.

8. The argument should not be interpreted to imply that good information processing is not only a necessary but also a sufficient condition for high-quality leadership.

9. In some cases intellectuals have attempted to play the role prophets played in the past, but they have rarely had the status and influence prophets had in traditional societies.

10. For the importance of creativity in emploting adversaries' actions in counterdeception, see Sarbin, 1982.

11. For a short discussion of the conditions that stimulate creativity, see Hogarth, 1980.

Bibliography

Abelson, R. P. 1982. "Three Modes of Attitude-Behavior Consistency." In M. P. Zanna, E. T. Higgins, and C. P. Herman, eds., *Consistency in Social Behavior: The Ontario Symposium*, vol. 2, pp. 131–46. Hillsdale, N.J.: Erlbaum.

———. 1980a. *Differences Between Belief and Knowledge Systems.* Cognitive Science Technical Report no. 1. New Haven, Conn.: Cognitive Science Program, Yale University.

———. 1980b. *The Psychological Status of the Script Concept.* Cognitive Science Technical Report no. 2. New Haven, Conn.: Cognitive Science Program, Yale University.

———. 1976a. "Social Psychology's Rational Man." In S. I. Benn and G. W. Mortimore, eds., *Rationality and the Social Sciences*, pp. 58–89. London: Routledge and Kegan Paul.

———. 1976b. "Script Processing in Attitude Formation and Decision Making." In J. S. Carroll and J. W. Payne, eds., *Cognition and Social Behavior*, pp. 33–45. Hillsdale, N.J.: Erlbaum.

———. 1972. "Are Attitudes Necessary?" In B. T. King and E. McGinnies, eds., *Attitudes, Conflict, and Social Change*, pp. 19–32. New York: Academic Press.

———. 1959. "Modes of Resolution of Belief Dilemmas." *Journal of Conflict Resolution*, 3: 343–52.

Abelson, R. P., E. Aronson, W. J. McGuire, T. M. Newcomb, M. J. Rosenberg, and P. H. Tannenbaum, eds. 1968. *Theories of Cognitive Consistency: A Sourcebook.* Chicago: Rand McNally.

Abelson, R. P., and A. Levi. 1985. "Decision Making and Decision Theory." In G. Lindzey and E. Aronson, eds., *Handbook of Social Psychology: Theory and Method*, vol. 1, pp. 231–309. 3d ed. New York: Random House.

Abelson, R. P., and M. J. Rosenberg. 1958. "Symbolic Psycho-Logic: A Model of Attitudinal Cognition." *Behavioral Science*, 3: 1–13.

Abramson, L. Y., and L. B. Alloy. 1980. "Judgment of Contingency: Errors and Their Implications." In A. Baum and J. Singer, eds., *Advances in Environmental Psychology*, vol. 2, pp. 111–30. Hillsdale, N.J.: Erlbaum.

Adelman, M. L. 1973. "Crisis Decision-Making and Cognitive Balance." *Sage Professional Papers in International Studies*, vol. 1, no. 02-002, pp. 61–94. Beverly Hills, Calif.: Sage.

Adomeit, H. 1982. *Soviet Risk-Taking and Crisis Behavior: A Theoretical and Empirical Analysis.* London: Allen and Unwin.

Adorno, T. W., E. Frenkel-Brunswick, D. N. Levinson, and R. N. Sanford. 1950. *The Authoritarian Personality.* New York: Harper.

Agranat Commission. 1975. *The Agranat Commission Report.* Tel Aviv: Am Oved. (In Hebrew.)

Ajzen, I. 1982. "On Behaving in Accordance with One's Attitudes." In M. P. Zanna, E. T. Higgins, and C. P. Herman, eds., *Consistency in Social Behavior: The Ontario Symposium*, vol. 2, pp. 3–15. Hillsdale, N.J.: Erlbaum.

———. 1977. "Intuitive Theories of Events and the Effects of Base-Rate Information on Prediction." *Journal of Personality and Social Psychology*, 35: 303–14.

Ajzen, I., C. A. Dalto, and D. P. Blyth. 1979. "Consistency and Bias in the Attribution of Attitudes." *Journal of Personality and Social Psychology*, 37: 1871–76.

Ajzen, I., and M. Fishbein. 1983. "Relevance and Availability in the Attribution Process." In J. Jaspars, F. D. Fincham, and M. Hewstone, eds., *Attribution Theory and Research: Conceptual, Developmental, and Social Dimensions*, pp. 63–89. London: Academic Press.

———. 1977. "Attitude-Behavior Relations: A Theoretical Analysis and Review of Empirical Research." *Psychological Bulletin*, 84: 888–918.

Akerlof, G. A. 1970. "The Market for 'Lemons': Quality Uncertainty and the Market Mechanism." *Quarterly Journal of Economics*, 84: 488–500.

Albert, S., and D. A. Whetten. 1985. "Organizational Identity." In L. L. Cummings and B. M. Staw, eds., *Research in Organizational Behavior*, vol. 7, pp. 263–95. Greenwich, Conn.: Jai Press.

Allison, G. T. 1971. *Essence of Decision: Explaining the Cuban Missile Crisis.* Boston: Little, Brown.

———. 1969. "Conceptual Models and the Cuban Missile Crisis." *American Political Science Review*, 63: 689–718.

Allison, G. T., and M. H. Halperin. 1972. "Bureaucratic Politics." In R. Tanter and R. H. Ullman, eds., *On Theory and Policy in International Relations*, pp. 40–79. Princeton, N.J.: Princeton University Press.

Alloy, L. B., and A. H. Ahrens. 1987. "Depression and Pessimism for the Future: Biased Use of Statistically Relevant Information in Predictions for Self Versus Others." *Journal of Personality and Social Psychology*, 52: 366–78.

Allport, G. W., and L. Postman. [1947] 1972. *The Psychology of Rumor.* New York: Russell and Russell.

Alter, R. 1973. "The Masada Complex." *Commentary*, 56 (1): 19–24.

Amos, J. 1982. "Deception and the 1973 Middle East War." In D. C. Daniel and K. L. Herbig, eds., *Strategic Military Deception*, pp. 317–34. New York: Pergamon Press.

Anderson, C. A. 1983. "Abstract and Concrete Data in the Perseverance of Social

Theories: When Weak Data Lead to Unshakeable Beliefs." *Journal of Experimental Social Psychology*, 19: 93–108.

Anderson, C. A., M. R. Lepper, and L. Ross. 1980. "Perseverance of Social Theories: The Role of Explanation in the Persistence of Discredited Information." *Journal of Personality and Social Psychology*, 39: 1037–49.

Anderson, P. A. 1983a. "Decision Making by Objection and the Cuban Missile Crisis." *Administrative Science Quarterly*, 28: 201–22.

———. 1983b. "Normal Failures in the Foreign Policy Advisory Process." *World Affairs*, 146: 148–75.

———. 1981. "Justification and Precedents as Constraints in Foreign Policy Decision-Making." *American Journal of Political Science*, 25: 738–61.

Apsler, R., and D. O. Sears. 1968. "Warning, Personal Involvement, and Attitude Change." *Journal of Personality and Social Psychology*, 9: 162–66.

Argyle, M. 1975. *Bodily Communication*. New York: International Universities Press.

Aronson, E., and B. W. Golden. 1962. "The Effect of Relevant and Irrelevant Aspects of Communicator Credibility on Opinion Change." *Journal of Personality*, 30: 135–46.

Aronson, E., J. A. Turner, and J. M. Carlsmith. 1963. "Communicator Credibility and Communication Discrepancy as Determinants of Opinion Change." *Journal of Abnormal and Social Psychology*, 67: 31–36.

Art, R. J. 1973. "Bureaucratic Politics and American Foreign Policy: A Critique." *Policy Sciences*, 4: 467–90.

Asch, S. E. 1958. "Effects of Group Pressure upon the Modification and Distortion of Judgments." In E. E. McCoby, T. M. Newcomb, and E. L. Hartley, eds., *Readings in Social Psychology*, pp. 174–83. New York: Holt, Rinehart, and Winston.

Ashford, D. E. 1972. *Ideology and Participation*. Beverly Hills, Calif.: Sage.

Atkin, C. 1973. "Instrumental Utilities and Information Seeking." In P. Clarke, ed., *New Models of Mass Communication Research*, pp. 205–42. Beverly Hills, Calif.: Sage.

Atkins, A. L., K. K. Deaux, and J. Bieri. 1967. "Latitude of Acceptance and Attitude Change." *Journal of Personality and Social Psychology*, 6: 47–54.

Audi, R. 1988. "Self-Deception, Rationalization, and Reasons for Acting." In B. P. McLaughlin and A. O. Rorty, eds., *Perspectives on Self-Deception*, pp. 92–120. Berkeley: University of California Press.

Auerbach, Y. 1986. "Turning-Point Decisions: A Cognitive-Dissonance Analysis of Conflict Reduction in Israel–West Germany Relations." *Political Psychology*, 7: 533–50.

Axelrod, R. 1979. "The Rational Timing of Surprise." *World Politics*, 31: 228–46.

———. 1977. "Argumentation in Foreign Policy Settings: Britain in 1918, Munich in 1938, and Japan in 1970." *J. of Conflict Resolution*, 21: 727–44.

———. 1976. "Results." In R. Axelrod, ed., *Structure of Decision: The Cognitive Maps of Political Elites*, pp. 221–48. Princeton, N.J.: Princeton University Press.

———. 1973. "Schema Theory: An Information Processing Model of Perception and Cognition." *American Political Science Review*, 67: 1248–66.

———. 1972. *Framework for a General Theory of Cognition and Choice*. Research Series no. 18. Berkeley: Institute of International Studies, University of California.

Back, K. W. 1961. "Decisions Under Uncertainty: Rational, Irrational, and Non-rational." *American Behavioral Scientist*, 4 (6): 14–19.

———. 1951. "Influence Through Social Communication." *The Journal of Abnormal and Social Psychology*, 46: 9–23.

Backman, C. W. 1970. "Role Theory and International Relations: A Commentary and Extension." *International Studies Quarterly*, 14: 310–19.

Bailey, F. G. 1969. *Strategems and Spoils*. Oxford: Basil Blackwell.

Ball, G. W. 1982. *The Past Has Another Pattern: Memoirs*. New York: Norton.

———. 1972. "Top Secret: The Prophecy the President Rejected." *Atlantic Monthly*, 230 (July): 35–49.

Barber, D. J. 1977. *The Presidential Character: Predicting Performance in the White House*. 2d ed. Englewood Cliffs, N.J.: Prentice-Hall.

Bar-Hillel, M. 1980. "The Base-Rate Fallacy in Probability Judgments." *Acta Psychologica*, 44: 211–33.

Baron, R. M. 1981. "Social Knowing from an Ecological Event Perspective: A Consideration of the Relative Domains of Power for Cognitive and Perceptual Modes of Knowing." In J. H. Harvey, ed., *Cognition, Social Behavior, and the Environment*, pp. 61–89. Hillsdale, N.J.: Erlbaum.

Baron, R. M., and J. H. Harvey. 1980. "Contrasting Perspectives on Social Knowing: An Overview." *Personality and Social Psychology Bulletin*, 6: 502–6.

Bar-Tal, D. 1983. *The Masada Syndrome: A Case of Central Belief*. Discussion Paper no. 3. Tel Aviv: International Center for Peace in the Middle East.

Bartov, H. 1978a. *Daddo-48 Years and Twenty More Days*. Vol. 1, *Forty-eight Years, 1925–1973*. Tel Aviv: Ma'ariv Book Guild. (In Hebrew.)

———. 1978b. *Daddo-48 Years and Twenty More Days*. Vol. 2, *Twenty Days, 6.10.73–25.10.1973, The War Diary*. Tel Aviv: Ma'ariv Book Guild. (In Hebrew.)

Bass, M. B., and D. G. Dunteman. 1963. "Biases in the Evaluation of One's Own Group, Its Allies and Opponents." *Journal of Conflict Resolution*, 7: 16–20.

Bastick, T. 1982. *Intuition: How We Think and Act*. New York: Wiley.

Beaumont, R. A. 1985. "Guideposts or Guesses? Is the 'Lessons of War' Concept Valid?" In J. Brown and W. P. Snyder, eds., *The Regionalization of Warfare*, pp. 243–67. New Brunswick, N.J.: Transaction Books.

Beck, A. T. 1963. "Thinking and Depression. I. Idiosyncratic Content and Cognitive Distortions." *Archives of General Psychiatry*, 9: 324–33.

Beer, F. A., A. F. Healy, G. P. Sinclair, and L. E. Bourne, Jr. 1987. "War Cues and Foreign Policy Acts." *American Political Science Review*, 81: 701–15.

Belloni, F. P., and D. C. Beller. 1976. "The Study of Factions as Competitive Political Organizations." *Western Political Quarterly*, 29: 531–49.

Bem, D. J. 1972. "Self-Perception Theory." In L. Berkowitz, ed., *Advances in Experimental Social Psychology*, vol. 6, pp. 1–61. New York: Academic Press.

———. 1967. "Self-Perception: An Alternative Interpretation of Cognitive Dissonance Phenomena." *Psychological Review*, 74: 183–200.

Bem, D. J., and A. Allen. 1974. "On Predicting Some of the People Some of the Time: The Search for Cross-situational Consistencies in Behavior." *Psychological Review*, 81: 506–20.

Bem, D. J., and D. C. Funder. 1978. "Predicting More of the People More of the Time: Assessing the Personality of Situations." *Psychological Review*, 85: 485–501.

Bennett, E. B. 1955. "Discussion, Decision, Commitment, and Consensus in 'Group Decision.'" *Human Relations*, 8: 251–73.

Bennett, J. P. 1975. "Foreign Policy as Maladaptive Behavior: Operationalizing Some Implications." *Papers of the Peace Science Society (International)*, 25: 85–104.

Bennett, W. L. 1982. "Rethinking Political Perception and Cognition." *Macropolitics*, 2: 175–202.

————. 1981. "Perception and Cognition: An Information-processing Framework for Politics." In S. L. Long, ed., *The Handbook of Political Behavior*, vol. 1, pp. 69–193. New York: Plenum Press.

————. 1975. *The Political Mind and the Political Environment*. Lexington, Mass.: Lexington Books.

Ben-Porat, Y. 1985. "The Yom Kippur War, Error in May and Surprise in October: New Facts on the Yom Kippur Surprise." *Ma'arachot*, 299: 2–9. (In Hebrew.)

————. 1983. "Evaluations of the Situation: Why Did They Fall Apart?" *Ma'arachot*, 289–90: 29–38. (In Hebrew.)

Ben-Zvi, A. 1976–77. "Misperceiving the Role of Perception: A Critique." *Jerusalem Journal of International Relations*, 2: 74–93.

————. 1976. "Hindsight and Foresight: A Conceptual Framework for the Analysis of Surprise Attacks." *World Politics*, 28: 381–95.

Berkowitz, B. D. 1985. "Intelligence in the Organizational Context: Coordination and Error in National Estimates." *Orbis*, 29: 571–96.

Berman, J. S., S. J. Read, and D. A. Kenny. 1983. "Processing Inconsistent Social Information." *Journal of Personality and Social Psychology*, 45: 1211–24.

Berman, L. 1982. *Planning a Tragedy: The Americanization of the War in Vietnam*. New York: Norton.

Berrington, H. 1989. "When Does Personality Make a Difference? Lord Cherwell and the Area Bombing of Germany." *International Political Science Review*, 10: 9–34.

Betts, R. K. 1982. *Surprise Attack: Lessons for Defense Planning*. Washington, D.C.: Brookings Institution.

————. 1980–81. "Surprise Despite Warning: Why Sudden Attacks Succeed." *Political Science Quarterly*, 95: 551–72.

————. 1978. "Analysis, War, and Decision: Why Intelligence Failures Are Inevitable." *World Politics*, 31: 61–89.

Beyth-Marom, R. 1982. "How Probable Is Probable? A Numerical Translation of Verbal Probability Expressions." *Journal of Forecasting*, 1: 257–69.

Bieri, J. 1966. "Cognitive Complexity and Personality Development." In O. J. Harvey, ed., *Experience, Structure and Adaptability*, pp. 13–37. New York: Springer.

Billings, R. S., T. W. Milburn, and M. L. Schaalman. 1980. "A Model of Crisis Perception: A Theoretical and Empirical Analysis." *Administrative Science Quarterly*, 25: 300–316.

Binion, R. 1969. "Repeat Performance: A Psychohistorical Study of Leopold III and Belgian Neutrality." *History and Theory*, 8: 213–59.

Bjork, R. A. 1978. "The Updating of Memory." In G. H. Bower, ed., *The Psychology of Learning and Motivation*, vol. 12, pp. 235–59. New York: Academic Press.

Björkman, M. 1984. "Decision Making, Risk Taking, and Psychological Time:

Review of Empirical Findings and Psychological Theory." *Scandinavian Journal of Psychology*, 25: 31–49.

Blachman, M. J. 1973. "The Stupidity of Intelligence." In M. Halperin and A. Kanter, eds., *Readings in American Foreign Policy: Bureaucratic Perspective*, pp. 328–34. Boston: Little, Brown.

Block, J., and P. Petersen. 1955. "Some Personality Correlates of Confidence, Caution, and Speed in a Decision Situation." *Journal of Abnormal and Social Psychology*, 51: 34–41.

Bloom, A. H. 1981. *The Linguistic Shaping of Thought*. Hillsdale, N.J.: Erlbaum.

Blumer, H. 1967. "Society as Symbolic Interaction." In J. G. Manis and B. N. Meltzer, eds., *Symbolic Interaction*, pp. 139–48. Boston: Allyn and Bacon.

Bobrow, D. B. 1977. "Communications, Command, and Control: The Nerve of Intervention." In E. P. Stern, ed., *The Limits of Intervention*, pp. 101–20. Beverly Hills, Calif.: Sage.

———. 1972. "Transfer of Meaning Across National Boundaries." In R. L. Merritt, ed., *Communication in International Politics*, pp. 33–61. Urbana: University of Illinois Press.

Bobrow, D. G., and D. A. Norman. 1975. "Some Principles of Memory Schemata." In D. G. Bobrow and D. A. Norman, eds., *Representation and Understanding: Studies in Cognitive Sciences*, pp. 131–49. New York: Academic Press.

Bodenhausen, G. V., and R. S. Wyer. 1985. "Effects of Stereotypes on Decision Making and Information Processing Strategies." *Journal of Personality and Social Psychology*, 48: 267–82.

Bogart, D. H. 1980. "Feedback, Feedforward, and Feedwithin: Strategic Information in Systems." *Behavioral Science*, 25: 237–49.

Bond, M. H. 1983. "A Proposal for Cross-cultural Studies of Attribution." In M. Hewstone, ed., *Attribution Theory: Social and Functional Extensions*, pp. 144–59. Oxford: Basil Blackwell.

Bonham, G. M. 1976. "Cognitive Process Models and the Study of Foreign Policy Decision-Making." In H. Bossel, S. Klaczko, and N. Muller, eds., *System Theory in the Social Sciences*, pp. 498–518. Basel: Birkhäuser Verlag.

Bonham, G. M., M. J. Shapiro, and T. L. Trumble. 1979. "The October War: Changes in Cognitive Orientation Towards the Middle East Conflict." *International Studies Quarterly*, 23: 3–44.

Booth, K. 1979. *Strategy and Ethnocentrism*. London: Croom Helm.

Borgida, E., and N. Brekke. 1981. "The Base Rate Fallacy in Attribution and Prediction." In J. H. Harvey, W. J. Ickes, and R. F. Kidd, eds., *New Directions in Attribution Research*, vol. 3, pp. 63–95. Hillsdale, N.J.: Erlbaum.

Borgida, E., and R. E. Nisbett. 1977. "The Differential Impact of Abstract vs. Concrete Information on Decisions." *Journal of Applied Social Psychology*, 7: 258–71.

Botwinick, J. 1984. *Aging and Behavior*. 3d ed. New York: Springer.

Boulding, K. E. 1969. "National Images and International Systems." In J. N. Rosenau, ed., *International Politics and Foreign Policy*, pp. 422–31. Rev. ed. New York: Free Press.

———. 1965. "The Learning and Reality-testing Process in the International System." In J. C. Farrell and A. P. Smith, eds., *Image and Reality in World Politics*, pp. 1–15. New York: Columbia University Press.

———. 1956. *The Image*. Ann Arbor: University of Michigan Press.

Bowers, K. S. 1981. "Knowing More Than We Can Say Leads to Saying More Than We Can Know: On Being Implicitly Informed." In D. Magnusson, ed., *Toward a Psychology of Situations: An Interactional Perspective*, pp. 179–94. Hillsdale, N.J.: Erlbaum.

———. 1973. "Situationism in Psychology: An Analysis and a Critique." *Psychological Review*, 80: 307–36.

Bozeman, A. B. 1985. "Statecraft and Intelligence in the Non-Western World." *Conflict*, 6: 1–35.

———. 1960. *Politics and Culture in International History*. Princeton, N.J.: Princeton University Press.

Bracken, P. 1983. *The Command and Control of Nuclear Forces*. New Haven, Conn.: Yale University Press.

Bradburn, N. M. 1963. "The Cultural Context of Personality Theory." In J. M. Wepman and R. W. Heine, eds., *Concepts of Personality*, pp. 333–60. Chicago: Aldine.

Bradley, G. W. 1978. "Self-serving Biases in the Attribution Process: A Reexamination of the Fact or Fiction Question." *Journal of Personality and Social Psychology*, 36: 56–71.

Brady, L. P. 1978. "The Situation and Foreign Policy." In M. A. East, S. A. Salmore, and C. F. Hermann, eds., *Why Nations Act*, pp. 173–90. Beverly Hills, Calif.: Sage.

Brandon, H. 1970. *Anatomy of Error: The Secret History of the Vietnam War*. London: Andre Deutsch.

Brecher, M. 1974. *Decisions in Israel's Foreign Policy*. London: Oxford University Press.

———. 1972. *The Foreign Policy System of Israel*. London: Oxford University Press.

Brecher, M., and H. Ben Yehuda. 1985. "System and Crisis in International Politics." *Review of International Studies*, 11: 17–36.

Brecher, M., with B. Geist. 1980. *Decisions in Crisis: Israel, 1967 and 1973*. Berkeley: University of California Press.

Brecher, M., B. Steinberg, and J. Stein. 1969. "A Framework for Research on Foreign Policy Behavior." *Journal of Conflict Resolution*, 13: 75–101.

Brehm, J. W. 1960. "A Dissonance Analysis of Attitude-Discrepant Behavior." In M. J. Rosenberg, C. I. Hovland, W. J. McGuire, R. P. Abelson, and J. W. Brehm, eds., *Attitude Organization and Change*, pp. 164–97. New Haven, Conn.: Yale University Press.

Brehmer, B. 1980. "In One Word: Not from Experience." *Acta Psychologica*, 45: 223–41.

Breslauer, G. W. 1983–84. "Do Soviet Leaders Test New Presidents?" *International Security*, 8 (3): 83–107.

Brewer, T. L. 1973. "Issue and Context Variations in Foreign Policy: Effects on American Elite Behavior." *Journal of Conflict Resolution*, 17: 89–114.

Brislin, R. W. 1981. *Cross-cultural Encounters: Face-to-Face Interaction*. New York: Pergamon Press.

Broad, W., and N. Wade. 1982. *Betrayers of the Truth*. New York: Simon and Schuster.

Brody, R. A. 1966. "Cognition and Behavior: A Model for International Relations." In O. J. Harvey, ed., *Experience Structure and Adaptability*, pp. 321–48. New York: Springer.

Bronfenbrenner, U. 1961. "The Mirror Image in Soviet-American Relations: A Social Psychologist's Report." *Journal of Social Issues*, 17 (3): 45–56.

Bronner, R. 1982. *Decision Making Under Time Pressure*. Lexington, Mass.: Lexington Books.

Brown, J. L., and N. M. Agnew. 1986. "Feedback Bias from Ignoring the Outcome of Rejected Alternatives." *Behavioral Science*, 32: 34–41.

Brown, R. W. 1965. *Social Psychology*. New York: Free Press.

Brown, R. W., and E. H. Lennenberg. 1954. "A Study in Language and Cognition." *Journal of Abnormal and Social Psychology*, 49: 454–62.

Bruner, J. S., and L. Postman. 1948. "Symbolic Value as an Organizing Factor in Perception." *Journal of Social Psychology*, 27: 203–8.

Brunsson, N. 1985. *The Irrational Organization*. Chichester, Eng.: Wiley.

Brzezinski, Z. 1983. *Power and Principle: Memories of the National Security Adviser, 1977–1981*. New York: Farrar, Straus and Giroux.

Budner, S. 1962. "Intolerance of Ambiguity as a Personality Variable." *Journal of Personality*, 30: 29–50.

Bull, H. 1969. "International Theory: The Case for a Classical Approach." In K. Knorr and J. N. Rosenau, eds., *Contending Approaches to International Politics*, pp. 20–38. Princeton, N.J.: Princeton University Press.

Bunch, M. E. 1958. "The Concept of Motivation." *Journal of General Psychology*, 58: 189–205.

Burke, J. P., and F. I. Greenstein. 1989. "Presidential Personality and National Security Leadership: A Comparative Analysis of Vietnam Decision-Making." *International Political Science Review*, 10: 73–92.

Burnstein, E. 1967. "Sources of Cognitive Bias in the Representation of Simple Social Structures." *Journal of Personality and Social Psychology*, 7: 36–48.

Burnstein, E., and M. L. Berbaum. 1983. "Stages in Group Decision Making: The Decomposition of Historical Narratives." *Political Psychology*, 4: 531–61.

Byrne, D. 1961. "Interpersonal Attraction and Attitude Similarity." *Journal of Abnormal and Social Psychology*, 62: 713–15.

Caldwell, D. 1977. "Bureaucratic Foreign Policy–Making." *American Behavioral Scientist*, 21: 87–110.

Calhoun, R., and S. L. Hutchison, Jr. 1981. "Decision-Making in Old Age: Cautiousness and Rigidity." *International Journal of Aging and Human Development*, 13: 89–98.

Callaway, M. R., R. G. Marriott, and J. K. Esser. 1985. "Effects of Dominance on Group Decision Making: Toward a Stress-Reduction Explanation of Groupthink." *Journal of Personality and Social Psychology*, 49: 949–52.

Cantor, N., and W. Mischel. 1979. "Prototypes in Person Perception." In L. Berkowitz, ed., *Advances in Experimental Social Psychology*, vol. 12, pp. 4–52. New York: Academic Press.

Carr, E. H. 1973. *What Is History?* Harmondsworth, Eng.: Penguin.

Carter, R. F. 1959. "Bandwagon and Sandbagging Effect: Some Measures of Dissonance Reduction." *Public Opinion Quarterly*, 23: 279–87.

Cervone, D., and P. K. Peake. 1986. "Anchoring, Efficacy, and Action: The Influence of Judgmental Heuristics on Self-Efficacy Judgments and Behavior." *Journal of Personality and Social Psychology*, 50: 492–501.

Chaiken, S. 1987. "The Heuristic Model of Persuasion." In M. P. Zanna, J. M.

Olson, and C. P. Herman, eds., *Social Influence: The Ontario Symposium*, vol. 5, pp. 3–40. Hillsdale, N.J.: Erlbaum.

———. 1980. "Heuristic Versus Systematic Information Processing and the Use of Source Versus Message Cues in Persuasion." *Journal of Personality and Social Psychology*, 39: 752–66.

Chaiken, S., and C. Stangor. 1987. "Attitudes and Attitude Change." In M. R. Rosenzweig and L. W. Porter, eds., *Annual Review of Psychology*, vol. 38, pp. 575–630. Palo Alto, Calif.: Annual Reviews.

Chan, S. 1982. "Expert Judgments Under Uncertainty: Some Evidence and Suggestions." *Social Science Quarterly*, 63: 428–44.

———. 1979. "The Intelligence of Stupidity: Understanding Failures in Strategic Warning." *American Political Science Review*, 73: 171–80.

Chanda, N. 1979. "The Black Book of Hatred." *Far Eastern Economic Review*, Jan. 19, pp. 19–22.

Chanowitz, B., and E. J. Langer. 1981. "Premature Cognitive Commitment." *Journal of Personality and Social Psychology*, 41: 1051–63.

Chapman, L. J., and J. P. Chapman. 1969. "Illusory Correlation as an Obstacle to the Use of Valid Psychodiagnostic Signs." *Journal of Abnormal Psychology*, 74: 271–80.

Child, I. L., and L. W. Doob. 1943. "Factors Determining National Stereotypes." *Journal of Social Psychology*, 17: 203–19.

Christiansen, B. 1959. *Attitudes Toward Foreign Affairs as a Function of Personality*. Oslo: Oslo University Press.

Cioffi-Revilla, C. A. 1979. "Diplomatic Communication Theory: Signals, Channels, Networks." *International Interactions*, 6: 209–65.

Clarke, M. 1974. "On the Concept of 'Sub-Culture.'" *British Journal of Sociology*, 25: 428–41.

Clarke, P., and J. James. 1967. "The Effects of Situation, Attitude Intensity, and Personality on Information-Seeking." *Sociometry*, 30: 235–45.

Close, P. M. 1979. "The Principle of Uncertainty as an Integrative Concept in International Crises Research." *International interactions*, 5: 331–50.

Cobb, R. W. 1973. "The Belief-Systems Perspective: An Assessment of a Framework." *Journal of Politics*, 35: 121–53.

Cohen, A. R. 1960. "Attitudinal Consequences of Induced Discrepancies Between Cognitions and Behavior." *Public Opinion Quarterly*, 24: 297–318.

Cohen, C. 1981. "Inferential Reasoning in Old Age." *Cognition*, 9: 59–72.

Cohen, G., and D. Faulkner. 1983. "Age Differences in Performance on Two Information-processing Tasks: Strategy Selection and Processing Efficiency." *Journal of Gerontology*, 38: 447–54.

Cohen, L. J. 1981. "Can Human Irrationality Be Experimentally Demonstrated?" *Behavioral and Brain Sciences*, 4: 317–31.

Cohen, M. D. 1984. "Conflict and Complexity: Goal Diversity and Organizational Search Effectiveness." *American Political Science Review*, 78: 435–51.

Cohen, R. 1988. "Intercultural Communication Between Israel and Egypt: Deterrence Failure Before the Six-Day War." *Review of International Studies*, 14: 1–16.

———. 1987. *Theatre of Power: The Art of Diplomatic Signalling*. London: Longman.

———. 1979. *Threat Perception in International Crisis*. Madison: University of Wisconsin Press.

Colby, W., and P. Forbath. 1978. *Honorable Men: My Life in the CIA.* New York: Simon and Schuster.

Cole, M., and S. Scribner. 1974. *Culture and Thought: A Psychological Introduction.* New York: Wiley.

Converse, P. E. 1964. "The Nature of Belief Systems in Mass Publics." In D. Apter, ed., *Ideology and Discontent,* pp. 206–61. New York: Free Press.

Cooper, C. L. 1970. *The Lost Crusade: America in Vietnam.* New York: Dodd, Mead.

Cooper, J., and R. T. Croyle. 1984. "Attitudes and Attitude Change." In M. R. Rosenzweig and L. W. Porter, eds., *Annual Review of Psychology,* vol. 35, pp. 395–426. Palo Alto, Calif.: Annual Reviews.

Corbin, R. M. 1980. "Decisions That Might Not Get Made." In T. S. Wallsten, ed., *Cognitive Processes in Choice and Decision Behavior,* pp. 47–68. Hillsdale, N.J.: Erlbaum.

Cottam, M. L. 1986. *Foreign Policy Decision Making: The Influence of Cognition.* Boulder, Colo.: Westview Press.

Cottam, R. W. 1977. *Foreign Policy Motivation.* Pittsburgh, Penn.: University of Pittsburgh Press.

Craig, G. A. 1964. *The Politics of the Prussian Army, 1640–1945.* Oxford: Oxford University Press.

Craik, F.I.M., and M. Byrd. 1982. "Aging and Cognitive Deficits: The Role of Attentional Resources." In F.I.M. Craik and S. Trehub, eds., *Aging and Cognitive Processes,* pp. 191–211. New York: Plenum Press.

Crocker, J. 1981. "Judgment of Covariation by Social Perceivers." *Psychological Bulletin,* 90: 272–92.

Crozier, M., and E. Friedberg. 1980. *Actors and Systems: The Politics of Collective Action.* Chicago: University of Chicago Press.

Culbertson, F. M. 1957. "Modification of an Emotionally Held Attitude Through Role Playing." *Journal of Abnormal and Social Psychology,* 54: 230–33.

Cummins, H. W. 1973. "Mao, Hsiao, Churchill, and Montgomery: Personal Values and Decision Making." *Sage Professional Papers in International Studies,* vol. 2, no. 02-021. Beverly Hills, Calif.: Sage.

Cuthbertson, G. M. 1975. *Political Myth and Epic.* Michigan: Michigan State University Press.

Cyert, R. M., and J. G. March. 1963. *A Behavioral Theory of the Firm.* Englewood Cliffs, N.J.: Prentice-Hall.

Daniel, D. C., and K. L. Herbig. 1982a. "Propositions on Military Deception." In D. C. Daniel and K. L. Herbig, eds., *Strategic Military Deception,* pp. 3–30. New York: Pergamon Press.

———. 1982b. "Deception in Theory and Practice." In D. C. Daniel and K. L. Herbig, eds., *Strategic Military Deception,* pp. 355–67. New York: Pergamon Press.

Davidson, A. R., and E. Thomson. 1980. "Cross-cultural Studies of Attitudes and Beliefs." In H. C. Triandis and R. W. Brislin, eds., *Handbook of Cross-cultural Psychology: Social Psychology,* vol. 5, pp. 25–71. Boston: Allyn and Bacon.

Davis, D. F. 1978. "Search Behavior of Small Decision-making Groups: An Information Processing Perspective." In R. T. Golembiewski, ed., *The Small*

Group in Political Science: The Last Two Decades of Development, pp. 221–38. Athens: University of Georgia Press.

Davis, W. L., and E. J. Phares. 1967. "Internal-External Control as a Determinant of Information-Seeking in a Social Influence Situation." *Journal of Personality*, 35: 547–61.

Dawes, R. M. 1976. "Shallow Psychology." In J. S. Carroll and J. W. Payne, eds., *Cognition and Social Behavior*, pp. 3–11. Hillsdale, N.J.: Erlbaum.

Dayan, M. 1976. *Story of My Life*. Jerusalem: Edanim Publishers in collaboration with Dvir Publishing House, Tel Aviv. (In Hebrew.)

Dean, J. 1976. *Blind Ambition: The White House Years*. New York: Pocket Books.

DeFleur, M. L., and F. R. Westie. 1971. "Attitude as a Scientific Concept." In K. Thomas, ed., *Attitude and Behaviour*, pp. 295–311. Harmondsworth, Eng.: Penguin.

DeLamater, J. 1974. "A Definition of 'Group.' " *Small Group Behavior*, 5: 30–44.

De Rivera, J. H. 1968. *The Psychological Dimension of Foreign Policy*. Columbus, Ohio: Merrill.

Destler, I. M. 1974. *Presidents, Bureaucrats, and Foreign Policy*. Princeton, N.J.: Princeton University Press.

Detweiler, R. A. 1980. "Intercultural Interaction and the Categorization Process: A Conceptual Analysis and Behavioral Outcome." *International Journal of Intercultural Relations*, 4: 275–93.

———. 1978. "Culture, Category Width, and Attributions: A Model-building Approach to the Reasons for Cultural Effects." *Journal of Cross-cultural Psychology*, 9: 259–84.

———. 1975. "On Inferring the Intentions of a Person from Another Culture." *Journal of Personality*, 43: 591–611.

Deutsch, M., and H. B. Gerard. 1955. "A Study of Normative and Informational Social Influences upon Individual Judgment." *Journal of Abnormal and Social Psychology*, 51: 629–36.

Deutsch, W. K., and R. L. Merritt. 1965. "Effects of Events on National and International Images." In H. C. Kelman, ed., *International Behavior*, pp. 132–87. New York: Holt, Rinehart, and Winston.

Diamond, M. A. 1985. "The Social Character of Bureaucracy: Anxiety and Ritualistic Defense." *Political Psychology*, 6: 663–79.

———. 1984. "Bureaucracy as Externalized Self-System: A View from the Psychological Interior." *Administration and Society*, 16: 195–214.

Diamond, M. A., and S. Allcorn. 1986. "Role Formation and Defensive Activity in Bureaucratic Organizations." *Political Psychology*, 7: 709–32.

———. 1985. "Psychological Responses to Stress in Complex Organizations." *Administration and Society*, 17: 217–39.

Dion, K. L., R. S. Baron, and N. Miller. 1978. "Why Do Groups Make Riskier Decisions Than Individuals?" In L. Berkowitz, ed., *Group Processes*, pp. 227–99. New York: Academic Press.

Dittes, J. E., and H. Kelley. 1956. "Effects of Different Conditions of Acceptance upon Conformity to Group Norms." *Journal of Abnormal and Social Psychology*, 53: 100–107.

Dixon, N. F. 1976. *On the Psychology of Military Incompetence*. London: Jonathan Cape.

Dolen, L. S., and D. J. Bearison. 1982. "Social Interaction and Social Cognition in Aging: A Contextual Analysis." *Human Development*, 25: 430–42.

Doran, C. F., K. Q. Hill, and K. Mladenka. 1979. "Threat, Status Disequilibrium, and National Power." *British Journal of International Studies*, 5: 37–58.

Dore, R. P. 1975. "The Prestige Factor in International Affairs." *International Affairs*, 51: 190–207.

Douglas, M. T., and A. Wildavsky. 1982. *Risk and Culture*. Berkeley: University of California Press.

Downs, A. 1967. *Inside Bureaucracy*. Boston: Little, Brown.

Dowty, A. 1984. *Middle East Crisis: U.S. Decision-Making in 1958, 1970, and 1973*. Berkeley: University of California Press.

Dray, W. H. 1964. *Philosophy of History*. Englewood Cliffs, N.J.: Prentice-Hall.

Dretske, F. I. 1981. *Knowledge and the Flow of Information*. Cambridge, Mass.: MIT Press.

Dror, Y. 1971. *Crazy States*. Lexington, Mass.: Heath Lexington Books.

Druckman, D., and L. D. Ludwig. 1970. "Consensus on Evaluative Descriptions of One's Own Nation, Its Allies, and Its Enemies." *Journal of Social Psychology*, 81: 223–34.

Duijker, H.C.J., and N. H. Frijda. 1960. *National Character and National Stereotypes*. Amsterdam, Neth.: North Holland.

Eagly, A. H. 1969. "Responses to Attitude-discrepant Information as a Function of Intolerance of Inconsistency and Category Width." *Journal of Personality*, 37: 601–17.

Eagly, A. H., and K. Telaak. 1974. "Width of the Latitude of Acceptance as a Determinant of Attitude Change." In S. Himmelfarb and A. H. Eagly, eds., *Readings in Attitude Change*, pp. 459–70. New York: Wiley.

East, M. A. 1972. "Status Discrepancy and Violence in the International System: An Empirical Analysis." In J. N. Rosenau, V. Davis, and M. A. East, eds., *The Analysis of International Politics*, pp. 299–319. New York: Free Press.

Eban, A. 1978. *My Life*. Tel Aviv: Ma'ariv Book Guild. (In Hebrew.)

Eckstein, H. 1975. "Case Study and Theory in Political Science." In F. I. Greenstein and N. W. Polsby, eds., *Handbook of Political Science*, vol. 7, pp. 79–138. Reading, Mass.: Addison-Wesley.

Egeth, H. 1977. "Attention and Preattention." In G. H. Bower, ed., *The Psychology of Learning and Motivation*, vol. 11, pp. 277–320. New York: Academic Press.

Ehrenhaus, P. 1983. "Culture and the Attribution Process: Barriers to Effective Communication." In W. B. Gudykunst, ed., *Intercultural Communication Theory: Current Perspective*, pp. 259–70. Beverly Hills, Calif.: Sage.

Einhorn, H. J. 1980. "Learning from Experience and Suboptimal Rules in Decision Making." In T. S. Wallstein, ed., *Cognitive Processes in Choice and Decision Behavior*, pp. 1–20. Hillsdale, N.J.: Erlbaum.

Einhorn, H. J., and R. M. Hogarth. 1986. "Judging Probable Causes." *Psychological Bulletin*, 99: 3–19.

———. 1978. "Confidence in Judgment: Persistence of the Illusion of Validity." *Psychological Review* 85: 395–416.

Elkin, A. J., and D. J. Murray. 1974. "The Effects of Sleep Loss on Short-term Recognition Memory." *Canadian Journal of Psychology*, 28: 192–98.

Ellsberg, D. 1971. "The Quagmire Myth and the Stalemate Machine." *Public Policy*, 19: 217–74.

Epstein, E. J. 1980. "Incorporating Analysis of Foreign Governments' Deception into the U.S. Analytical System." In R. Godson, ed., *Intelligence Requirements for the 1980's: Analysis and Estimates*, pp. 123–35. Washington, D.C.: National Strategy Information Center.

Erdelyi, M. H. 1974. "A New Look at the New Look: Perceptual Defense and Vigilance." *Psychological Review*, 81: 1–25.

Erickson, E. H. 1963. *Childhood and Society*. 2d ed. New York: Norton.

Etheredge, L. S. 1981. "Government Learning: An Overview." In S. L. Long, ed., *The Handbook of Political Behavior*, vol. 2, pp. 73–161. New York: Plenum Press.

———. 1979. "Hardball Politics: A Model." *Political Psychology*, 1: 3–26.

———. 1978. *A World of Men: The Private Sources of American Foreign Policy.* Cambridge, Mass.: MIT Press.

Etzioni, A. 1969. "Social-Psychological Aspects of International Relations." In G. Lindzey and E. Aronson, eds., *The Handbook of Social Psychology*, vol. 5, pp. 538–601. 2d ed. Reading, Mass.: Addison-Wesley.

Eysenck, H. J. 1954. *The Psychology of Politics*. London: Routledge and Kegan Paul.

Faber, K. G. 1978. "The Use of History in Political Debate." *History and Theory*, 17 (4), suppl. 17: 36–67.

Fairley, W. B. 1977. "Evaluating the 'Small' Probability of a Catastrophic Accident from the Marine Transportation of Liquified Natural Gas." In W. B. Fairley and F. Mosteller, eds., *Statistics and Public Policy*, pp. 331–53. Reading, Mass.: Addison-Wesley.

Falk, A. 1985. *Moshe Dayan, The Man and the Myth: A Psychoanalytic Biography.* Jerusalem: Cana. (In Hebrew.)

———. 1984. "Moshe Dayan: Narcissism in Politics." *Jerusalem Quarterly*, 30: 113–24.

Falkowski, L. S., ed., 1979. *Psychological Models in International Politics*. Boulder, Colo.: Westview Press.

Farrell, B. R. 1966. "Foreign Policies of Open and Closed Political Societies." In B. R. Farrell, ed., *Approaches to Comparative and International Politics*, pp. 167–208. Evanston, Ill.: Northwestern University Press.

Farrell, J. C., and A. P. Smith, eds., 1965. *Image and Reality in World Politics.* New York: Columbia University Press.

Fazio, R. H., M. P. Zanna, and J. Cooper. 1977. "Dissonance and Self-Perception: An Integrative View of Each Theory's Proper Domain of Application." *Journal of Experimental Social Psychology*, 13: 464–79.

Feis, H. 1967. "Some Notes on Historical Record-Keeping, the Role of Historians, and the Influence of Historical Memories During the Era of the Second World War." In F. L. Loewenheim, ed., *The Historian and the Diplomat*, pp. 91–122. New York: Harper and Row.

Feldman, M. S., and J. G. March. 1981. "Information in Organizations as Signal and Symbol." *Administrative Science Quarterly*, 26: 171–86.

Festinger, L. 1964. *Conflict, Decision, and Dissonance*. Stanford, Calif.: Stanford University Press.

———. 1957. *A Theory of Cognitive Dissonance*. Stanford, Calif.: Stanford University Press.

Festinger, L., H. W. Riecker, and S. Schachter. 1956. *When Prophecy Fails*. Minneapolis: University of Minnesota Press.

Finlay, D. J., O. R. Holsti, and R. R. Fagen, eds., 1967. *Enemies in Politics*. Chicago: Rand McNally.

Fischer, D. H. 1970. *Historians' Fallacies: Toward a Logic of Historical Thought*. New York: Harper and Row.

Fischhoff, B. 1983. "Strategic Policy Preferences: A Behavioral Decision Theory Perspective." *Journal of Social Issues*, 39 (1): 133–60.

———. 1982. "For Those Condemned to Study the Past: Heuristics and Biases in Hindsight." In D. Kahneman, P. Slovic, and A. Tversky, eds., *Judgment Under Uncertainty: Heuristics and Biases*, pp. 335–51. Cambridge, Eng.: Cambridge University Press.

———. 1977. "Perceived Informativeness of Facts." *Journal of Experimental Psychology: Human Perception and Performance*, 3: 349–58.

———. 1976. "Attribution Theory and Judgment Under Uncertainty." In J. H. Harvey, W. J. Ickes, and R. F. Kidd, eds., *New Directions in Attribution Research*, vol. 1, pp. 421–52. Hillsdale, N.J.: Erlbaum.

———. 1975. "Hindsight/Foresight: The Effect of Outcome Knowledge on Judgment Under Uncertainty." *Journal of Experimental Psychology: Human Perception and Performance*, 1: 288–99.

Fischhoff, B., and R. Beyth. 1975. "'I Knew It Would Happen'—Remembered Probabilities of Once-Future Things." *Organizational Behavior and Human Performance*, 13: 1–16.

Fischhoff, B. and R. Beyth-Marom. 1976. "Failure Has Many Fathers." *Policy Sciences*, 7: 388–93.

Fischhoff, B., S. Lichtenstein, P. Slovic, S. L. Derby, and R. L. Keeney. 1981. *Acceptable Risk*. Cambridge, Eng.: Cambridge University Press.

Fischhoff, B., P. Slovic, and S. Lichtenstein. 1978. "Fault Trees: Sensitivity of Estimated Failure Probabilities to Problem Representation." *Journal of Experimental Psychology: Human Perception and Performance*, 4: 330–44.

———. 1977. "Knowing with Certainty: The Appropriateness of Extreme Confidence." *Journal of Experimental Psychology: Human Perception and Performance*, 3: 552–64.

Fishbein, M. 1966. "The Relationship Between Beliefs, Attitudes, and Behavior." In S. Feldmann, ed., *Cognitive Consistency*, pp. 199–223. New York: Academic Press.

Fisher, G. H. 1972. *Public Diplomacy and the Behavioral Sciences*. Bloomington: Indiana University Press.

Fiske, S. T. 1986. "Scheme-based Versus Piecemeal Politics: A Patchwork Quilt, but Not a Blanket, of Evidence." In R. R. Lau and D. O. Sears, eds., *Political Cognition*, pp. 41–53. Hillsdale, N.J.: Erlbaum.

———. 1981. "Social Cognition and Affect." In J. H. Harvey, ed., *Cognitive Social Behavior and the Environment*, pp. 227–64. Hillsdale, N.J.: Erlbaum.

Fiske, S. T., D. R. Kinder, and W. M. Larter. 1983. "The Novice and the Expert: Knowledge-based Strategies in Political Cognition." *Journal of Experimental Social Psychology*, 19: 381–400.

Fiske, S. T., and P. W. Linville. 1980. "What Does the Schema Concept Buy Us?" *Personality and Social Psychology Bulletin*, 6: 543–57.

Fiske, S. T., and S. E. Taylor. 1984. *Social Cognition*. Reading, Mass.: Addison-Wesley.

Fitzgerald, F. 1973. *Fire in the Lake: The Vietnamese and the Americans in Vietnam.* New York: Vintage Books.

Flavell, J. H. 1981a. "Cognitive Monitoring." In W. P. Dickson, ed., *Children's Oral Communication Skills,* pp. 35–60. New York: Academic Press.

———. 1981b. "Monitoring Social Cognitive Enterprises: Something Else That May Develop in the Area of Social Cognition." In J. H. Flavell and L. Ross, eds., *Social Cognitive Developments: Frontiers and Possible Futures,* pp. 272–87. Cambridge, Eng.: Cambridge University Press.

Flavell, J. H., E. R. Flavell, and F. L. Green. 1983. "Development of the Appearance-Reality Distinction." *Cognitive Psychology,* 15: 95–120.

Flowers, M. J. 1977. "A Laboratory Test of Some Implications of Janis's Groupthink Hypothesis." *Journal of Personality and Social Psychology,* 35: 888–96.

Franck, T. M., and E. Weisband. 1974. "Dissemblement, Secrecy, and Executive Privilege in the Foreign Relations of Three Democracies: A Comparative Analysis." In T. M. Franck, and E. Weisband, eds., *Secrecy and Foreign Policy,* pp. 399–441. New York: Oxford University Press.

———. 1971. *Word Politics.* New York: Oxford University Press.

Fraser, B. 1979. "The Interpretation of Novel Metaphors." In A. Ortony, ed., *Metaphor and Thought,* pp. 172–85. Cambridge, Eng.: Cambridge University Press.

Freedman, L. 1976. "Logic, Politics, and Foreign Policy Processes: A Critique of the Bureaucratic Politics Model." *International Affairs,* 52: 434–49.

Frey, D. 1986. "Recent Research on Selective Exposure to Information." In L. Berkowitz, ed., *Advances in Experimental Social Psychology,* vol. 19, pp. 41–80. Orlando, Fla.: Academic Press.

Frey, D., and M. Rosch. 1984. "Information Seeking After Decisions: The Roles of Novelty of Information and Decision Reversibility." *Personality and Social Psychology Bulletin,* 10: 91–98.

Friedberg, A. L. 1988. *The Weary Titan: Britain and the Experience of Relative Decline, 1895–1905.* Princeton, N.J.: Princeton University Press.

Friedlander, S., and R. Cohen. 1975. "The Personality Correlates of Belligerence in International Politics: A Comparative Analysis of Historical Case Studies." *Comparative Politics,* 7: 155–86.

Frith, C. D., J.T.E. Richardson, M. Samuel, T. J. Crow, and P. J. McKenna. 1984. "The Effects of Intravenous Diazepam and Hyoscine upon Human Memory." *Quarterly Journal of Experimental Psychology: Human Experimental Psychology,* 36: 133–44.

Gaenslen, F. 1986. "Culture and Decision Making in China, Japan, Russia, and the United States." *World Politics,* 39: 78–103.

Gair, E. L. 1952. "Selected Personality Variables and the Learning Process." *Psychological Monographs: General and Applied,* 66 (17): 1–28.

Gallucci, R. L. 1975. *Neither Peace nor Honor: The Politics of American Military Policy in Vietnam.* Baltimore, Md.: Johns Hopkins University Press.

Galtung, J. 1968. "Small Group Theory and the Theory of International Relations." In M. Kaplan, ed., *New Approaches to International Relations,* pp. 270–302. New York: St. Martin's Press.

Galtung, J., and M. H. Ruge, 1965. "The Structure of Foreign News." *Journal of Peace Research,* 2: 64–91.

Garner, W. R. 1962. *Uncertainty and Structure as Psychological Concepts.* New York: Wiley.

Gazit, M. 1984. *The Peace Process.* Tel-Aviv: Hakibutz Hameuchad. (In Hebrew.)

Gazit, S. 1980. "Estimates and Fortune Telling in Intelligence Work." *International Security,* 4 (4): 36–56.

Geertz, C. 1973. *The Interpretation of Cultures.* New York: Basic Books.

Gelb, L. H. 1972. "The Pentagon Papers and the Vantage Point." *Foreign Policy,* 6: 25–41.

Gelb, L. H., with R. K. Betts. 1979. *The Irony of Vietnam: The System Worked.* Washington, D.C.: Brookings Institution.

George, A. L. 1984. "Criteria for Evaluation of Foreign Policy Decisionmaking." *Global Perspectives,* 2: 58–69.

_____. 1980a. *Presidential Decisionmaking in Foreign Policy: The Effective Use of Information and Advice.* Boulder, Colo.: Westview Press.

_____. 1980b. "Domestic Constraints on Regime Change in U.S. Foreign Policy: The Need for Policy Legitimacy." In O. R. Holsti, R. M. Siverson, and A. L. George, eds., *Change in the International System,* pp. 233–62. Boulder, Colo.: Westview Press.

_____. 1979a. "Case Studies and Theory Development: The Method of Structured, Focused Comparison." In P. G. Lauren, ed., *Diplomacy: New Approaches in History, Theory, and Policy,* pp. 43–68. New York: Free Press.

_____. 1979b. "The Causal Nexus Between Cognitive Beliefs and Decision Making Behavior: The 'Operational Code' Belief System." In L. S. Falkowski, ed., *Psychological Models in International Politics,* pp. 95–124. Boulder, Colo.: Westview Press.

_____. 1974. "Adaptation to Stress in Political Decision Making: The Individual, Small Group, and Organizational Context." In G. V. Coelho, D. A. Hamburg, and J. E. Adams, eds., *Coping and Adaptation,* pp. 176–245. New York: Basic Books.

_____. 1972. "The Case for Multiple Advocacy in Making Foreign Policy." *American Political Science Review,* 66: 751–85.

_____. 1969. "The 'Operational Code': A Neglected Approach to the Study of Political Leaders and Decision Making." *International Studies Quarterly,* 13: 190–222.

George, A. L., and J. L. George. 1964. *Woodrow Wilson and Colonel House: A Personality Study.* New York: Dover.

George, A. L., and R. Smoke. 1974. *Deterrence in American Foreign Policy: Theory and Practice.* New York: Columbia University Press.

Gerard, H. B. 1985. "When and How the Minority Prevails." In S. Mosovici, G. Mugny, and E. von Avermaet, eds., *Perspective on Minority Influence,* pp. 171–86. Cambridge and Paris: Cambridge University Press and Editions de la Maison des Sciences de l'Homme.

Gettys, C. F., C. Kelly, and C. R. Peterson. 1973. "The Best Guess Hypothesis in Multistage Inference." *Organizational Behavior and Human Performance,* 10: 364–73.

Geyle, P. 1970. *Use and Abuse of History.* New York: Archon Books.

Ghoneim, H. M., S. P. Mewaldt, and J. V. Hinrichs. 1984. "Dose-Response Analysis of the Behavioral Effects of Diazepam: Psychomotor Performance, Cognition, and Mood." *Psychopharmacology,* 82: 296–300.

Gibb, J. R. 1974. "Defensive Communication." In R. S. Cathcart and L. A. Samovar, eds., *Small Group Communication*, pp. 327–39. 2d ed. Dubuque, Iowa: Web.

Gibbons, W. C. 1986. *The U.S. Government and the Vietnam War: Executive and Legislative Roles and Relationships*. Part 2, *1961–1964*. Princeton, N.J.: Princeton University Press.

Gibson, J. W. 1988. *The Perfect War*. New York: Vintage.

Gick, M. L., and K. J. Holyoak. 1983. "Schema Induction and Analogical Transfer." *Cognitive Psychology*, 15: 1–38.

―――. 1980. "Analogical Problem Solving." *Cognitive Psychology*, 12: 306–55.

Gilbert, D. T., E. E. Jones, and B. W. Pelham. 1987. "Influence and Inference: What the Active Perceiver Overlooks." *Journal of Personality and Social Psychology*, 52: 861–70.

Gilbert, R. E. 1988. "Psychological Pain and the Presidency: The Case of Calvin Coolidge." *Political Psychology*, 9: 75–100.

Gilligan, S. G., and G. H. Bower. 1984. "Cognitive Consequences of Emotional Arousal." In C. E. Izard, J. Kagan, and R. B. Zajonc, eds., *Emotions, Cognition, and Behavior*, pp. 547–87. Cambridge, Eng.: Cambridge University Press.

Gilovich, T. 1981. "Seeing the Past in the Present: The Effect of Associations to Familiar Events on Judgments and Decisions." *Journal of Personality and Social Psychology*, 40: 797–808.

Gilpin, R. 1981. *War and Change in World Politics*. Cambridge, Eng.: Cambridge University Press.

Gladstein, D., and J. B. Quinn. 1985. "Making Decisions and Producing Action: The Two Faces of Strategy." In J. M. Pennings and Associates, eds., *Organizational Strategy and Change*, pp. 198–216. San Francisco, Calif.: Jossey-Bass.

Gladstone, A. 1959. "The Conception of the Enemy." *Journal of Conflict Resolution*, 3: 132–37.

Glass, D. C. 1968. "Theories of Consistency and the Study of Personality." In E. F. Borgatta and W. W. Lambert, eds., *Handbook of Personality Theory and Research*, pp. 788–854. Chicago: Rand McNally.

Glenn, E. S. 1966. "A Cognitive Approach to the Analysis of Cultures and Cultural Evolution." In L. von Bertalanffy and A. Rapoport, eds., *General Systems: Yearbook of the Society for General Systems Research*, vol. 11, pp. 115–32. Ann Arbor, Mich.: Society for General Systems Research.

Glenn, E. S., with C. G. Glenn. 1981. *Man and Mankind: Conflict and Communication Between Cultures*. Norwood, N.J.: Ablex.

Glenn, E. S., R. H. Johnson, P. R. Kimmel, and B. Wedge. 1970. "A Cognitive Interaction Model to Analyze Culture Conflict in International Relations." *Journal of Conflict Resolution*, 14: 35–48.

Goffman, E. 1969. *Strategic Interaction*. Philadelphia: University of Pennsylvania Press.

Gold, H. 1978. "Foreign Policy Decision-Making and the Environment: The Claims of Snyder, Brecher, and the Sprouts." *International Studies Quarterly*, 22: 569–86.

Golding, S. L., and L. G. Rorer. 1972. "Illusory Correlation and Subjective Judgment." *Journal of Abnormal Psychology*, 80: 249–60.

Goldman, A. I. 1986. *Epistemology and Cognition*. Cambridge, Mass.: Harvard University Press.

Goldman, E. F. 1974. *The Tragedy of Lyndon Johnson*. New York: Dell.

Goldstein, K. M., and S. Blackman. 1979. *Cognitive Style*. New York: Wiley.

Golembiewski, R. T., and G. J. Miller. 1981. "Small Groups in Political Science: Perspectives on Significance and Stuckness." In S. L. Long, ed., *The Handbook of Political Behavior*, vol. 2, pp. 1–71. New York: Plenum Press.

Gonen, J. Y. 1975. *A Psycho-History of Zionism*. New York: New American Library.

Gooch, J. 1980. "Clio and Mars: The Use and Abuse of History." *Journal of Strategic Studies*, 3 (3): 21–36.

Goodman, N. 1978. *Ways of Worldmaking*. Indianapolis, Ind.: Hackett.

Gordon, M. M. 1973. "The Concept of the Sub-Culture and its Application." In D. O. Arnold, ed., *Subcultures*, pp. 31–36. Berkeley, Calif.: Glendessary Press.

Gouran, D. S. 1986. "Inferential Errors, Interaction, and Group Decision-Making." In R. Y. Hirokawa and M. S. Poole, eds., *Communication and Group Decision-Making*, pp. 93–112. Beverly Hills, Calif.: Sage.

Graber, D. A. 1984. *Processing the News: How People Tame the Information Tide*. New York: Longman.

———. 1976. *Verbal Behavior and Politics*. Urbana: University of Illinois Press.

Graff, H. F. 1970. *The Tuesday Cabinet*. Englewood Cliffs, N.J.: Prentice-Hall.

Granot, O. 1987. "Intelligence Surprised Twice." *Ma'ariv*, June 5, p. 6. (In Hebrew.)

Gray, C. S. 1986. *Nuclear Strategy and National Style*. Lanham, Md.: Hamilton Press.

———. 1981. "National Style in Strategy." *International Security*, 6 (2): 21–47.

Greenstein, F. I. 1975. *Personality and Politics: Problems of Evidence Influence and Conceptualization*. New York: Norton.

———. 1967. "The Impact of Personality on Politics: An Attempt to Clear the Underbrush." *American Political Science Review*, 61: 629–41.

Greenwald, A. G. 1980. "The Totalitarian Ego: Fabrication and Revision of Personal History." *American Psychologist*, 35: 603–18.

———. 1969. "The Open-Mindedness of the Counterattitudinal Role Player." *Journal of Experimental Social Psychology*, 5: 375–88.

Grinspoon, L. 1969. "Psychosocial Constraints on the Important Decision-Maker." *American Journal of Psychiatry*, 125: 1074–80.

Gross, N., P. W. McEachern, and W. S. Mason. 1965. "Role Conflict and Its Resolution." In H. Proshansky and B. Seidenberg, eds., *Basic Studies in Social Psychology*, pp. 494–505. New York: Holt, Rinehart, and Winston.

Gross, S. J., and M. C. Niman. 1975. "Attitude-Behavior Consistency: A Review." *Public Opinion Quarterly*, 39: 358–68.

Groth, A. J. 1964. "On the Intelligence Aspect of Personal Diplomacy." *Orbis*, 7: 833–48.

Gudykunst, W. B., and Y. Y. Kim. 1984. *Communicating with Strangers*. Reading, Mass.: Addison-Wesley.

Gustafsson, G., and J. J. Richardson. 1979. "Concepts of Rationality and the Policy Process." *European Journal of Political Research*, 7: 415–36.

Hagafors, R., and B. Brehmer. 1983. "Does Having to Justify One's Judgments

Change the Nature of the Judgment Process?" *Organizational Behavior and Human Performance*, 31: 223–32.

Halberstam, D. 1972. *The Best and the Brightest*. New York: Random House.

Hall, E. T. 1976. *Beyond Culture*. New York: Doubleday.

Halperin, M. H. 1974. *Bureaucratic Politics and Foreign Policy*. Washington, D.C.: Brookings Institution.

Hamilton, D. L. 1981. "Illusory Correlation as a Basis for Stereotyping." In D.L. Hamilton, ed., *Cognitive Processes in Stereotyping and Intergroup Behavior*, pp. 115–44. Hillsdale, N.J.: Erlbaum.

———. 1979. "A Cognitive-Attributional Analysis of Stereotyping." In L. Berkowitz, ed., *Advances in Experimental Social Psychology*, vol. 12, pp. 53–84. New York: Academic Press.

Handel, M. I. 1984. "Intelligence and the Problem of Strategic Surprise." *Journal of Strategic Studies*, 7: 229–81.

———. 1981. *The Diplomacy of Surprise: Hitler, Nixon, Sadat*. Harvard Studies in International Affairs no. 44. Cambridge, Mass.: Center for International Affairs, Harvard University.

———. 1980. "Surprise and Change in International Politics." *International Security*, 4 (4): 57–85.

———. 1977. "The Yom Kippur War and the Inevitability of Surprise." *International Studies Quarterly*, 21: 461–502.

———. 1976. *Perception, Deception, and Surprise: The Case of the Yom Kippur War*. Jerusalem Papers on Peace Problems no. 19. Jerusalem: Leonard Davis Institute for International Relations, The Hebrew University.

Hansen, R. D. 1980. "Commonsense Attribution." *Journal of Personality and Social Psychology*, 39: 996–1009.

Hareven, A. 1978. "Disturbed Hierarchy: Israeli Intelligence in 1954 and 1973." *Jerusalem Quarterly*, 9 (Fall): 3–19.

Harkabi, Y. 1984. "The Intelligence-Policymaker Tangle." *Jerusalem Quarterly*, 30 (Winter): 125–31.

———. 1983. *The Bar Kokhba Syndrome: Risk and Realism in International Politics*. Chappaqua, N.Y.: Rossel Books.

Harris, R. J. 1981. "Inferences in Information Processing." In G. H. Bower, ed., *The Psychology of Learning and Motivation*, vol. 15, pp. 81–128. New York: Academic Press.

Harvey, O. J. 1967. "Conceptual Systems and Attitude Change." In C. W. Sherif and M. Sherif, eds., *Attitude, Ego-Involvement, and Change*, pp. 201–26. New York: Wiley.

———. 1966. "System Structure, Flexibility and Creativity." In O. J. Harvey, ed., *Experience, Structure and Adaptability*, pp. 39–65. New York: Springer.

Hass, R. G. 1981. "Effects of Source Characteristics on Cognitive Responses and Persuasion." In R. E. Petty, T. M. Ostrom, and T. C. Brock, eds., *Cognitive Responses in Persuasion*, pp. 141–72. Hillsdale, N.J.: Erlbaum.

Healey, M., R. Pickens, R. Meisch, and T. McKenna. 1983. "Effects of Closazepate, Diazepam, Lorazepam, and Placebo on Human Memory." *Clinical Psychiatry*, 44: 436–39.

Heckhausen, H., H. D. Schmalt, and K. Schneider. 1985. *Achievement Motivation in Perspective*. Orlando, Fla.: Academic Press.

Heider, F. 1958. *The Psychology of Interpersonal Relations*. New York: Wiley.

Heiner, R. A. 1983. "The Origins of Predictable Behavior." *American Economic Review*, 73: 560–95.

Heise, D. R. 1979. *Understanding Events: Affect and the Construction of Social Action*. Cambridge, Eng.: Cambridge University Press.

Helson, H. 1964. *Adaptation-Level Theory*. New York: Harper and Row.

Henderson, J. T. 1976. "Leadership Personality and War: The Cases of Richard Nixon and Anthony Eden." *Political Science*, 28: 141–64.

Hensley, T. R., and G. W. Griffin. 1986. "Victims of Groupthink: The Kent State University Board of Trustees and the 1977 Gymnasium Controversy." *Journal of Conflict Resolution*, 30: 497–531.

Heradstveit, D., and G. M. Bonham. 1986. "Decision-Making in the Face of Uncertainty: Attributions of Norwegian and American Officials." *Journal of Peace Research*, 23: 339–56.

Heradstveit, D., and O. Narvesen. 1978. "Psychological Constraints on Decision-Making. A Discussion of Cognitive Approaches: Operational Code and Cognitive Map." *Cooperation and Conflict*, 13: 77–92.

Herek, G. M. 1986. "The Instrumentality of Attitudes: Toward a Neofunctional Theory." *Journal of Social Issues*, 42: 99–114.

Herek, G. M., I. L. Janis, and P. Huth. 1987. "Decision-Making During International Crises: Is Quality of Process Related to Outcome?" *Journal of Conflict Resolution*, 31: 203–26.

Hermann, C. F. 1969. "International Crisis as a Situational Variable." In J. N. Rosenau, ed., *International Politics and Foreign Policy*, pp. 409–21. Rev. ed. New York: Free Press.

———. 1963. "Some Consequences of Crisis Which Limit the Viability of Organizations." *Administrative Science Quarterly*, 8: 61–82.

Hermann, C. F., and L. P. Brady. 1972. "Alternative Models of International Crisis Behavior." In C. F. Hermann, ed., *International Crises*, pp. 281–303. New York: Free Press.

Hermann, M. G. 1987. "Foreign Policy Role Orientations and the Quality of Foreign Policy Decisions." In S. G. Walker, ed., *Role Theory and Foreign Policy Analysis*, pp. 123–40. Durham, N.C.: Duke University Press.

———. 1984. "Personality and Foreign Policy Decision Making: A Study of 53 Heads of Government." In D. A. Sylvan and S. Chan, eds., *Foreign Policy Decision Making: Perception, Cognition, and Artificial Intelligence*, pp. 53–80. New York: Praeger.

———. 1979a. "Who Becomes a Political Leader? Some Societal and Regime Influences on the Selection of Head of State." In L. S. Falkowski, ed., *Psychological Models in International Politics*, pp. 15–48. Boulder, Colo: Westview Press.

———. 1979b. "Indicators of Stress in Policymakers During Foreign Policy Crises." *Political Psychology*, 1 (Spring): 27–46.

———. 1978. "Effects of Personal Characteristics of Political Leaders on Foreign Policy." In M. A. East, S. A. Salmore, and C. F. Hermann, eds., *Why Nations Act?* pp. 49–68. Beverly Hills, Calif.: Sage.

———. 1976. "When Leader Personality Will Affect Foreign Policy: Some Propositions." In J. N. Rosenau, ed., *In Search of Global Pattern*, pp. 326–33. New York: Free Press.

———. 1974. "Leader Personality and Foreign Policy Behavior." In J. N.

Rosenau, ed., *Comparing Foreign Policies*, pp. 201–34. Beverly Hills, Calif.: Sage.

Hermann, M. G., with T. W. Milburn, eds. 1977. *A Psychological Examination of Political Leaders*. New York: Free Press.

Hersh, S. 1983. *The Price of Power: Kissinger in the Nixon White House*. New York: Summit Books.

Herzog, C. 1975. *The War of Atonement*. Jerusalem: Edanim. (In Hebrew.)

Heuer, R. J., Jr. 1982. "Cognitive Factors in Deception and Counterdeception." In D. C. Daniel and K. L. Herbig, eds., *Strategic Military Deception*, pp. 31–69. New York: Pergamon Press.

———. 1980. "Analyzing the Soviet Invasion of Afghanistan: Hypotheses from Causal Attribution Theory." *Studies in Comparative Communism*, 13: 347–55.

Higgins, E. T., and J. A. Bargh. 1987. "Social Cognition and Social Perception." In M. R. Rosenzweig and L. W. Porter, eds., *Annual Review of Psychology*, vol. 38, pp. 369–425. Palo Alto, Calif.: Annual Reviews.

Hill, C. 1978. "Theories of Foreign Policy Making for the Developing Countries." In C. Clapham, ed., *Foreign Policy Making in Developing States*, pp. 1–16. Farnborough, Eng.: Saxon House.

Hilsman, R., Jr. 1961. "Intelligence and Policy Making in Foreign Affairs." In J. N. Rosenau, ed., *International Politics and Foreign Policy*, pp. 209–19. New York: Free Press.

———. 1956. *Strategic Intelligence and National Decisions*. Glencoe, Ill.: Free Press.

Himmelstrand, U. 1960. "Verbal Attitudes and Behavior." *Public Opinion Quarterly*, 24: 224–50.

Hiniker, P. J. 1969. "Chinese Reactions to Forced Compliance: Dissonance Reduction or National Character." *Journal of Social Psychology*, 77: 157–76.

Hirschman, A. O. 1968. "Underdevelopment, Obstacles to the Perception of Change, and Leadership." *Daedalus*, 97: 925–37.

Hochbaum, G. M. 1954. "The Relation Between Group Members' Self-Confidence and Their Reactions to Group Pressure to Uniformity." *American Sociological Review*, 19: 678–87.

Hoffman, L. R. 1978a. "Group Problem Solving." In L. Berkowitz, ed., *Group Processes*, pp. 67–100. New York: Academic Press.

———. 1978b. "The Group Problem Solving Process." In L. Berkowitz, ed., *Group Processes*, pp. 101–13. New York: Academic Press.

Hoffmann, S. 1968a. "Perceptions, Reality, and the Franco-American Conflict." In J. C. Farrell and A. P. Smith, eds., *Image and Reality in World Politics*, pp. 57–71. New York: Columbia University Press.

———. 1968b. *Gulliver's Troubles, or the Setting of American Foreign Policy*. New York: McGraw-Hill.

Hogarth, R. M. 1980. *Judgement and Choice: The Psychology of Decision*. Chichester, Eng.: Wiley.

———. 1975. "Cognitive Processes and the Assessment of Subjective Probability Distributions." *Journal of the American Statistical Association*, 70: 271–94.

Hoge, D. R., and J. T. Lanzetta. 1968. "Effects of Response Uncertainty and Degree of Knowledge on Subjective Uncertainty." *Psychological Reports*, 22: 1081–90.

Holland, J. H., K. J. Holyoak, R. E. Nisbett, and P. R. Thagard. 1986. *Induction: Processes of Inference, Learning, and Discovery*. Cambridge, Mass.: MIT Press.

Hollander, E. P. 1965. "Conformity, Status, and Idiosyncrasy Credit." In J. D. Singer, ed., *Human Behavior and International Politics*, pp. 169–77. Chicago: Rand McNally.

―――. 1960. "Competence and Conformity in the Acceptance of Influence." *Journal of Abnormal and Social Psychology*, 61: 365–69.

Holst, J. J. 1966. "Surprise, Signals, and Reaction." *Cooperation and Conflict*, 1: 31–45.

Holsti, K. J. 1978. "A New International Politics? Diplomacy in Complex Interdependence." *International Organization*, 32: 513–30.

―――. 1970. "National Role Conception in the Study of Foreign Policy." *International Studies Quarterly*, 14: 233–309.

Holsti, O. R. 1977. *The 'Operational Code' as an Approach to the Analysis of Beliefs Systems*. Final Report to the National Science Foundation, Grant no. SOC 75-15368. Durham, N.C.: Duke University.

―――. 1976. "Cognitive Process Approaches to Decision Making: Foreign Policy Actors Viewed Psychologically." *American Behavioral Scientist*, 20: 11–32.

―――. 1972a. *Crisis, Escalation, War*. Montreal: McGill–Queen's University Press.

―――. 1972b. "Time, Alternatives, and Communications: The 1914 and Cuban Missile Crises." In C. F. Hermann, ed., *International Crises*, pp. 58–80. New York: Free Press.

―――. 1971. "Crisis Stress and Decision Making." *International Social Science Journal*, 23: 53–67.

―――. 1969. "The Belief System and National Images: A Case Study." In J. N. Rosenau, ed., *International Politics and Foreign Policy*, pp. 543–50. Rev. ed. New York: Free Press.

―――. 1967a. "Cognitive Dynamics and Images of the Enemy: Dulles and Russia." In D. J. Finlay, O. R. Holsti, and R. R. Fagen, eds., *Enemies in Politics*, pp. 25–96. Chicago: Rand McNally.

―――. 1967b. "Cognitive Dynamics and Images of the Enemy." *Journal of International Affairs*, 21: 16–39.

―――. 1965a. "The 1914 Case." *American Political Science Review*, 59: 365–78.

―――. 1965b. "East-West Conflict and Sino-Soviet Relations." *Journal of Applied Behavioral Science*, 1: 115–30.

Holsti, O. R., R. A. Brody, and R. C. North. 1969. "Measuring Affect and Action in International Reaction Models: Empirical Materials from the 1962 Cuban Crisis." In J. N. Rosenau, ed., *International Politics and Foreign Policy*, pp. 679–96. Rev. ed. New York: Free Press.

Holsti, O. R., and A. L. George. 1975. "The Effects of Stress on the Performance of Foreign Policy Makers." In C. P. Cotter, ed., *Political Science Annual*, Vol. 6: *Individual Decision Making*, pp. 255–319. Indianapolis, Ind.: Bobbs-Merrill.

Holsti, O. R., R. C. North, and R. A. Brody. 1968. "Perception and Action in 1914 Crisis." In J. D. Singer, ed., *Quantitative International Politics*, pp. 123–58. New York: Free Press.

Holsti, O. R., and J. N. Rosenau. 1984. *American Leadership in World Affairs: Vietnam and the Breakdown of Consensus.* Boston: Allen and Unwin.

Holt, R. R. 1972. "On the Nature and Generality of Mental Imagery." In P. W. Sheehan, ed., *The Function and Nature of Imagery*, pp. 3–33. New York: Academic Press.

Holyoak, K. J. 1985. "The Pragmatics of Analogical Transfer." In G. H. Bower, ed., *The Psychology of Learning and Motivation*, vol. 19, pp. 59–87. Orlando, Fla.: Academic Press.

–––––. 1984. "Analogical Thinking and Human Intelligence." In R. J. Sternberg, ed., *Advances in the Psychology of Human Intelligence*, vol. 2, pp. 199–230. Hillsdale, N.J.: Erlbaum.

Holzner, B., and J. H. Marx. 1979. *Knowledge Application: The Knowledge System in Society.* Boston: Allyn and Bacon.

Hong, L. K. 1978. "Risky Shift and Cautious Shift: Some Direct Evidence on the Culture-Value Theory." *Social Psychology*, 41: 342–46.

Hoopes, T. 1969. *The Limits of Intervention.* New York: McKay.

Hughes, T. L. 1967. "Relativity in Foreign Policy." *Foreign Affairs*, 45: 670–82.

Hulnick, A. S. 1986. "The Intelligence Producer–Policy Consumer Linkage: A Theoretical Approach." *Intelligence and National Security*, 1: 212–33.

Humphrey, D. C. 1984. "Tuesday Lunch at the Johnson White House: A Preliminary Assessment." *Diplomatic History*, 8: 81–101.

Huntley, M. S. 1974. "Effects of Alcohol, Uncertainty, and Novelty upon Response Selection." *Psychopharmacologia*, 39: 259–66.

Hurst, P. M., M. F. Weidner, and R. Radlow. 1967. "The Effects of Amphetamines upon Judgments and Decisions." *Psychopharmacologia*, 11: 397–404.

Hveem, H. 1972. "Foreign Policy Opinion as a Function of International Position." *Cooperation and Conflict*, 7: 65–86.

Hybel, A. R. 1986. *The Logic of Surprise in International Conflict.* Lexington, Mass.: Lexington Books.

Ichheiser, G. 1970. *Appearances and Realities.* San Francisco, Calif.: Jossey-Bass.

Inkeles, A., E. Hanfmann, and H. Beier. 1958. "Modal Personality and Adjustment to the Soviet Socio-Political System." *Human Relations*, 11: 3–22.

Inkeles, A., and D. J. Levinson. 1969. "National Character: The Study of Modal Personality and Sociocultural Systems." In G. Lindzey and E. Aronson, eds., *The Handbook of Social Psychology*, vol. 4, pp. 418–506. 2d ed. Reading, Mass.: Addison-Wesley.

Insight Team of the Sunday *Times*. 1974. *The Yom Kippur War.* London: Andre Deutsch.

Insko, C. A., and J. Schopler. 1971. "Triadic Consistency: A Statement of Affective-Cognitive-Conative Consistency." In K. Thomas, ed., *Attitude and Behaviour*, pp. 22–33. Harmondsworth, Eng.: Penguin.

Iriye, A. 1979. "Culture and Power: International Relations as Intercultural Relations." *Diplomatic History*, 3: 115–28.

Isaacs, A. R. 1983. *Without Honor: Defeat in Vietnam and Cambodia.* Baltimore, Md.: Johns Hopkins University Press.

Ishida, T. 1969. "Beyond the Traditional Concepts of Peace in Different Cultures." *Journal of Peace Research*, 2: 133–45.

Jäättelä, A., P. Männistö, H. Paatero, and J. Tuomisto. 1971. "The Effects of Diazepam or Diphenhydramine on Healthy Human Subjects." *Psychopharmacologia*, 21: 202–11.

Jacobson, E., H. Kumata, and J. E. Gullahorn. 1960. "Cross-cultural Contributions to Attitude Research." *Public Opinion Quarterly*, 24: 205–23.

James, L. R., and S. B. Sells. 1981. "Psychological Climate: Theoretical Perspectives and Empirical Research." In D. Magnusson, ed., *Toward a Psychology of Situations: An Interactional Perspective*, pp. 275–95. Hillsdale, N.J.: Erlbaum.

James, L. R., J. J. Hater, M. J. Gent, and J. R. Bruni. 1978. "Psychological Climate: Implications from Cognitive Social Learning Theory and Interactional Psychology." *Personnel Psychology*, 31: 783–813.

Janis, I. L. 1989. *Crucial Decisions: Leadership in Policymaking and Crisis Management*. New York: Free Press.

_____. 1985. "Sources of Error in Strategic Decision Making." In J. M. Pennings and Associates, eds., *Organizational Strategy and Change*, pp. 157–97. San Francisco, Calif.: Jossey-Bass.

_____. 1982. *Groupthink: Psychological Studies of Policy Decisions and Fiascoes*. Rev. ed. Boston: Houghton Mifflin.

_____. 1962. "Psychological Effects of Warning." In G. W. Baker and D. W. Chapman, eds., *Man and Society in Disaster*, pp. 55–92. New York: Basic Books.

_____. 1954. "Personality Correlates of Susceptibility to Persuasion." *Journal of Personality*, 22: 504–18.

Janis, I. L., and L. Mann. 1977. *Decision Making: A Psychological Analysis of Conflict, Choice, and Commitment*. New York: Free Press.

Jaros, D. 1972. "Biochemical Desocialization: Depressants and Political Behavior." *Midwest Journal of Political Science*, 26: 1–28.

Jasińska-Kania, A. 1982. "National Identity and Image of World Society: The Polish Case." *International Social Science Journal*, 34: 93–112.

Jaspars, J., and M. Hewstone. 1982. "Cross-cultural Interaction, Social Attribution, and Inter-Group Relations." In S. Bochner, ed., *Cultures in Contact*, pp. 127–56. Oxford: Pergamon Press.

Jellison, J. M., and J. Mills. 1969. "Effect of Public Commitment upon Opinions." *Journal of Experimental Social Psychology*, 5: 340–46.

Jenkins, J. B. 1975. "Uncertainty and Uncertainty-Reduction in the Global Arena: Toward an Integrated Approach to International Politics." In W. O. Chittick, ed., *The Analysis of Foreign Policy Outputs*, pp. 74–110. Columbus, Ohio: Merrill.

Jennings, D. L., T. M. Amabile, and L. Ross. 1982. "Informal Covariation Assessment: Data-based Versus Theory-based Judgments." In D. Kahneman, P. Slovic, and A. Tversky, eds., *Judgment Under Uncertainty: Heuristics and Biases*, pp. 211–30. Cambridge, Eng.: Cambridge University Press.

Jensen, L. 1982. *Explaining Foreign Policy*. Englewood Cliffs, N.J.: Prentice-Hall.

Jervis, R. 1986. "Representativeness in Foreign Policy Judgments." *Political Psychology*, 7: 483–505.

_____. 1985a. "Introduction: Approach and Assumptions." In R. Jervis, R. N. Lebow, and J. G. Stein, eds., *Psychology and Deterrence*, pp. 1–12. Baltimore, Md.: Johns Hopkins University Press.

_____. 1985b. "Perceiving and Coping with Threat." In R. Jervis, R. N. Lebow, and J. G. Stein, eds., *Psychology and Deterrence*, pp. 13–33. Baltimore, Md.: Johns Hopkins University Press.

_____. 1982–83. "Deterrence and Perception." *International Security*, 7 (3): 3–30.

_____. 1980. "Political Decision Making: Recent Contributions." *Political Psychology*, 2 (Summer): 86–101.

_____. 1976. *Perception and Misperception in International Politics*. Princeton, N.J.: Princeton University Press.

_____. 1970. *The Logic of Images in International Relations*. Princeton, N.J.: Princeton University Press.

_____. 1969. "Hypotheses of Misperception." In J. N. Rosenau, ed., *International Politics and Foreign Policy*, pp. 239–54. Rev. ed. New York: Free Press.

Jervis, R., R. N. Lebow, and J. G. Stein, eds. 1985. *Psychology and Deterrence*. Baltimore, Md.: Johns Hopkins University Press.

Johnson, H. H., and J. A. Scileppi. 1969. "Effects of Ego-Involvement Conditions on Attitude Change to High and Low Credibility Communicators." *Journal of Personality and Social Psychology*, 13: 31–36.

Johnson, H. H., J. M. Toncivia, and M. A. Poprick. 1968. "Effects of Source Credibility on the Relationship Between Authoritarianism and Attitude Change." *Journal of Personality and Social Psychology*, 9: 179–83.

Johnson, L. B. 1971. *The Vantage Point: Perspectives of the Presidency, 1963–1969*. New York: Holt, Rinehart, and Winston.

Johnson, L. K. 1984. "Decision Costs in the Intelligence Cycle." *Journal of Strategic Studies*, 7: 318–35.

_____. 1983. "Seven Sins of Strategic Intelligence." *World Affairs*, 146: 176–204.

_____. 1977. "The Operational Code and the Prediction of Leadership Behavior: Senator Franck Church at Midcareer." In M. G. Hermann with T. W. Milburn, eds., *A Psychological Examination of Political Leaders*, pp. 82–119. New York: Free Press.

Johnson, R. T. 1974. *Managing the White House: An Intimate Study of the Presidency*. New York: Harper and Row.

Joint Intelligence Subcommittee, Joint Intelligence Committee, Offices of the War Cabinet, Great Britain. 1943. *Probabilities of a German Collapse*. J.I.C. (43) 367 (Final), Oct. 21. Public Records Office.

Jones, E. E. 1979. "The Rocky Road from Act to Dispositions." *American Psychologist*, 34: 107–17.

Jones, E. E., and K. E. Davis. 1965. "From Acts to Dispositions: The Attribution Process in Person Perception." In L. Berkowitz, ed., *Advances in Experimental Social Psychology*, vol. 2, pp. 219–66. New York: Academic Press.

Jones, E. E., and R. DeCharms. 1957. "Changes in Social Perceptions as a Function of the Personal Relevance of Behavior." *Sociometry*, 20: 75–85.

Jones, E. E., D. E. Kanouse, H. H. Kelley, R. E. Nisbett, S. Valins, and B. Weiner, eds. 1971. *Attribution: Perceiving the Causes of Behavior*. Morristown, N.J.: General Learning Press.

Jones, E. E., and R. E. Nisbett. 1971. "The Actor and the Observer: Divergent Perceptions of the Causes of Behavior." In E. E. Jones, D. E. Kanouse, H. H. Kelley, R. E. Nisbett, S. Valins, and B. Weiner, eds., *Attribution: Perceiving the Causes of Behavior*, pp. 79–94. Morristown, N.J.: General Learning Press.

Jones, R. A. 1977. *Self-fulfilling Prophecies*. Hillsdale, N.J.: Erlbaum.

Jönsson, C., and U. Westerlund. 1982. "Role Theory in Foreign Policy Analysis."

In C. Jönsson, ed., *Cognitive Dynamics and International Politics*, pp. 122–57. London: Frances Pinter.

Judd, C. M. 1978. "Cognitive Effects of Attitude Conflict Resolution." *Journal of Conflict Resolution*, 22: 483–98.

Kahin, G. M. 1986. *Intervention: How America Became Involved in Vietnam.* New York: Knopf.

Kahn, R. L., D. M. Wolfe, R. P. Quinn, J. D. Snoek, and R. A. Rosenthal. 1964. *Organizational Stress.* New York: Wiley.

Kahneman, D., P. Slovic, and A. Tversky, eds. 1982. *Judgment Under Uncertainty: Heuristics and Biases.* Cambridge, Eng.: Cambridge University Press.

Kahneman, D., and A. Tversky. 1982a. "On the Study of Statistical Intuitions," *Cognition.* 11: 123–41.

_____. 1982b. "Variants of Uncertainty." *Cognition*, 11: 143–57.

_____. 1982c. "The Simulation Heuristic." In D. Kahneman, P. Slovic, and A. Tversky, eds., *Judgment Under Uncertainty: Heuristics and Biases*, pp. 201–8. Cambridge, Eng.: Cambridge University Press.

_____. 1979a. "Intuitive Prediction: Biases and Corrective Procedures." *Tims Studies in the Management Sciences*, 12: 313–27.

_____. 1979b. "Prospect Theory: An Analysis of Decision Under Risk." *Econometrica*, 47: 263–91.

_____. 1973. "On the Psychology of Prediction." *Psychological Review*, 80: 237–51.

_____. 1972. "Subjective Probability: A Judgment of Representativeness." *Cognitive Psychology*, 3: 430–54.

Kaiser, F. M. 1980. "Secrecy, Intelligence, and Community: The U.S. Intelligence Community." In S. K. Tefft, ed., *Secrecy: A Cross-cultural Perspective*, pp. 273–96. New York: Human Sciences Press.

Kalb, M., and B. Kalb. 1974. *Kissinger.* Boston: Little, Brown.

Kam, E. 1988. *Surprise Attack: The Victim's Perspective.* Cambridge, Mass.: Harvard University Press.

Kantor, R. E., and W. G. Herron. 1968. "Paranoia and High Office." *Mental Hygiene*, 52: 507–11.

Kaplowitz, N. 1984. "Psychopolitical Dimensions of International Relations: The Reciprocal Effects of Conflict Strategies." *International Studies Quarterly*, 28: 373–406.

Karnow, S. 1983. *Vietnam: A History.* New York: Viking Press.

Kattenburg, P. M. 1980. *The Vietnam Trauma in American Foreign Policy, 1945–1975.* New Brunswick, N.J.: Transaction Books.

Katz, D. 1974. "Psychological Barriers to Communication." In J. M. Civikly, ed., *Messages: A Reader in Human Communication*, pp. 321–31. New York: Random House.

_____. 1960. "The Functional Approach to the Study of Attitudes." *Public Opinion Quarterly*, 24: 163–204.

Katz, D., and R. L. Kahn. 1966. *The Social Psychology of Organizations.* New York: Wiley.

Kearns, D. 1976. *Lyndon Johnson and the American Dream.* New York: Harper and Row.

Keinan, G., N. Friedland, and Y. Ben-Porath. 1987. "Decision Making Under Stress: Scanning of Alternatives Under Physical Threat." *Acta Psychologica*, 64: 219–28.

Kellerman, B. 1983. "Allison Redux: Three More Decision-making Models." *Polity*, 15: 351–67.

Kelley, H. H. 1967. "Attribution Theory in Social Psychology." In D. Levine, ed., *Nebraska Symposium on Motivation*, pp. 192–240. Lincoln: University of Nebraska Press.

———. 1965. "Two Functions of Reference Groups." In H. M. Proshansky and B. Seidenberg, eds., *Basic Studies in Social Psychology*, pp. 210–15. New York: Holt, Rinehart, and Winston.

Kelley, H. H., and A. J. Stahelski. 1970. "Error in Perception of Intentions in a Mixed-Motive Game." *Journal of Experimental Social Psychology*, 6: 379–400.

Kelley, H. H., and E. H. Volkart. 1952. "The Resistance to Change of Group-anchored Attitudes." *American Sociological Review*, 17: 453–65.

Kelman, H. C. 1975. "International Interchanges: Some Contributions from Theories of Attitude Change." *Comparative International Development*, 10: 83–99.

———. 1974. "Attitudes Are Alive and Well and Gainfully Employed in the Sphere of Action," *American Psychologist*, 29: 310–24.

———. 1970. "The Role of the Individual in International Relations: Some Conceptual and Methodological Considerations." *Journal of International Affairs*, 24: 1–17.

———, ed. 1965a. *International Behavior*. New York: Holt, Rinehart, and Winston.

———. 1965b. "Social-Psychological Approaches to the Study of International Relations: The Question of Relevance." In H. C. Kelman, ed., *International Behavior*, pp. 565–607. New York: Holt, Rinehart, and Winston.

———. 1958. "Compliance, Identification, and Internalization: Three Processes of Attitude Change." *Journal of Conflict Resolution*, 2: 51–60.

———. 1955. "Societal, Attitudinal, and Structural Factors in International Relations." *Journal of Social Issues*, 11 (1): 42–56.

Kelman, H. C., and R. M. Baron. 1968. "Determinant of Modes of Resolving Inconsistency Dilemmas: A Functional Analysis." In R. P. Abelson, E. Aronson, W. J. McGuire, T. M. Newcomb, M. J. Rosenberg, and P. H. Tannenbaum, eds., *Theories of Cognitive Consistency: A Sourcebook*, pp. 670–83. Chicago: Rand McNally.

Kelman, H. C., and A. H. Eagly. 1974. "Attitude Toward the Communicator, Perception of Communication Content, and Attitude Change." In S. Himmelfarb and A. H. Eagly, eds., *Readings in Attitude Change*, pp. 173–90. New York: Wiley.

Kennedy, P. 1987. *The Rise and Fall of the Great Powers: Economic Change and Military Conflict from 1500 to 2000*. New York: Random House.

Keohane, R. O. 1986. "Reciprocity in International Relations." *International Organization*, 40: 1–28.

———. 1984. *After Hegemony: Cooperation and Discord in the World Political Economy*. Princeton, N.J.: Princeton University Press.

Keohane, R. O., and J. H. Nye. 1977. *Power and Interdependence*. Boston: Little, Brown.

Kessler, D. C., R. H. Price, and C. B. Wortman. 1985. "Social Factors in Psychopathology: Stress, Social Support, and Coping Processes." In M. R. Rosenzweig and L. W. Porter, eds., *Annual Review of Psychology*, vol. 36, pp. 531–72. Palo Alto, Calif.: Annual Reviews.

Kets de Vries, M.F.R., and D. Miller. 1984. *The Neurotic Organization*. San Francisco, Calif.: Jossey-Bass.

Kiesler, C. A. 1971. *The Psychology of Commitment*. New York: Academic Press.

Kilpatrick, F. P. 1970. "Two Processes in Perceptual Learning." In H. M. Proshansky, W. H. Ittelson, and L. G. Rivlin, eds., *Environmental Psychology*, pp. 104–12. New York: Holt, Rinehart, and Winston.

———. 1969. "Problems of Perception in Extreme Situations." In R. R. Evans, ed., *Readings in Collective Behavior*, pp. 168–73. Chicago: Rand McNally.

Kinder, D. R., and J. A. Weiss. 1978. "In Lieu of Rationality: Psychological Perspectives on Foreign Policy Decision Making." *Journal of Conflict Resolution*, 22: 707–36.

Kinnard, D. 1980. *The Secretary of Defense*. Lexington: University Press of Kentucky.

Kirkpatrick, S. A., D. F. Davis, and R. D. Robertson. 1976. "The Process of Political Decision-Making in Groups: Search Behavior and Choice Shifts." *American Behavioral Scientist*, 20: 33–64.

Kissinger, H. 1982. *Years of Upheaval*. Boston: Little, Brown.

———. 1979. *White House Years*. Boston: Little, Brown.

———. 1978. "The Lesson of the Past." *Washington Review*, 1 (1): 3–9.

———. 1969. "Domestic Structure and Foreign Policy." In J. N. Rosenau, ed., *International Politics and Foreign Policy*, pp. 261–75. Rev. ed. New York: Free Press.

Kleck, R. E., and J. Wheaton. 1967. "Dogmatism and Responses to Opinion-Consistent and Opinion-Inconsistent Information." *Journal of Personality and Social Psychology*, 5: 249–52.

Kleinhesselink, R. R., and R. E. Edwards. 1975. "Seeking and Avoiding Belief-Discrepant Information as a Function of Its Perceived Refutability." *Journal of Personality and Social Psychology*, 31: 787–90.

Kleinknecht, R. A., and D. Donaldson. 1975. "A Review of the Effects of Diazepam on Cognitive and Psychomotor Performance." *The Journal of Nervous and Mental Disease*, 161: 399–411.

Klineberg, O. 1964. *The Human Dimension in International Relations*. New York: Holt, Rinehart, and Winston.

Knorr, K. 1979. "Strategic Intelligence: Problems and Remedies." In L. Martin, ed., *Strategic Thought in the Nuclear Age*, pp. 69–91. London: Heinemann.

———. 1976. "Threat Perception." In K. Knorr, ed., *Historical Dimensions of National Security Problems*, pp. 78–119. Lawrence: University Press of Kansas.

———. 1964. "Failures in National Intelligence Estimates." *World Politics*, 16: 455–67.

Knorr, K., and P. Morgan, eds. 1983. *Strategic Military Surprise: Incentives and Opportunities*. New Brunswick, N.J.: Transaction Books.

Komer, R. W. 1986. *Bureaucracy at War: U.S. Performance in the Vietnam Conflict*. Boulder, Colo.: Westview Press.

Koriat, A., S. Lichtenstein, and B. Fischhoff. 1980. "Reasons for Confidence." *Journal of Experimental Psychology: Human Learning and Memory*, 6: 107–18.

Krakau, K. 1984. "American Foreign Relations: A National Style?" *Diplomatic History*, 8: 253–72.

Krasner, S. D. 1976. "State Power and the Structure of International Trade." *World Politics*, 28: 317–47.

Kratochwil, F. V. 1978. *International Order and Foreign Policy*. Boulder, Colo.: Westview Press.

Krech, D., and R. S. Crutchfield. 1971. "Perceiving the World." In W. Schramm and D. F. Roberts, eds., *The Process and Effect of Mass Communication*, pp. 235–64. Rev. ed. Urbana: University of Illinois Press.

Kreitler, H., and S. Kreitler. 1976. *Cognitive Orientation and Behavior*. New York: Springer.

Krepinevich, A. F. 1986. *The Army and Vietnam*. Baltimore, Md.: Johns Hopkins University Press.

Kruglanski, A. W., and I. Ajzen. 1983. "Bias and Error in Human Judgment." *European Journal of Social Psychology*, 13: 1–44.

Kruglanski, A. W., M. W. Baldwin, and S. M. J. Towson. 1983. "The Lay-Epistemic Process in Attribution-Making." In M. Hewstone, ed., *Attribution Theory: Social and Functional Extensions*, pp. 81–95. Oxford: Basil Blackwell.

Kruglanski, A. W., N. Friedland, and E. Farkash. 1984. "Lay Persons' Sensitivity to Statistical Information: The Case of High Perceived Applicability." *Journal of Personality and Social Psychology*, 46: 503–18.

Kucharski, A. 1984. "On Being Sick and Famous." *Political Psychology*, 5: 69–81.

———. 1978. "Medical Management of Political Patients: The Case of Dwight D. Eisenhower." *Perspectives in Biology and Medicine*, 22: 115–26.

Kuhn, T. S. 1970. *The Structure of Scientific Revolutions*. 2d ed. Chicago: University of Chicago Press.

Kuipers, B., A. J. Moskowitz, and J. P. Kassirer. 1988. "Critical Decisions Under Uncertainty: Representation and Structure." *Cognitive Science*, 12: 177–210.

Kuiper, N. A. 1978. "Depression and Causal Attributions for Success and Failure." *Journal of Personality and Social Psychology*, 36: 236–46.

Kulik, J. A. 1983. "Confirmatory Attribution and the Perpetuation of Social Beliefs." *Journal of Personality and Social Psychology*, 44: 1171–81.

LaBier, D. 1983. "Emotional Disturbances in the Federal Government." *Administration and Society*, 14: 403–48.

Lachman, R., J. L. Lachman, and E. C. Butterfield. 1979. *Cognitive Psychology and Information Processing*. Hillsdale, N.J.: Erlbaum.

Lakoff, G., and M. Johnson. 1980. *Metaphors We Live By*. Chicago: University of Chicago Press.

Landau, M. 1961. "On the Use of Metaphor in Political Analysis." *Social Research*, 28: 331–53.

Langer, E. J. 1975. "The Illusion of Control." *Journal of Personality and Social Psychology*, 32: 311–28.

Lanir, Z. 1983. *Fundamental Surprise: The National Intelligence Crisis*. Tel Aviv: Hakibutz Hameuhad for the Center for Strategic Studies, Tel Aviv University. (In Hebrew.)

Lanzetta, J. T. 1965. "Group Behavior Under Stress." In J. D. Singer, ed., *Human Behavior and International Politics*, pp. 212–19. Chicago: Rand McNally.

Laqueur, W. 1985. *A World of Secrets: The Uses and Limits of Intelligence*. New York: Basic Books.

———. 1981. "Foreign Policy and the English Language." *Washington Quarterly*, 4 (1): 3–12.

Larson, D. W. 1985. *Origins of Containment: A Psychological Explanation.* Princeton, N.J.: Princeton University Press.

———. 1982. *Belief and Inference: The Origins of American Leaders' Cold War Ideology.* Ph.D. diss., Stanford University.

Lasswell, H. D. 1965. "The Climate of International Action." In H. C. Kelman, ed., *International Behavior*, pp. 339–53. New York: Holt, Rinehart, and Winston.

———. 1931. "Faction." In *Encyclopedia of the Social Sciences*, vol. 6, pp. 49–51. New York: Macmillan.

Laszlo, E. 1975. "The Meaning and Significance of General System Theory." *Behavioral Science*, 20: 9–24.

Lathem, A. 1976. "The CIA Report the President Doesn't Want You to Read." *Village Voice*, February 16, pp. 70, 72–92.

Lau, R. R., and D. O. Sears. 1986. "Social Cognition and Political Cognition: The Past, the Present, and the Future." In R. R. Lau and D. O. Sears, eds., *Political Cognition*, pp. 347–66. Hillsdale, N.J.: Erlbaum.

Lazarsfeld, P. F., and H. Menzel. 1961. "On the Relation Between Individual and Collective Properties." In A. Etzioni, ed., *A Sociological Reader on Complex Organizations*, pp. 499–516. New York: Holt, Rinehart, and Winston.

Lazarus, R. S. 1966. *Psychological Stress and Coping Process.* New York: McGraw-Hill.

Lazarus, R. S., J. Deese, and S. F. Osler. 1952. "The Effects of Psychological Stress upon Performance." *Psychological Bulletin*, 49: 293–317.

Lazarus, R. S., and S. Folkman. 1984. *Stress Appraisal and Coping.* New York: Springer.

Leana, C. R. 1985. "A Partial Test of Janis' Groupthink Model: Effects of Group Cohesiveness and Leader Behavior on Defective Decision Making." *Journal of Management*, 11: 5–17.

Lebow, R. N. 1987. *Nuclear Crisis Management: A Dangerous Illusion.* Ithaca, N.Y.: Cornell University Press.

———. 1985. "Conclusions." In R. Jervis, R. N. Lebow, and J. G. Stein, eds., *Psychology and Deterrence*, pp. 203–32. Baltimore, Md.: Johns Hopkins University Press.

———. 1981. *Between Peace and War: The Nature of International Crisis.* Baltimore, Md.: Johns Hopkins University Press.

Lebow, R. N., and J. G. Stein. 1987. "Beyond Deterrence." *Journal of Social Issues*, 43 (4): 5–71.

Lee, D.H.K. 1966. "The Role of Attitude in Response to Environmental Stress." *Journal of Social Issues*, 22 (4): 83–91.

Lefcourt, H. M. 1976. *Locus of Control: Current Trends in Theory and Research.* Hillsdale, N.J.: Erlbaum.

Leng, R. J. 1983. "When Will They Ever Learn? Coercive Bargaining in Recurrent Crises." *Journal of Conflict Resolution*, 27: 379–419.

Lennard, H. L., L. J. Epstein, and B. G. Katzung. 1967. "Psychoactive Drug Action and Group Interaction Process." *Journal of Nervous and Mental Disease*, 145: 69–78.

Lerner, A. W. 1982. "Decision Making by Organizations." *Micropolitics*, 2: 123–52.

L'Etang, H. 1980. *Fit to Lead?* London: Heinemann.

———. 1970. *The Pathology of Leadership*. London: Heinemann.

Levi, A., and J. B. Pryor. 1987. "Use of the Availability Heuristic in Probability Estimates of Future Events: The Effects of Imagining Outcomes Versus Imagining Reasons." *Organizational Behavior and Human Decision Processes*, 40: 219–34.

Levi, A., and P. E. Tetlock. 1980. "A Cognitive Analysis of Japan's 1941 Decision for War." *Journal of Conflict Resolution*, 24: 195–211.

Levine, J. M., M. G. Samet, and R. E. Brahlek. 1975. "Information Seeking with Limitations on Available Information and Resources." *Human Factors*, 17: 502–13.

Levinson, D. J. 1959. "Role, Personality, and Social Structure in the Organizational Setting." *Journal of Abnormal and Social Psychology*, 58: 170–80.

Levite, A. 1987. *Intelligence and Strategic Surprises*. New York: Columbia University Press.

Levy, J. S. 1986. "Organizational Routines and the Causes of War." *International Studies Quarterly*, 30: 193–222.

———. 1983. "Misperception and the Causes of War: Theoretical Linkages and Analytical Problems." *World Politics*, 36: 76–99.

Levy, M. J., Jr. 1966. *Modernization and the Structure of Societies: A Setting for International Affairs*. Princeton, N.J.: Princeton University Press.

Lewicki, P. 1985. "Nonconscious Biasing Effects of Single Instances on Subsequent Judgments." *Journal of Personality and Social Psychology*, 48: 563–74.

Lewis, A. M. 1976. "The Blind Spot of U.S. Foreign Intelligence." *Journal of Communication*, 26: 44–55.

Lewis, B. 1975. *History—Remembered, Recovered, Invented*. Princeton, N.J.: Princeton University Press.

Lewy, G. H. 1978. *America in Vietnam*. New York: Oxford University Press.

Lieberman, S. 1956. "The Effects of Changes in Roles on the Attitudes of Role Occupants." *Human Relations*, 9: 385–402.

Lin Piao. 1972. "Long Live the Victory of People's War!" In K. Fan, ed., *Mao Tse-tung and Lin Piao: Post Revolutionary Writings*, pp. 357–412. New York: Doubleday.

Lindsay, P. H., and D. A. Norman. 1977. Human Information Processing. 2d ed. New York: Academic Press.

Lipowski, Z. J. 1974. "Sensory Overloads, Information Overloads, and Behaviour." *Psychotherapy and Psychosomatics*, 23: 264–71.

Liska, A. E. 1974. "The Impact of Attitude on Behavior." *Pacific Sociological Review*, 17: 83–97.

Littauer, R., and N. Uphoff, eds. 1972. *The Air War in Indochina*. Boston: Beacon Press.

Livant, W. P. 1963. "Cumulative Distortion of Judgment." *Perceptual and Motor Skills*, 16: 741–45.

Lockhart, C. 1973. "The Efficacy of Threats in International Interaction Strategies." *Sage Professional Papers in International Studies*, vol. 2, no. 02-203. Beverly Hills, Calif.: Sage.

Loftus, E. F., and G. R. Loftus. 1980. "On the Permanence of Stored Information in the Human Brain." *American Psychologist*, 35: 409–20.

Longley, J., and D. G. Pruitt. 1980. "Groupthink: A Critique of Janis's Theory."

In L. Wheeler, ed., *Review of Personality and Social Psychology*, vol. 1, pp. 74–93. Beverly Hills, Calif.: Sage.

Lord, C. 1985. "American Strategic Culture." *Comparative Strategy*, 5: 269–93.

Lord, C., L. Ross, and M. R. Lepper. 1979. "Biased Assimilation and Attitude Polarization: The Effects of Prior Theories on Subsequently Considered Evidence." *Journal of Personality and Social Psychology*, 37: 2098–2109.

Lord, R. G. 1985. "An Information Processing Approach to Social Perception, Leadership, and Behavioral Measurement in Organizations." In L. L. Cummings and B. M. Staw, eds., *Research in Organizational Behavior*, vol. 7, pp. 87–128. Greenwich, Conn.: Jai Press.

Lovell, J. P. 1984. "'Lessons' of U.S. Military Involvement: Preliminary Conceptualization." In D. A. Sylvan and S. Chan, eds., *Foreign Policy Decision Making: Perception, Cognition, and Artificial Intelligence*, pp. 129–57. New York: Praeger.

Lowenthal, A. F. 1972. *The Dominican Intervention*. Cambridge, Mass.: Harvard University Press.

Lubit, R., and B. Russett. 1984. "The Effects of Drugs on Decision-Making." *Journal of Conflict Resolution*, 28: 85–102.

Lutzker, D. R. 1960. "Internationalism as a Predictor of Cooperative Behavior." *Journal of Conflict Resolution*, 4: 426–30.

McArthur, L. Z. 1981. "What Grabs You? The Role of Attention in Impression Formation and Causal Attribution." In E. T. Higgins, C. P. Herman, and M. P. Zanna, eds., *Social Cognition: The Ontario Symposium*, vol. 1, pp. 201–46. Hillsdale, N.J.: Erlbaum.

———. 1980. "Illusory Causation and Illusory Correlation: Two Epistemological Accounts." *Personality and Social Psychology Bulletin*, 6: 507–19.

McClintock, C. G. 1958. "Personality Syndromes and Attitude Change." *Journal of Personality*, 26: 479–93.

McClintock, C. G., A. A. Harrison, S. Strand, and P. Gallo. 1963. "Internationalism-Isolationism, Strategy of the Other Player and Two-Person Game Behavior." *Journal of Abnormal Social Psychology*, 67: 631–36.

McClosky, H. 1967. "Personality and Attitude Correlates of Foreign Policy Orientation." In J. N. Rosenau, ed., *Domestic Sources of Foreign Policy*, pp. 51–110. New York: Free Press.

McGarvey, P. J. 1973. "DIA: Intelligence to Please." In M. Halperin and A. Kanter, eds., *Readings in American Foreign Policy: Bureaucratic Perspective*, pp. 318–28. Boston: Little, Brown.

McGrath, J. E., and N. L. Rotchford. 1983. "Time and Behavior in Organizations." In L. L. Cummings and B. M. Staw, eds., *Research in Organizational Behavior*, vol. 5, pp. 57–101. Greenwich, Conn.: Jai Press.

McGuire, W. J. 1969. "The Nature of Attitudes and Attitude Change." In G. Lindzey and E. Aronson, eds., *The Handbook of Social Psychology*, vol. 3, pp. 136–314. 2d ed. Reading, Mass.: Addison-Wesley.

———. 1960. "Cognitive Consistency and Attitude Change," *Journal of Abnormal and Social Psychology*. 60: 345–53.

MacVane, J., N. Butters, K. Montgomery, and J. Farber. 1982. "Cognitive Functions in Men Social Drinkers: A Replication Study." *Journal of Studies on Alcohol*, 43: 81–95.

McWhirter, D. A. 1978. "Testing for Groupthink: The Effect of Anticipated Group Membership on Individual Decision Making." In R. T. Golembiewski, ed., *The Small Group in Political Science*, pp. 210–20. Athens: University of Georgia Press.

Madsen, D. 1982. "The Effect of Psychological Stress on Influence Distributions." *International Political Science Review*, 3: 91–106.

Mandel, R. 1987. *Irrationality in International Confrontation*. New York: Greenwood Press.

———. 1979. *Perception, Decisionmaking, and Conflict*. Washington, D.C.: University Press of America.

Manis, M. 1961. "The Interpretation of Opinion Statements as a Function of Recipient Attitude and Source Prestige." *Journal of Abnormal and Social Psychology*, 63: 82–86.

Mansbach, R. W., and J. A. Vasquez. 1981. *In Search of Theory: A New Paradigm for Global Politics*. New York: Columbia University Press.

Maoz, Z. 1985. "Foreign Policy Decision Making: A Progress Report." *Jerusalem Journal of International Relations*, 7: 28–63.

March, J. G. 1982. "Theories of Choice and Making Decisions." *Society*, 20 (November–December): 29–39.

March, J. G., and J. P. Olsen. 1980. *Ambiguity and Choice in Organization*. 2d ed. Bergen, Nor.: Universitetsförlaget.

March, J. G., and H. A. Simon. 1958. *Organizations*. New York: Wiley.

Marks, B. A. 1977. "Decision Under Uncertainty: The Narrative Sense." *Administration and Society*, 9: 379–94.

Markus, H. 1977. "Self-Schemata and Processing Information About the Self." *Journal of Personality and Social Psychology*, 35: 63–78.

Markus, H., and R. B. Zajonc. 1985. "The Cognitive Perspective in Social Psychology." In G. Lindzey and E. Aronson, eds., *Handbook of Social Psychology: Theory and Method*, vol. 1, pp. 137–230. 3d ed. New York: Random House.

Marmor, M. F. 1982. "Wilson, Strokes, and Zebras." *New England Journal of Medicine*, 307: 528–35.

May, E. R. 1984. "Conclusions: Capabilities and Proclivities." In E. R. May, ed., *Knowing One's Enemies: Intelligence Assessment Before the Two World Wars*, pp. 503–42. Princeton, N.J.: Princeton University Press.

———. 1973. *"Lessons" of the Past*. New York: Oxford University Press.

Mayer, A. J. 1968. "Vietnam Analogy: Greece, Not Munich." *The Nation*, March 25, pp. 407–10.

Mazlish, B. 1976. *Kissinger: The European Mind in American Policy*. New York: Basic Books.

———. 1965. "Historical Analogy: The Railroad and the Space Program and Their Impact on Society." In B. Mazlish, ed., *The Railroad and the Space Program*, pp. 1–52. Cambridge, Mass.: MIT Press.

Mead, M. 1970. "Bio-social Components of Political Process." *Journal of International Affairs*, 24: 18–28.

———. 1968. "The Importance of National Cultures." In A. S. Hoffmann, ed., *International Communications and the New Diplomacy*, pp. 89–105. Bloomington: Indiana University Press.

Meddis, R. 1982. "Cognitive Dysfunction Following Loss of Sleep." In A. Burton, ed., *The Pathology and Psychology of Cognition*, pp. 225–52. London: Methuen.

Mehle, T., C. F. Gettys, C. Manning, S. Baca, and S. Fisher. 1981. "The Availability Explanation of Excessive Plausibility Assessments." *Acta Psychologica*, 49: 127–40.

Mehrabian, A., and M. Wiener. 1967. "Decoding of Inconsistent Communications." *Journal of Personality and Social Psychology*, 6: 109–14.

Meir, G. 1975. *My Life*. Tel-Aviv: Ma'ariv Book Guild. (In Hebrew.)

Merek, G. M., I. L. Janis, and P. Huth. 1987. "Decision Making During International Crises." *Journal of Conflict Resolution*, 31: 203–26.

Mewaldt, S. P., J. V. Hinrichs, and M. M. Ghoneim. 1983. "Diazepam and Memory: Support for a Duplex Model of Memory." *Memory and Cognition*, 11: 557–64.

Midlarsky, M. I. 1975. *On War*. New York: Free Press.

Migdal, J. S. 1974. "Internal Structure and External Behavior: Explaining Foreign Policies of Third World States." *International Relations*, 4: 510–26.

Milburn, T. W. 1972. "The Management of International Crises." In C. F. Hermann, ed., *International Crises*, pp. 259–77. New York: Free Press.

Milburn, T. W., and R. Billings. 1976. "Decision-making Perspectives from Psychology: Dealing with Risk and Uncertainty." *American Behavioral Scientist*, 20: 111–26.

Milburn, T. W., R. S. Schuler, and K. H. Watman. 1983a. "Organizational Crisis." Part 1, "Definition and Conceptualization." *Human Relations*, 36: 1141–60.

———. 1983b. "Organizational Crisis." Part 2, "Strategies and Responses." *Human Relations*, 36: 1161–80.

Miller, D. T., S. A. Norman, and E. Wright. 1978. "Distortion in Person Perception as a Consequence of the Need for Effective Control." *Journal of Personality and Social Psychology*, 36: 598–607.

Miller, E. F. 1979. "Metaphor and Political Knowledge." *American Political Science Review*, 73: 155–70.

Miller, G. A. 1956. "The Magical Number Seven, Plus or Minus Two: Some Limits on Our Capacity for Processing Information." *Psychological Review*, 63: 81–97.

Miller, J. G. 1965. "The Individual as an Information Processing System." In J. D. Singer, ed., *Human Behavior and International Politics*, pp. 202–12. Chicago: Rand McNally.

Miller, L. W., and L. Siegelman. 1978. "Is the Audience the Message? A Note on LBJ's Vietnam Statements." *Public Opinion Quarterly*, 42: 71–80.

Miller, N. 1974. "Involvement and Dogmatism as Inhibitors of Attitude Change." In S. Himmelfarb and A. H. Eagly, eds., *Readings in Attitude Change*, pp. 251–59. New York: Wiley.

Miller, R. L. 1978. "Preferred Strategies for Resolving Belief Dilemmas." *Journal of Social Psychology*, 104: 133–34.

Mineka, S., and R. W. Hendersen. 1985. "Controllability and Predictability in Acquired Motivation." In M. R. Rosenzweig and L. W. Porter, eds., *Annual Review of Psychology*, vol. 36, pp. 495–529. Palo Alto, Calif.: Annual Reviews.

Minix, D. A. 1982. *Small Groups and Foreign Policy Decision-Making*. Washington, D.C.: University Press of America.

Mischel, W. 1977. "The Interaction of Person and Situation." In D. Magnusson and N. S. Endler, eds., *Personality at the Crossroads: Current Issues in Interactional Psychology*, pp. 333–52. Hillsdale, N.J.: Erlbaum.

_____. 1968. *Personality and Assessment*. New York: Wiley.

Modelski, G. 1970. "The World's Foreign Ministers: A Political Elite." *Journal of Conflict Resolution*, 14: 135–75.

Mongar, T. M. 1969. "Personality and Decision-Making: John F. Kennedy in Four Crisis Decisions." *Canadian Journal of Political Science*, 2: 200–225.

Moorhead, G. 1982. "Groupthink: Hypothesis in Need of Testing." *Group and Organization Studies*, 7: 429–44.

Moos, R. H. 1973. "Conceptualization of Human Environments." *American Psychologist*, 28: 652–65.

Morgan, P. M. 1983. "The Opportunity for a Strategic Surprise." In K. Knorr and P. Morgan, eds., *Strategic Military Surprise: Incentives and Opportunities*, pp. 195–245. New Brunswick, N.J.: Transaction Books.

_____. 1977. *Deterrence: A Conceptual Analysis*. Beverly Hills, Calif.: Sage.

Morris, L. W. 1979. *Extraversion and Introversion: An Interactional Perspective*. Washington, D.C.: Hemisphere.

Morris, R. 1977. *Uncertain Greatness: Henry Kissinger and American Foreign Policy*. New York: Harper and Row.

Moscovici, S. 1976. *Social Influence and Social Change*. London: Academic Press.

Moscovici, S., and C. Nemeth. 1974. "Social Influence II: Minority Influence." In C. Nemeth, ed., *Social Psychology: Classic and Contemporary Integrations*, pp. 217–49. Chicago: Rand McNally.

Moxlery, R. A., Jr. 1974. "Reduction of Uncertainty." *International Journal of General Systems*, 1: 175–82.

Moynihan, D. P. 1979. "Further Thoughts on Words and Foreign Policy." *Policy Review*, 8: 53–59.

_____. 1978. "Words and Foreign Policy." *Policy Review*, 6: 69–71.

Mueller, J. E. 1980. "The Search for the 'Breaking Point' in Vietnam: The Statistics of a Deadly Quarrel." *International Studies Quarterly*, 24: 497–519.

Mullen, B. 1983. "Egocentric Bias in Estimates of Consensus." *Journal of Social Psychology*, 121: 31–38.

Murray, J. B. 1984. "Effects of Valium and Librium on Human Psychomotor and Cognitive Functions." *Genetic Psychology Monographs*, 109: 167–97.

Myers, D. G., and H. Lamm. 1976. "The Group Polarization Phenomenon." *Psychological Bulletin*, 83: 602–27.

Nakdimon, S. 1982. *Low Probability*. Tel Aviv: Revivim. (In Hebrew.)

Naylor, J. C., R. D. Pritchard, and D. R. Ilgen. 1980. *A Theory of Behavior in Organizations*. New York: Academic Press.

Neisser, U. 1976. *Cognition and Reality: Principles and Implications of Cognitive Psychology*. San Francisco, Calif.: Freeman.

Nemeth, C. 1987. "Influence Processes, Problem Solving, and Creativity." In M. P. Zanna, J. M. Olson, and C. P. Herman, eds., *Social Influence: The Ontario Symposium*, vol. 5, pp. 237–46. Hillsdale, N.J.: Erlbaum.

_____. 1982. "Stability of Faction Position and Influence." In H. Brandstätter, J. H. Davis, and G. Stocker-Kreichgauer, eds., *Group Decision Making*, pp. 185–200. London: Academic Press.

Neubauer, D. 1977. "Lying and the Stress for Cognitive Consistency." In G. M. Bonham and M. J. Shapiro, eds., *Thought and Action in Foreign Policy*, pp. 190–225. Basel: Birkhäuser Verlag.

Neustadt, R. E. 1970. *Alliance Politics*. New York: Columbia University Press.

Neustadt, R. E., and E. R. May. 1986. *Thinking in Time: The Uses of History for Decision-Makers*. New York: Free Press.

Newsweek. 1978. Aug. 21, p. 48.

Nicholas, R. W. 1966. "Segmentary Factional Political Systems." In M. J. Swartz, V. W. Turner, and A. Tuden, eds., *Political Anthropology*, pp. 49–60. Chicago: Aldine.

———. 1965. "Factions: A Comparative Analysis." In M. Banton, ed., *Political Systems and the Distribution of Power*, pp. 21–61. London: Tavistock.

Nickerson, R. S., A. Baddeley, and B. Freeman. 1987. "Are People's Estimates of What Other People Know Influenced by What They Themselves Know?" *Acta Psychologica*, 64: 245–59.

Niebuhr, R. 1968. "The Social Myths in the 'Cold War.'" In J. C. Farrell and A. P. Smith, eds., *Image and Reality in World Politics*, pp. 40–56. New York: Columbia University Press.

Nisbett, R. E., and E. Borgida. 1975. "Attribution and the Psychology of Prediction." *Journal of Personality and Social Psychology*, 32: 932–43.

Nisbett, R. E., E. Borgida, R. Crandall, and H. Reed. 1976. "Popular Induction: Information Is Not Always Informative." In J. S. Carroll and J. W. Payne, eds., *Cognition and Social Behavior*, pp. 113–33. Hillsdale, N.J.: Erlbaum.

Nisbett, R. E., D. H. Krantz, C. Jepson, and Z. Kunda. 1983. "The Use of Statistical Heuristics in Everyday Inductive Reasoning." *Psychological Review*, 90: 339–63.

Nisbett, R. E., and L. Ross. 1980. *Human Inference: Strategies and Shortcomings of Social Judgment*. Englewood Cliffs, N.J.: Prentice-Hall.

Nisbett, R. E., and S. Valins. 1971. "Perceiving the Causes of One's Own Behavior." In E. E. Jones, D. E. Knouse, H. H. Kelley, R. E. Nisbett, S. Valins, and B. Weiner, eds., *Attribution: Perceiving the Causes of Behavior*, pp. 63–78. Morristown, N.J.: General Learning Press.

Nisbett, R. E., and T. D. Wilson. 1977a. "Telling More Than We Can Know: Verbal Reports on Mental Processes." *Psychological Review*, 84: 231–59.

———. 1977b. "The Halo Effect: Evidence for Unconscious Alteration of Judgments." *Journal of Personality and Social Psychology*, 35: 250–56.

Nixon, R. M. 1978. *The Memoirs of Richard Nixon*. London: Sidgwick and Jackson.

Norem, J. K., and N. Cantor. 1986. "Anticipatory and Post Hoc Cushioning Strategies: Optimism and Defensive Pessimism in Risky Situations." *Cognitive Therapy and Research*, 10: 347–62.

North, R. C. 1968. "Perception and Action in the 1914 Crisis." In J. C. Farrell and A. P. Smith, eds., *Image and Reality in World Politics*, pp. 103–22. New York: Columbia University Press.

Northrop, F.S.C. 1953. *The Taming of Nations: A Study of the Cultural Bases of Foreign Policy*. New York: Macmillan.

Novick, L. R. 1988. "Analogical Transfer, Problem Similarity, and Expertise." *Journal of Experimental Psychology: Learning Memory and Cognition*, 14: 510–20.

Nydegger, R. V. 1975. "Information Processing Complexity and Leadership Status." *Journal of Experimental Social Psychology*, 11: 317–28.

Oakeshott, M. 1983. *On History and Other Essays*. Oxford: Basil Blackwell.

Oberdorfer, D. 1984. *Tet!* New York: Da Capo.

Ogden, C. K., and I. A. Richards. 1972. *The Meaning of Meaning*. 10th ed. London: Routledge and Kegan Paul.

Okun, M. A. 1980. "The Role of Non-cognitive Factors in the Cognitive Performance of Older Adults." *Contemporary Educational Psychology*, 5: 321–45.

Oneal, J. R. 1988. "The Rationality of Decision-Making During International Crises." *Polity*, 20: 598–622.

_____. 1982. *Foreign Policymaking in Times of Crisis*. Columbus: Ohio State University Press.

O'Reilly, C. A. 1983. "The Use of Information in Organizational Decision Making: A Model and Some Propositions." In L. L. Cummings and B. M. Staw, eds., *Research in Organizational Behavior*, vol. 5, pp. 103–39. Greenwich, Conn.: Jai Press.

_____. 1982. "Variations in Decision Makers' Use of Information Sources: The Impact of Quality and Accessibility of Information." *Academy of Management Journal*, 25: 756–71.

Ortony, A. 1975. "Why Metaphors Are Necessary and Not Just Nice." *Educational Theory*, 25: 45–53.

Ortony, A., R. E. Reynolds, and J. A. Arter. 1978. "Metaphor: Theoretical and Empirical Research." *Psychological Bulletin*, 85: 919–43.

Osgood, C. E. 1960a. "Cognitive Dynamics in the Conduct of Human Affairs." *Public Opinion Quarterly*, 24: 341–65.

_____. 1960b. *Graduate Reciprocation in Tension Reduction*. Urbana: University of Illinois Press.

Oskamp, S. 1965. "Overconfidence in Case-Study Judgments." *Journal of Consulting Psychology*, 29: 261–65.

Ostorm, T. M., and T. C. Brock. 1969. "Cognitive Bonding to Central Values and Resistance to Communication Advocating Change in Policy Orientation." *Journal of Experimental Research in Personality*, 4: 42–50.

Ostow, M. 1980. "The Hypomanic Personality in History." In R. H. Belmaker and H. D. van Praag, eds., *Mania: An Evolving Concept*, pp. 387–93. New York: Spectrum.

Paige, G. D. 1972. "Comparative Case Analysis of Crisis Decisions: Korea and Cuba." In C. F. Hermann, ed., *International Crises*, pp. 41–55. New York: Free Press.

Pally, S. 1955. "Cognitive Rigidity as a Function of Threat." *Journal of Personality*, 23: 346–55.

Palmer, B., Jr. 1984. *The 25-Year War: America's Military Role in Vietnam*. Lexington: University Press of Kentucky.

Palmer, D. R. 1978. *Summons of the Trumpet*. San Rafael, Calif.: Presidio Press.

Park, B. E. 1986. *The Impact of Illness on World Leaders*. Philadelphia: University of Pennsylvania Press.

Parker, E. S. 1982. "Comments on 'Cognitive Functioning in Men Social Drinkers: A Replication Study.'" *Journal of Studies on Alcohol*, 43: 170–77.

Parker, E. S., and E. P. Noble. 1977. "Alcohol Consumption and Cognitive Functioning in Social Drinkers." *Journal of Studies on Alcohol*, 38: 1224–32.

Peabody, D. 1985. *National Characteristics*. Cambridge, Eng.: Cambridge University Press.

Pears, D. F. 1984. *Motivated Irrationality*. Oxford: Oxford University Press.

Pennings, J. M. 1985. "Introduction: On the Nature and Theory of Strategic Decisions." In J. M. Pennings and Associates, eds., *Organizational Strategy and Change*, pp. 1–34. San Francisco, Calif.: Jossey-Bass.

The Pentagon Papers. The Defense Department History of U.S. Decisionmaking on Vietnam. 1971. Vol. 3. Senator Gravel ed. Boston: Beacon Press.

Perlmutter, A. 1975. "Israel's Fourth War, October 1973: Political and Military Misperceptions." *Orbis,* 19: 434–60.

Perry, M. 1979. "Literary Dynamics: How the Order of a Text Creates Its Meaning." *Poetics Today,* 1: 35–64.

Pervin, L. A. 1963. "The Need to Predict and Control Under Conditions of Threat." *Journal of Personality,* 31: 570–87.

Peterson, C. R., and L. R. Beach. 1967. "Man as an Intuitive Statistician." *Psychological Bulletin,* 68: 29–46.

Peterson, S. 1979. "Foreign News Gatekeepers and Criteria of Newsworthiness." *Journalism Quarterly,* 56: 116–25.

Peterson, S. A. 1985. "Neurophysiology, Cognition, and Political Thinking." *Political Psychology,* 6: 495–518.

Pettigrew, T. F. 1958. "The Measurement and Correlates of Category Width as a Cognitive Variable." *Journal of Personality,* 26: 532–44.

Petty, R. E., and J. T. Cacioppo. 1986. "The Elaboration Likelihood Model of Persuasion." In L. Berkowitz, ed., *Advances in Experimental Social Psychology,* vol. 19, pp. 124–205. Orlando, Fla.: Academic Press.

———. 1977. "Forewarning, Cognitive Responding, and Resistance to Persuasion." *Journal of Personality and Social Psychology,* 35: 645–55.

Petty, R. E., J. T. Cacioppo, and R. Goldman. 1981. "Personal Involvement as a Determinant of Argument-based Persuasion." *Journal of Personality and Social Psychology,* 41: 847–55.

Phillips, L. D., and G. N. Wright. 1977. "Cultural Differences in Viewing Uncertainty and Assessing Probabilities." In H. Jungermann and G. de Zeeuw, eds. *Decision Making and Change in Human Affairs,* pp. 507–19. Amsterdam, Neth.: D. Reidel.

Pisor, R. 1983. *The End of the Line: The Siege of Khe Sanh.* New York: Ballantine Books.

Platt, W. 1961. *National Character in Action: Intelligence Factors in Foreign Relations.* New Brunswick, N.J.: Rutgers University Press.

Polzella, D. J. 1975. "Effects of Sleep Deprivation on Short-term Recognition Memory." *Journal of Experimental Psychology: Human Learning and Memory,* 104: 194–200.

Post, J. M. 1980. "The Seasons of a Leader's Life: Influence of the Life Cycle on Political Behavior." *Political Psychology,* 2 (3–4): 35–49.

———. 1973. "On Aging Leaders: Possible Effects of the Aging Process on the Conduct of Leadership." *Journal of Geriatric Psychiatry,* 6: 109–16.

Postman, L., and J. S. Bruner. 1948. "Perception Under Stress." *Psychological Review,* 55: 314–23.

Postman, L., J. S. Bruner, and E. McGinnies. 1948. "Personal Values as Selective Factors in Perception." *Journal of Abnormal and Social Psychology,* 43: 142–54.

Potter, D. M. 1954. *People of Plenty: Economic Abundance and the American Character.* Chicago: University of Chicago Press.

Potter, W. C. 1980. "Issue Area and Foreign Policy Analysis." *International Organization,* 34: 405–27.

Powell, F. A. 1966. "Latitudes of Acceptance and Rejection and the Belief-Disbelief Dimension: A Correlational Comparison." *Journal of Personality and Social Psychology,* 4: 453–57.

Pruitt, D. G. 1965. "Definition of the Situation as Determinant of International Action." In H. C. Kelman, ed., *International Behavior*, pp. 393–42. New York: Holt, Rinehart, and Winston.

Pryor, J. B., and M. Kriss. 1977. "The Cognitive Dynamics of Salience in the Attribution Process." *Journal of Personality and Social Psychology*, 35: 49–55.

Pye, L. 1981. *The Dynamics of Chinese Politics.* Cambridge, Mass.: Oelgeschlager, Gunn, and Hain.

———. 1961. "The Non-Western Political Process." In J. N. Rosenau, ed., *International Politics and Foreign Policy*, pp. 286–94. New York: Free Press.

Pyszczynski, T. 1982. "Cognitive Strategies for Coping with Uncertain Outcomes." *Journal of Research in Personality*, 16: 386–99.

Pyszczynski, T., and J. Greenberg. 1987. "Toward an Integration of Cognitive and Motivational Perspectives on Social Inference: A Biased Hypothesis-testing Model." In L. Berkowitz, ed., *Advances in Experimental Social Psychology*, vol. 20, pp. 297–340. San Diego, Calif.: Academic Press.

Raiffa, H. 1968. *Decision Analysis.* Reading, Mass.: Addison-Wesley.

Rapoport, J. L., M. S. Buchsbaum, H. W. Weingartner, T. P. Zahn, C. Ludlow, and E. J. Mikkelsen. 1980. "Dextroamphetamine: Its Cognitive and Behavioral Effects in Normal and Hyperactive Boys and Normal Men." *Archives of General Psychiatry*, 37: 933–43.

Raser, J. R. 1966. "Personal Characteristics of Political Decision Makers: A Literature Review." *Peace Research Society Papers (International)*, 5: 161–81.

Rastogi, P. N. 1975. *The Nature and Dynamics of Factional Conflict.* Delhi: Macmillan.

Raven, B. H. 1974. "The Nixon Group." *Journal of Social Issues*, 30: 297–320.

Ravenal, E. C. 1980. *Never Again.* Philadelphia: Temple University Press.

Read, S. J. 1983. "Once Is Enough: Causal Reasoning from a Single Instance." *Journal of Personality and Social Psychology*, 45: 323–33.

Reed, S. M. 1973. *Psychological Processes in Pattern Recognition.* New York: Academic Press.

Reese, W. 1982. "Deception Within a Communications Theory Framework." In D. C. Daniel and K. L. Herbig, eds., *Strategic Military Deception*, pp. 99–114. New York: Pergamon Press.

Reitman, W. R. 1964. "Heuristic Decision Procedures, Open Constraints, and the Structure of Ill-defined Problems." In M. W. Shelly, and G. L. Bryan, eds., *Human Judgment and Optimality*, pp. 282–315. New York: Wiley.

Reychler, L. 1979. *Patterns of Diplomatic Thinking.* New York: Praeger.

Reyes, R. M., W. C. Thompson, and G. H. Bower. 1980. "Judgmental Biases Resulting from Differing Availabilities of Arguments." *Journal of Personality and Social Psychology*, 39: 2–12.

Ridgeway, C. L. 1983. *The Dynamics of Small Groups.* New York: St. Martin's Press.

Rogow, A. A. 1969. "Private Illness and Public Policy: The Cases of James Forrestal and John Winant." *American Journal of Psychiatry*, 125: 1093–97.

Rokeach, M. 1973. *The Nature of Human Values.* New York: Free Press.

———. 1968a. "The Nature of Attitudes." In *International Encyclopedia of the Social Sciences*, vol. 1, pp. 449–57. New York: Macmillan.

———. 1968b. *Beliefs, Attitudes, and Values.* San Francisco, Calif.: Jossey-Bass.

———. 1966. "Attitude Change and Behavioral Change." *Public Opinion Quarterly*, 30: 529–50.

———. 1960. *The Open and Closed Mind*. New York: Basic Books.

———. 1956. "On the Unity of Thought and Belief." *Journal of Personality*, 25: 224–50.

———. 1954. "The Nature and Meaning of Dogmatism." *Psychological Review*, 61: 194–204.

Rokeach, M., W. C. McGovney, and M. R. Denny. 1955. "A Distinction Between Dogmatic and Rigid Thinking." *Journal of Abnormal and Social Psychology*, 51:87–93.

Rolle, A. 1980. "The Historic Past of the Unconscious." In H. D. Laswell, D. Lerner, and H. Speier, eds., *Propaganda and Communication in World History*, vol. 3, pp. 403–60. Honolulu: University of Hawaii Press.

Rosch, E. 1975. "Cognitive Reference Points." *Cognitive Psychology*, 7: 532–47.

Rosenau, J. N. 1984. "A Pre-Theory Revisited: World Politics in an Era of Cascading Interdependence." *International Studies Quarterly*, 28: 245–305.

———. 1970. "Foreign Policy as an Adaptive Behavior." *Comparative Politics*, 2: 365–87.

———. 1966. "Pre-Theories and Theories of Foreign Policy." In R. B. Farrell, ed., *Approaches to Comparative and International Politics*, pp. 27–92. Evanston, Ill.: Northwestern University Press.

Rosenberg, M. 1969. *Conceiving the Self*. New York: Basic Books.

———. 1957. "Misanthropy and Attitude Toward International Affairs." *Journal of Conflict Resolution*, 1: 340–45.

Rosenberg, M. J. 1960a. "A Structural Theory of Attitude Dynamics." *Public Opinion Quarterly*, 24: 319–40.

———. 1960b. "An Analysis of Affective-Cognitive Consistency." In M. J. Rosenberg, C. I. Hovland, W. J. McGuire, R. P. Abelson, and J. W. Brehm, eds., *Attitude Organization and Change*, pp. 15–64. New Haven, Conn.: Yale University Press.

Rosenberg, S. W., and G. Wolfsfeld. 1977. "International Conflict and the Problem of Attribution." *Journal of Conflict Resolution*, 21: 75–104.

Ross, L. 1981. "The 'Intuitive Scientist' Formulation and Its Developmental Implications." In J. H. Flavell and L. Ross, eds., *Social Cognitive Developments: Frontiers and Possible Futures*, pp. 1–42. Cambridge, Eng.: Cambridge University Press.

———. 1978. "Some Afterthoughts on the Intuitive Psychologist." In L. Berkowitz, ed., *Cognitive Theories in Social Psychology*, pp. 385–400. New York: Academic Press.

———. 1977. "The Intuitive Psychologist and His Shortcomings: Distortion in the Attribution Process." In L. Berkowitz, ed., *Advances in Experimental Social Psychology*, vol. 10, pp. 173–220. New York: Academic Press.

Ross, L., T. M. Amabile, and J. Steinmetz. 1977. "Social Roles, Social Control, and Biases in Social-Perception Processes." *Journal of Personality and Social Psychology*, 35: 485–94.

Ross, L., D. Greene, and P. House. 1977. "The 'False Consensus Effect': An Egocentric Bias in Social Perception and Attribution Processes." *Journal of Experimental Social Psychology*, 13: 279–301.

Ross, L., M. R. Lepper, and M. Hubbard. 1975. "Perseverance in Self Perception and Social Perception: Biased Attributional Processes in the Debriefing Paradigm." *Journal of Personality and Social Psychology*, 32: 880–92.

Ross, L., M. R. Lepper, F. Strack, and J. Steinmetz. 1977. "Social Explanation and Social Expectation: Effects of Real and Hypothetical Explanations on Subjective Likelihood." *Journal of Personality and Social Psychology*, 35: 817–29.

Ross, M., and F. Sicoly. 1979. "Egocentric Biases in Availability and Attribution." *Journal of Personality and Social Psychology*, 37: 322–36.

Roth, T., K. M. Hartse, P. G. Saab, P. M. Piccione, and M. Kramer. 1980. "The Effects of Flurazepam, Lorazepam, and Triazolam on Sleep and Memory." *Psychopharmacology*, 70: 231–37.

Rothbart, M., M. Evans, and S. Fulero. 1979. "Recall for Confirming Events: Memory Processes and the Maintenance of Social Stereotypes." *Journal of Experimental Social Psychology*, 15: 343–55.

Rotter, J. B. 1966. "Generalized Expectancies for Internal Versus External Control of Reinforcement." *Psychological Monographs: General and Applied*, 80 (609): 1–28.

Royce, R. R. 1974. "Cognition and Knowledge: Psychological Epistemology." In E. C. Carterette and M. P. Friedman, eds., *Handbook of Perception*, vol. 1, pp. 149–76. New York: Academic Press.

Rundell, O. H., H. L. William, and B. K. Lester. 1978. "Secobarbital and Information Processing." *Perceptual and Motor Skills*, 46: 1255–64.

Sacksteder, W. 1974. "The Logic of Analogy." *Philosophy and Rhetoric*, 7: 234–52.

Saenger, G., and S. Flowerman. 1954. "Stereotypes and Prejudicial Attitudes." *Human Relations*, 7: 217–38.

Salanick, G. R. 1982. "Attitude-Behavior Consistencies as Social Logics." In M. P. Zanna, E. T. Higgins, and C. P. Herman, eds., *Consistency in Social Behavior: The Ontario Symposium*, vol. 2, pp. 51–73. Hillsdale, N.J.: Erlbaum.

Salanick, G. R., and M. Conway. 1975. "Attitude Inference from Salient and Relevant Cognitive Content About Behavior." *Journal of Personality and Social Psychology*, 32: 829–40.

Salpeter, E., and Y. Elitzur. 1973. *Who Runs Israel?* Tel Aviv: Levin-Apstein. (In Hebrew.)

Sampson, M. W., and S. G. Walker. 1987. "Cultural Norms and National Roles: A Comparison of Japan and France." In S. G. Walker, ed., *Role Theory and Foreign Policy Analysis*, pp. 105–22. Durham, N.C.: Duke University Press.

Sarbin, T. R. 1982. "Prolegomenon to a Theory of Counter-Deception." In D. C. Daniel and K. L. Herbig, eds., *Strategic Military Deception*, pp. 151–73. New York: Pergamon Press.

Sarbin, T. R., and V. L. Allen. 1968. "Role Theory." In G. Lindzey and E. Aronson, eds., *The Handbook of Social Psychology*, vol. 1, pp. 488–567. 2d ed. Reading, Mass.: Addison-Wesley.

Saris, W. E., and I. N. Gallhofer. 1984. "Formulation of Real Life Decisions: A Study of Foreign Policy Decisions." *Acta Psychologica*, 56: 247–65.

Sarnoff, I. 1960. "Psychoanalytic Theory and Social Attitudes." *Public Opinion Quarterly*, 24: 251–79.

Sarnoff, I., and D. Katz. 1954. "The Motivational Bases of Attitude Change." *Journal of Abnormal and Social Psychology*, 49: 115–24.

Schaff, A. 1973. *Language and Cognition*. New York: McGraw-Hill.

Schandler, H. Y. 1977. *Lyndon Johnson and Vietnam: The Unmaking of a President*. Princeton, N.J.: Princeton University Press.

Schank, R. C. 1979. *Reminding and Memory Organization: An Introduction to MOPs*. Research Report no. 170. New Haven, Conn.: Department of Computer Science, Yale University.

Schank, R. C., and Ableson, R. P. 1977. *Scripts, Plans, Goals, and Understanding: An Inquiry into Human Knowledge Structures*. Hillsdale, N.J.: Erlbaum.

Schein, E. H. 1983. *Organizational Culture: A Dynamic Model*. Cambridge, Mass.: Sloan School of Management, Harvard University.

Schelling, T. C. 1970. *The Strategy of Conflict*. London: Oxford University Press.

Schieder, T. 1978. "The Role of Historical Consciousness in Political Action." *History and Theory*, 17 (4), suppl. 17: 1–18.

Schiff, Z. 1974. *Earthquake in October*. Tel Aviv: Zmora, Bitan, Modan. (In Hebrew.)

Schlenker, B. R., and R. S. Miller. 1977. "Egocentrism in Groups: Self-serving Biases or Logical Information Processing?" *Journal of Personality and Social Psychology*, 35: 755–64.

Schoen, D. A. 1973. *Beyond the Stable State*. Harmondsworth, Eng.: Penguin.

Schroder, H. M., M. J. Driver, and S. Streufert. 1967. *Human Information Processing*. New York: Holt, Rinehart, and Winston.

Schustack, M. W. 1988. "Thinking About Causality." In R. J. Sternberg and E. E. Smith, eds., *The Psychology of Human Thought*, pp. 92–115. Cambridge, Eng.: Cambridge University Press.

Schwartz, G. 1980. "Conflict Resolution as a Process." In T. Johnstad, ed., *Group Dynamics and Society*, pp. 149–64. Cambridge, Mass.: Oelgeschlager, Gunn, and Hain.

Scott, A. M. 1982. *The Dynamics of Interdependence*. Chapel Hill: University of North Carolina Press.

———. 1977. "The Logic of International Interaction." *International Studies Quarterly*, 21: 429–60.

———. 1969. "The Department of State: Formal Organization and Informal Culture." *International Studies Quarterly*, 13: 1–18.

Scott, W. A. 1969. "Structure of Natural Cognitions." *Journal of Personality and Social Psychology*, 12: 261–78.

———. 1966. "Flexibility, Rigidity, and Adaptation: Toward Clarification of Concepts." In O. J. Harvey, ed., *Experience Structure and Adaptability*, pp. 369–400. New York: Springer.

———. 1965. "Psychological and Social Correlates of International Images." In H. C. Kelman, ed., *International Behavior*, pp. 71–103. New York: Holt, Rinehart, and Winston.

———. 1963. "Cognitive Complexity and Cognitive Balance." *Sociometry*, 26: 66–74.

———. 1960a. "Personal Values and Group Interaction." In D. Wilner, ed., *Decisions, Values, and Groups*, vol. 1, pp. 154–70. London: Pergamon Press.

———. 1960b. "International Ideology and Interpersonal Ideology." *Public Opinion Quarterly*, 24: 419–35.

———. 1959. "Cognitive Consistency, Response Reinforcement, and Attitude Change." *Sociometry*, 22: 219–29.

———. 1958. "Rationality and Non-Rationality of International Attitudes." *Journal of Conflict Resolution*, 2: 8–16.

Searing, D. D., J. J. Schwartz, and A. E. Lind. 1973. "The Structuring Principle: Political Socialization and Belief Systems." *American Political Science Review*, 67: 415–32.

Sederberg, P. C. 1984. "Organization and Explanation: New Metaphors for Old Problems." *Administration and Society*, 16: 167–94.

Segal, E. M., and E. W. Stacy, Jr. 1975. "Rule-governed Behavior as a Psychological Process." *American Psychologist*, 30: 541–52.

Segal, G. 1985. "Defence, Culture, and Sino-Soviet Relations." *Journal of Strategic Studies*, 8: 180–98.

Sells, S. B. 1970. "On the Nature of Stress." In J. E. McGrath, ed., *Social Psychological Factors in Stress*, pp. 134–39. New York: Holt, Rinehart, and Winston.

Selznick, P. [1957] 1984. *Leadership in Administration: A Sociological Interpretation.* Berkeley: University of California Press.

Semmel, A. K. 1982. "Small Group Dynamics in Foreign Policy Making." In G. Hopple, ed., *Biopolitics, Political Psychology, and International Politics*, pp. 94–113. London: Frances Pinter.

Sexton, T. R., and D. R. Young. 1985. "Game Tree Analysis of International Crises." *Journal of Policy Analysis and Management*, 4: 354–69.

Shanteau, J. 1988. "Psychological Characteristics and Strategies of Expert Decision-Makers." *Acta Psychologica*, 68: 203–15.

Shapiro, M. J., and M. G. Bonham. 1973. "Cognitive Process and Foreign Policy Decision-Making." *International Studies Quarterly*, 17: 147–74.

Shaver, K. G. 1975. *An Introduction to Attribution Processes.* Cambridge, Mass.: Winthrop.

Shaw, B. F. 1979. "The Theoretical and Experimental Foundations of a Cognitive Model for Depression." In P. Pliner, K. R. Blankenstein, and I. M. Spigel, eds., *Perception of Emotion in Self and Others*, vol. 5, pp. 137–64 New York: Plenum Press.

Shawcross, W. 1979. *Sideshow: Kissinger, Nixon, and the Destruction of Cambodia.* London: Andre Deutsch.

Sheehan, N. 1988. *A Bright Shining Lie: John Paul Vann and America in Vietnam.* New York: Random House.

Sheehan, N., H. Smith, E. W. Kenworth, and F. Butterfield, eds. 1971. *The Pentagon Papers as Published by the New York Times.* New York: Bantam.

Shepard, G. H. 1988. "Personality Effects on American Foreign Policy, 1969–84: A Second Test of Interpersonal Generalization Theory." *International Studies Quarterly*, 32: 91–123.

Shephard, R. M. 1964. "On the Subjectively Optimum Selection Among Multi-Attribute Alternatives." In M. W. Shelly and G. L. Bryan, eds., *Human Judgment and Optimality*, pp. 257–81. New York: Wiley.

Sherif, M., and C. W. Sherif. 1967. "Attitude as the Individual's Own Categories: The Social Judgment-Involvement Approach to Attitude and Attitude Change." In C. W. Sherif and M. Sherif, eds., *Attitude, Ego-Involvement, and Change*, pp. 105–39. New York: Wiley.

Sherman, S. J., and E. Corty. 1984. "Cognitive Heuristics." In R. S. Wyre and T. K. Srull, eds., *Handbook of Social Cognition*, vol. 1, pp. 189–286. Hillsdale, N.J.: Erlbaum.

Sherwin, R. G. 1982. "The Organizational Approach to Strategic Deception:

Implications for Theory and Policy." In D. C. Daniel and K. L. Herbig, eds., *Strategic Military Deception*, pp. 70–98. New York: Pergamon Press.

Shibutani, T. 1967. "Reference Groups as Perspectives." In J. G. Manis and B. N. Meltzer, eds., *Symbolic Interaction*, pp. 159–70. Boston: Allyn and Bacon.

Shih, C. 1988. "National Role Conception as Foreign Policy Motivation: The Psychocultural Bases of Chinese Diplomacy." *Political Psychology*, 9:599–631.

Shlaim, A. 1976. "Failure in National Intelligence Estimates: The Case of the Yom Kippur War." *World Politics*, 28: 348–80.

Showers, C., and N. Cantor. 1985. "Social Cognition: A Look at Motivated Strategies." In M. R. Rosenzweig and L. W. Porter, eds., *Annual Review of Psychology*, vol. 36, pp. 275–305. Palo Alto, Calif.: Annual Reviews.

Shultz, R. H. 1982. "The Vietnamization-Pacification Strategy of 1969–1972: A Quantitative and Qualitative Reassessment." In R. A. Hunt and R. H. Shultz, eds., *Lessons from an Unconventional War: Reassessing U.S. Strategies for Future Conflict*, pp. 48–117. New York: Pergamon Press.

Sidanius, J. 1978. "Intolerance to Ambiguity and Socio-Politico Ideology: A Multidimensional Analysis." *European Journal of Social Psychology*, 8: 215–35.

Siegel, A. E., and S. Siegel. 1957. "Reference Group, Membership Groups, and Attitude Change." *Journal of Abnormal and Social Psychology*, 55: 360–64.

Siegelman, L., and L. Miller. 1978. "Understanding Presidential Rhetoric: The Vietnam Statements of Lyndon Johnson." *Communications Research*, 5: 25–56.

Simon, H. A. 1985. "Human Nature in Politics: The Dialogue of Psychology with Political Sciences." *American Political Science Review*, 79: 293–304.

———. 1981. *Sciences of the Artificial*. 2d ed. Cambridge, Mass.: MIT Press.

———. 1978a. "Rationality as Process and as Product of Thought." *American Economic Review*, 68: 1–16.

———. 1978b. "Information-processing Theory of Human Problem Solving." In W. K. Estes, ed., *Handbook of Learning and Cognitive Processes*, pp. 271–95. Hillsdale, N.J.: Erlbaum.

———. 1976. *Administrative Behavior*. 3d ed. New York: Free Press.

———. 1974. "How Big Is a Chunk?" *Science*, 183: 482–88.

———. 1969. "On the Concept of Organizational Goal." In A. Etzioni, ed., *A Sociological Reader on Complex Organizations*, pp. 158–74. 2d ed. New York: Holt, Rinehart, and Winston.

Singer, J. D. 1969. "Threat Perception and National Decision Makers." In D. G. Pruitt and R. C. Snyder, eds., *Theory and Research on the Causes of War*, pp. 39–42. Englewood Cliffs, N.J.: Prentice-Hall.

———. 1968. "Man and World Politics: The Psycho-Cultural Interface." *Journal of Social Issues*, 24: 127–56.

———. 1961a. "The Relevance of Behavioral Sciences to the Study of International Relations." *Behavioral Science*, 5: 324–35.

———. 1961b. "The Level-of-Analysis Problem in International Relations." In K. Knorr and S. Verba, eds., *The International System: Political Essays*, pp. 77–92. Princeton, N.J.: Princeton University Press.

Singer, J. E. 1968. "The Bothersomeness of Inconsistency." In R. P. Abelson, E. Aronson, W. J. McGuire, T. M. Newcomb, M. J. Rosenberg, and P. H. Tannenbaum, eds., *Theories of Cognitive Consistency*, pp. 393–99. Chicago: Rand McNally.

Sjöberg, L. 1979. "Strength of Belief and Risk." *Policy Sciences*, 11: 39–57.

Skemp, R. R. 1979. *Intelligence, Learning, and Action*. Chichester, Eng.: Wiley.

Skevington, S. M. 1983. "Social Cognition, Personality, and Chronic Pain." *Journal of Psychosomatic Research*, 27: 421–28.

Slovic, P. 1975. "Choice Between Equally Valued Alternatives." *Journal of Experimental Psychology: Human Perception and Performance*, 1: 280–87.

Slovic, P., and B. Fischhoff. 1977. "On the Psychology of Experimental Surprise." *Journal of Experimental Psychology: Human Perception and Performance*, 3: 544–51.

Slovic, P., B. Fischhoff, and S. Lichtenstein. 1982. "Facts Versus Fears: Understanding Perceived Risk." In D. Kahneman, P. Slovic, and A. Tversky, eds., *Judgment Under Uncertainty: Heuristics and Biases*, pp. 463–92. Cambridge, Eng.: Cambridge University Press.

———. 1977. "Behavioral Decision Theory." In M. R. Rosenzweig and L. W. Porter, eds., *Annual Review of Psychology*, vol. 28, pp. 1–39. Palo Alto, Calif.: Annual Reviews.

———. 1976. "Cognitive Processes and Societal Risk Taking." In J. S. Carroll and J. W. Payne, eds., *Cognition and Social Behavior*, pp. 165–84. Hillsdale, N.J.: Erlbaum.

Slovic, P., and S. Lichtenstein. 1971. "Comparison of Bayesian and Regression Approaches to the Study of Information Processing in Judgment." *Organizational Behavior and Human Performance*, 6: 649–744.

Smart, C., and I. Vertinsky. 1977. "Designs for Crisis Decision Units," *Administrative Science Quarterly*, 22: 640–57.

Smith, E. E., and D. L. Medin. 1981. *Categories and Concepts*. Cambridge, Mass.: Harvard University Press.

Smith, E. R., and F. D. Miller. 1979. "Salience and the Cognitive Mediation of Attribution." *Journal of Personality of Social Psychology*, 37: 2240–52.

Smith, M. B. 1949. "Personal Values as Determinants of a Political Attitude." *Journal of Psychology*, 28: 477–86.

Smith, R. J. 1984. "Crisis Management Under Strain." *Science*, 225: 907–9.

Smith, S. 1984–85. "Policy Preferences and Bureaucratic Position: The Case of the American Hostage Rescue Mission." *International Affairs*, 61: 9–25.

———. 1980. "Allison and the Cuban Missile Crisis: A Review of the Bureaucratic Politics Model of Foreign Policy Decision-Making." *Millennium*, 9: 21–40.

Smock, C. D. 1955. "The Influence of Psychological Stress on 'Intolerance to Ambiguity.'" *Journal of Abnormal and Social Psychology*, 50: 177–82.

Snepp, R. 1978. *Decent Interval*. New York: Random House.

Sniezek, J. A. 1980. "Judgments of Probabilistic Events: Remembering the Past and Predicting the Future." *Journal of Experimental Psychology: Human Perception and Performance*, 6: 695–706.

Snyder, C. R. 1985. "The Excuse: An Amazing Grace?" In B. R. Schlenker, ed., *The Self and Social Life*, pp. 235–60. New York: McGraw-Hill.

Snyder, C. R., and R. L. Higgins. 1988. "Excuses: Their Effective Role in the Negotiation of Reality." *Psychological Bulletin*, 104: 23–35.

Snyder, G. H., and P. Diesing. 1977. *Conflict Among Nations: Bargaining, Decision Making, and System Structure in International Crises*. Princeton, N.J.: Princeton University Press.

Snyder, J. 1984. *The Ideology of the Offensive: Military Decision Making and the Disasters of 1914.* Ithaca, N.Y.: Cornell University Press.

Snyder, J. L. 1978. "Rationality at the Brink: The Role of Cognitive Processes in Failures of Deterrence." *World Politics,* 30: 345–65.

Snyder, M. 1982. "When Believing Means Doing: Creating Links Between Attitudes and Behavior." In M. P. Zanna, E. T. Higgins, and C. P. Herman, eds., *Consistency in Social Behavior: The Ontario Symposium,* vol. 2, pp. 105–30. Hillsdale, N.J.: Erlbaum.

———. 1981. "On the Self-perpetuating Nature of Social Stereotypes." In D. L. Hamilton, ed., *Cognitive Processes in Stereotyping and Intergroup Behavior,* pp. 183–212. Hillsdale, N.J.: Erlbaum.

———. 1979. "Self-monitoring Processes." In L. Berkowitz, ed., *Advances in Experimental Social Psychology,* vol. 12, pp. 85–128. New York: Academic Press.

Snyder, M., and W. B. Swann, Jr. 1978. "Hypothesis-testing Processes in Social Interaction." *Journal of Personality and Social Psychology,* 36: 1202–12.

Snyder, R. C., H. W. Bruck, and B. Sapin. 1962. *Foreign Policy Decision Making.* New York: Free Press.

Somit, A. 1968. "Toward A More Biologically Oriented Political Science: Ethology and Psychopharmacology." *Midwest Journal of Political Science,* 12: 550–67.

Sorensen, T. C. 1964. *Decision-Making in the White House.* New York: Columbia University Press.

Spear, N. E. 1978. *The Processing of Memories: Forgetting and Retention.* Hillsdale, N.J.: Erlbaum.

Speier, H. 1980. "The Communication of Hidden Meaning." In H. D. Lasswell, D. Lerner, and H. Speier, eds., *Propaganda and Communication in World History,* vol. 2, pp. 261–300. Honolulu: University of Hawaii Press.

Spiro, H. J. 1966. "Foreign Policy and Political Style." *Annals of the American Academy of Political and Social Science,* 366: 139–48.

Spradley, J. P. 1972. "Foundations of Cultural Knowledge." In J. P. Spradley, ed., *Culture and Cognition,* pp. 3–38. San Francisco, Calif.: Chandler.

Sprock, J., D. L. Braff, D. P. Saccuzzo, and J. H. Atkinson. 1983. "The Relationship of Depression and Thought Disorder in Pain Patients." *British Journal of Medical Psychology,* 56: 351–60.

Sprout, H., and M. Sprout. 1969. "Environmental Factors in the Study of International Politics." In J. N. Rosenau, ed., *International Politics and Foreign Policy,* pp. 41–56. Rev. ed. New York: Free Press.

———. 1962. *Foundations of International Politics.* Princeton, N.J.: Van Nostrand.

———. 1956. *Man-Milieu Relationship Hypotheses in the Context of International Politics.* Princeton, N.J.: Center of International Studies, Princeton University.

Spyropoulos, T., and J. Ceraso. 1977. "Categorized and Uncategorized Attributes as Recall Cues: The Phenomenon of Limited Access." *Cognitive Psychology,* 9: 384–402.

Starbuck, W. H. 1985. "Acting First and Thinking Later: Theory Versus Reality in Strategic Change." In J. M. Pennings and Associates, eds., *Organizational Strategy and Change,* pp. 336–72. San Francisco, Calif.: Jossey-Bass.

———. 1983. "Organizations as Action Generators." *American Sociological Review*, 48: 91–102.

Stasser, G., N. L. Kerr, and J. H. Davis. 1980. "Influence Processes in Decision-making Groups: A Modeling Approach." In P. B. Paulus, ed., *Psychology of Group Influence*, pp. 431–77. Hillsdale, N.J.: Erlbaum.

Staudinger, U. M., S. W. Cornelius, and P. B. Baltes. 1989. "The Aging of Intelligence: Potential and Limits." *Annals of the American Academy of Political and Social Science,* 503: 43–59.

Staw, B. M. 1980. "Rationality and Justification in Organizational Life." In B. M. Staw and L. Cummings, eds., *Research in Organizational Behavior*, vol. 2, pp. 45–80. Greenwich, Conn.: Jai Press.

———. 1976. "Knee-Deep in the Big Muddy: A Study of Escalating Commitment to a Chosen Course of Action." *Organizational Behavior and Human Performance*, 16: 27–44.

Staw, B. M., L. E. Sandelands, and J. E. Dutton. 1981. "Threat-Rigidity Effects in Organizational Behavior: A Multilevel Analysis." *Administrative Science Quarterly*, 26: 501–24.

Stein, A. A. 1982. "When Misperception Matters." *World Politics* 34: 505–26.

Stein, J. G. 1988. "Building Politics into Psychology: The Misperception of Threat." *Political Psychology*, 9: 245–71.

———. 1985a. "Calculation, Miscalculation, and Conventional Deterrence I: The View from Cairo." In R. Jervis, R. N. Lebow, and J. G. Stein, eds., *Psychology and Deterrence*, pp. 34–59. Baltimore, Md.: Johns Hopkins University Press.

———. 1985b. "Calculation, Miscalculation, and Conventional Deterrence II: The View from Jerusalem." In R. Jervis, R. N. Lebow, and J. G. Stein, eds., *Psychology and Deterrence*, pp. 60–87. Baltimore, Md.: Johns Hopkins University Press.

———. 1982a. "Military Deception, Strategic Surprise, and Conventional Deterrence: A Political Analysis of Egypt and Israel, 1971–73." *Journal of Strategic Studies*, 5: 94–121.

———. 1982b. "The 1973 Intelligence Failure: A Reconsideration." *Jerusalem Quarterly*, 24: 41–54.

———. 1978. "Can Decision-Makers Be Rational and Should They Be? Evaluating the Quality of Decisions." *Jerusalem Journal of International Relations*, 3: 316–39.

———. 1977. "Freud and Descartes: The Paradoxes of Psychological Logic." *International Journal*, 32: 429–51.

Stein, J. G., and R. Tanter. 1980. *Rational Decision-Making: Israel's Security Choices, 1967*. Columbus: Ohio State University Press.

Steinberg, J. 1966. "The Copenhagen Complex." *Journal of Contemporary History* 1 (3): 23–46.

Steinbruner, J. D. 1974. *The Cybernetic Theory of Decision*. Princeton, N.J.: Princeton University Press.

Steiner, I. D. 1982. "Heuristic Models of Groupthink." In H. Brandstätter, J. H. Davis, and G. Stocker-Kreichganer, eds., *Group Decision Making*, pp. 503–24. London: Academic Press.

———. 1964. "Ethnocentrism and Tolerance of Trait 'Inconsistency.'" *Journal of Abnormal and Social Psychology*, 49: 349–54.

Steiner, I. D., and H. H. Johnson. 1963. "Authoritarianism and 'Tolerance of Trait Inconsistency.'" *Journal of Abnormal and Social Psychology*, 67: 388–91.

Steiner, M. 1983. "The Search for Order in a Disorderly World: Worldviews and Prescriptive Decision Paradigms." *International Organization*, 37: 373–413.

Sternberg, R. J. 1977. "Component Processes in Analogical Reasoning." *Psychological Review*, 84: 353–78.

Stewart, R. A., G. E. Powell, and S. J. Chetwynd. 1979. *Person Perception and Stereotyping*. Farnborough, Eng.: Saxon House.

Stix, A. H. 1974. "Chlordiazepoxide (Librium): The Effects of a Minor Tranquilizer on Strategic Choice Behavior in the Prisoner's Dilemma." *Journal of Conflict Resolution*, 18: 373–94.

Stoessinger, J. G. 1968. "China and America: The Burden of Past Misperceptions." In J. C. Farrell and A. P. Smith, eds., *Image and Reality in World Politics*, pp. 72–91. New York: Columbia University Press.

Strack, F., and R. Erber. 1982. "Effects of Salience and Time Pressure on Ratings of Social Causality." *Journal of Experimental Social Psychology*, 18: 581–94.

Stuart, D., and H. Starr. 1981–82. "The 'Inherent Bad Faith Model' Reconsidered: Dulles, Kennedy, and Kissinger." *Political Psychology*, 3 (3–4): 1–33.

Suedfeld, P., and A. D. Rank. 1976. "Revolutionary Leaders: Long-term Success as a Function of Changes in Conceptual Complexity." *Journal of Personality and Social Psychology*, 34: 169–78.

Suedfeld, P., and P. Tetlock. 1977. "Integrative Complexity of Communication in International Crisis." *Journal of Conflict Resolution*, 21: 169–84.

Summer, H. G. 1984. *On Strategy: A Critical Analysis of the Vietnam War*. New York: Dell.

Swann, W. B., Jr., and S. J. Read. 1981. "Acquiring Self-Knowledge: The Search for Feedback That Fits." *Journal of Personality and Social Psychology*, 41: 1119–28.

Swap, W. C. 1984a. "How Groups Make Decisions: A Social Psychological Perspective." In W. C. Swap and Associates, eds., *Group Decision Making*, pp. 45–68. Beverly Hills, Calif.: Sage.

———. 1984b. "Destructive Effects of Groups on Individuals." In W. C. Swap and Associates, eds., *Group Decision Making*, pp. 69–95. Beverly Hills, Calif.: Sage.

Sylvan, D. A., and S. Chan, eds., 1984. *Foreign Policy Decision Making: Perception Cognition and Artificial Intelligence*. New York: Praeger.

Taylor, M. D. 1972. *Swords and Plowshares*. New York: Norton.

Taylor, S. E. 1982. "The Availability Bias in Social Perception and Interaction." In D. Kahneman, P. Slovic, and A. Tversky, eds., *Judgment Under Uncertainty: Heuristics and Biases*, pp. 190–200. Cambridge, Eng.: Cambridge University Press.

———. 1981. "The Interface of Cognitive and Social Psychology." In J. H. Harvey, ed., *Cognition, Social Behavior, and the Environment*, pp. 189–211. Hillsdale, N.J.: Erlbaum.

Taylor, S. E., and J. Crocker. 1981. "Schematic Bases of Social Information Processing." In E. T. Higgins, C. P. Herman, and M. P. Zanna, eds., *Social Cognition: The Ontario Symposium*, vol. 1, pp. 89–134. Hillsdale, N.J.: Erlbaum.

Taylor, S. E., and S. T. Fiske. 1978. "Salience, Attention, and Attribution: Top of the Head Phenomena." In L. Berkowitz, ed., *Advances in Experimental Social Psychology*. vol. 11, pp. 249–88. New York: Academic Press.

Taylor, S. E., and S. C. Thompson. 1982. "Stalking the Elusive 'Vividness' Effect." *Psychological Review*, 89: 155–81.

Terhune, K. W. 1970a. "The Effect of Personality in Cooperation and Conflict." In P. Swingle, ed., *The Structure of Conflict*, pp. 193–234. New York: Academic Press.

———. 1970b. "From National Character to National Behavior: A Reformulation." *Journal of Conflict Resolution*, 14: 203–63.

Tetlock, P. E. 1985a. "Accountability: The Neglected Social Context of Judgment and Choice." In B. M. Staw and L. Cummings, eds., *Research in Organizational Behavior*, vol. 7, pp. 297–332. Greenwich, Conn.: Jai Press.

———. 1985b. "Toward an Intuitive Politician Model of Attribution Processes." In B. R. Schlenker, ed., *The Self and Social Life*, pp. 203–34. New York: McGraw-Hill.

———. 1985c. "Integrative Complexity of American and Soviet Foreign Policy Rhetorics: A Time-Series Analysis." *Journal of Personality and Social Psychology*, 49: 1565–85.

———. 1984. "Content and Structure in Political Belief Systems." In D. A. Sylvan and S. Chan, eds., *Foreign Policy Decision Making: Perception, Cognition, and Artificial Intelligence*, pp. 107–28. New York: Praeger.

———. 1983a. "Accountability and the Complexity of Thought." *Journal of Personality and Social Psychology*, 45: 74–83.

———. 1983b. "Cognitive Style and Political Ideology." *Journal of Personality and Social Psychology*, 45: 118–26.

———. 1979. "Identifying Victims of Groupthink from Public Statements of Decision-Makers." *Journal of Personality and Social Psychology*, 37: 1314–24.

Tetlock, P. E., and A. Levi. 1982. "Attribution Bias: On the Inconclusiveness of the Cognition-Motivation Debate." *Journal of Experimental Social Psychology*, 18: 68–88.

Tetlock, P. E., and C. McGuire, Jr. 1984. "Cognitive Perspectives on Foreign Policy." In S. Long, ed., *Political Behavior Annual*, vol. 1, pp. 255–73. Boulder, Colo.: Westview Press.

Tharp, V. K. 1978. "Sleep Loss and Stages of Information Processing." *Waking and Sleeping*, 2: 29–33.

Thies, W. J. 1982. *When Governments Collide: Coercion and Diplomacy in the Vietnam Conflict, 1964–1968*. Berkeley: University of California Press.

Thomas, E. J. 1968. "Role Theory, Personality, and the Individual." In E. F. Borgatta and W. W. Lambert, eds., *Handbook of Personality Theory and Research*, pp. 694–727. Chicago: Rand McNally.

Thompson, J. C. 1980. *Rolling Thunder: Understanding Policy and Program Failure*. Chapel Hill: University of North Carolina Press.

Thompson, J. D., and W. J. McEwen. 1969. "Organizational Goals and Environment." In A. Etzioni, ed., *A Sociological Reader on Complex Organizations*, pp. 187–98. 2d ed. New York: Holt, Rinehart, and Winston.

Thompson, M., and A. Wildavsky. 1985. "A Cultural Theory of Information Bias in Organization." Mimeograph.

Thomson, J. C. 1973. "How Could Vietnam Happen? An Autopsy." In M. Halperin and A. Kanter, eds., *Readings in American Foreign Policy: Bureaucratic Perspectives*, pp. 98–110. Boston: Little, Brown.

Thorne, C. 1983. "International Relations and the Promptings of History." *Review of International Studies*, 9: 123–35.

Thorngate, W. 1980. "Efficient Decision Heuristics." *Behavioral Science*, 25: 219–25.

Torre, M. 1964. "How Does Physical and Mental Illness Influence Negotiations Between Diplomats?" *International Journal of Social Psychiatry*, 10: 170–76.

Triandis, H. C. 1971. *Attitude and Attitude Change*. New York: Wiley.

———. 1964. "Cultural Influence upon Cognitive Processes." In L. Berkowitz, ed., *Advances in Experimental Social Psychology*, vol. 1, pp. 2–48. New York: Academic Press.

Triandis, H. C., and V. Vassiliou. 1967. "Frequency of Contact and Stereotyping." *Journal of Personality and Social Psychology*, 7:316–28.

Trope, Y., and Z. Ginossar. 1988. "On the Use of Statistical and Nonstatistical Knowledge: A Problem-Solving Approach." In D. Bar-Tal and A.W. Kruglanski, eds., *The Social Psychology of Knowledge*, pp. 209–30. Cambridge, Eng.: Cambridge University Press.

Truman, H. S. 1956. *Memoirs: Years of Trial and Hope, 1946–1952*, vol. 2. New York: New American Library.

Tseng, W.-S., and J. Hsu. 1980. "Minor Psychological Disturbances of Everyday Life." In H. C. Triandis and J. C. Draguns, ed., *Handbook of Cross-cultural Psychology: Psychopathology*, vol. 6, pp. 61–97. Boston: Allyn and Bacon.

Tuchman, B. W. 1984. *The March of Folly: From Troy to Vietnam*. New York: Knopf.

Tucker, R. C. 1968. "The Theory of Charismatic Leadership." *Daedalus*, 97: 731–56.

Turbayne, C. M. 1970. *The Myth of Metaphor*. Rev. ed. Columbia: University of South Carolina Press.

Turner, B. A. 1976. "The Organizational and Interorganizational Development of Disasters." *Administrative Science Quarterly*, 21: 378–97.

Tversky, A. 1977. "Features of Similarity." *Psychological Review*, 84: 327–52.

———. 1972. "Elimination by Aspects: A Theory of Choice." *Psychological Review*, 79: 281–99.

Tversky, A., and D. Kahneman. 1983. "Extensional Versus Intuitive Reasoning: The Conjunction Fallacy in Probability Judgment." *Psychological Review*, 90: 293–315.

———. 1982. "Judgments of and by Representativeness." In D. Kahneman, P. Slovic, and A. Tversky, eds., *Judgment Under Uncertainty: Heuristics and Biases*, pp. 84–98. Cambridge, Eng.: Cambridge University Press.

———. 1980. "Causal Schemata in Judgment Under Uncertainty." In M. Fishbein, ed., *Progress in Social Psychology*, vol. 1, pp. 49–72. Hillsdale, N.J.: Erlbaum.

———. 1974. "Judgment Under Uncertainty: Heuristics and Biases." *Science*, 185: 1124–31.

———. 1973. "Availability: A Heuristic for Judging Frequency and Probability." *Cognitive Psychology*, 5: 207–32.

———. 1971. "Belief in the Law of Small Numbers." *Psychological Bulletin*, 76: 105–10.

Underdal, A. 1979. "Issues Determine Politics Determine Policies: The Case for a 'Rationalistic' Approach to the Study of Foreign Policy Decision-Making." *Cooperation and Conflict*, 14: 1–9.

U.S. Foreign Broadcast Information Service. 1979. *Daily Report: People's Republic of China*, no. 113 (June 11): F/2.

Vasquez, J. A. 1983. "The Tangibility of Issues and Global Conflict: A Test of Rosenau's Issue Area Typology." *Journal of Peace Research*, 20: 179–92.

Verba, S. 1969. "Assumptions of Rationality and Non-Rationality in Models of the International System." In J. N. Rosenau, ed., *International Politics and Foreign Policy*, pp. 217–31. Rev. ed. New York: Free Press.

Verbrugge, R. R., and N. S. McCarrell. 1977. "Metaphoric Comprehension: Studies in Reminding and Resembling." *Cognitive Psychology*, 9: 494–533.

Vertzberger, Y.Y.I. 1986. "Foreign Policy Decisionmakers as Practical-Intuitive Historians: Applied History and Its Shortcomings." *International Studies Quarterly*, 30: 223–47.

———. 1984a. *Misperceptions in Foreign Policymaking: The Sino-Indian Conflict, 1959–1962*. Boulder, Colo.: Westview Press.

———. 1984b. "Bureaucratic-Organizational Politics and Information Processing in a Developing State." *International Studies Quarterly*, 28: 69–95.

Vincent, R. J. 1980. "The Factor of Culture in the Global International Order." In *The Year Book of World Affairs, 1980*, vol. 34, pp. 252–64. London: Stevens.

Volkan, V. D. 1980. "Narcissistic Personality Organization and 'Reparative' Leadership." *International Journal of Group Psychotherapy*, 30: 131–52.

von Bergen, C. W., Jr., and R. J. Kirk. 1978. "Groupthink: When Too Many Heads Spoil the Decision." *Management Review*, 67 (3): 44–49.

von Glahn, G. 1981. *Law Among Nations*. 4th ed. New York: Macmillan.

von Winterfeldt, D., and W. Edwards. 1986. *Decision Analysis and Behavioral Research*. Cambridge, Eng.: Cambridge University Press.

Vought, D. 1982. "American Culture and American Arms: The Case of Vietnam." In R. A. Hunt and R. H. Shultz, eds., *Lessons from an Unconventional War: Reassessing U.S. Strategies for Future Conflicts*, pp. 158–90. Oxford: Pergamon Press.

Vredenburgh, D. J., and J. G. Maurer. 1984. "A Process Framework of Organizational Politics." *Human Relations*, 37:47–66.

Walker, S. G. 1986. "Operational Codes and Content Analysis: The Case of Henry Kissinger." In I. N. Gallhofer, W. E. Saris, and M. Melman, eds., *Different Text Analysis: Procedures for the Studies of Decision Making*, pp. 13–28. Amsterdam, Neth.: Sociometric Research Foundation.

———. 1983. "The Motivational Foundations of Political Belief System: A Re-Analysis of the Operational Code Constraint." *International Studies Quarterly*, 27: 179–201.

———. 1979. "National Role Conceptions and Systemic Outcomes." In L. S. Falkowski, ed., *Psychological Models in International Politics*, pp. 169–210. Boulder, Colo.: Westview Press.

———. 1977. "The Interface Between Beliefs and Behavior: Henry Kissinger's Operational Code and the Vietnam War." *Journal of Conflict Resolution*, 21: 129–68.

Wallace, M. D. 1973. *War and Rank Among Nations*. Lexington, Mass.: Lexington Books.

Walsh, J. P., and L. Fahey. 1986. "The Role of Negotiated Belief Structures in Strategy Making." *Journal of Management*, 3: 325–38.

Walsh, J. P., C. M. Henderson, and J. Deighton. 1988. "Negotiated Belief Structures and Decision Performance: An Empirical Investigation." *Organizational Behavior and Human Decision Processes*, 42: 194–216.

Walster, E., E. Berscheid, and A. M. Barclay. 1967. "A Determinant of Preference Among Modes of Dissonance Reduction." *Journal of Personality and Social Psychology*, 7: 211–16.

Waltz, K. N. 1979. *Theory of International Politics.* Reading, Mass.: Addison-Wesley.

Ward, D. 1974. "Kissinger: A Psychohistory." *History of Childhood Quarterly*, 2: 285–348.

Wason, P. C., and P. N. Johnson-Laird. 1972. *Psychology of Reasoning: Structure and Content.* Cambridge, Mass.: Harvard University Press.

Wasserman, B. 1960. "The Failure of Intelligence Prediction." *Political Studies*, 8: 156–69.

Webb, W. B., and C. M. Levy. 1984. "Effects of Spaced and Repeated Total Sleep Deprivation." *Ergonomics*, 27: 45–58.

Wedge, B. 1966. "Nationality and Social Perception." *Journal of Communication*, 16: 273–82.

Weick, K. E. 1979. "Cognitive Processes in Organizations." In B. M. Staw, ed., *Research in Organizational Behavior*, vol. 1, pp. 41–74. Greenwich, Conn.: Jai Press.

Weldon, M. J., and R. Stagner, 1956. "Perceptual Rigidity and Closure as a Function of Anxiety." *Journal of Abnormal and Social Psychology*, 52: 354–57.

Wells, G. L. 1981. "Lay Analyses of Causal Forces in Behavior." In J. H. Harvey, ed., *Cognition, Social Behavior, and the Environment*, pp. 309–24. Hillsdale, N.J.: Erlbaum.

Westcott, M. R. 1968. *Toward a Contemporary Psychology of Intuition.* New York: Holt, Rinehart, and Winston.

Westmoreland, W. C. 1976. *A Soldier Reports.* New York: Doubleday.

Whaley, B. 1973. *Codeword Barbarossa.* Cambridge, Mass.: MIT Press.

White, R. K. 1970. *Nobody Wanted War.* Rev. ed. New York: Doubleday.

⸻. 1966. "Misperception and the Vietnam War." *Journal of Social Issues*, 22 (3): 1–164.

⸻. 1965. "Images in the Context of International Conflict." In H. C. Kelman, ed., *International Behavior*, pp. 238–76. New York: Holt, Rinehart, and Winston.

White, R. K., and R. Lippit. 1968. "Leader Behavior and Member Reaction in Three 'Social Climates.'" In D. Cartwright and A. Zander, eds., Group Dynamics, pp. 318–35. 3d ed. New York: Harper and Row.

White, R. W. 1964. *The Abnormal Personality.* 3d ed. New York: Ronald.

Whithey, S. F. 1962. "Reactions to Uncertain Threat." In G. W. Baker and D. W. Chapman, eds., *Man and Society in Disaster*, pp. 93–123. New York: Basic Books.

Whorf, B. L. 1956. *Language, Thought, and Reality.* Cambridge, Mass.: Technology Press of MIT.

Wickelgren, W. A. 1979. *Cognitive Psychology.* Englewood Cliffs, N.J.: Prentice-Hall.

Wicker, A. W. 1971. "Attitude Versus Actions." In K. Thomas, ed., *Attitude and Behaviour*, pp. 135–78. Harmondsworth, Eng.: Penguin.

Wicklund, R. A., and J. W. Brehm. 1976. *Perspectives on Cognitive Dissonance.* Hillsdale, N.J.: Erlbaum.

Wiegele, T. C. 1977. "Models of Stress and Disturbances in Elite Political Behaviors: Psychological Variables and Political Decision-Making." In R. S. Robins, ed., *Psychology and Political Leadership*, pp. 79–111. New Orleans, La.: Tulane University Press.

———. 1973. "Decision Making in an International Crisis: Some Biological Factors." *International Studies Quarterly*, 17: 295–335.

Wildavsky, A. 1983. "Information as an Organizational Problem." *Journal of Management Studies*, 20: 29–41.

———. 1962. "The Analysis of Issue Contexts in the Study of Decision-Making." *Journal of Politics*, 24: 717–32.

Wilder, D. A., and V. L. Allen. 1978. "Group Membership and Preference for Information About Others." *Personality and Social Psychology Bulletin*, 4: 106–10.

Wilensky, H. 1967. *Organizational Intelligence: Knowledge and Policy in Government and Industry.* New York: Basic Books.

Williamson, S. R. 1979. "Theories of Organizational Process and Foreign Policy." In P. G. Lauren, ed., *Diplomacy: New Approaches in History, Theory, and Policy* pp. 137–61. New York: Free Press.

Willner, A. R. 1984. *The Spellbinders: Charismatic Political Leadership.* New Haven, Conn.: Yale University Press.

———. 1968. *Charismatic Political Leadership: A Theory.* Princeton, N.J.: Center of International Studies, Princeton University.

Willner, A. R., and D. Willner. 1965. "The Rise and Role of Charismatic Leaders." *Annals of the American Academy of Political and Social Science*, 358: 77–88.

Wilson, S. R. 1978. *Informal Groups.* Englewood Cliffs, N.J.: Prentice-Hall.

Wish, N. B. 1987. "National Attributes as Sources of National Role Conception: A Capability Motivation Model." In S. G. Walker, ed., *Role Theory and Foreign Policy Analysis*, pp. 94–103. Durham, N.C.: Duke University Press.

———. 1980. "Foreign Policy Makers and Their National Role Conceptions." *International Studies Quarterly*, 24: 532–54.

Witkin, H. A. 1974. "Cognitive Styles Across Cultures." In J. W. Berry and P. R. Dasen, eds., *Culture and Cognition*, pp. 99–117. London: Methuen.

Wittgenstein, L. 1953. *Philosophical Investigations.* Oxford: Basil Blackwell.

Wohlstetter, R. 1979. "The Pleasure of Self-Deception." *Washington Quarterly*, 2 (4): 54–63.

———. 1965. "Cuba and Pearl Harbor: Hindsight and Foresight." *Foreign Affairs*, 43: 691–707.

———. 1962. *Pearl Harbor: Warning and Decision.* Stanford, Calif.: Stanford University Press.

Wolfenstein, E. V. 1974. "The Two Wars of Lyndon Johnson." *Politics and Society*, 4: 357–96.

Wolfson, R. J., and T. M. Carroll. 1976. "Ignorance, Error, and Information in the Classic Theory of Decision." *Behavioral Science*, 21: 107–15.

Wong, P.T.P., and B. Weiner 1981. "When People Ask 'Why' Questions, and the

Heuristics of Attributional Search." *Journal of Personality and Social Psychology*, 40: 650–63.

Wood, G. 1978. "The Knew-It-All-Along Effect." *Journal of Experimental Psychology: Human Perception and Performance*, 4: 345–53.

Wright, G. N., and L. D. Phillips. 1980. "Cultural Variation in Probabilistic Thinking: Alternative Ways of Dealing with Uncertainty." *International Journal of Psychology*, 15: 239–57.

Wright, P. 1974. "The Harassed Decision Maker: Time Pressures, Distractions, and the Use of Evidence." *Journal of Applied Psychology*, 59: 555–61.

Wyer, R. S. 1974. *Cognitive Organization and Change: An Information Processing Approach.* Potomac, Md.: Erlbaum.

Wyer, R. S., and D. E. Carlston. 1979. *Social Cognition, Inference, and Attribution.* Hillsdale, N.J.: Erlbaum.

Yinger, M. J. 1973. "Counterculture and Subculture." In D. O. Arnold, ed., *Subcultures*, pp. 121–34. Berkeley, Calif.: Glendessary Press.

Zadny, J., and H. B. Gerard. 1974. "Attributed Intentions and Informational Selectivity." *Journal of Experimental Social Psychology*, 10: 34–52.

Zajonc, R. B. 1980. "Feeling and Thinking: Preferences Need No Inferences." *American Psychologist*, 35: 151–75.

_____. 1960. "The Concept of Balance, Congruity, and Dissonance." *Public Opinion Quarterly*, 24: 280–96.

Zander, A. 1971. *Motives and Goals in Groups.* New York: Academic Press.

Zanna, M. P., J. M. Olson, and R. H. Fazio. 1980. "Attitude-Behavior Consistency: An Individual Difference Perspective." *Journal of Personality and Social Psychology*, 38: 432–40.

Zashin, E., and P. C. Chapman. 1974. "The Uses of Metaphor and Analogy: Toward a Renewal of Political Language." *Journal of Politics*, 36: 290–326.

Zimmerman, W. 1973. "Issue Area and Foreign Policy Process." *American Political Science Review*, 67: 1204–12.

Zimmerman, W., and R. Axelrod. 1981. "The 'Lesson' of Vietnam and Soviet Foreign Policy." *World Politics*, 34: 1–24.

Zinnes, D. A. 1976. "The Problem of Cumulation." In J. N. Rosenau, ed., *In Search of Global Patterns*, pp. 161–66. New York: Free Press.

_____. 1972. "Some Evidence Relevant to the Man-Milieu Hypothesis." In J. N. Rosenau, V. Davis, and M. A. East, eds., *The Analysis of International Politics*, pp. 209–51. New York: Free Press.

_____. 1968. "The Expression and Perception of Hostility in Prewar Crisis: 1914." In J. D. Singer, ed., *Quantitative International Politics*, pp. 85–119. New York: Free Press.

Zinnes, D. A., R. C. North, and H. E. Koch, Jr. 1961. "Capability, Threat, and the Outbreak of War." In J. N. Rosenau, ed., *International Politics and Foreign Policy*, pp. 469–82. New York: Free Press.

Zinnes, D. A., J. L. Zinnes, and R. D. McClure. 1972. "Hostility in Diplomatic Communication." In C. F. Hermann, ed., *International Crises*, pp. 139–62. New York: Free Press.

Index

....

In this index an "f" after a number indicates a separate reference on the next page, and an "ff" indicates separate references on the next two pages. A continuous discussion over two or more pages is indicated by a span of page numbers, e.g., "57–59." *Passim* is used for a cluster of references in close but not consecutive sequence.

Library of Congress Cataloging-in-Publication Data

Vertzberger, Yaacov.
  The world in their minds : information processing, cognition, and
perception in foreign policy decisionmaking / Yaacov
Y. I. Vertzberger.
    p.   cm.
Bibliography: p.
Includes index.
ISBN 0-8047-1688-9 (alk. paper) :
  1. International relations—Decision making. I. Title.
JX1291.V47 1989   89-30921
351.89—dc19   CIP

∞ This book is printed on acid-free paper.